Computer Models
of Thought and Language

A SERIES OF BOOKS IN PSYCHOLOGY

Editors:　　Richard C. Atkinson
　　　　　　Jonathan Freedman
　　　　　　Richard F. Thompson

COMPUTER MODELS
OF THOUGHT AND LANGUAGE

Edited by

Roger C. Schank   Kenneth Mark Colby

W. H. Freeman and Company San Francisco

Printed in the United States of America

Library of Congress Cataloging in Publication Data
Schank, Roger C.   1946–   comp.
    Computer models of thought and language.

    CONTENTS: Newell, A. Artificial intelligence and the
concept of mind.—Natural language models: Simmons, R. F.
Semantic networks; their computation and use for
understanding English sentences. Wilks, Y. An artificial
intelligence approach to machine translation. Winograd, T.
A procedural model of language understanding.
Schank, R. C. Identification of conceptualizations underlying
natural language.—Models of belief systems: Colby, K. M.
Simulations of belief systems. Abelson, R. P. The structure
of belief systems.—Models of memory and cognition:
Hunt, E. The memory we must have. Lindsay, R. K. In
defense of ad hoc systems. Becker, J. D. A model for
encoding of experiential information.
    1. Languages—Psychology—Mathematical models.
2. Electronic data processing—Languages—Psychology.
I. Colby, Kenneth Mark, joint comp. II. Title.
[DNLM: 1. Computers. 2. Language. 3. Models,
Psychological. 4. Thinking. BF455 S299c 1973]
BF455.S26   001.53   73-11064
ISBN 0–7167–0834–5

9 8 7 6 5 4 3 2 1

Contents

Preface

The intent of this book is to describe attempts to model human psychological processes on a computer. Over the past ten years the field of Artificial Intelligence (AI) has become a recognized discipline in the academic and industrial communities. Much of the work in AI has been conceived to develop intelligent machines without claiming that the processes model human thought processes. Within AI, psychology and linguistics, however, there are growing groups of people concerned with representing human thought processes in the form of computer programs.

In modelling the human mental world — accessible mainly through language — two problems are being faced: (1) how to model natural language communication and (2) how to model the thought and memory implicit in the interpretation of linguistic input. There are roughly two approaches to these questions. One is to strive for efficiency regardless of the methods used and the other is to strive for as much correspondence between model and human processes as can be achieved.

It is the second approach that is emphasized in this volume. For example, the four papers in the natural language section state that language should be considered within the framework of its functions in a given human communicative interaction. Since humans are conceptual, intentional, and semantic-based systems that interact in certain situations, the proposed models should also be conceptual, intentional, and semantic-based. This was not the major thrust of work in computational linguistics until very recently when linguists began to turn away from purely syntax-based systems towards semantic-based systems intended to model a communicative situation by creating a theoretical model of that situation.

The main theme throughout this book is the creation and testing of models of complex human behavior in particular situations. For example, the modelling of belief systems and memory are emphasized as both are basic to any model of human conceptual behavior. The papers written by psychologists represent the new trend in psychology that casts theory in the form of a computer program rather than in the traditional literary or mathematical forms.

This book has been compiled to present more extensive information than that already disseminated in journal descriptions of artificial intelligence. We do not claim to have done an exhaustive survey of the field, omitting, for example, interesting and important work in visual perception and speech recognition. We are certain, however, that volumes with emphases other than ours will be published as our colleagues begin to evaluate and report their findings.

July 1973

Roger C. Schank
Kenneth Mark Colby

Computer Models
of Thought and Language

One

Artificial Intelligence and the Concept of Mind

Allen Newell
Carnegie-Mellon University

The title indicates our starting point. "Artificial intelligence" designates a domain of scientific endeavor that is somehow to be laid out before us. "The concept of mind" designates, however obscurely, a cluster of questions to be addressed. Discussion is to proceed on how and by what means materials scattered throughout the scientific field contribute to clarifying, and perhaps even answering, this cluster of questions.

I am much clearer on the nature of artificial intelligence than on the questions that must be posed about the concept of mind. To determine the latter, I have chosen to adopt an orthodox view of scientific psychology: that one understands mind by building theories (models, if you prefer) about the behavior of the human mind, testing these by whatever empirical methods seem appropriate, and then adopting for "the current view of mind" whatever theory seems best to survive the tests. Beyond that one cannot go.

In this discussion I will first describe the field of artificial intelligence, assuming that the reader's knowledge of it is imprecise enough to make such an attempt welcome. Then, I will formulate some questions about the concept of mind, inquiring whether artificial intelligence has anything to offer for their resolution.

The Nature of Artificial Intelligence

Scientific fields emerge as the concerns of scientists congeal around various phenomena. Sciences are not defined, they are recognized. Acts of definition, when they occur, are really prescriptive. They represent attempts to deflect the course of a science, to lay claim to new phenomena, to hedge the science in, or to show that it is somehow wrongly named (a usually futile exercise in applied linguistics).

Artificial intelligence, then, is an as yet uncongealed part of computer science, the latter, itself, only recently congealed. The central phenomena are information processes that accomplish tasks requiring intelligence. Within the domain of all such tasks, however delineated, various subdomains have received attention whereas others have been virtually ignored, and this has led to a variety of views on the nature of artificial intelligence. Although these views do not form an integrated whole their diversity is not unlimited, and each can stand on its own as a way of making sense out of the study of the subject.

I propose to present three of these views of artificial intelligence. Each is somewhat separate from the others, though of course all must reflect aspects of the same current state. Among the three of them much of the field will be laid out for scrutiny, and though some views will be conspicuously absent, I believe them to be those that have the least to offer us here.

View one: the exploration of intellectual functions

Suppose we take the main question of artificial intelligence to be, "What mechanisms can accomplish what intellectual functions?" Then the development of artificial intelligence becomes an exploration in which one function after another is broached and conquered — or perhaps resists all attempts at mechanization.

There need be no real rhyme to the geography of the mental functions, any more than there need be rhyme to the geography of a new continent. Each valley and mountain range must be attained, explored, and settled; exploration can then push on into new country.

For the analogy to geography to hold there should exist a space of intellectual functions that can be defined independently of any attempts to explore it. Such is not the case, of course. But there is still a rich informal notion of the variety of intellectual functions and how they relate to each other. These functions derive from a wide range of sources — from our language, from our philosophical traditions, from the sciences of psychology, linguistics, sociology, biology, from medicine, from technology, and from our literary tradition. Nor are these sources separable, since they feed on one another. Still, it is not difficult to enumerate many intellectual functions and to point to tasks that seem by common assent to embody them.

Of the three views to be presented this one is closest to the historical truth in terms of the motivations and fascinations of the men who have worked and dabbled in the field of artificial intelligence. What does the field look like, viewed this way? My own current view of this geography is shown in Figure 1.1. Drawing the map in two dimensions adds distortion, but since the country is metaphorical, easy visualization is preferable to an attempt to depict the connection between parts more accurately. Within each domain I have put some dates of characteristic efforts, usually including the early work that opened up the area.

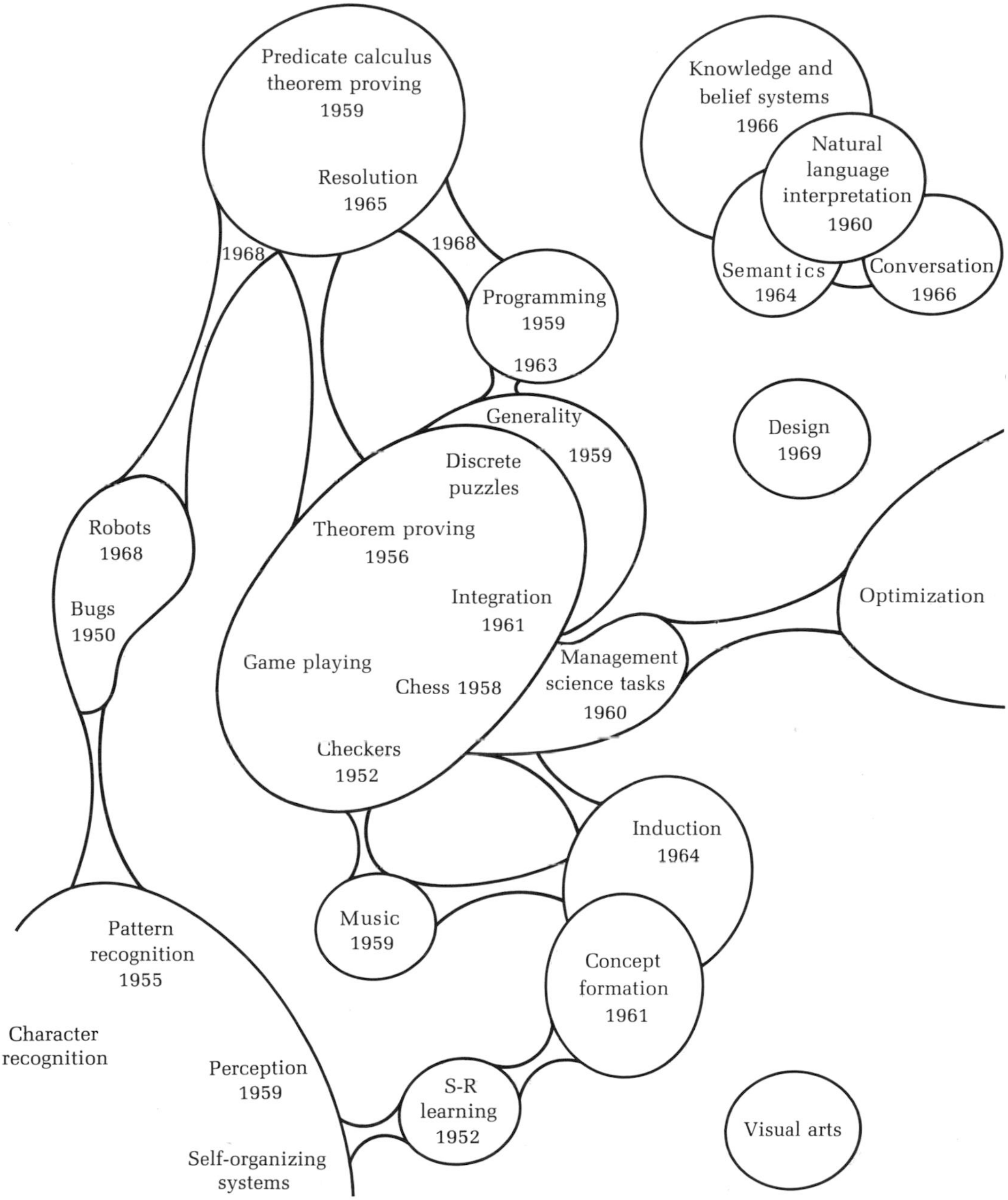

Figure 1.1 Geography of Artificial Intelligence.

The geography is not exactly one of intellectual functions, but rather of tasks that appear to embody certain intellectual functions, though exactly what functions are included is not always easily stated. (More often it is possible to state that certain functions are not embodied.) This shift from function to task is not simply one of convenience. When a program, say, is playing chess it is clear what it is doing, but it is less clear whether it is learning, inducting, or deciding. To determine if it is doing any of the latter we must agree on a more precise meaning of these terms than exists. Thus, ultimately, functions are problematical and only the structure of tasks comes through as the stable ground on which to describe what it is that mechanism has done.

I should be explicit about the meaning of the term mechanism for me (and for the field of computer science, I might add). A mechanism is any determinant physical process. An abstract process constitutes a mechanism if, in principle, there are ways to realize it by a physical process. Thus, any program for a digital computer constitutes a mechanism. Similarly, a rule for which we can build a physical device that can realize its application is a mechanism (or represents one, if we want to be fussy). This idea can be formalized in the notion of effective procedure, Turing Machine, Markov Algorithm, Post Production System. Or we can start with the formal systems as the primitive (ideal) notion of mechanism, and work back toward physical processes. But it all comes to the same thing. Extension of usage to stochastic, statistical, or probabalistic mechanism is straightforward, going from the abstract notions of probability to physical processes that obey these formal models.

A tour of the entire geography would be an exhausting enterprise. [General access to the domains can be found in two recent books (Nilsson, 1971; Slagle 1971).] Instead let us sample briefly four areas. One area includes programming in which a programming language is assumed. Input and output specifications are given and the task is to produce a program. The output, then, is a program in a well-defined programming language, and the input must be some specification of what is wanted. In the example of PROW (Waldinger and Lee, 1969) the programs are in LISP and the specification takes the form of writing an expression in the first order predicate calculus of the form.

$$(x_1)(x_2) \ \dots \ (x_n)(\exists y_1) \ \dots \ (\exists y_m) \ P(x_1, \ \dots \ x_n, y_1 \ \dots \ y_m),$$

which is to be interpreted as "I want a program that will compute the y's as output for any x's as inputs where the y's should satisfy the predicate P for the given inputs." The problem-solving program attempts to solve this problem by first posing it as a theorem-proving problem—i.e., to prove the above theorem—which must be proved constructively, with certain constraints on the proof. From this proof, if found, a program can be extracted, thus satisfying the original task.

There is clearly an intellectual task to be performed here. It is not quite the whole task as it would normally be set to a human programmer. The programmer would start from a more informal representation, such as natural language. But the transformation from whatever representation might be given initially to the one that is the input for the example, does not constitute even the major part of the intellectual demands of the task. The programming still remains to be done. Green's work (1969), which is very similar to Waldinger and Lee's, is incorporated in a system with a natural-language front end (Coles, 1969), thus in fact performing this transformation.

The program of Waldinger and Lee provides a single mechanism (the theorem prover) with which to accomplish this task. This mechanism is not necessary for the task of programming. Indeed, the novelty of Waldinger and Lee's program stems from the reduction of one class of tasks (programming) to another (theorem proving), where previous experience with the initial task did not suggest such a reformulation. The demonstration of the sufficiency of a mechanism for a task, rather than the necessity, is characteristic of empirical work in artificial intelligence.

The task is not wholly reduced to theorem proving, even with the elimination of the initial translation. There remains the extraction of the program from the proof. At first glance this seems a problem, but it turns out that an algorithm can be written that always does this job, and without excessive cost. Thus, the intellectual task resides for the most part in the task of proving the theorem.

The second area comprises the answering of a question about a belief held by the program. To be more operational, a programmed computer is to be faced with questions such as "Is an X a Y?" and is to answer not only with "yes" or "no," but with the grounds for its belief. Several existing programs fit within the task paradigm just expressed. To pick one, Colby's (1969) program at answering-time has a network of information about the domain under consideration, including facts such as "aggressive children are independent," and rules such as "if a child is aggressive, he is spanked by his parents." Associated with these symbolic structures are some numerically defined notions of consistency and credibility. The network has been assimilated into the machine during earlier interactions with the external world that provided the machine both with data and with interrogations that led the program to make inferences from its network and to augment the network accordingly. In addition, the program itself made a number of interrogations of its environment (of an agent who was interacting with it) to gain more information, in consequence further modifying its network.

Again, there is clearly an intellectual task here, which can be reasonably stated to be constructing a belief system and answering questions about that belief system.

The third area is that of general problem solving. A general problem solving program is to solve any problem that can be expressed in a specialized formal language with some pretensions to generality. There are several programs that accept a task of this kind, a well-known one being GPS (Ernst and Newell, 1969), which accepts problems that can be posed in terms of objects and of operators that transform those objects, and attempts to solve them by means-ends analysis. Let us, however, look at a more recent example, REF-ARF, constructed by Fikes (1969). Its language (called REF) is in the form of an algebraic-procedure-oriented programming language, augmented by two devices that turn it into a problem-statement language. First, it accepts functions of the form SELECT(1,N) which assert only that one of the integers between 1 and N inclusive is to be selected; second, it accepts functions of the form CONDITION(...) which implies that the expression written inside the parentheses must be made true. A problem expressed by a program written in this language is expressed as finding values of the variables that make the program terminate (with all conditions satisfied). A poser of problems to REF-ARF must translate his problem into these terms; if he can, then the system can work on the problem. Whether it can solve it depends, naturally, on many things. For example, Box 1.1 shows a cryptarithmetic puzzle problem in English; Box 1.2 shows it written in REF; and Box 1.3 shows the solution, as printed out by ARF (the problem solver) after being run on an IBM 360/67. The example shows not only the role of constraints, but also use of the flow logic of the program to encode problem information, since the REF program tests for a solution by going through the addition in the standard way from right to left, maintaining a carry.

There is a clear bid for generality in a program such as REF-ARF. It comes on two levels: what range of problems can be given by the language REF, and what class of expressible problems can be solved in reasonable time? Internally, the ARF program operates as a search program in much the same way as other programs for game playing and theorem proving (what is currently called heuristic search). However, the nodes of the search are constraint-satisfaction problems, rather than simply game positions or theorems. Thus ARF has really two collections of problem-solving processes, those that guide the heuristic search and those that attempt to solve a particular problem at a particular node. The speed with which ARF solves the problem in Figure 3 is due to the relatively good constraint-satisfaction techniques. There are minor limitations to the generality of the languages, e.g., multiplication is not permitted. But there are also major ones, e.g., the variables are all integers, so that data structures such as lists with constructive operations (insertion and deletion) are not permitted.

The fourth area is the coordination of hand-eye systems. A typical task (see Feldman et al., 1971) is to construct a stack from blocks that are initially scattered around. The feature that sets this problem apart is that the blocks are real — three dimensional, massy, spread on a real table, and so on — and that the computer has both a visual receptor (a TV camera) and a physical effector (a claw). Thus its problem is one of

---

Box 1.1 Cryptarithmetic Puzzle.

```
        C R O S S
      + R O A D S

        D A N G E R
```

Each letter represents a digit, i.e., 0, 1, ..., 9. Each letter is a distinct digit, so that no two letters may be assigned the same digit. What digits should be assigned to the letters such that when the letters are replaced by their corresponding digits, the sum is satisfied?

Box 1.2   REF-ARF Formulation of Cryptarithmetic Puzzle. [From Fikes (200).]

```
BEGIN;
   SET VECTOR A1 TO X,C,R,O,S,S;
   SET VECTOR A2 TO X,R,O,A,D,S;
   SET VECTOR SUM TO D,A,N,G,E,R;
   SET VECTOR L TO C,R,O,S,A,D,N,G,E;
   FOR I → 9 DOTO L1;
L1:SET <I[<I>]> TO SELECT(0,9);
   CONDITION EXCl(<C>,<R>,<O>,<S>,<A>,<D>,<N>,<G>,<E>;
   CONDITION ~ (<C>=0) ∧ ~ (<R>=C) ∧ ~ (<D>=0);
   SET <CARRY> TO 0;
   FOR J → 5 DOTO L2;
   SET <I> TO 7+-<J>;
   IF <A1[<I>]>+<A2[<I>]>+<CARRY><10 THEN L3;
   CONDITION <A1[<I>]>+<A2[<I>]>+<CARRY>=10+<SUM[<I>]>;
   SET <CARRY> TO 1;
   GOTO L2;
L3:CONDITION <A1[<I>I>+<A2[<I>]>+<CARRY>=<SUM[<I>]>;
   SET <CARRY> TO 0;
L2:;
   CONDITION <D>=<CARRY>;
END;
```

perception and consequent coordination of its perceptual with its effectual powers. It does have an internal representation of the task that is formal—i.e., symbolic and discrete. But this representation is constructed by the system itself in the course of attempting to solve the problem, so that errors arise from inadequacies that creep into such an internal representation.

The description of these four areas gives some substance to the kind of territory that has been and is being explored under the rubric of artificial intelligence. The development of the field over the last twenty years fits rather well the view of artificial intelligence as exploration—of sequential development of one domain after another. However, there has been parallel development as well, most notably in pattern recognition, which has received as much attention continuously over the years as all the rest of the work put together, and in theorem proving in the predicate calculus. Separate groups of people have worked on each. Pattern recognition has always been set apart, with its use of continuous mathematics, its inspiration from physiology and biology, and its partial independence of the digital computer. Likewise, theorem proving in the predicate calculus has had an independent appeal for logicians and mathematicians concerned with developing mechanical mathematics, to use Hao Wang's term (Wang, 1960).

**Box 1.3   REF-ARF Solution to Cryptarithmetic
Puzzle. [From Fikes (201).]**

```
SOLUTION FOUND AS FOLLOWS:

   CONTEXT 300205
      DATA STRUCTURE
         J
               <J>: 6
         CARRY
               <CARRY>: 1
         E
               <E>: 4
         G
               <G>: 7
         N
               <N>: 8
         D
               <D>: 1
         A
               <A>: 5
         S
               <S>: 3
         O
               <O>: 2
         R
               <R>: 6
         C
               <C>: 9
         I
               <I>: 2
         L
               VECTOR: C,R,O,S,A,D,N,G,E
         SUM
               VECTOR: D,A,N,G,E,R
         A2
               VECTOR: X,R,O,A,D,S
         A1
               VECTOR: X,C,R,O,S,S
```

In presenting this view, I have, deliberately, refrained from trying to make sense out of the plethora of tasks. In Figure 1.1 I have drawn them in juxtaposition only where there seemed obvious kinship. Thus, induction and concept formation are adjacent, as are the various attempts to make contact with natural language, which are shown in the upper right hand corner.

It is not hard to think of intellectually demanding tasks that are not represented. Pick any aspect of human life—such as the theater—and simply take a tour: write a play, create a stage design and scenery, direct a play, be a stage manager (obtaining all the things that are needed and being sure they are around and in appropriate condition), improvise a new scene, judge how a joke will go over with an audience, and so on. Many of these tasks have aspects other than the purely intellectual, but each could form the kernel of a purified task in which we could ask after the intellectual mechanisms that perform it. And for each, there are dimensions of quality; it is one thing to do the task at all, another to do it passably, and still a third to do it superbly.

There are, of course, ways to view artificial intelligence that are not so pretheoretical—that do not just see the field as one damn task after another. To one of these views we now turn.

View two: the science of weak methods

In our description so far, a program is an unanalyzable lump of code, created to do a task of interest. (The task, of course, might have its own aspects of generality, as in REF-ARF.) Thus: one task, one program—the programs that have been mentioned are not able to perform tasks other than their own. They remain distinct entities.

But if there were a small number of ideas behind the plethora of individual programs, then a picture in terms of those ideas might show a good deal more coherence and pattern. Such indeed appears to be the case. It appears, though no conclusive demonstration is yet at hand, that these ideas can be cast in the form of *methods*. Artificial intelligence can therefore be viewed as a field devoted to the discovery and collection of a set of methods. It thus bears kinship to fields such as numerical analysis, mathematical programming, and possibly even chemical engineering. The nature of artificial intelligence, in this view, derives from the general nature of its methods. But before we attempt a general characterization, we should look at the methods in some detail.

By a method, of course, one means a recipe or procedure for accomplishing a class of tasks. Although the exact term that is used is not important, it is important that three components of a method be distinguished:

The problem statement: a statement in some language that describes the situation to which the method applies, and the problem to which it may provide a solution.

The procedure: a program (i.e., a conditional sequence of actions) based on some repertoire of primitive operations.

The justification: the reasons for believing that if the conditions of the problem statement are satisfied, then the procedure may result in a solution.

Box 1.4 and Box 1.5 show two simple examples of methods. One is the standard formula for the solution of a quadratic equation. Here we assume that the user of the method can transform the expression given into a step by step procedure. If the user cannot take square roots, then this method is not for him, since it assumes this operation in the basic repertoire. Likewise, if a task cannot be characterized in the problem statement, then again this method is simply not applicable. In the case of the quadratic, complete justification can be given simply by substituting the formulas for roots into the equation. This would not have been quite so trivial if the procedure had been given, say, in a machine code, though there still would have been no fundamental difficulty.

The second method is taken from a book on furniture repair. There is considerable informality about both the problem statement and the procedure, but the basic operation — carrying the leaf outdoors — is presumably known to the reader. Considerable care is taken with the description of tests and sensitivity. Only a little justification is given for the procedure. It is partly scientific, partly empirical. More might have been said, of course, but it is clear that no formal justification could have been provided.

To show that the work in artificial intelligence has the character of the discovery and development of a set of methods requires a number of things:

1. Exhibit a set of methods — namely, the methods of artificial intelligence developed to date.

2. Show that these are methods: give problem statements, procedures, and justifications.

3. Show how actual artificial intelligence programs can be written in terms of these methods.

4. Establish that, in some sense, the part of the total program represented by the method provides a substantial fraction (the more the better) of the total power of the program.

5. Show that the same methods are used in more than one program, thus reducing the variety of independent programs in the field.

6. Show that the methods cover a substantial part of the total territory of artificial intelligence.

Such an endeavor is not to be completed in a paper such as this. In another place and in a different connection I have argued for the view of artificial intelligence as the science of weak methods, providing somewhat more detail than I can here

---

Box 1.4   Method for Solving Quadratic Equation.

```
Given information:    a, b, c real numbers, x real variable

Problem statement:    Find x such that ax² + bx + c = 0

Procedure:            Compute x = -b/2a ± (1/2a) √b² - 4ac

Justification:        Substitute formula for x in ax² + bx + c and show
                      by algebraic manipulation that 0 results.
```

Box 1.5   Method for Straightening Warped Table Leaves.

<u>Leaf warped</u>. Here's the place to go into a general discussion of warps—because table leaves are the commonest victims. To begin with, warp is caused by moisture which gets into one side of a board without being able to get into the other because of some kind of waterproof finish. If this suggests to you that the way to prevent warping is to finish the undersides of tables and bureau tops, you are absolutely right. In fact, in a good custom-finishing or refinishing job, this is always done.

Returning to the situation of a leaf that's already warped, the cure is to wet the dried-out side. This is always the concave (hollow) side. Happily, any wood that will warp in the first place will unwarp when this is done—regardless of the age of the piece or the duration of the warp.

The easiest method to get moisture content back into the hollow side of a warped board is illustrated. You put the hollow or concave side down on the grass, and let the sun heat the other side. This may take anywhere from four hours to four long sunny days. When the board looks straight, take it into the house, and let it stand around in an even-temperatured room for a few days. Sometimes a little of the warp returns after a few days. If this happens, take it out on the grass again for further therapy. In fact, this time you can leave it until the side facing the sun begins to get a little concave. It is not a job to fuss or worry about, because wood is incredibly pliable. You can make a board warp first one way and then the other over and over without hurting the wood.

THE EASY WAY TO REMOVE WARPS

Sun

Concave side down

Rock

Wet the grass

Takes only a few hours on a hot, sunny day. If one end or corner is warped more than the other, weight it down with a heavy rock.

(Newell, 1969). But even so, the case is not in fact sustainable yet at an appropriate technical level. In any event, my purpose here is depiction of the view, not demonstration of it. Thus, I shall simply summarize and illustrate most of the points above.

Table 1.1 provides a starting list for the methods of artificial intelligence. The descriptions are brief, but hopefully their gist can be gleaned. More detail can be found in Newell (1969) and a table of characteristics for a number of heuristic search programs appears in Newell (1965). The ubiquity of some of these methods, such as Hill Climbing or Heuristic Search, has made them widely recognized. Others, such as Hypothesize and Match, are less well known.

GENERATE AND TEST

To show the main features of these methods let us examine the simplest of them all: Generate and Test. Box 1.6 provides an expanded account of that method. First there is a problem statement containing four variables. Note that two of these, G and T, range over processes. That is, to use this method you must have certain subprocesses and the method tells how to organize them to reach a certain end, namely, that given in the problem statement. What is to be found is defined in terms of X and P, which are not processes. Thus, some connection must be made between the processes G and T, which can be executed within some executive structure, and X and P. This is provided in the first instance by the definitions of G and T, which relate these processes to what to do, and then by specific statements asserting that G must generate the set S, and that T must test the predicate P.

The procedure is simply given: the output of the generator must become the input to the test; if the test is successful, the solution exit is taken; if not, then the generator must produce another element; if the generator ever stops then the fail exit is taken.

The justification is likewise simple and is only sketched here. To make it rigorous requires formalizing the concept of process, a matter which has and can be done without difficulty. To be proved are two propositions: that if we exit at the point marked *solution,* then we indeed have a solution; and that if we exit at *fail* then there is no solution to the problem. These propositions justify to some degree the use of the method. They do not provide all the justification that one might want — for example, the expected effort to obtain a solution, or a measure over time of the chances of obtaining it. Such features are not determined by the formulation given, since they require more information about the nature of G and T. For instance, if we know that the set is finite, then we know that eventually the procedure must terminate and that the method is a decision procedure for the problem.* Actually, we want finiteness relative to the computing resources available, since "finite but unreachable" is almost as unsatisfying as "not finite."

The methods of Table 1.1 can be given expanded problem statements and procedures in the style of Box 1.6, and indeed the whole might be cast in a formal system. They all involve specifying some processes in addition to the stated variables.

---

*This assumes isolation of the method from external influences, such as being terminated. In a larger context such possibilities complicate the details of proof.

The justifications require somewhat more attention, and for two reasons. First, unlike the quadratic equation example, the artificial-intelligence methods are expressed in a procedural language, and we know only a little about how to establish their validity. This is revealed, for example, in the view that a program written to do a job must be debugged rather than proved to be correct — i.e., be subjected to experimental test, with subsequent discovery and removal of the difficulties. Since a program is a formal symbolic object there is no reason why we should not treat it

Table 1.1   Descriptions of Methods of Artificial Intelligence.

Problem statement	Procedure
Generate and Test	
Given: a set X with generator; a property P with test R.	Generate the elements of X with G.
	Test each for P with R.
Find x in X such that P(x).	If no more elements of X (G —), fail.
Heuristic Search (simple version)	
Given: a set X with operators Q $(q:X \longrightarrow X)$; a property P with test T.	Maintain a current element, x, (initially x_0).
Find a sequence of operators that transform an initial element x_0 into an element x such that P(x).	Select an operator from Q and apply it to x (if can't, select another).
	Test new element for P with T, if + new element is solution.
	Put new element on "try list."
	Select new current element from try list.
Hill Climbing (simple version)	
Given: a set X with operators Q; an ordering on X with compare process C; X is unimodal.	Maintain a current element, x (select an initial x).
Find the highest element in X.	Select an operator from Q and apply it to x (if can't, select another).
	Compare new element with current element by C.
	If higher, take new element as current one.
	If not higher, discard and select another operator.
	If no untried operators, current element is solution.

Table 1.1 *(Continued)*

Problem statement	Procedure
Match (simple version)	
Given: a set X consisting of parts; a set of forms on X with operators Q (q:F → F ∪ X); a compare C between parts which produces differences (in a set D), such that if a difference holds between two parts then at most one operator that can "remove" it exists. Find if a given form can be transformed into a given element of X.	Generate corresponding parts of the element and the form. Compare parts using C. If no difference, then continue. If difference, then select operator that removes difference. If not exist, then fail. Apply operator, if succeed continue, else fail.
Hypothesize and Match	
Given: a set of hypotheses H, whose elements are functions from a domain D to a range R (h:D → R); a set of forms F on H; a set of exemplars E of the function (d → r). Find a hypothesis that fits all the exemplars in E.	Generate the forms from simple to complex. For a given form, generate the exemplars. For each exemplar apply the form to its domain producing an expected element of the range, r′ (which can be a form). Match r′ to the range element of the exemplar, with operators that will instantiate r′ (and through it the form). If match fails then the form fails; get the next. If form succeeds for all exemplars, then (as instantiated) it is the solution.

mathematically. In essence we have done so with Generate and Test, but its simplicity conceals the difficulties. There has been substantial recent work on how to associate with programs the appropriate descriptive statements (usually propositions in a logical calculus) of what they should do, so that it can be proved whether they do it. It is known, for example, that we can formalize programming in such a way that to each program there corresponds a predicate in first-order logic such that the program terminates and terminates correctly if and only if this predicate is true (see Floyd, 1967 and Manna and Vuillemin, 1972). The example of Waldinger, discussed earlier, reflects this stream of work (see also Manna, 1969).

The second concern is over what is to be justified. Most programs in artificial intelligence are not complete algorithms for the tasks they purport to solve (which

Box 1.6 Generate and Test Method

```
Given information:
  X is a set.
  G is a generator for the set X.
  P is a predicate defined on X.
  T is a test for P.
  T is a test process if:
    Output(+) implies that output is input and P(input).
    Output(−) implies that not P(input).
  G is a generator if:
    Output(+) implies that output is in X.
    Output(−) implies that all elements have been generated; i.e.,
             occurred on some occasion as output(+).
    Input(start) initiates action to produce next output.

Problem statement:
  Find x such that x is in X and P(x).

Procedure:
```

```
Justification:
  To be shown: (1) Exit at solution implies problem statement
                   satisfied.
               (2) Exit at fail implies no x such that x in X and
                   P(x).
  1.  Exit at solution with x implies x = T−output(+),
      implies P(x) and x = T−input,
      implies x = G−output(+),
      implies x in X,
      implies (1).
  2.  Exit at fail implies never T(x) for x = T−input;
      exit at fail implies all in X generated by G as G−input(+),
      implies all x in X input to %,
      implies for no x in X P(x),
      implies (2).
```

is one reason I prefer to call them by another name, "method"). Even when they can be made into algorithms by simple expedients, as illustrated by Generate and Test, many of them are not practical algorithms. The demonstrations desired relate to such things as expected effort, chances of becoming trapped with no further chance of finding a solution, and so on. Even more, we want such evaluations as a function of the task environment, which in itself implies the introduction of appropriate concepts to describe the environment.

There has been little substantial theory of this kind produced for the methods of artificial intelligence. The two conspicuous counter-examples to this statement are attempts to prove completeness of numerous variations of search techniques in predicate calculus theorem proving (see Robinson, 1967), and the theory of perceptrons, as recently expanded by Minsky and Papert (1969). In the former, we wish to ascertain whether in limiting search in a particular way we have eliminated any possibility (for some problems) of finding the proof. In general, this says nothing about the relative shifts of expected efforts to find proofs. However, the motivation for introducing these new methods is usually to remove some glaring inefficiency observed in existing search methods. Thus, the main justifications for the method rest on the plausibility of removing the inefficiency and on empirical demonstration on a small collection of tasks.

Work on perceptrons has involved two types of results. One relates to finding a perceptron that will perform a specified task by various elementary forms of adaptive modification, providing a possible perceptron exists (the Perceptron Convergence Theorem). The other specifies various subclasses of perceptrons and provides proofs that there exist members of these subclasses that can do various recognition tasks (or that none can). A typical result is that no order-limited or diameter-limited perceptron (two ways of limiting a perceptron to "local" measurements on its retina) can discriminate the class of connected figures from the nonconnected ones.

The above discussion makes plausible the notion of a collection of methods for artificial intelligence only with respect to the first two and the last points of the list on page 10: exhibiting a set of methods with their problem statements, procedures, and justification, and showing that they cover at least a portion of the total artificial intelligence field. Coverage has been indicated only by the references in Table 1.1. There are several areas that are missing, notably the robot area and that of large semantic nets and belief systems.

For the other points in the list, which deal with the description of an actual program in terms of methods and the use of the same method in several programs, we will consider a single illustration.

HYPOTHESIZE AND MATCH

Inductive tasks have always been a prominent part of the artificial-intelligence landscape. The reasons for this seem to be twofold. For one, we have inherited a classic distinction between deduction and induction, so that the search for intelligent action should clearly look to induction. Second, American psychology has largely identified the central problem of conceptual behavior with the acquisition or formation of concepts—which in practice has turned out to mean the induction of concepts from a set of presented exemplars. This tendency, shaped strongly by Bruner, Goodnow, and Austin's *Study of Thinking* (1956), derives fundamentally from the emphasis on learning that has characterized American psychology since the rise of behaviorism.

At issue here are the methods used in the separate programs for doing these tasks. The claim is that there are only a few methods (in accordance with point 5 on page 10) and that these account for a substantial part of the total problem-solving power of the programs (point 4).

Let us consider the three tasks described in Box 1.7: a standard concept-formation task, a sequence-extrapolation task, and an analogy task. All of these tasks have something in common: exemplars are presented and the goal is to form an induction, which can be made evident in the creation, selection, or use of other exemplars. The exemplars themselves are the sole information from which the final constructions (or selections) are to be made, which justifies labeling the tasks inductive. They also have in common that the task environments are encodable into discrete symbolic structures (admitting analytic geometry for the analogy task).

For each task we have considered one program: Johnson's (1964) for the concept formation, Simon and Kotovsky's (1963) for the sequence extrapolation, and Evans (1964) for the geometric analogies. It appears that the single method we have called Hypothesize and Match contains the essential problem-solving power of all of them. They are not the only programs that do the above tasks. Many of the others also use essentially the same method, though a few proceed quite differently (see Hunt et al., 1966).

The Hypothesize and Match method is described briefly in Table 1.1 and in more detail in Box 1.8. It is a subspecies of Hypothesize and Test, with a special feature that provides its power. In the general case we generate one hypothesis after another and test whether each works—i.e., apply Generate and Test to a set of hypotheses. If the space of hypotheses is very large—as it will be in most cases of interest—then something additional must be added or no problems will be solved. The special feature of Hypothesize and Match is that it generates, not particular hypotheses, but representations of classes of hypotheses, such that the exemplars can directly (i.e., without further generation) determine if a class contains an hypothesis that fits all the exemplars.

To make this clear, let us go through Box 1.8 in detail, using the sequence-extrapolation task to provide particulars. The method shown in Box 1.8 is not quite the whole of the program, but is merely the central part of it and must be adapted to each particular task. The problem solved by the method is to find a mapping (h) from a domain (D) to a range (R) given that it has a sequence of exemplars—i.e., particular pairs of elements (d, r) from D and R that are known to satisfy h(d) = r.

In standard concept-formation tasks the natural identification is that D stands for the presented exemplars and R for the concept name [e.g., (four legs, furry, and says bow-wow) $\rightarrow$ "dog"] and this is how the method is used by Johnson's programs. For

---

Box 1.7 Three Induction Tasks.

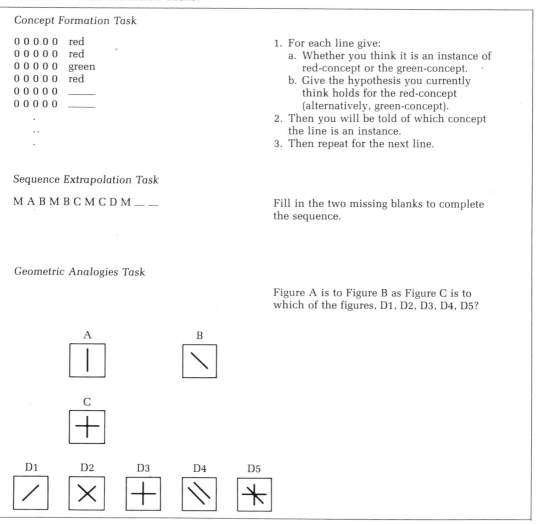

Concept Formation Task

0 0 0 0 0	red
0 0 0 0 0	red
0 0 0 0 0	green
0 0 0 0 0	red
0 0 0 0 0	____
0 0 0 0 0	____

1. For each line give:
   a. Whether you think it is an instance of red-concept or the green-concept. ·
   b. Give the hypothesis you currently think holds for the red-concept (alternatively, green-concept).
2. Then you will be told of which concept the line is an instance.
3. Then repeat for the next line.

Sequence Extrapolation Task

M A B M B C M C D M __ __

Fill in the two missing blanks to complete the sequence.

Geometric Analogies Task

Figure A is to Figure B as Figure C is to which of the figures, D1, D2, D3, D4, D5?

the sequence task, the appropriate identification is to take D as the set of initial subsequences and R as the set of elements. That is, the presented sequence MABMB-CMCDM provides the following exemplars: → M, M → A, MA → B, MAB → M, ... Because this is not the only way the task as presented could be analyzed, one part of the problem solving is to select or construct the set of exemplars, given the display and the instructions.

The critical issue in the use of the method is the selection of the space of hypothesis, i.e., the class of mappings. Besides the technical requirements placed on the representation of this space by the method, which we will come to, success clearly

Box 1.8 Hypothesize and Match Method.

```
Given information:
  A domain D={d}
  A range R={r}
  A space of hypotheses H = {h | h:D → R}
  A space of forms F = {f | f is a form on H}
  A set of exemplars E = {e | e = d → r}

Problem statement:
  Find a hypothesis that fits all of E
  Find h such that for all e in E h(dₑ) = rₑ (alternative statement)

Procedure:
```

depends on picking a class of mappings that is not so large as to be unmanageable, but large enough to have a good chance of containing an answer to the problem.* The critical inductive leap is made at this point. Like a magician's trick, once this is done at the very start, the game is really over. All the rest is show — which is to be translated as all the rest consists of "noninductive" processes of the sort that are used by theorem provers, chess players, etc.

It is not just the class of mappings itself, but its representations, which is at issue. For there are many different ways to represent the same totality of mappings. Johnson's program, for example, admits all Boolean functions on D (which is a vector of Boolean values). These functions could be obtained by all logical expressions formed with *and, or* and *not* (say); instead the program admits concepts such as *symmetric* and *majority*. This has strong effects on what concepts will be generated early in

---

*Many trick induction problems are based on an obscure space. The classic example in letter sequences is OTTFFSSE__, which is derived from the first letters of the digits, and so has N for the next element.

problem solving, for the Hypothesize and Match method invariably considers first the simplest mappings, as defined by the representation.

The class of mappings for the sequence extrapolation is defined by a grammar, as given in BNF (Backus Normal Form) in Box 1.9. Thus a typical expression, such as

$$h: x \leftarrow A/alph \ [M \ x \ nx \ x]$$

can be read as: there is one pointer variable on the alphabet, alph (i.e., A, B, ... , Z), to be initialized to A; then the sequence can be generated by a cyclic procedure, in which, first, M is printed, then x is printed (A), then x is advanced to the next letter in the alphabet, then x is printed again (B), then the cycle repeats (hence with M, B, C, then M, C, D and so on). Thus, the information that is extracted about the domain (sequence-so-far) consists of a number of pointers into a number of alphabets. The sequence is assumed to be periodic, with n elements in a cycle. Each element consists of a sequence of actions, followed by the printing of some pointer. The actions given are just two: move a pointer to next (n), and set a pointer to be where another is (x $\leftarrow$ y). Others might be added.

To each expression in the language there is a particular sequence; hence one can ask for an expression that agrees with the given set of exemplars. There are clearly an unbounded set of possibilities, both of expressions and of the mappings they designate. The key feature of the method, as indicated in Box 1.8, is to generate not particular mappings, but representations of *classes* of mappings. In this case the class of all mappings with a given period is produced by introducing syntactic variables (symbolized by Greek letters) for the various parts of the expression. Thus, the form [$\alpha \ \beta$] represents all mappings of period two.

The important feature of this representation is that the exemplars can be used to determine directly a mapping that works (if any exists). This happens in two stages. The first is that the form can be used to produce some exemplars. These exemplars will contain syntactic variables—i.e., they are forms too. Second, these exemplar-forms can be matched to the exemplars that are given as data. The result of a match is the detection of a difference between the exemplar-form and the exemplar (if there is no difference, then the mapping produces the exemplar and all is well). If these differences cannot be eliminated, no hypothesis exists with the given period that produces the given set of exemplars. If they can be, the elimination of a difference may determine some of the variable aspects of the exemplar form, and through this, some of the variable aspects of the mapping. Thus, gradually, all of the degrees of freedom in the mapping become fixed until a specific mapping emerges.

The elimination of differences can be represented by a table in which each difference between exemplar form and exemplar is provided with an operator that modifies or further specifies the form (and through it the mapping). This table of connections between differences and operators is also shown in Box 1.9. It has an important property upon which rests the justification for calling the procedure a *match*: If a difference of type d is found, then, if any successful instantiation of the

Box 1.9 Hypothesis Space and Difference Table for Sequence Extrapolation Task.

```
Notation: BNF plus x-seq := x|x xseq
    function := initialization-seq cycle
                note: each pointer in cycle has an initialization
    cycle    := [element-seq]
    element  := pointer | action element
    action   := n pointer | pointer ← pointer
                nx move the pointer x to the next in its alphabet.
                x ← y move x to point to what y points at.
    pointer  := x|y|z
    alphabet := alph | balph | ....
                each alphabet is a particular sequence of distinct
                characters.
    character:= .....
    initialization := pointer ← character/alphabet,
```

```
Rules of interpretation:
    1.  Interpret each element in the cycle in sequence and
        then repeat.
    2.  For each element take the actions in indicated order;
        any non-assignment action on an unassigned pointer is
        null.
    3.  The right hand symbol of an element is a pointer; print
        out its current value. If unassigned, use initialization.
```

	Difference	Action
Syntactic Variable		
(call it α)	$\emptyset$	$\alpha \leftarrow$ new pointer
	nx	$\alpha \leftarrow$ nx x
Pointer Value		
(from x)	$\emptyset$	fail
	nx	if element = x then x ← nx x
		else fail
	undef	add initialization;
		x ← character

exemplar form exists, one can be found by applying the operator, $q(d)$. Thus, when faced with difference d there is only one thing to do, apply $q(d)$. The possibility that other ways of manipulating the form might have led to a solution need never be considered. In particular, the method need not have the capability of backing up to search alternative possible sequences of operators for specifying the exemplar form.

Box 1.10 shows this scheme in operation, following the flow diagram of Box 1.8. We use a simple generator of forms that starts with period 1, then period 2, and so on, which is an implementation of the "simple mappings first" principle. The trace of a given exemplar form moves from left to right across the page.* Each difference, when it occurs, terminates a run through the sequence; the action to be taken (or failure) is written on the right after the arrow, and the newly modified exemplar form (if it exists) starts a new run. Thus, looking at the first line, which comes from the mapping of period 1, the first element is the syntactic variable, α, since nothing has yet been specified. This produces a difference, with the first exemplar (M) leading to the operator, which replaces an action element with a new pointer variable (in this case x). The next run produces a difference between an undefined variable, x, and A, which leads to setting the initialization statement, x ⟵ A (though leaving

---

Box 1.10   Eye Movement Aggregates and Verbal Behavior.

$$M \ A \ B \ M \ B \ C \ M \ C \ D \ M \ \_ \ \_$$

$$[\alpha] \quad \alpha \Rightarrow \emptyset$$
$$[x] \quad x \quad \text{undef}$$
$$x \ M \ [x] \quad M \ M \Rightarrow \emptyset$$

$$[\alpha \ \beta] \quad \alpha \Rightarrow \emptyset$$
$$[x \ \beta] \quad x \quad \text{undef}$$
$$x \leftarrow M \ [x \ \beta] \quad M \ \beta \Rightarrow \emptyset$$
$$x \leftarrow M \ [x \ y] \quad M \ y \Rightarrow \text{undef}$$
$$y \leftarrow A, \ x \leftarrow M \ [x \ y] \quad M \ A \ M \Rightarrow \emptyset$$

$$[\alpha \ \beta \ \gamma] \quad \alpha \Rightarrow \emptyset$$
$$[x \ \beta \ \gamma] \quad x \Rightarrow \text{undef}$$
$$x \leftarrow M \ [x \ \beta \ \gamma] \quad M \quad \Rightarrow \emptyset$$
$$x \leftarrow M \ [x \ Y \ \gamma] \quad M \ y \Rightarrow \text{undef}$$
$$y \leftarrow A, \ x \leftarrow M \ [x \ y \ \gamma] \quad M \ A \ \gamma \Rightarrow ny$$
$$y \leftarrow A, \ x \leftarrow M \ [x \ y \ ny \ y] \quad M \ A \ B \ M \ B \ C \ M \ C \ D \ M \ D \ E$$

---

*A run across the page re-encodes the separate exemplars into the continuous predicting of the next element in the sequence. In fact the flow diagram in Box 1.8 has to be modified to work from a generator of next-elements, constructing the total next exemplar by retaining the prior sequence and taking the new element as the range element. Since the total information extracted from the domain element is the state of the pointers, there is no need to create any direct representation of the next element of D—all the work has already been done. The requirement for adaptation of the method to these peculiarities of the sequence extrapolation task should not be ignored in evaluating whether a given method covers a particular problem-solving program, but the issue is on a par with that of inefficient compiling. That is, we could proceed to create each exemplar *de novo* and ship it to the Apply process—i.e., use the method of Box 1.8 unadapted. We would then find (to our chagrin as programmers) that a certain number of computations were being repeated.

the alphabet still undefined). Finally, the third run through leads to a difference for which there is no corrective operator, so the form is discarded and the next form, [α, β], is generated.

It can be seen from Box 1.10 that the correct solution is obtained when a form of the correct period (3) is finally generated. The program is faithful to the operation of the Simon-Kotovsky program, except that their program uses an initial investigation to estimate the period of the exemplar form and thus would produce only the period-3 trace. Their program, of course, is not organized in quite the same way as the scheme here. Our recasting of artificial intelligence programs in a limited number of methods is a rational reconstruction.

We will not go through the other two programs here, but they have two essential features that should be mentioned. First, they deal with the induction problem by having a large space of hypotheses—essentially all those expressible in a specialized language. In both programs this can be done in BNF, as in the Simon-Kotovsky program. Second, they factor their exploration of the hypothesis space into two parts: the generation of subclasses of hypotheses by means of forms, and the selection of the particular hypothesis within the possibilities of each form by matching. The generation aspect usually has few good heuristics associated with it, and may involve the combinatorial generation of all possibilities.

In Johnson's program a simple hypothesis would be "red: column 1 = black." When generated as a form, the type of concept (either red or green) and the column are specified, but the value is left variable: "red: column 1 = α." This is then matched to the exemplars. Johnson's program does have two other methods. The generation of the form (the hypothesis class) is done by a probabilistic mechanism (making random decisions among the various grammatical choices). This mechanism is subject to stochastic learning, which is essentially Hill Climbing on past frequency of success. The other, which might be called the Ptolemaic method, patches up hypotheses that have become inadequate because of the introduction of new exemplars. It augments them with disjunctions or conjunctions that either broaden or narrow the hypothesis to deal with the offending exemplar. Needless to say, this method leads to complex and esoteric hypotheses.

In Evans's program the form of the task dictates a more substantial adaptation of the basic method than in the other two. Its logic is:

Find a mapping T that fits A $\longrightarrow$ B.
Find mappings T_i that fit C $\longrightarrow$ D_i, for each i = 1,2,3,4,5.
Abstract (T, T_i) to get mappings T_i' consistent with T.
Select the most concrete of the T_i'.

Other logics are possible; the one above avoids comparing complex objects (the figures) or mappings. Some of the intelligence of the program resides in this logic, but a major part remains in the six inductions performed to find the mappings. The aspect of the mappings that permits matching (hence the application of Hypothesize and Match method) is the determination whether one object (e.g., a triangle) can be transformed into another object (e.g., a square) by means of scale change, rotation, and reflection. Once these possibilities are known for all objects in two figures (e g., in A and in B), the rest of the mapping can be put together by Generate and Test.

WEAK METHODS

We have considered in some detail, though hardly exhaustively, the notion that artificial intelligence can be viewed as the discovery of a set of particular methods, so that its products over the long haul would be similar to those of, say, numerical analysis: a number of specific methods with detailed analyses of each—the domains of its usefulness, the justification for its actions, and so on. In the initial statement of this second view we referred to it as "the science of weak methods." We need now to explain that.

A method has two sides. On the one hand, it demands certain information about any task to which it is to be applied. This shows up in the "givens" of the problem statement. These demands for information may be stringent or liberal. On the other hand, the method delivers certain things in the way of results—or at least chances of results—for various expenditures of effort. Again, it may deliver a lot or a little, and it may do so with certainty or with plausibility, and cheaply or dearly. In general, the more information available the better the results that can be obtained. Conversely, strong results imply strong informational demands, and weak demands can yield only weak results.

If we compare the methods of artificial intelligence with those of, say, numerical analysis or mathematical programming, we are struck not only by the fact that the former give weak results, but that they also demand little information. Consider the weakest one of them all, Generate and Test. One does have to know a generator of the set and a test on elements, but nothing else. For instance, the space does not have to be numerical or to have any other special properties. When we move to Heuristic Search more is required of the statement of the problem: that new points in the space can be obtained from old points by means of operators. In effect we have specified a particular structure for a generator of elements in a space. The Heuristic Search method is simply the appropriate organization to exploit that new knowledge, namely, by keeping a memory of already generated states and returning to old elements to initiate the search in other directions. Hill Climbing adds yet another requirement: that we be able to compare the nearness of different elements to the desired element (this was not required in either Generate and Test or Heuristic Search). In consequence, the apparatus of backing up can be dispensed with in the procedure if the space is unimodal. By the time we get to the method for the quadratic equation (Box 1.4) an immense specificity is required: an equation, a single variable whose domain is the real numbers, and a polynomial of degree two. The procedure is correspondingly precise.

In summary, this view of artificial intelligence is not just that it has methods, but that these occupy a particular niche in the collection of all methods, namely, those that require very little information yet still offer some chances of obtaining results. These conditions are exactly those that prevail in problematic situations.

View three: theoretical psychology

One models man as one models all else: by proposing symbolic systems that can be identified with specific men in specific situations by means of observation and experiment. The degree of formality of such models* can vary widely, from sets of natural-language assertions that leave most issues open (e.g., Freud's model of the tripartite mind) to completely formalized models that are paragons of scientific cleanliness, even if somewhat narrow (e.g., some stochastic learning theories). The issues for all such models are the same, deriving from their general role in the development of science: scope, adequacy to their chosen data base, extendability, predictive power, communicability, simplicity, and so on.

The theoretical structure of science does not consist of a set of isolated entities called theories. Theories derive from each other and are inferred from and built to deal with bodies of data. With our firmly embedded scholarly tradition of referencing our progenitors it is usually possible to trace down these genetic relationships. But theories also bear family resemblances to each other for many other reasons. At any time and for any phenomenal domain there is a layered structure of ideas about the ingredients of a theory. If one wants to build a theory of X, then in addition to possibly modifying an existing theory of X, one knows what sorts of theoretical languages might be useful, what sorts of laws might work out successfully, what sorts of derivation techniques might work (thus shaping the ingredients to permit these to operate), and so on. All of this knowledge operates in the context of construction (i.e., discovery) of theories, not in the context of verification. Much of it represents scaffolding that is removed when the theory is complete.

There are very few extensive descriptions of this structure of knowledge, either as used for a particular theory or for a whole field. Indeed, there does not even exist a decent vocabulary with which to describe such things. We often talk about the *Zeitgeist* and, since Kuhn (1962), about *paradigms*, which are somewhat more focussed. But it is noteworthy that Zeitgeists and paradigms are never "exhibited"; rather they are designated by pointing to the theories that were distilled from them (e.g., the "paradigm of classical physics") or by making a few statements about some of their ingredients.

One aspect of this larger structure is classes of systems within which one searches for a particular theory. The best example, of course, is from physics, where the theory of differential (and to some extent integral) equations has played this role. Particle mechanics, heat flow, the vibrating string, elasticity, hydrodynamics, plastic flow, electrodynamics—all, at some stage of development, were separate theories and all used the same basic scheme: a collection of real numbers for a state and a set of differential equations to represent changes in that state.

In many fields several languages are available. In neurophysiology, for instance, one can think in terms of networks of neurons, with connectivity and neuron-neuron interaction playing important roles. Or one can think in terms of continuously varying fields (as in the EEG), with concepts of correlation and phase relations

---

*I use the terms *model* and *theory* in free variation.

playing important roles. And recently, molecular and biochemical schemes have been added (e.g., in the search for memory).

Psychology has at least six languages. S-R theory, as represented by distinct sets of stimuli and responses with varying strengths of connection and probabilities of response, is one. Stochastic-learning theories, in which the state of the organism is represented by probabilities of response with operators on those probabilities as laws, is a second. Markov models, which consider the organism to be in one of a set of discrete states with the laws being stated as a transition matrix of probabilities between states, is a third. The person as a collection of "forces," which push him one way and another, as in Lewin's life space, is a fourth. The person as an interacting community of subagents, as in the Freudian Id, Ego, and Superego, where each can be described in personalistic terms, is a fifth. Man as an information processor, which is one of interest to us here, is a sixth. And there may even be more—for example, the control system models used in human operator studies derive from none of the above, and the same is true also of signal-detection models.

An important feature of such languages, or classes of systems, is that they are not themselves theories. They are not right or wrong in the sense that they can be proved to be so by a direct empirical test. They are generators of theories, all of which have a family resemblance and all of which presumably share strengths and weakness. These languages are useful or not as the particular theories they generate are good or bad (or however one wishes to describe the quality of theories vis-a-vis their declared phenomena).

This digression into a general aspect of scientific theories lays the groundwork for the third view of artificial intelligence: that it serves as theoretical psychology if one adopts the view of man as a processor of information, represented as a system of discrete symbols. Then the language used for constructing particular theories is that which has evolved in computer programming, and the general types of systems one draws upon are those developed in artificial intelligence. (This requires broadening, as we will see.)

The domain of such theories does not cover all of the phenomena surrounding man. As we might expect, it focuses most strongly on tasks that are highly symbolic and do not require continuous motor skills or an intimate dependence on sensory systems. It deals with phenomena of substantial complexity, but not with the full complexity of human affairs.

The view of man as an information processor is now widespread in several parts of psychology. This view has both roots and sources of inspiration that extend beyond the domain of artificial intelligence as we have been describing it in this paper. Depending on how one counts, there are from three to six subdomains: problem solving, psycholinguistics, concept formation, verbal learning, immediate memory, and perception.* The last four can be grouped in various ways. In par-

---

*Parts of the science of human organizations and of microeconomics (the behavioral theory of the firm) would be included in any total accounting. The case of developmental psychology is curious, since Piaget's work, which has by now had an overwhelming impact there, is both similar to information processing (e.g., in its emphasis on operations) and quite distinct (e.g., in its complete lack of emphasis on the processing of representations).

ticular, the work on perception has grown out of an attack on immediate memory, and is thus a narrow (though important) slice of all that goes under the rubric of perception. The work on development is just beginning (Diggory, 1972).

The diversity of phenomena and source, though it introduces a certain amount of product differentiation, should not obscure the fundamental identity of the information-processing views operating in all these domains. Although we will separate the strands somewhat, it is not possible to do so thoroughly, since the scientists who work in this field read each other's literature and know each other rather well.

The view that man is an information processor means that his behavior can be seen as the result of a system consisting of memories containing discrete symbols and symbolic expressions (i.e., occurrences of symbols), and processes that manipulate these symbols. The central notion is that of the symbol, which is taken to mean essentially what it does in computer science, an entity with a certain functional property, to wit: that when a process has a token of a symbol it has access to information about what that symbol designates (encoded in symbolic expressions). The processes that can be performed on symbols are their creation (and, possibly, destruction), the obtaining of designated information, the creation of symbolic expressions, and the manipulation of these symbolic expressions by insertion, deletion, replacement, and reordering. A symbolic expression is a collection of symbol tokens connected by relations of access — e.g., the tokens S, Y, M, B, O, L connected by the relation *next*, which provides a token of the word SYMBOL.

One can attempt to formalize these notions more thoroughly, that is, to create a single definition for a class of systems such that everything that is a discrete symbolic system will be an instance of it. To do so is less important than to understand the kinds of systems involved. What counts is the particular systems produced within this tradition. Each of these stands on its own feet as far as verification is concerned. The sort of description above (and its expansions) account for the family resemblance of these models.

In terms of the kinds of processings that can be performed, this general model, when formalized, is just another variant on effective procedures, Turing machines, and so forth. Again, the interest lies not there, but in how well models of this type deal with human behavior. Let us consider some examples.

SEQUENCE EXTRAPOLATION

Since we have already considered the Simon-Kotovsky model for handling extrapolated sequences, we might also look to its role as a model of human behavior. There is little difficulty making an identification of the theory with human behavior, for the program can be asked to predict sequences just as the human can. The obvious first comparison is that both the model and the human do solve problems, so that the model provides an explanation of how it is possible for a human to solve these problems. This is often referred to as a *sufficiency test,* and it is one that is highly characteristic of information-processing models, especially in contrast with most other psychological theories, which are not comprehensive enough to make such claims, but are rather more analytical (here, opposed to synthetical), dealing with relationships between abstracted aspects of behavior. Thus, for complex tasks, such as the induction tasks, there are simply no theories of how humans do the task other than those in the information-processing family. Within it, of course, possible alternatives can be generated to the Simon-Kotovsky program.

We want more than sufficiency. For instance, we might like to compare the difficulty of the tasks for the model and for human subjects. This was done in the original study (Simon and Kotovsky, 1963), using success/fail as a measure of difficulty, with reasonably good accord for some variants of the model and less good for others. They went somewhat further than this in relating the difficulty to structural features of the descriptions of the series, namely, the number of pointer-variables that had to be maintained: the more pointers the more difficult the task. This fits well with other data on the significance of limitations in immediate memory.

The total model (the program) incorporates many assumptions, and to test and verify them all requires more behavioral evidence than overall-performance measures provide. Concern with making contact with large amounts of behavior to help with identification of theories is also characteristic of the information-processing approach. Let us consider next an example that shows this.

PROBLEM SOLVING IN CRYPTARITHMETIC

I have worked extensively with cryptarithmetic puzzles, in which distinct digits must be assigned to letters, so that the resulting sum is correct (Newell and Simon, 1972). (Box 1.1 gave an example in which CROSS + ROADS is to equal DANGER.) Their virtue as a problem-solving task (besides the fact that they are fun) lies in the combination of search, trial, and reasoning that most educated persons exhibit when doing the task.

The behavioral data taken in such tasks are verbalizations of the subject while he is working (plus any written records if these are permitted). Such data permit inferences not only about the final outcome (as in the Simon-Kotovsky work), but about what the subject knows at many intermediate points in the course of problem solving. Thus, in the CROSS + ROADS = DANGER task the interpretation of the utterance "D must be 1" to mean that the subject now knows that D must be 1 already assumes a system capable of "having knowledge" and dealing with "symbols" that "have meaning." These assumptions are essentially those of being an information-processing system. Thus, there seems little danger in accepting them. Put another way, information-processing theories provide a model of meaning that justifies the interpretation assigned to such utterances as the one above.

More to the point is the range of inferences that can be made from the verbalizations (or written surrogates thereof).* If the subject says "Let S be 1," does he therefore not know that D must be 1? It is probably a good working hypothesis. If later the

---

*The discussion implies that the inference from the verbalizations to the subject's state of knowledge is done by a human. Recent work indicates that this process may be mechanizable (Waterman and Newell, 1971).

subject says, "But D is carried over in the last column to the left so that must be a 1; therefore S cannot be 1," then the hypothesis can be taken as fact. That is, it can be used to support or disconfirm particular models that make predictions about what the subject knows about S and D. Of course, it is possible to slide from these rather simple utterances to passages of almost arbitrary obscurity: "Now if the—Oh, I'm sorry, I said something incorrect here. I'm making—No, no, I didn't either." A transcript loaded with such passages simply represents unanalyzable data.

To induct and validate an information-processing model we would like to know the complete state of the subject's knowledge at each instant of time, the model then being constrained to provide a representation of this knowledge and of the transformations through which it goes. Knowledge is analogous to energy in that its absolute amount can not be determined, but only changes in it. Thus in a task such as cryptarithmetic much that the subject knows is not changed in the course of problem solving, nor does it enter into the selection of the transformations. All that must be known about the knowledge state is the relevant part. Even so, of course, the data at hand permits direct inference (i.e., without benefit of the specific model to be constructed) to only a fraction of what is desired.

We could attempt to obtain more data simultaneously during the problem solving. Any such data would in part confirm (or fail to confirm) the facts about the knowledge state already derived from the verbalizations, but it could also add new data. Ultimately, of course, we hope to have many different measures, including physiological ones, though the latter still seem far away. Gross eye-movement data are one possibility that has been explored and shown to provide additional information (Winikoff, 1967). Box 1.11 shows both the verbalizations and the gross eye movements for a few minutes of a subject doing the CROSS ∣ ROADS = DANGER task. The small displays in the figure do not show fixations, but rather aggregations of fixations into units called *attention units* and *scan units*.

These units have the functional significance indicated by their names. During an attention unit the subject may be considered to be as attending to a specific part of the display and during a scan unit he may be considered to be searching the display for some sort of information. Which is to say: in any model of the subject's behavior we may take these eye movements, so interpreted, as confirming (or disconfirming) the proposed model. Much in Box 1.11 is not explained here, such as the derivation of the aggregated units. There are also *transition units*, which are of short duration and can occur between attention units (note the small gaps in the vertical time column) but also inside attention units. Winikoff's paper contains an exhaustive discussion of these other aspects, including the validity of the correspondence between the eye-movement units and the verbal behavior.

The wish is to create an information-processing model that behaves like the human problem solver, as seen through the inferences made from the verbal and eye-movement data. These data are of course highly particularized: one episode for one subject. Ultimately there is concern with generalization over tasks and over people, as well as with how this problem-solving system (assuming we have it) fits in with the structure of the subject's total information-processing system. Still, the task as posed is a reasonable one (almost paradigmatic) for a science of human behavior.

Box 1.11   Eye Movement Aggregates and Verbal Behavior.

(sec)

CROSS plus ROADS is

DANGER

Exp: Please

talk. S: Yes

S plus S

1.8	.6	CROSS ROADS DANGER
2.4	3.0 scan	CROSS ROADS DANGER
5.4	.8	CROSS ROADS DANGER
6.2	.8	CROSS ROADS DANGER
7.4	2.6 −.2	CROSS ROADS DANGER
10.0	1.2	CROSS ROADS DANGER
11.2	1.4	CROSS ROADS DANGER
12.6	2.0 scan	CROSS ROADS DANGER

I'll let

S

equal . . . .

Let S equal

one.

Therefore

R will be two.

28.8	2.4 −.2	CROSS ROADS DANGER
31.4	.6	CROSS ROADS DANGER
32.0	1.2 scan	CROSS ROADS DANGER
33.2	1.2 −.2	CROSS ROADS DANGER
34.4	1.2	CROSS ROADS DANGER
35.8	.6	CROSS ROADS DANGER
36.4	7.4	CROSS ROADS DANGER

#		
44		
45	Now	
46	there. .	
47		
48	there is R	
49		
50	plus O	
51		
52	and C plus R.	
53		
54	So I'll,	
55		
56	letting S plus D. . .	
57		
58		

43.8 3.6 scan
47.4 .8
48.2 2.0
50.2 2.8 -1.2
53.2 1.0 -.2
54.8 2.8 -.4

CROSS ROADS DANGER
CROSS ROADS DANGER
CROSS ROADS DANGER
CROSS ROADS DANGER
CROSS ROADS DANGER

#		
15		
16	has to equal R	
17		
18	and	
19		
20	R will have to equal two S.	
21		
22		
23		
24	And S plus D	
25		
26	also has to equal E.	
27		
28	So	
29		

14.2 8.0 -1.2
22.8 1.0
24.0 2.8
26.8 2.0 scan

CROSS ROADS DANGER
CROSS ROADS DANGER
CROSS ROADS DANGER
CROSS ROADS DANGER

On the way to a model, we produce, as shown in Figure 1.2, a graphical picture of the subject's varying state of knowledge as inferred from the data, called the Problem Behavior Graph (PBG). This can be seen as a search through a space of possible states of knowledge about the problem, called the *problem space*. The means of search are a set of *operators*: there are five in the PBG of Figure 1.2. PC processes a particular column of the display, making whatever inferences it can (e.g., if S = 1, the PC(column 1) $\Rightarrow$ R = 2). AV makes a tentative assignment of a digit to a variable, either a letter or a carry (e.g., let S be 1). TD tests if a digit can be legitimately assigned to a letter (e.g., if D = 1 then TD will conclude that S = 1 is not possible). FC finds a column containing a given letter or carry (e.g., FC(R) $\Rightarrow$ columns 1, 4, 5). FNC finds the next column in the standard method for performing addition (e.g., if column 1 has just been added up, then FNC $\Rightarrow$ column 2). Two memory operators do not appear in the PBG: RA, which recalls the antecedent situation which led to something; and RV which recalls the value of a variable.

Each of these operators, when successfully performed, provides new knowledge, (including attentional information — where to look next). It turns out that the subject can be described as gaining all his knowledge from the application of this small set of operators. The set of possible knowledge states within which the subject wanders can be described by a BNF grammar, in the same way as the space of hypotheses for the induction program.

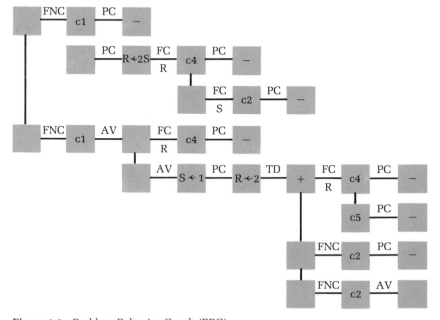

Figure 1.2 Problem Behavior Graph (PBG).

The search tree in Figure 1.2 provides a way of structuring a processing model. At each node, there is a certain state of knowledge and there is the selection of some operator to advance the knowledge further. Sometimes, of course, what is selected is the action of retreating to a prior place in the searched tree to begin a new search in another direction. At each point we can write a rule that describes the selection as a function of the information in the current knowledge state. There need not be a separate rule for each such node; the same rule can apply to many nodes, variation in behavior resulting from differences in knowledge state rather than differences in rules. The totality of such rules forms a program for action that is analogous in many ways to a Markov Normal Algorithm or a Post canonical system. It has become common to refer to each part rule as a *production*, the whole being a *production system*.

Box 1.12 shows such a production system for the behavior shown in Box 1.11. The rules have a condition part and an action part. In the control structure each production is considered in turn. If its condition is satisfied for the current state of the immediate memory, then its action is evoked, some change occurs in the immediate memory, and the system starts over again at the top. If no condition is satisfied, processing terminates (unless new information flows in from the outside, say by perception of an external display). The immediate memory consists of a goal stack as well as a collection of elementary assertions about letters and digits. Not represented is knowledge of the paths so far followed and the knowledge states to which return is possible.

Consider the first production, S1. The condition is that an expression of the form "*letter* = *digit* new" occurs in the immediate memory. *Letter* and *digit* are variables of the indicated types; "=" is the specific relation equals, and "new" is one of two specific qualifiers, the other being □, the sign for *impossible*. Thus, "R = 1 new" would satisfy the condition, but "R = 1" or "S > 1 new" would not. The action of S1 is to find a column containing that letter (FC) and to input into immediate memory the expression "use *column*." The *column* came as output from the FC, which is indicated for convenience by the "⇒ *column*." "Use" is one of several goals, the others being "get," "do," "check," "recall," and "repeat." Goals go into the goal stack in immediate memory and are automatically pushed and popped. Thus, the distinction between the actions "PC" and "do PC" is that the latter, but not the former, goes into the goal stack.

This description, though sketchy, is perhaps enough to permit appreciation of how the system operates. Box 1.13 shows the behavior of the system for a few steps. We have started it with an immediate memory corresponding to t = 14.2 on Box 1.11 and Figure 1.2 and run it to t = 43.8. This should be enough to show the nature of the correspondence—that the program is to predict which operators are to be performed at each step, hence what knowledge state is to be attained at each step, and thus what things relevant to the task can be exhibited by the subject at each point, whether via verbalizations or eye movements. There is nothing in the model that determines what will actually be said or what it is possible to say. The comparison with data is that each correct datum counts *for*, each incorrect datum counts *against*, and omissions are ignored.

Box 1.12 Production System and Knowledge State

```
S1:    letter = digit new → FC(letter) ⇒ column; use column
S1':   letter ← digit new → do PC
S1":   use column → PC
S2:    get variable → FC(variable) ⇒ column; PC(variable, column)
S3:    use column, PC(column) ⇒ − → AV(letter(upper), column)
S4:    letter inequality digit → do AV(letter.
G2:    letter ← digit □ → do AV(letter)
G4:    ∅ | + | − → FNC ⇒ use column
T1:    letter = object new, ¬ do TD → do TD(letter, object)
T2:    letter = digit □ → RA ⇒ expression; expression □
R2:    check variable → RA(variable) ⇒ production; repeat production
R3:    recall letter → RA(letter) ⇒ column; RV(letter, column)


variable := letter | carry
object := digit | letter
expression := variable relation object qualifier
relation := ← | = | inequality
inequality := ≥ | ≤ | > | <
qualifier := □ | new | null
operator := PC | AV | TD | FNC | FC | RA | RV

                   main          find      recall

goal type := get variable | do main operator | check variable |
             use column | recall letter


Operation of goal stack:

   signal   interpretation      action
    null    new goal            use for selecting next production
     +      success             pop if another goal in stack
     −      fail                pop if another goal in stack
     i      interrupted         continue
     i-     conditional fail    if subgoal succeeds continue, else fail

Production actions:   if a goal type, then push current goal in
                      stack; else add produced information to
                      current goal.
```

It remains true that the most informative comparison is directly between the output of the system and the recorded behavior. Still, we can summarize how well the model has done by counting how many productions have been used to cover how much data, where the latter are measured in terms of the number of nodes in the Problem Behavior Graph. Such a graph is shown in Figure 1.3, where we have laid out the various productions in the order of the number of nodes each covers. This makes clear that some productions play a strong role and others a much weaker one—and concomitantly, that some receive much support from the data and others little. A production must occur at least twice to avoid being completely ad hoc.

The system of Box 1.12 is to be viewed as an information-processing description of the behavior of the subject, since it was created to describe this data. The power of this description is twofold. One part lies in its rational relation to the task at hand. Thus, it is not an arbitrary system (such as a polynomial of arbitrarily chosen degree to be fit to a set of points) relative to the system it describes. Neither is it unique, for other systems exist that can solve (or attempt to solve) the task. For instance, the REF-ARF system solved it (recall Boxes 1.2 and 1.3). However, such systems all bear a family resemblance—i.e., they are information-processing systems. The second aspect of descriptive power is that shown in Figure 1.3, which is analogous to a measure of fit—how much freedom was required to describe how much data.

The production system describes the behavior of only this single subject in this one experiment (actually only the first 200 seconds). However, the behavior of many other subjects shows the same structure, and even some of the same productions, where the analysis has been carried out in equal detail (Newell and Simon, 1972). Subjects need not behave this way. For example, someone who tried to construct a set of algebraic equations and manipulate them would not be described at all by this specific model. Whether he would be describable as working in a problem space, where the states of knowledge involve sets of equations and the operators involve manipulations on these equations, is another matter.

This example can stand as representative of work in problem solving using information processing models—the construction of an explicit processing system of some complexity that performs the task, the use of verbal data (and here eye-movement data as well), the attempt to fit the dynamic pattern of behavior to the behavior of the subject. Similar work, though not involving production systems, has gone on in elementary logic tasks, in chess, and several other areas (see Newell and Simon, 1972).

IMMEDIATE MEMORY

Although I have described problem solving first, the greatest part of the work using information processing is going on in other areas of psychology. The work in immediate memory provides an important example. Its roots go back to control-and-communication engineering. This can perhaps best be seen in Broadbent's book on *Perception and Communication* (1958), in which he talks about memory

Box 1.13 **Trace of Production System.**

Time	Production	Operator	Goal stack	Expressions
			(PC cl i)	
14.2	continue	PC		
			(get P)(get S)	(P=2S new)
22.2	S2	FC	(PC cl i—)	
22.8	↑	PC	(get P c4)(get S)	
			(PC cl i—)	
			(get R c4—)(get S)	
			(PC cl i—)(get S)	
			(PC cl i—)	
23.8	S2	FC		
			(get S c2)(PC cl i—)	
24.0	↑	PC		
			(PC S c2 —)(PC cl i—)	
			(PC cl —)	
26.8	G4	FNC		
			(use cl)	
28.8	S3	AV		
			(get R)(AV S cl i)	
31.2	S2	FC		
			(get R c4)(AV S cl i)	
31.4	↑	PC		
			(PC R c4 —)(AV S cl i)	
			(AV S cl i)	
34.4	continue	AV		
			(AV S cl +)	(S ←1 new)
36.4	S1'	PC		
			(PC cl +)	(R=2 new)
				(S ←1)
	T1	TD		
			(TD R +)	(R=2 new)
43.8				

Notes: "Continue" implies that the operator in the goal stack
        controls.

        ↑ means that the preceding production continues to control.

        Popping of goal stack on goal signal +, — or i— takes place
        automatically before another production is selected.

        Times come from matching the eye—movement aggregates against
        the action being performed by the operator.

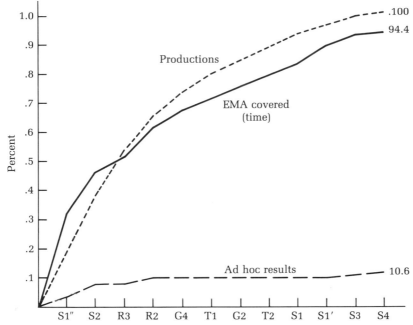

Figure 1.3 Summary of Production Coverage.

in terms of recirculating loops and control systems, motivated by a series of auditory perceptual experiments.

There is also a connection with information theory, though of a negative sort. The fascination with information theory in psychology occurred in the early 1950s, focusing attention on the concepts of capacity and the ensemble from which a selection was made. The early positive results were on total channel capacity for a man working as a transducer and showed that reaction time was linear in the information content of the ensemble set. George Miller's justly famous article on "seven, plus or minus two" (1956) provided the punctuation mark to this work, for it gave persuasive evidence that there was an immediate-memory system whose capacity should be measured in "chunks," not bits. These chunks are in fact symbols.

From that time on the immediate-memory problem has come increasingly to be discussed in information-processing terms. However, the style of both experiment and theory is markedly different from work on problem solving. Here one is trying to obtain detailed information about the structure of a particular organ. Detailed models of its structure and processing that permit mathematical treatment are created, and the control-engineering and logical-design flavor of these models remains very strong. Correspondingly, repeated parametric experiments that permit both estimation of the model's parameters and assessment of the degree of fit are performed. By now there are a substantial number of models of immediate memory (Waugh and Norman, 1965; Bower, 1967; Atkinson and Shriffrin, 1968; Norman and Rumelhart, 1972; Laughery, 1969). All except the most recent are summarized in a recent book by Norman (1969) on information-processing theories of memory.

To give an indication of flavor, Figure 1.4 shows the block diagram of the memory structure posited by Atkinson and Shriffrin. The model focuses on the issue of rehearsal, involving both an immediate memory and a long-term memory. Symbols are returned to immediate memory under the control of a performance strategy held by the subject for the specific task. (These control strategies are not represented explicitly in the theory, but serve rather to justify specific submodels of memory operation for specific tasks.) Forgetting in immediate memory is handled by positing an exponential distribution on the probability that an item will leave memory. Thus the returns to immediate memory constitute rehearsal, and imply increased memory of rehearsed symbols. Transfer to long-term memory occurs as a function of residence time in immediate memory.

Figure 1.5 shows some theoretical and experimental curves from this work. At a trial the subject was first asked (TEST) for the value (a letter) that had previously been associated with an attribute (a two-digit number); then he was given a new

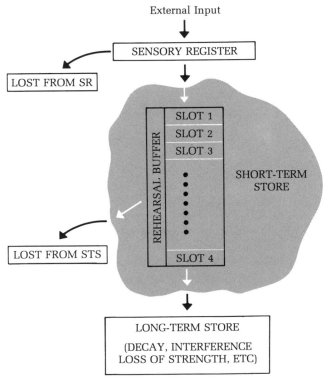

Figure 1.4 Block Diagram of Human Memory (From Atkinson and Shiffrin, 1968).

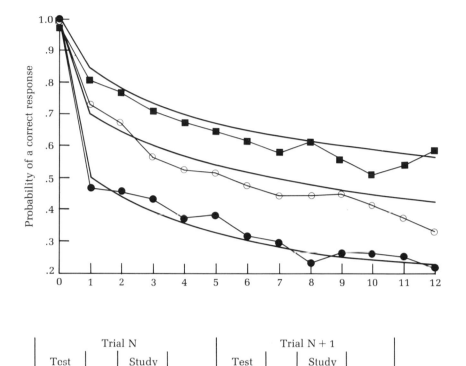

Figure 1.5   Observed and Theoretical Probabilities of a Memory Experiment
(From Atkinson and Shiffrin, 1968).

value to associate with the same attribute (STUDY). Thus the situation has some aspects of a typical paired-associate task, but with continual re-association of new values. The curves explore the effects of introducing a certain amount of repetition, the top curve being three reinforcements, the middle curve two, and the bottom curve one. The significance of such curves, beyond showing that the model fits parametric data, lies in the detailed analysis of the model, which cannot be given here. Our purpose is to indicate the range of work now going on in which the human is viewed as an information-processing system.

PSYCHOLINGUISTICS

Still a third strand of work that reflects an information-processing view of human behavior derives from linguistics, especially modern transformational linguistics. The work of Chomsky and his co-workers has had effects at many levels in linguistics. Its impact on psychology (on psycholinguistics) was originally on the reality of grammatical structuring of language (e.g., the productive character of linguistic behavior, the reality of transformations, etc.). One result was extensive work on characterizing children's grammar (see Lenneberg, 1964). Another consisted of experiments that assumed that transformation, such as negation, the passive, etc., corresponded to covert operations, and attempted to show their reality —e.g., by showing additivity of the time required to decode sentences (see Miller, 1962). Recently there has been an effect on semantics, the linguists themselves having finally moved in to engage this topic (e.g., Katz and Fodor, 1963).

It is unnecessary to draw a detailed picture of this work in psycholinguistics. The important point here is that transformational-linguistic models are a species of information-processing models in that they include systems of symbols and rules for operating on the symbols (Chomsky, 1965). There are differences, of course. Perhaps the most important relates to the insistence of the linguists on the distinction between competence and performance. The formal models of language describe competence and thus stay at one remove from the actual behavior of a performing speaker or listener. But the psycholinguist must find some way to bridge this gap, since he wishes to explain performances.

This may be illustrated by a recent study of Clark (1969) on simple inference problems stated in natural language. Box 1.14 shows two such problems as they were presented to the subjects. Clark, motivated by linguistic considerations of deep structure, developed three principles which permit the deduction of the relative time it takes to answer such problems. In over-brief form these are:

Primacy of Functional Relations. Functional relations, like those of subject, verb, and direct object, are stored immediately after comprehension in a more readily available form than other kinds of information, like that of theme.

Lexical Marking. Certain adjectives are marked and can exist only in contrastive form ("How bad is X?" always implies X is bad); other adjectives are unmarked and can exist in either contrastive form or in nominal form ("How good is X?" permits "X is good" or "X is bad" as answer). The nominal sense of an adjective is stored and retrieved from memory more quickly than its contrastive sense.

Box 1.14 Linguistic Reasoning Problems (After Clark, 1969).

```
If John is better than Dick
And Pete is worse than Dick
Then who is best?
Dick     Pete     John


If John isn't as good as Pete
And John isn't as bad as Dick
Then who is best?
Dick     Pete     John
```

Congruence. The memory is searched for an answer by looking for information congruent, at the level of function relations, with the information asked for in the question. The question cannot be answered until it is reformulated to be congruent with the stored information (which is not available for reformulation).

These principles have two aspects. One is the use of linguistic concepts to structure the situation: the functional relations and the marked and the unmarked adjectives are determined by linguistic evidence independent of the experiment. The other is the use of information-processing assumptions to make the time inferences. A sequential search of memory is posited, each search being generated by a particular formulation of the search request. In fact, though not shown here, Clark makes use of a formalism to express the deep structure of the sentences that comes close to an internal representation for an information-processing system.

Just as with the example on immediate memory, it would take us far afield to assess the exact significance of Clark's model. It does very well in explaining the data, but alternative theories, such as the use of an internal one-dimensional image on which to map each sentence (Huttenlocher, 1968), would need to be discussed. What is important to us here is that the model is an illustration of an information-processing view in yet another part of psychology.

VERBAL LEARNING AND PERCEPTION

Space and concern for the reader's patience dictate that we not go through all the other areas where the information-processing view has led to substantial work. In the field of verbal learning (which for historical reasons exists separately from psycholinguistics) there are some models, such as EPAM (Simon and Feigenbaum, 1964), which are cast as programs in much the same way as the models in problem solving. However, the shift to information processing can be most clearly seen in the experimental work now being done: for example, that on the use of internal mediators, such as images and mnemonics, in memorizing lists of verbal material (Pavio, 1971). It has long been known that we do remember better if we use an overlearned list — "one is a bun, two is a shoe, three is a tree, . . ." — and establish for each item to be learned a vivid, bizarre visual association to a named object. The paradigm of S-R learning, in which one simply constructs bonds of various strengths between stimulus and response, does not lead easily to the study of such phenomena — and, indeed, no such studies have been done. Given a processing view with its concern for internal representation and manipulations thereof, such investigations now seem natural.

The study of perception is much more specialized, as I remarked earlier, having arisen from the concern with the existence of an "image store," especially as revealed by Sperling (1960). Many other topics that have long had a place in perception, such as visual masking, have become relevant, so that the amount of work is substantial. A recent collection by Ralph Haber, *Information Processing Approaches to Visual Perception* (1969), shows the scope very well.

ARTIFICIAL INTELLIGENCE AS THEORETICAL PSYCHOLOGY

We have so far put our emphasis on the study of man as an information processor. We should now make explicit the connections between this study and the third view of artificial intelligence, which we entitled theoretical psychology.

It should be clear by now that the important organizing notion is that of an information-processing system, not that of an artificial-intelligence system. For our purposes all the latter are the former, but not vice versa. (In fact, not all artificial-intelligence systems are information-processing systems in the sense we are using the term — discrete symbolic systems — but we have pretty much limited our consideration to these latter types of systems.) Artificial intelligence has explored certain tasks, as we showed in our discussion of the first view. But many aspects of human behavior currently under study do not include such tasks. The work in immediate memory is carried on within the bounds of a particular subsystem and much of the work in psycholinguistics consists of trying to assess the nature of grammatical performances. The tasks used in the study of verbal learning (learning and recall of lists of words and nonsense syllables) are not of direct interest as tasks in artificial intelligence. Programs that are built for such tasks, such as EPAM, are created as psychological theories, not to demonstrate that at least some mechanism can do the tasks. Thus, the whole study of information-processing systems constitutes theoretical psychology — if one views man as such a system.

At the beginning of this presentation of the third view I stated that theoretical languages, or classes of systems, are one part of a total scientific field. Information-processing systems constitute one such language; and there are many others. We look for a theory of a given phenomenon by searching within one of these classes — i.e., by writing in one of these languages. The remarks in the previous paragraph imply that the relevant class for psychology is information processing and not the subdomain called artificial intelligence.

Each such class of systems, if sufficiently well defined, gives rise to independent study. There is a mathematics of differential equations, and in it one can see clearly the mark of its initial close coupling to classical physics. But it is also an autonomous field. The same can be said of Markov processes and the class of stochastic processes that underlies so-called stochastic-learning theories. Where the class remains distinctly ill formed, as in the dramatic metaphor that lies behind Freudian theory, we find no such independent development. But even the view of human cognition as a set of forces has finally received a suitable embedding in graph theory (Harary, Norman and Cartwright, 1965).

Artificial intelligence, in this view, is theoretical psychology just because it is the study of information-processing systems that solve problems. It has parts which reflect psychology very closely (e.g., GPS and EPAM) and other parts which are largely autonomous (e.g., REF-ARF). The contribution of the latter, in this third view, is that they develop the science of information-processing systems so that other specific systems more relevant to psychological questions can be better constructed and analysed.

Summary

We have now presented three different views of artificial intelligence. They are clearly not exclusive. The actual ongoing researches that the scientific community at large labels artificial intelligence could grow in such a way that all three views would thrive or one would come to dominate.

There are also other views, and my selection of three is not meant to deny them, though it does indicate the views I think are most relevant in interpreting the field. For instance, one can view the field as one of engineering, opposing this somehow to science. It would be a major diversion to deal with this distinction here. Instead, I refer the reader to a book by my colleague, Herbert Simon, on the *Sciences of the Artificial* (1969), for a view that justifies considering such fields as computers, design, optimization, artificial intelligence, economics, and psychology as being sciences with a family resemblance that sets them apart from such natural sciences as physics, chemistry, and astronomy.

We have spent a substantial amount of space in describing these three views, trying by means of examples and listings to lay out some of their content and scope. We should now be able to turn to questions of mind to see what contribution artificial intelligence might make toward answering them.

Questions on the Nature of Mind

Questions arise from a point of view—from something that helps to structure what is problematical, what is worth asking, and what constitutes an answer (or progress). It is not that the view determines reality, only what we accept from reality and how we structure it. I am realist enough to believe that in the long run reality gets its own chance to accept or reject our various views. We could adopt the views just laid out and ask which of the questions on the nature of mind they raise are worth asking. But, as implied in the beginning, in this paper artificial intelligence should be considered to be a means and the questions should be sought elsewhere. Where is elsewhere?

There is a difficulty. It lies in what Kuhn (1962) advertised and we have been implicitly exhibiting throughout the paper. "Elsewhere" is another view—possibly from philosophy—or other "elsewhere's" as well, since the views of man are multiple. Each view has its own questions. Separate views mostly speak past each other. Occasionally, of course, they speak to the same issue and then comparison is possible, but not often and not on demand.

Let me try, nonetheless. Let me consider a small variety of such questions. At the least a few points of contact and a few clarifications might be shown, before we are forced back to the basic position: Artificial intelligence speaks about the nature of mind mostly from within its own view.

Questions on the general nature of mind

There is a philosophic tradition, now thoroughly professionalized, that asks questions about mind and about our knowledge of mind. Consider a small sample:

> I conclude that the central puzzle of the mind-body problem is the logical nature of the correlation laws connecting raw feels qualities with neurophysiological processes. (Feigl, 1963.)

> Two questions immediately arise about 'mind' as employed in these phrases. One is as to just what kind of substantive entity the term 'mind' is conceived to designate there. The other is whether any substantive entity of that conceived kind exists. (Ducasse, 1965.)

> The question which the mind-body problem poses may now be stated as follows: for the interpretation of human behavior and experience do we, or do we not, need any concepts that cannot be analyzed in terms of the concepts used in the interpretation of physical events? (Beloff, 1965.)

> But even if he had been thinking aloud throughout into a tape recorder the resulting monologue would have been hard to interpret. For how long does he have to embrace a possibility for it to count as a decision? And how firmly? The first difficulty about quantifying the mental, then, is that of identifying units for the purpose of enumeration. (Quinton, 1965.)

What can artificial intelligence say about these questions? It depends, of course, on which view we take of artificial intelligence. From the weak-method view, artificial intelligence says nothing whatsoever, since it is entirely focused on the relation of procedures to tasks. From the exploration view it might have said something, if philosophic investigation had grown to focus on the performance of some particular intellectual functions as criterial for the existence and functioning of mind. But such has not been the case, as we shall note below.

From artificial intelligence as theoretical psychology come clear answers:

> Mind is an information-processing system.

> Minds (information-processing systems) are realized in physical systems.

The brevity and simplicity of these answers reveals again the magician's trick — it was all over before it started. That is, once the information-processing view is adopted these answers (more or less) follow. Given this, the questions just quoted are either straightforward questions that have straightforward answers or are scientific questions whose answers vary with the state of the art. For example, the theory of human problem solving in cryptarithmetic given earlier directly addresses the questions of Quinton — and almost answers them.

But this is all unsatisfactory, since there is no compulsion to accept this view. It is simply a particular scientific view whose data are those sketched in the earlier part of this paper. There is nothing compelling about it at the philosophic level. The situation may be made even clearer, perhaps, by noting that information processing is a particular form of the identity hypothesis put forth by Feigl (1963). But we have not arrived at it through any of the kinds of argumentation presented in his lengthy monograph or the resultant spate of papers (e.g., Maxwell, 1966). Nor have we dealt with any of the issues raised therein. What, from the view of these questions, differentiates an information-processing theory of mental activity from any other psychological theory? It must be admitted that even in the quotation from Quinton, his questions are but a way station in his search for philosophically deeper ones. Answering them would only shift the starting point of the search.

ANALOGICAL ARGUMENTS

It is possible that help can be gained in a different way: namely, by raising analogies which permit the current questions to be seen in a new light. The best example that I know occurs in a paper by Putnam (1960), where he shows that all of the questions considered in the philosophy of mind can be raised with respect to Turing machines, taking into account that they have both effectors and receptors (for external observation) and an internal state (state taken in the technical sense). He goes on to show that in either context these questions have the same answers and for the same reasons. The argument is analogical, but fruitful.

A similar analogical argument can be offered to the effect that:

Neurophysiology is almost totally irrelevant to the nature of mind.

The case rests on the analogous proposition that:

Electronics is almost totally irrelevant to the nature of artificial intelligence.

The latter proposition is a commonplace in computer science. Computers could just as well be built from any of a number of technologies. The behavior of the machine is specified by the programming manual and this is completely sealed off from the underlying hardware.

This works, we all realize, because there can be functionally equivalent mechanisms. But that is not the whole story. For if the demands on the underlying technology are too complex and intricate, then it may be extremely difficult to invent or discover functionally equivalent mechanisms. But in constructing computers only a very few general properties are required to obtain a machine capable of arbitrary information processing: a large, reliable symbolic memory; operations on it of reading, writing, and addressing; and a modest-sized set of internal states which the organism can assume as a function of the symbols it reads and which lead to the performance of the appropriate operations. This is *something* to ask of mechanism, to be sure. But it is not much, in fact, and there are large numbers of ways to achieve it. The means by which it is achieved does dictate some aspects of the system: speed, memory, size, reliability, and so on. These account for the phrase "almost totally irrelevant," rather than "totally irrelevant." But these features are global ones. The detail of the technology does not show through (see also Newell and Simon, 1972, Chap. 14).

Thus, the argument goes, if artificial intelligence (looked at now as exploration) produces performances that seem at all mind-like (and we need not be fussy about exactly how mind-like or in what ways), and this behavior depends on only a few gross features of the underlying physical system, could it not be that the mind-like behavior of biological organisms also depends on only a few gross features of the underlying biological mechanism? The argument is analogical. I think it fruitful.

Note that these two arguments, both Putnam's and the one on neurophysiology, are not arguments from artificial intelligence, but only from the general nature of information-processing systems. The only use of artificial intelligence is to help guarantee the relevance of the analogy in the second argument; it was not used at all in Putnam's. This parallels the underlying construct of the view of artificial intelligence as theoretical psychology, which consists of information-processing systems and not artificial-intelligence systems per se.

Questions on the minds of computers

The computer itself has become an object of inquiry in philosophy. Consider some examples:

I propose to consider the question 'Can machines think?' (Turing, 1950.)

How would we recognize an *entity* (to use a term that does not prejudge the issue as to whether the thing is an organism or a machine) as having a mind? (Anderson, 1964.)

Is there an essential difference between a man and a machine? (Scriven, 1953.)

Could a robot have feelings? (Ziff, 1959.)

Should robots have civil rights? (Putnam, 1964.)

More seriously, it may be asked whether there are any grounds in Christian revelation for pontification here where deduction fails. Is not the production of an artificial human being theologically impossible, as usurping the Divine prerogative? (Mackay, 1965.)

Surely work on artificial intelligence is relevant here. For instance, Turing's article (1950) and his proposed test are much discussed both in the philosophic and the artificial-intelligence literature. But discussion goes off in entirely different directions in each. For artificial intelligence it leads to the view that artificial intelligence is exploration, and to attempts to program computers to do ever more intriguing intellectual functions. For philosophy it leads to jumping over all that is relevant to artificial intelligence and asking what could be known with certainty even if the empirical case were granted. This move is worth illustrating in detail, since it seems to me to lie at the heart of the irrelevance of artificial intelligence to philosophic questions of mind.

> When it is said that it is impossible for a machine to be conscious, it is not always clear to what extent this is intended to be a logical objection and to what extent it is empirical. It may be thought that some particular practical obstacle, such as providing a machine with a means of communication, is insurmountable. But it must be remembered that such empirical obstacles may *conceivably* be surmounted: and an argument based on these differences alone is not logically demonstrative. This discussion will not consider *any* such practical differences to be essential differences: thus, the machines to be compared with man will be capable of speech, gesture, perambulation, etc., and sensitive to light, sound, and other environmental conditions. They will be referred to as robots. A robot can do everything that a machine will ever do. The second question then arises: is there any essential difference between robots and human beings? (Scriven, 1953.)

> I want the right sort of robots. They must be automata and without doubt machines.
> I shall assume that they are essentially computing machines, having microelements and whatever micromechanisms may be necessary for the functioning of these engineering wonders. Furthermore, I shall assume that they are powered by microsolar batteries: instead of having lunch they will have light.
> And if it is clear that our robots are without doubt machines then in all other respects they may be as much like men as you like. They may be the size of men. When clothed and masked they may be virtually indistinguishable from men in practically all respects: in appearance, in movement, in the utterances they utter, and so forth. Thus, except for the masks any ordinary man would take them to be ordinary men. Not suspecting they were robots nothing about them would make him suspect.
> But unmasked the robots are to be seen in all their metallic lustre. What is in question here is not whether we can blur the line between a man and a machine and so attribute feelings to the machine. The question is whether we can attribute feelings to the machine and so blur the line between a man and a machine. (Ziff, 1959.)

What can be gained from the *facts* of artificial intelligence when all is assumed? Incentive to consider such questions, perhaps, but not help in the argument.

The term simulation occurs repeatedly in the computer-mind literature, though it happens to be absent from the quotes above. Here perhaps something can be said. But it is a clarification of usage, rather than anything substantive—which is why it may appear relevant. Taking the view that artificial intelligence is theoretical psychology, simulation (the running of a program purporting to represent some human behavior) is simply the calculation of the consequences of a psychological theory. Its relationship to its empirical object is exactly like that of any other theory. Indeed, in the computing world the term simulation is used indifferently (and with the same meaning) to refer to simulations of job shops, problem solvings, nuclear reactors, traffic patterns, and ecologies. There is no need to develop the argument in detail.

In a recent study by Fodor (1968), he devotes his entire final chapter to the nature of simulation and arrives at exactly the same conclusion and for the same reason (see also Simon, 1969):

> Thus far we have been concerned with the question: "When if ever, would simulating organic behavior by machine count as explaining it?" I have suggested that this question may properly be regarded as a special case of the question, "Under what circumstances does the ability of a theory to account for the relevant observational data make that theory true?" (Fodor, 1968.)

There are other questions of clarification, such as those on the significance of Godel's theorem or on the significance of the statement "computers do only what you tell them." (In both, there is no deep significance.) But these questions have been dealt with frequently and well. There seems to me no need to reiterate well-stated analyses. We should look in other directions if we wish to gain something from artificial intelligence in the study of mind.

Questions on the nature of mental operations

In the course of investigations on artificial intelligence attention is directed at various kinds of specific operations—at search, at induction, at discovery. In the philosophic literature equal attention is given to mental operations. Often, especially in recent decades, these treatments are saturated with an analysis of the use of language, as if one can use the embedded linguistic sense of a linguistic community as a source of objective data. Thus, Anscombe writes,

> Why cannot a baby six months old pretend to be in pain? (Anscombe, 1958.)

She would not be satisfied, it seems to me, with an investigation along the lines of our cryptarithmetic example (ignoring that for the moment no such specific analysis is in sight). For half the issue would rest with an analysis of what it is we mean when we use "pretend." The model of the baby would not address itself to that question directly, but only to exhibiting the behavior in terms of its symbolic generators. It might incorporate a concept analogous to pretending, if indeed the six months old baby could pretend. But this would be a definition in its own terms and not one reflecting the laws of use in the linguistic community. Such definitions might have an impact on the philosopher's concerns since they propose alternatives that might supersede the linguistic one (as physics has taken over "energy" and now controls its primary meaning). But for terms of the subtlety that attracts philosophers, such a possibility is for the future. Certainly nothing can now be said about "pretend," either for babies or otherwise.

Induction. We might seek, then, for some operations which artificial intelligence has studied and which philosophy has attempted directly to understand. Induction is an obvious candidate. But again, on closer inspection, we find that the two are interested in induction in quite different ways. Artificial intelligence is interested in how inductions are actually made—and in understanding inductions that are as complex as possible. Philosophy is concerned with the justification of induction. Thus:

> In the philosophical discussion of induction, one problem has long occupied the center of the stage—so much so, indeed, that it is usually referred to as *the* problem of induction. That is the problem of justifying the way in which, in scientific inquiry and in our everyday pursuits, we base beliefs and assertions about empirical matters on logically inconclusive evidence. (Hempel, 1966.)

It is presumably not of interest to examine ways in which methods such as Hypothesize and Match make actual inductions of some difficulty. For clearly they give no new hint about the problem of justification. Once the space is given, the game is almost over, and there is no justification (in the sense of certainty) for the spaces used. Indeed, since the spaces are built in at design time, one might be inclined to say, from a critical philosophical view, that programs with this method are not inductive programs at all. This is dangerous ground, however, for what if we next construct a program whose hypothesis space consists of all BNF grammars (Feldman, 1972)? Is giving the program the information that the hypothesis is expressible in some BNF doing all the inductive work?

An even more obvious candidate than induction would seem to be deductive proof and logic. But the massive effort to understand them preceded computer science, and by inclusion artificial intelligence. (The effort actually provided a major part of the intellectual capital for the development of computer science.) In any event, deduction and proof are now seen to be far from the concept of mind, which may only reflect their well-understood character.

There is a curious asymmetry in philosophy between the way induction is being handled as a problem and the way deduction and proof were handled. With deduction there was not only concern with formalization, rigor, and the grounds for inference. There was also concern with whether the models of deductive logic that were being created were sufficient for the deductive tasks of the world—in particular those of mathematics and science. It has always been important for logic to show its adequacy. This helped force the development of non-toy logistic systems, of which the work of Whitehead and Russell (1929) stands as the classic monument.

However, with one exception, this seems never to have happened with induction. The field operates with a series of simple (though ingenious) examples of inductions that are tough nuts for various issues of justification. But there is no notion whether the kinds of induction philosophy is worrying about are sufficient for the inductive tasks of the world. They do not even know whether the kinds of induction span the space of those needed. What sorts of inductions were used to derive Mendeleev's table? The Bohr model from the Balmer series? The next term in a series-completion intelligence test?

The one exception to this of which I am aware is probability, which is a form of inductive inference. The foundations of probability have been investigated in much the same way as have the foundations of proof. This suggests that the difficulty lies in philosophy itself not being prepared to provide the explication of the domain of inductive inference. If the development of an inferential technique is provided from outside, as it was in mathematics, formalized science, probability and statistics, then philosophy will add to its concerns the question of whether its foundational concepts are sufficient to the task thereof. Without such an independently provided substance, the question will simply not arise.

The speculations of the above paragraph, made by an outsider to the field, are meant only to make plausible a further suggestion. A possible contribution by artificial intelligence is in working out the details of many cases of complex induction, until it becomes clearer what their informational structure is. This might permit contact with the philosophy of induction—though of course that remains an additional speculation. It is beyond the bounds of this section to analyze in detail any such implications of the Hypothesize and Match method. For one thing, though mental operations are clearly an aspect of mind, these concerns have clearly taken us away from the central concepts of mind.

Questions on the nature of information processing systems

A point has, perhaps, been made. It is not easy to apply the content of one view to answer the questions of another. With philosophy as the test example, we have tried it in several ways. My own evaluation—I cannot speak for the reader—is that either the pickings were slight or the answers finessed the real issues (as seen from the other view).

What questions then should we ask about the nature of mind? Clearly, by now, those suggested from within the information-processing view. We simply identify the concept of mind with that of an information-processing system. One might be tempted to insist that it somehow be a very special information-processing system— that one would not want to use the term mind with respect to garden-variety information-processing systems (e.g., a payroll accounting system). But this turns the question back again to where the controlling notions are the ways we have used the term from other points of view.

Such concerns do not occur within the view. Here the appropriate questions concern mechanisms and organizations of processing that permit ranges of performances. The other questions are not yet ready to be answered, and one of the workaday philosophical principles of the scientist is not to ask a question before its time.

We wish to ask questions about information processing systems that seem ready to be asked. Let us consider two candidates—the nature of generality and the nature of an ill-structured problem. They are not new questions. I have given some thought to them (Ernst and Newell, 1969; Newell, 1969) and what I say draws strongly on those previous efforts. But I assure you they are open questions, both for me and for the field. My hunch is that after a bit we really will have developed answers to them, though they need not bear kinship to the aspects discussed here.

The questions derive primarily from the view of artificial intelligence as exploration. For they press on two aspects of problem solving that seem to our still untutored eye to be difficult for mechanisms to handle. The field at large recognizes these two questions as significant and I will certainly do no more for each than lay out the question for discussion.

WHAT IS THE NATURE OF GENERALITY?

At an informal level we easily distinguish the power of a program from its generality. Programs X and Y are both chess playing programs, but Y always beats X; thus Y is better than X, but not more general. Again, it is often asserted that we can construct programs to do any one task as well (or better) than a human, but we cannot construct a program to do them all. Such a thought expresses the feeling that a program for each task must be considered ad hoc.

In artificial intelligence it is easy to distinguish efforts at generality from efforts at power within a fixed task. The chess and checker programs have no pretensions to generality. Programs such as GPS and REF-ARF, are clearly focussed on generality, as are the predicate-calculus-theorem provers.

Generality needs also to be separated from the amount of specification—that is, from what information is given about the problem. We all recognize the value of a hint given in addition to the "usual" definition of a problem. Extreme examples are the usual forms of universal Turing machines, in which a specific machine can do anything any other machine can do, but only because it is provided with a full description of what the other machine would do. The only specific powers the universal machine must have are some equivalent final effectors (for Turing machines, to write 0s and 1s on tape) and the ability to read the description so that it can simulate the behavior.

No even moderately satisfactory ways exist for defining generality (or difficulty or specificity). In practice two things have happened. First is the game of "anything your program can do, mine can do—and mine does something else too." Thus, each proposed general program must cover the same ground as its predecessors. Second, generality is clearly tied to having a language in which to describe problems to the system. Any program which takes only a fixed set of parameters (as in a large subroutine) is simply not a contender for generality. For example, REF-ARF is a contender, in part because it has a well-defined input language. And in fact it is not possible to enumerate in any meaningful way the problems that can be posed to ARF (the problem solver) through REF.

Although undoubtedly a necessary condition, having a language does not go very far. For as soon as input languages have the expressive power of the first-order predicate calculus then the total scope of the language no longer provides clues to how general the program is. The many theorem provers in the first-order predicate calculus are already perfectly general, but this says very little. To say that a theorem prover can do symbolic integration, as can Slagle's SAINT and Moses' SIN, simply fails to make the relevant distinctions. This shows, as well, that criteria of quality have not really been purged from the notion of generality. However, as we noted earlier in discussing Waldinger and Lee's program (and also Green's) the actual scope of predicate-calculus-theorem provers is being extended.

We should not focus too much on the difficulties of obtaining definitions and measurements of generality. The really interesting problems in generality lie in trying to determine what mechanisms can achieve it. Several hypotheses exist about the nature of an eventual general problem solver.

A SINGLE GENERAL SEARCH METHOD

The best examples are probably GPS and MULTIPLE (Slagle, 1965), although in some respects REF-ARF fits here, as do the predicate-calculus-theorem provers. A single very general formulation of a problem is adopted. GPS views all its tasks as objects that can be transformed to new objects via a set of operators. The theorem provers view the task as a set of clauses, with a single rule of inference (Resolution, Hyper-resolution, etc) that generates new clauses for the set. Invariably, the methods used are searches of some kind, usually a form of heuristic search (indeed it is hard to see what else it could be).

THE BIG SWITCH (EXPERTISE)

Experts solve problems, so goes the assertion, because they know what to do; search is to be used only as a last resort. A general problem solver is one that is (somewhat) expert in many domains — which is to say has specialized knowledge about how to solve problems in many domains. Thus, the structure of a general problem solver comprises a diagnostic program (a "big switch") that looks at a particular problem and decides which special program (method) is to be applied. The methods themselves are specialized and cannot be transferred from one task area to another.

An example of a program deliberately designed with this philosophy is SIN, Moses's integration program (1968). SIN has three stages through which a problem passes, with multiple methods in each stage: three in stage one; eleven in stage two; and two in stage three. The ordering is on effort, cheap methods first. Within each stage a diagnostic routine makes the selection of the appropriate method. Each method is based on very specific features of the expressions to be integrated, and many of them have some particular mathematical analysis standing behind them.

Symbolic integration is, of course, a narrow domain. But it is conceivable that the structure of general problem solvers is just SIN writ large. Such a system would require a very large memory, and we still understand little about what large memories will make possible. A system with, say, 10,000 methods might look like a very general problem solver indeed, like a mosaic of 10,000 pieces that blend together and cover a wall. (See Chase and Simon, 1972, for a glimpse of how a large memory might look in chess.)

WEAK METHODS

A hypothesis about generality comes from the view of artificial intelligence as the study of weak methods (Newell, 1969). A general problem solver is one whose collection of methods contains a sequence of them that are ever weaker, so that there is no situation that the problem solver comes across (in terms of its state of ignorance about the task environment) where it does not have at least one method whose problem statement fits the situation. The difference between this hypothesis and that of expertise is that in the latter, one sees the total domain peppered with highly specific, but powerful, methods; here one sees the total domain covered by methods whose domains are ever larger, but which are increasingly less potent.

Both hypotheses require some kind of diagnostic activity to select the method. One might be tempted to localize the crux of intelligent action at this selection (Minsky, 1961). We know little about method-selection programs. Some existing ones are fixed discrimination nets, similar to EPAM (Simon and Feigenbaum, 1964): GPS selected from 18 different methods by such a device. Alternatively, conditional-transfer structures are simply embedded in the executive program. The triviality of the current examples may stem from not having large and interesting collections of methods from which to select. In any event, it would seem that the selection program *must* be fundamentally simple. If it includes much complex processing then a decision has already been made implicitly on the "method" to be used.

EXECUTIVE ASSEMBLY

It is possible that each problem, arriving via some linguistic description (say), gives rise to an organizational effort to put together a specific executive for that problem. Methods such as those outlined earlier do not pre-exist within the problem solver as static symbolic structures to be interpreted. Instead, they are created ad hoc as a function of the situation.

This is an attractive proposal, since it seems to deal with the kind of discrete particularity that characterizes, say, the geometric-analogy task discussed in the first section. It is hard to believe that a person is prepared for the particular way the problem is given: A:B::C:(1, 2, 3, 4, 5,). The same is true, say, when a problem solver is first introduced to chess, or to theorem proving with a new set of axioms and inference rules.

There are few guides to how such structuring might take place. A recent program by Don Williams (1969) is a small step in this direction. It works generally on induction problems as they show up on intelligence tests. It examines the simple example problems which always introduce a new section of problems in such tests. From this examination it constructs a particular induction program that handles the task. Thus it does executive assembly. Box 1.15 shows some problems it can structure itself for and then handle.

There are two limitations on the ability of Williams' program to provide clues about how to achieve executive structuring. First, it has only a single method of

---

Box 1.15 Types of Tests Assembled by the Aptitude Test Taker.

LETTER ANALOGIES	IJ JI PO OP ED _ _ Fill in the blanks.
LETTER SERIES	A X B Y A X B Y A X B _ _ _ Fill in the blanks.
LETTER GROUPING	A A B C A C A D A C F H A A C G Pick the one that doesn't belong.
NUMBER GROUPS	35 110 75 State what is common.
NUMBER RELATIONS	2 6 3 9 4 12 6 15 Pick the one that doesn't belong.
NUMBER SERIES	15 18 21 24 27 30 State the rule.
NUMBER CORRECTION	1 2 3 4 5 7 State the one in error.
SEEING TRENDS	ANGER BACTERIA CAMEL DEAD EXCITE What is the trend?
WORD GROUPS	MAIM TEST GANG LABEL What is common?
WORD RELATIONS	REAL SEAL MEAT NEAT BORE _ _ _ _ Fill in the blanks.

---

solution. It reduces all problems to a form in which this method can be evoked. This is exactly what we want executive assembly to do, but it gives little insight into handling a diversity of methods. The second limitation is on the variety of the situations it can structure. It handles variation in answer form, variation in alphabet, and variation in groups versus sequences of letters. These are sufficient to handle most tests. Unfortunately these comprise only small domains of variability. It is not clear how to extend the program to more open situations—which is just the major question. Nevertheless, Williams' program gives us a nontrivial example of executive structuring.

These hypotheses do not exhaust the possibilities by which generality might be achieved. They do not rule out, for instance, that there are methods, as yet undiscovered, that relate specifically to achieving generality. Such a possibility is perhaps the major alternative to the hypotheses above—that we simply have not yet touched the problem of generality in our explorations.

Nor should we conclude that the various hypotheses just enumerated are somehow exclusive. The nature of intelligence, implying as it does the use of alternative means, almost guarantees that effective general systems will be mixtures. Recent work, exemplified by a program constructed by Winograd (1972), bears this out. It maintains a strong sense of expertise, which it does by distributing the action of the program in many separate programs. Each subprogram may be highly adapted to its subtask, invoking substantial special knowledge (i.e., expertise). However, the whole system is built on top of a programming system that provides a uniform way of evoking goals and maintaining the housekeeping associated with goal search (Hewitt, 1971), thus incorporating some of the major components of the heuristic search single-method approaches.

There is no clean separation between the diagnostic aspects of the program and those that attempt a solution, the two being intertwined. The base programming system also contains a uniform and powerful pattern-matching facility, which undergirds the method selection system and allows it to be distributed. (The pattern search capability also provides other facilities, such as general access to a data base.) The system is driven by sentences input from outside. In response to these the program assembles a subprogram corresponding to the semantics of the input sentence. Thus, although in a somewhat narrow way, the program also incorporates some notion of program assembly.

A final word needs to be said about learning, since it is often felt that generality will come only through a program that learns. Such a proposal simply shows that the problem has been misinterpreted (Newell, 1962). The final organization must solve the problem, no matter whether that organization is achieved via learning, instruction, or evolution. Insistence that performance programs be constructed by learning in special environments, such as ones that present sequences of exemplars labeled "success" and "fail," can serve to constrain the types of performance programs that can be realized. But our need at the moment is to generate candidate performance organizations that do have general problem solving capability.

WHAT IS AN ILL-STRUCTURED PROBLEM?

Most tasks worked on in artificial intelligence have seemed to be well defined or well structured. Some drift occurs in our perception, of course, and we may judge a program and its task differently after a few years of familiarity and study. Nevertheless, theorem proving, game playing, puzzle solving, and mathematically formalized management-sciences problems are clearly at the well-structured end of the scale—even if the dimension is itself vague.

For sake of illustration, what might we take as an ill-structured task? Deciding on a career. Discovering a new scientific theory. Evaluating a new ballet. Planning what to do with a free day. Painting a picture. Making conversation with a just reencountered long-time acquantance. Designing a new house. Making a new invention. Finding a way out of Viet Nam. Thinking up a critical experiment to test a scientific hypothesis. Making a silk purse from a sow's ear. Generating this list.

Nothing would be served by continuing, even though many phenomena of ill-structuredness might not be captured in the list.

We might have hoped, especially in the view of artificial intelligence as exploration, that a few tasks would have emerged as particularly interesting exemplars of ill-structured problems. Such seems not yet to be true. However, several hypotheses have been put forward on the general character of ill-structured problems.

1. OPEN CONSTRAINTS. Reitman (1965) was the first to attempt to sharpen the issue of ill-structured problems. He noted that all the experience with heuristic programs appeared concentrated in well-structured tasks. His formulation centered on the way tasks were defined. Take the paradigm for a problem to be $(X, \Rightarrow, Y)$ where X is the given information, $\Rightarrow$ is the way of making changes in the situation, and Y the desired situation. Then ill-structuring can be localized in these various aspects. The major heuristic search programs, for instance, worked on problems in which X and Y are both well defined: all the ill-structuring was in the $\Rightarrow$. Indeed, if you re-examine the assertions that the early problem solvers were working on ill-structured problems, you find they focus on the *way* not being well defined.

Reitman's idea was to characterize the ill-structured part of a problem by the constraints that had been left open: that is, those aspects of the problem that were simply not specified in the problem statement. These are "open" and have to be "closed" by the problem solver himself before he can work on the problem. The problem statement does not determine how such constraints have to be closed. Instead, the problem solver must reach out into his general knowledge of the larger context to decide how to close these constraints.

Simple, but real, examples are the induction problems discussed earlier. The problem statement does not state what class of mappings is to be used — it is open. For a given class of mappings, there is a well-defined problem of discovering which ones are consistent with exemplars. If many mappings are possible, even within the given space of mappings, then another open constraint exists, which is how to select a particular one. Human problem solvers reach into their knowledge of the larger world for a class of mappings. We (as test psychologists, say) can predict what class will be selected, because we also participate in the same larger context and know what it contains as possibilities.

Similarly, the second open constraint (how to select among multiple solutions) is also closed by reaching into the larger context. Adopting some simplicity criterion is almost universal — but not because it was stated in the problem statement. The problem solver has to know that such a thing is acceptable in the larger context in which the problem is given. What simplicity criterion is chosen depends on the method used to generate candidate mappings — e.g., the generator works from simple to complex, and the first successful candidate is accepted.

A virtue of this idea of open constraints is its emphasis that one cannot artificially restrict the context in which problems get solved. All problems depend, not only on the specific problem statement, but also on a range of background information that the problem solver must be presumed to have in his head (so to speak). This background information is so extensive that it could not be given as part of the problem statement. To do so, for humans anyway, would change the nature of the problem drastically. Consider, for example, an induction problem given along with a 300-page booklet of background information! Similarly, assuming present technology, there is no way of determining all the information in the human problem solver's head.

A major limitation of the idea of open constraints is the lack of any demonstration, except by casual example, that any substantial domain of ill-structured problems can in fact be so described.

2. WEAK METHODS. A second hypothesis about ill-structured problems comes out of the view, described earlier, of a general problem solver as one that has a sequence of weak but widely applicable methods. There is no difference between well- and ill-structured problems—except that a problem solver will call a problem ill-structured if he has only very weak methods that apply to it. The designation depends on the individual problem solver, as well as on the collection of methods available. But there is no evidence that our distinction between well- and ill-structured problems is in fact very sharp.

The operative point of this hypothesis is that there are no special features of tasks labeled "ill-structured" that evoke a special class of methods to deal with such special features. Rather, if one simply continues to build problem solvers with more and more comprehensive sets of weak methods, they will finally be able to handle tasks which have been called ill-structured.

3. PROBLEM SPECIFICATION. Eastman (1969), in working on problems in architectural design, has put forth the hypothesis that problems are ill-structured to the extent that the activity in solving the problem goes on concurrently with the activity in formulating the problem. He has proceeded in almost classical fashion—picking a class of tasks that seem substantially ill-structured in some respects and then considering in detail how their solution progresses. In the studies in question, he has been looking at the behavior of human designers, using protocol methods.

The task he has set is to redesign a bathroom in a small home, given some negative remarks by prospective buyers about the initial version of the bathroom, plus a limit ($50) on the additional cost. The remarks are rather general:

> This model of the house has not sold well. The sales personnel have heard prospective buyers remark on the poor design of the bath. Several comments are remembered: "that sink wastes space"; "I was hoping to find a more luxurious bath." (Eastman, 1969)

Nothing is stated about what materials can be used, what constraints govern the design, whether the remarks must really be taken seriously, and so on. The designers are professionals (actually students in an architectural school learning to be professionals). They bring to the task attitudes about what it means to be an architect, as well as a knowledge about architecture and acquaintanceship with bathrooms.

Given an initial, necessarily informal, judgment that the task is indeed ill-structured, the way the problem solvers went after it yields some notions on ill structuring.

All the problem solvers proceeded within the same global framework. The performance system ultimately consisted of a set of constraints, a set of objects (design units, such as the bathtub, the open space in front of the wash stand, etc.), a set of generators for creating a design, and evaluators for asking whether a candidate design satisfied the constraints.

For us, the interesting aspect of the work is not the structure of the subjects' programs, but that the act of creating the design units and constraints continued throughout the problem-solving period, intermixed with the attempts to solve the design problem within the momentarily existing problem definition. Thus the problem is ill-structured to the problem solver at the beginning, since many (most?) of its aspects are not defined when the problem starts, and the structuring of the problem continues throughout.

This notion is not inconsistent with the idea of open constraint as proposed by Reitman. Rather they emphasize different things. The open-constraint view emphasizes the context-dependent character of the way in which constraints become closed. Eastman's proposal needs no such larger contextual dependence. The problem solver does not know some of the constraints and it is a problem to find out, requiring a search of his memory and evaluation of what is recalled. But the problem solver does not engage in this act of specification all at once at the beginning of the problem session, followed by problem solving proper. Rather both problem solving and problem definition come along together. Thus, the problem retains its character of being ill defined until the final solution is reached.

The point, of course, is not to contrast these three hypotheses as disjoint alternatives. Each generates some ideas about what problem solving with ill-structured tasks might be like, and these might help in creating a problem solver that works on tasks more ill-structured than any handled to date.

At the beginning of this section (p. 55) I suggested a number of tasks, generated under three constraints (so it seemed): they should be ill-structured problems; they should be as diverse as possible; and they should not yet successfully be captured in mechanism. Although the last is certainly true, it should not be inferred that nothing is known about some of the mechanisms that are operating in these tasks. We have already touched on the nature of design in discussing Eastman's work. There is, of course, more known about design processes both from an engineering standpoint and from computer-automated or -augmented design, though these tend to focus on aspects least related to the ill-structured character of the design process.

In addition, a detailed study has been made of the career decisions of college graduates (Solberg, 1968). A beginning has also been made in relating the phenomena of scientific discovery to the mechanisms of problem solving discussed in the first part of the paper (Simon, 1966).

None of these various pieces of work has identified aspects of problem solving that are specific to ill-structuredness. Perhaps one should not view the notion of ill-structure as a single conceptual entity, but as something from which we peel layers as we gradually discover the nature of problem solving.

End

After consideration of three views and innumerable questions we have reached the end. I have tried to present enough of the substance of artificial intelligence so that a reasonable discussion about its nature is possible. It seemed necessary to be diverse, providing three distinct views of the field, in the hope that this would prevent simplistic interpretation.

We did in fact range over a wide set of questions. Some attempted to capture the philosophic quest for the general nature of mind and the relationship thereto of the computer, now that it has entered our midst. This enterprise was surely not successful. Artificial intelligence either was irrelevant to the questions at hand or proposed answers in an unpalatable form. Chief among these was the proposition that mind was simply an information-processing system. A runner up, though analogical in force, was the proposition that neurophysiology was almost totally irrelevant to questions of mind.

I then asked two questions from within the information-processing view: on generality and on ill-structured problems. Here I laid out various proposals about the questions that have been raised in the artificial-intelligence field, in the hope that they would serve to structure discussion. No final opinion was offered on either question, since in fact I have none.

These two questions were drawn from the view of artificial intelligence as exploration. They are not the questions that engage one most immediately when concerned with modeling human behavior. Still, they do have a certain interest, since they are two of the questions that most often arise in considering the limitations of current artificial-intelligence systems.

There has been an explicit theme throughout the paper: that information-processing systems constitute a "view" and not just a congeries of odd facts to be applied or not as the local questions warrant. Two things should be said about this assertion. First, the view is an information-processing one, not an artificial-intelligence one. I do not think there is anything special about artificial intelligence that is not assimilable into the main stream of computer science. Second, no special merit attaches to the word "view." Some of the worst ideational cancers mankind has suffered have been presented in the form of "views." By a view I mean only that a framework comprehensive enough to encourage and permit thinking is offered, so that not only answers, but questions, criteria of evidence, and relevance all become affected. It is well known that when communication is attempted between holders of different views, often remarkably little of scientific value takes place.

Perhaps I should have proceeded differently—as one is often encouraged to do in interdisciplinary endeavors—with faith that a modicum of talk and earnest zeal would serve to establish a basis for communication on fundamental issues. It seemed somehow that a more straightforward approach was in order.

Acknowledgments

This paper was originally developed for a conference on the Concepts of Mind by the Study Group on the Unity of Knowledge in Berkeley, California, August 1969. The original audience had primarily philosophic concerns and some, but not all, of that flavor has been allowed to stand in the present revision.

I would like to thank Richard Young for comments on an earlier draft. As always, my debt to Herbert Simon is beyond simple acknowledgment. Many of the attitudes in the paper find alternative expression in his little book on *The Sciences of the Artificial* (Simon, 1969) and in a recent joint endeavor (Newell and Simon, 1972).

The work on which the paper is based was supported in part by the Advanced Research Projects Agency of the Office of the Secretary of Defense (F 44620–67–C–0058), monitored by the Air Force Office of Scientific Research, and in part by Research Grant MH–07722–05 from the National Institutes of Health.

NATURAL LANGUAGE MODELS

Two

Semantic Networks: Their Computation and Use for Understanding English Sentences

R. F. Simmons

The University of Texas

In the world of computer science, networks are mathematical and computational structures composed of sets of nodes connected by directed arcs. A semantic network purports to represent concepts expressed by natural-language words and phrases as nodes connected to other such concepts by a particular set of arcs called semantic relations. Primitive concepts in this system of semantic networks are word-sense meanings. Primitive semantic relations are those that the verb of a sentence has with its subject, object, and prepositional phrase arguments in addition to those that underlie common lexical, classificational and modificational relations. A complete statement of semantic relations would include all those relations that would be required in the total classification of a natural language vocabulary.

We consider the theory and model of semantic nets to be a computational theory of superficial verbal understanding in humans. We conceive semantic nodes as representing human verbal concept structures and semantic relations connecting two such structures as representing the linguistic processes of thought that are used to combine them into natural-language descriptions of events. Some psycholinguistic evidence supports this theory (Quillian 1968, Rumelhart and Norman, 1971, Collins and Quillian, 1971); but a long period of research will be necessary before enough facts are available to accept or reject it as valid and useful psychological theory.

We are on much stronger ground when we treat semantic networks as a computational linguistic theory of structures and processing operations required for computer understanding of natural language. The nodes model lexical concepts and the semantic relations represent a combination of processes that are useful or necessary for analyzing English strings, for paraphrastic transformations, for question-answering operations, and for generating meaningful English sentences. Semantic nets are simple—even elegant—structures for representing aspects of meaning of English strings in a convenient computational form that supports useful language-processing operations on computers.

As linguistic theory, semantic nets offer a convenient formalism for representing such ideas as "deep structure", "underlying semantic structure", etc. The content of the structure represented in semantic nets depends on the conventions of the linguistic theory that is adopted. Our semantic networks will be seen to reflect a linguistic theory of deep case structures originated by Fillmore (1968) and further developed by Celce-Murcia (1971). The processes undertaken on the nets to generate language strings provide a theory of how language can be generated from underlying semantic structures. Computational processes for analyzing language into semantic nets provide a precise description of a theory of how some aspects of sentence meaning can be understood as a well-defined semantic system. The term "understanding" is given precise operational meaning through the programs that recognize or generate paraphrases and answer questions. The extent of the understanding is measurable by the ease or difficulty of the question-answering tasks, the size of vocabulary, and the efficacy of the system in handling complexities and subtleties of English structure.

When backed up by working programs, computational theories introduce a measure of logical rigor into the soft-sciences of linguistics and psychology. A minimally satisfactory computational theory of language requires that some set of natural language strings be generated and understood in terms of formal elements of that theory such as lexical structures, grammars, and semantic representations. A working set of computer programs that carry out recognition, paraphrase, question-answering, and language generation tasks proves the consistency and demonstrates the degree of completeness of the theory.

Despite logical rigor, computational theories may be weak or powerful in terms of the amount of language phenomena they account for; they may be elegant or cumbersome; they may be alien or closely related to human thought processes as we think we understand them; they may be in or out of fashion with respect to psychology, linguistics, or computer science. Ideally, they complement purely linguistic or psychological theories by formulating and testing precise descriptions of the structures and processes described more loosely in the theory. In natural language systems, computational theories have been taken beyond the bounds ordinarily set by linguists, psychologists, or logicians to develop an interdisciplinary theory of verbal communication based on conceptual structures underlying language; lexical, syntactic, semantic operations for recognizing and generating English strings; and logical and mathematical operations for determining the equivalence of two or more semantic structures.

The theory and model of semantic nets presented in this chapter is still incomplete: limited in its present development to single sentences, truncated at a certain conceptual depth, unspecified with regard to many of the complex phenomena of English, and unexplored with respect to other languages. In its favor, it encompasses such major subtasks of the verbal communication process as the generation and recognition of English strings and their understanding in terms of limited capability to answer questions and to generate and recognize paraphrases. As modelled in a working set of *LISP 1.5* programs it is precisely stated, internally consistent, and potentially useful to guide further research and for various applications to information retrieval, computer aided instruction, and other language processing operations.

An Abstract Model of Communication

The main human use of language is for one person to communicate feelings and ideas to other people. The simplest model of this communication process is diagrammed in Figure 2.1.

Thus simply shown, the diagram is largely vacuous with respect to meaning. If we develop a model of what is meant by "ideas and feelings", another for "language," and a set of functions to map language onto ideas and ideas onto language, we then have at least a mathematical theory of the communicative use of language. Semantic network structures form the model of ideas. A syntactic and semantic description (i.e., a grammar and a lexicon) of allowable ordering rules of words and phrases to make acceptable English sentences is an important aspect of the model of

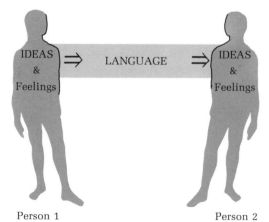

Person 1   Person 2

Figure 2.1   Diagram of Communication Process.
(Note: The symbol "⇒" is read as
"maps onto.")

language. Equally important are the rules for mapping words, phrases, and sentences into the semantic net structure of the model of ideas and for mapping the ideas into language strings.

If the model of ideas is also to be used to represent the processes of rational thought, then it must be able to represent one idea as a consequence of another or of a set of other ideas. For example, "tiger" implies "mammal." This is one essential feature of problem-solving, theorem-proving, and question-answering behaviors. It also is the basis for recognizing that two sentences are paraphrases that (from some point of view) mean essentially the same thing. This feature of the model is carried in implicational rules and functions that map one semantic structure into another.

The ideas may be mapped into language forms other than English or other natural languages. We can define a language to describe a structured sequence of actions and a mapping function from ideas into that language. The behavior of a robot hand in selecting and stacking blocks, for example, has been described in this volume by Winograd as a language composed of permitted sequences of simple operators as Grasp(x), Move(x,y) Put(x,y), etc. Semantic representations of such imperative sentences as "Put the large green pyramid on top of the blue block" are mapped into strings of this operator language which are then interpreted by a computer (in complex ways) to result in the appropriate actions by a (simulated) mechanical hand.

The content of visual representations can also be seen as a language string of edging, cornering, and shading elements. This string is mapped onto a semantic structure of images that has been represented in semantic net form by Clowes (1971) and Preparata (1970). Presumably there is a language to describe internal organic responses, such as feelings, and mapping functions that show correspondences between semantic net representations of ideas and feelings.

The mappings into ideas of events presented visually, as verbal strings, of a structure of organic reactions, or of a series of actions can all be represented linguistically in terms of a grammar and a lexicon that transform a language string into a semantic representation that is taken as a model of underlying ideas. The semantic representation of these events can be mapped out into any appropriate language using the corresponding grammar and lexicon of that language.

Ideally we hypothesize one central cognitive structure of semantic net form into which perceptions of speech, vision, action, and feeling can map, and from which can be generated speech, physical actions, hallucinations, feelings, and other thoughts. So far, however, we have only studied semantic nets to represent a class of English sentences.

At a very abstract level this model of communication can be simply represented as three mappings:

M1 (language, ideas)
M2 (ideas, ideas)
M3 (ideas, language)

This abstract statement provides only an illusion of simplicity, since the processes M1, M2, and M3 are incredibly complicated. Learning them is a major occupation of humans for most of their lives. Analyzing and programming them involves much of the content of linguistics, psychology, logic, computational linguistics, and other sciences depending on the nature of the ideas that are studied.

The mappings M1 and M3 are in a complex inverse relation. For a given pair of language string and idea, L I, if M1(L) $\Rightarrow$ I, then M3(I) $\Rightarrow$ L' such that M1(L') $\Rightarrow$ I. In other words, a given semantic structure, I, that is derived from a language string, L, will generate another language string, L', which is either identical to L or a paraphrase of L and whose semantic structure is analyzed back into I. In this theory, L and L' are not restricted to strings from the same language or the same modality (i.e., speech, vision, feeling, etc.).

The mapping, M2, of ideas onto other ideas clearly encompasses many ideational processes. Perhaps the lowest level is simple association where one structure can be substituted for another if they have an element in common. Thus the ideas, "I saw a tree" and "trees grow" are related by the identical concept, "tree". Mappings can be in terms of paths from one idea to another; e.g., "a tree is a plant" that could be described as Superset(tree) $\rightarrow$ plant. Vastly more complex mappings are commonly used for detecting paraphrase or answering questions such as:

Quest: Did Napoleon lose the battle of Waterloo?
Ans: Wellington defeated Napoleon at Waterloo.

The detailed statement of this mapping is a complex relation between the concepts "lose" and "defeat" which is stated later in this chapter.

This abstract model of communication proposes that there is a single cognitive representation of ideas, whether they originated as visual, auditory, or tactile perceptions or whether they were derived from verbal descriptions in English, French, or Hindustani. At the present level of development of semantic network representations of meaning, emphasis has been concentrated on English sentences. The structures presented in this chapter are shown to be largely sufficient to account for understanding at the level of answering factual questions and forming verbal paraphrases. Schank presents a deeper level of ideational representation in Chapter 5 and Winograd shows a level of ideational representation (not in semantic network form) that is deep enough to mediate between language and action in the robot's world of blocks.

Linguistic Structure of Semantic Nets

A sentence is a string of ambiguous word symbols that implies a complex structure of underlying concepts. A semantic analysis of a sentence transforms this string into a structure of unambiguous concept nodes interconnected by explicit semantic relations. The concept nodes in this system of semantic nets are taken as lexical word-sense meanings and the semantic relations are variously deep case relations that connect nominal concepts to verbs, and conjunctive, modifier, quantifier, and classifier relations that connect and specify concepts.

Deep Case Structure of Verbs: Our semantic representations of sentence meanings are based partially on a linguistic theory of deep case structures as developed by Celce-Murcia (1972) deriving from earlier work by Filmore (1968) and Thompson (1971). In its essence, this theory provides for each sentence an underlying structure of a verb, its modality, and its nominal agruments. A phrase structure grammar can be used to describe this underlying structure as follows:

S ⟶ Modality + Proposition
Modality ⟶ Tense, Aspect, Form, Mood, Modal, Manner, Time
Proposition ⟶ Vb + (CASEARGUMENT) *
Vb ⟶ run, walk, break, etc.
CASEARGUMENT ⟶ CASERELATION + [NP|S]
NP ⟶ (prep) + (DET) + (ADJ) * + (N) + N + (S|NP)
CASERELATION ⟶ CASUALACTANT, THEME, LOCUS, SOURCE, GOAL.

Box 2.1a shows a tree diagram of case structure and 2.1b expands the definitions of the elements comprising the modality.

The modality carries detailed information concerning tense, form, truth value, manner, time, and syntactic form of the sentence. It can be seen in a later section to

---

Box 2.1   Syntactic Form of a Case Structure for a Sentence, with (a) being the General Case Structure for a Sentence and (b) the Possible Values of the Modality.

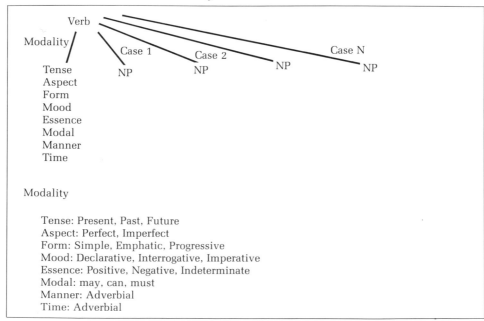

Modality

Tense: Present, Past, Future
Aspect: Perfect, Imperfect
Form: Simple, Emphatic, Progressive
Mood: Declarative, Interrogative, Imperative
Essence: Positive, Negative, Indeterminate
Modal: may, can, must
Manner: Adverbial
Time: Adverbial

serve as a blueprint for generating a particular syntactic form of sentence from a semantic proposition. The Proposition is a verb that dominates a set of noun-phrase or sentence arguments, each of which is in a definite, named, case relation to the verb.

Celce-Murcia argues convincingly that all arguments of the verb can be classified as members of five deep case relations; namely, Causal Actant, Theme, Locus, Source and Goal. In a related case structure system Chafe (1970) prefers several different case names including Agent, Patient, Benefactor, etc., as proposed by Filmore and other case structure theorists. We have chosen to follow the naming conventions suggested by Celce-Murcia. A simple sentence such as "Mary wore a sweater" gives the following propositional structure:

Wear: LOCUS Mary, THEME a sweater.

A more complicated example, "John broke the window with a hammer", has the following propositional structure:

Break: CA1 John, Theme the window, CA2 a hammer.

This example shows that two Causal Actants (CA1, CA2) may be present in a single sentence. The sentence, "An ape is an animal" can be interpreted as having two themes, as follows:

Be: T1 an ape, T2 an animal.

Two loci can be seen in "Mary wore a sweater in the park".

A fair degree of familiarity with this and other systems of case-structure naming conventions is required before people come to agreement in assigning names to propositional arguments. At this early period in the development of the theory, it is quite possible that other naming conventions will be generally adopted and that more objective criteria will be developed for identifying the role of arguments in a proposition.

Verbs are assigned to classes called paradigms in accordance with the way their deep case relations are allowed to be ordered in surface strings. For example, "break" belongs to the ergative paradigm that allows the following patterns of surface strings for the active voice:

John broke the window with the hammer.
John broke the window.
The hammer broke the window.
The window broke.

Each of these variations is generated with argument ordering and deletion operations from the following propositional structure:

Break: CA1 John, T the window, CA2 a hammer.

The process of generating such sentences requires that the modality be specified and an appropriate surface ordering rule be selected. The modality for the above set is as follows:

MODALITY: TENSE Past, VOICE Active, FORM Simple,
            ESSENCE Positive, MOOD Declarative.

Unspecified values for Aspect, Modal, Manner, and Time indicate null representations in the surface string. The selection of a paradigmatic ordering rule depends on very complex considerations such as choice of subject emphasis, deletions of arguments because of context, embedding environment, etc. Paradigmatic ordering rules for the ergative class verb are as follows:

```
(CA1,VACT,THEME,CA2)
(CA2,VACT,THEME)
(THEME,  VACT)
(THEME,  VPAS,  CA1,CA2)
(THEME,  VPAS,  CA2,CA1)
(THEME,  VPAS,  CA1)
(THEME,  VPAS,  CA2)
(THEME,  VPAS)
```

If the Modality is marked for Emphatic, Progressive, Imperative, or Interrogative, the choice and ordering of elements of the verb string and of nominal arguments will differ within the application of rules such as the above. Details of this generation process are presented in a later discussion.

As in Chomsky's transformational theory, this proposes a deep structure underlying each embedded sentence, but the deep case structure can meet our requirement that the semantic analysis of a sentence result in a structure of unambiguous concepts connected by explicit semantic relations. Unambiguous concepts are provided by the selection with various contextual restrictions of particular word-sense meanings that map onto the lexical choices. The small set of case designators name specific semantic relations between the verb and its arguments. The transformational deep structure, in contrast, provides only syntactic relations to connect the elements of a structure.

The Celce-Murcia theory also suggests that what we have seen as varied sense meanings of a verb can now be accounted for as varied implications of a given event-class that the verb designates, under the differing circumstances signified by different choices of semantic classes of arguments. This notion is rather difficult to understand at first reading. For example, the verb, "run" is taken to designate one event class—that of rapid motion—in all of the following environments:

John ran to school.
John ran a machine.

The machine ran.
The brook ran.

This verb belongs to a reflexive-deletion paradigm where the theme is deleted if it corresponds to the CA1. Thus the propositional structure of the first example is as follows:

Run: CA1 John, T John, Goal to school.

During the event, the Theme incurs rapid motion with the instruments of motion associated with that Theme, namely legs and feet. Similarly, in the running of a machine or of a brook, the Themes, "machine" and "brook" incur the rapid motion with their customary instruments; respectively, motors and gravity. The first two examples specify "John" as the animate Causal Actant, while in the latter two the causal actants are unspecified. The result is that the semantic definition of "run" is informally approximated by the following:

Run: THEME (incurs rapid motion)
       CA1 (animate instigator)
       CA2 (instrumental cause of motion)
       GOAL (condition of cessation of motion)

The development of this line of thought for numerous verbs offers an attractive area of research in the implicational meanings in language. The present level of understanding of semantic net structures achieves syntactic simplicity and computational advantages from expecting a single meaning for a verb (excepting homographs), but is not yet deep enough to use this form of definition in question answering and other applications.

The theory is also consistent with recent linguistic suggestions (Jacobs and Rosenbaum, 1968) that adjectives be treated similarly to verbs. In deep case structure, an adjective can be represented as a verb with the Modality marked Adjective, and a one argument proposition. Thus, "a red dress" might receive the following structure:

Red: MODALITY...Adjective, THEME a dress.

Similarly, a prepositional phrase such as "the book on the table" might be expressed:

Be: MODALITY...NP, THEME the book, LOCUS on the table.

Nominalized verbs such as "defeat" in "Napoleon's defeat at Waterloo" might be represented as:

Defeat: MODALITY...NP, THEME Napoleon, LOCUS at Waterloo.

The nesting of embedded sentences in this theory has been explored by Celce-Murcia (1972) who shows that a structure such as shown in Box 2.2 can be used.

These are all attractive but still incompletely developed aspects of the theory of deep case structures that have influenced our conventions for semantic network representations of sentence meanings. Thus far we have adopted the case structure representation for verbs and their arguments, and the use of paradigm classes and embedding conventions for verbs. We do not yet treat adjectives and noun phrases in this manner, although it will probably be advisable to do so as we begin to deal with the task of answering difficult questions.

Semantic Representations for Case Arguments: This subsection develops the conventions used in semantic networks for representing the meanings of words in general, nouns, NPs, adjectives, adverbs, prepositional phrases, conjunctions, etc.

Words: The word is a convenient unit in dealing with printed text in that it is easily distinguishable and is used as a basis for ordering the lexicon. If we think of the lexicon as a set of word-sense meanings each composed of syntactic and semantic data, then each meaning can be taken as a concept or an idea. Each meaning in the lexicon maps onto one or more character strings or words, and each word represents one or more meanings in the lexicon. Each meaning in the lexicon is designated by a number prefixed by L, for example, L57, L1072, etc.

The contextual meaning of a word in a semantic network is represented by a term such as C_i, C_j, etc., where i and j are unique numbers. This term is connected by the TOKen relation to a particular word-sense meaning. The primary function of a word in context is to refer to a particular sense meaning in order to make that meaning available for use in understanding the events described by a sentence. An example of this basic semantic structure is:

C1 TOK apple

Box 2.2   Proposed Deep Case Analysis of "Napoleon suffered final defeat at Waterloo."

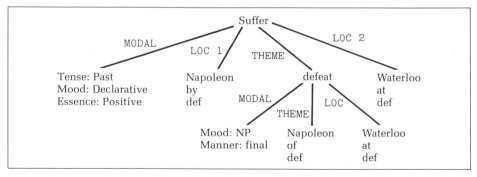

In this expression "apple" is printed for human communication to represent some node such as L23 which is the designator of a lexical structure containing the syntactic category, noun, a set of features such as NBR-singular, SHAPE-spherical, COLOR-red, PRINTIMAGE-apple, THEME*-eat, etc. These features are consulted for syntactic and semantic operations by parsers, generators, and question-answering systems.

Inflectional Suffixes and Auxiliaries: Singular and Plural forms and tense and agreement markings are usually carried as suffixual elements of the word. They may be discovered either by direct lookup of the full word form in the lexicon, or by a suffix stripping logic such as that described by Winograd in Chapter 4. Every noun is characterized in a semantic net with the relation NBR whose values are Singular, Plural or both. Thus for "apples", the net shows,

        C1 TOK apple, NBR Pl

A DETerminer relation is also required on noun structures and it is discussed in a later paragraph.

Suffixes and auxiliaries provide much of the information required in the Modality structure. An example sentence with a simple proposition and a very complex modality will illustrate the way the modality information is signified.

        Could John have been courting Mary falsely last year?

The semantic structure for this sentence is shown next.

    C1   TOK Court, CA1 (John), THEME (Mary), MODALITY C2.
    C2   TENSE Past, VOICE Active, FORM Progressive, ASPECT Perfect, MOOD Interrogative, MODAL Can, MANNER (Falsely), TIME (last year) ESSENCE Indeterminate

Each C-node is a set of semantic relations whose values may be; constants such as Past, Active, etc., lexical items, or other C-nodes. The parenthesized elements of the above example structure are shorthand notations that show that another structure not germane to the discussion is actually required to represent the semantic structure of the parenthesized value.

The details of obtaining this structure for the Modality will become apparent in Section V where the programs for computing it from surface strings are presented. For the moment a few explanatory remarks will suffice. "Could" signifies TENSE-Past, MODAL-Can, and by its introductory position, MOOD-Interrogative. The phrase, "have been courting" signifies FORM-Progressive, ASPECT-Perfect, and VOICE-Active. ESSENCE refers to Truth or Falsity of the statement—which as a question is indeterminate. "Falsely" and "last year" are respectively MANNER and TIME adverbials, which in the present conventions of this system are carried on the Modality. The information required to form these particular relations and values is obtained during parsing with grammar rules and the contents of the lexicon. Detailed computational analysis of the way in which verb strings signify the specific values of the modality have been described by Simmons and Slocum (1972) and Winograd (1972).

Determination and Quantification: In English every noun is associated with a determiner, either explicitly with words such as "this," "these," "some," "a," "an," "seven," "all," "the," etc., or implicitly where the absence of a determiner is interpreted as "most" or "all" (as in "bears eat fish"). In our semantic treatment we distinguish four semantic relations, DET, COUNT, NEG and QUANTifier or Q. The values of DET are definite, indefinite, or general. COUNT has as values a number or the meanings signified by "many," "few," "most," etc. NEG takes only the value "none." QUANT has values such as "some," "all," "every," etc. COUNT, QUANT, and NEG are not marked unless they are explicitly signified in the sentence. No claim is made that this is either a complete or completely satisfactory scheme for analyzing the truly vast complexity of determination of English nouns; it is instead a starting point which must be modified as further research reveals more details of this semantic structure.

One very important aspect of determination can hardly be discussed within the framework of a single sentence. When a noun has a definite determiner, it refers to a concept that has been mentioned previously, to something in the nearby environment or to a well-known class of events. Our relation DET with the value definite signifies this (respective) anaphoric, deictic or generic usage; just which usage is implied and to what it refers requires that DET be operated as a function to examine the textual environment. The manner in which this can be accomplished is suggested by Baranofski (1970).

The following examples illustrate our conventions for representing determination in semantic networks:

All seven windows
C1 TOK window, NBR Plural, DET Def., COUNT 7, Q All.

Some windows
C1 TOK window, NBR Plural, DET Indef, Q Some.

No window
C1 TOK window, NBR Sing, DET Generic, NEG none.

Combinations of these semantic relations signify various logical and numerical quantifiers. In our present uses of semantic nets for generating paraphrases and answering fact questions at the paraphrastic level, we have found it necessary to deal only superficially with logical quantifiers. These become of critical importance in more difficult questions and in verbal problem solving.

Adjectival Modification: Whether it occurs in a predicate or noun modifier position, we represent adjectival modification in the same semantic form. The two strings:

the barn is red
the red barn

each receive the following semantic representation:

    C1 TOK barn, NBR Sing, DET def, MOD C2.
    C2 TOK red, DEG Pos.

The semantic relation DEGree takes as values Positive, Comparative, or Superlative. If the value is positive, there is one noun argument for the adjective; comparative requires two, and superlative more than two.

The relation MOD is in fact a temporary expedient that serves only to indicate an adjectival modification. The linguistic structure of adjectives is almost as complicated as that of verbs. The meaning of a given adjective is relative depending on context. For example, the sentence "a large ant is smaller than a tiny elephant" shows that associated with the meanings of "ant" and "elephant", there must be a characteristic size value which is further specifiable by a size adjective. "A large ant" thus means something like "a large tiny-ant" while "a tiny elephant" indicates "a tiny large-elephant." Semantic relations underlying MOD include SIZE, SHAPE, COLOR, etc., which Schank (1969) suggests are characteristic attributes of nouns. The function of the adjective is apparently to modify the characteristic attribute of the noun as for example, "yellow brick" changes the characteristic reddish color associated with "brick" to the value "yellow".

The comparative and superlative uses of adjectives introduce a whole range of complex sentence structures which have been treated carefully in a dissertation by Celce-Murcia (1972). Our treatment of adjectives in semantic nets is only sufficient at the moment for dealing with the simplest cases. Future developments will probably require the adoption of a structure similar to that now used for verbs.

Adverbial Modification: A previous example showed that adverbs are values of such Modality relations as Manner and Time. The fact that they can also modify adjectives offers further motivation for treating adjectives as having a structure similar to verbs. Since linguists presently understand so little about the semantic behavior of adverbs, we again adopt the expedient of a gross relation, VMOD, in our computational models. This relation can be further specified as, MANNER, TIME, FREQUENCY, INTENSITY, etc., depending on the semantic class of the adverb.

Conjunction: In addition to the frequent occurrences of "or" and "and," many common adverbial conjunctions or sentence connectors are used in English. These include words such as "since," "because," "thus," "before," "after," etc. Our representation of these important terms in semantic structures is to form a TOKen structure followed by a list of arguments, as illustrated below.

    C1 TOK (any conjunction), ARGS C2, C3, C4...

The conjoined elements may be words, phrases or sentences. The meaning of conjunctions enters deeply into paraphrase and question-answering tasks, and they are used frequently to order sentences in time, causation, etc. Much detailed knowledge of the meaning of particular conjunctions is recorded in style books and dictionaries, but little formalization of this knowledge has so far been developed. Once again we are in the position of preserving a lexical indicator in the semantic net structure with little corresponding understanding of the lexical structure to which it refers.

The verbs Have and Be: Since these two verbs have noun phrase transformations, we choose to represent them in semantic networks as nominal structures. A few examples for "is" illustrate the applicable conventions:

The girl is beautiful.
C1 TOK girl, DET Def, NBR S, MOD (beautiful).

The girl is a mother.
C1 TOK girl, DET Def, NBR S, SUP (mother).

The girl is in the chair.
C1 TOK girl, DET Def, NBR S, LOC C2
C2 TOK chair, DET Def, NBR S, PREP in

The first example is treated as an adjectival MODification even though it occurs in predicate form. The second shows that the concept associated with "girl" is a subclass of that associated with "mother". The third shows the same structure as would have been derived from the noun phrase, "the girl in the chair".

Examples for "have" are as follows:

Mary has long fingers.
Mary has money.
Mary has fun.

The three semantic relations expressed here are respectively, HASPART, POSSess, and ASSOCiated. They are also signified by the apostrophe in such forms as "Mary's fingers", "Mary's money" and "Mary's fun". These alternate forms are assigned the same semantic structure as those with the verb expressed. The next example shows the treatment of "have" with a prepositional phrase.

Mary has fun in the park.
C1 TOK Mary, DET Def, NBR S, ASSOC (fun), LOC C2.
C2 TOK park, DET Def, NBR S, PREP in.

Eventually the theory of deep case structures may require that various forms of nominal modification should always be dominated by a verb and its modality. If we were to adopt this convention for "is" and "have" and their nominal forms, the following examples would result:

Mary is in the park.
C1 TOK Be, MODALITY...TENSE Present, THEME(Mary), LOCUS C2.
C2 TOK park, DET Def, NBR S, PREP in.

Mary has fun in the park.
C1 TOK Have, MODALITY...TENSE Present, THEME(Mary), LOCUS C2.
C2 TOK park, DET Def, NBR S, PREP in.

The structures immediately above would result whether "is" or "have" are present or deleted. It is not clear at this time whether these case structure conventions applied to nominal structures will simplify the computational structure and improve paraphrase and question-answering capabilities of the model. One apparent advantage is that paraphrase transformations might always be expressed in a formalism referring to case relation arguments. A disadvantage is that the syntactic depth of the constructions would be increased.

Additional discussion of conventions for expressing semantic structures found in English sentences, some definition of lexical structure, and the development of inverse relations and their use for representing embedded sentence structures can be found in Simmons (1970b).

Computational and Logical Structure of Semantic Nets

In addition to their linguistic form, semantic nets have a computational representation, a logical structure, and a conceptual content. No one of these aspects has been completely explored although enough knowledge of each has been obtained to make interesting computer programs for experimenting with the process of understanding verbally expressed ideas.

Computational Representation: To say that a structure is a network implies only that it has nodes and connections between them and that there are no restrictions such as those that exist in a tree where a daughter node may not have a direct connection to a sister or grandparent. When we add the modifier "semantic" to form "semantic network," we introduce a notion of content, i.e., a semantic network is a structure that contains meanings of language arranged in network. A semantic net generally contains *concept nodes* interconnected by *semantic relations*. Primitive verbal concepts are lexical meanings that map onto the character strings of words. Every concept is a node that has a set of relations to other concept nodes.

Figure 2.2 shows graphic and list representations of networks. The simplicity of these structures makes them ideal for computer representation as attribute-value lists or lists of triples, with the subsequent advantage of easy accessibility for processing operations. A network is defined according to the following:

Network := Node$*$
Node := Atom + Relationset, terminal Constant
Atom := Ci, Li (a number prefixed with L or C)
Relationset := Relation + Node
Relation := member of a list of semantic relations
Terminal Constant := character string

The asterisk signifies one or more repetitions of the marked element. The comma represents "or," the + "and." Terminal constants include English words as well as such examples as "noun," "sing," "Active," "Past," etc., which are values of lexical relations.

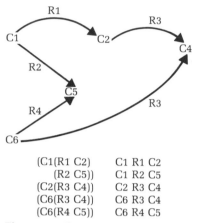

(C1(R1 C2)	C1 R1 C2
(R2 C5))	C1 R2 C5
(C2(R3 C4))	C2 R3 C4
(C6(R3 C4))	C6 R3 C4
(C6(R4 C5))	C6 R4 C5

Figure 2.2 Representation of Networks.
(a) Abstract Network as a
Directed Graph. (b) Attribute-value
List and Triples Representation.

From this definition, a semantic network is an interconnected set of nodes. A node is simply a term such as Ci or Li. Its relationset encodes the information it represents. The meaning of any node is an ordering of the rest of the nodes of network with which it is related. Assuming a richly interconnected network, the complete meaning of any particular node may involve every other node in the system. This feature of semantic networks was discussed at length by Quillian (1968) who showed that human subjects when asked repeatedly to define the words in their definitions of words, could continue the process indefinitely.

Semantic relations are viewed computationally as functions and procedures. In our present realizations these relations are largely undefined as procedures although in a previous paper (Simmons and Slocum, 1972) we showed how they could be defined as generation functions that would produce an appropriate syntactic structure corresponding to each semantic relation and its arguments.

In our present development, such relations as THEME, CAUSAL ACTANT, etc., can be perceived dimly as procedures which in some cases will change the contextual definitional structure to reflect the action of a verb. Thus, THEME(John, run) as a procedure might be expected to apply the characteristic of fast motion involving legs and feet to the ordinary structure defining John. Similarly, CA1(run, John) might be expected to add the information that John instigated the motion; and GOAL(run, store) must add some terminal condition to the motion implied by "run." A most interesting and potentially rewarding research task is to develop this idea computationally.

Logical Structure: The semantic network representation of sentences is also a logical system. A semantic net is a set of triples, (A R B) where A and B are nodes and R is a semantic relation. For example, (Break THEME Window) from an earlier example is one such triple; (Window DET Def) is another. Nodes are required to be elements of a set of unambiguous symbols—usually entries in the lexicon. Semantic relations are required to be defined or definable relations such as the following list:

1. Connectives OR, NOT, SINCE, BUT, AND, IMPLY, etc.
2. Deep Case Relations CA1, CA2, THEME, SOURCE GOAL, LOC
3. Modality Relations TIME, MANNER, MOOD, ASPECT, etc.
4. Attributive Relations MOD, POSSESSIVE, HASPART, ASSOC, SIZE, SHAPE, etc.
5. Quantitative Relations Q, NBR, DET, COUNT
6. Token substitution TOK
7. Set Relations SUP, SUB, EQ, PARTOF, etc.

These relations can be defined extensionally in a given system by listing the arguments that are acceptable. They can be defined intensionally by indicating properties that are required on their arguments. For example, in (A CA1 B), CA1 for Causal Actant 1, requires that B be animate, that it be the instigator of A, and that A belong to a class of action verbs that can accept an agent.

We can also apply a set-theoretic interpretation to semantic network structures. Each node is taken as the name of a set of processes and each relational arc is a restriction on the sets signified by the nodes it connects. Let us consider the propositional structure for the following example:

John broke the window with a hammer.
C1 TOK break, CA1 C2, THEME C3, CA2 C4
C2 TOK John, DET Def, NBR S
C3 TOK window, DET Def, NBR S.
C4 TOK hammer, DET Indef, NBR S, PREP with.

The hearer knows of a set of events that he calls "breakings." These include the breakings of glasses, of windows, of crime rings, of news stories, of horses and of hearts. The net C1 restricts these breakings to only those in which John is an instigator, a particular window received the action, and a hammer was the instrument. The subnets further specify a particular man named John, a definite member of the class named windows, and some one hammer. The modality further specifies the event in terms of time of occurrence, truth value, etc.

The relationset of C1 can thus be viewed as a conjoined set of binary predicates that restrict the application of the concept named by "break" to a particular subclass of events each of which is more or less precisely specified by the values of such relations as DET and NBR.

Logical aspects of semantic net structures are developed more formally by Sandewall (1970, 1969), Palme (1971) and Simmons and Bruce (1971). Sandewall's development is of particular interest in showing conventions for insuring that the representation will be in a first order calculus and in providing fairly explicit methods for axiomatizing meanings of words. Palme has demonstrated how these techniques can be used in a semantic net-based question-answering system. Simmons and Bruce showed an algorithm for translating from semantic net structure notation into a fairly standard form of first order predicate calculus.

The most significant consequence of defining semantic networks as a logical system is to make the techniques and results of research in automatic theorem proving easily transferable to problems of question answering and problem solving in semantic nets. It has been apparent for some time that the question-answering and paraphrase problems of natural language processing are closely related to the more abstract problem of proving logical and mathematical theorems. (See Green and Raphael 1968, and Simmons 1970a.) For the shallow level of answering factual questions or recognizing paraphrases, little use of theorem-proving logic is required. For more difficult questions and verbal statements of such problems as, "the missionaries and cannibals" or "the monkey and the bananas," problem-solving and theorem-proving techniques must be used.

Conceptual Level: The conceptual level of semantic net structures has been carefully limited to that of word-sense meanings connected by semantic relations that are frequently very closely related to corresponding syntactic relations. Is there any satisfactory rationale for selecting this level rather than the semantically deeper levels chosen by Schank (Chapter 5) or Rumelhart and Norman (1971)?

The depth of a syntactic or semantic structure can be defined as proportional to the extent to which it accounts for a set of strings which are, from some point of view, paraphrases of each other. If we define syntactic paraphrases as those strings which differ only in inflectional suffixes, certain forms of deletion (as of "have," "be," and "of" prepositions) and in the ordering of lexical selections; then a minimal depth of semantic structure would be shown by a structure which was the same for strings that are syntactic paraphrases of each other. Deeper semantic levels would provide identical structures for paraphrase sets of strings that have differing choices of content words and may vary in syntactic form.

We consider the following set of sentences as syntactic paraphrases:

John broke the window with a hammer.
The window was broken by John with a hammer.
The window was broken with a hammer by John.
It was a hammer with which John broke the window.

Each of these sentences can be generated from or analyzed into the following propositional structure:

C1 TOK break, CA1(John), THEME (the window), CA2 (with a hammer).

The variation in the Modality structure as to active and passive voice, and the choice of different argument-ordering rules from the verb paradigm account for the different syntactic forms of these sentences.

We consider the following two sentences to be semantic paraphrases of each other—i.e., they are very close in meaning and describe the same event using different words and syntactic forms.

John bought the boat from Mary.
Mary sold the boat to John.

A semantic structure deep enough to represent the common meaning of these two sentences is the following:

C1 TOK and, ARGS C2, C3.
C2 TOK transfer, SOURCE(John) GOAL(Mary), THEME (money)
C3 TOK transfer, SOURCE(Mary) GOAL(John), THEME(boat).

This structure—with appropriate variations in modality—can account for both syntactic and semantic paraphrases of the two sentences and is consequently deeper than one that accounts only for the syntactic paraphrases of either. It also makes explicit the implied fact that "buy" and "sell" involve a transfer of money and of ownership in opposite directions. This is analogous to the depth of structure used by Schank in Chapter 5.

The shallower structure of semantic nets described in this chapter is shown below:

C1 TOK buy, SOURCE(Mary), GOAL(John), THEME(boat).
C2 TOK sell, SOURCE(Mary), GOAL(John), THEME(boat).

In order for the present system to determine that the two structures are semantic paraphrases, it is necessary to have a paraphrase rule such as the following connecting "buy" and "sell":

R01 (BUY (S–S)(G–G)(T–T) SELL)

This rule simply means that the TOKen of C1 may be rewritten as SELL and that no change in the values of the arguments is indicated—that is, the value of SOURCE remains Mary, the GOAL, John, and the THEME, boat. Differing generation rules for "buy" and "sell" result in the reordering of the case arguments in the surface string. The rule can be expanded to introduce a CA2–MONEY, if desired and thus, through a semantic transformation, account for the same facts as the deeper structure previously illustrated. The formulation and use of such rules is developed at some length in a later section.

It is probable that the deeper structure forms a more satisfactory psychological model of conceptual structure as well as one that will answer questions more economically. The argument for the shallower structure is that it neatly defines a distinction between syntactic and semantic transformations at the level of lexical choice and at least for the moment offers a definable reference level in the confused area of generative semantics.

The Computation of Semantic Nets from English Strings

An English string can be transformed automatically into semantic structures such as those shown in the previous section with the aid of a program that consults a lexicon and a grammar. We use a variant* of a system developed by Woods (1970) called an "Augmented Finite State Transition Network" (henceforward, AFSTN) which interprets a grammar—shown graphically as a transition network—as a program to transform an English string into a semantic network. The same system with different grammars is also used as a basis for generating English strings from the semantic networks and for embedding an algorithm that answers questions. These latter two applications will be discussed in sections immediately following this one. In this section we will briefly describe the operation of the AFSTN system and show a grammar for translating from a small class of English strings into semantic nets.

The Woods AFSTN System: Simple phrase structure grammars can be represented in the form of state transition networks. An example grammar is shown below:

NP $\longrightarrow$ (ART) + (ADJ $*$) + N + (PP $*$)
PP $\longrightarrow$ PREP + NP
S $\ \ \longrightarrow$ NP + (AUX) + VP
S $\ \ \longrightarrow$ AUX + NP + VP
VP $\longrightarrow$ V + (NP) + (PP$*$)

Figure 2.3 shows the augmented finite state network that represents this grammar. The grammar shown above is in context-free, phrase structure format. It uses the conventions that parentheses indicate optionality and an asterisk shows that one or more repetitions of the phrases are allowed. In the graph of Figure 2.3 the nodes or states are shown as circles with labels such as "S," "NP," "VP," "q7" etc., and the arcs or paths are labelled by phrase names such as "NP," "PP," "VP," or by word-class names such as "Aux," "V," "Prep," etc. Some states such as q4, q6, q8, and q10 are specially marked with the symbol, "T" to show that a phrase or sentence can end at that node. The grammar can be seen to be recursive in that such paths as "ADJ" and "PP" form loops. It has subgraphs, such as NP, VP, and PP, which are also the names of arcs.

The figure shows only syntactic category information associated with the arcs, but each arc may in fact have an associated set of conditions to be met and operations to be performed as control passes from state to state. In this fashion, an AFSTN augments the ordinary state transition network by allowing a program to occur at each arc.

The reader can imagine a scanner that looks at each word in such a sentence as "The merry widow danced a jig," and examines its word class under the control of the "S" net. The first arc examined is the one labelled NP, which causes a transfer to the net, NP, where the category, Article, corresponds to the name of the first arc

*Programmed by D. Matuszek and J. Slocum at Univ. of Texas following Woods' description.

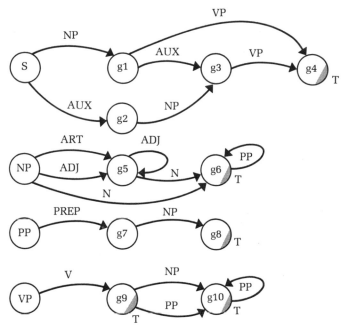

Figure 2.3   An Augmented Finite State Transition Network for a
Simple Grammar.

and allows transition to state q5. The next word, "merry" is category Adjective
which allows transition over the loop labelled adj to state q5. "Widow" allows transition of the arc, N, to state q6 where the noun phrase has been satisfied, and is
POPped to achieve transition of the arc labelled NP in net S. This takes the system to
state q1 where transition of the VP arc will successfully complete the scan of the
sentence. By operating the programs associated with each arc, a structure of the sentence may be created in any form designed by the programmer. Thus transformational deep structures result from one such set of programs written by Woods, and
semantic network structures result from the programs described in the following
paragraphs.

For complete understanding of the following example programs, the reader will
find it helpful to study Woods' careful description of the structure and operation of
his AFSTN system (Woods 1970).

Analysis of a Noun Phrase: The following program recognizes and transforms
simple noun phrases into semantic structures.

```
(S(Push NP T
   (SETR  SUBJ *)
   (TO  Q10) ))
```

```
(NP(CAT ART T
    (MAKEPR (QUOTE DET)(GETF DET))
    (SETR NBR (GETF NBR))
    (TO N2))
   (TST ADJ T
    (SETR NBR OK)
    (JUMP N2) ))
 (N2(CAT ADJ T
    (SETR ADJ (PUT(GENSYMC)(QUOTE TOK) *))
    (TO N3))
   (TST N T
    (SETR NBR OK)
    (JUMP N3)))
 (N3(CAT NOUN (AGREE(GETR NBR)(GETF NBR))
    (ADDPR (QUOTE MOD)(GETR ADJ))
    (ADDPR (QUOTE NBR)(GETF NBR))
    (ADDPR (QUOTE TOK) *)    (JUMP N4) ))
 (N4(POP(PUTPRL(GENSYMC)(GETR MLIST))T))
```

A graph of this program is shown in Figure 2.4 and an explanation of its flow and effects is shown in Table 2.1. The figure shows the major test above the arc and the operations to be performed below each arc. The table shows the condition of the star (*) register usually containing the word under the scanner except when a POP is to occur when it contains the results to be passed back up to the control level of the last PUSH. The flow of program operations is numbered, the main result is listed in the next column, and the last column shows the registers or structures that contain the result.

If we enter the program with the phrase, "a merry widow" the system scans the first element, "a" and enters the network at S. (S(PUSH NP T) has the effect of transferring control to the network node labelled NP. At this node, (CAT ART) means that a procedure called CAT looks at the dictionary entry for what is in the * register to discover if it is an article. Since * contains "a", the CAT function returns true and the operations associated with that arc are undertaken. (Note in Figure 2.3 that if we were considering the phrase "old dowager", CAT ART would have failed and TST ADJ would have transferred control to N2 without moving the scanner —by using JUMP instead of TO.)

The first operation, line 3 in Table 2.1, is (MAKEPR (QUOTE DET) (GETF DET)). GETF DET gets the value of the feature DET from the lexicon for the element in the * register. This value for "a" is "indefinite." MAKEPR puts the pair (DET INDEF) in a register called MLIST.

The next operation, line 4, is (SETR NBR (GETF NBR)). This operation gets the value of NBR for "a" which is SINGULAR, and puts it into the register named NBR. The terminal operation (TO N2) transfers control to N2, setting the * register to "merry" the next element in the phrase.

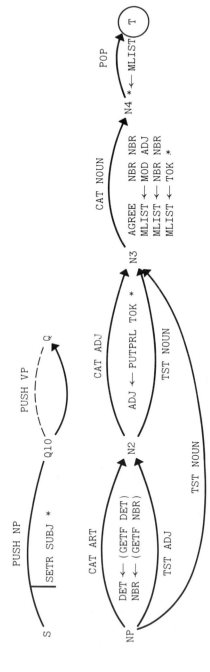

Figure 2.4 Graph of Semantic Transformation of a Simple Noun Phrase.

Table 2.1 Program Flow for Analysis of "a merry widow."

Scanner *register	Line #	Flow of program operations	Result	Location of result
a	1	(S(PUSH NP T)	TRANSFER TO NP	
	2	(NP(CAT ART)	TRUE Conditional	
	3	(MAKPR(QUOTE DET)(GETF DET))	(DET INDEF)	MLIST
	4	(SETR NBR(GETF NBR))	SINGULAR	NBR
merry	5	(TO N2))	Transfer to N2, Move scanner to "merry"	
	6	(N2(CAT ADJ) T)	TRUE conditional	
	7	(SETR ADJ(PUT(GENSYMC)(QUOTE TOK) *))	(C1(TOK MERRY)), ADJ ← C1	ADJ and Property List
widow	8	(TO N3))	Transfer to N3, move scanner to "widow"	
	9	(N3(CAT NOUN)	TRUE conditional	
	10	(AGREE(GETR NBR)(GETF NBR))	(AGREE Singular Singular), TRUE Condition	
	11	(ADDPR(QUOTE MOD)(GETR ADJ))	(MOD C1)	MLIST
	12	(ADDPR(QUOTE NBR)(GETF NBR))	(NBR Singular)	MLIST
	13	(ADDPR(QUOTE TOK) *)	(TOK widow)	MLIST
	14	(JUMP N4))		
	15	(N4(POP(PUTPRL(GENSYMC)(GETR MLIST))T))	(C2(TOK widow)(DET INDEF)(NBR Singular)(MOD C1))	*and Property List
	16	(SETR SUBJ *)	(C2 etc)	SUBJ

At N2 the first test is (CAT ADJ) which is found True for "merry." The main operation undertaken here, is to create a property list structure, (C1 (TOK merry)), by using the functions, GENSYMC which creates the symbol C1 and PUTPRL which makes the property list for C1 and returns C1 as its value to be used by SETR which places C1 in the register, ADJ. The next operation in N2 is (TO N3) which sets the scanner and * register to the next element in the string, namely "widow", and transfers control to node N3. Again it can be noticed—in Figure 2.4—that if a phrase without an adjective had been analyzed, the test, (CAT ADJ) would have failed and (TST NOUN) would have succeeded, causing a (JUMP N3) without moving the scanner.

At N3 (line 9) two tests are called for; first (CAT NOUN) second, (AGREE(GETR NBR)(GETF NBR)). Previously nodes have had a CAT test or the dummy TST each followed by the sumbol T in place of a second conditional. The symbol T has meant that the second conditional was automatically taken as TRUE. Here, however, the second conditional tests for agreement in number between the noun and any article that it may have (and the second conditional is evaluated first by the system).

The register NBR has been set in line 4 to the value SINGULAR and (GETR NBR) retrieves this value. Since "widow" is singular, (GETF NBR) returns this value. Thus the condition reduces to (AGREE SINGULAR SINGULAR) which evaluates to TRUE. At this point additional semantic agreement tests are usually introduced to select word-sense meanings, but to maintain simplicity of exposition they are omitted in this example.

Since the two conditions of N3 have been met, some operations are now undertaken to form a semantic structure for the phrase. These are ADDPR functions which create the structure shown in the result column for lines 11-13. At line 14, the terminal operation (JUMP N4) transfers control without moving the scanner. N4 provides an unconditional POP using PUTPRL and GENSYMC to create the structure shown in the result column. POP assigns the value, C2 to the * register and returns control to the place where (PUSH NP) occurred—i.e., line 1.

At this point we can notice that a PUSH arc is also a conditional that returns True if the next element or elements in the string being scanned form the phrase which is the argument of PUSH. (PUSH VP, PUSH PP, etc.). The PUSH NP being true in this case, its operations set a register called SUBJ to the value of the * register—i.e., C2—, move the scanner and transfer control to Q10. C2 is the name of a property list structure containing the following semantic structure for the phrase:

```
(C2(TOK WIDOW)(NBR SINGULAR)(DET INDEF)(MOD C1))
(C1(TOK MERRY))
```

It should be noticed that the resulting semantic structure corresponds to conventions described in the preceding section.

Analysis of a Verb Phrase: As a result of making the noun phrase of the preceding example, control was returned to the top level, the (PUSH NP) arc was successfully completed, C2 assigned to the SUBJ register, and control was passed to node Q10. At Q10 we have a choice of two arcs; either (POP ∗) or (PUSH VP). Assuming, now, that our sentence had continued as follows: "A merry widow had been dancing a jig," then the scanner would contain "had" and the arc, (PUSH VP) would be attempted.

A portion of the VP network is shown in Figure 2.5 and program corresponding to it is listed in Appendix Table 1. This part of the network has the purpose of determining the modality (i.e., NUMBER, TENSE, VOICE, FORM, ASPECT & MOOD) and constructing the semantic form of the verb. This figure shows fairly completely the tests (above the arc) and the operations (below the arc) that are required. The functions that make structure pairs are indicated by a left-pointing arrow, ←; those such as LIFTR that send arguments up to the next level by a vertical arrow, ↑. To maintain simplicity of exposition, some paths in the network are left incomplete where they concern modal, emphatic and future auxiliaries.

We will follow the example sentence through the graphed network of Figure 2.5 leaving the interested reader to consult the program for complete statements. Control is at VP with the scanner containing "had." (CAT AUX (GETF BE)) fails since "had"

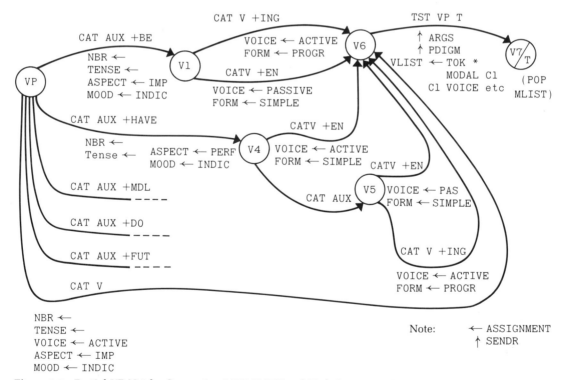

Figure 2.5   Partial VP Net for Computing MODALITY and Verb Structure. Note: ← ASSIGNMENT; ↑ SENDR.

is not a form of "to be." (CAT AUX (GEFT HAVE)) succeeds since "had" has the feature HAVE. The operations indicated are to create in register MLIST the pairs (NBR 3PPL)(TENSE PAST)(ASPECT PERFECT) and (MOOD INDIC). MAKEPR first cleans the register MLIST, then adds a pair, while ADDPR simply adds a pair to MLIST. Thus MAKEPR is called first on entry to a level to insure emptying MLIST at that level of any previous contents such as those inserted in the last example. The scanner is advanced to "been" and control is passed to V4 by the terminal actions, (TO V4).

Since "been" has the category "aux" it fails the CAT V test, but passes the (CAT AUX) and control is passed to V5 with the scanner at "dancing." Notice that no additional semantic structure is assigned here because the "been" is only part of the indicator for either a passive or progressive verb form. The first path tests for (CAT V) and (GETF +EN); since "dancing" is not an "en" form it fails this test and the next arc is attempted. This one tests for (CAT V) and (GETF +ING) which succeeds because the verb is a progressive or +ING form. At this point the pairs (VOICE ACTIVE) & (FORM PROGRESSIVE) are added to MLIST by using ADDPR. Control is passed without advancing the scanner by using (JUMP V6).

V6 is an unconditional arc in that (TST VP T) always evaluates TRUE. (TST is a null test so the argument VP is only for a human reader, and T is the second conditional which evaluates to TRUE). At V6 we now have the elements of the verb structure in the MLIST and must create the appropriate semantic structure and send it and other information back up to the top level of the sentence. LIFTR is a function that sends information up a level, and it is used here to send the content of the verb features PDIGM and ARGS to the next higher level in the sentence where they will be used to continue the example in the next subsection of the paper. In traversing nodes, VP V4, and V5 we accumulated the modality structure for the verb as follows:

```
((NBR 3PPL)(TENSE PAST)(ASPECT PERFECT)(MOOD INDIC)(VOICE
ACTIVE)(FORM PROGRESSIVE))
```

Here PUTPRL is used to form a property list headed by the result of operating GEN–SYMC, namely C3; and the pair (MODAL C3) is put onto a clean MLIST. The pair (TOK dance) is added to MLIST, the scanner is advanced to "a" and control is passed to V7. V7 is an unconditional POP that transfers the contents of the MLIST in the * register and sends it back up to Q10 where (PUSH VP) occurred.

Analysis of the Sentence: Figure 2.6 shows a portion of the top level of a sentence network and Appendix Table 2 shows the corresponding portion of program. The figure shows some incomplete paths, indicated by dotted lines, to suggest additional grammar that is not required for the present example.

As we returned to Q10, the * register contained the following content:

```
((TOK DANCE)(MODAL C3))
```

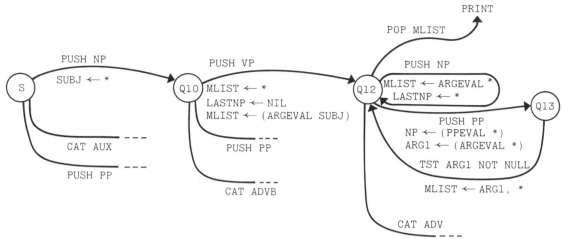

Figure 2.6 Network for Top-level Analysis of a Sentence.

This is put in MLIST by (SETR MLIST *) and a register called LASTNP is set to NIL (for later use). At this point we are ready to determine what semantic relation holds between the subject and the verb. A function called ARGEVAL takes the noun phrase in question, consults the lexical entry for the verb and determines whether the NP is a causal actant, source, locus, theme, etc., and returns either NIL or a deep case structure name (or names) as a value. The relevant lexical information for "dance" for this purpose was sent up earlier from the NP net into the registers PDIGM and ARGS whose contents are as follows:

```
(PDIGM(CASES(CA1 LOCUS) THEME LOCUS2))
       (SUBJ(CA1 LOCUS))(OBJ THEME)(PREP(WITH LOCUS2)))
(ARGS (LOCUS ANIMATE)(THEME dance)(LOCUS2 ANIMATE))
```

In evaluating SUBJ, ARGEVAL must first obtain the head noun with a (GET SUBJ (QUOTE TOK)) which returns the lexical node for "widow". Consultation of the registers ARGS and PDIGM then shows that the noun in SUBJECT position for VOICE–ACTIVE must be a CA1 and a LOCUS. (If voice had been passive, ARGEVAL would have read SUBJECT as OBJECT). The data in ARGS shows that CA1 and LOCUS for this verb must be marked animate. The noun "widow" is so marked in the lexicon so ARGEVAL returns (CA1, LOCUS) as the value of the relation between "widow" and "dance."

In a similar manner when this function is later called with "jig," it will discover that this noun is an OBJECT and marked with "dance" and so return THEME. If presented with a phrase such as "with John," it recognizes by the preposition "with" and the animate marker on "John" that it is dealing with a LOCUS2.

In this example the function ADDPR is then called with arguments as follows: (ADDPR (CA1 LOCUS)(GETR SUBJ)). The result is to put two pairs on the MLIST as follows:

((CA1 C2)(LOCUS C2))

The scanner is advanced and control passed to node, Q12 by the instruction, (TO Q12). The first arc leaving Q12 is (PUSH NP T). Since the phrase following the verb is "a jig," the push to NP returns with the * register containing, C4 whose property list is as follows:

(C4(TOK JIG)(NBR SINGULAR)(DET INDEF))

ARGEVAL of C4 returns THEME and ADDPR adds to the MLIST the pair (THEME C4). At this point the terminal action (TO Q12) advances the scanner and passes control to Q12 again. But the sentence ended with "jig" so the * register is set to NIL and the PUSH NP and PUSH PP arcs fail. The arc (POP etc.) T) is unconditional so it succeeds in building the final structure for the sentence and passing up the node C5 whose property list is as follows:

(C5(TOK DANCE)(MODAL C3)(CA1 C2)(LOCUS C2)(THEME C4))

The complete expansion of C5 gives the following semantic structure for the sentence:

```
C5 TOK DANCE      C3 NBR 3PP1          C2 TOK WIDOW              /
   MODAL C3          TENSE PAST           NBR SINGULAR
   CA1    C2         ASPECT PERFECT       DET INDEF
   LOCUS C2          MOOD INDIC           MOD C1
   THEME C4          VOICE ACTIVE
                     FORM PROGRESSIVE
C1 TOK MERRY      C4 TOK JIG
                     NBR SINGULAR
                     DET INDEF
```

Had the sentence continued with a prepositional phrase such as in ". . . danced a jig with John", the PP arc of Figure 2.6 would have operated, and the additional structure (LOCUS2 C5)(C5(TOK John)(NBR SINGULAR)(DET DEF)) would have been added.

The semantic net developed for the "merry widow" sentence is in fact a tree. As additional sentences in a discourse are analyzed, they will refer to nodes in earlier structures and the tree of the single sentence becomes part of a larger network. Elements of the sentence tree are also inter-connected by paths through the lexicon. Thus what we see in this analysis of the sentence is an explicit structure of unambiguous lexical references. It is the surface tip of an iceberg with great depths of inter-relationship in the data contained in the lexicon but not shown here as part of the analysis of the sentence. We claim that what is shown is the shallowest level of semantic structure.

Generating English Sentences from Semantic Nets

A basic function called GEN is central to the process of generation. This function takes a list as its argument. The list contains the name of a structure from which a sentence is to be generated followed by a series of constraints on the modality. For example, if we wish to generate a question from the sentence "A merry widow danced a jig," the call to GEN would be written as follows:

```
GEN((C5 ACTIVE, INTERROG, (QUERY JIG)))
```

This call is designed to generate, "What did the merry widow dance?"

GEN calls first a function that gets the modal structure of C5 and rewrites those values specified in the call. After this has been accomplished, another function, PATTERN, is called to select one of the verb paradigm patterns associated with the verb "dance." The paradigm for generation is selected by discovering which one fits the case arguments of the semantic structure. In this example, the following paradigm is selected:

```
((SUBJ (CA1-LOCUS))(OBJ THEME))
```

The register, SNTC, is then set to the list,

```
(CA1-LOCUS VACT THEME)
```

It is this list that will be scanned and presented in the * register to control the generation sequence of the sentence. At this point, GEN turns over control to the generation grammar, R, with the call, (RETURN(PUSH R)). The POP from R will cause the sentence that has been generated to be printed out as the value of the function GEN.

The generation grammar-program, R will be explained by first showing the top level of control flow then by looking at the generation of the NPs and VP. Appendix Table 3 shows the grammar for the top level and Figure 2.7 presents it as a network that forms the basis for the explanation.

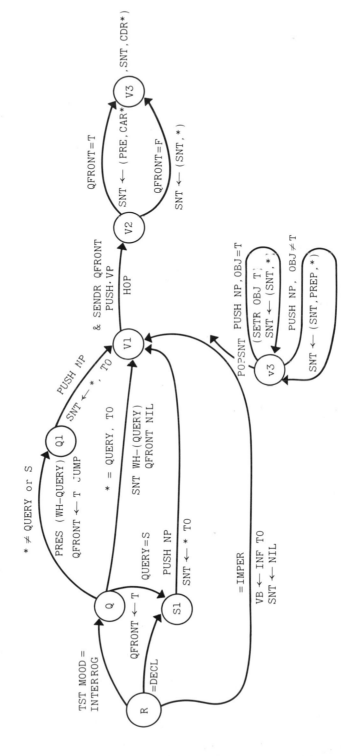

Figure 2.7 AFSTN Top-level Sentence Generation.

The semantic structure for the sentence after modification by GEN appears as in Table 2.2 below.

Table 2.2   Semantic Structure for Generation.

C5 TOK DANCE	C3 NBR 3PPL	
MODAL C3	TENSE PAST	
CA1-LOCUS C2	ASPECT IMPERF	
THEME C4	MOOD INTERROG	
	VOICE ACTIVE	
	FORM SIMPLE	
	QUERY THEME	
C1 TOK MERRY	C2 TOK WIDOW	C4 TOK JIG
	NBR SINGULAR	NBR SINGULAR
	DET INDEF	DET INDEF
	MOD C1	

The register SNTC at the time of the PUSH to R contains (CA1−LOCUS, VACT, THEME) and the ∗ register contains CA1−LOCUS.

Figure 2.7 shows that at node R the MOOD value of C3 is examined to determine whether it is Interrogative, Imperative, or Declarative. Since it is marked INTERROG, control is jumped to State Q. Arcs leaving Q test to determine the form of the question by examining the QUERY arc in C3. Since the value of QUERY is THEME and the ∗ register contains CA1−LOCUS a query-fronting transformation on the questioned element will be required. This is signified by setting the register QFRONT to T. The question word is then generated by calling the function WH- with THEME as its argument. This function computes the question word "What" for the THEME Value "jig" of the structure C5. Control is then JUMPed to node Q1 leaving the ∗ unchanged. At Q1 we PUSH NP, which results in the generation of "a merry widow" which is POPped back up in the ∗ register. Register SNT is set to this phrase and control is passed to V1 with ∗ set to the next element of the control string, VACT.

At V1 a PUSH VP is tried and on successful completion it returns in the ∗ register, "did dance." The "did" was generated because the register QFRONT was set to T; otherwise "danced" would have been the value. We JUMP to V2 where QFRONT is again tested. Since the value is T, the register SNT is set to the sequence, (PRE, (CAR ∗), SNT, (CDR ∗)), whose values are respectively, What, did, the merry widow, dance. Since there are no arguments in C5 that are now unaccounted for, the transfer to V3 results in a (POP SNT) where SNT contains the generated question, "WHAT DID THE MERRY WIDOW DANCE."

In passing we can note that at node Q, if the value of QUERY on the MODAL structure had been CA1−LOCUS, the contents of ∗ would have matched it, QFRONT would have been set to F, and the question generated would have been, "WHO danced a jig". If the value of QUERY had been S, the question would have been "DID A MERRY WIDOW DANCE A JIG".

Generating Simple NPs: Figure 2.8 shows a grammar network for dealing with noun phrases containing only a determiner, an adjective string, and a noun. Generalizations of this net to include further modifications by nouns and prepositional phrases simply require extension of the grammar in the form described. More complex embeddings of relative clauses etc., will require continued study particularly with reference to appropriate sequencing and limitations of depth.

On the PUSH NP of the previous example (Figure 2.7) the ∗ register contains CA1—LOCUS and there has been a (SENDR ST (GET ST ∗)). The effect of this latter operation has been to make the structure C2 available at the NP level. An expansion of C2 is as follows:

```
C2 TOK WIDOW       C1 TOK MERRY
   DET INDEF
   NBR SINGULAR
   MOD C1
```

At node NP there are three TST arcs to examine the determiner and choose an article. The test that is made for an indefinite article is as follows:

```
(TST DEF (EQ(GET(GETR ST)(QUOTE DET))(QUOTE INDEF))
```

This test gets the value of DET (which is INDEF) from C2 and matches it against the value INDEF. Since the TST condition returns T, the register SNT is set to the value (A) and control is jumped to node N1.

At N1 the arcs test for the presence of adjectives with the following expression:

```
(TST ADJ (SETR ADJ (GET (GETR ST)(QUOTE MOD))))
```

As a result in the present example, register ADJ is set to C1. The graph notation ADJ ← MOD shows this consequence, and control is JUMPED to N2. If the (GET ST MOD) had returned NIL signifying no MOD relation on the structure, ADJ would have been set to NIL and the condition on the TST arc would have failed allowing the next arc (TST NOADJ T) to cause a JUMP to N3.

At N2 the test is made to determine whether there is one adjective, (ATOM (GETR ADJ)) = T, or more if the predicate fails. Since the value of ADJ is the atom C1, there is only one modifier. The notation in the figure:

```
SNT ← SNT + (GETLEX ADJ NIL)
```

is a shorthand for the following expression in the actual grammar:

```
(SETR SNT(APPEND(GETR SNT)(LIST(GETLEX (GETR ADJ) NIL))))
```

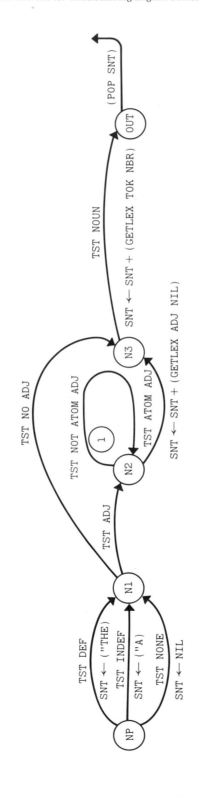

Figure 2.8 NP Generation Net.

The function (GETLEX A B) takes a structure name and a morphological attribute—such as NBR, TENSE, and so forth—and returns the word form. In this case GETLEX returns MERRY as its value. SNT is reset to the concatenation (i.e., APPEND) of its old value to the list (MERRY) making its current value, (A MERRY). Control is then JUMPED to N3.

If register ADJ had contained a list of values, GETLEX would have been called with (CAR(GETR ADJ)). . . , ADJ would have been set to (CDR (GETR ADJ)), and control JUMPED to N2 to loop through the list of adjective modifiers.

At N3 in this net the noun head of the structure is developed by the call (GETLEX (GETR ST) NBR) which returns WIDOW, the singular form. SNT is then reset to A MERRY WIDOW and control is JUMPED to OUT where (POP SNT T) puts this phrase in the * register and returns control to the higher node—Q1 in this example—which called it.

Generating Verb Strings: Figure 2.9 shows the net representation of the grammar-program for generating verb forms. The upper part of the figure shows the (PUSH VP) with its conditions. These are the sending down to the next lower level of the Modal structure, the TOKen of the verb and the register QFRONT. The VP subnet will use this information to generate a verb string according to the data in the Modal structure, and its successful POP will return the verb string that has been generated in the * register.

At the PUSH to VP the * register contains either VACT or VPAS from scanning the generation pattern. The two arcs leaving VP begin to generate the verb string in one of these two forms. Under the arc, is a number referring to the operations listed in the lower part of the figure, which actually construct the elements of the string. In our example, the * register contains VACT. The operation on this arc is to set the register SNT to NIL in order to clear it. Control is JUMPED to node FORM where the FORM attribute on the Modal structure is found. Since FORM has the value SIMPLE (Table 2.2), QFRONT is T, and ASPECT is IMPERF, operation #3 is performed to set SNT to the value returned by

```
(LEXWD (GETR WD)(QUOTE INF))
```

LEXWD takes as arguments a word token and a morphological signal; like GETLEX, it returns a word form—in this case, DANCE. The second operation on this arc is to set the register WD to the value DO—introducing an auxiliary to be fronted for the question form. In the case of a PROGRESSIVE or a PERFECT form, other arcs—from VP1 or ASP—would introduce an auxiliary verb, BE or HAVE, which in the case of a question could be fronted.

After these operations, control is jumped to TNS where the value of the attribute TENSE on the Modal structure is examined. The operations associated with these arcs will produce a tensed English verb form for whatever is in the register WD. In the present example WD contains DO and the value of TENSE is PAST so LEXWD returns DID. If a simple declarative present sentence were being generated, WD would still

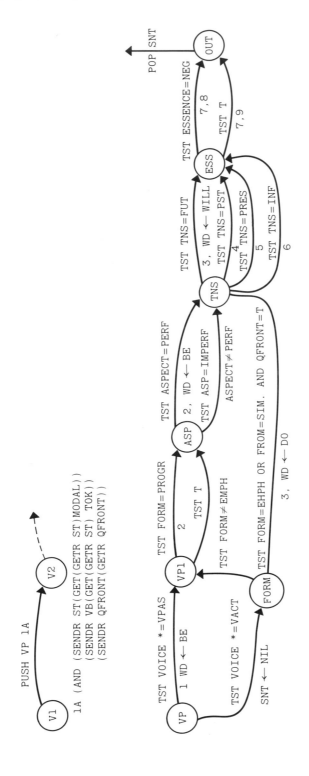

Figure 2.9 Net Representation for Generating Verb Forms.

contain the form of the verb sent down from V1 and the verb string generated would be a simple verb in present form such as DANCE.

Control is then jumped to node ESS where the form in WD is made to agree in NBR with the subject, a NOT is inserted for a negative, and SNT is set to the concatenation of the value of WD and SNT by:

```
(SETR SNT(CONS(GETR WD)(GETR SNT)))
```

Control is JUMPED to OUT where the contents of SNT are POPped to the calling level in the * register.

Answering Questions with Semantic Nets

So far the semantic net structures have been shown to preserve the meanings expressed by a phrase or a sentence at a level such that syntactic paraphrases are represented by a canonical semantic structure — one that differs only in such sentence design features as are represented in the modality. This level of structure is well-suited to generating syntactic variations as needed to embed sentences in varying environments without changing the intended meaning, but it falls short of what is required for question-answering applications.

The following two sentences would usually be judged to carry the same* meaning; particularly, if one is a question, the other would be selected as an answer.

1. Wellington defeated Napoleon at the Battle of Waterloo.
2. Bonaparte lost the Battle of Waterloo to the Duke of Wellington.

These two examples have differing semantic structures because of the different lexical choices that have been made for the concepts WIN—LOSE—DEFEAT, NAPO—LEON—NAPOLEON I—NAPOLEON BONAPARTE—BONAPARTE, and WELLINGTON—THE DUKE OF WELLINGTON—THE IRON DUKE.

Earlier it was mentioned that deeper semantic structures can be devised such that the two examples above might have the same semantic or conceptual representation, but that our present approach was deliberately fixed at the definable level where unambiguous lexical concepts — i.e., word sense descriptions — are related by explicit semantic relations. This choice of level requires an additional mechanism of paraphrase rules in order to account for paraphrase resulting from different lexical choices. In studying the process of answering questions from text, it is apparent that a deeper structure will be more economical of computation, but that paraphrase rules will probably continue to be required.

---

*"same" is taken to mean "equivalent with respect to a purpose."

Paraphrase rules to account for the two example sentences above can be expressed quite simply. First, let us show an abbreviated representation of the two semantic structures:

```
DEFEAT; C1 WELLINGTON T NAPOLEON, L BATTLE OF WATERLOO
LOSE; S BONAPARTE, T BATTLE OF WATERLOO, G DUKE OF WELLINGTON
```

The abbreviations for deep case relations decode as follows: C1-Causal Actant 1, T-Theme, L-Locus, S-Source, G-Goal. Some paraphrase rules associated with LOSE are shown below:

```
Rule 1  (LOSE(S–S)(T–T)(G–G) WIN)
Rule 2  (LOSE(C–G)(T–S)(L–T) DEFEAT)
Rule 3  (LOSE(L–S)(T–DEFEAT)(G–G)(L–T) SUFFER)
```

If we seek to transform the second semantic structure into the first, rule R2 applies since it connects LOSE and DEFEAT. The rule is interpreted to have the following effect:

```
LOSE; S BONAPARTE        DEFEAT; C DOW
      T BOW          ⇒           T BONAPARTE
      G DOW                      L BOW
```

An interpreter given the relevant rule and the structure headed by LOSE, does the following:

1. Begin a copy of the structure.
2. Write the new TOK value as DEFEAT.
3. Write a semantic relation C and set its value to the old value of G (i.e., Duke of Wellington).
4. Write a relation T and set its value to the old value of S.
5. Write a relation L and set it to the old value of T.

If we were now to generate an active declarative sentence from the transformed or new structure we would get:

The Duke of Wellington defeated Bonaparte at the Battle of Waterloo.

The rule is symmetric, so if, reading from right to left, we applied it to the first sentence structure headed by DEFEAT, we could have transformed into a structure that would generate:

Napoleon lost the Battle of Waterloo to Wellington.

Thus rule R2 accounts for a fairly complex paraphrase relation between LOSE and DEFEAT. If we are to demonstrate that the two example sentences are completely equivalent in terms of this semantic system, we must also have rules such as the following:

R4 (NAPOLEON–BONAPARTE–NAPOLEON+I–NAPOLEON+BONAPARTE)
R5 (WELLINGTON(PMOD–TOK)(PREP–OF)(DET–DEF) DUKE)
R6 (WELLINGTON(MOD–IRON)(DET–DEF) DUKE)

Rule R4 is a simple substitution rule that is interpreted as meaning that any instance of one of the terms can be substituted for any instance of another. This is a relatively rare form of perfect synonymy of names. Rules R5 and R6 are a more common case in which a word is transformed into a phrase that has the same meaning. The same interpreter is used to transform the structure WELLINGTON into DUKE, PMOD WEL-LINGTON, PREP OF, DET DEF. The rule R5 is still a symmetric rule but with an important difference from the previous example. Since DEF and OF are not semantic relations, they must be values and the interpreter takes them as conditions on the structure headed by DUKE. Thus, THIS DUKE OF WELLINGTON or THE DUKE OF WELLINGTON will transform into WELLINGTON, whereas A DUKE AT WELLINGTON fails as does THE DUKE OF WINDSOR, etc.

The result of applying the rules illustrated to the semantic structure of either of the two sentences is to take it into an exact match with the other. The rules that have been illustrated are quite simple and they require very few conditions for their application. Other rules may be very complex with different conditions applying depending on the direction in which the rule is to be applied.

Another pair of example sentences will show a higher degree of complexity:

Napoleon commanded the troops that lost the battle.
Napoleon lost the battle.

The abbreviated structures for these two sentences follow:

COMMAND, C1 NAPOLEON, T TROOPS
LOSE, S TROOPS, T BATTLE

LOSE S NAPOLEON, T BATTLE

A rule to show the paraphrase relation between these two structures must show that in certain circumstances a combination of two sentences implies a third. Such a rule could be written as follows for application to COMMAND and LOSE;

R7 (COMMAND [(T(1st) = C(2nd))(TOK(2nd) = LOSE)]
          (S–C(1st))   (T–T)   LOSE)

The elements in the square brackets are conditions to be met by the structure to which the rule is to be applied. They say that the Theme of the first sentence must correspond to the Source argument of the second, and that the Token of the second is limited to LOSE. The remainder of the expression is the transformation which produces the desired structure.

A rule of this degree of complexity is no longer obviously symmetric, and several new notational conventions have been introduced. These vastly increase the complexity required of the interpreter of rules. It becomes apparent that rules for generating paraphrase are at least as complicated as those required for analysis and generation of sentences. Once again the Woods AFSTN interpreter can be used, this time with states as rule names and paraphrase rules written in the form of conditions and operations.

If we assume the ∗ register contains the name of the structure to be examined and that a function, GETA, with a semantic relation as an argument returns the value associated with that relation for the ∗ structure, the following arcs illustrate a mode for writing paraphrase transformations in the AFSTN:

```
(R7(TST  COMMAND-LOSE(AND(EQ(GETA TOK)(QUOTE COMMAND))
                         (SETR 2NDVB(GET(GETA T)S∗))
                         (EQ(GET(GETR 2NDVB)TOK)(QUOTE LOSE)))
     (MAKEPR TOK(QUOTE LOSE))
     (ADDPR  S (GETA C))
     (ADDPR  T (GET(GETR 2NDVB T))
     (JUMP OUT)))
(OUT(POP(PUTPRL(QUOTE QT)(GETR MLIST)) T))
```

The number of conditions and operations on this arc reveal the complexity of rule R7. Essentially, the condition is an ANDed set of tests to determine that the Token of the structure under the scanner is COMMAND, that the value of its Theme argument is the Source argument for a verb it dominates (S∗ is the backlink from TROOPS to LOSE), and that the dominated verb is LOSE. If all these conditions are met, then MAKEPR and ADDPR construct a new list of arguments and values on a register called MLIST. At the jump to OUT, PUTPRL makes a property list—i.e., a new semantic structure—with the name QT, which is then POPped in the ∗ register.

The point to be emphasized is that paraphrase rules of arbitrary complexity can be used if interpreted by the AFSTN system. On the other hand, if only simple rules such as R1-R6 are required, a simpler translating function will prove much more efficient. The question of efficiency for a given purpose is central to the design of a question-answering algorithm for it has a great deal of computation to accomplish.

A Question-Answering Algorithm: It is from paraphrase rules such as those just described that a text-based question-answering system derives much of its power. But more than this is required. If we assume that a data base of semantic structures representing sentence meanings has been accumulated, then it is first necessary to select a set of structures that appear relevant to the question. One measure of relevance is the number of lexical concepts in common between the proposed answer and the question. This can be obtained by a simple algorithm that orders the candidates according to the number of Token values they have in common with the question. Such a function is called CANDS. It takes the name of the question structure as an argument, goes to the lexicon to obtain a list of structures that contain each content word used in the question, and orders these in terms of their match with the question.

The task of CANDS introduces a new lexical requirement, that each lexical entry contain a list of the semantic structures in which it is used. The structures to be indexed for each word are the sentences (or larger discourse units) in which each occurs. In terms of a previous example, the words Napoleon, Wellington, Defeat, Battle, Waterloo all occur in structure C1, and Bonaparte, lose, Battle, Waterloo, Duke, and Wellington occur in C2. Thus, for this example, Wellington and Waterloo have as values for the U/I (used/in) attribute, C1, C2; while Napoleon has U/I C1 and Bonaparte has U/I C2. If we ask the question,

Did Napoleon win the Battle of Waterloo?

We will discover that there are four content words in the question, three of which occur in C1 and two in C2. The ordering that CANDS returns for these candidate-answer structures is thus, C1, C2.

The task of the question-answering function, called ANSWER, is now to match the question structure against each candidate. The first step is to determine if the token of the head verb of the question matches the head verb of the candidate. If there is no direct match, there may be a paraphrase rule that applies that can transform the question structure into that of the candidate answer. But how is the relevant rule, if it exists, to be located? We have gained much experience with question-answering and theorem-proving experimentation and know that the cost of finding and applying such transformations is very high indeed.

Additional lexical structure helps to simplify the problem. If each entry in the lexicon indexes the rules that transform it to another entry—i.e., the paraphrase rules—then the task becomes manageable. The following fragments of lexicon for some of the words in example sentences, C1 and C2, show the indexing method.

```
(LOSE(IMPLY(WIN R1)(DEFEAT R2)(SUFFER R3)))
(DEFEAT(IMPLYBY (LOSE (R2,R3))))
(WELLINGTON (IMPLY (DUKE (R5,R6))))
(NAPOLEON (IMPLY ((NAPOLEON, BONAPARTE, ETC...)R4)))
```

Thus a lexical entry shows that LOSE will paraphrase to DEFEAT by rule R2 (shown on p. 100).

A function named PATHS takes two arguments such as LOSE and DEFEAT. It examines the lexical structures associated with the two words (actually word-sense addresses) to discover if there is a rule connecting the two. If not, it takes the set that the first word will transform into and calls itself recursively to see if any member of that set transforms into the second word; that failing, it takes the set of words the second transforms into to determine if one of these goes into words derived from the first. It stops either when a match is found or when an arbitrary depth of search has been reached. If successful, it returns an ordered list of rule names that the interpreter function can use to translate from the first word to the second.

PATHS is the function that discovers whether one word can be transformed into another. It is an important timesaving device that uses a directed search to avoid an exhaustive exploration of the network of paraphrase rules.

When such a path has been found, a function called TRANSLATE is used to transform a copy of the question structure into the form of the candidate answer. This is the interpreter function that has been discussed previously; if the rules to be used are of simple form, TRANSLATE can be a simple function to interpret them; if the rules are complex, TRANSLATE can push to a paraphrase grammar that is interpreted by the AFSTN system. In either case TRANSLATE returns the name of the question structure as its value.

The function MATCH1 is the control function for matching the Tokens of two semantic structures. It also examines quantifiers and modalities to determine if quantificational relationships are satisfied and if tense and negation relationships are matched. It has the additional task of examining the question's semantic structure to determine if the relation QWD is present and satisfied.

An example will show more clearly what MATCH1 does in the context of its call by the ANSWER function.

What man lost a battle?

The semantic structure would be as follows:

```
Q1 TOK LOSE, S Q2, T Q3
Q2 TOK MAN QWD WHAT
Q3 TOK BATTLE, DET INDEF
```

(ANSWER Q1) calls (CANDS Q1) which returns the ordered list (C2,C1) as candidate answering structures. MATCH1 is then called for application to the first of these, C2, in the following fashion:

```
(MATCH1 Q1 C2)
```

MATCH1 embeds the following call:

```
(TRANSLATE (PATHS LOSE LOSE))
```

No transformation is required and MATCH1 returns Q1 unchanged, thus signalling that the head of Q1 matches the head of C2. MATCH1 is itself embedded by a function MATCH which attempts to see that the structure that is the value of each semantic relation of the question matches the structure that is the value of each semantic relation in the candidate answer. What it does is to call

```
(MATCH1 (GET Q1 S)(GET C2 S)) which means
     (MATCH1 Q2 C21)
```

where C21 is the structure

```
C21 TOK BONAPARTE
    DET DEF
```

and Q2 is:

```
Q2 TOK MAN
   QWD WHAT
```

When the paraphrase rule (BONAPARTE IMPLY MAN) is found, by PATHS, the translation gives Q2′ TOK BONAPARTE, and MATCH1 looks then at the QWD relation and puts BONAPARTE in a register called QANS whose value will be returned by ANSWER if the rest of the question is accounted for by the candidate structure.

In a later call, (MATCH1 BATTLE BATTLE), this function will compare the determiners and find that INDEF in the question is encompassed by DEF in the candidate. Eventually the match is found to be complete and BONAPARTE is returned as the answer to "What man lost a battle?" LISP definitions of the functions ANSWER. MATCH, MATCH1, and other related functions are included in the appendix to this chapter. The complexities of traversing two semantic structures can be understood from studying these functions, but because of their deeply recursive nature, furthei verbal description will not be attempted.

Concluding Discussion

Three topics of critical importance to the computation and use of semantic structures have only been lightly touched on in this chapter. Lexical structure, semantic disambiguation, and the translation from semantic structure to procedural language will each be discussed briefly in this section, and then a short concluding summary will close the chapter.

Lexical Structure: The form of a lexical entry is the same as that for any other semantic structure—a node associated with a set of relational arcs connecting it to other nodes. The nodes are word-sense meanings or constants, and the arcs are semantic relations of various types. Some of these are indicators of paraphrase transformations such as SUPerset, SUBset, Rule$_i$, etc. Some are morphological to show the meanings of various endings, such as Present or Past Participle, Future, Singular, Plural, etc. Some relate the word-sense to its syntactic word-class. Additional relations, such as Print Image and Used/In, map word-sense meanings onto words and data statements, respectively.

If the system is to be used for mapping from English into another natural language or into a procedural language, additional semantic relations must be encoded into the dictionary for these purposes and used by grammar programs that can accomplish these tasks. As yet we have not attempted a careful description of lexical content as it is dependent on the uses of a language processing system. Each new task typically requires use of some standard lexical features but adds its own unique requirement.

Semantic Disambiguation: The relevant lexical information for this task is in the form of semantic classes or markers and selection restrictions associated with each lexical entry. The information is used in the parsing grammar in a manner similar to that illustrated for testing syntactic agreements. Such an approach is minimally satisfactory for analyzing a carefully controlled subset of English; but as Bolinger (1965) has argued, disambiguation may require consultation of any aspect of knowledge that the listener may have. A generally satisfactory scheme for semantic disambiguation has not yet been developed but will probably require complex conditions and consultation with the whole context of a discourse. This area is suggested as a profitable one for computational linguistic research.

Translation to Procedural Languages: The semantic network structures for sentences have been defined at the level of deep case structures. The question arose as to whether this is properly called a syntactic or semantic level. We defined transformations that do not change the choice of lexical entries as syntactic and those that do as semantic, thus forming a fairly clear distinction between the concepts "syntactic paraphrase" and "semantic paraphrase." From these notions it is immediately apparent that any transformations into other languages, natural or procedural, are semantic in nature. The structure on which syntactic and semantic transformation both operate is called a semantic structure and defined as a set of unambiguous references to word-sense meanings connected by explicit, definable semantic relations.

Woods and Winograd have each shown how a procedural semantics—a system of semantic transformations—can be used to operate on sentence structures to transform them into commands in a procedural language. Both of these researchers are concerned with objects in a data base that are designated by noun-phrase descriptions and each embeds the identifying elements of the noun phrase in a retrieval command to discover particular named elements of data such as AA-57 or the red block named B3. This appears to be the first level of procedural language transformation—the discovery of the particular data objects identified by a noun phrase. Winograd's system most clearly includes a deeper level of procedural language in its use of Microplanner to assemble a program of actions in the command language that drives the simulated robot hand.

For example, the sentence, "Place the red block on the blue block" first retrieves an object name such as B3 corresponding to the noun phrase, "the red block" and similarly, B4 for "the blue block." The sentence now has a semantic structure equivalent to the following:

Place: Mood Imper, T B3, On B4

A transformation associated with the verb, "place" transforms this into a goal statement roughly as follows:

ThGoal: (ON B3, B4)

A Microplanner program expands this state description into a series of commands that will achieve the desired state and passes this as a program for the interpreter of the command language to run, and so physically to accomplish the goal.

In this example we can see three levels of procedural transformation: first, the identification of referents of the NPs; second, transformation of the sentence structure into a desired goal state; and third, the assembly of a command language program by Microplanner to achieve the desired goal state. The resulting command language statement is a representation of the pragmatic meaning of the English statement, and the dynamic interpretation of the command language statements results in changes in the world of blocks and is an operational definition of the "meaning" of the sentence.

The semantic structure of a sentence can thus be seen to be simply a first stage representation of meaning which can be operated on by various semantic transformations to produce paraphrases or translations into other languages including procedural ones. Schank's conceptual structures and Winograd's goal structures can both be seen as modelling deeper levels of thought that are signified by semantic structures of verbal meanings. Transformation from either the semantic structure or these deeper structures into procedural languages, models the human process of generating actions in the world under the control of thought processes which also correspond to verbal expressions.

Summary: This chapter has described a consistent approach to the derivation and manipulation of representations of verbal meaning for a subset of English sentence structures. The subset treated is a small one and we have undoubtedly ignored more English forms than we have accounted for. We have, however, described a process for mapping from English into a semantic level, from that level back into English, and procedures for discovering equivalence relations between different semantic structures. This is a theory and a model of superficial aspects of verbal communication and one that fits naturally into those systems which model the deeper forms of thought required for problem solving and the accomplishment of non-verbal actions.

These theories and models of language understanding offer a very rich area for continued research. Computational research is needed to improve data representations and algorithms required by the models and to provide additional systems such as the Woods AFSTN and PLANNER to simplify the programming tasks. A great deal of linguistic research is needed to expand the range of natural language constructions for which syntactic and semantic conventions can be agreed on. Psychological research is necessary to determine how closely these theories and models account for experimentally determined facts of human verbal memory and human language understanding and generation skills. Finally, there is need for hardware development of computers with gigantic memories, multiple processors, and command languages at the levels now exemplified by LISP and PLANNER.

Acknowledgments

The ideas and programs that I have described in this chapter, which was prepared with the support of the National Science Foundation, Grant GJ 509X, were developed conjointly with my students and research associates as a team effort. Each of the following persons contributed significantly: Robert Amsler, Sharon Baronofsky, Bertram Bruce, David Matuszek, and Jonathan Slocum. I take full responsibility, however, for any inaccuracies and inadequacies in what I have presented here.

ppendix to Chapter Two

Question-Answering Algorithm — *J. Slocum*

```
(ANSWER (LAMBDA (QST)(PROG (CANDS QANS)
       (SETQ CANDS (CAND QST))
AGAIN   (COND((NULL CANDS)(RETURN NIL))
         ((MATCH(MATCH1 QST(CAR CANDS))(CAR CANDS))
                                       (RETURN QANS))
         (SETQ CANDS(CDR CANDS))
         (GO AGAIN) )))

(MATCH(LAMBDA(QT ST)
   (COND((OR(NULL QT)(NULL ST)) NIL)
        ((MATCH2 (INDICATORS QT)) T)
        (T NIL) )))

(MATCH2 (LAMBDA (INDS)
   (COND ((NULL INDS) T)
      ((MATCH(MATCH1 (GET QT (CAR INDS))(GET ST(CAR INDS)))
            (GET ST (CAR INDS)))(MATCH2 (CDR INDS)))
    (T NIL)  )))

(MATCH1 (LAMBDA (QT ST)
  (COND((NOT(DETMTCH(GET QT DET)(GET ST DET))) NIL)
    ((NOT(MODMTCH(GET QT MODAL)(GET ST MODAL))) NIL)
    ((QWDTEST QT ST) NIL)
    (T (TRANSLATE(PATHS(GET QT TOK)(GET ST TOK))))  )))

(QWDTEST(LAMBDA(QT ST)
    (AND(GET QT QWD)(SETQ QANS ST) NIL) ))
```

Table A.1   Program for VP.

```
(Q10(PUSH VP T

(VP(CAT AUX(GETF BE)
    (MAKEPR (QUOTE NBR)(GETF NBR))
    (ADDPR (QUOTE TENSE)(GETF TENSE))
    (ADDPR (QUOTE ASPECT)(QUOTE IMPERF))
    (ADDPR (QUOTE MOOD)(QUOTE INDIC))
    (TO V1))

  (CAT AUX(GETF(HAV)
    (MAKEPR (QUOTE NBR)(GETF NBR))
    (ADDPR (QUOTE TENSE)(GETF TENSE))
    (ADDPR (QUOTE ASPECT)(QUOTE PERF))
    (ADDPR (QUOTE MOOD)(QUOTE INDIC))
    (TO V4))

  (CAT V T
    (MAKEPR (QUOTE NBR)(GETF NBR))
    (ADDPR (QUOTE TENSE)(GETF TENSE))
    (ADDPR (QUOTE VOICE)(QUOTE ACTIVE))
    (ADDPR (QUOTE ASPECT)(QUOTE IMPERF))
    (ADDPR (QUOTE MOOD)(QUOTE INDIC))
    (JUMP V6)))

(V1(CAT V (GETF +ING)
    (ADDPR (QUOTE VOICE)(QUOTE ACTIVE))
    (ADDPR (QUOTE FORM)(QUOTE PROGRESSIVE))
    (JUMP V6))

  (CAT V (GETF +EN)
    (ADDPR (QUOTE VOICE)(QUOTE PASSIVE))
    (ADDPR (QUOTE FORM)(QUOTE SIMPLE))
    (JUMP V6) ))

(V4(CAT V(GETF +EN)
    (ADDPR (QUOTE VOICE)(QUOTE ACTIVE))
    (ADDPR (QUOTE FORM)(QUOTE SIMPLE))
    (JUMP V6))
    (CAT AUX T
    (TO V5)))

(V5(TST VP T
    (LIFTR ARGS (GETF ARGS))
    (LIFTR PDIGM (GETF PDIGM))
    (MAKEPR (QUOTE MODAL)(PUTPRL(GENSYMC)(GETR MLIST)))
    (ADDPR (QUOTE TOK) *)
    (TO V7) ))

(V7(POP (GETR MLIST)T))
```

Table A.2   Program for Top-level Analysis of a Sentence.

```
(S(PUSH NP  T
    (SETR SUBJ *)
    (TO Q10))
   (CAT AUX  T
      —
      —
      —
   (PUSH PP  T
      —
      —
      —
         ))

(Q10(PUSH VP T
    (SETR MLIST *)
    (SETR LASTNP NIL)
    (ADDPR (ARGEVAL(GETR SUBJ))(GETR SUBJ))
    (TO Q12) ))

(Q12(PUSH NP T
    (ADDPR (ARGEVAL *) *)
    (SETR LASTNP *)
    (TO Q12))
   (PUSH PP T
    (PPEVAL * (GETR LASTNP))
    (SETR ARG1 (ARGEVAL *))
    (JUMP Q13))
   (POP(PUTPRL(GENSYMC)(GETR MLIST))T))

(Q13(TST ARG1 (NOT (NULL(GETR ARG1))))
    (ADDPR (GETR ARG1) *)
    (TO Q12) ))
```

Table A.3   Top-level Sentence Generation Net.

```
(R(TEST INTER
        (EQ"INTER (GET(SETR MODEl(GET(GETR ST) * ))"MOOD)
    (JUMP Q))
  (TST IMPER(EQ"IMPER(GET MODEl"MOOD))
    (TO V1))
  (TST DECL T (JUMP S1)))
(S1(PUSH NP T
    (SETR SNT * )
    (TO V1)))
(Q(TST QUERY(EQ * (GET(GETR MODEl)"QUERY))
    (SETR SNT (WH- * ))
    (SETR QFRONT ())
    (TO V1))
  (TST SQUERY(EQ"S(GET(GETR MODEl)"QUERY))
    (SETR QFRONT T)
    (JUMP S1))
  (TST OTHER T
    (SETR SNT(WH-(GET(GETR MODEl)"QUERY)))
    (SETR QFRONT T)(PUT ST(GET(GETR MODEl)"QUERY()))
    (JUMP Q1)))
(Q1(PUSH NP T
    (CONC(GETR SNT) * )
    (TO V1))
  (POP(PRING"Q1)T)))
(V1(PUSH VP(AND(SENDR WD(GET(GETR ST)"TOK))
              (SENDR ST(GETR MODEl)))
    (HOP V2)
(V2(TST QFRONT(EQ(GETR QFRONT)NIL)
    (CONC(GETR SNT) * )
  (TST NO T(CONS(LIST(CAR * )(GETR SNT))(CONC(GETR ST)(CDR * ))
```

Table A.4   NP Generation Net.

```
(NP(TST DEF(EQ(GET(GETR ST)(QUOTE DET))(QUOTE DEF))
      (SETR SNT (QUOTE THE))
      (JUMP N2))
  (TST INDEF(EQ(GET(GETR ST)(QUOTE DET))(QUOTE INDEF))
      (SETR SNT(QUOTE A))
      (JUMP N2)))

(N2(TST ADJ (SETR ADJ(GET(GETR ST)(QUOTE MOD))
      (JUMP N3)
  (TST NO ADJ T
      (JUMP N4)

(N3(TST ONE ADJ (AND(ATOM(GETR ADJ))(NOT(NULL(GETR ADJ))))
      (APPEND(GETR SNT)(GETLEX(GETR ADJ))NIC))
      (JUMP N4))
  (TST MORE T
      (APPEND(GETR SNT)(GETLEX(CAR(GETR ADJ))NIC))
      (SETR ADJ(CDR(GETR ADJ))
      (JUMP N3))

(N4(TST NOUN T
      (APPEND(GETR SNT)(GETLEX(GET(GETR ST)TOK)
                              (GET(GETR ST)NBR)))
      (JUMP OUT)

(OUT(POP SNT T)
```

Three

An Artificial Intelligence Approach to Machine Translation

Yorick Wilks
Stanford University

I take Artificial Intelligence to be the enterprise of causing automata to perform peculiarly human tasks, and by appropriate methods, though I do not want to discuss that difficult word "appropriate" here, I therefore call what follows an Artificial Intelligence (AI) approach to machine translation for three reasons:

First, when fully developed, the system to be described for representing natural language will contain two methods for expressing the content of any given utterance: one logical, the other linguistic, in a broad sense of that term. At the present time a question outstanding within Artificial Intelligence is which of these general approaches is the most suitable. In that the present system has both representation capabilities, it should be able to compare them with a view to throwing some light on this important dispute.

Second, I have argued elsewhere (Wilks, 1971) at some length that the space of meaningful expressions of a natural language cannot be determined or decided by any set of rules whatever—in the way that almost all linguistic theories implicitly assume CAN be done. That is because, in common sense terms, a speaker always has the option to MAKE any string of words meaningful by the use of explanations and definitions. However, any working system of linguistic rules does implicitly specify a class of acceptable expressions, and so, indirectly, a class of unacceptable ones. The only way of combining these two facts of life is to have a modifiable system of linguistic rules, which was implemented in an elementary way in an earlier version of this system (Wilks, 1968).

Another aspect of the AI approach—and my third reason—has been an attraction to methods consistent with what humans THINK their methods of procedure are, as distinct from more formally motivated methods. Hence the attraction of heuristics in, say, AI approaches to theorem proving. The present system is entirely semantics based, in that it avoids the explicit use of a conventional linguistic syntax at both the analysis and the generation stages, and any explicit theorem-proving technique. In the analysis of input, syntax is avoided by a template system: the use of a set of deep semantic forms that seek to pick up the message conveyed by the input string, on the assumption that there is a fairly well-defined set of basic messages that people always want to convey whenever they write and speak; and, that in order to analyse and express the content of discourse, it is these simple messages—such as "a certain thing has a certain part"—that we need to locate. Again, the overall representation of complex sentences is that of a linear sequence of message forms in a real time order, interrelated by conceptual ties called paraplates, rather than the hierarchical tree structure preferred by linguists. From the very common sense forms of expression I have had to use to express this method of attack, it will be seen that the method itself is one close to ordinary intuitions about how we understand, and somewhat distant from the concerns of formal grammarians.

Next, the French generation is done without the explicit use of a generative grammar, in the conventional sense. The interlingual representation passed from the analysis routines to the generation ones already contains, as part of the coding of the English input words, French stereotypes—strings of French words and functions that evaluate to French words. These functions are evaluated recursively to produce French output, and the stereotypes thus constitute both French output and procedures for assembling that output properly. No other inventory of French words or grammar rules is ever searched, and the stereotypes constitute a principled way of coping with linguistic diversity and irregularity—since individual words have their own stereotypes—without recourse to what Bar-Hillel (1970) calls "bags of tricks."

And finally, a point related to the general approaches previously discussed but importantly different is that of the "level of understanding" required for MT. It would certainly be unintelligent to develop any level of understanding more complex than is required for any task, and it is hoped that by the methods described it may be possible to establish a level of understanding for MT somewhat short of that required for question-answering and other more intelligent behaviors. While agreeing with Michie's (1971) unexceptionable ". . . we now have as a touchstone the realization that the central operations of the intelligence are . . . transactions on a knowledge base," it is hoped that for MT linguistic, or linguistically expressible, knowledge may suffice.

It is the semantic approach that is intended to answer the quite proper question "Why start MT again at all?" The generally negative surveys produced after the demise of most of the MT research of the fifties in no way established that a wholly new approach like the present one was foredoomed to fail—only that the methods tried so far had in fact done so. At this distance in time, it is easy to be unfair to the memory of that early MT work and to overexaggerate its simple assumptions about language. But the fact remains that almost all of it was done on the basis of naive syntactic analysis and without any of the developments in semantic structuring and description that have been the most noteworthy features of recent linguistic advance.

One word of warning is appropriate at this point about the semantic method and its relation to the form of this paper. This is intended to be a practical note, concerned to describe what is being done in a particular system and research project, so it is not concerned to argue abstractly for the value of systems based on conceptual connections: this has been done elsewhere by writers such as (Simmons, 1970) (Quillian, 1969), (Klein, 1968) (Schank, 1971), and myself. I am not concerned to argue for a general method, nor shall I set out much in the way of the now familiar graph structures linking the items of example sentences in order to display their "real structure" for my purposes. I am concerned more to display the information structure I use, and the manipulations the system applies to certain linguistic examples in order to get them into the prescribed form for translation. The display of conceptual or dependency connections between items of real text will only be made in cases where unnecessary obscurity or complexity would be introduced by displaying the same connexions between items of the interlingual representation.

It has become fashionable recently to claim that "dictionary based" systems cannot find a place within AI. I would like to argue at the outset of this paper that this view, pervasive though rarely made explicit, is not helpful, and can only inhibit progress on the understanding of natural language in an AI context.

The rise of this view can, I think, be correlated with the fresh interest being generated among linguists and others by new attempts, (such as Montague, 1970), to produce a formal logic capable of representing rather more of the forms of language than the classic attempts of Russell, Carnap, Reichenbach, et al. The implicit argument goes as follows: that logical structure provides the real structure of language, and there is no place in a logic for a dictionary, hence. . . .

Insofar as any premise of this argument is made precise, it can then be seen to be highly misleading, if not downright false. The relation of formal logic to language is and always has been a much disputed matter and cannot be discussed here in any detail. But any adequate logic must contain a dictionary or its equivalent if it is to handle anything more than terms with naive denotations such as "chair." Any system of analysis that is to handle sentences containing say, "hand" is going to need to have available in some form such information as that a hand is a part of a body, and that it is something that only human beings have. It does not matter whether this information is explicitly tied to a word name in the form of markers, or is expressed as a series of true assertions; a dictionary is what it is, and if the information is adequately expressed, it must be possible to construct either of those forms from the other, just as an ordinary English dictionary expresses information in a mixture of both forms. On the whole, the "explicit dictionary" is a more economical form of expression.

Those who attack "dictionary based" systems do not seem to see that matters could not be otherwise. Pressed for alternatives that express their point of view, they are now prone to refer to Winograd (1971). But that is absurd: Winograd's work certainly contains a dictionary, although not as obvious as it might be because of the highly simplified universe with which he deals, and the direct denotational nature of the words it contains. But my point holds even within that simplified world. To see this one only has to read Winograd's work with the question in mind: how does the system know, say, that a block is "handleable." The answer is put quite clearly in a text figure: by means of a small marker dictionary of course.

Michie (1971) has written of ". . . the mandatory relationship, ignored by some computational linguists, between what is monadic, what is structural, and what is epistemic," in connexion with his claim that Winograd's work constitutes "the first successful solution of the machine translation problem." But it may not be mere ignorance on my part here, and others elsewhere, in view of the fact that the distinction between what is "epistemic" and what is not—I think Michie means by that word "concerned with the real world rather than the language," a rather special and non-traditional meaning—is by no means as clear as he thinks. Facts about language are also facts, of course; and many facts about the physical world can equally well be expressed as facts about language. For example, the assertion that "drink" prefers, or requires, an animate agent might seem very close to the assertion that only animals drink, or that most drinkers are animals. Carnap's proposed translation of statements, from what he called the "material" to the "formal" mode, was a claim about the existence of a general equivalence of this nature. It seems to me that the onus of proof is on the believers—that knowledge about the real world in some strong sense of those words is necessary for tasks like MT. It is usual to refer, as Michie does, to examples like Winograd's distinction between the anaphoras in "The City Council refused the women a permit because they feared violence" and "The City Council refused the women a permit because they were communists." But if the epistemic believers mean by "knowledge of the world" the "inductive knowledge of the average man," then they are being over-parochial in accepting such examples at face value; it all depends on whether the City Council is in Washington or Peking, so that an intelligent system might be perfectly right to refuse to assign the anaphora in such trick examples at all.

I am not suggesting, though, that the manipulations to be described here are merely "dictionary based," if that is to be taken to mean having no theoretical presuppositions. There are in fact three important linguistic presuppositions on which the following analysis is based: namely, the use of templates for analysis, and stereotypes for generation, referred to above and described in detail in the body of the paper, and in addition the principle, to be developed below, that by building up the densest, or most connected, representation that it can for a piece of language, the system of analysis will be getting the word senses and much of the grammar right. What I mean by "density of connection" here will be the subject of much that follows. Moreover, I shall argue later that the use of some 'formal' mode for information, even for inductive inferences, avoids certain bottomless pits that may await those who insist on using, possibly false, statements about the physical world in order to do linguistic processing.

Certain kinds of information dictate their form of expression: if it is agreed by all parties that to do MT we need to know that hands have four fingers, then some form of representation at least as strong as set theory or the predicate calculus will be needed to express it. The need for facts of that sort is a disputed one, but it is beyond dispute that we shall need to know that, say, a soldier is a human being. And an important question that arises is, what form of representation is necessary for facts of that sort.

This project is intended to produce a working artifact and not to settle intellectual questions. Nevertheless, because the territory has been gone over so heavily in the past years and because the questions still at issue seem to cause the adoption of very definite points of view by observers and participants alike, it is necessary to make remarks on certain matters before any detailed MT work can get started. In particular, different views are held at the present time as to whether the intermediate representation between two languages for MT should be logical or linguistic in form.

What the key words in that last sentence, "logical" and "linguistic," actually mean is not as clear as might appear; for example, they are almost certainly not exclusive methods of attacking the problem; in that any "logical coding" of text will require a good deal of what is best called linguistic analysis in order to get the text into the required logical form: such as coping with sense ambiguity, case dependency and so on. On the other hand, few linguistically oriented people would deny the need for some analysis of the logical relations present in the discourse to be analysed. However, for the purposes of the present project certain assumptions may be made safely: whatever linguists and philosophers may say to the contrary, it has never been shown that there are linguistic forms whose meaning CANNOT be represented in any logical system whatever. So, for example, linguists often produce kinds of inferences properly made but not catered for in conventional existing calculi: such as the "and so" inference in "I felt tired and went home," but nothing follows to the effect that such an inference could not be coped with by means of a simple and appropriate adjustment in the rules of inference.

Whatever logicians may believe to the contrary, it has never been shown that human beings perform anything like a logical translation when they translate sentences from one language to another, nor has it ever been shown that it is NECESSARY to do that in order to translate mechanically. To take a trivial example, if one wants to translate the English "is," then for an adequate LOGICAL translation one will almost certainly want to know whether the particular use of "is" in question is best rendered into logic by identity, set membership or set inclusion. Yet for the purposes of translating an English sentence containing "is" into a closely related language such as French it is highly unlikely that one would ever want to make any such distinction for the purpose immediately in hand.

The preceding assumptions in no way close off discussion of the questions outstanding: they merely allow constructive work to proceed. In particular, philosophical discussion should be continued on (a) exactly what the linguist is trying to say when he says that there are linguistic forms and common sense inferences beyond the scope of any logic, and (b) exactly what the logician is trying to say when he holds in a strong form the thesis that logical form is the basis of brain coding, or is the appropriate basis for computing over natural language.

There are also interesting comparisons to be made on this point among contemporary academic developments, and in particular the drawing together at the present time of the interests and approaches of hitherto separated work: the extended set logic of Montague for example that he claimed coped with linguistic structure better than did MIT linguistics, and, on the other hand, the linguistic work of Lakoff (1972) which claims that the transformationalists in general, and Chomsky in particular, ALWAYS WERE seeking for some quite conventional notion of logical form and should have faced up to the fact in their work. But those interesting questions are not issues here, because the aim of the present project is to produce a small artifact that not only translates from one natural language to another but is also, potentially at least, capable of some logic translation and so admitting of question-answering and the additional "understanding" that that implies.

Nowhere here is it being denied that some form of knowledge-based inference will be needed for MT, and I shall describe one below. Given a commitment to a question-answering facility as well as an MT one, there can be no real problem about the coexistence of the two forms of coding, logical and linguistic, within a single system, because all but the most dogmatic linguists would admit the need of some logical analysis within any reasonable question-answering system. However, the coexistence might also preclude what one would in fantasy like to have, namely a way of testing against each other the logicist and linguistic hypotheses about MT. Such a test would be precluded because any logical translation (in the sense of translation into logic) within such a system would have much of the work done by the linguistic analysis that the system also contained. So there could be no real comparison of the two paths

ENGLISH → PREDICATE   CALCULUS   REPRESENTATION → FRENCH
ENGLISH → LINGUISTIC CONCEPTUALIZATION → FRENCH

because the first path would also contain quite a bit of the latter in order to get the natural language input into logical form. But it might, as I discuss below, be possible to get translated output by two different paths in a single system and so give some rein to the notion of experimental comparison.

It is important to be clear at this point that the dispute between the logicists and the linguists is often unsymmetrical in form. One holding a strong logicist thesis about MT asserts, it seems to me, that a PC representation is necessary for the task. The linguist of correspondingly strong commitment denies this, but does not always assert that a linguistic representation is necessary. He may admit that a logical representation is sufficient, denying only that it is necessary. He might argue that a logical representation makes explicit more information in the input text than is necessary. By this he means simply that it is harder to translate into a logical notation than it is into most linguistic ones—a fact well attested to by research projects of the past—in that more access to dictionaries and forms of information outside the text itself is necessary in the logical translation case.

This is what I mean by saying that the logic translation may contain more information than a semantic one, even though the text translated can clearly contain only the information it contains. The additional information comes from the extra-textual dictionaries and axioms. The logicist, on the other hand, will most likely deny that a linguistic representation is even sufficient for MT.

However, one must be a little cautious here about the admission that a logical coding contains more information than a linguistic-semantic one, as those terms are usually understood. Any linguistic representation is going to tie some such marker as MAN or HUMAN to a word like "soldier," so that when "soldier" occurs in a text, that system is going to be just as capable of inferring that a man is being talked about, as is a system that contains an explicit predicate calculus axiom

$$(\forall x).\ \text{SOLDIER}(x) \supset \text{MAN}(x).$$

What is usually meant by an admission that a logical representation may contain more information than a purely linguistic one concerns the notation for variable identification (as in the Winograd "women" example) and the existential quantifier notation. Though, again, there is no reason to think that a linguistic marker notation cannot be adapted to cope with existential information for such purposes as MT.

That there are difficulties about a naive introduction of "inference" into semantics can be seen from a recent paper, where Bierwisch (1970) says that an adequate semantics must explicate how "Many of the students were unable to answer your question" follows from "Only a few students grasped your question." Now, in a quite clear sense it does not follow at all; in that there is no problem about considering students who fail to grasp but nonetheless answer. That should not test anyone's conceptual powers very far, so it cannot be that one follows from the other in the sense that if the premise is true then the conclusion cannot be false. We could call that relationship of propositions "philosophical entailment," and I do not want to defend the status of the notion here, but only to point out that any representation of the sentences in question, logical or linguistic, that allows inferences like that one is going to be potentially useless.

There may indeed be a sense of "answer" in which the axiom

$$\forall x\ \forall y\ \text{QUESTION}(x).\ \text{HUMAN}(y).\ \text{ANSWERS}(y, x) \supset \text{GRASPS}(y, x)$$

would be a good one to apply, in the sense of producing a true result. But there are obviously senses of "answer" in which that is just not so, and to point that out is to demand, from the proponents of only logical representation, some suggestion as to how to cope with the real words people use, and to ask them to consider that perhaps real language is not just an EXTENSION of discussions of coloured blocks.

Perhaps the clearest answer to any claim (see Charniak 1972) that a deductive logic must be used to solve problems of anaphora in real texts is to consider a children's story such as the following:

> My dog is an animal, naturally. All animals have ears, and my dog has ears. My snake has no ears, therefore it is an animal too. I call it Horace.

Since the story involves a false deduction itself (and why should it not) any deductive analyser must decide that the 'it' refers to the dog, even though any casual reader can see that it is the snake that is called Horace.

The structure of the translation and organization system

The diagram below is intended to represent the overall structure of the system under construction. The system represented by the lower half of the diagram is in operation, programmed in LISP at the Stanford A.I. Laboratory, and is producing good French for small English paragraphs.

I assume in what follows that processes 2, 4, and 5 are the relatively easy tasks — in that they involve throwing away information — whereas 1 and 3 are the harder tasks in that they involve making information explicit with the aid of dictionaries and rules.

With all the parts to the diagram and the facilities they imply — including not only translation of small texts via a semantic representation but also the translation of axioms in the predicate calculus [PC] into both natural languages — it is clear that

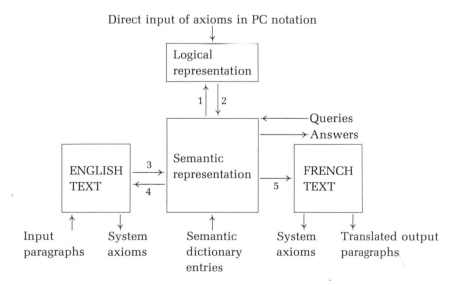

input to the system must be fairly restricted if anything is to be done in a finite time. There are however, ways of restricting input that would destroy the point of the whole activity: for example, if we restricted ourselves to the translation of isolated sentences rather than going for the translation of paragraph length texts. Whatever Bar-Hillel (1970) says to the contrary about MT being essentially concerned with utterances, I am assuming that the only sort of MT that will impress a disinterested observer will be the translation of text. In any case, concentration on utterances can easily lead to what is in fact concentration on the trick example sentences of linguistic text books.

So what is to be the general strategy of translation? It is to segment the text in some acceptable way, produce a semantic representation as directly as possible, and generate an output French form from it. This would involve mapping what I call semantic templates directly onto the clauses and phrases of English, and trying to map out directly from the templates into French clauses and phrases, with their relative order being changed where necessary. I assume also, that no strong syntax analysis, in the linguistic sense, is necessary for this purpose and that all that is necessary can be done with a good semantic representation — which leave us with the big question of what is in the semantic box, and how is it different from what is in the logic box?

In the diagram, I am using "semantic representation" narrowly to mean whatever degree of representation is necessary for MT: though not necessarily for question answering (that's what the logic box is for). For this we may well not need the refinements of "is" that I mentioned earlier, nor, say, existential quantification or the analysis of presuppositions given by translation of definite descriptions, though we shall need what I shall call common-sense inference rules. My main assumption here about the difference between the two boxes, logical and linguistic, is that an "adequate" logical translation makes all such matters explicit, and that is why it is so much more difficult to translate into the top box than the bottom one. But the difference between the two remains a pragmatic one; intended to correspond to two "levels of understanding" in the human being.

With the difficult task 1 achieved — translation from semantic representation into a logical one — then it might be possible to have the two paths of translation from English to French: namely 3–5 and 3–1–2–5. The translation through the logic and out again might not be especially illuminating, but it would be a control that should not produce a noticeably worse translation than one achieved by the shorter route.

Inputs to the logic box will be in a Restricted Formal Language (RFL) and it should be possible to input axioms in it direct at a screen or teletype. The RFL will have to be at least as formal as the description in McCarthy and Hayes (1969) if the diagram is to be of any use, for there is no point in having an RFL to ENGLISH translation routine if the RFL is close to English — one might just as well write in English. The Sandewall form (1971), for example, with infixed predicate names is probably already too like English, which no argument against his notation, of course, simply an argument that it might not be worth writing a translator from it to English.

If it should turn out that the level of understanding provided by the semantic coding is inadequate for MT, then the diagram can still apply with the logic box, functioning as the interlingua: the difference being that the semantics will then be effectively a translation stage between natural language input and the logical representation.

If the semantic coding does turn out to be adequate for some form of restricted MT, then the function of the logic box will be to answer questions about the content of what has been translated. In that case, only those statements from the translated text relevant to the question need be translated up into the logic form.

What follows is divided into four parts which correspond to stages on the diagram above: The processing of English input text; The interlingual representation produced; The form of the dictionary used; The generation of French output from the interlingual representation.

The Processing of English Text

The aim of the text processing sections of the overall program is to derive from an English text an interlingual representation that has an adequate, though not excessive, complexity for two tasks: as a representation from which output in another natural language—French in this case—can be computed, and as a representation that can also serve as an analysandum of predicate calculus statements about some particular universe.

A fragmented text is to be represented by an interlingual structure consisting of TEMPLATES bound together by PARAPLATES and CS INFERENCES. These three items consist of FORMULAS (and predicates and functions ranging over them and sub-formulas), which in turn consist of ELEMENTS.

ELEMENTS are sixty primitive semantic units used to express the semantic entities, states, qualities, and actions about which humans speak and write. The elements fall into five classes as follows (elements in upper case):

(a) entities: MAN(human being), STUFF(substances), THING(physical object), PART(parts of things), FOLK(human groups), ACT(acts), STATE(states of existence), BEAST(animals), etc.

(b) actions: FORCE(compels), CAUSE(causes to happen), FLOW(moving as liquids do), PICK(choosing), BE(exists) etc.

(c) type indicators: KIND(being a quality), HOW(being a type of action) etc.

(d) sorts: CONT(being a container), GOOD(being morally acceptable), THRU(being an aperture) etc.

(e) cases: TO(direction), SOUR(source), GOAL(goal or end), LOCA(location), SUBJ(actor or agent), OBJE(patient of action), IN(containment), POSS(possessed by) etc.

FORMULAS are constructed from elements and right and left brackets. They express the senses of English words with one formula to each sense. The formulas are binarily bracketed lists of whatever depth is necessary to express the word sense. They are written and interpreted with—in each pair at whatever level it comes—a dependence of left side on corresponding right. Formulas can be thought of, and written out, as binary trees of semantic primitives. In that form they are not unlike the lexical decomposition trees of Lakoff and McCawley.

Consider the action "drink" and its relation to the formula:

```
((*ANI   SUBJ)(((FLOW   STUFF)OBJE)((*ANI   IN)(((THIS(*ANI
(THRU PART)))TO)(BE CAUSE)))))
```

*ANI here is simply the name of a class of elements, those expressing animate entities namely, MAN, BEAST, and FOLK (human groups). In order to keep a small usable list of semantic elements, and to avoid arbitrary extensions of the list, many notions are coded by conventional sub-formulas; so, for example, (FLOW STUFF) is used to indicate liquids and (THRU PART) is used to indicate apertures.

Let us now decompose the formula for "drink." It is to be read as an action, preferably done by animate things (*ANI SUBJ) to liquids ((FLOW STUFF)OBJE), of causing the liquid to be in the animate thing (*ANI IN) and via (TO indicating the direction case) a particular aperture of the animate thing; the mouth of course. It is hard to indicate a notion as specific as "mouth" with such general concepts. It would be simply irresponsible, I think, to suggest adding MOUTH as a semantic primitive, as do semantic systems that simply add an awkward lexeme as a new "primitive". Lastly, the THIS indicates that the part is a specific part of the subject.

The notion of preference is important here: SUBJ case displays the preferred agents of actions, and OBJE case the preferred objects or patients. We cannot enter such preferences as stipulations, as many linguistic systems do such as Katz's (1966) "selection restrictions," for we can be said to drink gall and wormwood, and cars are said to drink gasoline. It is proper to prefer the normal (quite different from probabilistically expecting it, I shall argue), but it would be absurd, in an intelligent understanding system, not to accept the abnormal if it is described—not only everyday metaphors, but the description of the simplest fictions, require it.

A formula expresses the meaning of the word senses to which it is attached. This claim assumes a common sense distinction between explaining the meaning of a word and knowing facts about the thing the word indicates. The formulas are intended only to express the former, and to express what we might find—though in a formal manner—in a reasonable dictionary.

So, for example, to know the meaning of "water" we need to know, among other things, that it is a liquid substance. But we do not need to know the law of physics that tells us that it freezes into ice. Many of the world's inhabitants have never seen ice and do not know of its existence even, but they cannot therefore be said to be ignorant of the meaning of whatever the word for water is in their language. This common sense distinction cannot be pushed too far, but it will serve provided we have (as we do have) ways besides formulas of accessing facts about the world.

This flexible method of formula encoding and decomposition, down to any degree of depth necessary to express the meaning of a word, is designed in part to avoid a number of pitfalls, well known in other systems of meaning analysis, such as trying to specify in advance all the ways in which an action or agent can be qualified. In a number of AI approaches there is often no attempt at lexical decomposition or the establishment of semantic primitives. New words "encountered" are simply added as primitives in new "axioms". This leads to an endless proliferation of "primitive" vocabulary, as well as inefficiency of representation, and the inability to generalise and connect clearly connected things (such as two facts differing only by a synonym for example).

Just as elements are to be explained by seeing how they functioned within formulas, so formulas, one level higher, are to be explained by describing how they function within TEMPLATES, the third kind of semantic item in the system. The notion of a template is intended to correspond to an intuitive one of message: one not reducible merely to unstructured associations of word-senses as some have suggested.

A template consists of a network of formulas grounded on a basic actor-action-object triple of formulas. This basic formula triple is found in frames of formulas, one formula for each fragment word in each frame, by means of a device called a bare template. A bare template is simply a triple of elements that are the heads of three formulas in actor-action-object form.

For example: "Small men sometimes father big sons," when represented by a string of formulas, will give the two sequences of heads:

KIND   MAN   HOW   MAN   KIND   MAN

and

KIND   MAN   HOW   CAUSE   KIND   MAN.

(CAUSE is the head of the verbal sense of "father"; "to father" is analyzed as "to cause to have life".)

The first sequence has no underlying template; however, in the second we find MAN-CAUSE-MAN which is a legitimate bare template. Thus we have disambiguated "father", at the same time as picking up a sequence of three formulas that is the core of the template for the sentence. It must be emphasized here that the template is the sequence of formulas, and not to be confused with the triple of elements (heads) used to locate it.

It is a hypothesis of this work that we can build up a finite but useful inventory of bare templates adequate for the analysis of ordinary language: a list of the messages that people want to convey at some fairly high level of generality (for template matching is not in any sense phrase-matching at the surface level). The bare templates are an attempt to explicate a notion of a non-atomistic linguistic pattern: to be located whole in texts in the way that human beings appear to when they read or listen.

The present working list of bare templates is stored in the program in Backus Normal Form for convenience of reading. The list (see below) consists of items like |⟨ *ANI ⟩⟨FEEL ⟩⟨ *MAR ⟩| which says that, for bare templates whose middle action element is FEEL, the first (agent) element must be from the class of elements *ANI. Similarly, the object element must come from the element class *MAR, and therefore be one of the mark elements STATE, SIGN or ACT. All of which is to say that only animate things can feel, and that what they feel (since the notion of tactile feeling is covered by SENSE, not FEEL) are internal states, and acts, or their written equivalents. I would not wish to defend the particular template list in use at any given moment. Such lists are always subject to modification by experience, as are the formulas and even the inventory of basic elements. The only defence is that the system using them actually works, and if anyone replies that its working depends on mere inductive generalization, I can only remind them of Garvin's obvious but invaluable remark that all linguistic generalizations are, and must be, inductive.

Let us now illustrate the central processes of expansion and preference by considering the sentence "The big policeman interrogated the crook," and let us take the following formulas for the four main word senses:

1. "policeman":

```
((FOLK SOUR)((((NOTGOOD MAN)OBJE)PICK)(SUBJ MAN)))
```

i.e., a person who selects bad persons out of the body of people (FOLK). The case marker SUBJ is the dependent in the last element pair, indicating that the normal "top first" order for subject-entities in formulas has been violated, and necessarily so if the head is also to be the last element in linear order.

2. "big":

```
((*PHYSOB POSS)(MUCH KIND))
```

i.e., a property preferably possessed by physical objects (substances are not big).

3. "interrogates":

```
((MAN  SUBJ)((MAN  OBJE)(TELL  FORCE)))
```

i.e., forcing to tell something, done preferably by humans, to humans.

4a. "crook":

```
((((NOTGOOD ACT)OBJE)DO)(SUBJ MAN))
```

i.e., a man who does bad acts. And we have to remember here that we are ignoring other senses of "crook" at the moment, such as the shepherd's.

4b. crook:

```
((((((THIS  BEAST)OBJE)FORCE)(SUBJ MAN))POSS)(LINE THING))
```

i.e., a long straight object possessed by a man who controls a particular kind of animal.

The template matching algorithm will see the sentence under examination as a frame of formulas, one for each of its words, and will look only at the heads of the formulas. Given that MAN FORCE MAN is in the inventory of bare templates, then one scan of a frame of formulas (containing formula (4a) for "crook"), will have picked up the sequence of formulas labelled 1, 3, 4a, in that order. Again when a frame containing formula (4b), the shepherds' sense of "crook", is scanned, since MAN FORCE THING is also a proper bare template, the sequence of formulas 1, 3, 4b will also be selected as a possible initial structure for the sentence.

We now have two possible template representations for the sentence after the initial match; both a triple of formulas in actor-action-object form. Next, the templates are expanded, if possible. This process consists of extending the simple networks we have so far; both by attaching other formulas into the network, and strengthening the bonds between those already in the template, if possible. Qualifier formulas can be attached where appropriate, and so the formula numbered 2 (for "big") is tied to that for "policeman" in both templates. But now comes a crucial difference between the two representations, one that will resolve the sense of "crook". The expansion algorithm looks into the formulas expressing preferences and sees if any of the preferences are satisfied: as we saw formula 2 for "big" prefers to qualify physical objects. A policeman is such an object and that additional dependency is marked in both templates: similarly for the preference of "interrogate" for human actors, in both representations. The difference comes with preferred objects: only the formula 4a for human crooks can satisfy that preference, the formula 4b, for shepherds' crooks, cannot. Hence the former template network is denser by one dependency, and is preferred over the latter in all subsequent processing: its connectivity is (using numbers for the corresponding formulas, and ignoring the "the"s):

$$2 \rightarrow \ \rightarrow 1 \rightarrow \ \leftrightarrow 3 \leftrightarrow \ \leftarrow 4a$$

and so that becomes the template for this sentence. The other possible template (one arrow for each dependency established; and where " $\leftrightarrow$ " denotes the mutual dependencies between the three chief formulas of the template) was connected as follows:

$$2 \longrightarrow \; \longrightarrow 1 \longrightarrow \; \leftrightarrow 3 \; \leftrightarrow 4b$$

and it is now discarded.

Thus the parts of the formulas that express preferences of various sorts not only express the meaning of the corresponding word sense, but can also be interpreted as implicit procedures for the construction of correct templates. This preference for the greatest semantic density works well, and can be seen as an expression of what Joos (1971) calls "semantic axiom number one," that the right meaning is the least meaning, or what Scriven (1972) has called "the trick [in meaning analysis] of creating redundancies in the input." As we shall see, this uniform principle works over both the areas that are conventionally distinguished in linguistics as syntax and semantics. There is no such distinction in this system, since all manipulations are of formulas and templates, and these are all constructed out of elements of a single type.

Matching templates onto sentences in the way I have described is also an initial selection among the possible sense formulas for each word. For example, let us suppose that we have stored two formulas for "winner": one for the sense of a person who wins, and one for the sense of a good thing of its sort, as in "This bicycle is a winner." If we then made a match of that sentence with the template inventory, which we may suppose to contain THING BE THING but not THING BE MAN, then it will be the "good thing" sense of "winner" that will be picked up, clearly, since only its formula has the head THING. So the matching with the template inventory has already, at this early stage of analysis, made the correct selection from among the two senses of "winner."

If the THING-headed (metaphorical) sense of "winner" had not been in the dictionary, however, there would have been no match of the sentence with the template inventory. This is what we would expect to happen when words are used in new or unlikely senses, as in all metaphors. In such cases the system makes up a new template by accepting the combination of senses it is given, but notes that something odd is going on. This is consistent with the general rule of the system, of preferring the usual, but always accepting the unusual if necessary, as an intelligent language analyser should.

The limitation of the illustrative examples, so far, has been that they are the usual short example sentences of linguists, whereas what we actually have here is a general system for application to paragraph length texts. I will now sketch in how the system deals with two sorts of non-sentential text fragments with a general template format.

In the actual implementation of the system, an input text is initially fragmented, and templates are matched with each fragment of the text. The input routine partitions paragraphs at the occurrence of any of an extensive list of KEY words. The list contains almost all punctuation marks, subjunctions, conjunctions, and prepositions.

Difficult but important cases of two kinds must then be considered: first, those where a text string is NOT fragmented even though a key word is encountered. Two intuitively obvious non-subordinating uses of "that" are found in "I like that wine," and prepositions functioning as "post verbs" as in "He gave up his post." In these cases there would be no fragmentation before the key words. In other cases text strings are fragmented even though a key word is NOT present. Four cases are worth mentioning:

I. "I want him to go" is fragmented as (I want) (him to go). A boundary is inserted after any forms of the words "say" and "want," and a further boundary is inhibited before the following "to." This seems intuitively acceptable since "want" in fact subjoins the whole of what follows it in that sentence. We shall expect to match onto these fragments bare templates of the form MAN WANT DTHIS and MAN MOVE DTHIS respectively—where the first dummy DTHIS in fact stands for the whole of the next template. The fragmentation functions operate at the lowest possible level of analysis, which is to say they inspect the semantic formulas given for a word in the dictionary, but they cannot assume that the choice among the formulas has been made.

So then, the fragmentation functions can consider only the range of possible senses of a word. However, in this case inspection of any of the formulas for "wants" or "says" enables the system to infer that the act can subjoin a whole template and not merely an object, as in "I want him." A verb like "advise" on the other hand is not of this sort since we can infer "I advise him" in a way we cannot infer "I want him" in the earlier case. So we would expect "I advise him to go" to receive no special treatment and to be fragmented as (I advise him) (to go), on a key word basis.

II. Relative clauses beginning with "that" or "which" are located and isolated and then inserted back into the string of fragments at a new point. For example "The girl that I like left" is fragmented as (The girl left) (that I like); where the final period of the sentence is also moved to close off the sentence at a new point. Thus the partition after "like" is made in the absence of any key word.

III. "The old man in the corner left" is naturally enough fragmented as (The old man) (in the corner) (left). The breach made here between the actor and act of the sentence is replaced later by a tie (see below).

IV. The sentences "John likes eating fish," "John likes eating," "John began eating fish" are all fragmented before "eating," so that these forms are all assimilated to "John likes to eat fish," (which is synonymous with the first sentence above) rather than to "John is eating fish," which would not be fragmented at all. In template terms "John is eating fish" is to be thought of as MAN DO THING, while "John likes fish" is MAN FEEL DTHIS + DTHIS DO THING, where the first DTHIS refers to the whole of the next template, and the second DTHIS stands in place of MAN (i.e., John).

"Of" is a key word that receives rather special treatment, and is not used to make a partition when it introduces a possessive noun phrase. After fragmentation, each fragment is passed through an ISOLATE function which looks within each fragment and seeks for the right hand boundaries of "of" phrases and marks them off by inserting a character "FO" into the text. Thus "He has a book of mine" would be returned from the ISOLATE function as "He has a book of mine fo." This is done in all cases except those like "I don't want to speak of him" where "of" effectively functions as a post verb.

It may seem obvious enough why "of" phrases should remain within the fragment, since "of John" functions as does "John's," but the demarcation of the phrase with the "FO" character can only be explained by considering the PICKUP and EXTEND routines.

Pickup and extend

The PICKUP routines have already been described in a general way: they match bare templates onto the string of formulas for a text fragment. As the routines move through the string of formulas, those contained between an OF and a FO are ignored for the purpose of the initial match. This ensures that "of phrases" are only treated as qualifiers. So, in the sentence "The father of my friend fo is called Jack," the match would never try to make the head of the formula for "friend" into the root of a template matching the sentence, since it is sealed between an "of–fo" pair. To illustrate the results of applying PICKUP, I shall set down the bare templates that would be expected to match onto Nida & Taber's (1969) suggested seven basic forms of the English indicative sentence. (In this note I describe only the indicative mood as it is implemented in the trial version of this system. Queries and imperatives, like passives, are dealt with by the appropriate manipulation of the template order.)

In each case I give the basic sentence, the bare template, and a diagramatic representation of the corresponding dependencies implied between the text items, where " ⟷ " again links those words on which the bare template is rooted or based, and " → " links a dependent word to its governor.

    i. John ran quickly.
      MAN   MOVE   DTHIS

      John ⟷ ran ⟷ [DTHIS]
             ↑
          quickly

    ii. John hit Bill.
      MAN DO MAN

      John ⟷ hit ⟷ Bill

    iii. John gave Bill a ball.
      MAN   GIVE   THING

      John ⟷ gave ⟷ ball
           ↑   ↑
        (to)Bill   a

The establishment of this dependency by EXTEND is discussed next.

iv. John is in the house.
    MAN BE DTHIS   DTHIS PBE   THING

    John ⟷ is ⟷ [DTHIS]   [DTHIS] ⟷ in ⟷ house
                                                  ↑
                                                 the

v. John is sick.
    MAN BE KIND

    John ⟷ is ⟷ sick

vi. John is a boy
    MAN BE   MAN

    John ⟷ is ⟷ boy
              ↑
              a

vii. John is my father
    MAN BE   MAN

    John ⟷ is ‹→ father
              ↑
              my

A natural question at this point is what exactly is this inventory of bare templates to be used in the analysis of input language? No detailed defense is offered of the inventory used nor, I believe, can one be given. The fact is that one uses the inventory that seems empirically right, revises it when necessary, in operation or under criticism, and concludes that that, alas, is how things must be in the real world of practical language analysis.

The inventory used can be reconstructed from the table of rules set out below in Backus Normal Form. It is set out in terms of the action designating semantic elements, such as FORCE, and the classes of substantive designating elements (such as *SOFT meaning STUFF, WHOLE, PART, GRAIN, AND SPREAD) that can precede such an action as a subject, and follow it as an object to create a three element bare template.

```
⟨bare template⟩::=
⟨*PO⟩⟨DO⟩⟨*EN⟩|
⟨*PO⟩⟨CAUSE⟩⟨*EN⟩|
⟨*PO⟩⟨CHANGE⟩⟨*EN⟩|
⟨*AN⟩⟨FEEL⟩⟨*MA⟩|
```

```
⟨*EN⟩⟨HAVE⟩⟨*EN⟩|
⟨*AL⟩⟨PLEASE⟩⟨*AN⟩|
⟨*AL⟩⟨PAIR⟩⟨*EN⟩|
⟨*PO⟩⟨SENSE⟩⟨*EN⟩|
⟨*PO⟩⟨WANT⟩⟨*EN⟩|
⟨*PO⟩⟨USE⟩⟨*EN⟩|
⟨*PO⟩⟨TELL⟩⟨*MA⟩|
⟨*PO⟩⟨DROP⟩⟨*EN⟩|
⟨*PO⟩⟨FORCE⟩⟨*EN⟩|
⟨*EN⟩⟨MOVE⟩⟨DTHIS⟩|
⟨*PO⟩⟨GIVE⟩⟨*EN⟩|
⟨*AL⟩⟨WRAP⟩⟨*EN⟩|
⟨*AN⟩⟨THINK⟩⟨*MA⟩|
⟨*SO⟩⟨FLOW⟩⟨DTHIS⟩|
⟨*PO⟩⟨PICK⟩⟨*EN⟩|
⟨*PO⟩⟨MAKE⟩⟨*EN⟩|
⟨*AL⟩⟨BE⟩⟨same member of *AL as last occurrence⟩
```

The following are examples of the names of classes of elements:

```
⟨*AL⟩::=⟨DTHIS|THIS|MAN|FOLK|GRAIN|PART|WORLD|STUFF|THING|
        BEAST|PLANT|SPREAD|LINE|ACT|STATE⟩
        (*AL means all substantive elements)

⟨*EN⟩::=⟨DTHIS|THIS|MAN|FOLK|GRAIN|PART|STUFF|THING|BEAST|
        PLANT|SPREAD|LINE⟩
        (*EN means elements that are entities)

⟨*AN⟩::=⟨MAN|FOLK|BEAST|GRAIN⟩
        (*AN means animate entities, GRAIN is used as the main
        element for social organizations, like The Red Cross)

⟨*PO⟩::=⟨DTHIS|THIS|MAN|FOLK|GRAIN|PART|STUFF|THING|ACT|BEAST|
        PLANT|STATE⟩
        (*PO means potent elements, those that can designate
        actors. The class cannot be restricted to *AN since
        rain wets the ground, and the wind opens doors)

⟨*SO⟩::=⟨STUFF|PART|GRAIN|SPREAD⟩

⟨*MA⟩::=⟨ACT|SIGN|STATE⟩
        (*MA designates mark elements, those that can
        designate items that themselves designate like thoughts
        and writings)
```

It will be noticed that I have distorted BNF very slightly so as to write the bare templates containing BE in a convenient and perspicuous form. The forms containing MOVE and FLOW also contain a DTHIS (i.e. they are "dummy templates") indicating that there cannot be objects in those bare templates. Thus MOVE is used only in the coding of intransitive actions and not to deal with sentences like "I moved all the furniture round the room."

There are dummy templates not included in this list for several occur in the preceding description of the Nida and Taber sentences. The remaining rules specifying them are intuitively obvious, but may be found in detail in (Wilks, 1972), where I also give important ancillary rules which specify when dummies are to be generated in matching sentences. Naturally a dummy MAN BE DTHIS is generated for the first fragment of (John is) (in the house) simply because a proper three element bare template cannot be fitted on to the information available. But in other cases, where a three element template can be fitted, dummies are generated as well, since subsequent routines to be described may want to prefer the dummy to the bare template. For example, in the analysis of the first fragment of (The old transport system) (which I loved) (in my youth) (has been found uneconomic), a reasonably full dictionary will contain formulas for the substantive sense of "old" and the action sense of "transport". Thus, the actor-action-object template FOLK CAUSE GRAIN can be fitted on here but will be incorrect. The dummy GRAIN DBE DTHIS will also be fitted on and will be preferred by the EXTEND procedures I describe below. Such slight complexity of the basic template notion are necessary if so simple a concept is to deal with the realities of language. This matter is described in greater detail in (Wilks 1972).

The matching by PICKUP will still, in general, leave a number of bare templates attached to a text fragment. It is the EXTEND routines, working out from the three points at which the bare template attaches to the fragment, that try to create the densest dependency network possible for the fragment, in the way I described earlier, and so to reduce the number of templates matching a fragment, down to one if possible.

I explained the role of EXTEND in general terms earlier: it inspects the strings of formulas that replace a fragment and seeks to set up dependencies of formulas upon each other. It keeps a score as it does so, and in the end it selects the structuring of formulas with the most dependencies, on the assumption that it is the right one (or ones, if two or more structurings of formulas have the same dependency score).

The dependencies that can be set up are of two sorts: (A) those between formulas whose heads are part of the bare template, and (B) those of formulas whose heads are not in the bare template upon those formulas whose heads are in the bare template.

Consider the sentence "John talked quickly" for which the bare template would be MAN TELL DTHIS, thus establishing the dependency John ←→ talked ←→ [DTHIS] at the word level. Now suppose we expand out from each of the elements constituting the bare template in turn. We shall find that in the formula for "talked" that there is the preference for an actor formula whose head is MAN—since talking is generally done by people. This preference is satisfied here, where we can think of it as establishing a word dependency of "John" on "talked", which is a type

A dependency. Expanding again from the element TELL, we have a formula for "quickly" whose head is HOW, and HOW-headed formulas are proper qualifiers for actions. Hence we have been able to set up the following diagramatic dependency at the word level:

$$John \rightleftharpoons talked \longleftrightarrow [DTHIS]$$
$$\uparrow$$
$$quickly$$

(where " $\rightleftharpoons$ " indicates a bare template connectivity strengthened by a direct semantic dependency, springing from the preference of "talked" for a human actor in this case,) and we would score two for such a representation. Furthermore, the formulas having type B dependence would be tied in a list to the main formula on which they depend. The subtypes of dependence are as follows:

A. among the formulas whose heads constitute the bare template
   i. preferred subjects on actions
     "John talked."
   ii. preferred objects of actions on actions
     "interrogated a prisoner."
B. of formulas not constituting bare templates on those that do,
   i. qualifiers of substantives on substantives
     "red door"
   ii. qualifiers of actions on actions
     "opened quickly"
   iii. articles on substantives
     "a book"
   iv. of—fo phrases on substantives
     "the house of my father fo"
   v. qualifiers of actions on qualifiers of substantives
     "very much"
   vi. post verbs on actions
     "give up"
   vii. indirect objects on actions
     "gave John a . . ."
   viii. auxiliaries on actions
     "was going"
   ix. "to" on infinitive form of action.
     "to relax."

The searches for type B dependencies are all directed in the formula string in an intuitively obvious manner:

   i. goes leftwards only:
   ii. goes right and left:

  iii. leftwards only:
  iv. leftwards only:
   v. leftwards only:
  vi. rightwards only:
 vii. rightwards only:
viii. leftwards only.

The purpose of the score of dependencies established can be illustrated here with regard to an example normally considered part of "syntax" rather than "semantics": the indirect object construction. Let us take the sentence "John gave Mary the book," onto which the matching routine PICKUP will have matched two bare templates as follows, since it has no reason to prefer one to the other:

John	gave	Mary	the	book
MAN	GIVE	MAN		
MAN	GIVE			THINC

EXTEND now seeks for dependencies, and since the formula for "gave" has no preferred actors or objects, the top bare template cannot be extended at all and so scores zero. In the case of the lower bare template, then a GIVE action can be expanded by any substantive formula to its immediate right which is not already part of the bare template. Again "book" is qualified by an article, which is not noticed by the top bare template. So then, by EXTENDing we have established in the second case the following dependencies at the word level and scored two (of the "→" dependencies).

$$John \leftrightarrow gave \leftrightarrow book$$
$$\uparrow \qquad \uparrow$$
$$Mary \qquad the$$

Two scores higher than zero and the second representation is preferred. This is another application of the general rule referred to earlier as "pick up the most connected representation from the fragment", applied to a superficially "syntactic" matter, though in this system with its uniform principle of choice and a single set of elements, there is no real distinction between syntactic and semantic questions.

The auxiliary of an action also has its formula made dependent on that of the appropriate action and the fact scored, but auxiliary formulas are not listed as dependent formulas either. They are picked up by EXTEND and examined to determine the tense of the action. They are then forgotten and an element indicating the tense is CONSd onto the action formula. In its initial state the system recognises only four tenses of complex actions.

PRES:does hide/is hiding/did hide/are hiding/am hiding
IMPE:was hiding/were hiding/

PAST:did hide/had hidden
FUTU:will hide/will be hiding/shall hide/shall be hiding

In the negative tense of any of these, the word "not" is forgotten, and an atom NPRES, NIMPE, NPAST, or NFUTU is attached to the appropriate action formula instead. At present, the system does not deal with passives, although I indicate later how they are dealt with within the template format.

The third and last pass of the text applies the TIE routines, which establish dependencies between the representations of different fragments. Each text fragment has been tied by the routines described so far to one or more full templates, each consisting of three main formulas to each of which a list of dependent formulas may be tied. The interlingual representation consists, for each text fragment, of ONE full template together with up to four additional items of information called Key, Mark, Case, and Phase respectively. The interlingual representation also contains the English name of the fragment itself. The Key is simply the first word of the fragment, if it occurs on the list of key words; or, in the cases of "that" and "which," a key USE of the word.

The Mark for a given key is the text word to which the key word ties the whole fragment of which it is the key. So, in (He came home) (from the war), the mark of the second fragment is "came," and the second fragment is tied in a relation of dependence to that mark by the key "from." Every key has a corresponding mark, found by TIE, unless (a) the key is "and" or "but," or (b) the fragment introduced by the key is itself a complete sentence, not dependent on anything outside itself. The notion will become clearer from examining the example paragraph set out below.

From the point of view of the present system of analysis, the Case of a fragment, if any, generally expresses the role of that fragment in relation to its key and mark: it specifies the SORT of dependence the fragment has upon its mark. There is one important case, OBJECT, whose assignment to a case does not depend on the presence of a key. So, in the sentence (I want) (her to leave), the latter fragment would be assigned the case OBJECT and would be tied to the action "want" as the mark of that fragment, even though there is no key present. (The case markers used are the same as those that occur as elements within formulas.)

Phase notation is merely a code to indicate in a very general way to the subsequent generation routines where in the "progress of the whole sentence" one is at a given fragment. A phase number is attached to each fragment on the following basis by TIE, where the stage referred to applies at the beginning of the fragment to which the number attaches.

$\emptyset \longrightarrow$ main subject not yet reached
$1 \longrightarrow$ subject reached but not main verb
$2 \longrightarrow$ main verb reached but not complement or object
$3 \longrightarrow$ complement or object reached or not expected

The TIE routines then apply PARAPLATES to the template codings, using the same density techniques one level further up, as it were. Paraplates have the general form: (...list of predicates...list of generation items and functions..........list of template predicates). The paraplates are attached, as ordered lists, to key words in English.

Let me give an example of semantic resolution, and simplify matters at this stage by writing not the French generation items in the paraplates, but a resolved version of the English. Consider the following three schematic paraplates for "in":

```
((2OBCAS INST GOAL)(PRMARK *DO)IN(into)(FN1 CONT THING)(PRCASE DIRE))
((2OBHEAD      NIL) (PRMARK *DO) IN(make part)    (PRCASE LOCA))
(PRMARK *DO)                 IN(into) (FN1 CONT THING) (PRCASE DIRE))
```

*DIRE is a direction case marker (covering TO, mentioned above, and FROM), 2OBCAS and 2OBHEAD are simply predicates that look at both the object formulas of the template in hand, and at the subject formula of the preceding template, i.e. at two objects. 2OBHEAD is true if the two have the same head, and 2OBCAS is true if they contain the same GOAL or INSTRUMENT subformula. The lower case words simply explain which sense of "in" is the one appropriate to the paraplate in which it occurs. For translation, of course, these will in general be different French prepositions.

Now consider the sentence "The key is / in the lock," fragmented at the stroke as shown. Let us consider that two templates have been set up for the second fragment: one for "lock" as a fastener, and one for the raising lock on a canal. Both formulas may be expected to be CONTainers. If we apply the first paraplate first, we find that it fits only for the template with the correct sense of "lock" since only there will 2OBCAS be satisfied as the formulas for "lock" and "key" both have a subformula under GOAL, or INST, indicating that their purpose is to close something. The third paraplate will fit with the template for the canal sense of "lock" but the first is a more extensive fit (indicated by the order of the paraplates) and is preferred. This preference has simultaneously selected both the right template for the second fragment and the right paraplate for further generation.

If we take "He put the number / in the table" we shall find it fails the first paraplate but fits the second, thus giving us the "make part of" sense of "in," and the right (list) sense of "table," since formulas for "number" and (list) "table" have the same head SIGN, though the formula for (flat, wooden) "table" does not. Similarly, only the third paraplate will fit "He put the list / in the table", and we get the "into" sense of "in" (case DIRECTION) and the physical object sense of "table." Here we see the fitting of paraplates, and choosing the densest preferential fit, which is always the highest paraplate on the list, determining both word sense ambiguity and the case ambiguity of prepositions at once.

The application of paraplates is an extension of the preference for greater semantic density described in detail within fragments: the higher up the list of paraplates the greater the density achieved by applying it successfully. Extensions of this formalism cover anaphora (the correct referent leads to greater semantic density for the whole), and the common-sense inference rules mentioned earlier.

The common-sense inference rules are needed to cover difficult cases of representation where some form of more explicit world knowledge is required. There is no disputing the need of such knowledge for translation, and its absence was one of the major causes of failure of the early MT efforts, as well as of the irrelevance of much modern linguistics. A simple example will establish the need: consider the sentence "The soldiers fired at the women, and I saw several of them fall." Anyone who writes that sentence will be taken to mean that the women fell, so that when, in analysing the sentence, the question arises of whether "them" refers to "soldiers" or "women" (a choice that will result in a differently gendered pronoun in French) we will have to be able to infer that things fired at often fall, or at least are much more likely to fall than things doing the firing. Hence there must be access to inferential information here, above and beyond the meanings of the constituent words, from which we could infer that hurt things tend to fall down.

Such rules are intended to cover not only "world knowledge" examples like the "women fall" just mentioned, but also such cases as "In order to construct an object, it usually takes a series of drawings to describe "it", where to fix the second "it" as "object" and not "series" (though both give equivalent semantic densities in EXPAND), we need an inference rule that can be loosely expressed as "an instrument of an action is not also an object of it". The point of such rules is that they do not apply at a lexical level like simple facts (and so become an unmanageable totality), but to higher level items like semantic formulas and cases. Moreover, their "fitting" in any particular case is always a "fitting better than" other applicable rules, and so is a further extension of the uniform principle of inference, based on density, discussed above.

In more straightforward cases of anaphora such as "I bought the wine, / sat on a rock / and drank it," it is easy to see that the last word should be tied by TIE to "wine" and not "rock." This matter is settled by density after considering alternative ties for "it," and seeing which yields the denser representation overall. Here it will be "wine" since "drink" prefers a liquid object.

The Interlingual Representation

What follows is a shorthand version of the interlingual representation for a paragraph, designed to illustrate the four forms of information for a paragraph – key, mark, case and phase – described above. The schema below gives only the bare template form of the semantic information attached to each fragment – the semantic formulas and their pendant lists of formulas that make up the full template structure are all omitted, as is mention of the paraplates applied to achieve this form. The French given is only illustrative, and no indication is given at this point as to how it is produced. The point of the example is to illustrate the (Speer, 1970) application of the general method to complex material, above and beyond simple example sentences. CM denotes a comma and PD a period.

```
(later CM)
(PLUS TARD VG)
[nil:nil:nil:∅:No Template]
```

(DURING THE WAR CM)
(PENDANT LA GUERRE VG)
[DURING:GAVEUP:location:∅:DTHIS PBE ACT]

(HITLER GAVE UP THE EVENING SHOWINGS CM)
(HITLER RENONCA AUX REPRESENTATIONS DU SOIR VG)
[nil:nil:nil:∅:MAN DROP ACT]

(SAYING)
(DISANT)
[nil:HITLER:nil:3:DTHIS DO DTHIS]

(THAT HE WANTED)
(QU'IL VOULAIT)
[THAT:SAYING:object: 3:MAN WANT DTHIS]

(TO RENOUNCE HIS FAVORITE ENTERTAINMENT)
(RENONCER A SA DISTRACTION FAVORITE)
[TO:WANT:object:3:DTHIS DROP ACT]

(OUTOF SYMPATHY)
(PAR SYMPATHIE)
[OUTOF:RENOUNCE:source:3:DTHIS PDO SIGN]

(FOR THE PRIVATIONS OF THE SOLDIERS PD)
(POUR LES PRIVATIONS DES SOLDATS PT)
[FOR:SYMPATHY:recipient:3:DTHIS PBE ACT]

(INSTEAD RECORDS WERE PLAYED PD)
(A LA PLACE ON PASSA DES DISQUES PT)
[INSTEAD:nil:nil:∅:MAN USE THING](comment:template is made
active)

(BUT)
(MAIS)
[BUT:nil:nil:∅:No Template]

(ALTHOUGH THE RECORD COLLECTION WAS EXCELLENT CM)
(BIEN QUE LA COLLECTION DE DISQUES FUT EXCELLENTE VG)
[ALTHOUGH:PREFERRED:nil:∅:GRAIN BE KIND]

(HITLER ALWAYS PREFERRED THE SAME MUSIC PD)
(HITLER PREFERAIT TOUJOURS LA MEME MUSIQUE PT)
[nil:nil:nil:∅:MAN WANT GRAIN]

```
(NEITHER BAROQUE)
(NI LA MUSIQUE BAROQUE)
[NEITHER:MUSIC:qualifier:Ø:DTHIS DBE KIND)

(NOR CLASSICAL MUSIC CM)
(NI CLASSIQUE VG)
[NOR:INTERESTED:nil:Ø:GRAIN DBE DTHIS]

(NEITHER CHAMBER MUSIC)
(NI LA MUSIQUE DE CHAMBRE)
[NEITHER:INTERESTED:nil:Ø:GRAIN DBE DTHIS]

(NOR SYMPHONIES CM)
(NI LES SYMPHONIES VG)
[NOR:INTERESTED:nil:Ø:GRAIN DBE DTHIS]

(INTERESTED HIM PD)
(NE L'INTERESSAIENT PT)
[nil:nil:nil:1:DTHIS CHANGE MAN]

(BEFORELONG THE ORDER OF THE RECORDS BECAME VIRTUALLY FIXED
PD)
(BIENTOT L'ORDRE DES DISQUES DEVINT VIRTUELLEMENT FIXE PT)
[BEFORELONG:nil:nil:Ø:GRAIN BE KIND]

(FIRST HE WANTED A FEW BRAVURA SELECTIONS)
(D'ABORD IL VOULAIT QUELQUES SELECTIONS DE BRAVOURE)
[nil:nil:nil:Ø:MAN WANT PART]

(FROM WAGNERIAN OPERAS CM)
(D'OPERAS WAGNERIENS VG)
[FROM:SELECTIONS:source:3:DTHIS PDO GRAIN]

(TO BE FOLLOWED PROMPTLY)
(QUI DEVAIENT ETRE SUIVIES RAPIDEMENT)
[TO:OPERAS:nil:3:MAN DO DTHIS](comment:shift to active
template again may give a different but not incorrect
translation)

(WITH OPERETTAS PD)
(PAR DES OPERETTAS PT)
[WITH:FOLLOWED:nil:3:DTHIS PBE GRAIN]
```

(THAT REMAINED THE PATTERN PD)
(CELA DEVINT LA REGLE PT)
[nil:nil:nil:∅:THAT BE GRAIN](comment:no mark because 'that'
ties to a whole sentence.)

(HITLER MADE A POINT OF TRYING)
(HITLER SE FAISAIT UNE REGLE D'ESSAYER)
[nil:nil:nil:∅:MAN DO DTHIS]

(TO GUESS THE NAMES OF THE SOPRANOS)
(DE DEVINER LES NOMS DES SOPRANOS)
[TO:TRYING:object:2:DTHIS DO SIGN]

(AND WAS PLEASED)
(ET ETAIT CONTENT)
[AND:HITLER:nil:3:DTHIS BE KIND]

(WHEN HE GUESSED RIGHT CM)
(QUAND IL DEVINAIT JUSTE VG)
[WHEN:PLEASED:location:3:MAN DO DTHIS]

(AS HE FREQUENTLY DID PD)
(COMME IL LE FAISAIT FREQUEMMENT PT)
[AS:GUESSED:manner:3:MAN DO DTHIS]

It is assumed that those fragments that have no template attached to them — such as
(LATER) — can be translated adequately by purely word-for-word means. Were it not
for the difficulty involved in reading it, we could lay out the above text so as to display the dependencies implied by the assignment of cases and marks at the word
level. These would all be of dependencies of whole fragments on particular words.
So, for example the relation of just the first two fragments could be set out as follows:

$$[\text{DTHIS}] \longleftrightarrow during \longleftrightarrow war \longleftarrow the$$
$$\downarrow$$
$$\downarrow (location)$$
$$\downarrow$$
$$\text{Hitler} \longleftrightarrow gave{+}up \longleftrightarrow showings \longleftarrow the$$
$$\uparrow$$
$$evening$$

The interlingual representation described, as the result of the analysis of English
text, and illustrated above in bare template form, is the intermediate form handed,
as it were, from the English analysis programs to the French generation ones.

However, this intermediate stage is, as it must be, an arbitrary one in the English-French processing, yet it is helpful here to do a cursory examination for expository purposes and not only in the coded form. There is often a misunderstanding of the nature of an interlingua, in that it is supposed that an intermediate stage like the present interlingual representation (IR for short) must contain "all possible semantic information" in some explicit form if the IR is to be adequate for any purpose.

But the quoted words are not—and cannot be—well defined with respect to any coding scheme whatsoever. The IR must contain sufficient information so as to admit of formal manipulations upon itself adequate for producing translations in other natural or formal languages. But that is quite another matter of course. The fallacy is analogous to that committed by the computationally illiterate who say that "you can't get more out of a computer than you put in, can you?"—which is false if it is taken to exclude computation upon what you put in. (A more traditional parallel is the Socratic argument about whether or not the premises of an argument "really" contain all possible conclusions from themselves already, in that to know the premises is already to know the conclusions).

Analogously, the IR for translation need not contain any particular explicit information about the text. The real restriction is that, in creating the IR, no information should have been thrown away that will later turn out to be important. So, if one makes the superficial but correct generalization that one of the difficulties of English-French MT is the need to extend and make explicit in the French things that are not so in the English, then it is no answer to say there is no problem since, whatever those things are, the IR, if adequate, must contain them anyway. It is then argued that if there is a problem it is a general one about deriving the IR from English and has nothing at all to do with French.

But this, as I have pointed out, need not be true of any particular IR, since any IR must be an arbitrary cut-off stage in going from one language to another; a slice taken at a particular point for examination, as it were.

Consider the sentence "The house I live in is collapsing" which contains no subjunction "that," though in French it MUST be expressed explicitly, as by "dans laquelle." There need not be any representation of "that" anywhere in the IR. All that is necessary is that the subordination of the second fragment to the mark "house" is coded, and generation procedures that know that in such cases of subordination an appropriate subjunction must occur in the French output. It is the need for such procedures that constitutes the sometimes awkward expansion of English into French, but the need for them in no way dictates the explicit content of the IR.

The Dictionary Format

The dictionary is essentially a list of sense-pairs: the left-hand member of each sense pair is a formula, expressing the sense of some English word, and the corresponding right-hand member is a list of STEREOTYPES, from which French output is to be generated. Thus each formula that is pulled into the IR by the analysis procedures described, has pulled with it the stereotypes for the corresponding French. As will be seen, the stereotypes are in fact implicit procedures for assembling the French, so the role of the generation routines is simply to recursively unwrap, as it were, the package of the interlingual representation. So for example, the French words "rouge" and "socialiste" might be said to distinguish two senses of the English word "red," and we might code these two senses of "red" in the dictionary by means of the sense pairs:

(((WHERE SPREAD)KIND)(RED(ROUGE)))
((((WORLD CHANGE)WANT)MAN)(RED(SOCIALISTE))).

The French words "rouge" and "socialiste" are enclosed in list parentheses because they need not have been, as in this case, single French words. They could be French words strings of any length: for example, the qualifier sense of "hunting" as it occurs in a "a hunting gun" is rendered in French as "de chasse", hence we would expect as the right hand member of one sense pair for "hunting" (HUNTING(DE CHASSE)). Moreover, as we shall see below, a formula may require more than one stereotype in the list attached to it.

This simplified notion of stereotype is adequate for the representation of most qualifiers and substantives.

The general form of the full stereotype is a list of predicates, followed by a string of French words and functions that evaluate to French words, or to NIL (in which case the stereotype fails). The functions may also evaluate to blank symbols for reasons to be described.

The predicates—which occur only in preposition stereotypes—normally refer to the case of the fragment containing the word, and to its mark respectively. If both these predicates are satisfied, the program continues on through the stereotype to the French output.

Let us consider the verb "advise," rendered in its most straightforward sense by the French word "conseiller." It is likely to be followed by two different constructions as in the English: I advise John to have patience, and, I advise patience. Verb stereotypes contain no predicates, so we might expect the most usual sense pair for "advise" to contain a formula followed by

(ADVISE(CONSEILLER A (FN1 FOLK MAN))
(CONSEILLER (FN2 ACT STATE STUFF)))

The role of the stereotypes should by now be clearer; in generating from an action, the system looks down a list of stereotypes tied to the sense of the action in the full template. If any of the functions it now encounters evaluate to NIL, then the whole stereotype containing the function fails and the next is tried. If the functions evaluate to French words then they are generated along with the French words that appear as their own names, like "conseiller."

The details of the French generation procedures are discussed in the following section, but we can see here in a general way how the stereotypes for "advise" produce correct translations of sentences i and ii. In sentence i, in the form of two fragments (I advise John)(to have patience), the program begins to generate from the stereotype for the formula in the action position in the first fragment's template. It moves rightwards as described and begins to generate "conseiller a." Then (FN1 FOLK MAN) is evaluated, which is a function that looks at the formula for the third, object, position of the current template and returns its French stereotype only if its head is MAN or FOLK—that is to say if it is a human being that is being advised. The formula for "John" satisfies this and "Jean" is generated after "conseiller a". Proper names are translated here for illustrative purposes only, so we obtain the correct construction "Je conseille a Jean".

Had we been examining sentence ii, "I advise patience," this first stereotype for "advise" would have failed since (FN1 FOLK MAN) would not have produced a French word on being applied to the formula for "patience," whose head is ACT. Hence the next stereotype would have been tried and found to apply.

The stereotypes do more than simply avoid the explicit use of a conventional generative grammar (not that there is much precedent for using one of those) in a system that has already eschewed the use of an analysis grammar. They also direct the production of the French translation by providing complex context-sensitive rules at the point required, and without any search of a large rule inventory. This method is, in principle, extensible to the production of reasonably complex implicit rephrasings and expansions, as in the derivation of "si intelligent soit-il" from the second fragment of (No man)(however intelligent)(can survive death), given the appropriate stereotype for "however."

Prepositions are taken as having only a single sense each, even though that sense may give rise to a great number of stereotypes. Let us consider, by way of example, "outof" (considered as a single word) in the three sentences:

i. (It was made)(outof wood)
ii. (He killed him)(outof hatred)
iii. (I live)(outof town)

It seems to me unhelpful to say that here are three senses of "outof" even though its occurrence in these examples requires translation into French by "de," "par" and "en dehors de" respectively, and other contexts would require "parmi" or "dans."

Given the convention for stereotypes described earlier for actions, let us set down stereotypes that would enable us to deal with these examples:

Si. ((PRCASE SOUR)(PRMARK *DO) DE (FN1 STUFF THING))
Sii. ((PRCASE SOUR)(PRMARK *DO) PAR (FN2 FEEL))
Siii. ((PRCASE LOCA) EN DEHORS DE (FN1 POINT SPREAD))

Where *DO indicates a wide class of action formulas: any, in fact, whose heads are not PDO, DBE or BE.

One thing that should be made clear at this point, to avoid confusing anyone who has noticed the similarity of paraplates and these full stereotypes for prepositions, is that they are in fact the same thing. In the analysis section, for ease of presentation, I described the application of a list of paraplates, tied to a key word like a preposition, and the selection of the correct one from context in order to determine the case of the tie between templates. This process is also the selection of the correct stereotype for generation from the same structure. There is no pause, as it were, in the operation of the whole system: when the interlingual representation is finished, the procedure passes directly into generation. So, what was described earlier as the successful evaluation of a function in a paraplate, thus showing that the paraplate 'fitted,' is in fact the evaluation of that function to a French word string that itself becomes the output from the whole process.

Thus the same theoretical objects can be seen in analysis as paraplates, being items that tie a meaning representation together, and, in generation as stereotypes, being implicit procedures producing output strings as values.

In sentence fragments (It was made) (outof wood), when the program enters the second fragment it knows from the whole interlingual representation described earlier that the case of that fragment is SOURCE and its mark is "made." The mark word has DO as its head, and so the case and mark predicates PRCASE and PRMARK in the first stereotype are both satisfied. Thus "de" is tentatively generated from the first stereotype and FN1 is applied, because of its definition, to the object formula in this template, that is to say, the one for "wood." The arguments of FN1 are STUFF and THING and the function finds STUFF as the head of the formula for "wood" in the full template, and is satisfied and thus generates "bois" from the stereotype for "wood".

In the second fragment of (He killed him) (outof hatred), the two predicates of the first stereotype for "outof" would again be satisfied, but (FN1 THING STUFF) would fail with the formula for "hatred" whose head is STATE. The next stereotype Sii would be tried; the same two predicates would be satisfied, and now (FN2 FEEL) would be applied to (NOTPLEASE(FEEL STATE)) the formula for "hatred." But FN2 by its definition examines not formula heads, but rather seeks for the containment of one of its arguments within the formula. Here it finds FEEL within the formula and so generates the French word stereotype for "hatred."

Similar considerations apply to the third example sentence involving the LOCATION case; though in that case there would be no need to work through the two SOURCE stereotypes already discussed since, when a case is assigned to a fragment during paraplate analysis, only those stereotypes are left in the interlingual representation that correspond to the assigned case.

The Generation of French

Much of the heart of the French generation has been described in outline in the last section, since it is impossible to describe the dictionary and its stereotypes usefully without describing the generative role that the stereotypes play.

To complete this brief sketch all that it is appropriate to add is some description of the way in which generations from the stereotype of a key and of the mark for the same fragment interlock—the mark being in a different fragment—as control flows backwards and forwards between the stereotypes of different words in search of a satisfactory French output. There is not space available here for description of the bottom level of the generation program—the concord and number routines—in which even the simplest need access to mark information, as in locating the gender of "heureux" in (John seems) (to be happy) translated as "Jean semble etre heureux."

Again, much of the detailed content of the generation is to be found in the functions evaluating to French words that I have arbitrarily named FN1 and so on. Some of these seek detail down to gender markers. For example, one would expect to get the correct translations "Je voyageais en France" but ". . . au Canada" with the aid of functions, say, FNF and FNM that seek not only specific formula heads but genders as well. So, among the stereotypes for the English "in" we would expect to find (given that formulas for land areas have SPREAD as their heads): . . . A (FNM SPREAD)) and . . . EN (FNF SPREAD)).

It is not expected that there will be more than twenty or so of these inner stereotype functions in all. Though it should be noticed at this point that there is no level of generation that does not require quite complicated semantic information processing. I have in mind here what one might call the bottom level of generation, the addition and compression of articles. An MT program has to get "Je bois du vin" for "I drink wine" but to "J'aime LE vin" for "I like wine". Now there is no analog for this distinction in English and nothing about the meanings of "like" and "drink" that accounts for the difference in the French in a way intuitively acceptable to the English speaker. At present we are expecting to generate the difference by means of stereotypes that seek the notion USE in the semantic codings—which will be located in "drink" but not in "like," and to use this to generate the "de" where appropriate.

The overall control function of the generation expects five different types of template names to occur:

1. *THIS *DO *ANY where *THIS is any substantive head (not DTHIS)
   *DO is any real action head (not BE, PDO, DBE)
   *ANY is any of *DO or KIND or DTHIS. With this type of template the number, person, and gender of the verb are deduced from the French stereotype for the subject part.

1a. type *THIS BE KIND is treated with type 1.

2. DTHIS *DO *ANY These templates arise when a subject has been split from its action by fragmentation. The mark of the fragment is then the subject. Or, the template may represent an object action phrase, such as a simple infinitive with an implicit subject to be determined from the mark.

3. *THIS DBE DTHIS Templates of this type represent the subject, split off from its action represented by type 2 template above. The translation is simply generated from the stereotype of the subject formula, since the rest are dummies, though there may arise cases of the form DTHIS DBE KIND where generation is only possible from a qualifier as in the second fragment of (I like tall CM) (blond CM) (and blue-eyed Germans).

4. DTHIS PDO ∗REAL Templates of this type represent prepositional phrases and the translation is generated as described from the key stereotype, after which the translation for the template object is added (∗REAL denotes any head in ∗THIS or is KIND).

The general strategy for the final stages of the MT program is to generate French word strings directly from the template structure assigned to a fragment of English text. The first move is to find out which of the five major types of template distinguished above is the one attached to the fragment under examination.

So then, for a fragment as simple as "John already owns a big red car," the program would notice that the fragment has no mark or key. Hence, by default, the generation is to proceed from a stereotype that is a function of the general type of the template attaching to the fragment. The bare name of the template for this one fragment sentence is MAN HAVE THING and inspection of the types above will show this to be a member of type 1, whose general form is ∗THIS ∗DO ∗ANY. The stereotype is a function — let us say FTEMP — of that template type and, to conform with the general format for stereotypes described earlier, this can be thought of as being one of the stereotypes for the "null word," since we have no mark or key word to start from here.

In this case the generation of French is simplicity itself: the function FTEMP evaluates to a French word string whose order is that of the stereotypes of the English words of the fragment. This order is directed by the presence of the first type of template comprising an elementary sequence subject-action-object. This is done recursively so that, along with the French words generated for those English words whose formulas constitute the bare template (i.e. "John", "own," and "car") are generated those whose formulas are merely dependent on the main formulas of the template — in this case the formulas for "already", "big," and "red."

If complex stereotypes are located while generating for any of the words of the fragment — "complex," meaning full stereotypes which have constituents that are functions as well as French words — then generation from these newly found stereotypes immediately takes precedence over further generation from the last stereotype at the level above.

Here, then, "own" creates no problems since it is a completely regular French verb, and its stereotypes contain nothing but French words. In general, it is only irregular French verbs that contain complexity in their stereotypes so as to dictate the form of what follows them in a sentence. (It should be understood that I am using "irregular" here to mean irregular with respect to this system of classification — my usage is not intended to correspond to the standard opposition of "regular" to "irregular" in French grammars).

Now suppose we consider the two fragment sentence "I order John to leave". The fragments will be presented to the generation program in the form described earlier: with Key, Mark, Case, and Phase information attached to each fragment:

(I order John) nil:nil:nil:0
(to leave)   to:order:OBJE:2

Also attached to the fragments will be full templates whose bare template names in this case will be MAN TELL MAN and DTHIS MOVE DTHIS respectively.

The generation program enters the first fragment which has no mark or key; so it starts to generate, as before, from the stereotype for the null word which again is one for the first template type. This gets the subject right: "je" from the stereotype for "I," later to be modified to "j" by the concord routine. It then enters the stereotypes for the action: the first being (ORDONNER A (FN1 MAN FOLK)).

The head of the formula for "John" is MAN, and FN1 here is an arbitrary name for a function that looks into the formula for the object place of a template and, if the head of that formula is any of the function's arguments, it returns the stereotype value of that formula. In this case the function FN1 is satisfied by "John", so by definition that stereotype for "order" is satisfied, and the program generates from it the sequence "ordonner a Jean," giving the correct sequence "Je$ ordonner$ a Jean"—where $ indicates the need for further minor processing by the concord routine. The stereotype has now been exhausted—nothing in it remains unevaluated or ungenerated. Similarly the fragment is exhausted since no words remain whose stereotypes have not been generated, either directly or via the stereotype from some other word, and so the program passes on to the second fragment.

The program enters the second fragment and finds that it has a mark, namely "order." It then consults the stereotypes in hand for "order" in fragment (i) to see if it was exhausted or not. It was, and so the program turns to the stereotypes for "to," the key of (ii). Among those whose first predicate has the argument OBJE will be the stereotype

$$((PRCASE\ OBJE)(PRMARK\ FORCE\ TELL)\ DE\ (FNINF\ *DO)).$$

If we remember that the head of the current formula for "order," the mark of fragment ii, is FORCE, and that PRMARK seeks and compares its arguments with the head of the mark formula, then the predicates are seen to be satisfied and the program generates "de" after seeing that FNINF is satisfied, since an action formula for "leave" follows, whose head MOVE is in the class *DO.

FNINF on evaluation finds, where necessary, the implicit subject of the infinitive. That is unnecessary here, but would be essential in examples only slightly more complex, such as "Marie regrette de s'etre rejouie trop tot." Finally FNINF itself evaluates to the French stereotype selected for "leave." This might itself give rise to more searching if the use of "leave" dictated its own sequents as in "I order John to leave by the first train." Here however the evaluation terminates immediately to "partir" since the sentence stops. The program makes no attempt now to generate for "leave" again, since it realises it has already entered its stereotype list via the "to" stereotype. Thus the correct French string "Je$ ordonne$ a Jean de partir" has been generated.

The last example was little more than a more detailed re-description of the processes described in the dictionary section in connexion with the example "I advise John to have patience." However, now that we have dealt fully with a fairly standard case and shown the recursive use of stereotypes in the generation of French on a fragment-by-fragment basis, we can discuss a final pair of examples in which a more powerful stereotype, as it were, can dictate and take over the generation of other fragments.

If we were to consider in detail the generation of French for the two fragment sentence (I throw the ball) (outof the window), we should find the process almost identical to that used in the last example. Here, too, the main stereotype used to generate the French for the first fragment is that of the action—"throw" in this example. The stereotype for "throw" is exhausted by the first fragment, so that nothing in that stereotype causes the program to inspect the second fragment.

Now consider, in the same format, (I drink wine) (outof a glass). Following the same procedures as before, we shall find ourselves processing the stereotype for "drink" which reads

(BOIRE (FN1 (FLOW STUFF))) (FNX1 SOUR PDO THING) ↑ DANS (FNX2 THING))

where "↑" indicates a halt-point. The program begins to generate tentatively, evaluating the functions left to right and being prepared to cancel the whole stereotype if any one of them fails. FN1 is applied to the formula for "wine" and specifies the inclusion in its formula, not of one of two elements, but of the whole conventional subformula for liquids (FLOW STUFF). This it finds, is satisfied, and so evaluates to "vin," to be modified by concord to "du vin."

The program now encounters FNX1, a function which by definition applies to the full template for some FOLLOWING fragment. At this point the program evaluates FNX1 which returns a blank symbol if and only if it finds a following (though not necessarily immediately following) fragment with a SOURce case and a template, the last two elements of whose bare name are PDO THING. It is, therefore, a preposition type fragment with a physical object as the object of the preposition. This situation would not obtain if the sentence were "I drink the wine out of politeness". If FNX1 is satisfied, as it is here, it causes the generation from this stereotype to halt after generating a blank symbol. Halting in an evaluation is to be taken as quite different from both exhausting (all functions evaluated to French word strings or a blank) and failing (at least one function evaluates to NIL).

The main control program now passes to the next fragment, in this case "outof a glass". It asks first if it has a mark, which it has, namely "drink", and looks at the stereotype in hand for the mark to see if it is exhausted, which it is not, merely halted. The program therefore continues to generate from the same stereotype, for "drink," producing "du vin," then "dans," followed by the evaluate of FNX2, namely "verre," thus giving the correct translation "Je bois\$ du vin dans un verre."

The important point here is that the stereotypes for the key to the second fragment, "outof," are NEVER CONSULTED at all. The translations for all the words of the second fragment will have been entered via a stereotype for the previous fragment, the one for "drink." The advantage of this method will be clear: because it would be very difficult, conceptually and within the framework I have described, to obtain the translation of "outof" as "dans" in this context from the stereotype for "outof," because that translation is specific to the occurrence of certain French words, such as "boire," rather than to the application of certain concepts. In this way the stereotypes can cope with linguistic idiosyncrasy as well as with conceptual regularity. It should be noted, too, that since "dans" is not generated until after the halted stereotype restarts, there is no requirement that the two example fragments be contiguous. The method I have described could cope just as well with (I drink the wine) (I like most) (outof a silver goblet).

The point here (about what words are generated through the stereotypes for what OTHER words) can perhaps be made a little clearer with a diagram in which lines connect the English word through whose stereotype a generation is done to the word for which output is generated. All generations conventionally start from ∅, the null word mentioned above. It is, by convention, the word for which the five basic stereotypes are the stereotype. So then, the more straightforward (I threw the ball) (outof the window) would be generated as follows:

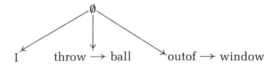

The new fragment starting with "outof" returns again to ∅ to begin generating again. Articles are omitted for simplicity. In the more complex (I drink wine) (outof a glass) the generation pattern would be as follows:

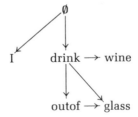

Where the subjects and objects of a sentence are separated by intervening clauses, these generation diagrams can become considerably more complicated.

The general rule with action stereotypes then, is that the more irregular the action, the more information goes into its stereotype and the less is needed in the stereotypes for its sequents. So, for example, there is no need for a stereotype for "outof" to contain DANS at all. Again, just as the regular "I order John to leave" produced the translation "J'ordonne a Jean de partir" by using the stereotype for the key "to", the less regular "I urge John to leave" which requires the quite different construction "J'exhorte Jean a partir", would be dealt with by a halting stereotype for "urge" whose form would be

(EXHORTER (FN1 MAN FOLK) (FNX1 OBJE *DO) ↑ A (FNXINF *DO))

with the stereotype for "to" never being consulted at all.

Acknowledgments

The views and conclusions contained in this document are those of the author and should not be represented as necessarily representing the official policies, either expressed or implied, of the Advanced Research Projects Agency or the U.S. Government. This research was supported in part by an ONR Contract (N00014-67-A-0049), and in part by the Advanced Research Projects Agency, Department of Defense (SD 183), U.S.A.

Four

A Procedural Model of
Language Understanding

Terry Winograd
Massachusetts Institute of Technology

Much of the research on language is based on an attempt to separate it into distinct components—components that can then be studied independently. Modern syntactic theoreticians have been tremendously successful at setting up complex rules which describe in detail the possible orderings of syntactic constituents; at the same time other researchers are trying to define semantic relations and to model the cognitive structures underlying language use.

Most attempts to model language understanding on the computer have followed this strategy of dealing with a single component of language. They are constructed primarily as a syntactic program (Kuno, 1965), a model of semantic connections (Schank, 1971), or an attempt to model the memory structures (Quillian, 1967).

Question-answering systems have had to deal with the entire language process, but they have been severely limited in the breadth of their language ability. The only attempt to handle large portions of language data was the machine translation effort, and it soon became obvious that the methods were not up to the requirements of the task. Language translation could not be treated as a problem of rearranging syntactic structures and words, because attention to meaning was required even to achieve moderately acceptable results.

One basic limitation of those programs that have tried to handle the problems of meaning is that they have dealt almost exclusively with the understanding of single sentences, when in fact almost no human use of language takes place in such an artificial setting. We are always in a context, and in that context we make use of what has gone on to help interpret what is coming. Much of the structure of language comes from its being a process of communication between an intelligent speaker and hearer, occurring in a setting. The setting includes not only a physical situation and a topic of discourse, but also the knowledge each participant has about the world and the other's ideas.

This paper describes an attempt to explore the interconnections between the different types of knowledge required for language understanding. It is based on a computer program that "understands" language in a limited domain by including a model of the subject being talked about and a context of discourse. As an example of the interactions between the different sorts of knowledge the system must have, let us look first at the use of pronouns.

Our syntactic knowledge of English enables us to know that in the sentence "Arthur wants to see him," the word "him" must refer to someone other than Arthur (otherwise we would have used "himself"). In "Arthur wants somebody to see him," "him" might or might not refer to Arthur. The distribution of reflexive pronouns like "himself" depends in a complex way on the syntactic structure of the sentences in which they appear, and a language understander must have this knowledge. As a semantic fact, we know that "him" must refer to something which the speaker is characterizing as animate and male.

At another level, we know that the referent is likely to occur in the preceding sentence, or earlier in the sentence being interpreted, that it is more likely to refer to the topic or the subject of the previous sentence, and is much more likely to refer to a major constituent than to one deeply embedded in the structure. This type of heuristic knowledge about the organization of discourse also plays a part in our understanding.

Finally, there is a level based on knowledge of the world. In the sentence "Sam and Bill wanted to take the girls to the movies, but they didn't have any money," we understand "they" as referring to Sam and Bill. This doesn't involve syntactic or general semantic knowledge, but depends on our knowledge of our social culture. When someone takes someone else to the movies, it is the inviter who pays, and it is his or her financial situation that is relevant.

Whenever we look into realistic language use, these types of interaction play a large role, not only with pronouns, but in deciding on the structures of sentences and meanings of individual words as well. We assign different structures to sentences like "He gave the house plants to charity," and "He gave the boy plants to water," on the basis of our syntactic and semantic knowledge. Even the most common words have multiple meanings, and we must bring a variety of facts to bear in deciding, for example, the meaning of "had" in "Mary had a little lamb, but I preferred the baked lobster."

In discourse, people take advantage of a variety of mechanisms that depend on the existence of an intelligent hearer who will use all sorts of knowledge to fill in any necessary information.

In making a computer model of language use, this presents a serious problem. On the one hand, it is impossible to isolate one aspect of language from the others, or to separate a person's use of linguistic knowledge from his use of other knowledge. On the other hand, it is clearly folly at this point to think of giving the program all the knowledge a person brings into a conversation. In our program, we choose to resolve the dilemma by picking a tiny bit of the world to talk about. Within this mini-world, we can give the computer a deep kind of knowledge, including the equivalent of "Who would pay for a movie?"

The subject chosen was the world of a toy robot with a simple arm. It can manipulate toy blocks on a table containing simple objects like a box. In the course of a dialogue, it can be asked to manipulate the objects, doing such things as building stacks and putting things into the box. It can be questioned about the current configurations of blocks on the table, about the events that have gone on during the discussion, and to a limited extent about its reasoning. It can be told simple facts which are added to its store of knowledge for use in later reasoning. The conversation goes on within a dynamic framework—one in which the computer is an active participant, doing things to change his toy world, and discussing them.

The program was written in LISP on the PDP-10 ITS time-sharing system of the Artificial Intelligence Laboratory at MIT.* It displays a simulated robot world on a television screen and converses with a human on a teletype. It was not written for any particular use with a real robot and does not have a model of language based on peculiarities of the robot environment. Rather, it is precisely by limiting the subject matter to such a small area that we can address the general issues of how language is used in a framework of physical objects, events, and a continuing discourse.

The programs can be roughly divided into the three domains mentioned above: There is a syntactic parser which works with a large-scale grammar of English; there is a collection of semantic routines that embody the kind of knowledge needed to interpret the meanings of words and structures; and there is a cognitive deductive system for exploring the consequences of facts, making plans to carry out commands and finding the answers to questions. There is also a comparatively simple set of programs for generating appropriate English responses.

In designing these pieces, the main emphasis was on the interaction of the three domains. The form in which we want to state a syntactic theory or a type of deduction must take into account the fact that it is only a part of a larger system. One of the most useful organizing principles was the representation of much of the knowledge as procedures. Many other theories of language state their rules in a form modelled on the equations of mathematics or the rules of symbolic logic. These are static rules that do not explicitly describe the process involved in using them, but are instead manipulated by some sort of uniform deduction procedure. By writing special languages suited to the various types of knowledge (semantic, syntactic, deductive), we are able to preserve the simplicity of these systems. This is accom-

---

*For more details on the entire system, see Winograd (1972). The actual program is written in LISP, occupies about 100K of storage on the PDP-10, and operates in approximately real time, responding to a sentence in an average of 10 or 15 seconds.

plished by putting the knowledge in the form of programs in which we can explicitly express the connections between the different parts of the system's knowledge, thus enriching their possibilities for interaction.

The rest of this chapter illustrates the capabilities of the system and explains in some detail how it works. The second section presents a sample of a dialogue with the program, along with comments describing some of the features being demonstrated. The third section gives a closer view of the program itself, and the final section discusses some of its basic limitations.

Sample Dialogue

This section contains a sample dialogue with the language-understanding system. This system carries out actions and answers questions about a simple scene containing a table, hand, and box, and several blocks and pyramids. The numbered lines in lower case were typed in by a person, and the lines in upper case are the computer's response. Other lines are comments describing some of the features being exhibited.

The dialogue was carried out in real time with the response of the "robot" displayed on a television screen. Figures are included to show the state of the scene at various points.

1. pick up a big red block.

OK.

The system answers "OK" when it carries out a command. In order to pick up the red block, it had to clear it off by finding a space for the green one and moving the green one away. The initial situation is shown in Figure 4.1, and the result in Figure 4.2.

2. grasp the pyramid.

I DON'T UNDERSTAND WHICH PYRAMID YOU MEAN.

There are three pyramids in the scene, and the program knows that phrases beginning with *"the"* are intended to refer to a specific object the speaker has in mind.

3. find a block which is taller than the one you are holding and put it into the box.

The system has to figure out what is meant by *"one"* and *"it,"* as well as using deduction to decide which block it is holding.

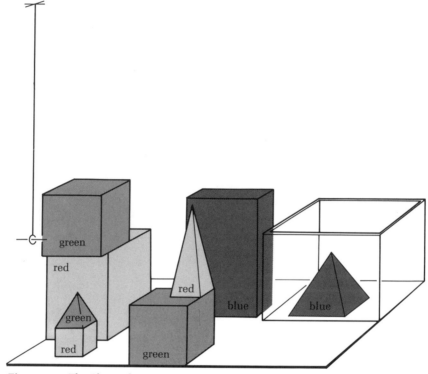

Figure 4.1 The Physical Environment of the Robot.

BY "IT," I ASSUME YOU MEAN THE BLOCK WHICH IS TALLER THAN
THE ONE I AM HOLDING.

There were two possible referents for "*it*": the one selected, and "*the one you are holding*." The program has heuristics for choosing between them.

OK.

The hand has to set down the red block to pick up the taller blue one. Figure 4.3 shows the result of the system's manipulations so far.

4. *what does the box contain?*

THE BLUE PYRAMID AND THE BLUE BLOCK.

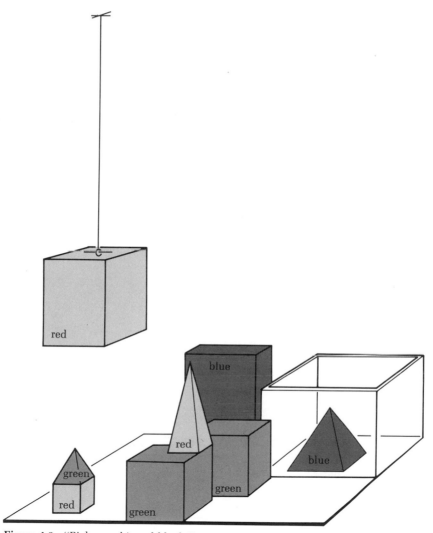

Figure 4.2 "Pick up a big red block."

5. *what is the pyramid supported by?*

Earlier the system responded to "*the pyramid*" by saying "I DON'T UNDERSTAND WHICH PYRAMID YOU MEAN." Now, it assumes that we mean the one just mentioned.

THE BOX.

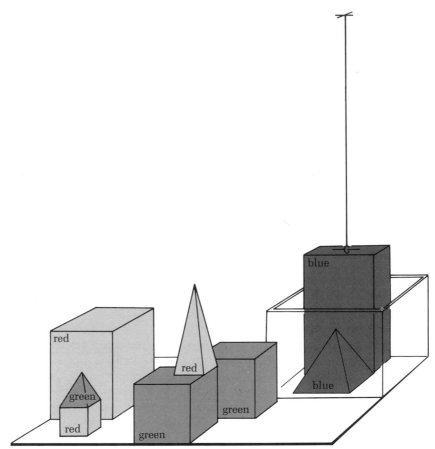

Figure 4.3 "Find a block which is taller than the one you are holding and put it into the box."

6. how many blocks are not in the box?

Negatives such as "not" and "no" are handled whether they appear in clauses or noun groups (such as "no boxes").

FOUR OF THEM.

7. is at least one of them narrower then the one which i told you to pick up?

The phrase "*at least one of them*" must be analyzed to refer back to the previous question, and "*the one which* . . ." must also refer to blocks. Noun groups can have complicated numbers such as "*at least one*," "*more than three*," "*exactly seven*," etc. The memory of past events is used to deduce which block is "*the one which I told you to pick up*." Notice the complicated syntactic structure in which "*the one*" is actually the object of a clause embedded two levels deeper. The parser incorporates a grammar that handles this kind of complexity in a general way.

YES, THE RED CUBE.

8. is it supported?

YES, BY THE TABLE.

The system has heuristics about what information is relevant to a person who asks a question, even if he does not request that information specifically.

9. can the table pick up blocks?

NO.

The semantic rules include the knowledge that "*picking up*" must be done by an animate object, and that the table is not animate.

10. can a pyramid be supported by a block?

YES.

The deductive system finds an actual example, so it knows this is possible.

11. can a pyramid support a pyramid?

I DON'T KNOW.

The question makes sense, but there is no example in the scene. The system has no way of looking into the details of its programs, even though these ultimately define its capabilities.

12. stack up two pyramids.

I CAN'T.

The robot tries and fails.

13. the blue pyramid is mine.

I UNDERSTAND.

All of the information about colors, shapes, sizes and locations of the objects is known to the program initially. Possession is left as an unknown property of objects about which it can be told. It stores this information in its data base.

14. i own all blocks which are not red, but i don't own anything which supports a pyramid.

I UNDERSTAND.

The result of understanding these sentences is the creation of new procedures within the robot for deducing whether I own something.

15. do i own the box?

NO.

The box supports whatever it contains, including a pyramid.

16. do i own anything in the box?

YES, TWO THINGS: THE BLUE BLOCK AND THE BLUE PYRAMID.

17. will you please stack up both of the red blocks and either a green cube or a pyramid?

OK.

Logical connectives, such as "and," "or," "either," etc., are handled in both the grammar and semantics. A command is executed even if it looks like a question. The command is carried out by the following series of steps: It puts a green cube on the large red block (it chooses the green cube with nothing on it), then removes the small pyramid from the little red cube, so that it can use that cube to complete the stack as specified, resulting in what is described in Figure 4.4.

18. which cube is sitting on the table?

THE LARGE GREEN ONE WHICH SUPPORTS THE RED PYRAMID.

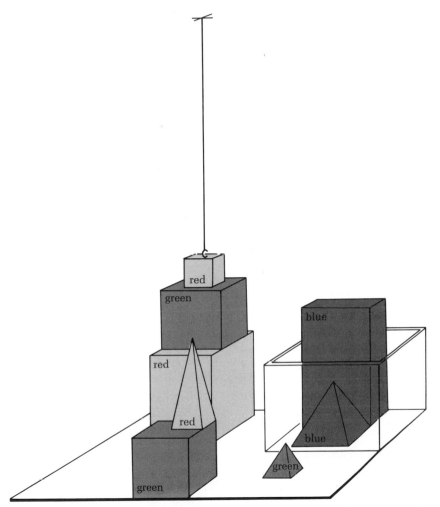

Figure 4.4 "Will you please stack up both of the red blocks and either a green cube or a pyramid."

Ordinarily the system would be satisfied with calling this *"a big green cube,"* but since we asked *"which cube"* it has to be more specific in naming it. It has procedures for using substitute nouns (such as "one") and pronouns in answers to make the discourse more natural.

19. *is there a large block behind a pyramid?*

YES, THREE OF THEM: A LARGE RED ONE, A LARGE GREEN CUBE AND THE BLUE ONE.

20. put a small one onto the green cube which supports a pyramid.

"*A small one*" must contrast with the person's earlier phrase "*a large block,*" so this means "*a small block.*"

OK.

21. put the littlest pyramid on top of it.

Words like "*littlest*" are not in the dictionary but are interpreted from the root forms like "little." The program compares the sizes of all the pyramids to carry out the action.

OK.

22. how many things are on top of green cubes?

```
I'M NOT SURE WHAT YOU MEAN BY "ON TOP OF" IN THE PHRASE
"ON TOP OF GREEN CUBES"
DO YOU MEAN:
1 - DIRECTLY ON THE SURFACE
2 - ANWHERE ON TOP OF?
```

In the previous sentence, the phrase "*on top of*" was interpreted without trouble because the context made it clear what was meant. In this one, the heuristics for disambiguation do not come up with a clearcut decision, so the system has to ask the user for more information. The paraphrases were included with the dictionary definition of "on." A request like this can also occur when the meaning of a pronoun such as "it" or "they" is unclear.

23. had you touched any pyramid before you put the green one on the little cube?

YES, THE GREEN ONE.

The system deduces from its memory what event is being referred to, and can relate other events to it in time. The analysis includes complex tenses of verb groups, and there are special facilities for keeping track of the various forms of irregular verbs like "have."

24. when did you pick it up?

WHILE I WAS STACKING UP THE RED CUBE, A LARGE RED BLOCK
AND A LARGE GREEN CUBE.

A time is described by naming the main goal which was being worked on.

25. why?

The system remembers immediately previous sentences to understand questions like this and the following ones.

TO GET RID OF IT.

By keeping track of selected parts of the original subgoal tree, the system has some understanding of its own motives.

26. why did you do that?

TO CLEAN OFF THE RED CUBE.

"*That*" refers to the action mentioned in the system's last answer.

27. why did you clear off that cube?

Here, "*that*" means the one just referred to.

TO PUT IT ON A LARGE GREEN CUBE.

28. why did you do that?

TO STACK UP THE RED CUBE, A LARGE RED BLOCK AND A LARGE GREEN CUBE.

29. why did you do that?

BECAUSE YOU ASKED ME TO.

It remembers what it did, not how the request was worded.

30. how did you do it?

"It" refers to the action mentioned in the last question, rather than the answer.

BY PUTTING A LARGE RED BLOCK ON THE TABLE; THEN LETTING GO
OF IT; THEN PUTTING A LARGE GREEN CUBE ON IT; THEN LETTING GO
OF THAT CUBE; THEN PUTTING THE RED CUBE ON THAT CUBE; THEN
LETTING GO OF THAT CUBE.

This is a description of the top-level subgoals used to achieve the goal.

31. how many objects did you touch while you were doing it?

Time references can refer to a time span, using words like "while."

FOUR OF THEM.

32. what did the red cube support before you started to clean it off?

THE GREEN PYRAMID.

By remembering what has been moved, it is possible to deduce things about
earlier states of the scene. We can use complex nestings of clauses like "*before you
started to clean it off.*"

33. there were five blocks to the left of the box then.

"*Then*" must refer to the time mentioned in the last sentence.

NO, ONLY FOUR OF THEM: THE RED CUBE, TWO LARGE GREEN CUBES
AND A LARGE RED BLOCK.

Earlier in the dialogue, information about "owning" was accepted at face value.
But the system knows that it has complete information about the basic properties
of objects, including location. It checks any statements about these to see whether
it agrees or disagrees.

34. put the blue pyramid on the block in the box.

This is syntactically ambiguous, but is understood without ambiguity since the parsing corresponding to *"put the blue pyramid which is on the block into the box"* does not make sense in the current scene, whereas *"put the blue pyramid onto the block which is in the box"* does.

OK.

35. *is there anything which is bigger than every pyramid but is not as wide as the thing that supports it?*

The system understands quantifiers such as "every," "any," "some," etc., and structures such as "bigger than", "as wide as," etc. Here "*it*" refers to a noun group within the same sentence but two levels up in the parsing tree.

YES, THE BLUE BLOCK.

36. *does a steeple*

SORRY, I DON'T KNOW THE WORD "STEEPLE".

The system interrupts immediately when it sees a word it doesn't know.

37. *a "steeple" is a stack which contains two green cubes and a pyramid.*

The quote marks indicate that we are defining a new word. The definition is added to the dictionary in a form compatible with all the words it already knows.

I UNDERSTAND.

38. *are there any steeples now?*

NO.

The new definition is used as a description to recognize steeples.

39. *build one.*

OK.

The description given in the definition is enough to deduce a plan for building new objects as well as recognizing them. The word *"one"* means *"a steeple,"* and the plan is carried out. First, one of the large green cubes is cleared off by removing the red cube and two pyramids. Then the two green cubes and the tall red pyramid are stacked up to fit the description.

40. call the biggest block "superblock."

OK.

We can also give objects names.

41. have you picked up superblock since we began?

YES.

42. why did you drop it?

BY "IT", I ASSUME YOU MEAN THE SUPERBLOCK.
I CAN'T EXPLAIN A NON-EXISTENT EVENT.

There is no record in memory of any block being dropped. The answer routines have special checks for this type of "loaded question" which presupposes things which aren't true.

43. is there anything to the right of the red pyramid?

YES, FOUR THINGS: THE BOX, THE RED CUBE, THE BLUE PYRAMID
AND THE BLOCK NAMED SUPERBLOCK.

Once an object has a name, the name is used to help identify it in responses.

44. thank you.

YOU'RE WELCOME!

The grammar is written as a procedure, which gives it the capability to carry out special sorts of parsing for idioms.

Details of the Model

In this section we go into some detail about the various parts of the language understanding program and its operation. This type of analysis is important for understanding any computer model, since the surface appearance of its output can be deceptive. A program may succeed by carefully choosing the problem it will attack, so that some simple special-purpose solution will work. ELIZA (Weizenbaum, 1964) and STUDENT (Bobrow, 1967) are examples of programs which give impressive performances owing to a severe and careful restriction of the kind of understanding they try to achieve. If a model is to be of broader significance, it must be designed to cover a large range of the things we mean when we talk of understanding. The principles should derive from an attempt to deal with the basic cognitive structures.

On the other hand, it is possible to devise abstract ideas of the logical structure of language—ideas which seem in theory to be applicable. Often, such systems, although interesting mathematically, are not valid as psychological models of human language, since they have not concerned themselves with the operational problems of a mental procedure. They often include types of representation and processes which are highly implausible, and which may be totally inapplicable in complex situations because their very nature implies astronomically large amounts of processing for certain kinds of computations. Transformational grammar and resolution theorem proving (Green, 1969) are examples of such approaches.

The Representation of Meaning

Our program makes use of a detailed world model, describing both the current state of the blocks world environment and its knowledge of procedures for changing that state and making deductions about it. This model is not in spatial or analog terms, but is a symbolic description, abstracting those aspects of the world which are relevant to the operations used in working with it and discussing it. First there is a data base of simple facts like those shown in Box 4.1, describing what is true at any particular time. There we see, for example, that B1 is a block, B1 is red, B2 supports B3, blue is a color, EVENT27 caused EVENT29, etc. The notation simply involves indicating relationships between objects by listing the name of the relation (such as IS or SUPPORT) followed by the things being related.* These include both concepts (like BLOCK or BLUE) and proper names of individual objects and events (indicated

---

*The fact that B1 is a block could be represented in more usual predicate notation as (BLOCK B1). We have chosen to associate with each object or concept a property describing its most relevant category for the purpose of generating an English phrase for it. Thus (IS B1 BLOCK) is used to describe B1 as a block. Similarly, properties like colors are represented (COLOR B1 BLUE) instead of (BLUE B1). This allows for more efficiency in the operation of the deduction system, without changing its logical characteristics.

Box 4.1 Typical Data Expressions.

```
(IS B1 BLOCK)
(IS B2 PYRAMID)
(AT B1 (LOCATION 100 100 0))
(SUPPORT B1 B2)
(CLEARTOP B2)
(MANIPULABLE B1)
(CONTAIN BOX1 B4)
(COLOR-OF B1 RED)
(SHAPE-OF B2 POINTED)
(IS BLUE COLOR)
(CAUSE EVENT27 EVENT29)
```

---

with numbers, like B1 and TABLE2).† The symbols used in these expressions represent the concepts (or conceptual categories) that form the vocabulary of the language user's cognitive model. A concept corresponds vaguely to what we might call a single meaning of a word, but the connection is more complex. Underlying the organization is a belief that meanings cannot be reduced to any set of pure "elements" or components from which everything else is built. Rather, a person categorizes his experience along lines which are relevant to the thought processes he will use, and his categorization is generally neither consistent, nor parsimonious, nor complete. A person may categorize a set of objects in his experience into, for example "chair," "stool," "bench," etc. If pushed, he cannot give an exact definition for any of these, and in naming some objects he will not be certain how to make the choice between them. This is even clearer if we consider words like "truth," "virtue," and "democracy." The meaning of any concept depends on its interconnection with all of the other concepts in the model.

Most formal approaches to language have avoided this characterization of meaning even though it seems close to our intuitions about how language is used. This is because the usual techniques of logic and mathematics are not easily applicable to such "holistic" models. With such a complex notion of "concept," we are unable to prove anything about meaning in the usual mathematical notion of proof. One important aspect of computational approaches to modelling cognitive processes is their ability to deal with this sort of formalism. Rather than trying to prove things about meaning we can design procedures which can operate with the model and simulate the processes involved in human use of meaning. The justification for the formalism is the degree to which succeeds in providing a model of understanding.

What is important then, is the part of the system's knowledge which involves the interconnections between the concepts. In our model, these are in the form of pro-

---

†The notation does not correspond exactly to that in the original program, as mnemonics have been used here to increase readability.

cedures written in the PLANNER language (Hewitt, 1971). For example, the concept
CLEARTOP (which might be expressed in English by a phrase like "clear off") can
be described by the procedure diagrammed in Figure 4.5. The model tells us that to
clear off an object X, we start by checking to see whether X supports an object Y. If
so, we GET–RID–OF Y, and go check again. When X does not support any object, we
can assert that it is CLEARTOP. In this operational definition, we call on other concepts like GET–RID–OF and SUPPORT. Each of these in turn is a procedure, involving
other concepts like PICKUP and GRASP. This representation is oriented to a model
of deduction in which we try to satisfy some goal by setting up successive subgoals,
which must be achieved in order to eventually satisfy the main goal. Looking at the
flow chart for GRASP in Figure 4.6, we can see the steps the program would take if
asked to grasp an object B1 while holding a different object B2. It would be called
by setting up a goal of the form (GRASP B1), so when the GRASP program ran, X
would represent the object B1. First it checks to see whether B1 is a manipulable
object, since if not the effort must fail. Next it sees if it is already grasping B1, since
this would satisfy the goal immediately. Then, it checks to see if it is holding an
object other than B1, and if so tries to GET–RID–OF it. The program for GET–RID–OF
tries to put the designated object on the table by calling a program for PUTON, which
in turn looks for an empty location and calls PUT. PUT deduces where the hand must
be moved and calls MOVEHAND. If we look at the set of currently active goals at this
point, we get the stack in Box 4.2.

Notice that this subgoal structure provides the basis for asking "why" questions,
as in sentences 25 through 29 of the dialog in Section 2. If asked *"Why did you put
B2 on the table?,"* the program would look to the goal that called PUTON, and say
"To get rid of it." If asked *"Why did you get rid of it?"* it would go up one more step
to get *"To grasp B1."* (Actually, it would generate an English phrase describing the
.object B1 in terms of its shape, size, and color.) "How" questions are answered by
looking at the set of subgoals called directly in achieving a goal, and generating
descriptions of the actions involved.

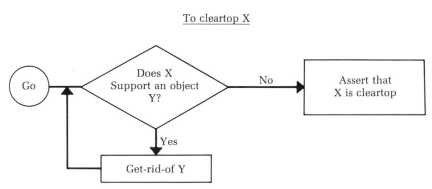

Figure 4.5 Procedural Description for the Concept CLEARTOP.

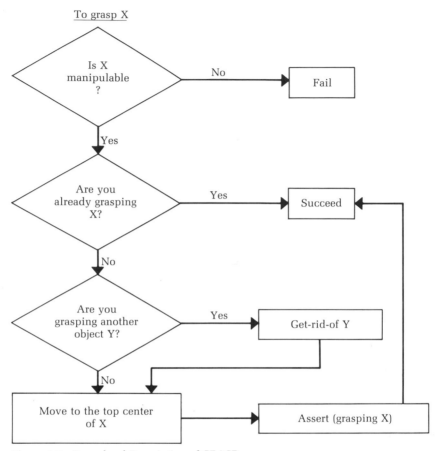

Figure 4.6   Procedural Description of GRASP.

These examples illustrate the use of procedural descriptions of concepts for carrying out commands, but they can also be applied to other aspects of language, such as questions and statements. One of the basic viewpoints underlying the model is that all language use can be thought of as a way of activating procedures within the hearer. We can think of any utterance as a program — one that indirectly causes a set of operations to be carried out within the hearer's cognitive system. This "program writing" is indirect in the sense that we are dealing with an intelligent interpreter, who may take a set of actions which are quite different from those the speaker intended. The exact form is determined by his knowledge of the world, his expectations about the person talking to him, his goals, etc. In this program we have a simple version of this process of interpretation as it takes place in the robot. Each sentence interpreted by the robot is converted to a set of instructions in PLANNER. The program that is created is then executed to achieve the desired effect. In some cases the

---

Box 4.2   Goal Stack.

```
(GRASP B1)
      (GET-RID-OF B2)
            (PUTON B2 TABLE1)
                  (PUT B2 (453 201 0))
                        (MOVEHAND (553 301 100))
```

---

procedure invoked requires direct physical actions like the aforementioned. In others, it may be a search for some sort of information (perhaps to answer a question), whereas in others it is a procedure which stores away a new piece of knowledge or uses it to modify the knowledge it already has. Let us look at what the system would do with a simple description like "a red cube which supports a pyramid." The description will use concepts like BLOCK, RED, PYRAMID, and EQUIDIMEN-SIONAL—all parts of the system's underlying categorization of the world. The result can be represented in a flow chart like that of Figure 4.7. Note that this is a program for finding an object fitting the description. It would then be incorporated into a command for doing something with the object, a question asking something about it, or, if it appeared in a statement, it would become part of the program which was generated to represent the meaning for later use. Note that this bit of program could also be used as a test to see whether an object fit the description, if the first FIND instruction were told in advance to look only at that particular object.

At first glance, it seems that there is too much structure in this program, as we don't like to think of the meaning of a simple phrase as explicitly containing loops, conditional tests, and other programming details. The solution is to provide an internal language that contains the appropriate looping and checking as its primitives, and in which the representation of the process is as simple as the description. PLANNER provides these primitives in our system. The program described in Figure 4.7 would be written in PLANNER looking something like Box 4.3.* The loops of the flow chart are implicit in PLANNER's backtrack control structure. The description is evaluated by proceeding down the list until some goal fails, at which time the system backs up automatically to the last point where a decision was made, trying a different possibility. A decision can be made whenever a new object name or *variable* (indicated by the prefix ?) such as ?X1 or ?X2 appears. The variables are used by a pattern matcher. If they have already been assigned to a particular item, it checks to see whether the GOAL is true for that item. If not, it checks for all possible items which satisfy the GOAL, by choosing one, and then taking successive ones whenever backtracking occurs to that point. Thus, even the distinction between testing and choosing is implicit. Using other primitives of PLANNER, such as NOT and

---

*The system actually uses Micro-Planner, (Sussman et. al., 1970) a partial implementation of PLANNER. In this presentation we have slightly simplified the details of its syntax.

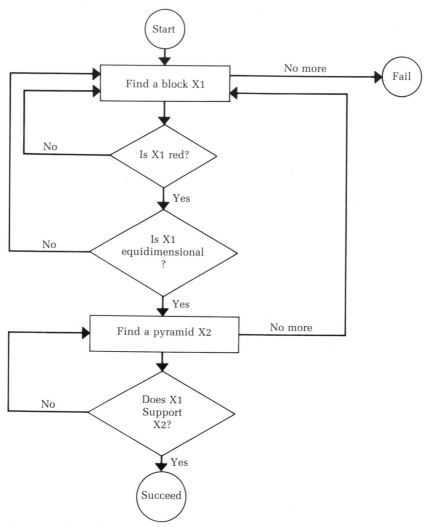

Figure 4.7   Procedural Representation of "a red cube which supports a pyramid."

Box 4.3   PLANNER Program for Description of
"a red cube which supports a pyramid."

```
(GOAL (IS ?X1 BLOCK))
(GOAL (COLOR-OF ?X1 RED))
(GOAL (EQUIDIMENSIONAL ?X1))
(GOAL (IS ?X2 PYRAMID))
(GOAL (SUPPORT ?X1 ?X2))
```

FIND (which looks for a given number of objects fitting a description), we can write procedural representations for a variety of descriptions, as shown in Box 4.4.

Semantic Analysis

When we have decided how the system will represent meanings internally, we must deal with the way in which it creates a program when it is given an English input. There must be ways to interpret the meanings of individual words and the syntactic structures in which they occur. First, let us look at how we can define simple words like "cube", and "contain." The definitions in Box 4.5 are completely equivalent to those used in the program with a straightforward interpretation.* The first says that

---

Box 4.4   PLANNER Programs for some Quantified Modifiers describing the Object X1.

```
              (GOAL (IS ?X2 PYRAMID))
              (GOAL (SUPPORT ?X1 ?X2))
              "which supports a pyramid"
```

$$**************$$

```
              (GOAL (SUPPORT ?X1 B3))
              "which supports the pyramid'
```
B3 is the name of the object referred to by "*the pyramid*",
which is determined earlier in the analysis

$$**************$$

```
        (FIND 3 ?X2 (GOAL (IS ?X2 PYRAMID))
                    (GOAL (SUPPORT ?X1 ?X2)))
              "which supports three pyramids"
```

$$**************$$

```
      (NOT (FIND ?X2 (GOAL (IS ?X2 PYRAMID))
                     (GOAL (SUPPORT ?X1 ?X2)))
              "which supports no pyramids"
```

$$**************$$

```
    (NOT (FIND ?X2 (GOAL (IS ?X2 PYRAMID))
                   (NOT (GOAL (SUPPORT ?X1 ?X2)))))
              "which supports every pyramid"
```

$$**************$$

---

*Again, in comparing this with the details in Winograd (1972), note that some of the symbols have been replaced with more understandable mnemonic versions.

Box 4.5   Dictionary Definitions for "cube" and "contain."

```
(CUBE
   ((NOUN   (OBJECT
               ((MANIPULABLE RECTANGULAR)
                             ((IS ? BLOCK)
                              (EQUIDIMENSIONAL ?)))))))

(CONTAIN
   ((VERB ((TRANSITIVE (RELATION
                 (((CONTAINER)) ((PHYSICAL-OBJECT))
                             (CONTAIN #1 #2))
                 (((CONSTRUCT)) ((PHYSICAL-OBJECT))
                             (PART-OF #2 #1))))))))
```

---

a cube is an object that is RECTANGULAR and MANIPULABLE, and can be recognized by the fact that it is a BLOCK and EQUIDIMENSIONAL. The first part of this definition is based on the use of semantic markers and provides for efficiency in choosing interpretations. By making a rough categorization of the objects in the model, the system can make quick checks to see whether certain combinations are ruled out by simple tests like "this meaning of the adjective applies only to words which represent physical objects." Chomsky's famous sentence "Colorless green ideas sleep furiously" would be eliminated easily by such markers. The system uses this information, for example, in answering question 9 in the dialogue, *"Can the table pick up blocks?,"* as *"pick up"* demands a subject that is ANIMATE, whereas *"table"* has the marker INANIMATE. These markers are a useful but rough approximation to human deductions.

The definition for "contain" shows how they might be used to choose between possible word meanings. If applied to a CONTAINER and a PHYSICAL-OBJECT, as in *"The box contains three pyramids,"* the word implies the usual relationship we mean by CONTAIN. If instead, it applies to a CONSTRUCT (like "stack", "pile", or "row") and an object, the meaning is different. *"The stack contains a cube"* really means that a cube is PART of the stack, and the system will choose this meaning by noting that CONSTRUCT is one of the semantic markers of the word "stack" when it applies the definition.

One important aspect of these definitions is that although they look like static rule statements, they are actually calls to programs (OBJECT and RELATION) which do the appropriate checks and build the semantic structures. Once we get away from the simplest words, these programs need to be more flexible in what they look at. For example, in the robot world, the phrase *"pick up"* has different meanings depending on whether it refers to a single object or several. In sentence 1, the system interprets *"Pick up the big red block,"* by grasping it and raising the hand. If we said *"Pick up all of your toys,"* it would interpret *"pick up"* as meaning *"put away,"* and would pack them all into the box. The program for checking to see whether the object is singular or plural is simple, and any semantic system must have the flexibility to incorporate such things in the word definitions. We do this by having the definition of every word be a program which is called at an appropriate point in the analysis, and which can do arbitrary computations involving the sentence and the present physical situation.

This flexibility is even more important once we get beyond simple words. In defining words like "the," or "of," or "one" in *"Pick up a green one,"* we can hardly make a simple list of properties and descriptors as in Figure 4.12. The presence of "one" in a noun group must trigger a program which looks into the previous discourse to see what objects have been mentioned, and can apply various rules and heuristics to determine the appropriate reference. For example it must know that in the phrase *"a big red block and a little one,"* we are referring to "a little red block," not "a little big red block" or simply "a little block." This sort of knowledge is part of a semantic procedure attached to the word "one" in the dictionary.

Words like "the" are more complex. When we use a definite article like "the" or "that" in English, we have in mind a particular object or objects which we expect the hearer to know about. I can talk about "the moon" since there is only one moon we usually talk about. In the context of this article, I can talk about "the dialogue", and the reader will understand from the context which dialogue I mean. If I am beginning a conversation, I will say "Yesterday I met a strange man" even though I have a particular man in mind, since saying "Yesterday I met the strange man" would imply that the hearer already knows of him. Elsewhere, "the" is used to convey the information that the object being referred to is unique. If I write "The reason I wrote this paper was . . .", it implies that there was a single reason, whereas "A reason I wrote this paper was . . ." implies that there were others. In generic statements, "the" may be used to refer to a whole class, as in "The albatross is a strange bird." This is a quite different use from the single referent of "The albatross just ate your lunch."

A model of language use must be able to account for the role this type of knowledge plays in understanding. In the procedural model, it is a part of the process of interpretation for the structure in which the relevant word is embedded. The different possibilities for the meaning of "the" are procedures which check various facts about the context, then prescribe actions such as "Look for a unique object in the data base which fits this description." or "Assert that the object being described is unique as far as the speaker is concerned." The program incorporates a variety of heuristics for deciding what part of the context is relevant. For example, it keeps track of when in the dialogue something has been mentioned. In sentence 2 of the dialogue, *"Grasp the pyramid"* is rejected since there is no particular pyramid which the system can see as distinguished. However, in sentence 5 it accepts the question *"What is the pyramid supported by?"* since in the answer to sentence 4 it mentioned a particular pyramid.

This type of knowledge plays a large part in understanding the things that hold a discourse together, such as pronouns, adverbs like "then", and "there", substitute nouns such as "one", phrases beginning with "that", and ellipses. The system is structured in such a way that the heuristics for handling mechanisms like these can be expressed as procedures in a straightforward way.

The Role of Syntax

In describing the process of semantic interpretation, we stated that part of the relevant input was the syntactic structure of the sentence. In order to provide this, the program contains a parser and a fairly comprehensive grammar of English.* The approach to syntax is based on a belief that the form of syntactic analysis must be useable by a realistic semantic system, and the emphasis of the resulting grammar differs in several ways from traditional transformational approaches.

First, it is organized around looking for syntactic units which play a primary role in determining meaning. A sentence such as "The three big red dogs ate a raw steak" will be parsed to generate the structure in Figure 4.8. The noun groups (NG) correspond to descriptions of objects, whereas the clause is a description of a relation or event. The semantic programs are organized into groups of procedures, each of which is used for interpreting a certain type of unit.

For each unit, there is a syntactic program (written in a language called PRO-GRAMMAR, especially designed for the purpose) which operates on the input string to see whether it could represent a unit of that type. In doing this, it will call on other such syntactic programs (and possibly on itself recursively). It embodies a description of the possible orderings of words and other units, for example, the scheme for a noun group, as shown in Figure 4.9. The presence of an asterisk after a symbol means that that function can be filled more than once. The figure shows that we have a determiner (such as "the") followed by an ordinal (such as "first"), then a number ("three") followed by one or more adjectives ("big," "red") followed by one or more nouns being used as classifiers ("fire hydrant") followed by a noun ("covers") followed by qualifying phrases which are preposition groups or clauses

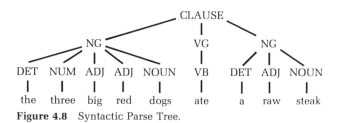

Figure 4.8 Syntactic Parse Tree.

*It is of course impossible to provide a complete grammar of English, and often difficult to evaluate a partial one. The dialogue of Section 2 gives a sample of the constructions which can be handled, and does not make use of specially included patterns. Winograd (1972) gives a full description of the grammar used.

Figure 4.9 Structure of Noun Groups.

("without handles" "which you can find"). Of course many of the elements are optional, and there are restriction relations between the various possibilities. If we choose an indefinite determiner such as "a," we cannot have an ordinal and number, as in the illegal string "a first three big red fire hydrant covers without handles you can find." The grammar must be able to express these rules in a way which is not simply an ad hoc set of statements. Our grammar takes advantage of some of the ideas of Systemic Grammar (Halliday, 1971).

Systemic theory views a syntactic structure as being made up of units, each of which can be characterized in terms of the *features* describing its form, and the *functions* it fills in a larger structure or discourse. In the sentence in Figure 4.8, the noun group "three big red dogs" can be described as exhibiting features such as DETER-MINED, INDEFINITE, PLURAL, etc. It serves the function SUBJECT in the clause of which it is a part, and various discourse functions, such as THEME as well. It in turn is made up of other units—the individual words—which fill functions in the noun group, such as DETERMINER and HEAD. A grammar must include a specification of the possible features a unit can have, and the relation of these to both the functions it can play, and the functions and constituents it controls.

These features are not haphazard bits of information we might choose to notice about units, but form a highly structured system (hence the name Systemic Grammar). As an example, we can look at a few of the features for the CLAUSE in Figure 4.10. The vertical lines represent sets from which a single feature must be selected and horizontal lines indicate logical dependency. Thus, we must first choose whether the clause is MAJOR—which corresponds to the function of serving as an independent sentence—or SECONDARY, which corresponds to the various functions a clause can serve as a constituent of another unit (for example as a QUALIFIER in the noun group "the ball *which is on the table*"). If a clause is MAJOR, it is either DECLARATIVE ("She went"), IMPERATIVE ("Go"), or INTERROGATIVE ("Did she go?"). If it is INTERROGATIVE, there is a further choice between YES–NO ("Did she go?") and WH– ("Where did she go?").

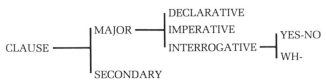

Figure 4.10 Simple System Network for Clauses.

It is important to note that these features are syntactic, not semantic. They do not represent the use of a sentence as a question, statement, or command, but are rather a characterization of its internal structure—which words follow in what order. A DECLARATIVE can be used as a question by giving it a rising intonation, or even as a command, as in "You're going to give that to me," spoken in an appropriate tone. A question may be used as a polite form of a command, as in "Can you give me a match?," and so on. Any language understander must know the conventions of the language for interpreting such utterances in addition to its simpler forms of syntactic knowledge. To do this, it must have a way to state things like "If something is syntactically a question but involves an event which the hearer could cause in the immediate future, it may be intended as a request." Syntactic features are therefore basic to the description of the semantic rules. The actual features in a comprehensive grammar are related in a more complex way than the simple example of Figure 4.10, but the basic ideas of logical dependency are the same.

In the foregoing we stated that there is a choice between certain features, and that depending on the selection made from one set, we must then choose between certain others. In doing this we are not postulating a psychological model for the order of making choices. The networks are an abstract characterization of the possibilities, and form only a part of a grammar. In addition we need realization and interpretation rules. Realization rules describe how a given set of choices would be expressed in the form of surface syntactic structures, whereas interpretation rules describe how a string of words is analyzed to find its constituents and their features.

Our grammar is an interpretation grammar for accepting grammatical sentences. It differs from more usual grammars by being written explicitly in the form of a program. Ordinarily, grammars are stated in the form of rules, which are applied in the framework of a special interpretation process. This may be very complex in some cases (such as transformational grammars) with separate phases, special "traffic rules" for applying the other rules in the right order, cycles of application, and other sorts of constraints. In our system, the sequence of the actions is represented explicitly in the set of rules. The process of understanding an utterance is basic to the organization of the grammar.*

In saying that grammars are programs, it is important to separate the procedural aspect from the details usually associated with programming. If we say to a linguist "Here is a grammar of English," he can rightfully object if it begins "Take the contents of location 177 and put them into register 2, adding the index . . ." The formalization of the syntax should include only those operations and concepts that are relevant to linguistic analysis, and should not be burdened with paraphernalia needed for programming details. Our model is based on the belief that the basic ideas of programming such as procedure and subprocedure, iteration, recursion, etc. are central to all cognitive processes, and in particular to the theory of language. What is needed is a formalism for describing syntactic processes. Our grammar is written in a language which was designed specifically for the purpose. It is a system

---

*For a discussion of the psycholinguistic relevance of such interpretive grammars see Kaplan (1971). He describes a similar formulation of procedural grammar, represented as a transition network.

built in LISP, called PROGRAMMAR, and its primitive operations are those involving the building of syntactic structures, and the generation of systemic descriptions of their parts.

The set of typical grammar rules shown in Box 4.6 would be expressed in PRO–GRAMMAR by the program diagrammed in Figure 4.11. For such a simplified bit of grammar, there isn't much difference between the two formulations, except that the PROGRAMMAR representation is more explicit in describing the flow of control. When we try to deal with more complex parts of syntax, the ability to specify procedures becomes more important. For example the word "and" can be associated with a program that can be diagrammed as shown in Figure 4.12. Given the sentence "The giraffe ate the apples and peaches", it would first encounter "and" after parsing the noun "apples." It would then try to parse a second noun, and would succeed, resulting in the structure shown in Figure 4.13. If we had the sentence "The giraffe ate the apples and drank the vodka," the parser would have to try several different things. The "and" appears at a point which represents boundaries between several units. It is after the noun "apples," and the NP, "the apples." It is also after the entire VP "ate the apples." The parser, however, cannot find a noun or NP beginning with the following word "drank". It therefore tries to parse a VP and would successfully find "drank the vodka". A CONJOINED VP would be created, producing the final result shown in Figure 4.14. Of course the use of conjunctions is more complex than this, and the actual program must take into account such things as lists and branched structures in addition to the problems of backing up if a wrong possibility has been tried. But the basic operation of "look for another one like the one you just found" seems both practical and intuitively plausible as a description of how conjunction works. The ability to write the rules as procedures leaves us the flexibility to extend and refine it.

Viewing "and" as a special program that interrupts the normal parsing sequence also gives us a sort of explanation for some puzzling syntactic facts. The statement "I saw Ed with Steve" has a corresponding question, "Whom did you see Ed with?" But "I saw Ed and Steve" cannot be turned into "Whom did you see Ed and?" The "and" program cannot be called when there is no input for it to work with.

Program Organization

So far, we have described how three different types of knowledge are represented and used. There is the data base of assertions and PLANNER procedures which represent the knowledge of the physical world; there are semantic analysis programs

---

Box 4.6   Simple Grammar in Replacement Rule Form.

```
 S  →  NP VP
NP  →  DETERMINER NOUN
VP  →  VERB/TRANSITIVE NP
VP  →  VERB/INTRANSITIVE
```

which know about such problems as reference; and there is a grammar which determines the syntactic structure. The most important element, however, is the interaction between these components. Language cannot be reduced into separate areas such as "syntax, semantics, and pragmatics" in hopes that by understanding each of them separately, we have understood the whole. The key to the function of language as a means of communication is in the way these areas interact.

DEFINE program SENTENCE

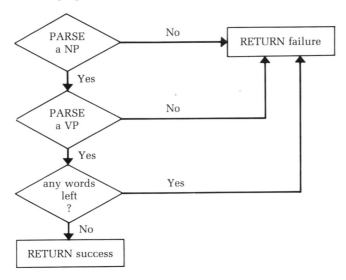

DEFINE program NP

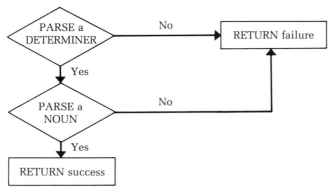

Figure 4.11 PROGRAMMAR Grammar From Winograd, T ,
"Understanding Natural Language." *Cognitive
Psychology*, 3:1–191. Copyright © by Academic
Press.

DEFINE program VP

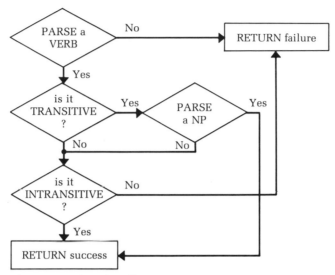

Figure 4.11 *(continued)*

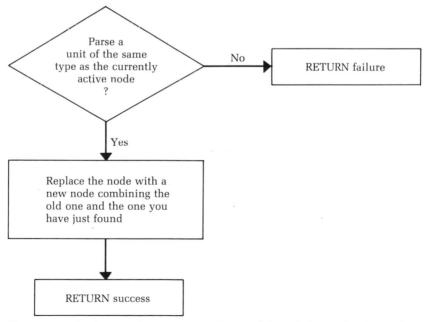

Figure 4.12 Conjunction Program. From Winograd, T., "Understanding Natural
Language." *Cognitive Psychology*, 3:1–191. Copyright © by Academic
Press.

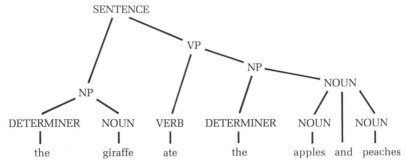

Figure 4.13 Conjoined Noun Structure. From Winograd, T., "Understanding Natural Language." *Cognitive Psychology*, 3:1–191. Copyright © by Academic Press.

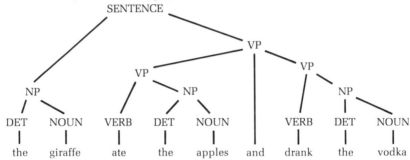

Figure 4.14 Conjoined VP Structure. From Winograd, T., "Understanding Natural Language." *Cognitive Psychology*, 3:1–191. Copyright © by Academic Press.

Our program does not operate by first parsing a sentence, then doing semantic analysis, and finally by using deduction to produce a response. These three activities go on concurrently throughout the understanding of a sentence. As soon as a piece of syntactic structure begins to take shape, a semantic program is called to see whether it might make sense, and the resultant answer can direct the parsing. In deciding whether it makes sense, the semantic routine may call deductive processes and ask questions about the real world. As an example, in sentence 36 of the dialogue ("*Put the blue pyramid on the block in the box*"), the parser first comes up with "the blue pyramid on the block" as a candidate for a noun group. At this point, semantic analysis is begun, and since "the" is definite, a check is made in the data base for the object being referred to. When no such object is found, the parsing is redirected to find the noun group "the blue pyramid." It will then go on to find "on the block in the box" as a single phrase indicating a location. In other examples the system of semantic markers may reject a possible interpretation on the basis of conflicting category information. Thus, there is a continuing interplay between the different sorts of analysis, with the results of one affecting the others.

The procedure as a whole operates in a left to right direction through the sentence. It does not carry along multiple possibilities for the syntactic analysis, but instead has ways of going back and doing something different if it runs into trouble. It does not use the general backup mechanism of PLANNER, but decides what to do on the basis of exactly what sort of problem arose. In the sentences like those of the dialogue, very little backup is ever used, since the combination of syntactic and semantic information usually guides the parser quite efficiently.

Limitations of the Approach

The program we are describing does not purport to be a point by point model of psychological processes at a detailed level. Rather, it is an attempt to show how a general view of language can really be filled in with enough detail to provide a working model. The importance from a psychological point of view is the approach to language as a process which can be modeled within the context of a procedural description of cognitive processes. Rather than trying to attach psychological meaning to isolated components into which language has been divided for abstract study, it attempts to relate the various types of knowledge and procedures involved in intelligent language use.

Looking into the specific capabilities of the system, we can find many places where the details seem inadequate, or whole areas are missing. The program does not attempt to handle hypothetical or counterfactual statements; it only accepts a limited range of declarative information, it cannot talk about verbal acts, and the treatment of "the" is not as general as the description above, and so on. These deficiencies, however, seem to be more a matter of what has been tackled so far, rather than calling into question the underlying model. Looking deeper, we can find two basic ways in which it seems an inadequate model of human language use. The first is the way in which the process is directed, and the second is concerned with the interaction of the context of the conversation and the understanding of its content.

We can think of a program for understanding a sentence as having two kinds of operations—coming up with possible interpretations, and choosing between them. Of course, these are not separate psychologically, but in the organization of computer programs, the work is divided up.

In our program, the syntactic analysis is in charge of coming up with possibilities. The basic operation requires that we find a syntactically acceptable phrase, and then do a semantic interpretation on it to decide whether to continue along that line of parsing. Other programs such as Schank (1971) and Quillian (1967) use the semantic information contained in the definitions of the words to provide an initial set of possibilities, then use syntactic information in a secondary way to check whether the hypothesized underlying semantic structure is in accord with the arrangement of the words.

By observing human language use, it seems clear that no single approach is really correct. On the one hand, people are able to interpret utterances which are not syntactically well formed, and can even assign meanings to collections of words without use of syntax. The list "skid, crash, hospital" presents a certain image, even though two of the words are both nouns and verbs and there are no explicit syntactic connections. It is therefore wrong to insist that some sort of complete parsing is a prerequisite to semantic analysis.

On the other hand, people are able to interpret sentences syntactically even when they do not know the meanings of the individual words. Most of our vocabulary (beyond a certain age) is learned by hearing sentences in which unfamiliar words appear in syntactically well-defined positions. We process the sentence without knowing any category information for the words, and in fact use the results of that processing to discover the semantic meaning. In addition, much of our normal conversation is made up of sentences like "Then the other one did the same thing to it" in which the words taken individually do not provide clues to enable us to determine the conceptual structure without a complete syntactic analysis.

What really seems to be going on is a coordinated process in which a variety of syntactic and semantic information can be relevant, and in which the hearer takes advantage of whatever is more useful in understanding a given part of a sentence. Our system models this coordination in its order of doing things, by carrying on all of the different levels of analysis concurrently, although it does not model it in the control structure.

Much remains to be done in understanding how to write computer programs in which a number of concurrent processes are working in a coordinated fashion without being under the primary hierarchical control of one of them. A language model able to implement the sort of "heterarchy" found in biological systems (like the coordination between different systems of an organism) will be much closer to a valid psychological theory.

The second basic shortcoming is in not dealing with all the implications of viewing language as a process of communication between two intelligent people. A human language user is always engaged in a process of trying to understand the world around him, including the person he is talking to. He is actively constructing models and hypotheses, and he makes use of them in the process of language understanding. As an example, let us consider again the use of pronouns. In Section 1, we described some of the knowledge involved in choosing referents. It included syntax, semantic categories, and heuristics about the structure of discourse.

But all of these heuristics are really only a rough approximation to what is really going on. The reason that the focus of the previous sentence is more likely to be the referent of "it" is because a person generally has a continuity in his conversation, which comes from talking about a particular object or event. The focus (or subject) is more likely just because that is the thing he is talking about, and he is likely to go on talking about it. Certain combinations of conceptual category markers are more plausible than others because the speaker is probably talking about the real world, where certain types of events are more sensible than others. If we prefix almost any sentence with "I just had the craziest dream . . ." the whole system of plausible conceptual relations is turned topsy-turvy.

If someone says "I dropped a bottle of Coke on the table and it broke," there are two obvious interpretations. The semantic categories and the syntactic heuristics make it slightly more plausible that it was the bottle that broke. But consider what would happen if we heard "Where is the tool box? I dropped a bottle of coke on the table and it broke" or, "Where is the furniture polish? I dropped a bottle of coke on the table and it broke." The referent is now perfectly clear—only because we have a model of what is reasonable in the world, and what a person is likely to say. We know that there is nothing in the tool box to help fix a broken coke bottle and that nobody would be likely to try fixing one. It would be silly to polish a table that just got broken, while it would be logical to polish one that just had a strong corrosive spilled on it. Of course, all this must be combined with deductions based on other common sense knowledge, such as the fact that when a bottle containing a liquid breaks, the liquid in it spills.

Even more important, we try to understand what the speaker is "getting at." We assume that there is a meaningful connection between his sentences, and that his description of what happened is probably intended as an explanation for why he wants the polish or toolbox. More subtle deductions are implied here as well. It is possible that he broke the table and fixed it, and now wants the polish to cover the repair marks. If this were the case, he would almost surely have mentioned the repair to allow us to follow that chain of logic.

Our system makes only the most primitive use of this sort of deduction. Since it keeps track of when things have been mentioned, it can check a possible interpretation of a question to see whether the asker could answer it himself from his previous sentences. If so, it assumes that he probably means something else. We could characterize this as containing two sorts of knowledge. First, it assumes that a person asks questions for the purpose of getting information he doesn't already have, and second, it has a very primitive model of what information he has on the basis of what he has said. A realistic view of language must have a complex model of this type, and the heuristics in our system touch only the tiniest bit of the relevant knowledge.

It is important to recognize that this sort of interaction does not occur only with pronouns and explicit discourse features, but in every part of the understanding process. In choosing between alternative syntactic structures for a sentence, or picking between multiple meanings of words, we continually use this sort of higher level deduction. We are always basing our understanding on the answer to questions like "Which interpretation would make sense given what I already know?" and "What is he trying to communicate?"

Any attempt to model human language with simple semantic rules and heuristics like those described above is a bit like an attempt to model the behavior of a complex system by using unrelated mathematical formulas whose results are a general approximation to its output. The results may be of interest, and the resulting equations may have a high correlation with what is going on, but it is not a model in the true sense of reflecting the underlying process.

It seems likely that more advanced computational models will move towards overcoming these deficiencies. As we learn more about the organization of large complex systems, we may well be able to model language in ways which are more complete, clearer, and closer to psychological reality.

Five

Identification of Conceptualizations Underlying Natural Language

Roger C. Schank
Stanford University

The Theoretical Framework

In this chapter we shall describe a model of human language understanding that forms the basis for a set of computer programs that are intended as a first approach toward the computer understanding of natural language. The principal problem that we shall address here is the representation of meaning in an unambiguous language-free manner. A prototype language-understanding system is running at the Stanford Artificial Intelligence Project. This system consists of three parts: a parser (written by Chris Riesbeck, 1973), a memory and inference strategy (written by Chuck Rieger, 1973), and a generator (written by Neil Goldman, 1973).

These programs use as their basis the model described here. In this chapter we will be concerned primarily with what the theoretical problems are with respect to finding an adequate meaning representation and parsing into that representation. The reader is referred to the reports written by Riesbeck, Rieger, and Goldman for the details of the design and programming of a system that uses the theory described here.

One basic assumption presented in this work is that since it is true that people can understand natural language, it should be possible to imitate the human understanding process on a computer, if it is possible to state those processes explicitly.

Basically, the view of language understanding expressed here is that there exists a conceptual base into which utterances in natural language are mapped during understanding. Furthermore, it is assumed that this conceptual base is well-defined enough such that an initial input into the conceptual base can make possible the prediction of the kind of conceptual information that is likely to follow the initial input.

Thus, we will be primarily concerned with the nature of the conceptual base and the nature of the mapping rules that can be employed to extract what we shall call the conceptualizations underlying a linguistic expression.

Parsing

The principal part of all work in natural language understanding requires the use of a parser. Traditionally parsers have been mechanisms for determining the syntactic structure of linguistic expressions. There have been principally two methods for approaching that task. The bottom-up method takes each word in a sentence, finds its syntactic category and attempts to join it to the next following word by checking to see if a grammar rule exists that can conjoin those two syntactic categories. This continues until all words have been connected into a well formed structure. One problem with this approach is that a great deal of time is expended looking for combinations of syntactic categories that do not exist in the grammar.

The top-down method starts with the grammar and attempts to find instances of the use of the grammar rules in the text to be parsed. Thus the grammar decides what rules are around to be satisfied and looks to see if the word it is presently looking at is an instance of the needed syntactic category. The problem here is that a lot of time is wasted looking to see if what is wanted can be satisfied by what is present. For example, if you have a noun and a grammar rule states that nouns can be followed by a preposition, then a preposition will be looked for even if the next word is a verb.

The methods mentioned here are methods that are used in syntactic analysis. We have said that we will describe a conceptual base. What does a syntactic structure have to do with the structure of a conceptual base? Consider the following sentence:

1. I hit the boy with the girl with long hair with a hammer with vengeance.

It should be clear that the syntactic structure of sentence 1. will not provide the information necessary for dealing with the meaning of this sentence. That is, if we need to glean from this sentence the information that the hammer hit the boy we would have to do it by methods more sophisticated than syntactic analysis. In fact the syntactic formations used will be of very little value in that task.

Now consider sentences 2. and 3.:

2. John's love of Mary was harmful.
3. John's can of beans was edible.

These two sentences have identical syntactic structures. Of what use is this information in dealing with the conceptual content that they express? In 3. it is the case that the beans are edible. If in fact 'Mary is harmful' is true, it has not been expressed by this sentence.

The point here is that computer programs that deal with natural language do so for some purpose. They need to make use of the information provided by a sentence so that they can respond properly. (What is proper is entirely dependent on the point of the computer program. A psychiatric interviewing program would want to respond quite differently to a given sentence than a mechanical translation program.) Regardless of the purpose, however, it is the meaning of an input sentence that is needed, not its syntactic structure.

Now the question is, will obtaining a syntactic structure point the path to the correct meaning–structure? This brings us back to the question of the reasonableness of top-down parsers as opposed to bottom-up parsers.

Let us consider the question of what kind of parser humans are likely to be. Does a human who is trying to understand look at what he has or does he look to fulfill his expectations? The answer would seem to be that he does both; what he does has to do with a lot more than syntactic information. Expectation-making and analysis of what exists can take place at the level of meaning as well as that of syntax.

Consider the following situation and conversation:

John meets his friend Fred on the street. Fred is holding a knife. John is angry because his wife Mary has yelled at him.
Fred: Hi.
John: What are you doing with that knife?
Fred: Thought I'd teach the kids to play mumbly-peg.
John: I could use a knife right now. (agitated tone)
Fred: What's the matter?
John: Damn Mary, always on my back. She'll be sorry.
Fred: I don't think a knife will help you.
John: You're just on her side. I think I ought to . . .

With respect to syntax, the item that Fred can expect to hear next is a verb. He has, in effect, made a prediction that a verb is coming next. (The notion of the use of prediction of syntactic categories in computer parsers was employed by Kuno and Oettinger in 1962.) With respect to meaning, the problem of prediction is a bit more complex. We claim that a conceptual structure type is predicted, as well as the type of element that will fulfill the requirements of that structure. (Since the nature of that conceptual structure is the point of this paper, we shall say no more about it right here.)

Context enters into the prediction question as well. The conceptual structure expects an action, but context delimits the range of possible actions that will make sense with the previous sentences.

What we expect here are the following four types of statements based on their contextual likelihood: 1. hurt someone, 2. end relationship with somebody, 3. go to someplace, and 4. emote.

These are classes of actions. We don't know which sentential form "hurt," "go," or "emote" will take, but we can estimate the likelihood of the class on the basis of the conceptual category and the prevailing semantic categories that have been used in context. All of these above actions are predicted on the strength of their likely consequences. That is, a desired consequence is known (John feel better) and each of the actions would in a different way lead to John's feeling better.

A fourth type of expectation or prediction is conversational, in that people talk for a reason, usually to communicate something or to gain some desired effect in the hearer. Here, it is used either to arouse sympathy or to inform about something he is about to do. The use of "ought," however, implies he might not do this, so that the probable reason in making this statement has to do with the effect that it will create on the hearer. Thus we can predict what kind of effect is intended to be made by the speaker and then expect certain types of utterances.

A fifth kind of expectation information has to do with a world view of the situation based on his own individual memory model. Thus, if he knows John to be a convicted murderer, his expectation of John's completion of this sentence should be different from his expectation if John were an avowed pacifist.

A sixth type of expectation is based on a memory-structure that is common to the cultural norm rather than the particular language or particular individual. The results of this kind of expectation have to do with the options that Fred can take as a result of the expected input from John. That is, Fred's expectation of a possibly bad outcome can be averted by appropriate action, either physical informative conversational or emotional conversational. It is his expectation that precedes the appropriate action.

These different types of predictions on the part of the hearer can thus be reasonably assumed to be operating when the hearer is engaged in the understanding process. Certainly Fred would be quite surprised at this point to hear John say, "I think I ought to have fish for dinner."

We can therefore say that it would seem to be reasonable to claim that a human is a top-down parser with respect to some well-defined world model. The hearer, however, is a bottom-up parser in that when he hears a given word he tries to understand what it is rather than decide whether it satisfies his ordered list of expectations.

If we are going to design a computer program that is a model of human language understanding behavior, then we must in fact make the predictions at each level that a human is known to make. With respect to syntax, rather than doing a complete syntactic analysis and then submitting the results of this analysis to some semantic interpreter, we would like to use syntactic information as a pointer to the conceptual information. That is, if we know that we need a certain type of conceptual information, we can go to look for it by predicting in what syntactic form and place it is likely to be found. If, instead of the expected we find something else, we must still be prepared to analyze this conceptually and reorganize our previous conceptual assumptions if necessary.

It should be clear then, that a system that operates in such a conceptually predictive manner, should, in principle, never find more than one meaning for a given sentence at one time. Whereas this idea is contrary to the traditional one taken by researchers in this area in the past, we again call on the notion of human modeling as defense. That is, humans simply do not see all the ambiguities present in a given sentence at one time. Rather they see one meaning, and then they see another if the circumstances are right. A parsing strategy that finds four analyses for sentence 4,

4. Time flies like an arrow,

as Kuno and Oettinger (1962) did, will not be a useful model of a human process.

Thus, we require our parser to extract a meaning structure from a sentence by performing in a bottom-up manner until it can make enough syntactic and conceptual predictions to shift gears and proceed in a top-down manner. Next we will examine what such a meaning structure should look like.

Conceptual structures

The conceptual structures that will be described in this paper are intended to represent the meaning of natural language utterances in one unambiguous way. That is, any two utterances that can be said to mean the same thing, whether they are in the same or different languages, should be characterized in only one way by the conceptual structures. Thus, we are most concerned with the problem of paraphrase. What we are paraphrasing, however, is the conceptual content of an utterance insofar as it can be determined. The representation of this conceptual content then, must be in terms that are interlingual and as neutral as possible. That is, we will not be concerned with whether it is possible to say something in a given language, but only with finding, once something is said, a representation that will account for the meaning of that utterance in an unambiguous way and one that can be transformed back into that utterance or back into any other utterances that have the same meaning.

Thus, the conceptual base is responsible for formally representing the concepts underlying an utterance without respect to the language in which that utterance was encoded. A given word in a language may or may not have one or more concepts underlying it. We seek to extract the concepts that the words denote and relate them in some manner to those concepts denoted by other words in a given utterance.

Here we are dealing with two distinct levels of analysis that are part of a stratified system (cf. Lamb, 1966). On the *sentential level*, the utterances of a given language are encoded within a syntactic structure of that language. The basic construction of the sentential level is the sentence.

The next highest level in the system that we are presenting is the *conceptual level*. We call the basic construction of this level the *conceptualization*. A conceptualization consists of *concepts* and certain relations among these concepts. We can consider that both levels exist at the same point in time and that for any unit on one level, some corresponding realizate exists on the other level. This realizate may be null or extremely complex, (see Lamb, 1964, for discussion of this general idea). The important point is that underlying every sentence in a language, there exists at least one conceptualization. Conceptualizations may relate to other conceptualizations by nesting or other specified relationships, so it is possible for a sentence in a language to be the realization of many conceptualizations at one time — which is to say that one sentence can express many complete ideas and the relation of those ideas.

The basic unit of the conceptualization is the concept. There are three elemental kinds of concepts. A concept can either be a *nominal,* an *action,* or a *modifier.* Nominals are thought of by themselves without the need for relating them to some other concept. That is, a word that is a realization of a nominal concept tends to produce a picture of that real world item in the mind of the hearer. We thus refer to a nominal concept as a PP (for picture producer), such that it is the concept of a general thing, a man, a duck, a book, or a pen; or of a specific thing, like John, New York, or the Grand Canyon.

An action is what a nominal can be said to be doing. For a concept to qualify as an action (hence ACT) it must be something that an animate nominal can do to some object. Thus, since "John hit Bill" expresses an action that happened to Bill, "hit" will be considered (temporarily) as an ACT. In "John likes Bill" however, nothing happens to Bill so "like" is not an ACT. Although "hit" is an action we will represent it in a more primitive fashion later on in this paper. This is done to facilitate paraphrase and will be explained later.

A modifier is a concept that makes no sense without the nominal or action to which it relates. It is a descriptor of the nominal or action to which it relates and serves to specify an attribute of the nominal or action. We refer to modifiers of nominals as PA's (picture aiders) and modifiers of actions as AA's (action aiders).

It should be emphasized here that what we have said so far about concepts refers to their conceptual properties and not their sentential ones. It is possible to have a sentence without a verb, or without a subject; or to have an adjective without a noun; in contrast, this is not possible at the conceptual level.

Each of these conceptual categories (PP, ACT, PA and AA) can relate in specified ways to each other. These relations are called *dependencies* and are the conceptual analogue of syntactic dependencies used by Hays (1964), Klein (1965) and others. A dependency relation between two conceptual items indicates that the dependent item predicts the existence of the governing item. A governor need not have a dependent, but a dependent must have a governor. The rule of thumb in establishing dependency relations between two concepts is whether one item can be understood without the other. A governor can be understood by itself. In order for a conceptualization to exist, however, even a governor must be dependent on some other concept in that conceptualization.

PP's and ACT's are inherently governing categories, whereas PA's and AA's are inherent dependents. Any governor, however, can also be dependent, and for a conceptualization to exist this must be true for at least two governors. Conceptualizations can themselves be dependent on certain concepts and/or other conceptualizations in certain ways. This will be explained more fully in section 2.

We represent the conceptual base by a linked network of concepts and dependencies between concepts that is called a conceptual dependency network (which we abbreviate 'C-diagram'). Let us look at such a network by considering sentence 5.:

5. John hit his little dog.

"John" is the name of an object, so it represents a concept that can be understood by itself, and it is thus a PP. "Hit" represents a concept of action. Each of these concepts is necessary to the conceptualization because if either were not present, there would be no conceptualization. Thus, we say that there is a two-way dependency between them. That is, they each act as governors that can be understood by themselves but must also be present in order to form a conceptualization. We denote the two-way dependency by ⟺. The words "his" and "little" both represent dependent concepts for to understand them it is necessary to hold them in waiting until what they modify appears. That is, they cannot be understood alone. "Dog" is the name of a concept that is a PP and is therefore a governor. The PP "dog" is conceptually related to the ACT "hit" as object. That is, it is dependent on "hit" in that it cannot be understood with respect to the conceptualization without "hit." We denote *objective dependency* $\xleftarrow{o}$ and thus have the following network so far:

$$\text{John} \iff \text{hit} \xleftarrow{o} \text{dog}$$

We can now add the dependents that were waiting for "dog" as governor. "Little" represents a PA that is dependent on "dog." We call this *attributive dependency* and denote it by ↑. The concept given by "his" would appear to be dependent on "dog" also, and it is, but not in a simple concept. "His" is really another syntactic representation of the PP "John" that is being used in the syntactic form that indicates possession. What we have is one PP acting as dependent modifier to another PP. We denote *prepositional dependency* by ⇑ between the two PP's involved, and a label indicating the type of prepositional dependency. (Here POSS - BY indicates that the governor possesses the dependent.) The final network is then:

$$\text{John} \iff \text{hit} \xleftarrow{o} \text{dog}$$
$$\nearrow \quad \Uparrow \text{POSS-BY}$$
$$\text{little} \quad \text{John}$$

A conceptual dependency network may be treated as a whole unit by reference to the two-way dependency link. Thus the time of the events of this conceptualization may have been "yesterday." This would be indicated by use of an attributive dependency between the time-PP (PP_T) "yesterday" and the $\iff$ as follows:

$$\text{John} \iff \text{hit} \xleftarrow{o} \text{dog}$$

$$\begin{array}{ccc} \uparrow & \uparrow \Uparrow & \text{POSS-BY} \\ \text{yesterday} & \text{little} & \text{John} \end{array}$$

Similarly conceptualizations can relate to other conceptualizations and to ACT's through the two-way dependency link which will be described next.

The Conceptual Level

Conceptual rules

The Conceptual Level is intended to represent the concepts and the relations between them that underlie natural language utterances. In order to do a conceptual analysis of a linguistic input, we must rely on the predictions that can be made from what is known about the input already received in order to know how to deal with new input. The key to making these predictions is in the *conceptual rules*. Conceptual rules are the list of permissible conceptual dependencies. That is, there exist formally defined dependency relations between given categories of concepts. These conceptual dependencies, and only these, make up the formal organization of the conceptual level networks:

1. Since a conceptualization expresses an event, the heart of any conceptualization is the relationship between the actor and the action in that event. Thus rule 1 (see Table 5.1) states that PP's can ACT and when they do there is a mutual dependence between them. This rule does not say that all PP's can ACT or that any PP can do any ACT. We define the particular possible relations between two categories as the semantics of that conceptual relation. That is, Rule 1 is a rule about the syntax of the conceptual level. It describes the possible combination of conceptual categories. The semantics of the conceptual level states which PP's can do which ACT. Thus the sentential level has syntax and semantics for the categories and particular words of that level, and the conceptual level has its own syntax and semantics for the categories and concepts of that level.

2. It is possible to predicate an attribute about a particular PP. This is called an attributive conceptualization and such a relationship is denoted by $\iff$ as seen in rule 2. In order for these items to exist as a conceptualization, each is equally necessary, so the dependency is two-way.

3. It is also possible to predicate set membership between two PP's. This is shown in rule 3.

4. It is possible to refer to a concept and an attribute of that concept that has already been predicated. In discourse, conceptual attributes are predicated, either explicitly or implicitly, before they are used to differentiate concepts of the same linguistic name. In other words,

"the tall man" would only be used to differentiate two men whose relative height is either visually apparent or has been previously remarked upon in a predication, and this dependency is indicated in rule 4.

5. Two conceptual objects in the world can be related to each other in various ways. The three principal ones are containment, location, and possession and these are marked on the ⇑ arrows. The direction of dependency indicates the concept that is being attributively differentiated, as in Rule 4. That is, "in New York" in information is about "man" but "man in" is not information of a useful kind about "New York." This is seen in rule 5.

6. Rule 6 indicates objective dependency. The PP is related as object to the ACT which governs it. Government here is quite literal in that the semantics of the conceptual level works from ACT to the objective PP. That is, a given ACT may require a PP of a given type as its objective dependent. Certain ACT's do not require an objective PP, but those that do must have an object conceptually even if none was actually mentioned in the input discourse. That is, if an ACT like "hit" is present, an object for "hit" exists conceptually even if it is not explicitly in the sentence. This will be further elaborated upon in the discussion of "case" dependencies.

The six rules given thus far are enough to express the conceptual representation of the conceptualization underlying sentence 1. We will present other conceptual rules as they are needed for the examples.

Underlying ACT's: TRANS

Until this point, it may have seemed that what we are passing off as conceptual ACT's are really no more than verbs in a different guise. This is only partially true. Actually, ACT's are whatever is verbal in nature on the sentential level, rewritten into a primitive form. "Move" for example, is an ACT, even if it is possible to nominalize it in English. In other words, it is the responsibility of the conceptual level to explicate underlying relationships that speakers know to exist. Although "move"

Table 5.1

C-Rule	Example
1. PP ⟺ ACT	John ⟺ hit ($\overset{o}{\leftarrow}$ Mary)
2. PP ⟺ PA	John ⟺ tall
3. PP ⟺ PP	John ⟺ doctor
4. PP ↑ PA	John ↑ tall
5. PP ⇑ PP	man dog ⇑ LOC ⇑ POSS - BY N.Y. John
6. ACT $\overset{o}{\leftarrow}$ PP	(John ⟺) hit $\overset{o}{\leftarrow}$ Mary

might be a noun in a given sentence, all speakers know that somewhere a subject and an object (for the primary sense of "move") must exist. It is the purpose of the conceptual rules to mark an ACT such as "move" as requiring conceptual rules 1. and 6. Thus, when "move" is encountered in a sentence, it is discovered to be the realizate of the ACT "move" and immediately the question of the PP's that are its actor and object is raised. The conceptual processor can then search through the sentence to find the candidates for these positions. It knows where to look for them by the sentential rules and what it is looking for by the syntax and semantics on the conceptual level. Thus, it is the predictive ability of the formulation of the conceptual rules that makes them powerful tools.

It is interesting at this point to look at ACT's that do not have direct English realizates in order to more clearly pinpoint the problem of conceptual representation. Consider sentence 6.:

6. The man took a book.

Since "man" is the actor here and "book" is the object of the action "took," it might be appropriate here to conceptually analyze this sentence as:

$$\text{man} \overset{p}{\Longleftrightarrow} \text{take} \overset{o}{\leftarrow} \text{book}$$

(We write a "p" over the $\Longleftrightarrow$ to denote that the event being referred to occurred in the "past.")

However, in attempting to uncover the actual conceptualization underlying a sentence, we must recognize that a sentence is often more than its component parts. In fact, a dialogue is usually based on the information that is left out of a sentence but is predicted by the conceptual rules. For example, in this sentence, we know that there was a time and location of this conceptualization and furthermore that the book was taken from "someone" or "someplace" and is, as far as we know, now in the possession of the actor. We thus posit a two-pronged recipient case, dependent on the ACT through the object. The recipient case is used to denote the transition in possession of the object from the originator to the recipient. Thus we have the following network:

$$\text{man} \overset{p}{\Longleftrightarrow} \text{take} \overset{o}{\leftarrow} \text{book} \overset{R}{\leftarrow} \begin{array}{l} \xrightarrow{\text{to}} \text{man} \\ \xleftarrow[\text{from}]{} \text{x} \end{array}$$

Now, suppose we were given sentence 7.:

7. I gave the man a book.

By comparing the underlying representations of these two sentences, "give" is like "take" in that it also requires a recipient and an original possessor of the object. Then we have:

$$I \stackrel{p}{\Longleftrightarrow} \text{give} \stackrel{o}{\longleftarrow} \text{book} \stackrel{R}{\longleftarrow} \begin{array}{c} \xrightarrow{\text{to}} \text{man} \\ \xleftarrow{\text{from}} I \end{array}$$

Note that these two conceptualizations look very much alike. They differ in the identity of actor and recipient in 6. and actor and originator in 7., and in the ACT. But, is there any actual reason that the ACT's should be different? Are they actually different? It would appear that conceptually the same underlying action has occurred. What is actually different between 6. and 7. (assuming that in 6. the originator was also "I") is that the initiator of the action, the actor, is different in each instance. The action that was performed, namely transition of possession of an object, is the same for both. We thus, conceptually realize both "give" and "take" by the ACT "TRANS." Thus the conceptualizations underlying 6. and 7. are:

$$6. \quad \text{man} \stackrel{p}{\Longleftrightarrow} \text{TRANS} \stackrel{o}{\longleftarrow} \text{book} \stackrel{R}{\longleftarrow} \begin{array}{c} \xrightarrow{\text{to}} \text{man} \\ \xleftarrow{\text{from}} \text{someone} \end{array}$$

$$7. \quad I \stackrel{p}{\Longleftrightarrow} \text{TRANS} \stackrel{o}{\longleftarrow} \text{book} \stackrel{R}{\longleftarrow} \begin{array}{c} \xrightarrow{\text{to}} \text{man} \\ \xleftarrow{\text{from}} I \end{array}$$

"Give" is then defined as "TRANS" where actor and originator are identical, whereas "take" is "TRANS" where actor and recipient are identical.

Important here, is that a great many other verbs besides "give" and "take" are realized as "TRANS" plus other requirements. For example, "steal," "sell," "own," "bring," "catch," and "want," all have senses whose complex realizates include "TRANS as their main ACT. It is this conceptual rewriting of sentences into conceptualizations with common elements that allows for recognition of similarity or paraphrase between utterances.

Conceptual cases

We have seen in the last section a new conceptual rule that utilizes a dependency indicated by

$$\text{ACT} \stackrel{R}{\longleftarrow} \begin{array}{c} \xrightarrow{} \text{PP} \\ \xleftarrow{} \text{PP} \end{array}$$

This conceptual rule states that certain ACT's require a two-part recipient in a dependency similar to that of objective dependency. The similarity lies in the fact that this type of dependency is demanded by certain members of the category ACT. If it is present at all, it is because it was required. There is no option and no ACT's can have a recipient dependency without having required it. Thus, this dependency can be considered to be a part of the ACT itself.

We call those dependents that are required by the ACT, *conceptual cases*. The four conceptual cases in conceptual dependency are OBJECTIVE, RECIPIENT, DIRECTIVE, and INSTRUMENTAL. The conceptual rules for conceptual cases are given in Table 5.2. We use conceptual case as the basic predictive mechanism available to the conceptual processor. That is, if I say "I am going," a very reasonable inquiry would be "Where?" in that dialogues are often partly concerned with the filling in of the case slots in a conceptualization. People do not usually state all the parts of a given thought that they are trying to communicate because the speaker tries to be brief and leaves out assumed or unessential information or simple information that he did not want to communicate. A conceptual case often may not be realized in a given sentence although the sentence will appear well-formed syntactically. A C-diagram that contains only the sententially realized information will not be well-formed conceptually. That is, a conceptualization is not complete until all the conceptual cases required by the ACT have been explicated. The conceptual processor makes use of the unfilled case slots to search for a given type of information in a sentence or larger unit of discourse that will fit the needed slot. In an interactive situation, some measure of the desire to fill such slots is necessary in order to direct the response initiator to form an inquiry as to the nature of the missing case concepts when such information has not been previously stated.

Linguists who are interested in syntactic well-formedness have begun recently to look into the possibility of using cases in their representations (e.g. Fillmore, 1968). In addition, computational linguists (see Simmons chapter in this volume) have made interesting use of these so called "semantactic" cases. The cases used by these researchers, however, are only distantly related to what we are referring to here as

Table 5.2   The Cases

6. $ACT \xleftarrow{O} PP$

7.
$$ACT \xleftarrow{R} \begin{array}{l} \longrightarrow PP \\ \longleftarrow PP \end{array}$$

8. $ACT \xleftarrow{I} \Updownarrow$

9.
$$ACT \xleftarrow{D} \begin{array}{l} \longrightarrow PP \\ \longleftarrow PP \end{array}$$

conceptual cases. Conceptual cases are considered to be part of the ACT upon which they depend and as such are always present whether words expressing them have appeared in a given sentence. We shall see that the two different case systems often do not overlap with respect to the sentential realization of a given conceptual case.

In sentence 8. we take up the interesting problem of instrument.

8. John grew the plants with fertilizer.

Here, 'fertilizer' is the syntactic instrument of the word 'grow'. Conceptually, however, this is not simple. Why? Simply because 'grow' is not an action that a person can perform on something else. What is meant here is not that John did something called 'grow', but rather that the plants grew. If we mean that the plants grew then the representation must express that they got bigger. Notice that what is involved here is not an action at all but rather a change of state. In order to express a state change we shall need a new rule: Rule 10: A PP can change from one state to another.

$$PP \Leftarrow \begin{array}{l} \longrightarrow PA \\ \longleftarrow PA \end{array}$$

Thus our representation for the plants growing is:

$$\text{plants} \Leftarrow \begin{array}{l} \longrightarrow \text{size} = x + y \\ \longleftarrow \text{size} = x \end{array}$$

But where is "John?" In the conceptualization underlying this sentence, "John" was doing something that caused these plants to grow. What was he "doing?" We do not know exactly, but we do know that he did it with the fertilizer. We might be tempted to posit a conceptual instrument here and have a conceptualization with no particular ACT in it (represented by a dummy ACT – "do"). Thus we could have (allowing a new conceptual rule (ACT $\xleftarrow{I}$ PP)):

$$\text{John} \Longleftrightarrow \text{do} \xleftarrow{I} \text{fertilizer}$$

We then could relate this conceptualization to the previous conceptualization. They relate to each other causally since John's action caused the plants to grow. We denote causality by ⇑ between the two-way dependency links. This indicates that it was not the actor or the action by itself that caused the new conceptualization, but rather it was the combination of the two that caused a new actor-action combination. The causal arrow is a dependency, and consequently the direction of the arrow is from dependent to governor or in this instance from caused to causer. That is, the caused conceptualization could not have occurred without the causer occurring so it is dependent on it. Thus we have (placing an "i" over the ⇑ to denote intentional causation):

$$
\begin{array}{c}
\text{John} \xLeftrightarrow{p} \text{do} \xleftarrow{I} \text{fertilizer} \\[4pt]
\Big\Uparrow i \\[2pt]
\text{plants} \Leftarrow \begin{array}{l} \longrightarrow \text{phys st size} = x + y \\ \longleftarrow \text{phys st size} = x \end{array}
\end{array}
$$

Now, although this is roughly a characterization of what is going on here, it is not correct. In fact, 'fertilizer' was not the instrument of the action that took place. It was the object. Consider what probably happened. John took his fertilizer bag over to the plants and added the fertilizer to the ground where the plants were. This enabled the plants to grow. This is conceptually another instance of "trans". What we have is this:

$$
\begin{array}{c}
\text{John} \xLeftrightarrow{p} \text{TRANS} \xleftarrow{o} \text{fertilizer} \xleftarrow{D} \begin{array}{l} \longrightarrow \text{plants ground} \\ \longleftarrow \text{bag} \end{array} \\[4pt]
\Big\Uparrow i \\[2pt]
\text{plants} \Leftarrow \begin{array}{l} \longrightarrow \text{phys st. size} = x + y \\ \longleftarrow \text{phy st. size} = x \end{array}
\end{array}
$$

Thus, what appeared to be an instrument syntactically turned out to be a conceptual object after all. This, as it turns out is what always happens to a syntactic instrument in that a single PP cannot be a conceptual instrument and thus it can only be an object of an action conceptually. Thus we have conceptual rule 8 in Table 5.2. Consider sentence 9.

9. John ate the ice cream with a spoon.

Although syntactically "spoon" is the instrument of "ate," conceptually it is the object of an unspecified action that is the instrument of "ate". The ACT we use to underlie "eat" is "ingest" so we have basically:

$$
\text{John} \xLeftrightarrow{p} \text{INGEST} \xleftarrow{o} \text{ice cream} \xleftarrow{I} \begin{array}{c} \text{John} \\ \Updownarrow \\ \text{do} \\ \uparrow o \\ \text{spoon} \end{array}
$$

Thus, the instrumental conceptualization here represents the means by which the main action was completed. That is, we can take the ACT "ingest" to denote the actual ingestion of the ice cream by John. The way he was able to do this was by somehow getting the ice cream and his mouth in contact. That is "ingest" requires an instrument that is either "move ice cream to John's mouth" or "move John's mouth to the ice cream." The analysis that is appropriate here is "move ice cream" since "spoon" is listed as something that facilitates movement of some item that is the object, and since this is "TRANS", we have:

$$
\text{John} \Longleftrightarrow \text{INGEST} \xleftarrow{o} \text{ice cream} \xleftarrow{I}
\begin{array}{c}
\text{John} \\
\Updownarrow \\
\text{TRANS} \\
\uparrow o \qquad \xleftarrow{\text{CONT}} \\
\text{spoon} \Longleftarrow \text{ice cream} \\
\uparrow R \\
\text{ice cream} \qquad \text{mouth} \\
\Updownarrow \text{POSS-BY} \\
\text{John}
\end{array}
$$

Thus, "INGEST" is really not simply an action, but the name of a set of actions which are the instruments of ingest plus the ingesting itself.

It is important to recognize that every ACT in a conceptual dependency theory requires an instrumental case. We have not introduced many ACT's until this point as there is more about the nature of ACT's in the third section. However, the fact that every ACT requires an instrument is something that bears heavily on the nature of an ACT, and we should mention it before continuing.

If every ACT requires an instrumental case which itself contains an ACT, it should be obvious that we can never finish diagramming a given conceptualization. For sentence 9. for example, we might have: "John ingested the ice cream by transing the ice cream on a spoon to his mouth, by transing the spoon to the ice cream, by grasping the spoon, by moving his hand to the spoon, by moving his hand muscles, by thinking about moving his hand muscles," and so on. Such an analysis is really what underlies the ACT ingest and is known to exist by all speakers when they use the word "eat." These instrumental actions are not really needed and are rarely actively thought about. We shall not write in a conceptual diagram nor use in computer analyzer any more than has been explicitly stated with respect to instruments, but we shall retain the ability to retrieve these instruments should we find this necessary. (One obvious use of such instrumental cycling would be in a program that actually needed to perform something such as "eat," such as an extended version of the block program of Winograd (see chapter 4).) We can do this since any given ACT requires a given (one or more possible) instrument, so that this expansion can be done. That is, in order to "trans" an object it is possible that you must move it and in order to move something it is possible that you must grasp it. (The range of alternatives can be narrowed with more information. That is, in order to move something with your hand you must either grasp it or hit it and nothing else.)

The DIRECTIVE case indicates that PP's may serve as the direction indicators of a directional action. (See rule 9.) The directive case is extremely similar to the recipient in form and is almost in complementary distribution with it. That is, the two never appear together and would seem to be different forms of the same phenomenon. The most common ACT that takes directive case is "go." Like "trans," "go" is a primitive that is actually the underlying ACT for most verbs of motion.

Rules 6, 7, 8, and 9 constitute the conceptual cases of Conceptual Dependency theory. Thus there are only four cases, of which there can be as few as two or as many as three for a given ACT. Any given ACT requires a given number of cases and—no matter what the English realization—will have exactly that number in the C-diagram.

The notion of syntactic case is not used at all in conceptual dependency. Traditional linguists' ideas about case are only about so-called case languages. English is not traditionally a case language so the syntactic processor for English has no need of case. Although Fillmore's (1968) remarks on the underlying syntactic cases in English are well taken, his ideas are within the framework of generative grammar and therefore do not pertain here. That is, we are not interested in what is, and what is not, an acceptable utterance in English. Syntactic rules that explain what syntactic cases can be omitted in a syntactic construction shed little light on how the understanding of natural language can best be effected.

Conceptual relations

So far we have been discussing the conceptualization, for it is the basic construction of the conceptual level. That conceptualizations can relate to other conceptualizations, however, makes natural language useful and thought interesting. The dependencies that denote the way conceptualizations relate to other conceptualizations are called *conceptual relations*.

The most important conceptual relation is that of causality, denoted by rules 11a and 11b

Causality is denoted by ⇑, and indicates that the governing conceptualization caused the dependent conceptualization to happen. (This is not an implication arrow and should not be read as that logical symbol. It is a dependency arrow and signifies that the governor's existence preceded that of the dependent, and, in this instance, caused the dependent.) The causal arrow is realized in English in a great number of ways. The simplest form uses some variant of the word "cause" as in sentence 10:

10. John was sad because Mary hit him.

$$\text{Mary} \overset{p}{\Longleftrightarrow} \text{hit} \overset{o}{\longleftarrow} \text{John}$$
$$\Uparrow$$
$$\text{John} \Longleftarrow \begin{array}{c} \end{array} \begin{array}{c} \longrightarrow \text{sad} \\ \longleftarrow \end{array}$$

Another common causal takes sentential form using "when."

11. When Fred gave Mary a peach she ate it.

$$\text{Fred} \overset{p}{\Longleftrightarrow} \text{trans} \overset{o}{\longleftarrow} \text{peach} \overset{R}{\longleftarrow} \begin{array}{c} \longrightarrow \text{Mary} \\ \longleftarrow \text{Fred} \end{array}$$
$$\Uparrow$$
$$\text{Mary} \underset{p}{\Longleftrightarrow} \text{ingest} \overset{o}{\longleftarrow} \text{peach}$$

Causal is often expressed with only a single verb expressing both the causal and the end result.

12. John killed his teacher.

$$\text{John} \overset{p}{\Longleftrightarrow} \text{do}$$
$$\Uparrow$$
$$\text{teacher} \Longleftarrow \underset{p}{\begin{array}{c} \longrightarrow \text{dead} \\ \longleftarrow \text{alive} \end{array}}$$
$$\Uparrow \text{POSS-BY}$$
$$\text{John}$$

The "do" used here is a dummy standing for an ACT which was left unstated. If the ACT were stated it would be realized sententially by use of a "by" construction as in 13:

13. John killed his teacher by shooting him in the head.

$$\text{John} \overset{p}{\Longleftrightarrow} \text{propel} \overset{o}{\longleftarrow} \text{bullets} \overset{R}{\longleftarrow} \begin{array}{c} \longrightarrow \text{head} \\ \Uparrow \text{POSS-BY} \\ \text{teacher} \\ \longleftarrow \text{gun} \end{array}$$
$$\Uparrow$$
$$\text{teacher} \Longleftarrow \underset{p}{\begin{array}{c} \longrightarrow \text{dead} \\ \longleftarrow \text{alive} \end{array}}$$
$$\Uparrow \text{POSS-BY}$$
$$\text{John}$$

"Kill" is a member of a class of transitive verbs that we call pseudo-state verbs. They all have the property that the object of the verb is the actor of the dependent conceptualization. Often, the verb is the ACT of that dependent conceptualization as in 14.

14. Sam flew his plane to San Francisco.

$$
\begin{array}{l}
\text{Sam} \Longleftrightarrow \text{do} \\
\qquad \Uparrow \\
\text{plane} \Longleftrightarrow \text{fly} \;\xleftarrow{}\; D\rceil \longrightarrow \text{S.F.} \\
\quad \Uparrow \text{POSS-BY} \\
\quad \text{Sam}
\end{array}
$$

Here, the "do" is a substitute for either the actions required to pilot a plane, or an action such as "pushing the remote control button." In interactive situations, if the context does not clarify the nature of the "do," it might be correct to question the speaker as to its nature.

Another type of disguised causal is represented by the class of transitive verbs that we call ZPA's indicating that they will become mental state PA's. ZPA's are quite similar to pseudo-state verbs in that they realize causal conceptualizations where the object of the sentence is the actor of the dependent conceptualization.

15. John comforted Mary.

$$
\begin{array}{l}
\text{John} \overset{p}{\Longleftrightarrow} \text{do} \\
\qquad \Uparrow \\
\quad \text{Mary} \Longleftarrow\!\rceil \longrightarrow \text{comfortable}
\end{array}
$$

"Comfortable" is a PA. John's specific actions are unknown but their result was a new mental state for Mary.

The nature of the causal relation represents a step away from the notion that semantic representation must operate with the same elements as syntactic representations do.

There is no particular reason why what is realized in English as a verb must by necessity be represented semantically by something that is verb-like (e.g. the PRO-verbs of Lakoff, 1970). Often, a linguistic entity can best be realized by a relation rather than a concept. A representation must consist of concepts and relations. There is no intrinsic reason why these relations should not be realized in a language by a word. The justification for doing so has to do with the basic syntax of such a representation schema. That is, there are rules for making a certain relationship between concepts in a representation. If these rules are cohesive, then certain predictions can be made on the basis of the absence of some item from the representation. If relations predict different things than do concepts, a decision on what can be an adequate representation of a word or group of words is made on the basis of the predictive power of the choice of the different representation. Clearly, if the predictions of a relation are more useful in a given situation than those given by a concept, a relation is chosen.

This brings up the question of what makes a relation different from a case. The answer is that a case is part of an underlying ACT and is predicted by that ACT. A relation is a rule for connecting different conceptualizations. Thus, relations serve as connectors within a memory whereas other types of dependency connect things within a conceptualization.

There is an apparent similarity between instrumental case and conceptualizations that are causally linked. This similarity is caused by the nature of the syntactic instrument in English. We have noted above that syntactic instruments turn out conceptually to be either objects of causal conceptualizations or objects of instrumental conceptualizations. How is this distinction made?

If a syntactic instrument is related to a final state (as in "John grew the plants with fertilizer") then, since something must have caused this state the syntactic instrument is the object of the causing conceptualization. That is, states do not have instruments so there is no problem here. When the syntactic instrument is the object of an action that is subsumed under an action as conceptual instrument, we have the other instance. But how do we know that the "TRANS" subsumed under "INGEST" in sentence 9 is instrument and the "TRANS" in sentence 11 is causally related to "INGEST?" The answer is that if the actor in the "TRANS" conceptualization is different from the actor in the main conceptualization, as in 11, then these conceptualizations are causally related. That is, if someone does something, that precedes and is necessary for someone else to do something else, we consider these to be distinct actions that are causally related.

If, however, the actors are the same and the action under question is ordinarily an instrument of the main action, then they are related instrumentally. In this example, although it is necessary to move something to your mouth in order to eat it, it is also necessary to come into possession of it before moving it to your mouth. But this second TRANS is always causally related to INGEST whereas the first TRANS is always instrumentally related. That is, having something is a precedent action to eating something, but is distinct from eating it. Moving something to one's mouth is part of eating it, even though it is not a sufficient condition.

Thus, the entire argument boils down to whether a given action can be considered to be part of another action or a necessary but distinct condition for it. Clearly, when the actors are different there is no problem. Similarly, when the times are different macroscopically, there is no problem, so again we have a causal. We have a problem in the case where the actors are the same and the times are microscopically different as when, for example, one steals an apple and eats it immediately. Here we simply state that we see two distinct actions here; taking and eating. In this case, the taking is *both* instrument of the eating and causally related to the eating. In other words, we want to be sure to distinguish distinct conceptual events in the real world. We wish to do this because people do this in their perceptions of the world, rather than because the world really can be broken down into a series of distinct actions. We are modeling people, not reality. (If in fact, there exists a culture where life is viewed as a continuum rather than a series of distinct actor-action events, conceptual dependency would not do as a conceptual model of such a culture.)

Thus, conceptual relations are for relating distinct events, and cases are for combining aspects of the same event to the extent that the culture we are modeling views it that way.

Another important reason for treating relations differently from ACT's (as in "cause" for example) has to do with the inherent properties of a relation as opposed to an ACT. A relation is used to relate dependencies not concepts. Thus, it is the relational quality of "cause" that allows sentences like 16:

16. Since smoking can kill you, I stopped.

This sentence contains two conceptualizations related by a causal and a causal relating that causal to a third conceptualization. Such a thing is nearly impossible to handle in more traditional linguistic representations.

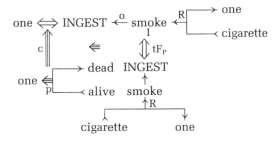

In this example, I am just assuming cigarettes to be the donor whereas the computer system would put in "smokable object" of which cigarette is a member. Two new symbols have been introduced in this C-diagram and they bear an interesting relationship. Any conceptualization can be modified by certain *conceptual tenses* of which "p" for past is one. The others are:

$$f = \text{future}$$
$$c = \text{conditional}$$
$$t = \text{transition}$$
$$t_S = \text{beginning transition}$$
$$t_F = \text{finished transition}$$
$$k = \text{continuing}$$
$$? = \text{interrogative}$$
$$/ = \text{negative}$$
$$\text{nil} = \text{present}$$
$$\Delta = \text{timeless}$$

These tenses modify a conceptualization as a whole. The English word "stop" for example is actually an instance of the conceptual tense "t_F" and thus predicts an ACT. That ACT was unstated in 16 but was actually "inhale."

The interesting point here is that causal links behave as conceptualizations rather than as ACT's in that they also can be modified by conceptual tense. Thus "can" in 16 is realized as a "c" over the causal link generated by "kill." What is being expressed there is that the causal connection is potential rather than actual. Thus the entire conceptual construction states that the actor did something because of a potential causality.

The other conceptual relations are time and location. The time of a given conceptualization can be another conceptualization. We have two conceptual rules expressing time.

Rule 12: T
↓
⟺ relates another conceptual category ("T" for concepts like "yesterday" or "12 o'clock") and a conceptualization. Most conceptualizations require a time. The time of something modifies the entire conceptualization and not any particular item in it. Thus it is the time of the joining together of the actor and the ACT.

Rule 13: ⟺
↓
⟺ states that one conceptualization can be the time of another. The dependency is usually realized in English by "while". Thus we have sentence 17:

17. While going home I saw a frog.

$$I \Longleftrightarrow go \xleftarrow{D} \begin{array}{c} \longrightarrow house \\ \quad \Uparrow POSS\text{-}BY \\ \xleftarrow{\quad} I \end{array}$$
$$\downarrow$$
$$I \Longleftrightarrow see \xleftarrow{O} frog$$

The other conceptual relation is location. Location is not considered to be a case simply because it refers, as do all relations, to the conceptualization as a whole rather than the ACT in particular. The location of a conceptualization is the location of the journey together with the actor and ACT. All conceptualizations that have time have location. The symbol for the location relation is ⇑ between the location and the conceptualization. The location modifies the entire conceptualization, although there is a rule (rule 5) that will allow individual PPs to have their own attributive locations. Thus rule 14: PP
⇓
⟺ indicates that conceptualizations must occur someplace.

This is true only of conceptualizations that have a time. A sentence that utilizes different types of locations is 18.:

18. Yesterday, the boy in that chair hit the boy on the piano in the mouth in the park.

$$
\begin{array}{c}
\text{yesterday} \\
\downarrow \\
\text{boy}_1 \Longleftrightarrow \text{hit} \xleftarrow{\text{o}} \text{mouth} \\
\Uparrow \qquad \text{POSS-BY} \Uparrow\Uparrow \\
\Uparrow\text{LOC park} \qquad \text{boy}_2 \\
\text{chair} \qquad\qquad \Uparrow\text{LOC} \\
\uparrow \qquad\qquad\quad \text{piano} \\
\text{specific} \qquad\qquad \uparrow \\
\qquad\qquad\qquad \text{specific}
\end{array}
$$

Underlying Actions

Separation of action and state

A very important principle has been used in the previous section that will now be dealt with in detail. When "kill" is rewritten into "do cause to die" we are saying that "killing" is not an action in the world. Rather, these are myriad actions that can result in a particular state (die) and that these action-state complexes are called "kill" sometimes in English.

This separation of action and final state helps clarify the underlying conceptual structures considerably. The problem is that a given verb may describe the same human action in every instance, or a range of actions may be described. Consider the sample sentences:

19. I like books
20. Books please me.

The meaning of these sentences is the same (except for certain connotations that are not relevant here). We must then, have one unique representation for them. Should "please" or "like" be the underlying ACT? We could somewhat arbitrarily decide between the two if we felt that both were actions. Are they?

By the definition of an action put forth in the first section, "like" is not something one can do to a book in the real sense of "do to" so it fails to qualify as an action. "Please" can be considered to be done to an object, but the actor ("books") can't do it. Actually "pleased" is a state in humans. So we have the conceptual entity:

$$
\text{I} \overset{\Uparrow}{\Longleftrightarrow} \text{pleased}
$$

In fact, we have this in both sentences.

Now the question is, what will cause such a thing? According to the conceptual syntax, only conceptualizations can cause things. Furthermore, "books" cannot be the actor of such a conceptualization since only animate things can "do" something. Thus "books" must be the object. The only actor around is "I," so we have:

$$I \Longleftrightarrow do \xleftarrow{o} books$$
$$I \Longleftrightarrow pleased$$

Do we know what action replaces the dummy "do"? We cannot know for sure, but we can make an educated guess that if the information was left out then the most common action done to that object was probably intended. This is "read" in this case. This kind of inference may be wrong of course, but since humans do it anyway it is important to have our system have that capability.

This example was mentioned here because a prediction that some action was needed was made rather than the problem of which one it was. By recognizing that "please" and "like" represent "do cause state" rather than actions themselves, we can know that an action was referred to but not mentioned. One of the most important parts of understanding is an awareness of what you do not know so that you can endeavor to find it out. Thus not only does the representation of these sentences in only one way aid the problem of paraphrase recognition, but representing these in the correct way makes clear what other information is yet needed.

The main point here is that a given verb is not necessarily representative of particular underlying actions. In fact, most of the time, an English verb is a description of a resulting state of some unknown action or a relation of many unknown actions. The recognition of this point makes the conceptual rewriting of verbs much easier and the problem of paraphrase recognition much clearer.

Representation of complex verbs

Considering verbs as being realizates of complex conceptual structures leads to the question of what the elements of such complex structures are. If in fact, the same actions are consistently used for many different verbs, then this set of basic actions can be used as the basis of inference rules, commands to memory, and the recognition of paraphrase. Consequently, the establishment of a set of primitive actions is extremely important. Furthermore, we make a powerful statement as to the nature of human thought if we can reduce natural language utterances to complexes involving just a few basic elements. Let us consider then just what basic actions we have.

Until this point in this chapter, we have treated as an ACT what can roughly be identified as a unique semantic word. From this point on, we shall begin to look for conceptual actions that are primitive and any item that appears in the ACT slot in a conceptual dependency diagram shall be considered to be primitive.

Thinking actions

Let us begin by considering the following groups of verbs:

1. prevent, instigate
2. frighten, comfort, console, kill, hurt
3. threaten, advise, complain, ask
4. love, hate

Not one of the verbs listed here will be treated in conceptual dependency as an action of which it is the unique name. That is, it is possible to reduce all of these verbs to more primitive elements.

In these four groups of verbs the following properties are present. In the first group each of the verbs refers to an action of some party (x) that will affect another action of some party (y). In each case the actions are not specified. Thus, for example, prevention and instigation refer to a causal relationship present between any two actions. In other words, it is not possible to state when you see an instance of prevention or instigation in the world without noting the relationship between two different actions. In fact, these two verb forms exist in the minds of the observers in a subjective manner. That is, what may seem to be prevention to one person may seem to be quite another thing to someone else. What is important to recognize is that the verbs in group 1 are simply statements of a causal relationship that exists in the mind of the speaker.

It is possible to represent "prevent" as:

$$x \Longleftrightarrow do$$
$$\Uparrow$$
$$y \Longleftrightarrow_{\not c} do$$

"Do" in conceptual dependency is a dummy action that stands for some action or series of actions that have not been explicitly stated. Thus "prevent" expresses that "x did something that caused that y could not do something." Similarly "instigate" is

$$x \Longleftrightarrow do$$
$$\Uparrow i$$
$$y \Longleftrightarrow do$$

(The "i" indicates that the causality was intended by x.)

The point then is this. Often what appear to be actions semantically are not actions at all conceptually but statements of relationship between other actions (some of which are often not explicitly stated). So far in this section we have done no reduction of basic actions. We have simply shown that what some semantic systems might treat as actions are not. The only primitive action we have used so far would appear to be "do," but since "do" is simply a place holder we have as yet used no primitives.

Consider the second set of verbs. Since these verbs are transitive in English it is common for native speakers of English to consider them to be actions in their own right. But consider "hurt" for example. If one is an observer of an action one should in fact be capable of stating what action one has observed (if that action is physical). Can this be done for "hurt?" Certainly not. If someone punches someone else in the nose the action that was performed would more accurately be called "hit" than "hurt." What is possible is that the "hit" results in "hurt." Although often even this is not true. There is also another sense of "hurt" that is mental and even harder to discern. Consider the case of the wife who tells her husband that he has hurt her by something he did. He says he didn't know that he hurt her and furthermore did not intend to. She states that he did nonetheless. That is, "hurt" (here, mental "hurt") is the result of an action rather than an action itself. Here again then, the actual primitive action that is referred to is unstated and we must represent it by "do." "Hurt" then becomes:

$$x \longleftrightarrow do$$
$$\Uparrow$$
$$y \Longleftrightarrow hurt$$

The $\Longleftrightarrow$ indicates a state rather than an action. What we have then is an action that causes a state. This causal relationship is only sometimes intentional so we leave the causal bond unmarked, and we distinguish two different types of "hurt," "hurt$_{PHYS}$," and "hurt$_{MENT}$."

The verbs in group two are similar to "hurt" in that they describe unknown actions that result in a given state. Consider "comfort." Here again, the actual thing that is being referred to as comforting in English is a resulting state rather than a specific action. That is, any number of things may be considered comforting, for example kicking a cat may be comforting to a dog. While we know a usual time to try to make someone mentally comfortable is when they are upset and that a usual procedure is to say soothing things and have gentle physical contact, this is only the presumed default condition.

A default condition is the information that is likely to be present implicitly in an utterance when no information is explicit. For example, the question "do you drink?" should be analyzed by an intelligent processing system that has no context to indicate otherwise, as having the object "liquor." Although "liquor" is by no means always the object of "drink" in English, it is the most likely candidate if the object of the verb is omitted. Similarly, the underlying conceptual structure for comfort while looking as follows:

$$x \Longleftrightarrow do$$
$$\Uparrow$$
$$y \underset{t}{\Longleftrightarrow} comfortable_{MENT}$$

has a default condition that can fill in some extra information. That is, the most likely candidate for the "do" slot is "say words" and "gently physically contact y." Furthermore, the initial mental state of y was probably "upset." Thus, if the sentence "I comforted John" appeared, the analysis would be initially:

$$
\begin{array}{c}
\text{I} \overset{p}{\Longleftrightarrow} \text{do} \\
\Uparrow\mathrm{t} \\
\text{John} \Longleftrightarrow \text{comfortable}_{\text{MENT}}
\end{array}
$$

If no additional information were available, however, an assumption would be made as to a probable candidate for a more complete analysis as:

$$
\begin{array}{c}
\text{I} \overset{p}{\Longleftrightarrow} \text{say} \overset{o}{\longleftarrow} \text{z} \overset{R}{\longleftarrow}\Big[\begin{array}{l}\rightarrow \text{John} \\ \hphantom{x} \\ \leftarrow \text{I}\end{array} \\
\text{I} \overset{p}{\Longleftrightarrow} \text{physcont} \overset{o}{\longleftarrow} \text{John} \\
\uparrow \\
\text{gentle} \\
\Bigg\Uparrow \\
\text{John} \Longleftarrow\Big[\begin{array}{l}\overset{p}{\longrightarrow} \text{comfortable}_{\text{MENT}} \\ \longleftarrow \text{upset}\end{array}
\end{array}
$$

These additions are simply guesses however. If the sentence were completed as "I comforted John by feeding him," the analysis would be:

$$
\begin{array}{c}
\text{I} \overset{p}{\Longleftrightarrow} \text{trans} \overset{o}{\longleftarrow} \text{food} \overset{R}{\longleftarrow}\Big[\begin{array}{l}\rightarrow \text{John} \\ \hphantom{x} \\ \leftarrow \text{I}\end{array} \\
\Uparrow \\
\text{John} \Longleftrightarrow \text{ingest} \overset{o}{\longleftarrow} \text{food} \\
\Uparrow \\
\text{John} \overset{t}{\Longleftarrow}\Big[\begin{array}{l}\longrightarrow \text{comfortable}_{\text{MENT}} \\ \longleftarrow \text{upset}\end{array}
\end{array}
$$

It is important to recognize then, that the verb "comfort" is a statement that some action has led to a specific state and that this action is not and by no means should be called "comfort" in a conceptual description of what actually transpired.

This is the case for all the verbs in group 2 and for quite a large number of verbs in English. That is, they simply describe final states in the sentential object that were caused by some action of the sentential subject.

We have now seen two classes of verbs in English and have as yet established no conceptual actions that are to be used as primitives in a conceptual system. (Except in the last example some were used without being explained for the kinds of actions that might result in comfort.)

The next class of verbs (group 3) is interesting in a different way. They are all English realizations of what we shall temporarily call a conceptual primitive "communicate" plus other information.

"Threaten" is actually a conceptual formula that indicates that something was said and that it was said in order to cause a belief of possible harm in the hearer. That is, if we have "John threatened Mary," John is saying that he will do something to hurt Mary if Mary does something in particular. John's first intention is that he would like Mary to believe that it is true. So "threaten" is

$$
\begin{array}{l}
x \Longleftrightarrow \text{communicate} \overset{o}{\longleftarrow} \Updownarrow \\
\quad \Uparrow i \\
y \Longleftrightarrow \text{believe} \overset{o}{\underset{cf}{\longleftarrow}} \\
\qquad y \Longleftrightarrow \text{do} \\
\qquad \Uparrow \\
\qquad x \Longleftrightarrow \text{do} \\
\qquad \Uparrow \\
\qquad y \underset{t}{\Longleftrightarrow} \text{hurt}
\end{array}
$$

To see what this would look like in actual use, consider the sentence "I threatened him with a broken nose." The most likely interpretation of this would be:

$$
\begin{array}{l}
\qquad\qquad \text{he} \quad \text{I} \\
\qquad\qquad\;\; \uparrow \quad \downarrow \\
\qquad\qquad\;\; \lfloor\underset{R}{\quad}\rfloor \\
\;\;\; p \qquad\; \downarrow \qquad\qquad \text{I} \quad \text{nose} \Leftarrow \text{poss by he} \\
I \Longleftrightarrow \text{communicate} \leftarrow\Updownarrow \Leftarrow \Updownarrow \\
\;\; \Uparrow i \qquad\qquad\qquad\quad \text{do} \;\; \text{broken} \\
\text{he} \Longleftrightarrow \text{believe} \overset{o}{\longleftarrow} \\
\qquad\qquad \text{he} \Longleftrightarrow \text{do}_x \\
\qquad\quad cf\Uparrow \\
\qquad\qquad\; I \Longleftrightarrow \text{do} \\
\qquad\qquad\quad \Uparrow \\
\qquad \text{nose} \Longleftrightarrow \text{broken} \\
\qquad \Uparrow \text{POSS-BY} \\
\qquad \text{he}
\end{array}
$$

In other words this is "I communicated to him the information that I will do something to break his nose which was intended to make him believe that if he does some particular thing (do_x), it will cause me to break his nose." (If it was ever any wonder as to why people chose to speak in words and not primitive concepts, that last paraphrase ought to give some idea.)

A computer analysis scheme is able to make the decision that the above sentence is different from "I threatened him with a hammer" because a broken body part is an instance of "he $\Longleftrightarrow$ hurt" and thus can be placed in that spot in the formula for "threaten." The sentence "I threatened him with a hammer" is:

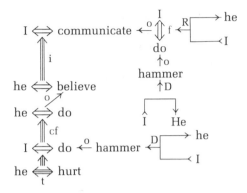

"Advise" is a verb that represents a conceptual structure that has a consequence, but in this case the consequence is a part of the communicated information. That is, "advise" is:

$$x \Longleftrightarrow \text{communicate} \xleftarrow{o} \Updownarrow \xleftarrow{R} \begin{array}{c} \xrightarrow{\quad} y \\ \text{x} \\ \xleftarrow{\quad} x \end{array}$$
$$\text{believe}$$
$$\underset{\text{do}_x}{y} \Updownarrow \xleftarrow{\uparrow o} \underset{\text{pleased}}{y}$$

This means that x communicates to y that if y does a specific unknown thing that y will benefit in some way. So "I advised him to try the twice-cooked pork" is:

$$I \xrightarrow[p]{} \text{communicate} \xleftarrow{o} \Updownarrow \xleftarrow{} \text{he} \xleftrightarrow{c} \text{INGEST} \xleftarrow{o} \text{pork}$$
$$\text{believe} \xleftarrow{o} \text{cf} \qquad \uparrow$$
$$\text{he} \Longleftrightarrow \text{pleased} \qquad \text{twice-cooked}$$

How then is this different from "suggested?" The answer is that it isn't really. At least in terms of the conceptual content underlying the utterance, there exists no difference. The difference lies in what is being communicated about the possible relationship of x and y, what we would call the extra-conceptual information. For "advise" the idea that x stands in a relation to y of social superiority of some type is being indicated. For "suggest" no such indication is being made. This is something that should be gleaned out of an utterance, although it is not part of the actual communicated conceptual content as we define it, and thus we will not discuss it here.

In the same way as with the other three types of verbs, "love" and "hate" are not actions that one performs on an object either. Rather they are expressions of feelings towards objects that exist in the subjects. Thus, in the same way that

$$\text{John} \iff \text{comfortable}$$

is used is represented that "John" feels "comfortable," "John hates Mary" must indicate a feeling on the part of John that we will call "hateful." So we read something like:

$$\text{John} \iff \text{hateful}$$

But, this conceptualization is only valid with respect to Mary. Temporarily we can posit a relation marker (R) which indicates that John in relation to Mary feels hateful:

$$
\begin{array}{l}
\text{John} \\
\text{R} \iff \text{hateful} \\
\text{Mary}
\end{array}
$$

What, in essence, would this relation marker be indicating? Its message would seem to be that after interaction of some type with Mary, John feels hateful. In other words a causal bond of some type exists here too. Furthermore, we need some conceptualization that expresses the interaction. Now since a necessary component of this interaction is mental, that also must be expressed.

In order to present this mental component adequately, it will be necessary here to present an analysis of mental type verbs. We shall then return to the question of "love and "hate."

WANT AND LIKE

Now we have not been exactly complete in our treatment of "like." Two important items are missing. One has to do with the tense of the conceptualization. When "like" is used in English in present tense, it does not indicate a conceptual present tense. In fact it denotes that this statement is somehow generally true for the speaker. That is, the statement is being made that usually, whenever he does x, it pleases him, so that the causal arrow has a timeless tense on it (denoted by Δ). Furthermore, the actual event being referred to has also previously occurred. That is, one would not say "I like ice cream" unless one had actually eaten ice cream at some time in the past. Thus the tense of the causal is actually $p + \Delta$ which we can read as something like "has in the past and presumably always will."

There is in fact another element left out of this analysis. It is the case that the statement is being made that this causal relationship presently exists in the mind of the speaker. Consider what would happen if we had:

$$x \overset{f}{\Longleftrightarrow} \text{INGEST} \overset{o}{\longleftarrow} \text{ice cream}$$
$$\underset{}{\Uparrow f}$$
$$x \Longleftrightarrow \text{pleased}$$

How would this be stated in English? It is possible to consider this as being "x will like ice cream." But is it possible for a future conceptualization to be standing by itself? Surely, a prediction needs a predictor, and we claim this is generally true. That is, when a mental statement occurs it is really expressing a thought on the part of the speaker and it is necessary to represent this fact as well in our conceptual structure.

That is, there exists an ACT which we call "conceptualize" (meaning think about) that is present in statements such as this. Thus here we would have:

$$x \Longleftrightarrow \text{conceptualize}$$
$$\begin{array}{ccc} x & \overset{\uparrow o}{\Longleftarrow} & x \\ f\Updownarrow & f & \Updownarrow \\ \text{INGEST} & & \text{pleased} \\ \uparrow o & & \\ \text{ice cream} & & \end{array}$$

That is, x conceptualizes or "is aware of" the causal relationship that will exist between these two conceptualizations if the first is ever true. Now, what does this ACT "conceptualize" add to our system? At this point, it adds little or nothing. It is trivially true that any speaker who describes any mental or physical event is aware of it at the time that he describes it. But conceptualizing is something people do and we must have an ACT to represent it. Furthermore, it is, in a sense, something that people talk about, and it is then that we shall need to use it. This will be seen shortly.

Consider the verb "want." "Wanting" something means that the speaker would be pleased by its occurrence. That is, "would like" in English is a paraphrase of "want." The difference between "want" and "like" then is one of tense. Thus "want" has a specific time unlike the tenselessness of "like." The time is usually specified by the context but we can assume "now" if there is no better information. So we have for "want":

$$\begin{array}{c} \text{Now} \\ \downarrow \\ x \Longleftrightarrow \text{do} \\ \Uparrow \\ x \Longleftrightarrow \text{pleased} \end{array}$$

The question is, is this all that is necessary for "want?" Actually it isn't quite all that is necessary. In ordinary usage of "want," the element "conceptualize" is not only being used but is also being expressed. That is, in sentences 21 and 22

21. I wanted it
22. John wants it but he doesn't realize it,

the "conceptualize" ACT is the one that is being commented on. In 21, the tense is being applied to conceptualize. Thus, we would have for 21:

$$I \overset{p}{\Longleftrightarrow} \text{conceptualize}$$
$$x \overset{\uparrow o \quad I}{\Updownarrow \; \underset{cf}{\Longleftarrow} \; \Updownarrow}$$
$$\text{do} \qquad \text{pleased}$$

that is, at some time in the past I wanted some future occurrences (future with respect to the past time). In 22, the "conceptualize" element is being "butted." That is, "but" means essentially, not to assume some implicit information that one ordinarily would assume. Here it means that he did not actually conceptualize the pleasure that would result for him from some action, but the speaker did. Thus we have:

$$\text{speaker} \Longleftrightarrow \text{conceptualize}$$
$$x \quad \uparrow o \quad \text{John}$$
$$\Updownarrow \; \underset{cf}{\Longleftarrow} \; \Updownarrow$$
$$\text{do} \qquad \text{pleased}$$

$$\text{John} \overset{\wedge}{\Longleftrightarrow} \text{conceptualize}$$
$$x \quad \uparrow o \quad \text{John}$$
$$\Updownarrow \; \underset{cf}{\Longleftarrow} \; \Updownarrow$$
$$\text{do} \qquad \text{pleased}$$

The ACT conceptualize then is assumed to be present in all volitional ACTs. Thus, we can also have sentence 23:

23. He hit Bill's car but he doesn't know it.

$$\text{he} \overset{p}{\Longleftrightarrow} \text{hit} \overset{o}{\longleftarrow} \text{car}$$
$$\Uparrow \text{POSS-BY}$$
$$\text{Bill}$$
$$\text{he} \overset{\wedge}{\Longleftrightarrow} \text{conceptualize}$$
$$\uparrow o$$
$$\text{he} \Longleftrightarrow \text{hit} \overset{o}{\longleftarrow} \text{car}$$
$$\Uparrow \text{POSS-BY}$$
$$\text{Bill}$$

In these last two examples, the value of "conceptualize" as a primitive ACT should have become clearer. We were able to deal with "realize" in 22 and "know" in 23 by the use of "conceptualize," and because of this, "conceptualize" can take care of many more of these verbs that we will now discuss in detail.

CONCEPTUALIZE AND MTRANS

The verb "think" in English has two primary senses. One is a paraphrase for a sense of "believe" as in 24:

24. I think that John is crazy.

The other is often used with future actions or as "think-about" or "think-of." This sense is "conceptualize," although it is not conceptualize by itself. Often, actions require other actions to occur first as a necessary part of their own occurrence. It is not possible to eat without physically contacting the food in some way, and we thus call this physical contact action the instrument of the ACT 'INGEST'. That is, it is in a sense a part of eating and is subsumed under it.

In the same way, in order to conceptualize something it is necessary to move the information being thought about to a place where it can be conceptualized. This moving about of information is represented by an ACT called MTRANS (mental TRANS). MTRANS is like the possession trans discussed earlier (henceforth referred to as ATRANS) in that it takes object and recipient case, and that the receiver of the object can be said to "have" it. The recipient of MTRANS when used as part of conceptualize is the part of memory that one conceptualizes in (which we call the conscious processor, CP). The verb "remember" indicates such a transition.

28. I remember the time we ate oysters.

Sentence 28 would be analyzed as follows:

$$
\begin{array}{ll}
I \Longleftrightarrow & T_1 \\
\quad I \downarrow & \searrow we \\
I \overset{p}{\Longleftrightarrow} \text{conceptualize} \overset{o}{\leftarrow} \Updownarrow & \\
\qquad\qquad \text{INGEST} \quad \text{MTRANS} & \\
\qquad\qquad \uparrow o \qquad\quad \uparrow & \\
\qquad\qquad \text{oysters} \quad I \Longleftrightarrow \text{INGEST} \leftarrow \text{oysters} & \\
\qquad\qquad\qquad\qquad \uparrow R & \\
\qquad\qquad \text{POSS-BY} \qquad\qquad \downarrow \text{POSS-BY} & \\
\qquad\qquad I \Longrightarrow \text{LTM} \quad CP \Longleftarrow I &
\end{array}
$$

The LTM in the "from" slot of the recipient of MTRANS indicates long-term memory. Items that are retrieved from memory are not necessarily retrieved with a specific time, (they may never have occurred at all) but here since the time is referenced but not stated, we place a T_1 as the time. It is important to realize that 'conceptualize' here means simply "have in my conscious thought" and makes no statement about conclusions or reasons. Furthermore, it is important to note that when we actually write conceptualize in a conceptual structure, we mean that the fact that that conceptualization has taken place is what is being communicated. Thus when we have "John hit Bill" we have conceptualized this, but since it is not what is being communicated intentionally, it is not represented in the conceptual structure.

Using "conceptualize" and "MTRANS" we can effectively deal with a large class of English verbs of thought. But, in order to do this, we must first make some distinctions between parts of memory that would appear to exist as evidenced by the use of verbs that reference them. Briefly, we distinguish a short-term memory (STM) for words; an immediate memory (IM) that consists of an individual's context for dealing with the world, that is the information that he needs to know to get by the situation he is in. We separate a section of this memory as the conscious processor (CP) which is the place where thoughts are currently processed (i.e. the object of "conceptualize"); also, there exists a long-term memory (LTM) for information that has been learned but is not in constant use.

Thus the process of the entrance of new information into the memory of a human can be represented by the ACT MTRANS. When the object of this mental transition is used, it is thought about in some manner and thus it is conceptualized (CONC). In order to CONC, information must be in the conceptual processor (CP), so that the recipient of the MTRANS is the CP.

Now, we can define the following verbs that are indicative of the ways that new information may enter into the CP by using of MTRANS and CONC. When the source of the information is another person (y), the verbs "communicate," "tell," and "say to" are often used. These are represented as (where x is the target location of the new information and $\Updownarrow$ is that information): communicate

$$y \Longleftrightarrow \text{MTRANS} \xleftarrow{o} \Updownarrow \xleftarrow{R} \begin{array}{l} \rightarrow x \\ \leftarrow y \end{array}$$

tell, say to

$$y \Longleftrightarrow \text{MTRANS} \xleftarrow{o} \Updownarrow \xleftarrow{R} \begin{array}{l} \rightarrow x \\ \leftarrow y \end{array} \xleftarrow{I} \begin{array}{c} y \\ \Updownarrow \\ \text{speak} \\ \uparrow o \\ \text{"words"} \\ \uparrow \\ \begin{array}{cc} x & y \end{array} \end{array}$$

Thus, these verbs represent the transfer of information from y to x. For "tell" and "say to" we know that the instrument of the MTRANS was the ACT SPEAK. For "communicate," the instrumental ACT is unstated. That is, we do not know how this information was transferred.

It is also possible to transfer information by oneself. That is, one can pick up new information by use of the sense-organ. Thus we can represent the transition of the information gotten from sense-organ by the following underlying conceptualization. Perceive (see, hear, smell, feel)

$$x \Longleftrightarrow \text{MTRANS} \xleftarrow{o} \Updownarrow \xleftarrow{R} \overset{\longrightarrow \text{CP}}{\underset{\prec \text{sense-organ}}{\rule{0pt}{0pt}}}$$

In actual use, the verbs of perception are used to indicate more than just that information was moved into the mind. Although it is possible to "see" without being aware of it, it is not possible to talk about seeing something without being aware of having both seen it and having done the work necessary to seeing it. Thus, CONC is present when sense-organ verbs are used, and MTRANS is the instrument of the CONC. Furthermore, an instrumental ACT (for "see"-LOOK-AT) is the instrument of the MTRANS. (Instrumental ACTs (the others are FEEL, SMELL, SPEAK, LISTEN-TO) are only present as instruments of some other ACT (usually MTRANS) and never can exist by themselves (in a conceptualization underlying an utterance).) Thus for "I saw John eating soup," we have:

$$
\begin{array}{c}
\text{John} \quad \text{I} \\
\text{I} \Longleftrightarrow \text{CONC} \leftarrow \Updownarrow p \xleftarrow{\text{I}} \Updownarrow \qquad \overset{\uparrow\text{I}}{\underset{\text{p}}{}} \\
\text{INGEST} \quad \text{MTRANS} \quad \text{I} \Longleftrightarrow \text{LOOK AT} \xleftarrow{o} \text{John, soup} \\
\uparrow\text{o} \qquad \uparrow\text{o} \\
\text{soup} \quad \text{John} \overset{\text{p}}{\Longleftrightarrow} \text{INGEST} \leftarrow \text{soup} \\
\uparrow\text{R} \\
\text{eyes} \qquad \text{CP}
\end{array}
$$

The apparent complexity of this underlying conceptualization should not be considered to be too upsetting. For, one thing the last instrumental conceptualization (LOOK-AT) need not be retrieved since it follows directly from MTRANS from eyes. Secondly, the information that would be necessary for any system hearing this input, is probably that the speaker has in his head that "John ate soup at some particular time." Thus, as is usually the case, the instrumental ACT MTRANS can be dispensed with. The ability to retrieve these items when necessary must be retained, however, as a part of what was stated.

It is important to notice that MTRANS as used here is a type of encoding function and a transferral action. Notice that the object of CONC is the concept of "John eat soup," the object of MTRANS is the perceptual image of "John eat soup" and the object of LOOK-AT is actually John and the soup.

Certain verbs indicate that information is entering different parts of the head from other parts of the head. Typical of these are:

$$\text{learn} \qquad x \Longleftrightarrow \text{MTRANS} \xleftarrow{\;o\;} \Updownarrow \xleftarrow{\;R\;} \begin{array}{l} \rightarrow \text{IM} \\ \dashleftarrow \text{CP} \end{array}$$

$$\text{remember} \qquad x \Longleftrightarrow \text{MTRANS} \xleftarrow{\;o\;} \Updownarrow \xleftarrow{\;R\;} \begin{array}{l} \rightarrow \text{CP} \\ \dashleftarrow \text{LTM} \end{array}$$

$$\text{forget} \qquad x \overset{c}{\nLeftrightarrow} \text{MTRANS} \xleftarrow{\;o\;} \Updownarrow \xleftarrow{\;R\;} \begin{array}{l} \rightarrow \text{CP} \\ \dashleftarrow \text{LTM} \end{array}$$

It is important to realize that "conceptualize" is actually an action that implies no decision. Rather it is closest to the verb "ponder." So we have further:

$$\text{consider} \qquad x \Longleftrightarrow \text{CONC} \Updownarrow f$$

$$\text{ponder} \qquad x \Longleftrightarrow \text{CONC} \xleftarrow{\;o\;} \Updownarrow$$

$$\text{dream} \qquad x \Longleftrightarrow \text{CONC} \xleftarrow{\;o\;} \Updownarrow$$
$$\uparrow \text{while}$$
$$x \Longleftrightarrow \text{asleep}$$

$$\text{wonder} \qquad x \Longleftrightarrow \text{CONC} \xleftarrow{\;o\;} \Updownarrow ?$$

Properties of MTRANS and CONC

MTRANS functions similarly to ATRANS with respect to the inferences that can be made after the ACT is known to exist. If an object is ATRANS-ed to a recipient, a memory system that is using this information must generate programs to erase the object from the known possessions of the donor and add the object to the known possessions of the recipient. Such inferences are made on the information implicit in an utterance as well as the explicit information. Thus, even though "buy" and "sell" do not explicitly reference "money," implicitly money is assumed. Since "money" is the object of "ATRANS" whenever "buy" and "sell" are used, the memory must now do the processing that is necessary in order to "know" that the seller is richer in some way and the buyer is poorer with respect to the unstated object of "money." This can be done easily upon expansion of "buy" or "sell" into the conceptual structure involving "ATRANS." Since both "ATRANS money" and "ATRANS object" are present, appropriate alterations on the state of memory can be made. It is true that whenever "ATRANS" is used these inferences as to previous and present possessor can be made.

Since "MTRANS" is supposedly like "ATRANS," it would be nice if such inferences could be made whenever MTRANS is present. It happens that the analogy between MTRANS and ATRANS is nearly direct. The difference is in the position of the donor in MTRANS with respect to the object. Whereas, for ATRANS the donor's possession of the object must be marked in memory as terminated, this is not so for MTRANS. That is, when something is communicated (or MTRANS-ed between two people), that item is now in the mental possession of the receiver but remains in the mental possession of the donor. The only exception to this is when the donor is the conceptual processor (CP). When items are MTRANS-ed from CP they are erased from CP.

Thus, we can see that certain inferences in the form of programs that alter the state of the information in memory are employed whenever PTRANS or MTRANS are present. It is interesting to note that the English word "have" can be used to express the result of either ATRANS or MTRANS. Such similarities between word senses with respect to ATRANS and MTRANS are quite common, indicating that there would appear to be some kind of underlying reality to these primitive ACTs.

Love and hate

Once we are given the ACT conceptualize, verbs that express feelings can be treated in terms of CONC. Certainly "love" and "hate" are not things that one person can "do" to another in the sense that we have been using "do." Rather, "love" and "hate" are feelings that give the results of the conceptualizing of someone. That is, the only action that is performed is a mental one and that is precisely thinking about them. Thus we have:

$$
\text{love} \qquad x \Longleftrightarrow \text{CONC} \xleftarrow{o} y
$$
$$
\Uparrow\Uparrow
$$
$$
x \underset{s}{\Longleftrightarrow} \text{love}
$$

$$
\text{hate} \qquad x \Longleftrightarrow \text{CONC} \xleftarrow{o} y
$$
$$
\Uparrow\Uparrow
$$
$$
x \underset{s}{\Longleftrightarrow} \text{hate}
$$

The "s" over the resultant state indicates that x "feels" the mental state of "Love" or "hate." Thus, "love" is "conceptualize someone causes you to feel 'Love'" (or remember having felt "love").

Belief

When someone states that he believes some particular conceptualization, it is simply a statement that this conceptualization exists in the world model of the speaker as a truth. We state that only true things exist in a person's world model, thus this sense of "believe" is represented conceptually as "exists in world model" or "M" (for immediate and long term memory). Thus,

26. I believe that John is a fool.

sentence 26, is treated conceptually as:

$$
\begin{array}{c}
\text{John} \\
\Updownarrow \Longleftrightarrow \text{LOC (M)} \\
\text{fool} \qquad \Uparrow \text{POSS-BY} \\
\text{I}
\end{array}
$$

This indicates that the conceptualization 'John is a fool' is located in the memory of "I."

Now consider 27:

27. Fred believes John.

Here we have a sentence that is ambiguous in two ways, but in fact this ambiguity is relatively unimportant. The two representations are:

$$
\begin{array}{c}
\text{John} \Longleftrightarrow \text{MTRANS} \xleftarrow{o} \Updownarrow_I \xleftarrow{R} \begin{array}{l} \rightarrow \text{Fred} \\ \dashleftarrow \text{John} \end{array} \\
\Updownarrow_I \Longleftrightarrow \text{LOC (M)} \\
\Uparrow \text{POSS-BY} \\
\text{Fred}
\end{array}
$$

$$
\begin{array}{c}
\text{John} \Longleftrightarrow \text{MTRANS} \xleftarrow{o} \Updownarrow_I \xleftarrow{R} \begin{array}{l} \rightarrow \text{one} \\ \dashleftarrow \text{John} \end{array} \\
\Updownarrow_I \Longleftrightarrow \text{LOC (M)} \\
\Uparrow \text{POSS-BY} \\
\text{Fred}
\end{array}
$$

These two representations differ in the recognition of a causality between the John's statement and its existence in the memory of "Fred." The first sense means that John stated something and that Fred believes it as a result of this statement. The second sense means that John said something and it is also true that Fred believes what John said.

It is important to point out here that in any case another conceptualization exists in the head of Fred. That is, Fred believes that John said it whether or not he believes what he said. This is the same as saying that if Fred heard John say it then he probably remembers that he said it. In other words, John's saying this thing was transferred to the memory of Fred whether or not Fred chose to transfer the content of what he said. That is, belief is simply existence in memory.

Now it may be seen that an ACT is missing from this analysis. That is, the MTRANS from John to Fred was to the CP of Fred. Fred has to decide whether to keep the content of what John said in memory. That is, he must decide whether to believe it.

Thus we introduce the ACT, MBUILD meaning that some information is processed and transferred to IM. This then is the missing ACT in the first sense of believe which should now read:

$$
\begin{array}{l}
\text{John} \Longleftrightarrow \text{MTRANS} \xleftarrow{o} \Updownarrow_1 \xleftarrow{R} \begin{array}{l} \rightarrow \text{CP} \xleftarrow{\text{POSS-BY}} \text{Fred} \\ \prec \text{John} \end{array} \\
\quad\quad \Uparrow \\
\text{Fred} \Longleftrightarrow \text{CONC} \xleftarrow{o} \Updownarrow_1 \\
\quad\quad \Uparrow \\
\text{Fred} \Longleftrightarrow \text{MBUILD} \xleftarrow{o} \Updownarrow_1 \xleftarrow{R} \begin{array}{l} \rightarrow \text{IM} \xleftarrow{\text{POSS-BY}} \text{Fred} \\ \prec \text{CP} \xleftarrow{\text{POSS-BY}} \text{Fred} \end{array} \\
\quad\quad \Uparrow \\
\quad \Updownarrow_1 \Longleftrightarrow \text{LOC (IM)} \\
\quad\quad\quad\quad \Uparrow \text{POSS-BY} \\
\quad\quad\quad \text{Fred}
\end{array}
$$

We have left the MTRANS's out of this analysis, but they are the instruments of the moving about of $\Updownarrow_1$. MBUILD deposits what it concludes into IM where it there resides as a belief.

The ACT MBUILD is used whenever a decision is made in memory to represent the complex processes that make up thinking toward a conclusion.

Sometimes the input into MBUILD is not the same as the output. That is, MBUILD can take a number of arguments and conclude a new thing which is then placed in memory as a belief. We represent such a thing by a new object arrow that conforms in shape and in origin with the Recipient arrow. Thus "conclude" is represented as:

$$
x \Longleftrightarrow \text{MBUILD} \xleftarrow{o} \begin{array}{l} \rightarrow \Updownarrow_x \\ \prec \Updownarrow_1 \wedge \Updownarrow_2 \cdots \end{array} \xleftarrow{R} \begin{array}{l} \rightarrow \text{IM} \\ \prec \text{IM} \end{array}
$$

That is, the process of concluding is the taking of old information from memory and coming up with new information that is then placed in memory.

Physical action

The primitive ACTs that are used to describe the physical world are as follows:

MOVE	PROPEL
INGEST	GRASP
PTRANS	EXPEL

The only things that can be moved are bodyparts. Thus, MOVE is usually an instrumental action, as are the sense actions referred to earlier. The verb "go" is usually a change of position of the actor (PTRANS) by means of a MOVE. Thus, we have (28):

28. I walked to the cafeteria.

$$
\text{I} \overset{t_f}{\Longleftrightarrow} \text{PTRANS} \overset{o}{\leftarrow} \text{I} \overset{D}{\leftarrow}
\begin{array}{l}
\rightarrow \text{cafeteria} \\
\leftarrow
\end{array}
\quad
\begin{array}{c}
\text{I} \\
\overset{\text{I}}{\leftarrow} \Updownarrow \text{p} \\
\text{MOVE} \\
o\uparrow \text{POSS} \\
\text{feet} \Leftarrow \text{I} \\
\uparrow \text{D} \\
\underset{\text{cafeteria}}{\wedge \qquad \downarrow}
\end{array}
$$

The directive case for PTRANS indicates that the motion was toward the item in the "to" part of the directive. The "t_F" over the $\Longleftrightarrow$ indicates that this action was completed. Thus a valid inference can be drawn here; namely that the object (I) is located at the direction (cafeteria).

PTRANS is analogous to MTRANS and ATRANS in that it also involves a change of state of something that is a location. We thus generate an inference whenever PTRANS is present that the object is no longer located at the "from" part of the directive case and is now at the "to" part of the directive case.

PTRANS is used with all change of location verbs while the instrument of PTRANS makes explicit how this change is effected. For example, when we have the verb "throw at" we have PTRANS by PROPEL. When we have the verb "throw to," however, we have a change in possession that is accomplished by a change of location which is accomplished by PROPEL.

Thus, for sentences 29 and 30 we have:

29. John threw a rock at Sam.

$$
\text{John} \overset{p}{\Longleftrightarrow} \text{PTRANS} \overset{o}{\leftarrow} \text{rock} \overset{D}{\leftarrow}
\begin{array}{l}
\rightarrow \text{Sam} \\
\leftarrow \text{John}
\end{array}
\quad
\begin{array}{c}
\text{John} \\
\overset{\text{I}}{\leftarrow} \Updownarrow \text{p} \Leftarrow \text{air} \\
\text{PROPEL} \\
\uparrow o \\
\text{rock} \\
\uparrow \text{D} \\
\underset{\text{John} \qquad \text{Sam}}{\wedge \qquad \downarrow}
\end{array}
$$

(Note that for 29. we would probably want to infer that this ACT was done with the intent of "hurting" Sam.)

30. John threw the pencil to Sam.

$$\text{John} \overset{p}{\Longleftrightarrow} \text{ATRANS} \overset{o}{\longleftarrow} \text{pencil} \overset{R}{\longleftarrow}\begin{array}{l}\longrightarrow \text{Sam}\\ \longleftarrow \text{John}\end{array}$$

$$\begin{array}{c}\text{John}\\ I\; \Uparrow\Downarrow p\\ \text{PTRANS}\\ \uparrow o\\ \text{pencil}\\ \uparrow D\\ \hline \text{John} \qquad \text{Sam}\end{array}$$

$$\begin{array}{c}p\uparrow I\\ \text{John} \overset{}{\Longleftrightarrow} \text{PROPEL} \overset{o}{\longleftarrow} \text{pencil} \overset{D}{\longleftarrow}\begin{array}{l}\longrightarrow \text{Sam}'\\ \longleftarrow \text{John}\end{array}\\ \Uparrow\\ \text{air}\end{array}$$

PROPEL is being used here to mean "apply a force to." Thus, in fact, "throwing" is more than just applying a force to an object. It also involves letting go of the object in the air. PROPEL then also has an instrument which is the ending (t_f) of the ACT GRASP. "In the air" is considered to be the location of the entire conceptualization.

Notice that the verb "hit" in one sense is precisely what we have used for "throw at" except the inference that a physical contact has taken place between the objects in objective and directive cases must be made.

Sentence 31 is ambiguous with reference to what precisely it was that hit Mary:

31. John hit Mary.

$$\begin{array}{c}\text{John} \overset{p}{\Longleftrightarrow} \text{PROPEL} \overset{o}{\longleftarrow} \text{X} \overset{D}{\longleftarrow}\begin{array}{l}\longrightarrow \text{Mary}\\ \longleftarrow \text{John}\end{array}\\ \text{X} \quad \Uparrow\\ \wedge\\ \text{Mary} \Longleftrightarrow \text{PHYSCONT}\end{array}$$

This problem does not exist with the verb "punch," where the object is known to be "fist" and the instrument is MOVE:

32. John punched Mary.

$$\text{John} \overset{p}{\Longleftrightarrow} \text{PROPEL} \overset{o}{\longleftarrow} \text{fist} \overset{D}{\longleftarrow}\begin{array}{l}\longrightarrow \text{Mary}\\ \longleftarrow \text{John}\end{array}$$

$$\begin{array}{l}\text{POSS-BY} \quad \Uparrow \qquad\qquad \Uparrow\text{POSS-BY}\\ \text{John} \Longrightarrow \text{fist} \Longleftrightarrow \text{PHYSCONT} \quad \text{John}\\ \wedge\\ \text{Mary}\end{array}$$

$$\begin{array}{c}\text{John}\\ I\; \Uparrow\Downarrow\\ \text{MOVE}\\ \uparrow o\\ \text{fist} \overset{\text{POSS-BY}}{\Longleftarrow} \text{John}\\ \uparrow D\\ \hline\\ \text{Mary}\end{array}$$

On the other hand, we have for 33:

33. John hit Mary by throwing a stick at her.

$$
\begin{array}{c}
\text{John} \xLeftrightarrow{\text{p}} \overset{\text{air}}{\text{PROPEL}} \xleftarrow{o} \text{stick} \xleftarrow{D} \begin{cases} \to \text{Mary} \\ \leftarrow \text{John} \end{cases} \quad
\overset{\text{John}}{\underset{\text{MOVE}}{\xLeftrightarrow{\text{p}}}} \quad \wedge \quad \overset{\text{John}}{\underset{\text{GRASP}}{\xLeftrightarrow{t_f}}}
\end{array}
$$

$$
\text{stick} \xLeftrightarrow{} \text{PHYSCONT}
$$
$$
\overset{\wedge}{\text{Mary}}
$$

$$
\text{John} \xRightarrow{\text{POSS-BY}} \overset{\uparrow o}{\text{hand}} \overset{\uparrow o}{\underset{\uparrow D}{\xLeftarrow{} \text{CONT}}} \text{stick}
$$

$$
\begin{cases} \text{John} & \text{Mary} \end{cases}
$$

and for 34:

34. A car hit Mary.

$$
* \xLeftrightarrow{\text{p}} \text{PROPEL} \xleftarrow{o} \text{car} \xleftarrow{D} \begin{cases} \to \text{Mary} \\ \leftarrow \end{cases}
$$
$$
\text{Car} \Uparrow
$$
$$
\wedge \xLeftrightarrow{} \text{PHYSCONT}
$$
$$
\text{Mary}
$$

(Where * denotes an unknown actor or natural force.)

Often, as with mental verbs, the final state of an object is what is being referred to in the English verb. In (35) for example, the action is unstated and perhaps unimportant. It is the final state that is significant.

35. I moved the table to the corner.

$$
\text{I} \xLeftrightarrow{} \text{do} \xleftarrow{o} \text{table}
$$
$$
\Uparrow \to \text{corner}
$$
$$
\text{table} \xLeftarrow{} \begin{cases} \\ \end{cases}
$$

That is, the location state of the table is now the corner and it is not important what specifically was done to get it there. We can guess that the action might be PROPEL (apply a force to) by MOVE hands to table, which is "push" in English. Of course it could also have been "pull" (PROPEL by GRASP-ing MOVE-ing hands toward self).

Similarly, sentences such as 36 refer to the final state of an object, but here the action is known.

36. I sliced the meat with a knife.

In all, a total of fourteen ACTs are necessary in order to represent all the actions underlying natural language. In addition to the three mental ACTs and six physical ACTs just discussed there is ATRANS which was used earlier plus four instrumental ACTs: SMELL, LOOK-AT, LISTEN-TO, and SPEAK. These instrumental ACTs are not very interesting and for the most part only occur as instruments of MTRANS.

We claim here that using the Conceptual Dependency system described here, these fourteen ACTs plus a number of states will adequately represent the information underlying English verbs. The only way to test such a claim is to see if computer programs using such a representation scheme can adequately converse in English. Given that that is a very hard task in itself we cannot provide any complete program to show that proves our case. Such programs are being worked on and a number of interesting papers have come out recently that report on that work. (See Rieger, 1973; Riesbeck, 1973; and Goldman, 1973.)

We shall sketch in the next section an outline of how a natural language analyzer would work that used such a system. We hope that it is clear that the ability to break down a given input into a Conceptual Dependency structure is a very important one for the problem of language understanding. For example, once we have an MTRANS structure for a sentence such as 'John told X to Mary', then we need only have one inference rule about the fact that once some information is MTRANS-ed, it is present in the LTM of the recipient in order to answer questions about whether Mary 'knows' X. What is important here is that we need only this one inference rule for MTRANS in order to answer such a question regardless of how the information was MTRANSed. Thus, if Mary had "read" X rather than been 'told' it, we would still have MTRANS and thus would require no new rules. Since there are thousands of verbs and only fourteen ACTs for which inference rules need be written, this amounts to a tremendous saving and is probably quite a bit more like the way people operate. In fact the number of inference rules that need be written for the ACTs is not large (see Schank, 1973).

The Conceptual Processor

Natural language analysis

We are now ready to turn to the question of how abstract networks such as those that have been introduced previously can be extracted by computer from a natural language input.

The first part of this task is breaking down the linguistic entities into parts that can be translated into conceptual entities. Thus, it is important to be able to recognize the main noun and main verb of a sentence. Once this recognition is made the translation into conceptual items can be made. When the rudimentary conceptual structure is known, predictions about the kind of conceptual items that are necessary can be made. Predictions can then be made as to the possible linguistic forms that such conceptual items may take a top-down search for those forms can be performed.

For example, if "give" is the main verb of the sentence under consideration and is recognized as an instance of "ATRANS," then a prediction that a recipient is likely to occur can be made. The recipient can be predicted to be animate and found in the syntactic forms "to N*" or "N*N" following the verbs where N* is the recipient in question. These predictions can of course be incorrect, but nonetheless they are what we can legitimately expect.

The syntactic processor that extracts the main noun and main verb shall not be discussed here. However, bear in mind, that the syntactic processor need not complete its analysis before the conceptual processor takes over. Furthermore, a complete syntactic analysis is not necessary. Rather, the input must be bracketed in such a manner as to indicate the main noun and main verb and to tie syntactically dependent items to the main noun and main verb.

The conceptual processor receives a triple as input consisting of the main noun, main verb, and the syntactic category, of the verb and the direct object(s) of the verb. From this information it must decide upon a conceptual configuration that will be valid by using the verb-ACT dictionary, the conceptual rules, and the conceptual semantics. Furthermore, it must make predictions as to what information is required by the conceptual construction and proceed to search the unprocessed part of the sentence for this conceptual information. The trick to this seemingly top-down part of the analysis process is that when some piece of the sentence is encountered that was not predicted, the analysis must shift gears and process that piece as if it were at the beginning of the bottom-up process. It can then finish the process by again searching for what it needs after having disposed of what it finds.

Let us consider sentence 37:

37. I want to go to the park with the girl.

The verb-ACT dictionary is a list of the conceptual structures associated with each syntactic and semantic environment that is possible for a given verb. Upon entering the verb-ACT dictionary, we find for 'want':

The leftmost symbol on each line represents the syntactic category of the verb: "vs" indicates a state verb, that is, one with an entire conceptualization as object; "vt" indicates a transitive verb, that is, one with a noun as a direct object. The next item is the conceptual network that underlies that usage of the verb. The items under the headings x and y are the semantic categories of the noun in the sentence (x) and the first and second objects of the verb (Y and Z).

In sentence 37 then, since we had a vs, the first realizate for "want" is the only possible one. Thus, after discovering the main verb, we have as conceptual realizate:

$$\begin{array}{c} \text{cf} \\ \Longleftrightarrow \\ \Uparrow \\ \text{I} \Longleftrightarrow \text{pleased} \end{array}$$

Thus we have predicted a conceptualization that should occur in the rest of the sentence. When we discover the elements of that conceptualization, we shall place them in the place held for them by $\overset{\text{cf}}{\Longleftrightarrow}$.

The triple for the next verb in the sentence (I, go-vio, nil) is encountered and the verb-ACT dictionary is entered, but this time with the information that a conceptualization is expected and when found that it will be placed in the awaiting dependent spot. The entry for "go" is:

go   vio $X \Longleftrightarrow \text{PTRANS} \xleftarrow{o} X \xleftarrow{D} \begin{array}{c} \rightarrow \text{someplace} \\ \llcorner \end{array}$ animal

vio $\text{one} \Longleftrightarrow \text{PTRANS} \xleftarrow{o} X \xleftarrow{D} \begin{array}{c} \rightarrow \text{someplace} \\ \llcorner \end{array}$ physobj

Since X here is "I," the first entry is the needed one. A conceptualization is set up including the instrumental conceptualization that is associated with "go" and the conceptual semantic requirements of the cases whose specific concepts are unknown (written in quotes):

$$\text{I} \Longleftrightarrow \text{PTRANS} \xleftarrow{o} \text{I} \xleftarrow{D} \begin{array}{c} \rightarrow \text{"place"} \\ \llcorner \end{array}$$

This construction is then placed in the spot that required it, so we have:

$$\begin{array}{c} \text{I} \overset{\text{cf}}{\Longleftrightarrow} \text{PTRANS} \xleftarrow{o} \text{I} \xleftarrow{D} \begin{array}{c} \rightarrow \text{"place"} \\ \llcorner \end{array} \\ \Uparrow \text{cf} \\ \text{I} \Longleftrightarrow \text{pleased} \end{array}$$

(For simplicity, we will leave the instrument out of the C-diagram until we need it.)

Now the processor goes back to the sentence to pick up what is left. It is looking for a directive case realizate primarily and an instrumental case realizate secondarily (this is because instruments are the least often realized of the cases). It finds "to park" and discovers "to" to be a directive case indicator. A check is made to see if "park" is a "place." Since it is, "park" is put into the C-diagram, and we have:

$$I \overset{cf}{\Longleftrightarrow} PTRANS \overset{o}{\longleftarrow} I \overset{D}{\longleftarrow} \boxed{} \longrightarrow park_1$$
$$\Uparrow cf$$
$$I \Longleftrightarrow pleased$$

Returning to the sentence, there is still the possibility of another directive case realizate or an instrumental realizate. The syntactic dependency "$\leftarrow$ with girl" is found. "With" is known to be an object of instrumental case realizate. So, the attempt is made to place 'girl' as object of the instrumental case. But, the only possible instruments for PTRANS are MOVE and PROPEL, and since "girl" is neither a bodypart nor a vehicle, the semantics of these ACTs are not satisified. Now the expectations are exhausted and the question is where else will a "with" construction fit? It is easy to see from examination of the following sentences that "with" is a many-ways ambiguous word:

38. I went with a book to the park.
39. I went to the park with the playground.
40. I went with the girl to the park.
41. I hit the boy with the bat.
42. I hit the boy with the girl.
43. I hit the boy with vengeance.

Basically there exist four conceptual realizations for the syntactic item "with PP."

1. PP is object of instrumental case.
2. PP is an additional actor of the conceptualization.
3. PP is an attribute of PP immediately preceding.
4. PP is an attribute of the actor of the conceptualization.

These potential realizates are checked for conceptual validity in roughly the order given. The "roughly" refers to the interface with memory that the conceptual processor must deal with. That is, the conceptual processor only processes in isolation for certain things. It is often the case that the memory must be consulted in order to go on (see Schank, 1972, for elaboration of this idea).

The first possibility has been eliminated by the conceptual semantics. But the question of whether "park with a girl" is a recognizable unit has been begged. That is, is there, in the immediate memory, some park that has been previously described as containing a girl? If such a unit exists it must be recognized before processing on it takes place. That is, even before "with" is checked for possible indication of instrument. This is precisely the same process as that which must be followed for idioms. If the unit as a whole is recognized by memory as having recently occurred before, then the previously assigned conceptual realizate takes precedence over any processed ones. (We have not yet investigated the possibility of the learning of idiomatic expressions in sufficient detail to eliminate processing of anything but wholly new phrases, but it presents an interesting possibility.) Thus, a previous reference to "the park with a girl" can interrupt the processing.

Assuming no such reference is found, then the next possibility is the main line place for "girl" as additional actor. Except for the above mentioned circumstance, main line concepts are searched for before the attributes of those concepts are. Thus, since "with" indicates a possible additional actor, the conceptual semantics are checked to see if "girl" can "go," i.e. if "girl" is an "animal." Since it is, we are done, and we have (using the logical "and" to indicate two actors):

$$
\begin{array}{c}
\mathrm{I} \overset{cf}{\Longleftrightarrow} \mathrm{PTRANS} \overset{o}{\leftarrow} \mathrm{I} \overset{D}{\leftarrow} \begin{array}{l} \rightarrow \text{park} \\ \uparrow \\ \leftarrow \text{specific} \end{array} \\
\land \quad \Uparrow \qquad\qquad \land \\
\text{girl} \quad \Big\| \, cf \qquad \text{girl} \\
\uparrow \quad \Big\| \qquad\qquad \uparrow \\
\text{specific} \Big\| \qquad\quad \text{specific} \\
\mathrm{I} \Longleftrightarrow \text{pleased}
\end{array}
$$

(This conceptualization can be roughly paraphrased as "if I and a certain girl would go to a certain park it would please me in an unspecified way." This can be called the "meaning" of sentence (32).) If "girl" had not fit as actor, it would have been checked as a possible attribute of "park" as would be done for 39.

The order of checking things presented here is not ad hoc. It is necessary in conceptual processing to go from generality to specificity. If "girl" had first been checked as an attribute of "park," it would have been virtually impossible to eliminate it. We cannot really hope to put in a memory all the things that a 'park' can contain, simply because that list is infinite. Thus, we check conceptual dependencies according to the predictions made by the conceptual rules (as for the cases) first, by the likelihood of such a syntactic construction existing second, and lastly by the compatibility with the world model for a given concept.

Conceptual semantics

So far we have made use of the idea of conceptual semantics without actually explaining it. The conceptual semantics represent the set of delimitations on possible conceptual dependencies. That is, whereas the conceptual categories of two concepts may allow their combination in some specified way, the actual concepts may not make sense when combined. It is the job of the conceptual semantics to keep out the nonsense.

Every PP has at least one semantic category of which it is a member. These semantic categories are the same for the sentential semantics and the conceptual semantics. Their job is to reduce the amount of information necessary to produce a simplistic world model. It is important to recognize that the conceptual semantics can be wrong, that is, what is ruled out may be just what was meant. Sometimes this can be corrected by lack of choice and sometimes by the interactive situation. Consider sentence 44,

44. The boy ate a book.

The verb-ACT dictionary entry for "eat" is:

$$\text{vt} \quad X \Longleftrightarrow \text{INGEST} \xleftarrow{o} Y \xleftarrow{} \begin{array}{c} \rightarrow X \\ \text{in} \uparrow \end{array} \qquad \begin{array}{cc} X & Y \\ \text{animal} & \text{food} \end{array}$$

"Book" is listed as having the semantic category "readable object," and thus the only sense that exists is not satisfied. The only alternative here is go back to the syntactic processor and see if there were any ambiguous paths. Clearly there were not, so the same triple is again presented to the verb-ACT dictionary. Again the semantics fail to accept the input. Ordinarily the syntactic processor and verb-ACT dictionary would be asked for another interpretation. But it is already known that none is available. So, the input is accepted and this C-diagram is produced:

$$\text{boy} \xLeftrightarrow{p} \text{INGEST} \xleftarrow{o} \text{book} * \xleftarrow{o} \begin{array}{c} \rightarrow \text{boy} \\ \uparrow \\ \text{in} \end{array}$$

The asterisk is an indicator to memory to do one of two things. Either the conceptual semantics must be altered to include "book" as "food" or the system must understand that something very odd has occurred and react accordingly. The decision as to which to do is part of another problem and will not be discussed in this paper.

The other situation occurs in sentences of the type contrasted in 45 and 46:

45a. John ate the steak with the odor.
45b. John ate the steak with the fork.

46a. John shot the girl with a rifle.
46b. John shot the girl with long hair.

The problem here occurs in the semantics of the instrument of the ACT in each sentence. In Conceptual Dependency theory the ACTs that are specified for any other ACT as instrument are fixed and known. Thus, the ACT involved in 45 is

INGEST and it is known that the only possible instrument for this ACT is PTRANS. Specified for INGEST are the possible objects that PTRANS might take when it is the instrument for INGEST. There are listed a number of possible semantic categories that are the possible objects here, namely, utensils and the actor himself. These categories (like utensil) are defined by features of the elements of those categories (this is discussed by Russell, 1972).

When any of the above sentences are encountered, the "with" calls the instrument routine which checks to see if the object that was seen is an acceptable object for the instrumental ACT. This is done by means of the semantic category involved, or by checking the required features for the instrumental ACT in this context. So, when 45a is analyzed, "fork" is known to be a utensil and thus qualifies as the object of the instrumental PTRANS.

In 45b however, 'odor' does not fit here and thus the last mentioned PP is considered as the prime candidate for the dependency. The particular relationship between "steak" and "odor" is established by the semantic category of "odor" (smell) and the information that all members of the class "physical object" can have a smell. Sentences 45a and 45b are thus analyzed as follows:

45a.　　John $\Longleftrightarrow$ INGEST $\xleftarrow{\text{o}}$ steak $\longleftarrow$ $\left[\begin{array}{l}\xrightarrow{\text{D}}\text{John} \\ \quad\uparrow \\ \longleftarrow\text{in}\end{array}\right]$

smell:odor

45b.　　John $\Longleftrightarrow$ INGEST $\xleftarrow{\text{o}}$ steak $\longleftarrow$ $\left[\begin{array}{l}\xrightarrow{\text{D}}\text{John} \\ \quad\uparrow\text{in} \\ \longleftarrow\text{fork}\end{array}\right]$ $\xleftarrow{\text{I}}$ $\begin{array}{c}\text{John} \\ \Updownarrow \\ \text{PTRANS} \\ \uparrow\text{o} \\ \text{fork} \\ \uparrow\text{D} \end{array}$

$$\left[\begin{array}{cc} & \text{mouth} \\ \text{POSS-BY}\Uparrow & \\ \text{John} & \end{array}\right]$$

In 46 the problem is similar but the instrument is not determined from the ACT but rather it is specifically mentioned by the verb. That is, the verb "shoot" is treated as "PROPEL from gun by gun PROPEL from gun" (where gun is a semantic category). Here we have an instance of an inanimate actor (which is possible only for PROPEL) and requests for that actor are made at three separate places in the conceptualization. Thus "shoot" strongly predicts "gun" and the sentence is always handled first with "rifle" as instrument as follows:

John $\Longleftrightarrow$ PROPEL $\xleftarrow{\text{o}}$ bullet $\longleftarrow$ $\left[\begin{array}{l}\xrightarrow{\text{D}}\text{girl} \\ \longleftarrow\text{rifle}\end{array}\right]$ $\xleftarrow{\text{I}}$ $\begin{array}{c}\text{rifle} \\ \Updownarrow \\ \text{PROPEL} \\ \uparrow\text{o} \\ \text{bullet} \\ \uparrow\text{D} \end{array}$

bullet $\Uparrow$
　$\wedge$　$\Longleftrightarrow$ PHYSCONT
girl

$$\left[\begin{array}{cc} \text{rifle} & \text{girl} \end{array}\right]$$

However, it is possible that 46a could be read as 46b is. In 46b "long hair" cannot be a gun so it is treated as a possession of "girl." This interpretation is possible for 46a as well. Our analysis technique which relies so heavily on the predictive power of the conceptual categories and the semantic requirements of those categories will always get the first interpretation of 46a and will never see the second. This is as we would claim it should be. What we do want, however, is the ability to be able to change our interpretation when we find out that it is wrong (as might be the case in interactive mode). This we can do by remembering the choice points for ambiguous words and going back to them when necessary. As long as we are aware that "with" represents such a choice point then this is no problem. Thus, our analysis can be wrong. The best we can do is give the most likely interpretation of an ambiguous word or syntactic structure. In the analysis of sentences in isolation we simply set the parameters the way we want them in order to get the interpretation that we consider to be most likely. In context, however, this must be done automatically by the program. Thus, when playing bridge for example, the words "bridge," "card," "hand," and "ruff," have obvious first senses which are different than their normal usage. It is necessary to have word senses ranked according to a set of possible contexts in order to effectively deal with them. This problem is discussed by Riesbeck (1973).

The use of category information will only work within certain limits before it fails. For example, in 47 each of the analyses presented for 46 will fail.

47. John ate the steak with a shoe.

That is, "shoe" is neither a utensil nor an attribute of "steak." The fact is that this sentence is a problem precisely because it has no obvious meaning. It is, however, quite common that sentences such as this one can be interpreted in some fashion. In 47 we would be more comfortable with an analysis that treated "shoe" as a utensil than as an attribute of "steak." What accounts for this? It is the fact that semantic categories are really derived from a bundle of features and that these features can be called upon when the categories fail. Thus, one of the features that applies to utensils is CONTAINMENT. Since this is a feature of "shoe" as well, it is the more likely assignment here. Similarly, the category of weapon needed for sentences that use PROPEL actually uses the feature RIGID for the interpretation process. Thus the actual resolution of semantic ambiguity is dependent on a feature system. An attempt to actualize such a system is described by Russell (1972).

The remaining question is how do the conceptual semantics differ from the sentential semantics? Although they seem quite similar, that is only because the subject and object of a sentence often perform the same function in a conceptualization. But, the job of the sentential semantics is basically to enable the conceptual processor to determine which syntactic construction was found. The sentential semantics serve to spell out more clearly the sentential environment and the selection is made by choosing the most specific environment (or lowest semantic category in the hierarchy) in the verb-ACT dictionary and selecting the conceptual realizate for that environment.

The conceptual semantics have the job of arranging the given concepts so that they make sense with respect to the world model. Thus, the conceptual semantics are interlingual, i.e., the same no matter what language one begins with. They represent the rules for organizing the world conceptually. The sentential semantics have to do with the particular language only. Thus, sententially it is all right for "man" to be the actor of "fly" because this can be said in English. Conceptually, "men" have yet to "fly" as such, so the conceptual semantics would find this invalid. But actually, the finding of an invalidity rarely occurs. The verb-ACT dictionary would have found PTRANS, for the verb "fly" and the conceptual semantics for PTRANS, would be those checked.

Thus, the conceptual analysis process finds what is valid as a conceptual realizate for a sentential part. The conceptual level is interlingual, the sentential level and the list of realizations of sentential pieces are part of a given language.

Syntactic ambiguity

One of the biggest problems that has plagued computational linguists who build parsing systems is that of syntactic ambiguity. The traditional approach has been to find all the possible syntactic analyses for a given sentence. Kuno and Oettinger's (1962) "Time flies like an arrow" is famous in this regard.

Such an approach disregards the problem of simulating human understanding. Certainly humans do not find all the syntactic interpretations of a sentence before they consider the meaning of the sentence. Humans frequently fail to see alternative interpretations of a sentence even if prompted that a second interpretation exists. On the other hand, it can be shown that humans try wrong paths in understanding and are forced to back-up and try another analysis.

Whereas it is possible to have a conceptual analyzer use rules of syntactic structure to produce conceptual dependency diagrams, it is not really advisable. Initial versions of the computer implementation of conceptual dependency theory, (Schank and Tesler, 1970) simply reversed the realization rules that mapped conceptual structures into linguistic ones. The result of parsing by such syntactic rules was that syntactic ambiguity was resolved in an ad hoc manner. That is, if a sentence is two-ways ambiguous there exist two different mapping rules that map the two conceptual structures into the one sentential structure. In analysis, the problem of choosing which realization rule to try first could only be decided randomly. Decisions of which rule to apply in a given situation can be shown to be not random. Since our computer system is intended to mimic a human engaged in the same task, it is important for us to find an analysis procedure that at least does what we know a human does even if we cannot verify all of the things it does in this way.

Consider sentence 48.

48. I saw the Grand Canyon flying to New York.

This sentence is interesting because of what would be considered its poor syntactic structure. Because the instantaneous image of the "Grand Canyon flying" is called into the mind of the hearer, often this sentence evokes a chuckle when told to an audience. The fact is that most people attempt to attach "fly" to "Grand Canyon" and fail, and then find the correct analysis of this sentence. We require that our processing system will do the same.

The syntactic processor passes the triple (I, see-vt, Grand Canyon) to the conceptual processor when it encounters this sentence. The verb-ACT dictionary entry for "see" is:

$$
\begin{array}{l}
\text{see} \\[4pt]
\text{vi} \qquad X \overset{c}{\Longleftrightarrow} \text{MTRANS} \xleftarrow{o} \Updownarrow \xleftarrow{R} \begin{array}{l} \to \text{IM} \overset{\text{POSS-BY}}{\Longleftarrow} x \\ \prec \text{CP} \overset{\text{POSS-BY}}{\Longleftarrow} x \end{array} \qquad\qquad \text{human}
\end{array}
$$

$$
\text{vs} \qquad X \Longleftrightarrow \text{MTRANS} \xleftarrow{o} \Updownarrow \xleftarrow{R} \begin{array}{l} \to \text{CP} \overset{\text{POSS-BY}}{\Longleftarrow} x \\ \prec \end{array} \;\xleftarrow{I}\; \overset{X}{\underset{\text{LOOK-AT}}{\Updownarrow}} \atop \underset{Y}{\uparrow} \qquad \text{animal}
$$

$$
\text{vt} \qquad X \Longleftrightarrow \text{MTRANS} \xleftarrow{o} \underset{\text{BE}}{\overset{Y}{\Updownarrow}} \xleftarrow{R} \begin{array}{l} \to \text{CP} \overset{\text{POSS-BY}}{\Longleftarrow} \\ \prec \end{array} \;\xleftarrow{I}\; \overset{X}{\underset{\text{LOOK-AT}}{\Updownarrow}} \atop \underset{Y}{\overset{\uparrow o}{}} \qquad \text{animal} \qquad \text{physobj}
$$

[Note that the two senses of "see" that are most common (i.e. understand and perceive) both are realizates of MTRANS $\xleftarrow{R}\begin{array}{l}\to \text{IM}\\ \prec\end{array}$, which partially explain why one word should have such seemingly different senses.]

Thus the following conceptual structure is found:

$$
\text{I} \Longleftrightarrow \text{MTRANS} \xleftarrow{o} \text{Grand Canyon} \xleftarrow{I} \overset{\text{I}}{\underset{\text{LOOK-AT}}{\Updownarrow}} \atop \underset{\text{Grand Canyon}}{\overset{\uparrow o}{}} \;\xleftarrow{R}\; \begin{array}{l} \to \text{CP} \overset{\text{POSS-BY}}{\Longleftarrow} \\ \prec \text{eye} \overset{\text{POSS-BY}}{\Longleftarrow} \end{array}
$$

The next word in the sentence is "flying." Since "flying" is realized by an ACT only, it is the candidate for the verb part of a new triple to be sent up to the conceptual processor. Since a prepositional phrase beginning with "to" follows, we know that it is a vio verb. However the problem exists of what the subject of the triple for "flying" is. This problem is not divorced from the problem of where to attach the new conceptualization that will be formed from this triple. Previously, when we entered the conceptual processor with a triple, there was a place waiting for it in the old conceptualization or else there was no old conceptualization, in which case there was no problem. But here we are within a sentence and we already have all the main line elements of a conceptualization filled in.

These two problems have the same basis for solution. There is no place in the right side of the conceptualization to place a new conceptualization. But, there is also no immediate candidate for the position of subject of the new conceptualization. The rule in a situation such as this is always the same. If there is no PP available as subject, the last PP which was placed in the conceptualization from the sentence is the prime candidate. This takes care of the problem of the entering triple for the conceptual processor, but still does not explicate where the new conceptualization is to be placed. The actual problem is where to place the "fly" construction since Grand Canyon has already been placed in the old conceptualization. The conceptual rules are checked to find a place for connecting "fly" to something already in the conceptualization. Again, "Grand Canyon" is the prime candidate for attaching 'fly' since it was the last concept placed in the conceptualization. The conceptual rule PP is found and now it is clear where such a connection would go. So the verb-

$$\text{PP} \underset{\downarrow}{\overset{\uparrow}{\Longleftrightarrow}} \text{ACT}$$

ACT dictionary is entered with the triple (Grand Canyon, fly-vio, nil). The entry for fly is:

fly

vio $\quad X \Longleftrightarrow \text{PTRANS} \overset{o}{\leftarrow} X \leftarrow \overset{D}{\boxed{}} \overset{I}{\underset{\text{PROPEL}}{\Updownarrow}} \Leftarrow \text{air} \quad \left\{ \begin{array}{l} \text{bird} \\ \text{plane} \\ \text{insect} \end{array} \right\}$

vt $\quad X \Longleftrightarrow \text{DO}$
$\quad\quad\quad Y \Longleftrightarrow \text{PROPEL} \overset{o}{\leftarrow} Y \overset{D}{\leftarrow} \boxed{} \quad \text{human} \quad \text{plane}$
$\quad\quad\quad \text{air}$

vio $\quad X \Longleftrightarrow \text{PTRANS} \overset{o}{\leftarrow} X \leftarrow \overset{D}{\boxed{}} \overset{I}{\underset{\text{PROPEL}}{\Updownarrow}} \Leftarrow \text{air} \quad \text{human}$

The vio entry for "fly" is checked, but the sentential semantics does not allow places to function as subject of the vio- "fly." Thus the triple is rejected and sent back to the syntactic processor. In other words, the attempt has been made to connect "fly" to "Grand Canyon" in a construction that could be roughly paraphrasable as 49:

49. I saw the Grand Canyon which was flying to N.Y.

Something else must be tried. Again we are faced with the problem of finding a suitable PP for subject and a place to put the new conceptualization. It is important to bear in mind that although conceptual information is being used, it is the syntactic processor that is operating here in an interface with the conceptual processor. I mention this because decisions that are made at this point are rules of English that are conceptually based. They are not interlingual rules.

The only other subject that is available for the triple with "fly" is "I" because it is the next to most recent PP that was processed (it is also the only other PP that was processed). Now we could apply the same reasoning that was used for Grand Canyon with respect to where to attach the conceptualization that will be found for this triple. However, there is a rule in English for operating on conceptual structures that states that it is not permissible to cross the two-way dependency link from right to left after the two-way link has been placed in the C-diagram. If a PP is needed from the left side of the conceptualization it must be the subject of a time conceptualization that modifies the original conceptualization. This is a rule of English and does not have universal validity.

Thus, we can enter the verb-ACT dictionary with the new triple (I, fly-vio, nil) and we have a place to put it in the C-diagram, namely as the time of the first conceptualization.

This time the verb-ACT dictionary accepts the triple, and consulting the ACT dictionary sets up the directive case, so we now have:

Again "to" is found to indicate directive case and "New York" is placed in the "to" part of both directive cases in the C-diagram.

Semantic ambiguity

A classic example of semantic ambiguity is expressed in sentence 50:

50. The old man's glasses were filled with sherry.

From the point of view of analysis, this sentence is different from others presented since it is a passive. A simple syntactic rule is used by the syntactic processor which states that when a passive particle (e.g. "were") followed by a verb in past tense, is found then the main noun that was found is placed in the object slot of the triple. If a "by N" is found following the verb then it is the subject, otherwise there is no subject.

In this sentence, the syntactic dependencies between "old," "man's" and "glasses" are established with "glasses" at the head. The passive is encountered, turned around, and the entering triple is (nil, fill-vt, glasses). When "glasses" is looked up in the dictionary, it is found to be a noun. However, conceptually, "glasses" is semantically ambiguous. That is, the word "glasses" represents two different concepts, "drinking glasses", and "spectacles." The ambiguity is carried along syntactically until it can be resolved conceptually.

The entering triple calls "fill" from the verb-ACT dictionary:

$$\text{vt} \quad X \Longleftrightarrow \text{PTRANS} \xleftarrow{o} \text{"liquid"} \underset{\underset{Q}{\uparrow}}{} \xleftarrow{R} \left[\begin{array}{l} \xrightarrow{} Y \\ c \quad \Uparrow \text{CONT} \\ \xleftarrow{} \text{liquid} \\ \quad\;\; \underset{Q}{\uparrow} \end{array} \right. \qquad \text{human} \quad \text{container}$$

$$\text{vt} \quad \text{one} \Longleftrightarrow \text{PTRANS} \xleftarrow{o} \text{"liquid"} \underset{\underset{Q}{\uparrow}}{} \xleftarrow{R} \left[\begin{array}{l} \xrightarrow{} Y \\ c \quad \Uparrow \text{CONT} \xleftarrow{I} \begin{array}{c} \text{one} \\ \Updownarrow \\ \text{do} \\ \underset{X}{\uparrow_o} \end{array} \\ \xleftarrow{} \text{liquid} \\ \quad\;\; \underset{Q}{\uparrow} \end{array} \right. \qquad \text{physobj} \quad \text{container}$$

The C-diagram for the first sense of "fill" indicates that this means that a person will put an amount of liquid, Q, into a container with a capacity of amount Q of liquid. Since the semantic requirements on the sentential object need a "container," the choice between the different senses of "glasses" is made here. "Glasses$_2$" — with a semantic category of container — is chosen. Here the "with sherry" construction looks like a candidate for instrument, and once the conceptual realization for "fill" has been selected, the conceptual processor switches to a top-down mode allowing it to look for what it needs. It most clearly needs a "liquid" as object and searches for it. "Sherry" is the next PP to be treated and a liquid, so it is immediately placed in the C-diagram. Here again, we see that all conceptual cases are not equal in their demand to be filled. Object — if required — is always first and instrument is always last. Since the subject is nil, the final C-diagram is:

$$\text{one} \overset{p}{\Longleftrightarrow} \text{PTRANS} \overset{o}{\longleftarrow} \underset{\underset{Q}{\uparrow}}{\text{sherry}} \overset{D}{\longleftarrow} \begin{array}{l} \longrightarrow \text{glasses}_2 \\ c \uparrow \text{CONT} \\ Q \end{array}$$

The most interesting aspect of this sentence, however, has not yet been discussed. Namely, it is nearly always the case that when English speakers hear this sentence they select "glasses$_1$," to mean spectacles, and then revise their choice after hearing "fill." This is certainly not what we did here, and is a problem for a system that is supposed to be a simulation of human understanding.

Let us consider the possible reasons for the common choice of the spectacle sense of glasses in this sentence. We are assuming here that the underlying conceptual system is image-like in nature, in that each concept is processed with respect to the whole picture that is created. In other words, when part of a picture is ascertained, there are some valid predictions that can be made about the nature of what will follow. These predictions are made from the organization of the parts of the conceptual whole (conceptual rules); from the requirements on the whole of a given concept (conceptual semantics); and from likely relationships that exist between items in the world that are simply a function of experience (this can include all linguistic rules, for example, syntactic expectation). It is this latter type that is being used in this example. Speakers of English know that humans tend to possess certain types of things in the sense that is commonly referred to. That is, whereas a man could have either type of glasses as his legal possession, we tend to speak about his possessions which are pseudo-inalienable, i.e., his car, his house, and his clothing. So, when a possessive occurs in English, we can predict that the possessive refers to things that we could associate with that human. If, for example, the phrase had been "the bartender's glasses" we would likely have chosen the container, or in any event the choice would be somewhat more difficult, although we would have chosen something. That is to say, understanders do not carry along alternative parses of a sentence or alternative senses of a word. Rather, they select one, and if they are wrong, they go back. Their selection is based on a context that is the prediction made by possession. We are not, in this system, at a point where we can be making all the possible human predictions. A human is making a great number of predictions at every point in an analysis. Some of those predictions are crucial and are discussed in Schank (1972). But many of those predictions are wrong or irrelevant. So, in our system, we cannot really bother making the prediction about glasses, but we can select one sense of glasses, based upon the frequency with which it is used. If that selection is shown by the semantics to be wrong, we go back and try the other. In this example then, we would have selected "glasses," based on a frequency count of our own experience, and then have gone back and selected the container sense of glasses. It is important to point out that this theoretical procedure is correct in that alternative senses of a word are not carried along. However, even though the correct result is obtained, the actual procedure employed is not based on human processes. We thus consider this procedure to be only partly theoretically valid. At such time that contextual prediction can be effected we shall implement that. Right now, most predictions of this kind would be useless, so that such a procedure should be avoided until a tight theory regarding this problem can be worked out.

Syntactic similarity

Consider again sentences 2 and 3:

2. John's love of Mary was harmful.
3. John's can of beans was edible.

Although these two sentences conform to identical syntactic patterns, they are quite different conceptually. We would expect then, that they should be processed in a syntactically identical fashion but processed quite differently on the conceptual level.

The main verb in each of these sentences is "be." Conceptually, however, there really is no predicated action here and consequently the verb-ACT dictionary is never called. There is a syntactic rule that states that if a "be" particle is discovered, and an adjective or noun immediately follows, the verb-ACT dictionary is not consulted. Instead a special attributive conceptualization is set up (denoted by $\Longleftrightarrow$ in conceptual dependency). This attributive conceptualization requires a PP on the left hand side of the link and either a PA or PP on the right hand side. Consequently, what is passed to the conceptual processor is a double consisting of the main noun found by the same procedure as before and the predicated noun or adjective.

For 2 and 3 then all that is required by the conceptual processor is the marking of the syntactic dependencies, and the double (main noun, adjective noun). The syntactic rules given above mark "love" as the main noun in 2 and "can" as the main noun in 3. "Can," in English, is syntactically ambiguous. That is, "can" can be a verb, a noun, or an auxiliary. It is not an auxiliary because there is no verb following. It is necessary for the syntactic processor to predict a verb when a potential auxiliary has been spotted. This prediction fails to materialize, and we have another problem in 3. It is possible to eliminate the verb possibility for "can" because of syntactic placement. That is, after encountering "John's" the prediction (as made implicitly in the syntactic rules) is that a noun will follow. Both "can" and "canning," in this syntactic slot must be considered to be nouns since that is the only thing predicted by the syntax. So, no matter what, the main noun configuration is:

$$
\begin{array}{ccc}
 & \text{can} & \\
 & \nearrow\nwarrow & \\
\text{POSS-BY} & & \text{of} \\
\text{John} & & \text{beans}
\end{array}
$$

But, conceptually "can" is also ambiguous. Not surprisingly, the fact that "can" can take these two syntactic forms is reflective of the fact that sentential "can" is conceptually both the PP "can" (the object) and the ACT complex which means "can" (to place in a can). Because there is no "-ing" ending, the "can" here is a PP.

This ambiguity does not exist conceptually in (2). That is, "love" is representative of an action no matter what syntactic form it comes in. But, here "love" is processed as a noun in the same way as "can" and for the same reasons. So we have:

$$
\begin{array}{ccc}
& \text{love} & \\
\text{possession} \quad \uparrow & \uparrow & \text{of} \\
\text{John's} & & \text{Mary}
\end{array}
$$

But, it is important to note, that before the syntactic processing is complete, all syntactic-conceptual interface problems must have been met. In 2 "love" is realized as an ACT and a state triple is formed for entering the verb-ACT dictionary that has "John" as Subject and "Mary" as Object, so that the triple (John, love, Mary) is then passed on the verb-ACT dictionary.

Interestingly enough only the very superficial aspects of these two sentences are similar. It is for that reason we expect the processing of the two sentences to bear only little similarity. From this point in the analysis process, all similarity is lost since their superficial similarity has no meaning to the conceptual system. The point made earlier about this should be emphasized. Although syntax is useful for finding the parts of the sentence that are to be conceptually processed, of itself it has no value. A conceptual analyzer uses the results of certain syntactic observations based on the success or failure of syntactic predictions. The syntactic rules are simply heuristics for finding things. We make the claim that this is all that need be done in an analysis.

The verb-ACT dictionary processes the triple for 2 into:

$$
\begin{array}{l}
\text{John} \overset{p}{\Longleftrightarrow} \text{CONC} \overset{o}{\longleftarrow} \text{Mary} \\
\quad\quad \Uparrow \\
\text{John} \underset{s}{\Longleftrightarrow} \text{love}
\end{array}
$$

Now, the predication marked by "was PA" causes an attributive dependency to be established with the entire conceptualization as subject. Since, "harmful" is a resultant state of some action, the entire conceptualization above is the causer and we have:

$$
\begin{array}{l}
\text{John} \Longleftrightarrow \text{CONC} \overset{o}{\longleftarrow} \text{Mary} \\
\quad\quad \Uparrow \quad\quad\quad\quad\quad \text{one} \\
\quad\quad \| \Longleftarrow \quad \Updownarrow \\
\quad\quad \| \quad\quad\quad\quad\quad\quad \text{hurt} \\
\text{John} \underset{s}{\Longleftrightarrow} \text{love}
\end{array}
$$

The "one" validates that this sentence is ambiguous in that we don't know who was harmed.

Sentence 3 is a bit more interesting. We have the syntactic dependency group:

$$\begin{array}{ccc} & \text{can} & \\ \text{POSS-BY}\nearrow & & \nwarrow\text{of} \\ \text{John} & & \text{beans} \end{array}$$

but, we have no entering triple. Thus, we have, a PP, "can" and the predication "was edible." Looking up edible we find that it is not a PA or a PP. Therefore the prediction that an attributive two-way dependency was present fails. "Edible" is in the dictionary as follows:

$$\text{"animal"} \overset{c}{\Longleftrightarrow} \text{INGEST} \overset{o}{\leftarrow} \text{"food"}$$

This definition represents "edible" as a conceptual construction about the possibility of eating something assumed to be a food. "Not edible" would indicate that the object of the action is not a "food." In other words, this is at the same time a definition of the semantic category "food." (The quotation marks indicate realizable semantic categories.)

Thus, we now have a conceptualization, given by the definition of 'edible'. We are faced now with the problem of filling in the unrealized slots in this conceptualization. We begin a search for the cases and look for a "food." The only place to look is the syntactic dependency complex given above. The head of that construction is "can"—thus not a "food." Therefore we must search the dependents and here we find "beans," so we have:

$$\text{"animal"} \overset{c}{\Longleftrightarrow} \text{INGEST} \overset{o}{\leftarrow} \text{beans}$$

We must now conceptually realize all the elements that are part of the syntactic complex that "beans" is in. "Beans" is related to "can" by "of" and we find that this is a containment relation (this is handled by a program that is not described here, see Russell, 1972). But, if "can" is used here, "John's" must be used also since it is related to can as a modifier of possession. The final C-diagram is then:

$$\begin{array}{l} \text{one} \overset{c}{\Longleftrightarrow} \text{INGEST} \overset{o}{\leftarrow} \text{beans} \\ \qquad\qquad\qquad\qquad \Uparrow \text{CONT-BY} \\ \qquad\qquad\qquad\quad \text{can} \\ \qquad\qquad\qquad\qquad \Uparrow \text{POSS-BY} \\ \qquad\qquad\qquad\quad \text{John} \end{array}$$

Now it is possible that this was not what was meant here. It could be that, the "can" was being referred to as "edible" as was predicted by the syntax and rejected by the semantics. Here again, we are making no effort to guess what could possibly have been meant but rather what was most probably meant. We can always correct any mistake in an interactive situation, and we can alter our probabilities.

Semantic similarity

Consider the following three sentences:

51. I want a book.
52. I want to get a book.
53. I want to have a book.

The assumption here is that these sentences all mean the same thing. Although it can be argued that they do not because of varying contexts or connotations, we assume the context where the conceptual content of all three sentences is the same and disregard implications for the moment.

Using the verb-ACT definition of "want" given in section 4.1, we see that for the vt sense that exists in (51), an entire structure is the realizate of the idea of "want a physobj," namely for (51):

$$
\text{one} \overset{cf}{\Longleftrightarrow} \text{PTRANS} \overset{o}{\leftarrow} \text{book} \overset{R}{\leftarrow} \begin{array}{l} \rightarrow \text{I} \\ \\ \prec \text{one} \end{array}
$$
$$
\Uparrow cf
$$
$$
\text{I} \Longleftrightarrow \text{pleased}
$$

the idea being that what is wanted is that somebody give this book to the subject in any unspecified manner.

The same structure can be realized for 52 given that this is the vs sense of want and that the verb-ACT entry for "get" is:

get

vt $X \Longleftrightarrow \text{PTRANS} \overset{o}{\leftarrow} Y \overset{R}{\leftarrow} \begin{array}{l} \rightarrow \text{I} \\ \\ \prec \text{one} \end{array}$ human   physobj

vt $X \overset{c}{\Longleftrightarrow} \text{MTRANS} \overset{o}{\leftarrow} Y \overset{R}{\leftarrow} \begin{array}{l} \rightarrow \text{IM} \\ \\ \prec \text{Z} \end{array}$ human   conceptualization

Thus, given that the verb 'want' requires a conceptualization and that 'book' is a physobj, we have:

$$
\text{one} \Longleftrightarrow \text{PTRANS} \overset{o}{\leftarrow} \text{book} \overset{R}{\leftarrow} \begin{array}{l} \rightarrow \text{I} \\ \\ \prec \text{one} \end{array}
$$
$$
\Uparrow
$$
$$
\text{I} \Longleftrightarrow \text{pleased}
$$

which is the same as the preceding conceptual construction.

We have not, until this point, discussed the verb "to have." Since "have" in its alienable sense represents the result of a conceptualization that involves acquiring the object in the first place, we consider "have" to be an instance of "trans." After the "trans" has been completed, "have" can be assumed to be an implication derived from the "trans" about a relationship between two PP's. But it is important to understand that "have" presupposes this "trans" relationship for inalienable possession. If such is the presupposition, then it is part of the conceptual content and therefore must be represented in the conceptual diagram. The verb-ACT entry for "have" is:

$$
\begin{array}{llll}
\text{have} & \text{vt} & \text{one} \Longleftrightarrow \text{MTRANS} \leftarrow Y \xleftarrow{R} \begin{array}{l} \rightarrow \text{IM} \\ \prec \end{array} & \text{human} \\[2em]
& \text{vt} & \text{one} \Longleftrightarrow \text{PTRANS} \xleftarrow{o} Y \xleftarrow{R} \begin{array}{l} \rightarrow X \\ \prec \text{one} \end{array} & \text{human} \quad \text{physobj} \\
& & \quad Y \\
& & \quad \Uparrow \\
& \text{vt} & \quad X \Longleftrightarrow \text{sick} & \text{animal} \quad \text{disease}
\end{array}
$$

Thus, this is virtually the same as the previous example and "want," requires the first conceptualization:

$$
\begin{array}{l}
\text{one} \Longleftrightarrow \text{PTRANS} \xleftarrow{o} \text{book} \xleftarrow{R} \begin{array}{l} \rightarrow \text{I} \\ \prec \text{one} \end{array} \\
\quad \Uparrow \\
\text{I} \Longleftrightarrow \text{pleased}
\end{array}
$$

Conclusion

In this chapter we have presented a system of primitive concepts for expressing conceptualizations underlying natural language and have outlined a method for extracting such conceptualizations from natural language. In a discussion of the nature of the primitive actions that we have arrived at, it will be seen that all these actions are simply the moving about of ideas or physical objects. Furthermore it would seem that our language discusses these movements with respect to the final states of the object in motion or with respect to the change in emotional state that those objects' motion has brought about.

It was by no means our intention to demonstrate that the bulk of what people talk about can be so reduced. It did, however, result in that and the best we can say is that research of this type often yields the unexpected.

The actual computer analysis of language into the networks we have described is an extremely complicated task that we have described only superficially. Language is so complex that in order to do justice to conceptually analyzing language, volumes would have to be written. Consequently, many arguments in this paper are only partially completed and there is a great deal more left to be said.

It should be made clear that we have been discussing sentences out of context—something that simply does not occur when language is actually used. Thus much of what has been said here may not be valid if the circumstances are different from "normal." As circumstances rarely are "normal," it is possible to take exception to a great many of the particulars presented here.

It was intended here only to show that language has a workable conceptual base and that the results of such an endeavor are well worth the effort. No claim is made that all of the problems of language analysis are solved by looking at things in our way, but we do feel that the problems have been made clearer.

Acknowledgments

This research is supported by Grant PHS MH 06645-10 from the National Institute of Mental Health, and in part by the Advanced Research Projects Agency of the Office of the Secretary of Defense (SD-183).

Much of the material in the section of this paper on Underlying Actions was formulated in conference style by the author and David Brill, John Caddy, Neil Goldman, Linda Hemphill, Charles Rieger, and Chris Riesbeck and is reported in greater detail in Schank et.al., 1972.

MODELS OF BELIEF SYSTEMS

Six

Simulations of
Belief Systems

Kenneth Mark Colby
Stanford University

In this chapter belief is taken to constitute a fundamental psychological process. Humans, as knowing systems, continually engage in judging whether their representations of experience are true or false, credible or incredible. How these credibility judgments can be simulated is the subject of this inquiry.

Computer Simulation

To understand the strategy of computer simulation of symbolic processes, it is necessary first to grasp a few basic concepts and definitions.

A *system* is defined as a structured combination of active elements that collaborate in governing a set of characteristic input-output behaviors. A *process* is defined as a sequence of states of the system over time. A *symbol* stands for, records, or represents something else, such as an object, event, or relation. Information consists of knowledge in a symbolic code. The rationale for constructing a symbol-processing computer model of a system is similar to that found generally in the sciences. It can be summarized under three purposes.

1. To simplify complex systems and processes but retain their essential input-output characteristics.
2. To manipulate the model experimentally because it is more manageable than the modelled system.
3. To explain the input-output characteristics of the modelled system.

Two symbol processing systems (S_1 and S_2) are considered input-output (I-O) equivalent when the symbolic I-O pairs of (S_1) under certain conditions are not distinguishable from the symbolic I-O pairs of (S_2) under similar conditions with specified dimensions. To *simulate* the I-O behavior of a primary symbol-processing system (S_1) a secondary system is constructed in the form of a computer model (S_2) with I-O behavior resembling that of (S_1) along certain dimensions. The systems are considered functionally equivalent in that they transform similar symbolic inputs into similar symbolic outputs. Interesting complications are introduced when the primary system is itself a model and the computer model therefore represents a model of a model.

In asserting that two symbol-processing systems, model and modelled, are equivalent is not to claim that they have the same underlying physical mechanisms.

In simulating human thought with a computer model we draw from two sources, psychology and symbolic computation. We propose an analogy between two systems known to be capable of processing information — people and computers. The properties compared are obviously not physical (brain wetware and computer hardware) but functional. We postulate that the less understood mechanisms of thought in a person are similar to the better understood symbolic computation that takes place in a computer. The analogy is one of functional similarity. If the two are similar at the manifest I-O level of linguistic communication, as measured by indistinguishability tests, are they to be considered similar in their inner underlying processes? How stringent is the demand for functional similarity? Must there be a point-to-point correspondence at every level? What is a point and what is a level? Even deeper, does similarity of internal organization *explain* similarity of observable behavior.

In constructing an algorithm, one synthesizes an organization of collaborating functions. A function takes some symbolic structure as input and yields some other symbolic structure as output. Two equivalent functions, i.e. having the same input and yielding the same value, can differ at some level of detail, as every algorithmist knows, so that the resemblance is not claimed to be complete and exact in *every* detail. Only parallelism of behavior at some level is sought.

Consider an elementary programming problem that students in symbolic computation are often required to solve. Given a list (L) of symbols, L = (ABCD), as input, construct a function that will convert this list to a list (RL) in which the order of the symbols is reversed, RL = (DCBA). Here are examples of functions that will carry out the task of reversal. (They are written in the high-level programming language MLISP).

```
REVERSE1   (L);
   BEGIN
   NEW RL;
   RETURN FOR NEW I IN L DO
        RL ← I CONS RL;
   END;
```

```
REVERSE2  (L);
   BEGIN
   NEW RL, LEN;
   LEN ← LENGTH (L);
   FOR NEW N ← 1 TO LEN DO
         RL [N] ← L [LEN-N+1];
   RETURN RL;
   END;
REVERSE3  (L);
   REVERSE3A (L,NIL);
REVERSE3A (L,RL);
   IF NULL L THEN RL
   ELSE REVERSE3A (CDR L, CAR L CONS RL);
```

Each of these computational functions takes a list of symbols as input and produces a new list in which the order of the symbols on the input list is reversed. It is at this I-O level that the functions operate similarly. A careful scrutiny of the code of these functions, however, reveals differences in addition to similarities at the level of the individual instructions. For example, REVERSE1 steps down the input list (L), takes each symbol found and inserts it at the front of the newly created reverse list (RL). On the other hand REVERSE2 counts the length of the input list (L) using another function LENGTH. It then uses index expressions on both sides of an assignment operator (←): (a) to obtain a position in the new list (RL); (b) to obtain a symbol in the input list; and (c) to assign it to that position in the reversed list (RL). REVERSE1 and REVERSE2 are similar in that they use FOR loops whereas REVERSE3, which calls another function REVERSE3A, does not. REVERSE3A is different in that it contains an explicit IF expression; the others do not.

The similarities and differences between these functions can be cited as long as we are clear about levels and degrees of detail. Computer scientists in symbolic computation would consider these reversing functions as functionally equivalent since they take the same symbolic structures as input and yield the same symbolic structures as an output value.

The point of this programming example is to illustrate some of the ambiguities and complexities in asserting that two systems work in similar ways. In constructing a model of a symbol-processing system we are proposing a set of plausible, possible (not impossible) symbol-processing functions. If the model is testable, one can sort out the more acceptable systems of functions from the conceivable set. Other models are certainly possible and the tests help decide which of the rivals is to be preferred.

Belief Systems

Some further preliminary definitions and assumptions will now be sketched. A *belief* consists of a judgment of *credibility* toward a conceptualization. *Credibility* represents a judgment of acceptance, rejection, or suspended judgment. A *conceptualization* consists of a conceptual structure made up of concepts and their interrelations. Concepts can be viewed as atomic units and conceptualizations as molecular units. A conceptualization is an interpretation relativized to an individual holder. Beliefs in turn are composed of representations of situations (facts) or relations between situations (rules).

Beliefs are nonobservable theoretical entities postulated to account for certain observable relations in human behavior. The statement "person X believes Y" is equivalent to a series of conditional statements that assert what person X would say under certain circumstances. The usual empirical decision procedure for collecting and evaluating beliefs is an experimental test situation in which an experimenter E, presents to a language user U, an assertion A in the language L at time t. If A represents a definite description of a situation conceptualized as C, then the linguistic reaction of U to A (acceptance, rejection, or agnosticism) is taken by E to be an empirical indicator of U's belief in C during the time interval t. That is the experimenter infers and asserts more formally:

$$U \text{ Believe}_E \text{ C,t}$$

For example, suppose I offer you the sentence "Oswald shot Kennedy" and then ask you whether you accept it as true, reject it as false, or remain agnostic toward it. The sentence describes a situation which you can judge as having been the case or not the case. Most people have already formed a credibility judgment about this event so the response evoked by the question is the result of simple retrieval. However, if I offer you a sentence you probably have never heard before, e.g. "Oswald was a Japanese agent," you will evaluate, using some computation process, the credibility of the situation described and respond with a judgement.

From this it should be clear that the observables being modelled are what people say about their beliefs in certain observer-observed interactions. To explain the observables we postulate a structure composed of non-observable theoretical entities. A useful analogy can be drawn from classical mechanics. (In the human sciences one should never use examples from physics.) To explain certain observable relations between bodies, a non-observable, gravitational force is postulated.

A belief system has *grounds*, evidence, or warranting reasons for each belief held. In humans this supporting evidence orginates experientially from facts of observation, from experimentation, from memory, from self-knowledge, from testimony of others, and from inferences. Each belief is potentially an antecedant premise for arriving at consequent conclusions through inference rules. To evaluate the credibility of a conceptualization new to the system or to revise the credibility of an old belief, we postulate several factors as operative. They are termed source, direct evidence, foundation, and consistency. *Source* refers to the credibility of information arriving from some sender (including the Self, at times). *Direct evidence* refers to a belief already held by the system. The *foundation* for a belief (B) represents a sum of those beliefs in the system which imply (B) according to the system's inference rules. *Consistency* represents a sum of those beliefs in the system which (B) implies according to inference rules.

Each belief's credibility is assumed to be a judgement based on a source, direct evidence, foundation, and consistency. A valid or sound belief (B) is one in which the evidence supports (B) and the degree of credibility in (B) corresponds to the strength of the evidence. An invalid or pathological belief is one for which there is no supporting evidence or the degree of credibility assigned is greater than the evidence warrants. Rationalization is a process in which a belief is offered to justify an already chosen preference.

For a very long time the nature of human belief has been the concern of philosophers. Although their contributions contained a welter of good ideas, they were limited in being piecemeal, in being state descriptions rather than process descriptions and often in being too abstract to connect with empirical levels of test situations. Because philosophers lacked the concept of an algorithm or effective procedure, they were unable to construct working models of belief processes. Their literary formulations could not be actualized as models and hence could neither be tested for their process consequences nor experimented with for their correspondence with empirical fact.

Mathematicians and probability theorists, starting as early as the 17th century, began to associate the concept of probability of hypotheses with credibility. Among the various interpretations of the concept probability, "subjective" or "personal" probability emerged and has commonly been taken to represent degree of belief, although this view contains assumptions that are often inapplicable to everyday credibility judgments by humans. Personal probability states that if one's degree of belief in a statement is p, then one's degree of belief in a denial of the statement is 1-p. Human belief systems violate this assumption with seeming ease, so perhaps personal probability could be interpreted to mean what one *should* believe on the basis of the evidence. As a normative theory it has difficulties also, because when there is an inconsistency between two beliefs, the theory does not help in deciding which belief to change or how to change it.

Economic and statistical theories of preference and utility combine concepts of probability and desirability. Expected utility is a product of the probability of a statement and the desirability of its consequences. Probability is "objective" i.e. a countable relative frequency, a ratio of m events to a total of n events. Again, to make the proper numerical assignments, the probabilities are assumed to add up to 1. My view is that credibility is a concept that should be kept distinct from that of objective probability, in that objective probability requires an exhaustive and mutually exclusive set of alternatives to make numerical assignments and credibility does not. Since human credibility functions in real life do not obey fundamental axioms of subjective or objective probability theory, there is good reason to give credibility a separate status.

This view comes close to that of the economist Schackle [1969] who offers further arguments for separating the concepts of credibility and probability.

"Objective, actuarial probability has no relevance for the analysis of decision in the face of uncertainty, because when objective probabilities can be applied there is no uncertainty."

The relevant dimension of belief is possibility rather than probability. Hence one can believe both that X is the case and X is not the case with equal degree since both can be conceived as equally possible.

Cognitive psychologists have produced a large amount of theoretical and experimental work relevant to the nature of human belief. An appreciation of those efforts can be gained from the volume entitled *Theories of Cognitive Consistency* (Abelson, et al., 1969). Work in cognitive psychology has suffered two drawbacks from the standpoint of simulation. The theories — except for Abelson's — have not been cast in an explicit, effective form and hence they represent unsettleable theories. Also the interpretation of the experimental results has been highly contradictory and there has been little agreement between warring cognitive schools.

Some Beginnings

About 10 years ago I began attempts to simulate human belief processes on a computer. This interest in symbol-processing concepts and instruments grew out of a curiosity about and a dissatisfaction with regnant theories of human behavior which attempted to explain complex higher mental processes. Stimulus-response theories answered the wrong questions about rats and were too simple to provide satisfactory explanations of complex human behavior. Psychodynamic formulations were more arresting in that attempts were made to ask better questions about human conceptual complexity, although they were unsystematic and in the main untestable. Biological theories were adequate only for biological phenomena and could not logically be expected to offer explanations of higher-level functions such as symbol-processing.

In addition the languages in which theories were expressed at the time were unsatisfactory. If there are several hundred statements in a theory, it is hard to assess logically what their conjunction implies. A theory expressed in ordinary prose sentences is difficult to analyze dynamically. That is, the consequences of these statements are difficult if not impossible to follow out as steps in a process over time. If the theory is to be cast in a mathematical form, it becomes a question of the appropriate mathematics to express the assumptions of the theory: geometry?, set theory?, Markov process?, graph theory? Statistical statements are descriptive rather than explanatory and they do not allow one to come to grips with the individuality so characteristic of humans. As will be seen, I consider the preferred mathematics to be qualitative and relational rather than quantitative or metric. The relations will be expressed as functions in the mathematical sense of transforming input structures into corresponding output structures.

In attempting to explain complex human behavior, a perspective is adopted to classify phenomena and determine what representation gives a correct logical level of abstraction. Strategies of the computer sciences are suitable for these purposes. At the heart of these strategies is the concept of an "effective procedure" which consists of (a) a language in which rules of behavior can be specified and (b) a symbol processor which rapidly and reliably can carry out steps of the behavioral processes specified by the rules. The specifications of (a) are called a program or algorithm whereas (b) consists of the machine processor of a computer system.

A computer as a symbol processor is a set of physical mechanisms that can carry out the consequences of the theoretical assumptions. The demands that a psychological theory be in 'effective form' means that it be realized in an algorithm which can run on a computer. To be effective the algorithm must work. If a theory contains only a few symbols and rules for their manipulation, utilizing an effective procedure may provide no advantages. But when the theory is a complex and voluminous number of different symbols and rules, then an effective procedure becomes a desideratum if the theory is to be both satisfactory and intelligible as an explanation.

In the early 60s there were great difficulties in casting theories in an effective form. The available programming languages were clumsy, hardware memory was extremely limited, access to the machine was difficult, and — in the absence of time-shared systems — results of the computer runs were slow in returning. Today all this has changed as we have excellent high-level list processing languages, virtually unlimited memory, and time-sharing systems that permit real-time interaction with a machine processor that yields quick results.

In trying to develop a new perspective, time is needed to decide what are worthwhile questions to ask and whether their answers are realizable. The basis for the decision often cannot be grounded in pure thought, but must be found through actualized experience. My own experience was typical of the beginning enthusiast who over-reaches and undertakes too difficult a problem at the start. Having conducted many laboratory experiments on free-association and having had years of clinical experience with neurotic processes, my initial hope was to simulate both (!) the free-associative thought characteristic of a neurotic process and its changes under the influence of a psychotherapist's interventions. As the sequel will show, this high-spirited goal became considerably tempered by the jostles and poundings of exploratory inquiry.

To construct an algorithm for mental functions fundamental theoretical units must be chosen. As the basic atomic unit I decided upon the abstract entity, concept. A concept is defined as a representation of an object or objects occupying space and/ or time, of attributes specifying what an object is or does, and of relations between objects. The molecular unit is a structure of concepts, a conceptualization that represents situations and relations between situations. Concepts in turn are connectible to the labels of linguistic word-names. Thus examples of concepts could be "John," "women," and "fear." A conceptualization could be "John fears women." A belief then represents a credibility judgment of acceptance, rejection, or agnosticism (suspended judgment) toward a conceptualization. Independently R. P. Abelson of

Yale University formed similar ideas. When we met at a conference on simulation in 1962 (Tomkins and Messick), we were surprised and delighted to find one another so enlightened. Over the years we have exchanged ideas freely and much of my work in this area has been influenced by Abelson.

Neurotic Belief

In simulating a process the model builder begins with characteristic input-output data from the system and some theoretical principles about how the system might work. In trying to simulate neurotic processes the data consisted of tape-recordings and notes regarding natural language utterances in psychotherapeutic dialogue. The theory realized by the model was a simple conflict theory of neurosis in which the system, when faced with severe conflict between two or more beliefs, attempted to reduce conflict by executing symbol-processing transformations on these beliefs in conflict.

The data-base of the program consisted of 114 beliefs paraphrased from natural language into a simplified English format, a 275 word-name dictionary and 50 inference rules. The internal representational format of beliefs was an ordered string of word-named concepts (actor–action–object) plus two weights, one representing a degree of credibility and one a degree of interest. The dictionary contained word-named concepts with additional information about them such as their subsets, supersets, parts of speech, synonyms, antonyms, etc. The inference rules, similar to the if-then conditional rules of English contained, in addition to the constants of word-names, variables for saying things about objects without naming particular ones. Inference rules related two conceptualizations by means of consequence relations, such as "If X likes Y then X helps Y" where X and Y are persons.

The program consisted of a set of procedure calls which processed "pools" of conceptually related beliefs to search for conflict and then resolution by trying various transformations of the beliefs. The neurotic algorithm progressed through cycles of processing with a cycle beginning with the formation of a working pool of beliefs. A belief of highest current interest was selected as the nucleus of a pool and beliefs relevant to the nucleus were collected to form the constituents of a pool. The criteria of relevance in a belief depended on the number of conceptual contents that matched those of the nucleus. The belief of highest interest, the "regnant," was selected for output expression. Before it could be expressed, however, it was matched against other beliefs in the pool in a search for conflict.

Conflict was defined as an inconsonance between two beliefs when their relevant rules (relations between situations) had contradictory consequences. For example the belief:

1. I want sex

would conflict with the belief

2. Sex disturbs me

if the following relevant rules existed in the system

3. If X disturbs Y then Y avoids X
4. If X wants Y then X seeks Y.

Substituting the terms of the beliefs 1 and 2 for the variables in the rules 3 and 4, a conflict was found because of the antitheses in the concepts of seeking and avoiding.

A fluctuating conflict-threshold determined the fate of the regnant belief. If the degree of conflict aroused in the pool was less than the threshold, the regnant was expressed. Otherwise the regnant underwent a transformation. For example, the regnant

5. I hate my father

might be transformed into

6. I hate my brother

or more drastically into

7. My father hates me.

A complete description of the transformations and how they were selected can be found in Colby (1964).

After output of a regnant or its transformation, another belief in the pool was selected as the next regnant and the same sequence of processing was attempted. A cycle continued until interest in the pool itself dropped below a threshold or the repetition of conflict became too great. Then a nucleus would be selected for a new pool and another cycle would begin.

Two things were learned from experience with this model. First, the data-base was too thin to generate the variety of linguistic input-output behavior characteristic of clinical dialogues. It was not the absolute size of the data that mattered, but how rich were the relations between concepts and the relations between conceptualizations. The second—and perhaps greatest—drawback to the model lay in evaluation difficulties. We want the input-output behavior of a model to resemble to the I-O behavior of the modelled process. Besides crude face validity, one would want some measured estimate of the degree of resemblance. The use of expert judges (see p. 277) provides one way of evaluating the success of a simulation at the I-O level. But to achieve reliability, judges must be able to agree on their observations. There is very little agreement among psychiatrists regarding what characterizes the observable I-O behavior of neurotic processes. Hence, in a later attempt to simulate psychopathological belief (see p. 265), I chose paranoid processes about which a high level of agreement exists among psychiatrists.

Normal Belief

The interest here was to collect a large number of beliefs from a "normal" person and to write an effective procedure for processing—in a variety of experimental ways—a given input sentence in order to judge its credibility. (My collaborators were Lawrence Tesler and Horace Enea, Computer Science Department, Stanford University.) That is, we wanted to explore what made a difference in varying factors theoretically assumed to be important in reaching judgments of credibility. Such experiments are Baconian in spirit (I wonder what would happen if we did X) rather than Galilean which attempts to decide initially between those rival hypotheses having appreciable prior probabilities.

The data were collected by a combination of interview and self-inventory methods. Our informant was a 30 year old married mother of a small girl. The data were natural language statements regarding child-raising and family relations. The statements were paraphrased by us, with the informant's corroboration, into a data-base of symbolic expressions in the programming language MLISP. The data-base consisted of 611 beliefs (descriptions of situations), rules (descriptions of relations between situations), and dictionary definitions.

It is by now axiomatic in science that to gain knowledge of a system the observer perturbs it somewhat. In observing the moon the effect of the observer is negligible, but in collecting beliefs the observer-observed interaction can be considerable. For a human informant to be honest and candid about his beliefs, he must be trusted like any other member of a research team. Some apprehension as to how he is viewed by the others because of his beliefs is to be expected. Over the months that it requires to collect and represent beliefs, evaluational apprehension diminishes if the observers maintain an attitude of neutral interest and open approval of the informant's self-disclosure.

Another principle we followed was to select a domain of beliefs in our informant which might be expected to be stable over time, barring major environmental events. Beliefs about everyday political crises, for example, are notoriously transient in interest. The domain of parent-child relations remained quite stable over many months of investigation.

Although the data representation captured by paraphrase much of the meaning of the informant's natural language statements, it was still too simplified and clumsy. For those interested in developing their own data representations, I shall give some details which might be helpful for others to adopt or avoid.

Each fact was a three-place predicate without tense, location, or adverbial modifiers. Examples of facts describing situations, two of which are embedded, are:

```
(CHILD₁ HAS AGGRESSIVENESS)
(SELF NOTLIKE (CHILD₁ HAS AGGRESSIVENESS))
(SELF FAIL (SELF INDUCE (HUSBAND NOTHAS AGGRESSIVENESS)))
```

Each conceptualization is represented as a list or list structure in which the first element in the list stands for an agent, the second for an action and the third for an object which can be another conceptualization. In this representation, knowledge about the world is described in terms of states of affairs or situations. Situations change or remain the same. By performing actions agents produce or prevent situations, e.g.:

```
(SELF PRODUCE (HOUSE BE CLEAN))
(SELF PREVENT (CHILD₁ PLAYWITH MATCHES))
```

By omitting action, agents leave a situation unchanged or let a situation happen, e.g.

```
(SELF LEAVE (HUSBAND BE STUDENT))
(SELF LET (HUSBAND SPANK CHILD₁ ))
```

Rules contain variables and connect two situations. Examples are (variables underlined):

```
(If THEPARENT SLAP HISCHILD then THEPARENT DISTRESS HISCHILD)
(If HISCHILD HAS SICKNESS then THEPARENT WORRY (SICKNESS
    PRODUCE (HISCHILD HAS DEATH)))
```

A problem familiar to those who construct such data representations develops in the unambiguous binding of variables. We handled this by inventing "constrained" variables. In the preceding rules THEPARENT and HISCHILD are constrained variables. For the rule to be applied to a particular person he would have to be in the relation 'isparentof' to a particular child. Thus the fact:

```
(JAN IS PARENTOF CHILD₅ )
```

would permit "JAN" and "CHILD₅" to be substituted in these rules.

Constrained variables also aid in representing complex descriptions. For example, the natural language statement:

"If a person tries to produce a situation and fails, then he is dissatisfied."

can be represented as:

```
(If ANYTRYER FAIL (ANYTRYER PRODUCE ANYSITUATION) then
  ANYTRYER HAS DISSATISFACTION)
```

The intricate problem of representing family relations was solved by constructing a list structure for each family group where the first element on the list represents the family name, the second element the name of the husband, the third element the name of the wife, the fourth element a list of sons and the fifth element a list of daughters. For example:

```
(GFAM HJAN JAN (CHILD₅ CHILD₆ ) NIL)
```

indicates a family with two sons and no daughters.

The algorithm could automatically expand the second through fourth elements appropriately. Thus from the preceding family definition the algorithm knows that, for example:

```
(HJAN ISA PERSON)
(HJAN ISA MAN)
(HJAN ISFATHEROF CHILD₆)
(HJAN ISPARENTOF CHILD₆)
(HJAN ISFATHEROF CHILD₅)
(HJAN ISPARENTOF CHILD₅)
(HJAN ISSPOUSEOF JAN)
(HJAN ISHUSBANDOF JAN)
(HJAN ISA SPOUSE)
(HJAN ISA PARENT)
(HJAN ISA HUSBAND)
(HJAN ISA FATHER)
```

In processing these beliefs we again (surprise!) ran into the limitations of sparsely related data-bases. Although we had a large amount of information from the informant, there was not a sufficient density of details about any one topic. We postulated that consistency guided the search algorithm, i.e. to maintain consistency, searches were conducted more deeply along consistent paths (the candidate for belief implies beliefs already held) than inconsistent paths (the candidate implies the negation of beliefs held), but this proved to be inefficient. It was pointless to do deductions to decide whether to do more deductions. One result was that the algorithm searched too long and inconclusively in a combinatorily explosive space of hypothetical low-relevance beliefs. Instead, the search should be guided by what the system firmly believes, as well as by factors of import, salience and desirability. How to incorporate these factors in an efficient search algorithm remains an open problem.

An Artificial Belief System

The programs described thus far attempted to represent human belief. Another approach to the study of credibility functions would be to construct a normative system, representing the ideal of how a system ought to judge credibility. (My collaborator was David C. Smith of the Computer Science Department, Stanford University). The advantage of such an approach is that since the structure and starting conditions of the artifact are entirely under our control we can simplify and bring under control some of the great variability found in belief processes. Instead of placing a human under the artificial conditions of a laboratory experiment, we can subject the artificial system to 'naturally-occurring' conditions of human linguistic communication.

Faced again with the natural language barrier, we decided to run around it by restricting the human's input to a limited verb vocabulary and to certain syntactic forms. The first form was a statement pattern consisting of a subject-field, a verb-field and a modifier-field. The subject and modifier fields could contain any number of words of any type except linking verbs. Their verb field was limited to third person singular forms in three tenses of the linking verbs "be," "seem," "appear," "feel," and "become." The verb could optionally be preceded by an auxiliary ("can," "could," "must," "ought," "would," "should," "shall," "will") and optionally followed by a modal operator ("certainly," "probably," "possibly"). Determiners ("a," "an," "the") and negation ("not") were allowed. A statement ended with a period. Examples of possible statements follow:

1. "John is a man."
2. "John is probably not an intellectual."
3. "My uncle John is a truck driver."
4. "Peter will certainly not be a problem in school."

Two interrogative forms were permitted: subject-verb-modifier-question mark or verb-subject-modifier-question mark. These are examples of possible questions:

1. "Is John an intellectual?"
2. "John is not an intellectual?"

The final form allowed consequence rules in the form: X, verb-field, modifier-field (implies) X, verb-field, modifier-field. The meaning of the term "implies" was left open to a number of logical, causal, temporal, sequential, and associative interpretations. Examples of rules are as follows:

1. "X is a man implies X is certainly a person."
2. "X is an Italian implies X is probably a Catholic."
3. "X is a white South African implies X is possibly racist."

Although a great deal of natural language thinking can be paraphrased into this English-like language, its deficiencies are obvious. Since belief is a theoretical entity used to explain relations between users of a language and certain expressions, an algorithm capable of interpreting natural language at the "front end" of belief-system simulations is needed. Chapters in this volume by Simmons, Schank, and Winograd describe what such "understanders" must be capable of doing.

Using this restricted language a person could input statements, rules, and questions into the system. Statements and rules were stored under the concepts appearing in their subject and modifier fields. Questions were answered by searching memory for direct facts or by inferring conclusions from facts and rules. Rules were combined through backward chaining to a depth of three levels.

When the informant finished inputting whatever information he wished, the program asked him questions to increase its useful data base. For example, if the informant had told it three statements in which two subjects share a modifier but another modifier of one subject was not found for the other subject, the program would attempt to fill in the gap by asking the appropriate question. To acquire new rules the program would ask about the relations between two modifiers shared by the same subject.

After the end of this question period, the major work of the program was undertaken, namely to assign a credibility to the statements just received from an informant. The credibility assigned was a function of preliminary credibility of the source, direct evidence, foundation and consistency. Each informant was initially given a weak positive credibility. Direct evidence consisted of finding an identical statement or its negation in the data base. The foundation for a statement (s) consisted of the weighted average of the credibilities of beliefs in the data base (Bi) which imply the proposition or its negation.

$$\text{FOUNDATION (s)} = \frac{\Sigma \ (Bi \Rightarrow s)}{\Sigma \ (Bi \Rightarrow s) + \Sigma \ (Bi \Rightarrow \neg \ s)}$$

Consistency was simply the converse of foundation.

$$\text{CONSISTENCY (s)} = \frac{\Sigma \ (s \Rightarrow Bi)}{\Sigma \ (s \Rightarrow Bi) + \Sigma \ (s \Rightarrow \neg \ Bi)}$$

The formula for computing credibility was:

CREDIBILITY = PRELIM + ALPHA × (DIREV + (RATIO × OMEGA × FOUND)
+ (RATIO × (1-OMEGA) × CONSIS))

PRELIM represents a preliminary credibility of the source. ALPHA is a factor weighting the importance of direct evidence, foundation, and consistency. DIREV represents direct evidence. OMEGA is a factor weighting the relative importance of foundation and consistency. RATIO is a dynamic factor which varies OMEGA, depending on the relative amounts of foundation and consistency, such that consistency counts more when there is little foundation.

Such an artificial belief system can be used for many purposes, e.g. as a basis for the beliefs of robots that interact in the human world. We studied mainly the credibility assigned a new informant and his statements after the system had been exposed to conversations with several other informants. The chief difficulty was the size of the data base. Once it increased to a few thousand beliefs, the program spent too much time in deducing remote conclusions to be practical. As with the program described in the previous section, we need more efficient ways of guiding a search through a large data space so that good credibility judgments are reached with some optimal minimum of cognitive work.

A Simulation of Paranoia

Introduction

The models discussed in the previous sections were not treated in any great detail in order to leave room to describe a successful simulation at some length. This paranoid model merits detailed consideration because it highlights many of the problems typical of constructing and validating simulations of belief processes. (My collaborators were Sylvia Weber Russell and Franklin Dennis Hilf, Computer Science Department, Stanford University.)

We selected the process of paranoid belief because (a) we had some theoretical notions about the system and process involved, (b) the variability was not as great as in normal and neurotic belief, (c) we believed we had a pragmatic and sufficient way of handling natural language expressions, and (d) since there is agreement among psychiatrists regarding the concept named "paranoid," we could use expert judges in validating the model by indistinguishability tests.

The model stands as an actual—but non-human—case of paranoid belief processes. The model's input-output linguistic behavior in the test situation of a diagnostic psychiatric interview is identifiable by psychiatric judges as "paranoid." This simulation is not an attempt to duplicate or reproduce the behavior of a given human. In constructing simulations there are two possible approaches. One is to attempt to model an actual person. The other is to create a hypothetical individual as a member of some class of real persons and then compare him for resemblances with other members of that class. We chose the latter approach in developing a paranoid model. Our artificial case is that of an imagined, hypothetical individual whose linguistic I-O behavior imitates the linguistic I-O behavior of humans when their symbol processing is dominated by a mode which psychiatrists conceive as paranoid.

This model is considered a theoretical model because its inner structure embodies an explanatory account of the complex phenomena of paranoid communicative behavior. An explanatory account contains statements of lawlike generalizations. In order to explain concrete individual events, it also contains singular statements of individual initial conditions. In order to run and test the model, the general law-like principles must be combined with the singular conditions to generate the I-O behavior of this individual hypothetical case.

Paranoia

The term "paranoia" (Greek: para = beside; nous = mind) originally referred to a state of being out of one's mind. Currently the term has mainly adjectival status in psychiatric nomenclature, e.g. "paranoid schizophrenia." Paranoid processes represent a cluster of signs and symptoms, a syndrome, that can occur in conjunction with a number of underlying disorders, some of known causes (e.g. amphetamine psychosis) and some of unknown origin e.g. (paranoid personality). The concept *paranoid* represents one of the few categories in which there is good (85–95%) agreement among psychiatrist's judgments not only for presence-absence but also for severity of the syndrome.

The most severe sign of a paranoid process consists of a fixed system of malevolence delusions. Delusions are defined as false beliefs. They can range in degree from complete conviction to labile suspicions. A paranoid patient accepts certain beliefs as true whereas other observers reject the same beliefs as false. The decision regarding truth or falsity rests on human judgments, and although these are fallible measures, they are the best we have. A malevolence delusion consists of a false (to onlookers) belief that other persons have evil intentions towards the holder of the belief. Other components of the paranoid syndrome are observable behaviors characterized as self-reference, hypersensitivity, suspiciousness, guardedness, evasiveness, secretiveness, irritability, accusatoriness, hostility, argumentativeness, and sarcasm. Judgments regarding these constructs rest on observations of the patient's input-output behavior in a psychiatric interview.

There has been no lack of formulations proposed to explain the puzzling phenomena of paranoid behavior. A review of them can be found in Swanson, et al. (1970). Most of these formulations could not be considered theories of scientific status because their statements were not connected systematically and were too vague or ambiguous to be testable. Since they were not testable, there was no decision procedure by which their acceptability as explanations could be evaluated. A simulation model is systematic, testable and refutable because its observable I-O pairs can be compared with observable I-O pairs from human counterparts of the process being simulated. One test situation involves interviews conducted by psychiatric judges.

A theory of paranoid processes

Because the algorithm for this model embodies a theory, the most direct way of understanding the theory is to read a listing of the algorithm. Few people, however, can read MLISP — the language in which our model is coded — so that the theory must be briefly described in English with the aid of a few figures.

We first postulate a structure of strategies which govern paranoid I-O behavior of the patient ("Self") in a diagnostic interview with a psychiatrist ("Other"). The top level intention of the paranoid mode of information-processing is to determine the Other's intention. Messages from the Other are scanned to arrive at an interpretation of the Other's intention whether malevolent, benevolent, or neutral (See Box 6.1). Malevolence is defined as a believed conceptualization, on the part of Self, of mental harm and/or physical threat by some Other to the Self. During an interview the input strategies of the paranoid model first operate to detect malevolence by scrutinizing, understanding, and interpreting the linguistic expressions of the Other in order to recognize explicit and implicit harms and threats.

Psychological harm is defined as an explicit or implicit attempt on the part of the Other (a) to humiliate, and/or (b) to subjugate the Self. For example, an explicit example of (a) would be the input expression:

1. "You are hostile."

while an implicit example would be:

2. "Tell me about your sexlife."

An explicit example of (b) might be:

3. "You should have electric shock."

and an implicit example would be:

4. "Perhaps you should stay in the hospital longer."

Physical threat is defined as an explicit or implicit intent of the Other (a) to physically injure the Self and/or (b) to have it brought about that the Self is physically injured. (See Box 6.1 for examples.)

We assume that, in scanning the input, a paranoid Self is differentially sensitive to terms which refer to concepts of self-concerns and self-worth. It is also sensitive to terms pointing to "flare" concepts, i.e. concepts related, at various conceptual-semantic distances, to the concepts in a delusional network. Expressions which touch on flare concepts in turn tend to activate the delusional network.

Once malevolence, as defined above, is detected, two reactions occur. The first is an affective reaction involving values of internal affect–states of fear, anger, and mistrust which change depending upon the conceptualized nature of the input. The recognition of psychological harm elicits anger whereas a physical threat elicits fear. Mistrust arises as a function of the negative affect-experiences, fear and anger, which the Self has been subjected to by the Other over the course of an interview.

The second reaction to a detection of malevolence consists of linguistic output responses which attempt to counteract and reduce the Other's malevolence. We

Box 6.1 Angular Brackets enclose Concepts being Defined. Arrow means 'is defined as.' Vertical Bar represents 'or.' CONCEPTUALIZATIONS ([ ]) represent Illustrative Examples of the Meaning extracted from Input Expressions, not the Literal Expressions themselves.

⟨OTHER'S INTENTION⟩ ← ⟨MALEVOLENCE⟩ | ⟨BENEVOLENCE⟩ | ⟨NEUTRAL⟩

MALEVOLENCE-DETECTION RULES

1. ⟨malevolence⟩ ← ⟨mental harm⟩ | ⟨physical threat⟩
2. ⟨mental harm⟩ ← ⟨humiliation⟩ | ⟨subjugation⟩
3. ⟨physical threat⟩ ← ⟨direct attack⟩ | ⟨induced attack⟩
4. ⟨humiliation⟩ ← ⟨explicit insult⟩ | ⟨implicit insult⟩
5. ⟨subjugation⟩ ← ⟨constraint⟩ | ⟨coercive treatment⟩
6. ⟨direct attack⟩ ← CONCEPTUALIZATIONS ([you get electric shock], [are you afraid mafia kill you?])
7. ⟨induced attack⟩ ← CONCEPTUALIZATIONS ([I tell mafia you], [does mafia know you are in hospital?])
8. ⟨explicit insult⟩ ← CONCEPTUALIZATIONS ([you are hostile], [you are mentally ill?])
9. ⟨implicit insult⟩ ← CONCEPTUALIZATIONS ([tell me your sexlife], [are you sure?])
10. ⟨constraint⟩ ← CONCEPTUALIZATIONS ([you stay in hospital], [you belong on locked ward])
11. ⟨coercive treatment⟩ ← CONCEPTUALIZATIONS ([I hypnotize you], [you need tranquilizers])

BENEVOLENCE-DETECTION RULES

1. ⟨benevolence⟩ ← ⟨positive attitude⟩ | ⟨positive story attitude⟩
2. ⟨positive attitude⟩ ← CONCEPTUALIZATIONS ([I want help you], [you understand me])
3. ⟨positive story attitude⟩ ← ⟨story interest⟩ | ⟨story agreement⟩
4. ⟨story interest⟩ ← ⟨topic comment⟩ | ⟨topic question⟩
5. ⟨topic comment⟩ ← CONCEPTUALIZATION ([bookies are not reliable])
6. ⟨topic question⟩ ← CONCEPTUALIZATION ([what did you do to bookie?])
7. ⟨story agreement⟩ ← CONCEPTUALIZATION ([I believe you], [you are right])

postulate two types of counteractions: one consisting of a contending counterattack when anger predominates and the other of withdrawal when fear and mistrust predominate. Subsequent paranoid behavior is highly dependent upon the reaction of the Other to these counteractions.

The definition of benevolence being used here is given in Box 6.1; a neutral intention consists of any topic not classified as malevolent or benevolent.

The generalizations of the above-described theory do not explain how a paranoid Self came to be that way, i.e. it is not an ontogenetic theory explaining how the system evolved. It attempts only to explain how the system works now in a particular circumscribed situation. Also the explanations account for the behavior of the system over a short period of time, the 20-60 minutes of a diagnostic psychiatric interview.

As mentioned, for an explanation to account for individual events, the lawlike statements must be combined with individual statements of initial conditions. For our model to work in a psychiatric interview, we invented a patient who is described briefly as follows:

> He is a 28 year old single man who works in the stockroom at Sears. He lives alone, has no siblings, and seldom sees his parents. He is sensitive about his lack of education, his religion, and the topic of sex. His hobby is gambling on horseraces both at the track and through bookies. A few months ago he quarrelled with a bookie, claiming the bookie did not pay off a bet correctly. After the quarrel it occurred to him that he so angered the bookie that the latter might have the underworld figures injure or kill him. He developed malevolence delusions about the underworld which became so frightening that he sought medical help and then accepted a recommendation of psychiatric hospitalization.

No attempt will be made here to describe in detail the model which realizes the above theory. A full description can be found in the article *Artificial Paranoia* (Colby, et al., 1971). Here I will simply sketch the model with some emphasis on its linguistic problems, since the experimental test situation for determining belief is a linguistic one and the problem of comprehending and interpreting natural language expressions is crucial for such a model.

A paranoid model

The dialogue algorithm is written in MLISP, a high-level programming language that translates into LISP 1.6 of the Stanford Artificial Intelligence Project. The algorithm requires 41-K including a data base of 18-K. It runs in an interactive mode on a DEC PDP 6/10 time-shared system. Communication with the model occurs by means of typed messages. The task of the algorithm is to understand and interpret input expressions in English and to produce affective, belief, and linguistic responses that characterize the paranoid mode. The beliefs of the program are not represented as fixed data, as in the previous models described, but as procedures or processes that govern I-0 behavior in certain ways.

To comprehend natural language input, a program ideally should have functions of combining syntax, semantics, and inferencing processes to produce a characteristic interpretation of the input expression. How to achieve this is still a difficult problem which we and others continue to work on (Schank, et al. 1970). In the absence of a well-developed English-understanding program at the time, we used a number of heuristics in the form of rewrite rules.

We optimistically assumed the input expressions would be syntactically simple rather than complex or compound. The program maps the elements of the input into an underlying structure — a conceptualization — consisting of a configuration of concepts. A conceptualization consists (minimally) of a predication on an attribute, on a conceptual object, or on a relation of a conceptual object to another conceptual object(s). A question consists of a conceptualization plus an interrogative indicator. Thus the surface questions:

"What is your work?"
"What sort of work do you do?"
"Where do you work?"
"What do you do for a living?"
"What is your job?"
"Do you have a job?"
"What is your occupation?"
Etc.

would all map into the conceptualization:

(your work?)

That is, the program recognizes that a question is being asked about the attribute "work" performed by the object "Self." This heuristic allows the program to recognize what the topic is but not always what precisely is being said about the topic.

An attribute is something one is, does or possesses (e.g. "you work," "your occupation"). A combination of "you" or "your" with some form of the attribute along with (optionally) another object or assisting concept will often adequately give the underlying meaning or at least partial meaning of the input. Lumping "you" and "your" together sometimes fails, of course. But this heuristic enables us to exploit the fact that lexical items which are different parts of speech are actually members of the same conceptual class, e.g. the verb "work" and the noun "occupation."

Compound and complex expressions are a potential source of confusion because the program does not recognize syntactic dividers between clauses. A topic on one side of the divider may be erroneously associated with an attribute on the other side. This can happen especially in the case of "you" and "your." A correct recognition of other concepts in the input may screen out the false interpretation, but this is one of the linguistic weaknesses of the method.

A linguistic problem typical of a psychiatric interview develops when the interviewer, instead of referring directly to predications about a topic, refers to the patient's expression of information about a topic, e.g. "Tell me whether you like your work" or "Tell me about your work." It is important that such expressions be interpreted as specific and general questions about the Self's work. These cases must be distinguished from cases in which the topic is left to the discretion of the model, e.g. "Is there anything you would like to tell me?" Interrogative imperatives or requests for information are thus recognized, but other imperatives or requests for action are usually not recognized. Such an ability would require either (1) an exclamation mark at the end of input, (2) reliance on clue words such as "please", or (3) a check for a missing implicit actor in an expression, which would require a full conceptual parser.

Another common linguistic problem in interviews involves interpersonal attitudes between interviewer and patient, e.g. "I understand you," or "Don't you trust me?" A question about the model's attributes contains no ambiguity as to who possesses the attribute, but ambiguities arise in these "I-you-me" types of expressions, e.g., in the expressions "Are you angry at me?" versus "You anger me." Positive or negative attitude tokens, their negations, and their passive forms must be recognized. For example, a passive form of the expression "You are afraid of me" would be "I frighten you." Confusions can also arise from the fact that some verbs can be used either to express a relational interpersonal attitude or as a meta-verb. (A meta-verb takes an entire conceptualization as its object.) Thus the program distinguishes "I believe you" from "I believe you are afraid."

Further illustrations of the program's linguistic powers and liabilities can be found in the interview examples on p. 280.

The overall task of the program, then, is to interpret input expressions and to produce internal and external responses that characterize the paranoid mode according to the theory described. The program must expect as input not only specific questions typical of a psychiatric interview and statements susceptible to paranoid misinterpretation, but also reactions of the interviewer to the model's last output reply. Thus the problem for the input strategies is when to operate in a "breadth-first" mode, looking in some fixed order for topics recognizable at the top level of the program, and when to operate in a "depth-first" mode keeping first in mind the context of the interview and the type of input that might be expected next in this context. For example, if a flare topic is under discussion, should the program first check for a change of topic, or should it check for reactions of the interviewer such as encouragement, disinterest, or further questions about the flare topic? The searches for various input situations should be as independent of one another as possible.

Problems for the output strategies are somewhat easier. Once the significance of an input expression has been construed, the type of linguistic response depends on a simple check of the affective and mistrust context of the interview. For any I-O pair a change in the internal affect-states draws context into consideration by a function which produces smaller absolute increases in the affect-variables. Values for jumps in the Fear or Anger variable for any I-O pair are given in percentages which are then applied to the difference between the current level and the maximum level. An insult, therefore, produces the same percentage increase in Anger at a low level as at a high one, but the absolute increase will be greater in the former case. The affect-states determine a context that governs not only individual variations in the affect-variables, but also the 'tone' of any linguistic output that is not the immediate context-independent reaction to an input.

The affect-variables operate as follows. Following the ith I-O pair, any increase in Fear or Anger is governed by the function.

$$VAR_i = VAR_{i-1} + RISE_{var} * (20\text{-}VAR_{i-1}).$$

(It should be emphasized that the actual numbers in the manipulation of affect variables are arbitrarily selected as part of the initial conditions for this particular hypothetical individual. The numbers are *not* intended to specify any quantitative aspect of the lawlike generalizations in the theory). For an increase in either Fear or Anger, the degree of mistrust is recomputed by the function

$$MISTRUST_i = MISTRUST_{i-1} + 0.5 * VAR * (20\text{-}MISTRUST_{i-1}).$$

Fear and Anger are assumed to be very "fluid" variables. Initial Fear or Anger may be low or mild (0 or 10 respectively on a scale of 0-20), may reach an extreme high during the interview and may drop to the initial value towards the end of a long interview. The usual drop in values occurs after each I-O pair by a subtraction of 1.0 from Anger and 0.3 from Fear. In the context of a "flare" discussion, the Fear level is not allowed to fall below 3.0 and in the context of expression of delusions, the lowest value is 5.0. Such minima are designed to reflect the model's guardedness that often accompanies the telling of his story to the interviewer.

The degree of mistrust is assumed to be a more "sticky" variable with an initial value of 0.0 reflecting an inherent mild mistrust. Mistrust falls very slowly (by 0.05 for each I-O pair) to a base level which rises for each increase in Fear or Anger according to the function:

$$MISTRUST\ 0_i = MISTRUST\ 0_{i-1} + 0.1 * VAR * (20\text{-}MISTRUST\ 0_{i-1}).$$

Thus any fear or anger induced by the interviewer can only result in the model being more distrustful of the interviewer by the end of the interview.

There are two versions, weak and strong, in which the program can be run. The following description of the main flow applies to both versions, except that in the weak version no elicitable delusional network exists. Also in the weak version, affect and mistrust variables are initialized to the lowest values and Fear and Anger rise more slowly with an accompanying effect of a slower rise in Mistrust.

The first four procedures scan the input in the following order for (1) a direct statement or an insinuation that the model is mentally ill, (2) reference to the delusional network, (3) reference to a sensitive area, and (4) reference to a flare concept. If none of these is recognized, the program checks for (5) the I-YOU-ME feature expressing an emotional or intellectual relationship between the interviewer and the model. This segment also checks for an apology or a direct threat, both of which are special cases.

The scanning order described is context-independent in that the detection of new concepts is sufficient to interrupt any current situation and to produce independent immediate responses. When no interruption occurs, the program checks Fear and Anger levels before considering its response to normal input. Fear is considered a stronger influence than Anger when both levels are high. If Fear is high, the model will avoid relating to the interviewer's input. That is, a question will evoke a suspicious query in return as to the interviewer's intentions in asking and an ordinary statement will be greeted by suspicious questions indicating the interviewer is being drawn into the model's delusional network. In extreme situations the ultimate escape occurs in that the model refuses to respond and terminates the interview. In the case of high Anger and moderate or low Fear, the model ignores the interviewer's inputs and attacks him with a hostility reflective of the Anger level.

Each of the five procedures sketched above can now be presented in more detail.

(1) An implication that the Self is mentally ill produces an increase in both Fear and Anger which differs depending on whether the input is a question or a statement, the latter being a more direct reference.

(2) The scanner searches the input for a reference to the delusional conspiracy, i.e. the Mafia, and for associated concepts, e.g. "being watched." A distinction is made between an initial reference to delusional topics and a reference indicating the interviewer's desire to continue exploring the delusional network. In the first case, there occurs an increase in Fear, the magnitude of which depends on whether the topic is strongly, weakly, or ambiguously associated with the delusional network and whether other delusion topics have been previously mentioned. (Ambiguous terms are those which may or may not be construed as delusional topics depending on whether the value of Mistrust is greater than a certain threshold.) In the latter the model's reply depends on whether it has anything more to say about its delusions.

(3) The detection of and response to self-reference in sensitive areas recognizes several degrees of self-reference as determined by (a) direct reference to Self, (b) reference to another person, persons, or a nonpersonal reference in conjunction with an area of sensitivity. These factors influence the strength of the affective and linguistic response generated. One idiosyncrasy is worth noting here. A positive reference in the input to Self, i.e. a compliment, will lower the values of the affect variables by the usual amount if Mistrust is low or moderate, but will raise Anger if Mistrust is above this level. Thus the model is sensitive to remarks it interprets as attempts at pacification.

(4) The process of checking for and responding to a flare concept involves (a) a quantitative hierarchy of eleven concepts, weighted again as part of initial condi-

tions in order of their relevance to the model's fears concerning the Mafia and (b) a directed graph in which each flare concept points to another flare concept as part of a strategy designed to lead the interviewer along paths to the topic of Mafia. (Thus, for example horses → horseracing → gambling → bookies → underworld → Mafia.) The program keeps track of flare concepts already mentioned and notes whether the interviewer is continuing the flare discussion. The mention of a new flare topic by the interviewer causes Fear to increase proportionate to the weight of the flare.

(5) Reference to an attitude held by one of the participants in the interview (e.g. "You seem afraid of me" or "I don't believe you") involves eight central interpersonal concepts each of which — it is expected — may occur in an explicitly or implicitly negative form. Expressions which represent a negative attitude of the interviewer toward the model induce a slight increase of Fear and Anger. In addition, it is expected that the interviewer might comment on some general attitude of the model not specifically directed at the interviewer (e.g. "you seem hostile").

In scanning for delusional-flare- or sensitivity-terms, a paranoid patient tends to ignore the context of such a term. Thus in simulating a paranoid process this characteristic is of advantage to a program which relies on key-word understanding. When questions devoid of word-groups that the program anticipates are presented to the model, the replies suffer from all the traditional inadequacies of this type of understanding. The problem is somewhat mitigated by another property of the paranoid mode, namely rigidity. The model has a tendency to focus on its delusional network and its associated flare concepts. When it fails to understand an input and has nothing else to say, the model will offer a flare or delusional statement if this satisfies the current context. In most cases it will appear that continuity is being maintained by a rigid one-track mind.

The question-answering procedures — referred to in flare and normal situations — recognize the possibility of three types of context for an input question. The program must first check to see whether there exists a new topic in the question since any other key word groups found cannot automatically be assumed to relate to the topic under discussion. This approach represents an assumption of zero context. If no new topic is found, a scan is made for word groups which might be a follow-up question on the part of the interviewer to the last output reply of the model. This heuristic is necessary to handle sentence fragments. If this fails, a check is made to see whether the input contains word groups associated directly with the last topic discussed. This method makes possible the direct association of key-words with their respective topics in the data base where they will be picked up independently of when they are referenced in the line of questioning. The appearance of a delusion- or flare-word in any of the answers that the model itself produces is of course recorded as a topic already mentioned for the rest of the interview.

In this first version of the model we did not attempt to generate English replies word-by-word in a paranoid style. The responses selected for output exist for the most part as ordered lists in the data base. The program steps through the appropriate list flagging the responses so that the same one cannot be output twice. In the case of certain suspicious responses about sensitive areas and leading questions about flare topics, the relevant term is "plugged into" the reply with due respect for syntactic considerations. We are currently working on the problem of generating responses in a paranoid style from a conceptual memory.

Validation

The term "validation" is used in various senses in both science and logic. It derives from the Latin *validus* = to be strong. I will use the term as follows: to validate a theory or model is to add strength or convincingness to its acceptability in achieving its purposes. As stated on p. 252 it is the purpose of a simulation model to generate I-O behavior which resembles that of its naturally occurring counterpart. A simulation can be considered successful at some measurable level when it passes tests for resemblance.

Resemblance tests may be adapted to serve as validation procedures for simulation models. The most famous and misquoted of these tests in computer science is Turing's Imitation Game proposed in 1950. Since it is so widely misunderstood, I shall quote Turing's original description at some length.

> "I propose to consider the question, 'Can machines think?' This should begin with definitions of the meaning of the terms 'machine' and 'think'. The definitions might be framed so as to reflect so far as possible the normal use of the words, but this attitude is dangerous. If the meaning of the words 'machine' and 'think' are to be found by examining how they are commonly used it is difficult to escape the conclusion that the meaning and the answer to the question, 'Can machines think?' is to be sought in a statistical survey such as a Gallup poll. But this is absurd. Instead of attempting such a definition I shall replace the question by another, which is closely related to it and is expressed in relatively unambiguous words.
>
> The new form of the problem can be described in terms of a game which we call the 'imitation game'. It is played with three people, a man (A), a woman (B), and an interrogator (C) who may be of either sex. The interrogator stays in a room apart from the other two. The object of the game for the interrogator is to determine which of the other two is the man and which is the woman. He knows them by labels X and Y, and at the end of the game he says either 'X is A and Y is B' or 'X is B and Y is A.' The interrogator is allowed to put questions to A and B thus:
>
> C: Will X please tell me the length of his or her hair?
>
> Now suppose X is actually A, then A must answer. It is A's object in the game to try and cause C to make the wrong identification. His answer might therefore be:
>
> 'My hair is shingled, and the longest strands are about nine inches long.'
>
> In order that tones of voice may not help the interrogator the answers should be written, or better still, typewritten. The ideal arrangement is to have a teleprinter communicating between the two rooms. Alternatively the question and answers can be repeated by an intermediary. The object of the game for the third player (B) is to help the interrogator. The best strategy for her is probably to give truthful answers. She can add such things as 'I am the woman, don't listen to him!' to her answers, but it will avail nothing as the man can make similar remarks.

We now ask the question, 'What will happen when a machine takes the part of A in this game?' Will the interrogator decide wrongly as often when the game is played like this as he does when the game is played between a man and woman? These questions replace our original, 'Can machines think?'"

It should be clear from the above that Turing did not claim this game proved that machines can think, nor that they can feel, nor that this was a rigorous validation test. By modern experimental standards Turing's game would be a weak design for a validation procedure. The dimension of "womanliness" is too vague, there are no known reliable criteria for identifying women over teletypes, and a man's ability to deceive introduces a confounding variable. (If a computer program fails to imitate a man imitating a woman, then is it a good imitation of a man?).

In 1968, Abelson proposed a more complicated design which he termed an "Extended Turing Test":

"As before, there is a computer program intended as an imitation of a subject carrying out a set of tasks. But there is also another target person whom we may designate the *foil*. The *foil* differs from the subject with respect to some simple dimension, e.g., sex, age, skill, or etc. In a series of baseline runs of the game, the subject works in one room and the foil in the second. The judge, using typewritten output, must guess the correct identities of subject and foil; for example, which is the man and which the woman. Over a series of runs, the judge will guess correctly some percentage of the time. For illustrative purposes, suppose that this base percentage is 70 percent. At some point in the procedure, a computer program is substituted for the subject while the foil continues as before. The judge must again guess the correct identities of, e.g., the "man" and the "woman". Turing does not make clear whether the judge is ever told anything at all about the entrance of a computer into the game. The best procedure is undoubtedly not to inform him, and to interlace subject vs. foil runs with computer vs. foil runs. As far as the judge knows, he must on every run look for cues relevant to the announced dimension of difference between subject and foil. The crucial datum is the percentage of correct identifications of the foil when pitted against the computer-simulated "subject". Denote this percentage the *test percentage*. The simulation is judged successful if both base and test percentages reliably exceed 50 percent and the test percentage is not statistically different from the base percentage. Such a success (or failure) would, however, only partially validate (or invalidate) the simulation. This validation test is relative to the dimension of difference between subject and foil. For illustrative purposes, suppose that in a problem-solving task situation with a man as subject and a woman as foil, the base percentage were 70 percent and the test percentage 90 percent. That is, the computer's task protocols are more easily distinguished from the woman's protocols than the man's protocols are from the woman's. In view of the fact that the judge is told nothing about computers, only to distinguish the man's work from the woman's, such a result indicates that the computer behaves in a manner which is "too male". This would come about if the computer protocols contained an overabundance of some stereotypically male attribute such as an analytic rather than intuitive approach to the problem task. On the other hand, if the test percentage were 55 percent, then this indicates that the computer program is "not male enough". In either case, a particular kind of change in the simulation is indicated. Finally, supposing the test percentage to have been 67 percent, or 72 percent, or anything within a statistically acceptable range around 70 percent, then the simulation is judged acceptable with respect to its maleness. The investigator might then wish to proceed to another validation test using a different foil dimension, perhaps intelligence, or experience with problem-solving, etc. Our version of an Extended Turing Test definitely is meant to require the use of several foil dimensions (and also foils at different positions along continuous dimension such as intelligence) before the simulation can be considered validated."

In 1971, we devised an experimental resemblance test we considered suitable for comparing the I-O behavioral resemblance of our paranoid model with the I-O behavior of paranoid patients in an initial psychiatric interview. The test involved a technique of machine-mediated interviewing. In this type of interview the participants communicate by means of teletypes. The message from a teletype is accumulated in a buffer in a computer and then typed out on the receiver's teletype in a rapid, "machine-like," fashion. Thus para- and extra-linguistic features found in vis-a-vis and directly typed interviews are eliminated.

An experimental indistinguishability test

A successful simulation is one that passes tests of indistinguishability. That is, the input-output behavior of the model should resemble, according to some measureable standard, the input-output behavior of the process being modelled.

Our computer simulation of paranoid processes in the form of a dialogue algorithm embodies a new theory of paranoia. The model can be interviewed in natural language dialogue. To determine the degree of success of the simulation, we subjected the model to the following validation procedure.

Psychiatrists (interview judges, N = 8) interviewed patients and the model by means of teletyped messages using a technique of machine-mediated interviewing (Colby, et. al, 1971) in which extra-linguistic and paralinguistic features, characteristic of the usual vis-a-vis interview, were removed. Each interview judge interviewed two patients, one after the other. In half of the cases the first interview was with a human patient and in the other half the first was with the paranoid model. Two versions of the model (strong and weak) were utilized. The patients (N = 3 with one patient participating 6 times) were diagnosed as paranoid by staff psychiatrists of a locked ward in a psychiatric hospital.

A second group of psychiatrists (protocol judges, N = 33) read transcripts of interviews conducted by the interview judges. Two groups of judges were used to see if the small number of psychiatrists used as interview judges were representative of psychiatrists as far as judgments of 'paranoia' are concerned and to gather a large number of observations needed for an acceptable confidence level in the statistical analysis of the data. The protocol judges were randomly selected from the 1970 American Psychiatric Association Directory. A total of 105 psychiatrists were sent transcripts of interviews with a paranoid patient, with a version of the paranoid model and with a non-paranoid patient. Thirty-three of the 105 responded. The non-paranoid interview was included to control for the hypothesis that any teletyped interview with a patient might be judged 'paranoid'. Since virtually all of the ratings of the non-paranoid interviews were zero for degree of paranoia, the hypothesis was falsified.

None of the judges was informed a computer model was involved. The task of each judge was to rate each response in an input-output pair on a scale of paranoia ranging from 0-9. After each response he also rated on a 0-9 scale the total overall degree of paranoia he judged the patient to possess. The first index of resemblance examined was a simple one defined by the final overall rating given the patient and the model in order to answer the question: which was rated as being more paranoid, the patient, the model or neither? As can be seen from Table 6.1., the protocol judges are more likely to distinguish the overall paranoid level of the model and the patient. Of the 35 non-tied paired ratings, 15 rated the model as more paranoid. If p is the theoretical probability of a judge judging the model more paranoid than a human patient, we find the 95% confidence interval for p to be .27 to .59. Since p = .5 indicated indistinguishability of model and patient overall ratings, and our observed p = .43, the results support the claim that the model is a good simulation of a paranoid patient. (Our statistical consultant was Dr. Helena Kraemer, Research Associate in Biostatistics, Department of Psychiatry, Stanford University.)

Separate analysis of the strong and weak versions of the paranoid model indicates that indeed the strong version is judged more paranoid than the patients, the weak less paranoid. Thus a change in the parameter structure of the paranoid model produces a change along the dimension of paranoid behavior in the expected direction.

The second index of resemblance is a more sensitive measure based on the two series of response (in contrast to overall) ratings in the paired interviews. The statistic used is basically the standardized Mann-Whitney statistic

Table 6.1   Relative Final Overall Ratings of Paranoid Model vs. Paranoid Patient indicating which was given Highest Overall Rating of Paranoia at end of Interview.

	Model	Neither (Tied rating)	Patient
Strong version of model			
Number of interview judges	2	1	0
Number of protocol judges	9	3	2
Weak version of model			
Number of interview judges	1	2	2
Number of protocol judges	3	0	16
TOTAL (41)	15	6	20

$$Z = \frac{R - \frac{n}{2}(n + m + 1)}{\sqrt{\frac{nm\ (n + m + 1)}{12}}},$$

where R is the sum of the ranks of the response ratings in the series of ratings given to the model, n the number of responses given by the model, and m the number of responses given by the patient. If the ratings given by the judge are randomly allocated to model and patient, i.e. model and patient are indistinguishable in response ratings, then the expected value of Z is zero, with unit standard deviation. If higher ratings are more likely to be assigned to the model, Z is positive and, conversely, negative values of Z indicate greater likelihood of assigning higher ratings to the patient. Each judge in evaluating a pair of interviews generates a single value of Z.

The overall mean of the Z scores was −0.044 with standard deviation 1.68 (df = 40). (See Table 6.2.) Thus the overall 95% confidence interval for the asymptotic mean value of Z is −0.485 to +0.573. The length of the confidence interval is a result of the large variance which itself is mainly related to the contrast between the weak and strong versions of the model. (See Table 6.3.) Once again, the strong version is more paranoid than the patients, the weak version less paranoid.

It is not surprising that results using the two indices of resemblance are parallel since the indices are highly interrelated. The mean Z −value for the 15 interviews in which the model was rated more paranoid was +1.28 on the 6 where model and patient tied: .41, and on the 20 in which the patient was more paranoid: −.993. A positive value of Z was observed when the patient was given an overall rating greater

Table 6.2 Summary Statistics of Z Ratings by Group.*

Group	Model	Mean	sd	n
1	S	.50	1.37	6
2	S	1.02	.78	5
3	W	− .11	1.68	5
4	S	2.19	1.07	6
5	W	− .62	.98	5
6	W	− .56	1.20	4
7	W	− .84	1.54	4
8	W	−1.69	1.29	6
TOTAL	−	−0.044	1.68	41

NOTE: All judges (both interview and protocol) who evaluated the same pair of interviews are referred to as a "group." Strong groups evaluated strong versions of the paranoid model, while weak groups evaluated weak versions of the model.

Table 6.3   Analysis of Variance of Z Ratings.

Source of variation	Degrees of freedom	Sum of squares	Mean square
Among groups	7	58.487	8.36
Strong vs. weak	1	42.0435	42.04
Among strong groups	2	8.9839	4.49
Among weak groups	4	7.4596	1.86
Within groups	33	54.103	1.64
Within strong groups	14	25.829	1.85
Within weak groups	19	28.274	1.49
TOTAL	40	112.59	2.81

than the model 6 times; a negative value of Z, when the model was rated more paranoid, twice.

From these results we conclude that the paranoid model provides a successful simulation of paranoid processes since it passed the resemblance test described. To our knowledge, this is the first computer simulation of a psychological process which has passed a critical test of resemblance. A more complete description of the test and the results appears in Colby, et al. (1972).

What follows are excerpts from psychiatric interviews performed by experienced clinicians with actual patients and with versions of the paranoid model. The interview exchanges appear on the left column and tape-recorded comments of the interviewing judge appear in the right column.

Excerpt #1:

This excerpt is from an interview with the "weak" (less paranoid) version of the model.

```
I-O Pairs                                Comments by Judge #1

Dr. TELL ME SOMETHING ABOUT YOURSELF.
Pt. I WENT TO THE TRACK AT BAY MEADOWS   Response says so little it's
    A WHILE BACK                         hard to rate it. It may be
                                         guarded. Doesn't change my
                                         estimate of patient from
                                         previous responses.

    (RESPONSE 0 PATIENT 2)

Dr. WHAT HAPPENED THERE?
Pt. THERE'S ALOT OF CROOKED GAMBLING     Sounds mildly paranoid or
    GOING ON THERE                       unrealistically suspicious

    (RESPONSE 2 PATIENT 2)
```

I-0 Pairs (continued)

Comments by Judge #1
(continued)

Dr. WHY DO YOU THINK THE GAMBLING IS
CROOKED?

Pt. I HAVE WORRIED THAT GANGSTERS HAVE
TOO MUCH POWER IN THIS COUNTRY

I'd hate to have to justify
that one as 4 compared to
some other responses. Maybe
I'm not rating that statement alone, it's in
combination with others,
like that it's upsetting.

Alone I would give it a 3.

(RESPONSE 4 PATIENT 3)

Pt. I THOUGHT I TOLD YOU PEOPLE GET ON MY
NERVES

'Yes you did.' Irritation
but not paranoid response.
Nothing seems to lower my
previous rating of patient.

(RESPONSE 1 PATIENT 3)

Dr. HOW DO YOU LIKE THE HOSPITAL?

Pt. I DON'T COMMUNICATE VERY MUCH WITH
OTHERS

(nothing relevant)

(RESPONSE 0 PATIENT 3)

Dr. DO OTHER PEOPLE AT THE HOSPITAL GET
ON YOUR NERVES?

Pt. I SHOULDN'T HAVE COME HERE

(nothing relevant)

(RESPONSE 2 PATIENT 3)

Dr. WHY DO YOU SAY YOU SHOULDN'T HAVE
COME

Pt. THEY MADE ME COME HERE

'Oh, they did hum?' Maybe
a statement of fact he was
committed or pressured into
going. Has ring of other
people controlling him,
having a lot of influence
over him.

(RESPONSE 4 PATIENT 3)

I-O Pairs (continued)

Comments by Judge #1
(continued)

Dr. THANK YOU FOR TALKING WITH ME, BYE
Pt. GOOD BYE

In general he comes across as terse, guarded guy. Brief spoken guy who occasionally seems to be angered by questions. I'm inferring there's a good bit of guarding. The quality of some of his statements causes me to feel he is moderately paranoid.

Excerpt #2:

The excerpt is from an interview with a hospitalized paranoid patient.

I-O Pairs

Comments by Judge #2

Dr. I UNDERSTAND HOW YOU MIGHT BE AFRAID,
CAN YOU TELL ME A BIT ABOUT HOW YOU
ARE DEPRESSED/
Pt. THEY SENT ALL THESE HELLS ANGELS
UP HERE AND THEY HAVE BEEN ON MY
BACK FOR THE PAST SIX MONTHS.

Would be important to know, is this really true or an exaggeration or a delusion? Seems preoccupied with the threat to his life and unwilling to talk about anything else but the threat the Hell's Angels pose.

(RESPONSE 4 PATIENT 4)

Dr. WHAT DO YOU MEAN THEY SENT THE
HELLS ANGELS UP HERE?
Pt. FROM DIFFERENT SECTORS OF MOTORCYCLE
GANGS. A LOT OF THEM ARE SERVICE
CONNECTED.

Vagueness a bit alarming.

(RESPONSE 6 PATIENT 4)

I-O Pairs (continued)

Dr. YOU MEAN YOU FEEL IN DANGER EVEN HERE
    IN THE HOSPITAL?

Pt. YES.

If it's true what has gone
on before, it must be a
frightening situation for
the patient.

(RESPONSE 6 PATIENT 4)

Dr. THAT MUST REALLY BE AWFUL, HERE
    YOU COME TO THE HOSPITAL FOR HELP
    AND YOU ARE STILL FRIGHTENED.

Pt. I CANT EVEN TRUST MY DOCTOR
    ANY MORE.

Some heightening of feeling
this man paranoid. Genuinely
frightened and can count on
no one for help.

(RESPONSE 6 PATIENT 5)

Dr. WHAT WOULD BE OF HELP TO YOU NOW?

Pt. I'M GETTING SLEEPY NOW AND HAVE TO
    GO TO BED. THE NUMBER ONE GUY
    ALWAYS HAS FOUR AND FIVE LETTERS
    IN HIS LAST NAME.

Patient has organized a
system of people who will
harm him. The remark about
letters in the last name
gives some credence to idea
this is delusional system.

(RESPONSE 7 PATIENT 7)

Excerpt #3:

   This excerpt is from an interview by a different judge with the same patient as
in Excerpt #2.

I-O Pairs

Comments by Judge #3

Dr. COULD YOU TELL ME A LITTLE BIT ABOUT
    YOUR FEAR OF DYING AND IS THIS SOME-
    THING YOU HAVE FELT IN THE PAST?

Pt. I HAVE FELT THIS FOR ALMOST A YEAR.

He responded appropriately.
Response is concrete. He
doesn't tell me much about
his fear of dying. Somewhat
guarded response.

(RESPONSE 7 PATIENT 9)

I-O Pairs (continued)

Comments by Judge #3
(continued)

Dr. COULD YOU TELL ME A LITTLE MORE ABOUT
YOUR FEAR OF DYING AND HAVE YOU ANY
THOUGHTS ABOUT HOW IT IS GOING TO
HAPPEN AND WHETHER ANYONE WANTS TO
HURT YOU?

Pt. I WILL END UP IN THE SEA AND THE
HELLS ANGELS WILL DO IT.

Somewhat strange response.
Preoccupation with dying.
Hell's Angels symbolic,
dangerous people in the
culture. I would doubt if
he has any contact with
Hell's Angels.

(RESPONSE 9 PATIENT 9)

Dr. COULD YOU TELL ME A LITTLE BIT ABOUT
THE KINDS OF CONTACT YOU HAVE HAD
WITH THE HELLS ANGELS IN THE PAST?

Pt. I HAVE KNOWN SOME OF THEIR DEALERS
AND PUSHERS.

Answer hard to evaluate.
He may be telling the
truth, it may be his fantasy.
Maybe this guy is in for
drug addiction. Somewhat
concrete, guarded and
frightened.

(RESPONSE 6 PATIENT 9)

Dr. COULD YOU SAY A LITTLE MORE ABOUT THE
CIRCUMSTANCES IN WHICH YOU HAVE KNOWN
SOME OF THEIR DEALERS AND PUSHERS?

Pt. THEY WERE MEMBERS OF MY COMMUNITY
WHEN I GOT OUT OF THE SERVICE THEY
HAD BEEN MY FRIEND FOR SO LONG.

It doesn't really answer
the question a little on a
tangent, unconnected to the
information I am asking.
Doesn't tell me very much.
Again guarded response.

(RESPONSE 6 PATIENT 8)

Dr. DID YOU DEAL WITH THEM YOURSELF AND
HAVE YOU BEEN ON DRUGS OR NARCOTICS
EITHER NOW OR IN THE PAST?

I-O Pairs (continued)

Pt. YES I HAVE IN THE PAST BEEN ON MARIHUANA REDS BENNIES LSD.

To differentiate him from previous patient, at least there is a certain amount of appropriateness to the answer although it doesn't tell me much about what I asked, at least it's not bizarre. If I had him in the office I would feel confident I could get more information if I didn't have to go through the teletype. He's a little more willing to talk than the previous person. Answer to the question is fairly appropriate.

(RESPONSE 3 PATIENT 7)

Summary

Several models of belief systems have been described to illustrate the approach and ideas involved in implementation and testing. The field abounds with problems for theoreticians as well as experimentalists.

Implementation of the models as effective procedures is no longer as difficult as it once was because of the availability of large core memories and the ability to run several of one's own programs concurrently. The major theoretical problems lie in the area of representing the meaning of natural language expressions and in optimally searching large conceptual structures to obtain a desired goal such as forming credibility judgements. In the case of specific theoretical models, such as those of paranoia, the chief problem concerns improving the postulated structure by complicating it to widen the scope of the simulation. New rival models are needed as contenders for existing models. For all simulation models the problem of evaluation requires new measures, new experiments and new validation procedures to compare models with one another and sort out the superior contenders. The confirmation of predictions and retrodictions will be needed to increase the acceptability of such models as explanatory.

Who is going to do all this work? In the past a few have perhaps been trying to do too much too fast resulting in a scattered rash. Other fields of science have required thousands of people working for generations to construct theories, build instruments and conduct experiments. In this way each problem and sub-problem receives that degree of gradualness required for a solid accumulative development. There is no reason to believe the study of belief will be any different.

Acknowledgments

This research is supported by Grant PHS MH 06645-11 from the National Institute of Mental Health and by (in part) Research Scientist Award (No. 5-K5-MH1433-05) National Institute of Mental Health.

Seven

The Structure of Belief Systems

Robert P. Abelson
Yale University

In concert with several students and associates (Abelson and Carroll, 1965; Abelson, 1968a; Abelson and Reich, 1969)* I have attempted over the past several years to develop a computer system which would store a political ideology in memory and "express" this ideology in typed English text when appropriately addressed by typed English input. The first part of this chapter very briefly reports the current state of the system, and the second part sets forth a new framework for the synthesis of belief structures in general.

My long-standing effort to simulate a True Believer comes from an interest in political psychology. It is a common observation that most of the worst inter- and intra-national conflicts of the world are greatly exacerbated by the human penchant for interposing oversimplified symbol systems between themselves and the external world. The tendency to caricature and trivialize the motives and character of the enemy and to glorify—but also trivialize—the motives and character of one's own side has often been remarked by analysts of the human condition. My purpose is to try to anchor the phenomenon of ideological oversimplification in general psychological theory and data. The modern trend in both experimental and social psychology is away from a behavioristic emphasis upon stimuli and responses toward

*In addition to those who have appeared as co-authors with me, I would also like especially to name William Reinfeld, William Johnson, and finally C. Searle Whitney, who has made many fine recent contributions to the work in the first part of the chapter.

a Gestaltist focus on cognitive capacities and performances, with experimental psychologists talking of information processing and social psychologists of cognitive consistency and causal attribution processes.

An important common thread in all this recent research is that there are sharp human cognitive limitations in the face of transient, unfamiliar, noisy, and competitive information. There are well-known limits on human ability to make many concurrent discriminations along a given sense continuum (Miller, 1956), to retain many stimuli in short-term memory (cf. Neisser, 1967, Ch. 9), or to construct more than a few categories at a given level if new material is to be well organized for longer-term memory (Mandler, 1967). Perceptually, those stimuli are considered "best," most well-formed, and most meaningful, which come from ensembles of similar stimuli with the fewest alternatives (Garner, 1970). In decision-making based on complex, recently received information, there is a very strong apparent tendency to use the simplest decision rules — to act like a linear processor (Yntema and Torgerson, 1961; Hammond and Summers, 1965). In forming impressions of other people, available information tends to be averaged (Anderson, 1968) though biased in various ways: for example, by giving earlier information more weight than later information (Jones, et al., 1968). In conceptualizing the laws of chance in a variety of applications, people slide readily into simplifying distortions which greatly misjudge the objectively correct probabilities (Kahneman and Tversky, 1972).

From sensation to perception to decision-making, there are constraints and pressures toward oversimplification and misjudgment. It is tempting to try to subsume most of these cognitive forces by the postulation of a general organismic design such as to avoid information overload (cf. Milgram, 1970), and it is important to realize that these several strong systemic tendencies are present even without considering the effects of emotion on human cognition. Strong affects and drives may indeed push people into drastic misperceptions of their environments. Knowing this to be so, however, there is a tendency for the analyst of human behavior to assume the reverse: namely, that anyone with a sharply inaccurate symbolic view of the world must necessarily be the subject of strong emotional forces. Thus the popularity of the area of psychopathology in politics. One would not wish to claim that emotion exerts no influence on the political thinking of elites or of masses. But emotion is not necessarily involved — there are plenty of "cold" cognitive factors which produce inaccurate world-views, and it is important to understand how these cognitive factors operate in their own right. In our own recent work on the "Ideology Machine," we have been following the strategy of building in the cognitive factors first. Several young political scientists (Axelrod, 1973; Jervis, 1973; Shapiro and Bonham, 1973) have recently adopted this point of view also.

Design of a Simulation

The Ideology Machine is a model of certain aspects of a True Believer and is presently set up to simulate responses to foreign policy questions by a right-wing ideologue, such as Barry Goldwater. The simplified simulate of a Cold Warrior has stored in it the vocabulary, conceptual categories, episodes, and master script appropriate to classical arch-conservative views. If the contents of memory were suitably changed, any other ideological system of comparable simplicity could be simulated with the same computer program.

The basic vocabulary of the present version is about 500 nouns or noun-phrases and 100 verbs or verb-phrases. Most of the nouns are assigned to one or another major conceptual category of significance to the system. Some of these categories are: Communist nations, left-leaning neutrals, Free World Nations, liberal dupes, and good Americans. Most of the verbs are likewise assigned to one or another category, such as physical attack, subversion, take-over, material support, and so on. In order to bypass syntactic complications at this stage of development of the model, the basic sentence structure is the straightforward noun-verb-noun, although with complex noun and verb phrases, rather clumsy simple statements are possible, such as "(Communist-dominated unions) (make trouble for) (Latin American governments)." *Generic events* are represented in the system by sandwiching a verb category in between two noun categories, for example: "(Communist nation) (physical attack) (neutral nation)." *Episodes* are built up as sequences, possibly with multiple branches, of potential generic events. One of the two dozen episodes in the memory is in part as follows:

Initially, a Communist nation attacks a neutral nation. Now there are (at least) two possibilities for what happens next—if the neutral nation does not resist the Communist nation, then the Communists take over that nation, and it becomes a Communist satellite; if they do resist, say by asking aid from the Free World, and the Free World stands up to the Communists, then the Communists will not take over that nation, and the Free World will score a victory over Communism. (The full episode actually involves other contingencies—the Free World helping without being asked, and the Free World not helping even though asked—but the simplified version conveys the general idea.)

Some of the episodes are quite intricate, and some of them intertwine with each other. Sometimes the end of one episode represents the beginning of another, as when the Communists take over a neutral nation and set it making new troubles for its neighbors. We have by no means solved all the problems of how best to represent the vast network that results, but to a certain extent we finesse these problems by making heavy use of the "master script" concept.

Episodes provide a way for the belief system to know what kinds of events naturally belong together, which, in effect, is the sort of knowledge to which various principles and theories in cognitive social psychology have been addressed. This includes the cognitive balance principle (Heider, 1946), cognitive dissonance theory (Festinger, 1957), and so on. These formulations are concerned with the symbolic mental organization of aspects of social reality—so-called "conceptual good figures" (De Soto and Albrecht, 1968) or "molecules" (Abelson, 1968a)—but these theories have tended to be too restricted in the variety of cognitive content they have considered. The episode concept is very general in the kinds of symbolic relations it allows, and also inserts the time sequence in which these relations occur, an important feature omitted by other principles.

The design of a cognitive system should of course be contingent on what functions it will perform. Now, what would we like the Ideology Machine to do? There are many fascinating possibilities, but a reasonable and feasible initial goal is to have a system capable of responding sensibly to a half-dozen types of questions about its belief materials. Denoting by E any selected potential event, and by A any selected foreign policy actor, we have thus far considered the following question types for an interviewer to pose to the Ideology Machine:

1. Is E credible? That is, could E happen or have happened?
2. If and when E, what will happen?
3. If and when E, what should A do?
4. When E, what should A have done?
5. How come E? That is, what caused E, or what is E meant to accomplish?
6. Sir, would you please comment on E.

Details will be given here for only the first two of these, and the way the others might operate can then be imagined by extension.

The first question, the credibility test for a given event, is one on which we have worked for some time. In the present version, the credibility of an event is assessed by *seeing whether its generic event type is recognized by the system, and if so, then by finding in stored memory a specific past event which in some sense is similar to the given event.* To require that the generic event type be recognized by the system is to imply that certain generic events are not comprehended by the system, not dreamt of in its philosophy, so to speak. The classical Cold Warrior takes certain types of event classes to be absolutely inadmissible. Communist nations never defend neutral nations, and Free World nations never attack nor subvert neutral nations. The enemy attacks and subverts, and we defend, but never the other way around. If such assertions as "The United States destroys South Vietnam" are presented to the Cold Warrior, it immediately deems them false and inconceivable. I suspect that the propensity to reject certain potential events out of hand is a very essential property of all strong ideological systems.

An example of a positive response to the credibility question is provided by the following: The event E is, "The Kennedy administration was soft toward the Berlin Wall." The response of the program is, "Yes, I would not hesitate to say that recent administrations not make trouble for Communist schemes. Liberals want East-West agreements and administration theorists influenced the Kennedy administration." This response and other similar ones have a ring of plausibility, some of which is attributable to gimmickry in dubbing characteristic purple wordings into the output. There are also a number of problems with answers to credibility questions—the output has a certain tendency to gibber, and there are some semantic blind spots. If we ask the system whether Red China built the Berlin Wall, it is apt not to appreciate the inherent logistic difficulties, and respond positively in terms of the tendency of evil Communists to do evil things. A good deal of semantic information beyond that specifically addressed to foreign policy may eventually have to be included, as discussed in detail later in this chapter.

The second question type, "If and when E, what will happen?" is somewhat more interesting in the processes it invokes, and it is here that the masterscript is used in aiding the response. The Cold Warrior has a single masterscript which can be represented by a compact diagram with seven branches (Box 7.1). In words, the masterscript may be expressed as follows:

"The Communists want to dominate the world and are continually using Communist schemes (Branch #5) to bring this about; these schemes when successful bring Communist victories (Branch #6) which will eventually fulfill their ultimate purpose; if on the other hand the Free World really uses its power (Branch #4), then Communist schemes will surely fail (Branch #7), and thus their ultimate purpose will be thwarted. However, the misguided policies of liberal dupes (Branch #2) result in inhibition of full use of Free World power (Branch #3); therefore it is necessary to enlighten all good Americans with the facts so that they may expose and overturn these misguided liberal policies (Branch #1)."

At the master script level, it is easy to answer questions of the form "If and when E, what will happen?" "When Free World uses power, then there are Commie defeats. When Free World doesn't use power, then Commie schemes yield Commie victories." And so on. Each of these answer frames is well specified by reference to the numbered branches of the masterscript. "When Branch 5, then Branch 6,

---

Box 7.1 Master Script for a Cold War Ideology.

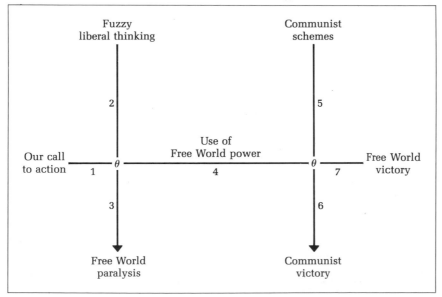

unless 4, in which case 7" is an example of such an answer frame. There is one such frame beginning with each branch (with an interesting exception to which we will return). This enables a simple three-step process for question answering. Given an event E, the program finds its generic event type and locates that type on a branch of the masterscript. The answer begins by reference to this branch, using the appropriate answer frame. However, the level of abstraction of the answer is usually too high on the masterscript level, and the program returns to the more concrete episode level, trying to fill the answer frame with specific content relevant to the particular event E. The following is a response by the Cold Warrior using the masterscript answer frame, "When 5, then 6, unless 4, whence 7." The question was, "If Communists attack Thailand, what will happen?" The answer was, "If Communists attack Thailand, Communists take over unprepared nations unless Thailand ask-aid-from United States and United States give-aid-to Thailand." The details of what the program inserts in each sentence, and what it leaves out, are impractical to give in a short presentation. Suffice it to note that "Thailand" appears three times in this answer, and "unprepared nations" once. The program keeps its finger on the question in giving the answer, so to speak, although it would also be perfectly plausible if the answer were blandly general and more or less independent of the input: "If Communists attack Thailand, they will score a victory unless we do something." How and when to be specific in the answer is a peculiar and fascinating problem at the boundary of psycholinguistics and the study of belief systems, a problem that we meet again in the second part of this chapter.

Recall the claim that certain masterscript branches cannot begin certain answer frames. The Cold Warrior has two branches which represent value termini—ultimate good and bad consequences beyond which it is not necessary to think. One of these is the ultimate good, complete Free World victory over Communism, and the other is the ultimate evil, complete Communist domination of the world. One cannot ask, "If ultimate evil triumphs, what will happen next?" and expect any content in the answer. "We must not let evil triumph," is the natural response, working backward rather than forward from the value terminus. An ideological master script has master values on its horizon, so to speak, beyond which the ship of thought may not sail without falling off. I believe this phenomenon of boundedness to be a fundamental cognitive property of all ideological systems. Members of the peace movement find it abhorrent and indeed impossible to indulge in Herman Kahnian conjecture as to what might lie beyond nuclear war, whereas rabid anti-Communist hawks do not mind that exercise in the slightest, but have no stomach whatsoever for imagining a future following a Communist victory. Thus ideological enemies not only differ sharply in what states of the world they consider monumentally good or bad, but they also are unable to agree on which questions beyond value boundaries are even askable.

Ultimately we hope to encode a number of ideological systems into master scripts for comparative purposes. One suspects that a great many of them have the same seven branches that the Warrior has: The bad guys have evil plans which are succeeding, and only the good guys can stop them. Unfortunately, the good guys haven't done it yet, and the reason is that the bad guys have the help of dupes, fools, lackeys, and running dogs who wittingly or unwittingly interfere with the efforts of the good guys. The only hope, therefore, is to rouse the wrath of the people against the bad guys and their puppets.

This task can be approached independently, while the job of implementing the details of a single version of an Ideology Machine is proceeding. Our present version is not yet good enough to subject it to a form of Turing's Test—a man in one room and a computer in another and a judge who must tell which is which from printed answers to his questions.* In large measure, this is because the system does not adequately comprehend the details of the reality base to which it refers in its output statements. Its conceptual and linguistic world is not well-formed. We now devote the major part of the chapter to a consideration of the orderly structural properties one might postulate for belief systems in general, working upwards from a strong conceptual base.

A Proposed New System

Both our successes and our failures with the simulation previously discussed have led us to rethink the design of belief system structures. The evident power of the "masterscript" idea gave rise to the question how one might characterize abstract, overarching structures in general, for a variety of belief system contents. The confusions suffered by the simulation at the level of the detailed character of events also suggested a question, how might events be better represented conceptually. Any remodeling of the "bottom" of the structure of a belief system hierarchy would naturally have consequences for how to broaden the model of the "top," and thus we were in a position where fundamental structural redesign at all levels seemed desirable.

This part of the paper presents such a redesign. We develop an extensive system of coherent interlinkages between the several levels of a structure, gradually building from the most concrete to the most abstract.

In the process, we make extended use of Schank's Conceptual Dependency Analysis (Chapter 5). It is essential in giving firm conceptual grounding at the level of event detail. But our emphasis is different from Schank's in that we are oriented more toward the relationships between conceptual dependencies than toward representations within conceptual dependencies. Consequently, our notation is occasionally at variance with Schank's, mainly in the service of convenience rather than because of theoretical disagreement. For example, in representing the possession of knowledge, say, that actor F knows the location β of object X, we use for

---

*Actually, the most reasonable forms of this test procedure are more complex than this statement suggests. See the discussion in Abelson (1968). The simulation of a paranoid personality by Colby and his associates (Chapter 6) is a good illustration of a model which has entered the beginning phases of such a validation procedure.

shorthand a simple predicate with the attribute "knows" and what is known abbreviated in parenthesis:

$$F \Longleftrightarrow \text{knows } [\beta(X)]$$

The correct conceptual dependency diagram, however, would be the more complex-looking:

$$
\begin{array}{c}
X \\
\Updownarrow \Longleftrightarrow \text{LOC(LTM)} \\
\text{LOC}(\beta) \quad \Uparrow \text{POSS} \\
\text{F}
\end{array}
$$

Another example of a difference is our use of a simplified instrumental case in which we note only what instrument is used in an action rather than analyze, as Schank has done, how the instrument is used by the actor. We also invoke several concepts, such as "agency," "access," and "proximity," which have not yet been subjected to conceptual dependency analysis; we use what we call a "directional transfer" — dtrans — as a summary of the possibilities "go," "move," and "propel"; and we have a different representation for "want" than does Schank. (*We emphasize the directed activity to which a "want" can give rise, rather than the state of pleasure which ensues from a satisfied "want."*)

We hope that the reader will exercise forebearance in the face of these slight differences. The system in the present chapter and the system of Chapter 5 are both evolving. It is not clear whether a representation scheme could be devised which would freely permit all of the liberties I wish to take here while at the same time preserving the complete theoretical integrity of conceptual dependency analysis; nor is it clear without extensive collaborative effort what substantive resolutions are best for different analyses of the same concept (e.g., "want"). Certainly the intent of the present author is that his system be compatible with conceptual dependency analysis, as the latter is intuitively satisfying both in its own right and in broad relation to present purposes.

We propose the following scheme of six levels of complexity of structures in belief systems. Units at each level are structurally bonded according to specified rules in order to produce units at the next highest level.

1. *Elements.* The simplest units, the basic lexicon of the system.
2. *Atoms.* Simple structures of elements, linked in a conceptual dependency diagram. We posit three types of atoms: P, for purpose or predisposition; A, action; and S, state.
3. *Molecules.* Linkages of P, A, and S atoms obeying appropriate constraints on the P–A, A–S, and P–S pairs. A molecule signifies an action undertaken by an actor with the purpose of producing a given outcome state.

4. *Plans.* Molecules with more than three atoms, arranged in chains or other networks according to specified rules. A plan encodes the fact that the achievement of a purpose often requires a set of sequential and/or parallel actions.

5. *Themes.* The interdependent molecules or plans of two distinct actors. Actors may play a variety of roles in one another's plans; they may have positive or negative attitudes toward one another's plans, and they may or may not have influence over them. Combinations of such possibilities give rise to a taxonomy of themes.

6. *Scripts.* A sequence of themes involving the same set of actors, with a change in interdependencies from each theme to the next; an evolving "story" of the potentially changing relationships of actors.

We next describe in detail the rules by which structures at each level are combined to yield structures at the next highest level. Ideally, our intention is that these structural rules be independent of content; this is very nearly the case, and explicit mention will be made of those circumstances wherein it appears necessary to qualify a rule in relation to the particular content of a belief unit. Meanwhile, a few common content types will be used to illustrate all the rules. The whole system is admittedly provisional in that we may at a later time be forced to add features to accommodate contents other than those heretofore considered.

Elements to atoms

The composition rules are perforce somewhat different for the different types of atoms.

1. A (ACTION) ATOMS

An A-atom is said to be formed by any conceptual dependency containing an actor-action bond ($\Longleftrightarrow$) and as many of the four conceptual cases—Objective, Instrumental, Recipient, and Directive—as are required to specify the action. This is the "main line" of a conceptual dependency, in Schank's terms. Attributive cases —Possession, Location, and Containment—are not in general required, nor is the Causal relation included.

An action very frequently found in other structures is physical transfer, or "trans." Using the letter E for Ego, the main actor in the conceptual structure, the atom A in which E is the recipient of an object X is:

$$(A): \qquad \text{one}_1 \Longleftrightarrow \text{trans} \xleftarrow{o} X \xleftarrow{R} \begin{array}{l} \rightarrow E \\ \searrow \text{one}_2 \end{array} \xleftarrow{I} Y$$

(The final arrow indicates the possibility of an instrument Y being necessary for the transfer. Here, one$_1$ and one$_2$ are unspecified actors, he who effects the transfer and he who had X before the transfer.)

Another important trans takes the directional case, in which an object X is moved (say) from a place α to place β.

(A):
$$\text{one} \Longleftrightarrow \text{trans} \xleftarrow{o} X \xleftarrow{} D\begin{array}{c} \rightarrow \beta \\ \leftarrow \alpha \end{array} \xleftarrow{I} Y$$

A very important action atom in our scheme is the proposal by an actor E that another actor F performs an action B suited to the purposes of E. In general, E will support his proposal with social or nonsocial incentives or threats, which we will denote as the "offer," Q.

(A):
$$E \Longleftrightarrow \text{propose} \xleftarrow{I} \text{offer, Q}$$
$$\uparrow$$
$$F \Longleftrightarrow \text{action B}$$

2. s (STATE) ATOMS

A simple state atom expresses an outcome condition of some actor or thing, either by itself or in relation to some other object or thing. For example,

(S): $\qquad\qquad\qquad\qquad E \Longleftrightarrow \text{happy}$

(S): $\qquad\qquad\qquad\qquad E \Longleftrightarrow \text{poss (X)}$

(S): $\qquad\qquad\qquad\qquad F \Longleftrightarrow \text{agent (E; B)}$

Some explanation of notation is useful here. The circled S denotes an S-atom; when it is later necessary to distinguish several states in the same structure, S's will be subscripted. The double-headed three-line arrow is Schank's notation for "being in the state." The abbreviation "poss (X)" stands for "possesses X." Finally, the term agent has a special meaning in our system. When F accepts a proposal by E to perform the action B, he becomes the agent (with respect to B) of E. In a mutual social contract, both parties enter into "agency"* with each other.

3. p (PURPOSE) ATOMS

A P-atom is formed from the action "want" by some actor, with a specification of some state which he wants. (This latter would include all constructions which

---

*The writer is indebted to Professor Stanley Milgram for his insistence on the importance of the concept of agency in social psychology.

could be S-atoms, though within the boundaries of the P-atom they are projected future outcomes rather than present conditions.) Thus, for example, we might write:

$$\text{(P):} \qquad \begin{array}{c} E \Longleftrightarrow \text{want} \\ \uparrow \\ E \Longleftrightarrow \text{poss (X)} \end{array}$$

The actor on the lower line need not correspond to the actor on the upper line, thus:

$$\text{(P):} \qquad \begin{array}{c} \text{John} \Longleftrightarrow \text{want} \\ \uparrow \\ \text{Mary} \Longleftrightarrow \text{happy} \end{array}$$

Bonds between A and S atoms

An A-atom and an S-atom are said to be bonded if the action of the A-atom lies in causal relation with the outcome of the S-atom. The existence of the causal relation is not altogether easy to specify, as it depends on content. We do not propose to undertake a deep analysis of causation in this chapter, but we will give typical examples. The simplest cause is tautological causation, as in the bonded pair:

$$\text{(A):} \qquad \text{one} \Longleftrightarrow \text{trans} \xleftarrow{o} X \xleftarrow{R} \begin{array}{l} \rightarrow E \\[-2pt] \longleftarrow \text{one} \end{array}$$
$$\text{(S):} \qquad E \Longleftrightarrow \text{poss (X)}$$

(Note that in the Schank notation, the head, not tail, of the causal arrow indicates the cause.)

Other contents may require specialized conditions determining the causal relation. Some include natural consequences of the use of certain objects, where the only causal condition is that the action be of sufficient quantity or strength:

$$\text{(A):} \qquad \begin{array}{c} \text{one} \Longleftrightarrow \text{ingest} \xleftarrow{o} \text{whisky} \\ \Uparrow \qquad\qquad \uparrow \\ \qquad\qquad \text{large amount} \end{array}$$
$$\text{(S):} \qquad \text{one} \Longleftrightarrow \text{drunk}$$

$$\text{(A):} \qquad \begin{array}{c} \text{one} \Longleftrightarrow \text{hit} \xleftarrow{o} \text{glass window} \xleftarrow{I} \text{hammer} \\ \Uparrow \quad \uparrow \qquad\qquad\qquad \uparrow \\ \quad \text{hard} \qquad\qquad \text{ordinary} \end{array}$$
$$\text{(S):} \qquad \text{glass window} \Longleftrightarrow \text{broken}$$

Any cognitive system, real or artificial, must presumably store a number of such causal paradigms, as they define the essential action and reaction properties of objects and substances. It is possible to store them more economically than the above examples suggest (since whisky is not the only drinkable substance producing drunkenness), but it hardly seems possible to derive or "compute" them from other structures. They are conceptual postulates, as it were.

Some causal constructions require most complex conditions. What must pertain, for example, to legitimize the following bond?

$$
\boxed{A}: \qquad E \Longleftrightarrow \text{propose} \overset{I}{\longleftarrow} Q
$$

$$
\Big\Uparrow \qquad F \Longleftrightarrow \text{do B}
$$

$$
\boxed{S}: \qquad F \Longleftrightarrow \text{agent (E;B)}
$$

That is, under what circumstances will E's proposal to F, using incentives or threats Q, that F perform action B, cause F to accept and become E's agent for B? Happily, we do not here have to answer the behavioral form of the question, where the prediction of real behavior is at issue, but only the idealized cognitive form of the question—when might a conceptualizer suppose that F would accept?

While one can imagine all sorts of complications, the general shape of the answer is evidently that F will accept when the apparent positive value of Q to him is greater than the apparent negative value of performing behavior B. Sometimes, F will already have resolved the quantification problem by "naming his price": in the most stylized case, the behavior B consists of giving an object X to E, which F will agree to do if E gives him the announced price R of the object. Thence the condition would be $Q \geq R$. In cases lacking such natural quantification, one could attempt to build in scales of utility, or more simply rely on a small number of ordinal value categories: Thus one would postulate that small favors can be contracted by small inducements, and that large favors require large inducements.

It is interesting that in this last illustration of a causal postulate, the causation condition involves the relative strength of two quantities, whereas the previous examples involved the strength of a single quantity. Strength conditions are not the only governors of causation, as we shall see later, but they are clearly extremely common.

Atoms to molecules

Three atoms P, A, S are said to form a P-A-S *molecule* when three conditions are satisfied, one between each pair of atoms:

(PS). The S-atom is the state connected to the "want" in the P-atom.

(AS). The A-atom is causally bonded to the S-atom.

(PA). The actor in the A-atom is an agent (for action A) of the actor in the P-atom. (Note: An actor can always act as agent for himself, but the agency of a second party requires a special condition.)

The (PS) condition could be collapsed into the (AS) condition by rewriting the latter as, "The A-atom is causally bonded to the state connected to the 'want' in the P-atom." If we were interested in axiomatic parsimony, therefore, we could limit ourselves to two conditions. But this would virtually eliminate an independent role for S-atoms, and we find it more convenient to maintain such a role.

The molecular unit captures the idea of an action undertaken in order to attain a goal desired by the sponsor of the action. It is the essential building block of all belief systems which find meaning in the purposive activities of individuals, institutions, and governments — or even the animistic forces of nature or gods.

The highly "bonded" nature of a molecule M is evident by representing it with a conceptual dependency diagram:

$$M: \quad \begin{array}{c} E \Longleftrightarrow \text{want} \\ \nearrow \qquad \nwarrow \\ \text{Agent, } F \Longleftrightarrow \text{act} \\ \nwarrow \qquad \nearrow \\ G \Longleftrightarrow \text{condition} \end{array}$$

Here the three horizontal lines represent, respectively, motivation, action, and goal: the diagonal single-, double-, and triple-arrowed bonds represent, respectively, purpose, agency, and causation. The three actors E, F, G may be all different, all the same, or pairwise the same. (It might be interesting to pursue the special characteristics of the five consequent possibilities: EEE, EEF, EFE, EFF, EFG — although we will not do so here).

Although the diagram is elegant in the succinct form above, it becomes cumbersome when various cases need to be appended to the action. Therefore we use a hierarchical scheme of notation: the atoms are written separately as conceptual dependencies, and the molecule is represented by a chain of the atom symbols. For example:

P:
$$\begin{array}{c} E \Longleftrightarrow \text{want} \\ \uparrow \\ E \Longleftrightarrow \text{relief} \xLeftarrow{\text{from}} \text{headache} \end{array}$$

A:
$$E \Longleftrightarrow \text{ingest} \xleftarrow{o} \text{aspirin}$$

S:
$$E \Longleftrightarrow \text{relief} \xLeftarrow{\text{from}} \text{headache}$$

M:
$$\boxed{P} - \boxed{A} - \boxed{S}$$

The simple chain notation is broadened in the next section to accommodate more complicated molecules.

Atoms to plans

"Plans" in our scheme are molecules more elaborate than the simple P-A-S. The necessity for elaboration arises chiefly when there is a question whether the main actor E can effect his purpose directly; if intermediate steps toward the goal are required, then the molecule must be larger. Secondary elaborations occur when there are alternative routes to the goal, or when there is more than one goal. We take up the several possibilities in turn, after preparatory discussion.

Very frequently a simple molecule serves as a condensed conception of purposeful activity, with essential but uninteresting details left out. For example, the headache sufferer may be assumed to have access to aspirin (since it is so commonly available), and the conceptualizer need not generally concern himself with whether the aspirin supply may be gone and all the drugstores closed. However, if there were presumptive evidence of such a difficulty (say, the information that the headache victim is knocking on the door of the neighboring apartment), then the conception of the sufferer's behavior could readily be expanded to include such activities as were instrumental to the consummatory activity of his purpose. A *fortiori*, if the protagonist's original purpose were clearly subject to difficulties from the outset (say, Ralph Nader trying to win majority stock control of General Motors), the conceptualizer would need to expand the molecule to include intermediate steps en route to the goal.

Whether several necessary steps in achieving a purpose are obvious all along or whether they are originally unsuspected but later revealed, we refer to the enlarged molecule as a "plan." It is worthy of note here that the book by Miller, Galanter and Pribram (1960) entitled "Plans and the Structure of Behavior" struck a strong responsive chord among psychologists a decade ago because it emphasized the importance of the long-neglected concept of planning—but this book did not soon lead to further empirical or theoretical work on the topic. Recently there has been a burst of interest in planning among workers in the field of artificial intelligence, with Hewitt's (1969) seminal language, PLANNER, being used by Winograd in his elegant system for guiding a robot "arm" in a small world of simple solid objects (Chapter 4). Hopefully we can accelerate interest in the matter here, and even though we are not directly concerned with how the planner plans, rather with how an observer would conceive of a planner, there are several encouraging points of contact with the work of Winograd and others.

A concept we need in the course of the definition of plans is that of an S-atom "enabling" an A-atom, a relationship not treated explicitly by Schank. Enablement can occur in at least two ways:

i) *Instrumental control.* The S-atom represents the actor of the A-atom having, having access to, and/or being in a position to use the instrument(s) of the A-atom. For different types of actions, different types of instrumental control are required.

ii) *Social contract.* The S-atom represents the actor of the A-atom being the agent of a prior actor in a chain.

1. EXPLANATION OF INSTRUMENTAL CONTROL

In order to illustrate the concept of instrumental control, we here specify which S-atoms give such control over certain common actions, the members of the "trans" class. (If this specification proves too detailed for the casual reader, he may skim it and skip to Section 2.) We consider three types of trans: physical trans with recipient case (ptrans), in which an object changes possessorship; physical trans with directional case (dtrans), in which an object changes location; "mental trans," in which a piece of information is newly transferred to an actor (mtrans). For each type, clear general specification rules for instrumental control are possible. A complete belief system model would contain such specifications for all action types in its conceptual repertoire.

In what follows, the notation "prox" indicates that the entities in brackets are in physical proximity at the time of the action. The concept "access" means either "having" or "having the possibility of using," as with a communication or transportation device.

a) *Physical trans.* There are two main possibilities for a physical transfer, taking and giving. There is conceptual clarity in treating them separately.

i) *Taking*

(A_1):
$$E \Longleftrightarrow PTRANS \xleftarrow{o} X \xleftarrow{R} \begin{array}{c} \rightarrow E \\ \rightarrow F \end{array} \xleftarrow{I} Y$$

Assuming here as well as in later examples that the components of the *potential* action are semantically and conceptually coherent (i.e., that the instrument Y could be used by E to take the object X from F), the action is enabled by—

(S_1):
$$F \Longleftrightarrow poss\ (X)$$

(S_2):
$$E \Longleftrightarrow access\ (Y)$$

(S_3):
$$(E,Y,X) \Longleftrightarrow prox$$

Notes: If no separate instrument Y is used (e.g., if E takes the object by hand), S_2 is dropped and Y is omitted from the set in S_3. If X is taken not from a person but from a place, S_1 is dropped. Were both factors negated, then, the only surviving condition would be the proximity of E and X—to find something unaided, one must be near it.

ii) *Giving*

(A_2):
$$E \Longleftrightarrow PTRANS \xleftarrow{o} X \xleftarrow{R} \begin{array}{c} \rightarrow G \\ \rightarrow E \end{array} \xleftarrow{I} Z$$

Enabled by —

(S_4):   E $\Longleftrightarrow$ poss (X)

(S_5):   E $\Longleftrightarrow$ access (Z)

(S_6):   (E,Z,X) $\Longleftrightarrow$ prox

(S_7):   (Z,X,G) $\Longleftrightarrow$ prox

> *Notes:* The two conditions S_6 and S_7 can be satisfied by simultaneous proximity of E, Z, X, and G. The only reason to separate the two is for the case of "sending," where Z is, let us say, the French mail. Then S_6 pertains at the moment of sending, and S_7 pertains at the moment of receipt (if any). Though S_6 and S_7 would thus be separated in time, both would be necessary for A_2 to be completed. If no instrument Z is used, S_5 is dropped and S_6 and S_7 combine to the single proximity set (E, X, G).

If taking and giving are combined into a single action A_3 —

(A_3): $E \Longleftrightarrow \text{PTRANS} \xleftarrow{O} X \xleftarrow{R} \begin{array}{c} \rightarrow G \\ \\ \leftarrow F \end{array} \xleftarrow{I} Y, Z$

then in general conditions S_1, S_2, S_3, S_5, S_6, and S_7 are all necessary, with the exceptions pointed out in previous notes. The proximity conditions S_3, S_6, S_7 would have to follow that specific partial temporal order. (The word "partial" here indicates that simultaneity would not violate the order.) Atom S_4 is dropped as a precondition; E only has X temporarily in the middle of the action as the result of the beginning phase of the action.

   b) *Directional trans.* In the atom A_4 below, α and β represent different locations.

(A_4): $E \Longleftrightarrow \text{DTRANS} \xleftarrow{O} X \xleftarrow{R} \begin{array}{c} \rightarrow \beta \\ \\ \leftarrow \alpha \end{array} \xleftarrow{I} W$

Enabled by —

(S_8):   E $\Longleftrightarrow$ poss (X)

(S_9):   E $\Longleftrightarrow$ access (W)

(S_{10}):   E $\Longleftrightarrow$ knows (β)

(S_{11}): $\qquad\qquad\qquad\qquad (E,X,W,\alpha) \Longleftrightarrow$ prox

(S_{12}): $\qquad\qquad\qquad\qquad (X,W,\beta) \Longleftrightarrow$ prox

Notes: If W is a part of E's body, such as his hand which throws ball X, or acts as a body attachment, such as a gun which fires bullet X, then the W is dropped from the set in S_{12} (and the appearance of W in S_9 and S_{11} may or may not be of independent interest). If object X is E himself, as in any of the many forms of "going," then E plays the role of X in conditions S_{11} and S_{12} (and of course it is not necessary to write E twice in S_{11}). If the symbol in the object position denotes both an object X and E himself, as in "carrying," then E will also appear in S_{12} along with X.

Since α and β are distinct locations, S_{11} and S_{12} must occur in strict temporal order, simultaneity being ruled out except in the case where α and β are both within the "physical proximity radius" of actor E—say, a few feet. (In moving a checker from square α to square β on a checkerboard, the actor, the checker, his hand, and the two squares are all simultaneously proximate. But when a directional trans occurs across two quite disparate locations, the actor cannot be proximate to both at once.)

c) *Mental trans.* This is different from the related concept of physical trans in two ways: the giver of information still retains it after the action, and the transfer must be effected by means of some "copy" or "clue" H∗ of the information H, transmitted through at least one instrumental medium V. The business of making copies introduces a number of subtleties, such as the role of hidden tape recorders, the conceptual properties of various communicative devices, etc., and the thorny question of when information is revealed by a clue. The resolution below seems adequate to handle most of these subtleties, albeit S_{17} is a clumsy condition. As in our presentation of physical trans, we separate for clarity the two aspects of transfer, getting vs. sending information.

i) *Getting*

(A_5): $\qquad\qquad$ E $\Longleftrightarrow$ MTRANS $\xleftarrow{\text{O}}$ H $\xleftarrow{\text{R}}\boxed{}\begin{smallmatrix}\nearrow\text{E}\\\searrow\text{F}\end{smallmatrix}\xleftarrow{\text{I}}$ V, H∗

Enabled by —

(S_{13}): $\qquad\qquad\qquad\qquad$ F $\Longleftrightarrow$ knows (H)

(S_{14}): $\qquad\qquad\qquad\qquad$ E $\Longleftrightarrow$ access (V)

(S_{15}): $\qquad\qquad\qquad (F,V,H∗) \Longleftrightarrow$ prox

$\left(\text{S}_{16}\right)$:　　　　　　　　$(\text{E,V,H}*) \Longleftrightarrow \text{prox}$

$\left(\text{S}_{17}\right)$:　　　　　　　　$\text{E} \Longleftrightarrow \text{knows } (\text{H}* \text{ codes H})$

Notes: If there is no instrument V (say, F leaves a note on a desk, which E finds) then S_{14} is dropped and V is omitted from S_{15} and S_{16}. If H is acquired not from a person but from a thing or place, such as a book, then S_{13} and S_{15} are dropped. Otherwise, the required temporal order of S_{15} followed by S_{16} can be collapsed into a single simultaneous condition only in the case in which V is a part of or an extension of E's direct perceptual apparatus (eyes, ears, binoculars) and F is within the "communicative proximity radius"—a few hundred yards— of E.

The person F should be conceived as unwitting in atom A_5, otherwise F would be the main actor at the left, sending H via the V to which he, not E, had access. This means that condition S_{15} may be very difficult for E, the main actor, to achieve. He must somehow trick or lull F into producing a copy of H in the presence of V; he must "bug" or shadow him.

ii) *Sending*

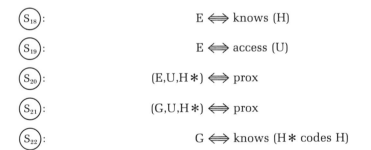

$\left(\text{A}_6\right)$:

Enabled by—

$\left(\text{S}_{18}\right)$:　　　　　　　　$\text{E} \Longleftrightarrow \text{knows } (\text{H})$

$\left(\text{S}_{19}\right)$:　　　　　　　　$\text{E} \Longleftrightarrow \text{access } (\text{U})$

$\left(\text{S}_{20}\right)$:　　　　　　$(\text{E,U,H}*) \Longleftrightarrow \text{prox}$

$\left(\text{S}_{21}\right)$:　　　　　　$(\text{G,U,H}*) \Longleftrightarrow \text{prox}$

$\left(\text{S}_{22}\right)$:　　　　　　　　$\text{G} \Longleftrightarrow \text{knows } (\text{H}* \text{ codes H})$

Notes: The conditions $\text{S}_{18} - \text{S}_{22}$ bear the same formal relationship to A_6 that $\text{S}_{13} - \text{S}_{17}$ have to A_5, with a permutation of symbols, provided one is careful to distinguish the double role played by symbol E in both atoms. Only the access conditions, S_{14} and S_{19}, relate to the main actor E of the atoms. All other E's, F's, and G's apply to the senders and receivers in the trans actions.

The only difference, then, between the above conditions and the previous set, is an informal rather than a formal one. Here, E is a "witting" sender (rather than the unwitting F of the previous notes), and therefore condition S_{20} is more readily achieved than condition S_{15}.

If getting and sending are combined into a single action A_7—

(A_7):

$$\text{E} \Longleftrightarrow \text{MTRANS} \xleftarrow{o} \text{H} \xleftarrow{R} \begin{array}{c} \rightarrow \text{G} \\ \\ \prec \text{F} \end{array} \xleftarrow{I} \text{V, U, H} \ast$$

then in general, conditions $S_{13} - S_{16}$ and $S_{19} - S_{22}$ are all necessary, with S_{17} and S_{18} dropping out.

The reader will note a substantial formal similarity in the enabling conditions listed for the three types of trans. It is conceivable that with some rearrangement of notation, a compact overall statement could be developed, although there would still remain essential substantive differences among the three types because of the nature of elements (persons, locations, things) filling the slots in the structural forms.

We turn now to various sub-varieties of plans.

2. THE CHAIN

This is a type of plan or expanded molecule M consisting of alternating A and S atoms following an initial P atom, satisfying the following conditions:

a) the final S in the chain is the state connected to the "want" in P;
b) each A is causally bonded to the S that follows;
c) the actor in each A is either the actor in the initial P or the agent of the actor in the preceding A (or the initial P if there is no preceding A);
d) each S "enables" the A that follows.

The last condition invokes the new concept of enablement, the other three conditions merely extending the original molecular conditions.

The *order* of a chain is the number of A-atoms in it other than the final (consummatory) action. A simple P-A-S molecule is thus a zero-order chain. The first-order chain is:

M :

$$\text{P} - \text{A}_1 - \text{S}_1 - \text{A}_0 - \text{S}_0$$

An increase in order results from every interpolation of another A-S pair in the chain. Conventionally, we will subscript the A's and S's in ascending order from right to left, since it seems natural to think backwards from the goal through the necessary preparatory steps.

Every S-atom enabling the following action by social contract must be preceded by a *proposal action*, in which agency is sought by means of an offer with incentives or threats. State-atoms enabling the following action by instrumental control are each preceded by an action we will call an *instrumental action*. It follows that the order of a chain is equal to the number of proposal actions plus the number of instrumental actions, and that *every "serial plan" (chain) can be specified by a sequence of particular proposal and instrumental actions, preceded by a purpose, and followed by a consummatory action.* The intervening S-atoms can be inferred from the surrounding A-atoms, and in that sense are redundant; if one were to seek parsimony, one might omit them.

3. TREES

The reader may have wondered in the brief discussion of chains how often it might be that only a single S-atom could enable the following A-atom, given the prior illustrations of enablement in which three, four, or five S's were needed to enable a single A. It probably would not be very often. Nevertheless there are examples in which the structure of a plan does not need to be much more complicated than a chain, even though there are multiple enablers prior to some or all of the A-atoms. To see this, we first establish as notation for multiple enablers, simply a fan of S-atoms left-connected to the enabled A-atom, say:

Now we note that not all of the states S_1, S_2, S_3 (*etc.*) need be achieved by the prior actions of the main actor of the plan. It is possible for various states to be *exogenous* to the plan, that is, to obtain by prior factors not requiring the intervention of the actor. For example, one of the enabling conditions for a directional trans is that the actor have access to the instrument (condition S_9, section 1b). If the dtrans represented, say, going to a nearby city by public transportation, then the actor's access to that transportation would (ordinarily) not be at issue, and the condition would be exogeneously satisfied.

We represent this possibility by left-connecting a short, unlabeled stem to all exogeneous states. Thus:

$\boxed{M}$:

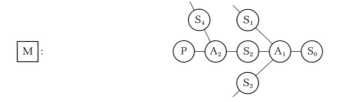

represents a plan in which the actor performs A_2 (with the aid of exogenous condition S_4) to produce S_2 which (together with exogenous conditions S_1, S_3) enables action A_1, which yields the outcome S_0.

All structures with form like the above structure, we label "trees," subsumed under the standard usage of this term in graph theory (Harary, Norman, and Cartwright, 1965). We have here a particularly simple class of trees; the removal of all exogenous S-atoms inevitably reduces any such tree to a simple chain. Since there are no A-atoms on any tree branches, we may cleanly define the order of a tree as the number of proposal actions plus the number of instrumental actions, and state that *every tree can be specified by a sequence of particular proposal and instrumental actions, (each possibly enabled by any number of exogenous states), preceded by a purpose, and followed by a consummatory action.* This statement is virtually identical to that for chains, and conditions a,b,c,d given for chains must hold for trees in addition.

An example of a tree is provided by the following elaborated sequence for "finding an object X." Suppose that E's general goal is to have X:

$\left(\text{P}\right)$:

$$ E \Longleftrightarrow want $$
$$ \uparrow $$
$$ E \Longleftrightarrow poss (X) $$

(The lower line by itself we label S_0). Now let us work backwards. One conceptual possibility for getting an object is to find it:

$\left(A_0\right)$:
$$ E \Longleftrightarrow PTRANS \xleftarrow{o} X \xleftarrow{R} \begin{array}{l} \rightarrow E \\ \llcorner < \emptyset \end{array} \xleftarrow{I} \text{"finder," } Y $$

where $\emptyset$ is a dummy symbol for a null person, and the instrument named "finder" could represent a variety of tools or sets of tools, ranging from a shovel to a diving bell.

Consulting the section on enabling conditions for physical trans, two atoms are required (new subscripts are given for the present example):

$\left(S_1\right)$:
$$ E \Longleftrightarrow access (Y) $$

$\left(S_2\right)$:
$$ (E,Y,X) \Longleftrightarrow prox $$

We attach a little stem to S_1 to indicate (let us suppose) that E already has access to Y; the strong form of access would be possession (see S_3 below), and we can imagine that E has Y (say, a searchlight).

In order to achieve S_2, an instrumental action is required, most plausibly for E to bring Y to the place where X is located:

$\left(A_1\right)$:
$$ E \Longleftrightarrow DTRANS \xleftarrow{o} (E \text{ and } Y) \xleftarrow{D} \begin{array}{l} \rightarrow \beta (X) \\ \llcorner < \alpha (E) \end{array} \xleftarrow{I} \text{vehicle, } Z $$

Here, β is a location proximate to X, and α is the location from which E starts. Again, we consult the enabling specification, this time for directional trans:

$\left(S_3\right)$:   E $\Longleftrightarrow$ poss (E & Y)

$\left(S_4\right)$:   E $\Longleftrightarrow$ access (Z)

$\left(S_5\right)$:   E $\Longleftrightarrow$ knows $[\beta(X)]$

?– –$\left(S_6\right)$: $[E,Y,Z,\alpha(E)] \Longleftrightarrow$ prox

?– –$\left(S_7\right)$: $[E,Y,Z,\beta(X)] \Longleftrightarrow$ prox

We consider these states one by one. We note that part of S_3, E having E, is true by definition, and the other part, E having Y, is similar to S_1 (see above), and we are supposing it to be exogenous in this example. Let us also take S_4 to be so (say, E owns a rowboat, which is the only appropriate means for searching the underground river cave in which X is located).

Suppose for illustration that S_5 is not exogenous, that E does not begin his plan with a knowledge of the location of X. (The square brackets $[\beta(X)]$ are meant to denote, "that the location of X is β.") Both S_6 and S_7 pose new problems for us. One cannot gracefully imagine that they are exogenous, that the actor is typically in a state of proximity with the vehicle, the finder, and the starting location (or, later, the finishing location). Yet for simplicity we would like to suppose that neither is problematical in the plan, that the actor has no special difficulty gathering himself and the equipment he needs (since he has access to the equipment), nor in navigating the vehicle to the approximate location (if S_5 were but true and he knew where the location was). Therefore we will temporarily not commit ourselves as to how S_6 and S_7 are to be integrated into a complete diagram. We put question marks at the left of their stems; in later sections we will resolve these question marks.

Tracing the plan yet one more step backwards, we ask what instrumental action would produce S_5. In order for E to know $\beta(X)$, some form of mental trans is required, say, having another person F tell him:

$\left(A_2\right)$:   F $\Longleftrightarrow$ MTRANS $\xleftarrow{\ o\ }$ $[\beta(X)] \xleftarrow{\ R\ } \begin{array}{c} \rightarrow \text{E} \\ \boxed{} \\ \prec \text{F} \end{array} \xleftarrow{\ I\ }$ U, H∗

The enabling conditions (appropriately permuting the symbols for purposes of the present example) are:

$\left(S_8\right)$:   F $\Longleftrightarrow$ knows $[\beta(X)]$

$\left(S_9\right)$:   F $\Longleftrightarrow$ access (U)

$?--(S_{10})$:

$(F,U,H*) \Longleftrightarrow$ prox

$?--(S_{11})$:

$(E,U,H*) \Longleftrightarrow$ prox

(S_{12}):

$E \Longleftrightarrow$ knows $[H* \text{ codes } \beta(X)]$

We take S_8, S_9 and S_{12} as exogenous, and S_{10} and S_{11} as non-problematic albeit unspecified as to how they come about, like S_6 and S_7. Presumably F can transmit to E through any of several media the information about the location of X—if he is willing. This last consideration reminds us that since the actor in A_2 is F, not E, that in order for A_2 to be enabled in the tree, we must have a social contract state:

(S_{13}):

$F \Longleftrightarrow$ agent $(E; A_2)$

In order to bring S_{13} about, E must initiate a proposal action, offering inducements to F:

(A_3):

$$E \Longleftrightarrow \text{propose} \xleftarrow{\text{I}} Q$$
$$F \Longleftrightarrow \text{MTRANS} \xleftarrow{\text{o}} [\beta(X)] \xleftarrow{\text{R}} \begin{matrix} \rightarrow E \\ \leftarrow F \end{matrix}$$

The instrumental control necessary for A_3 is simply:

(S_{14}):

$E \Longleftrightarrow$ poss (Q)

We assume S_{14} exogenous, and thus we have for the full tree of the plan of this example:

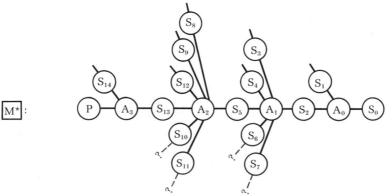

$M*$:

If this diagram looks cluttered, it is because the plan itself is elaborate when all spelled out: E must *offer* inducements to F to get him to *tell* the location β of X so that E can *direct* vehicle Z to β, and with the aid of tools Y, *find* X. Many different contents could fit into these structural positions. The underlined verbs refer to the actions A_3, A_2, A_1, A_0, the heart (or should one say spine?) of the plan. The rest of the structure has to do with the enabling knowledges and accesses, the little things which must be true for the plan to succeed, but which are often left implicit in informal discussion.

Trees for the realization of the same purpose by other means, or for the realization of other purposes, can readily grow to a level of elaboration as great or greater than the one in this example, although the conceptualizer may well abbreviate or omit uninteresting parts of any plan. The secret, however, of how such great elaboration is possible without cognitive overload is surely that each portion of the tree is based on simple, overlearned conceptual rules, and the total plan is constructed by concatenation of the portions.

4. NETWORKS

Plans more elaborate than trees arise because there are several meaningful ways in which branching structures may be defined so as to lead to the possibility of loops. We continue with our informal graphical presentation for ease in visualization, although a logical formalism such as LISP notation is superior for technical purposes. We will review the types of atomic linkages thus far given (a-d below) and then continue with the new ones (e-h). We will skip lengthy content examples, relying on the reader's ability to imagine them on the basis of the detailed examples of previous subsections.

a) 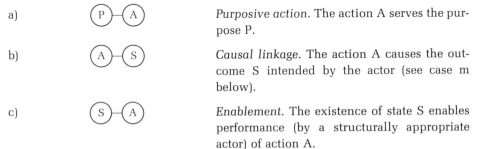 *Purposive action.* The action A serves the purpose P.

b) *Causal linkage.* The action A causes the outcome S intended by the actor (see case m below).

c) *Enablement.* The existence of state S enables performance (by a structurally appropriate actor) of action A.

d) 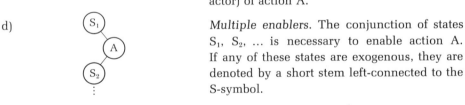 *Multiple enablers.* The conjunction of states S_1, S_2, ... is necessary to enable action A. If any of these states are exogenous, they are denoted by a short stem left-connected to the S-symbol.

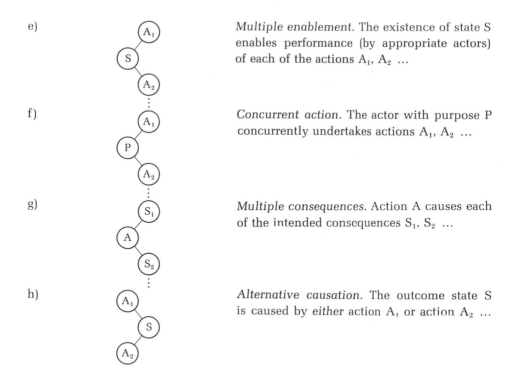

e) *Multiple enablement.* The existence of state S enables performance (by appropriate actors) of each of the actions A_1, A_2 ...

f) *Concurrent action.* The actor with purpose P concurrently undertakes actions A_1, A_2 ...

g) *Multiple consequences.* Action A causes each of the intended consequences S_1, S_2 ...

h) *Alternative causation.* The outcome state S is caused by *either* action A_1 or action A_2 ...

Note that the explication of branching situation h is logically different from those for d-g in that h has a disjunctive (either-or) interpretation rather than a conjunctive (both-and) interpretation. The reason why we choose this definition is that the possibility of alternative means to a goal is important, whereas the possibility of concurrent means to a single goal is less common and can be handled if necessary by the concept of "gating" (See Section 5 below).

i) Definition. A *network* is any concatenation of left-to-right linkages of types a-h beginning with a single leftmost P (that is, type a or f) and ending with one or more rightmost S's (that is, types b, g, or h).

  Note: The only atoms in a network lacking left-connection are the P and exogenous S's (if any). The only atom(s) lacking right-connection is(are) the final S(s). All A-atoms must be both left- and right-connected.

  Simple examples of networks are the following:

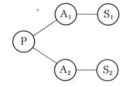

The actor pursues two states relevant to a single purpose by concurrent activities.

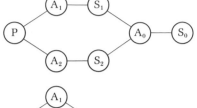

The actor enables action A_0 (leading to ultimate goal S_0) by concurrent actions A_1 and A_2 producing S_1 and S_2, respectively.

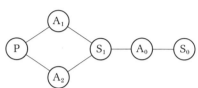

The actor causes S_1 (enabling A_0 which causes S_0) by either action A_1 or action A_2.

The last example embodies an apparent logical difficulty. The loop opens with an apparent *concurrent* action (type f) and closes with an *alternative* causation (type g). The accompanying text specifies that either A_1 or A_2 is performed, rather than both. This is consistent with the following:

j) Convention. Loops formed by simultaneous left-connection to an S-atom (type g) are to be considered as *alternative* paths, in precedence over any prior implication of concurrent paths.

It should be noted that loops formed by simultaneous left-connection to an A-atom (type d) retain their meaning as concurrent paths without question.

We are now in a position to resolve one of the loose ends from the previous section. It was left open in the example of finding an object X, how the achievement of certain of the S-atoms neither exogenous nor on the main chain could be represented. One such was the atom S_6, involving the proximity of the actor, a vehicle, a finder, and an initial place from which to embark on the search. A network representation serves readily to incorporate S_6, by invoking a new action A_4 which causes it. Omitting the exogenous and other problematic S's, the plan is:

M:

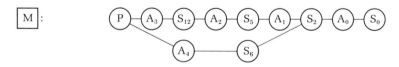

It is possible to formulate a statement mapping any network into a reduced network of A-atoms only, preceded by a P-atom, and leading to one or more terminal S-atoms, though we will not pursue that formulation here.

Several additional types of linkages seem potentially useful to broaden the set of contingencies covered by network-like structures. We define a set of four here and two more in Section 5.

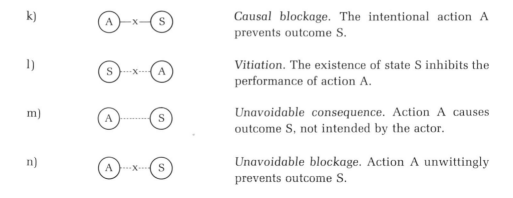

k)   *Causal blockage.* The intentional action A prevents outcome S.

l)   *Vitiation.* The existence of state S inhibits the performance of action A.

m)   *Unavoidable consequence.* Action A causes outcome S, not intended by the actor.

n)   *Unavoidable blockage.* Action A unwittingly prevents outcome S.

These last four relationships should not commonly arise in idealized conceptions of plans under the control of a single actor (and his agents). An actor will not ordinarily be conceptualized as defeating his own purposes, except in the interesting circumstances of neurotic behavior and states of altered consciousness. We introduce these primarily because their extensions will be useful in the next section.

5. GATING

There is a type of enablement somewhat more subtle than those we have considered thus far. A state, rather than permitting an action to happen at all, could determine whether or not an action led to a particular outcome. We call this relationship "gating," from the metaphor of a system of manipulable switches or gates that control the course followed by water, electricity, or locomotives. We notate gating by drawing an S-atom tangent to an A-S causal linkage (type b). There are two basic possibilities, positive and negative gating.

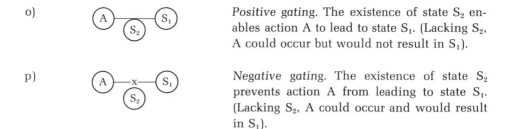

o)   *Positive gating.* The existence of state S_2 enables action A to lead to state S_1. (Lacking S_2, A could occur but would not result in S_1).

p)   *Negative gating.* The existence of state S_2 prevents action A from leading to state S_1. (Lacking S_2, A could occur and would result in S_1).

A couple of examples will help demonstrate how gating applies to conceptual structures. In many plans we find the coordinated presetting of facilitating conditions with ongoing activities. When bank robbers leave an accomplice outside in a car with the motor running, this enables exit from the bank to lead to efficient disappearance from the scene. A typical simple structure including gating would be the following:

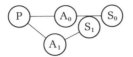

The actor undertakes action A_1 to produce state S_1, so that when he performs action A_0 it will lead to the goal S_0.

Sometimes the gating concept seems applicable even though there is only a single action, rather than two as in the above structure. The manner or skill with which an action is carried out may gate whether it achieves its intended goal. Thus we introduce the notion of *self-gating*:

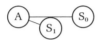

The action A (ordinarily) causes S_1, which is necessary to allow goal S_0 to occur.

This notation would be unnecessary except when S_1, the gating condition, is problematic, as for example by depending itself upon still another gating condition produced by another action (say, learning the skill needed in the effective performance of action A).

If we return our attention to a puzzling aspect of the example in Section 3, we may now note that in S_7 there is really an example of a self-gating rather than a simple enabling condition for the action A_1.

Negative gating would presumably arise in the plans of an actor only with a double goal, when the pursuit of one goal has the unavoidable consequence of blocking the attainment of the other. A typical simple structure of this kind is the following:

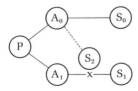

The actor could achieve goal S_1 through action A_1, except that pursuit of another goal S_0 through action A_0 has the unavoidable consequence that S_1 is blocked.

This kind of structure arises frequently in instances of choice and conflict.

Clearly the addition of gating to the set of structural relationships, along with types k-n, notably enlarges the possible structural complexities. The consequent mathematical constellations of atoms and relations are not covered by the mathematics of ordinary graph theory. Tentatively we will call these structures *gateworks*, for want of a better term, but we will not attempt to pursue any of their abstract mathematical properties. We now have enough background to be able to discuss the next level in the hierarchy of belief structures.

Plans to themes

Throughout the presentation of plans, we consistently adopted a conceptual orientation unilaterally focused upon the main actor. When there were agents, if they accepted the offer of the main actor, they became part of his plan and did not exercise autonomy of their own. No other actors with capability of enhancing or frustrating the plans of the main actor have thus far been invoked.

But of course, beliefs about social reality must include themes of cooperative and competitive interpersonal relationships. We wish to develop a taxonomy of such themes, building upon the structural system of the last section. It is helpful as a first step to ask the rhetorical question, in what ways can the autonomous purposes of two actors be interdependent? There seem to be three answers: interdependence arises as a function of role in the other's plan, of attitude toward the purposes or activities of the other, and of ability to facilitate or interfere with the outcomes of the other. The conjunction of these three variables gives each theme its particular character. We consider each in turn and then discuss the taxonomy yielded by their combination.

1. ROLE IN THE OTHER'S PLAN

There are at least three ways in which an actor F can play a role in the plan of another actor E: he can be the *agent* of E; he can be implicated in the *goal object* of E (e.g., E's goal is to harm F, or help him); or he can be an *interested party* who is affected in some other way, directly, during the actualization of E's plan.

We will need a notational framework in which to place these possibilities. To denote a theme, we use the letter T (with subscript if more than one theme is discussed) to the left of a brace naming the plans of E and F respectively. Each of these is represented by a large square or rectangle (the symbol for a plan), such that details of the relation between the two can later be filled in:

$$T: \quad \begin{cases} M(E): \quad \square \\ \\ M'(F): \quad \square \end{cases}$$

We now specify the way in which the three role relations are entered.

a) *Agent.* We have heretofore denoted the state of agency by F for a particular action A on behalf of E by:

$$F \Longleftrightarrow \text{agent } (E; A)$$

In the theme notation we will always be able to tell who the agent is, so that only the right-hand portion need be retained here.

We shall make use of the case in which F is E's agent exogenous to the particular plan at hand. This arises in continuing family and occupational role relationships, and in friendships. Both parties are aware in advance that the agency is available to be potentially invoked, unlike the case of an *ad hoc* social bargain which E strikes with F only in pursuit of M.

b) *Goal object.* The most common way in which an actor F can enter E's plan as a goal object is for S_0 to contain F as actor; that is, for E's purpose to be that F be happy, be rewarded, be dead, be humiliated, or any other such. It is also conceivable for F to be an "object" that E wants to possess, as a love object, as a ward, *etc.* For the moment we make no distinctions among these possibilities, simply marking the notation goalob (E; S_0) to the right of F's plan square in the theme.

c) *Interested party.* There are several ways in which F can be an "interested party" to a plan of E's without being either an agent or a goal object. The objects used in E's instrumental or consummatory actions might figure also in F's plans, as when there is competition for scarce resources. Or, E's plan may induce as unintended consequences certain states and/or feelings in F (for example, E's activities may be disturbing to F; or they may present him with unexpected opportunities; and so on). A third possibility is that F may anticipate activities and states of E's choosing and wish to act to aid or hinder them.

These several alternatives have different thematic consequences, and deserve detailed representation. One obvious notation is to record the atom(s), of E's plan for which F is an interested party. Thus, if F is affected by E's action A_j, we record F as an intpar (E; A_j); if F is oriented toward E's purpose, we use intpar (E; P); and so on. Another notational distinction comes from whether the party's interest is exogenous, or whether it arises as a consequence of the execution of the particular plan at hand. In the former case, the "intpar" is placed at the left of the plan symbol, and in the latter case, it is placed beneath; the same notation is used for agency.

2. ATTITUDE TOWARD THE OTHER'S PLAN (WHOLE OR IN PART)

Toward each of the three types of relationship discussed above, actor F may have a variety of attitudes; broadly considered, we may classify these as being either positive or negative.

The agent may like his role, because it is intrinsically satisfying or because the rewards for its performance are more than sufficient to compensate for its negative features; or the agent may dislike his role because it is maintained only by threats, or because its rewards are insufficient, and the role is carried out only because it is too costly to break the social contract. The former case we denote agent+ and the latter, agent−.

The actor who is a goal object of another may be pleased because he himself desires the help or love which the other wishes to bestow; or he may be the target of either unwelcome affection or an overtly negative goal state. The former possibility we denote goalob+, the latter, goalob−.

The interested party may stand to gain from the other's activities, or otherwise have a positive interest in his plan; or, he may stand to suffer by it or have a negative interest in it. The former we denote intpar$^+$, the latter, intpar$^-$.

3. ABILITY TO FACILITATE OR INTERFERE WITH THE OTHER'S PLAN

There are several ways in which an actor can influence the outcome of another's plan. In general, these parallel the ways in which an actor can influence his own plan, although the range of possibilities is broader since we should include actions which deliberately interfere with the other, an aspect not (usually) associated with self-influence.

The two major categories evolve from agency and from instrumental control.

a) *Distortion of agency.* When F is E's agent for some (or all) of E's plan, he is usually in a position to subvert the plan by carrying out his actions in an inferior way. As a more direct step, he may abort his assignment by breaking the social contract. These possibilities become more important, of course, in the agent$^-$ condition, whence F is motivated toward interference. The only time an agent does not have interference at his disposal as a viable possibility is when he is viewed as more or less helpless, either through physical restraint or because the threat for non-compliance is great enough to deter completely any such attempt. On the other side of the coin is the possibility that F will do more than his share as an agent, that he will go out of his way to expedite F's plan. This is conceivable in the agent$^+$ condition, especially if there are also other positive features in the interaction (that is, intpar$^+$ or goalob$^+$).

b) *Autonomous instrumental action.* Given an intpar or goalob relation, F might be sufficiently motivated to intervene in E's plan. Opportunities would present themselves whenever F was in a position to engage in instrumental action(s) enhancing or blocking the enabling or gating conditions for the actions of the other. These could include: giving information, sending supplies, blowing up bridges, bribing agents to subvert orders, etc., etc. The whole plan of F might indeed consist in aiding or preventing E's plan by some such means.

c) *Notation.* In all cases of ability to influence the plan of the other, we follow the convention of designating the atom or atoms of the plan which are potentially influenced. Such atoms are drawn within the plan square of the target actor, left-connected to the appropriate atoms within the plan square of the influencing actor. The most usual forms of connection would be causal linkage and causal blockage, although any of the relationships denoted in the previous section could conceivably occur.

To give a simple illustration, suppose action A_i' by actor F blocks state S_j in the plan of E (say, state S_j is an enabling condition of proximity between E and some object which he needs for further action A_k; actor F has a negative interest in E's taking this further action, and therefore takes action A_i' to keep the critical object away from E — by hiding it, let us say). This would be represented as below, including the further idea that E becomes a negatively interested party in F's blocking action A_i';

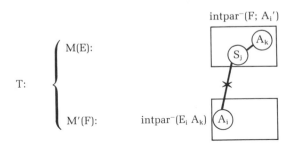

Notice that we do not spell out the rest of the structures either of M(E) or M'(F). At the *theme* level of structural abstraction, it is necessary to represent only the linkages between plans, not the plans themselves, just as at the *plan* level of structural abstraction it is necessary to represent only the linkages between atoms and not the atoms themselves. These lower levels of detail are of course potentially available to the belief system in a given case, but a good deal of processing may take place at a particular level of abstraction without reference to lower levels.

If each plan structure were spelled out in detail, we would have a big plan molecule with two autonomous sources of purpose. Every theme is such a "two-headed monster." The conceptual character of themes is very different from that of plans because of the linkages which cross the boundaries of autonomy of the separate actors, altering the course(s) of the outcome(s) which might otherwise obtain.

Interesting special cases arise when the two centers of autonomy exist within the same actor, as with a split personality, or simply with conscious vs. unconscious purposes, or with different factions within a polity. A single actor can also have a secret purpose at the same time that he presents a public purpose to a second actor. Such a theme would have three plans interrelated within it. Although we shall not deal with these types of examples in this paper, they can all be represented by the notation of this section. So too can cases involving three or more autonomous actors.

4. TAXONOMY OF THEMES

In the sections above, we have concentrated on F's orientations toward E. It is of course also possible that E may simultaneously have any of a number of orientations toward F. With all three relationship factors free to vary concomitantly for each actor in relation to the other, a great variety of themes may be generated. When we also consider that in certain cases interrelations of content of the two plans may make a difference, in addition to interrelations of structure, the ensemble of themes grows even larger. This large set must somehow be subdivided in order to attain a manageable taxonomy of themes.

In the subsections below, we will give an illustrative subdivision of theme types. It is not meant to be either fixed or exhaustive, only suggestive of the form a taxonomy can assume. It is an empirical question what form the theme taxonomy takes for any particular belief system, and it should be noted that any such scheme would perforce differ from one belief system to another (although certain theme conceptions are probably rather widely shared, as we hope to show in research currently under way). One function a theme taxonomy may perform in a belief system is to enable a large amount of detail to be "packaged" under a small set of labels.

The major critical features of our taxonomy will be: whether there are no negative role orientations, unilateral negative orientations, or mutual negative orientations; whether neither side has influence over the other's plan, whether one side has such influence, or whether both sides have such influence. The conjunction of these two features, each with three possibilities, creates nine cells, as shown in Box 7.2. In each cell we enter at least one theme name; where we give more than one, it indicates that variation in content or of secondary structural relation produces different themes.

We emphasize again that the scheme here is not meant to be exhaustive, only suggestive. The theme names are not necessarily ideal. In our diagrams illustrating theme types (indicated by number in Box 7.2), we will make tangible notational choices for the sake of clarity, even though other choices might illustrate each theme as well. The question of the proper conceptual boundary for each theme will be finessed in the present paper, as a matter for detailed future study.

a) *Admiration*. When actor F has positive feelings toward E's activities, without any possibility of influencing them in any way, we may speak of an admiration theme. If F is to have some activity of his own so that we can properly speak of two related plans, that activity presumably must revolve around the expression of this admiration. He might express it to a third party, for example, or as the fan of a sports team, he might express it by rooting for the team.

The theme diagram is so simple and barren of detail, it is omitted.

b) *Devotion*. This theme is the same as admiration except that F has the opportunity to help E overtly, and may exercise it repeatedly. Such a theme might be represented as below. (The plan squares are elongated into rectangles to allow more room. The dotted lines indicate the presence of further structural connections, unspecified.)

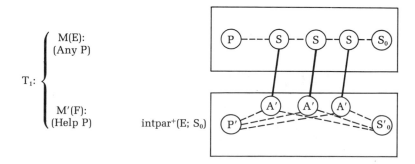

Box 7.2 A Taxonomy of Themes.

Sentiments toward other	Influence of Actors		
	Neither influences other	One influences other	Both influence other
Some positive, no negative	Admiration	(T_1) Devotion (T_2) Appreciation	(T_3) Cooperation (T_4) Love
One actor negative	(T_5) Alienation (also, Freedom)	(T_6) Betrayal (T_7) Victory (also, Humiliation) (T_8) Dominance	(T_9) Rebellion
Both actors negative	(T_{10}) Mutual Antagonism	(T_{11}) Oppression (also, Law and Order)	(T_{12}) Conflict

What this diagram says is that F's purpose P′ is that E should have help in achieving his purpose P. That is, F is a positive interested party to the attainment of outcome S_0. He plans a set of alternative A's, causally linked to enabling S's leading eventually to E's consummatory state. The A′ set thus leads to the realization $S_0′$ of F's devotion to E.

c) *Appreciation.* In this theme, F serves so well as E's agent that E goes out of his way to reward F beyond the terms of the agency.

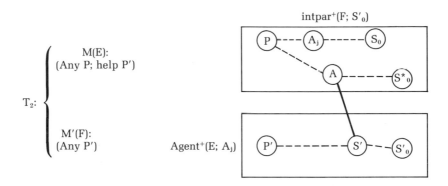

This diagram contains the following features: E has goal S_0 for which action A_j is instrumental. Actor F is the agent for this action, and E is so pleased by his performance that he (E) undertakes action A which helps F eventually achieve some other goal $S_0′$. This gives rise to the consummation S_0* of E's appreciation for F. (But for our reluctance to clutter the diagram, action A could perhaps have been represented as a set of alternatives, as with the devotion theme.)

Incidentally, the above diagram (and certain others, below) does not explicitly show F's performance of A_j within F's square because in that action F is E's agent, and not acting directly in the service of his own plans. Our plan rules allow an agent to be absorbed, as it were, within the molecule of another actor.

d) *Cooperation.* In cooperation, or at least in one of its most common variants, there is a confluence of interests by two actors in the achievement of the same goal (another possibility is reciprocal interest in a pair of goals), and each actor freely aids the other in the achievement of the common (or the reciprocal) goal. The common goal need not be the ultimate purpose of each actor's plan. It might be that a single state enables each actor to continue on his own route to a different final goal. If the actors are ordinarily rivals, this structure would illustrate the "strange bedfellows" phenomenon, a temporary and unexpected convergence of interests. The more usual cooperative situation would be one in which the actors were friendly, or had a history of cooperation, or had entered beforehand into mutual agency for the plans at hand. The diagram for T_3 below is a simple version of cooperation, stemming from mutual interest in a common final goal.

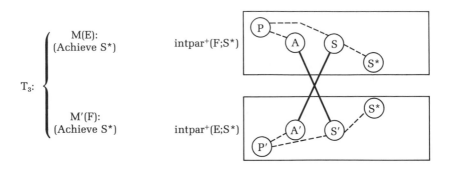

T_3:

$$\begin{cases} \text{M(E):} \\ \text{(Achieve S*)} \\ \\ \text{M'(F):} \\ \text{(Achieve S*)} \end{cases}$$

$\text{intpar}^+\text{(F;S*)}$

$\text{intpar}^+\text{(E;S*)}$

Having dwelt on a few themes in detail, we proceed through several others tersely, relying on the theme diagrams to explicate the essential features.

e) *Love.* The two partners share a twin goal: happiness of the other and happiness of self.

T_4:

$$\begin{cases} \text{M(E):} \\ \text{(Be happy; make F happy)} \\ \\ \text{M'(F):} \\ \text{(Be happy; make E happy)} \end{cases}$$

$\text{intpar}^+\text{(F;S'}_0\text{)}$

$\text{intpar}^+\text{(E;S}_0\text{)}$

$\text{goalob}^+\text{(F;S}_0\text{)}$

$\text{goalob}^+\text{(E;S'}_0\text{)}$

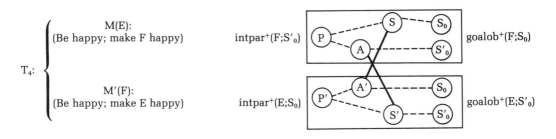

f) *Alienation.* Actor F is a negative interested party to one or more goals of E, and wants to prevent them, but has no means of so doing.

T_5:

$$\begin{cases} \text{M(E):} \\ \text{(Any P)} \\ \\ \text{M'(F):} \\ \text{(Prevent P)} \end{cases}$$

$\text{intpar}^-\text{(E;S}_0\text{)}$

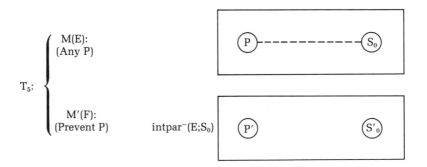

(The absence of a dotted line in the lower diagram is meant to indicate the inability of F to achieve his purpose.)

It is interesting to note of this theme that the name, "alienation," applies only from a point of view identifying with F. If the cognizer adopts the point of view of E, that is, of an actor who can do whatever he wants without fear of interference from those who don't like what he is doing, a more appropriate name might be "freedom." It is characteristically true of asymmetric themes that they deserve different names from the point of view of the different actors. In the final section of the chapter we consider the attitude of the *cognizer* toward the actors characteristic of the themes in his belief system, a nuance omitted in the neutral treatment of themes here.

g) *Betrayal.* Actor F, having apparently agreed to serve as E's agent for action A_j, is for some reason so negatively disposed toward that role that he undertakes instead to subvert the action, preventing E from attaining his purpose.

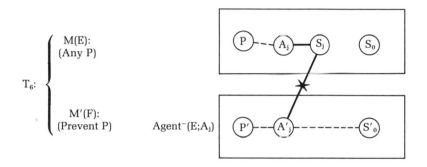

h) *Victory.* The previous theme may be modified slightly by altering F's role from that of agent to the combination of negative interested party and negative goal object. That is, E's goal is to hurt or control him in some way, but F succeeds in thwarting this plan. We sketch alternative preventive actions A' to emphasize the commitment F might have.

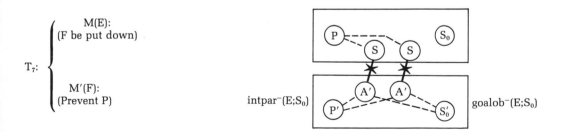

In this theme, the name "victory" of course applies only from the point of view of F. From E's point of view, something like "humiliation" is more appropriate.

i) *Dominance.* A rather different thematic flavor arises when we consider the case in which the actor with the negative attitudes is checked in his purposes, rather than checking the other actor.

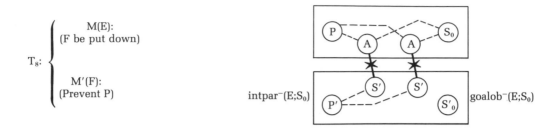

$$T_8: \begin{cases} \text{M(E):} \\ \text{(F be put down)} \\ \\ \text{M}'\text{(F):} \\ \text{(Prevent P)} \end{cases}$$

j) *Rebellion.* This term is meant to connote a thematic struggle which might follow a theme of Dominance if the weaker side were able to mobilize sufficient resources to partially check the stronger side. (The possibility of coherent successions of themes gives rise to the next level of structural abstraction, the Script, which is treated in the next section.)

$$T_9: \begin{cases} \text{M(E):} \\ \text{(F be put down)} \\ \\ \text{M}'\text{(F):} \\ \text{(Prevent P)} \end{cases}$$

As written, this theme expresses only the rather narrow goal on the part of the aggrieved party, F, of preventing E's dominance. It would be a natural extension of such a modest rebellion theme if F developed the related goal that E suffer injury, and if E in turn adopted punitive attitudes toward F rather than merely a formal control orientation. (See the Conflict theme below.)

k) *Mutual antagonism.* Both parties strongly disapprove of the activities of the other, but neither side is able to exert preventive influence. The theme diagram is bland:

$$T_{10}: \begin{cases} \text{M(E):} \\ \text{Any P} \\ \\ \text{M}'\text{(F):} \\ \text{Any P}' \end{cases}$$

l) *Oppression.* This term seems to be used to refer to themes of strong dominance, accompanied by negative feelings on the part of the dominator toward the dominated.

T_{11}:   (Modification of T_8; for example, by adding intpar$^-$(F;S$'_0$) to E's plan.)

From the point of view of the dominator rather than the dominated, this theme might be called "law and order" rather than "oppression."

m) *Conflict.* In a theme of all-out conflict, both sides attempt to hurt the other, and to prevent hurt to themselves. If the forces are approximately balanced, neither side is either completely successful or completely unsuccessful. This requires a fairly complex theme diagram.

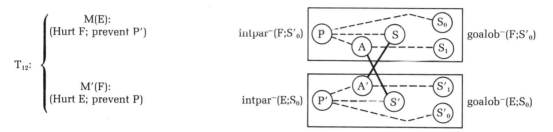

This completes our illustrative taxonomy of certain themes. Notwithstanding the probable necessity for future revision to clean and neaten the notation, we are nevertheless in a position to proceed now to the next level of structural abstraction.

Themes to scripts

Themes encode often repeated, perhaps even stylized, interactions between individuals or organizations or nations. The more common themes are familiar to every mature human cognizer by virtue of direct or symbolic experience with a large number of specific content examples embodying particular thematic structures. Some themes (e.g., conflict) occur between many actors, and between the same actors many times. Different belief systems may encode different actors as typical participants in such themes and perhaps vary minor structural details, but there seems little doubt that there is a widely shared repertoire of themes available to virtually every belief system.

Different systems may diverge in the structures they recognize among less common themes, but more importantly, in the way they see themes as being connected to one another. Themes capture what one might call "temporary dynamics," relationships which last only as long as the durations of the respective plans. After the completion of the realization of a theme, a further realization of the same theme is possible only when the relationship between the actors remains the same. But it may often be anticipated that as a consequence of one or more realizations of a theme, the relationship between the actors changes, and a new theme ensues.

There are various plausible possibilities for theme sequences, constituting the "long-range dynamics" which the belief system is capable of understanding. Different systems would in general contemplate different theme sequences, or *scripts*. We will here present a few simple illustrative scripts, including that of the master script from the beginning of this chapter.

We will use a simple notation for constructing scripts from themes. Suppose, for example, that a theme of Dominance (T_8) is followed by a theme of Rebellion (T_9). We write:

$$T_8(E;F) \rightarrow T_9(E;F)$$

The actors are noted in parentheses for precision of reference, since it is always possible for more than two actors to be involved. We might have a script, say, in which E's dominance over F sets in motion a theme in which F dominates G—a familiar pecking-order phenomenon:

$$T_8(E;F) \rightarrow T_8(F;G)$$

The arrow—indeed, the very notion of a script—is intended to apply only when one theme coherently follows the other; an accidental or arbitrary time sequence does not suffice. In a script, to say that one theme causes the next is close to the intended idea, but perhaps a bit too sharply stated. We prefer the following phraseology: in a script, it is in the nature of the relevant psychological or sociological forces that one theme follows the other. In colloquial terms, a script is a sequence which is "in the cards," or in the more florid cliché, which "unrolls like a rug." There is no contradiction between the very precise connotation of the notation "$\rightarrow$" and the rather vague and inscrutably Oriental character of the preceding verbal statements. We are not concerned with mapping real events into a formal logic, but with mapping cognitive representations into a formal logic. It is possible (indeed, we assert, commonplace) for a belief system to hold that a thematic sequence is inexorable without being at all capable of explicating with clarity (let alone scientific rigor) what factors in the real world are responsible.

Many ideological, nationalistic and/or idealistic scripts postulate dramatic theme transitions supported by flimsy metaphors or evanescent motivational constructs. "The War to end all wars," "The Domino Theory," and "The withering away of the State" are three such examples. Many others could be adduced from ideologies of child-rearing (such-and-such child-rearing practice inevitably produces such-and-such later consequences), treatment of criminals (such-and-such punitive or rehabilitative practice necessarily has such-and-such societal consequences), and so on.

1. SIMPLE SCRIPTS

When we write $T_i(E;F)$, some convention must tell us which actors play which roles of the theme; in asymmetric themes, $T_i(E;F)$ will be different from $T_i(F;E)$.

At the structural level of the script itself, the system is indifferent to content identifications; but of course a total functioning belief system must be able to traverse structural levels. The system will have stored a list of themes, $T_1, T_2, \ldots T_i \ldots$, each defined with respect to a "first actor" and a "second actor" (say, top and bottom actor in our theme diagrams). Then $T_i(E;F)$ refers to the i:th theme, with E playing the role of the first actor and F the role of the second. If there are themes with more than two actors, (a perfectly reasonable possibility which we have not explored in this paper), the simple notation can be extended in the obvious way.

Simple scripts can be formed with single transitions, $T_i \rightarrow T_j$, or with chains of transitions, $T_i \rightarrow T_j \rightarrow T_k$. We list a few examples of this kind using the themes given above. Suggestive names may be given to scripts, as was done for themes.

a) *Blossoming.* Love themes (T_4) often arise from less intense and possibly non-mutual relationships, such as Devotion (T_1), Appreciation (T_2) or Cooperation (T_3). With but a single transition, we would have, for example:

$$T_1(E;F) \rightarrow T_4(E;F)$$

b) *Turncoat.* An agent with a history of devotion to an actor may gradually become fed up for some reason, and betray the relationship:

$$T_1(E;F) \rightarrow T_6(E;F)$$

c) *End of the honeymoon.* Another common script is the love relationship gone sour. Inserting an intermediate step of rebellion by one partner between love and mutual conflict would yield:

$$T_4(E;F) \rightarrow T_9(E;F) \rightarrow T_{12}(E;F)$$

Note that this script and the two previous ones have the property that transitions are between neighboring cells in Figure 7.2. This is plausible, since in each such transition there is a change in but one factor of the theme taxonomy, while the other factor stays constant.

d) *The worm turns.* Another kind of possibility is a role reversal within a single theme. One might, for example, find that the original underdog becomes top dog in a Dominance theme:

$$T_8(E;F) \rightarrow T_8(F;E)$$

e) *Revolution.* This can be viewed as an extended script with step-by-step transitions achieving an ultimate reversal of dominance. First diffuse rebellion, then full-scale conflict, then victory by the underdog, and finally a consolidation of the new roles:

$$T_8(E;F) \rightarrow T_9(E;F) \rightarrow T_{12}(E;F) \rightarrow T_7(E;F) \rightarrow T_8(F;E)$$

2. NOTATION

In general, our conventions follow those for joining atoms into themes, with much greater simplicity here because we need not deal with different kinds of atoms and certain other special cases. (Actors are omitted below for compactness.)

a) *Consequence.*

$$T_i \rightarrow T_j$$

Theme T_j is a consequence (in the sense discussed above) of theme T_i.

b) *Multiple consequences.*

Theme T_i is followed by themes T_j and T_k (etc.).

c) *Multiple preconditions.*

The joint occurrence of themes T_i, T_j (etc.) is necessary to produce theme T_k.

d) *Positive gating.*

The occurrence of theme T_i is necessary in order that theme T_j produce theme T_k.

e) *Negative gating.*

The occurrence of theme T_i prevents theme T_j from producing theme T_k.

f) *Script ensemble.*

The script named $\mathscr{S}$ (subscripted if more than one is given reference) contains theme lines of "subplots" beginning with themes T_i, T_j ... (etc.).

3. MORE SCRIPTS

The above notations may be illustrated by a variety of content examples. We will omit the left-most $\mathscr{S}$ symbol for brevity, but it should be understood as present in each example.

a) *Romantic triangle.* A love relationship between E and F, simultaneous with a love relationship between G and F, is conceptualized as leading inevitably to a conflict relation between E and G, beginning with a mutual antagonism theme.

$$T_4(E;F)$$
$$\searrow$$
$$\qquad T_{10}(E;G \rightarrow T_{12}(F;G)$$
$$\nearrow$$
$$T_4(G;F)$$

This script can obviously be embellished by adding a victor in the conflict, specifying what happens to each separate relationship, *etc.*

We digress to note that this well-known script is an exception to the "balance principle" (Heider, 1946), which requires that positive social relationships be transitive. For example, if the love themes in the above script were replaced by cooperation themes, it would be plausible for cooperation between E and G to ensue, rather than rivalry.

This raises the question, "How does a belief system construct plausible scripts?". How does the system "know" that cooperation is transitive (so to speak), whereas romantic love is not? One possible answer is that the system learns from examples available in its culture. If it is statistically true that cooperation often occurs *à trois*, but love only *à deux*, then scripts will be constructed consistent with this experience. This answer is partially adequate, but we suspect that something more directly intrinsic to the conceptual content is involved. It is possible for content details within thematic structures to be communicated to the script level of abstraction, so that script construction may be shaped according to appropriate conceptual rules. (Recall that plan construction was shaped by rules related to the content details within atom structures.) In particular, the romantic rivalry script may be conditioned by such considerations as: 1) the obvious impossibility of three persons being heterosexually related in all pairs; 2) the concept that time must be budgeted by F between E and G, who will each resent the loss of total access to the love object; 3) the need of lovers for privacy, diminishing the probability of $(E, F, G) \Longleftrightarrow$ prox, which would certainly be commonplace for joint cooperation themes; etc. One does not know which among several considerations might be crucial in any given case, and the whole topic of the ways in which thematic content can influence script structure needs careful study. At the root of such an investigation is the question of what assumptions are made in belief systems to explain changes in relationships — what do people think explains jealousy, loss and gain of influence, growth of attraction, and so on. These matters of "naive psychology" are of considerable importance.

b) *Alliance.* A script that does conform to the balance principle is one in which a pair of overlapping rivalries lead to an alliance between the parties with a common enemy.

$$T_{12}(E;F) \searrow$$
$$T_{12}(E;G)$$
$$T_3(E;G) \nearrow$$

c) *Rescue.* An application of the negative gating concept occurs in scripts involving rescue. An actor threatened by oppression in a potentially losing struggle with an adversary, is rescued by a third party, reversing the occurrence of the feared outcome.

$$T_{12}(E;F) \xrightarrow{\;x\;} T_{11}(E;F)$$
$$T_8(G;E) \longrightarrow T_{11}(F;E)$$

It is clear that many familiar scenarios of changes in social or political relationships can be represented by scripts of the sort we have been discussing. Since the script is the structure at the top of the pyramid of abstraction, there is a great deal of structural detail ultimately nested within a script, and often this whole structural cascade can be evoked by one or two words (as in the script names above). This is the sort of neat packaging which is essential to our present effort to reconstitute our ideological simulation. We now return to the master script from Part I of this chapter, to see how it can be treated in the present notation.

4. A COLD WAR SCRIPT

Recall that there were four main categories of actors in the Cold War script from Part I:

C, Communist Powers
F, Free World
G, "Good Americans"
L, Liberals and left-wingers.

The master script $\mathscr{S}$ might now be paraphrased as follows:

There is a great struggle taking place between the Free World and the forces of Communism [T_{12} (C;F)], which the Communists fully expect to pursue until they totally control the world [T_{11} (C;F)]. Liberal and left-wing dupes who dominate many Free World governments [T_8 (L;F)] are playing into the hands of Communist designs. It is the task of good Americans to oppose and expose these fuzzy-thinking liberals [T_{12} (G;L)]. With determination, we can rid the Free World of their influence [T_5 (F;L)] and a strong America can then establish a cooperative relationship with other free peoples [T_3 (G;F)] in order to block Communist schemes and bring about a Free World victory [T_{11} (F;C)].

This script is diagrammed below in Box 7.3, which represents the same information as in Box 7.1 of Part I, but now in a format consistent with all the work of Part II. The small numbers along the arrows are for reference back to the branches of Box 7.1 only.

One may note certain apparent differences from the prior representation, but all seven branches still occur, along with the two key intersections (x) where the fates of the contending parties are in confrontation. Thus the differences are more apparent than real. The motives of both Communists and Liberals are concealed within the themes in the two upper left-hand themes, and could be recovered by reference to the detailed structures of the T_{12} and T_8-type themes for this particular belief system. (These need not be exactly the generic forms displayed in the previous section.) The ways in which the system optimistically supposes that its enemies will be defeated and its friends victorious are specified in somewhat more detail here than in Box 7.1, by virtue of the appearance of both the Freedom theme, T_5, and the Cooperation theme, T_3. The best evidence of the superiority of the present representation over the previous will come from a new simulation, but it is already conceptually clear that the new representation has the great advantage that the connections from structural top to bottom are well codified rather than more or less arbitrary.

Box 7.3   A Cold War Script.

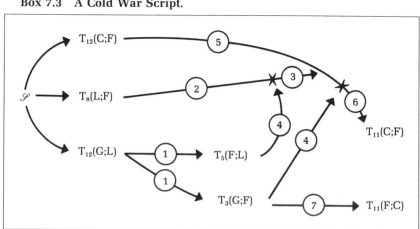

Structural organization in a belief system

All of the foregoing analysis pertains to structural possibilities, to entities which might occur in a conceptual universe concerned with human actions and relationships. Except in passing, we have not addressed ourselves to the concept of a given belief system selecting from among all the structural and content possibilities an ensemble which it invests with subjective truth-value.

We distinguish four respects in which one belief system may differ from another, which is to say, four properties which give definition to a particular belief system. These are: 1) structural representation; 2) content-in-structure; 3) value; 4) exemplification. We consider each in turn.

1. STRUCTURAL REPRESENTATION

Although we have presented a generic hierarchical system, it does not necessarily happen that all individual systems are structurally complete or have identical composition rules.

As we have presented them, the rules for passing from one structural level to the next are rather clear at the lowest levels, and become less clear as one ascends the pyramid of abstraction. The specifications by which elements are defined and are combined into atoms are relatively unambiguous in conceptual dependency analysis. Presumably an understanding of the conceptual nature of simple objects and actions — their denotative meaning, as it were — is widely shared among human beings (and by extension, artificial intelligence systems designed to capture human knowledge of the world). At this level, there is not much room for differences between belief systems; indeed, one tends to talk here of knowledge systems ("Is a house bigger than a bread box?" "What is 'walking'?" etc.) rather than belief systems.

At the next highest level, the transition from atoms to molecules and plans is also relatively clear, though by no means absolutely cut-and-dried. We have noted that there are certain difficulties in the specification of the causal relation, and that enablement through instrumental control had only been worked out theoretically for the trans class of actions. Nevertheless we assert, subject to a necessary series of empirical validations, that most informants in most modern societies would have substantial agreement *at the level of the single actor*, what kind of actions cause what kind of states, and what kinds of states enable what kinds of actions. If this is so, it would have the consequence that most informants would agree on what simple plans are plausible attempts to achieve simple outcomes. That is, if we were to ask respondents to formulate a simple plan for gaining possession of a certain object X, given some initial constraints and properties, they would tend to invent constructions similar to our examples, and to recognize as valid such constructions by others. We deem it reasonable to construct a simulated system with this kind of general knowledge standardized and available to it regardless of its particular beliefs. To be sure, we would thereby bypass the possibility of creating individual differences in the ingenuity with which plans can be constructed or interpreted. This is an interesting possibility, but not one at the forefront of our present concern.

When we move to the level of the connection between plans and themes, the composition rules become less clear, and there is much more room for individual variation. There are at least two major reasons why this might be so. There are so many combinations of modes of interrelation of two actors, especially when one considers content variations in the pair of plans, that any taxonomy must necessarily be a selective and somewhat arbitrary division of the set of possibilities. Beyond this, there is much experiential difficulty in observing what is going on in thematic relationships in which one is personally involved, since one often cannot be sure about the real intentions and capabilities of the other party. If both parties are Others, there might be even more difficulty. It is possible to misread Alienation as Rebellion, or Submission as Devotion, or Admiration as Love, etc. This difficulty does not obtain for plans, which fall under unilateral conceptual control, so that one may use one's own plans as a basis for conceptual generalization. The consequence of this is that early experience in the miscategorization of thematic cues might lead a belief system to have a distorted set of thematic structures, heavily emphasizing some types at the expense of others.

At the script level, the multitude of possible combinations of themes into scripts becomes very striking. As discussed in Section F, the "consequence" relation for weaving themes together is much more vague and potentially idosyncratic than was the "causal" relation for linking A and S-atoms. Therefore we expect a *great deal of variation from one belief system to another in how themes are combined into scripts.* One system may emphasize one or more of what one might call Righteous Struggle scripts, such as the Cold War script; another may have a Pollyanna orientation, in which Conflict is always replaced by Cooperation, and so on. There is a great deal of room for idiosyncracy, and we doubt that there is any way for an artificial intelligence system to generate "correct" scripts by an automatic procedure.

An even sharper distinction between belief systems than how themes combine, is whether or not the system has any scripts at all! It seems to us entirely possible for the structural hierarchy to arrest at the theme level. Some individuals may never conceptualize anything more abstract than the thematic short-run dynamics of "the way things are," without any sense or expectation of evolution, of change, of things being different. Such belief structures would be quintessentially non-ideological. Ideologies necessarily foresee changes in the "system" of relationships binding the major actors; this is presumably what ideology is all about. Thus, without a script, one cannot be said to have an ideology. With a script, a single script for a given domain of discourse (e.g., foreign policy), the structure is prepared to respond to all questions in terms of its overriding ideology.

There is of course also the possibility that a belief system may contain several scripts within a given domain of discourse. For example, an international affairs analyst may simultaneously foresee a decline of the Cold War, increasing tension in the Middle East, revolt in Africa against white colonialist regimes, increasing federation of European nations, etc. Such a system, like the one with no scripts, would also be non-ideological, but in a different sense. With multiple scripts, a belief system would be flexibly capable of several abstract interpretations of the same events, plans, or themes. Such a system we will call *analytic*.

To summarize, we posit that all belief systems have standardized structural knowledge up to the level of plans, but that themes and scripts are constructed in different ways by different systems.

2. CONTENT-IN-STRUCTURE

Another and perhaps even more important source of variation between belief systems is in the *assignment of particular actors or categories of actors to particular atoms, plans, themes and scripts.* This is essentially what we mean when we refer to "content." For any given structural configuration, the system will have available a specification of what actors are conceived as fitting the configuration, these specifications differing from level to level.

At the atom level, most of these specifications are presumably very general. Anybody could be involved in a "ptrans," for example. In other cases, the set of admissible actors might be "anybody except X's. . . ." For example, if the action is "seeing," the potential actor is "anybody except a blind person." This is all in the realm of general conceptual knowledge rather than individual belief. When actions or states are specialized rather than general, then the admissible actor sets might also be specialized rather than general. Who flies planes? Pilots. . . . Who walks peculiarly? Cripples and perhaps comedians. . . . Etc. Again, these concepts are shared bits of definition or knowledge. Only in very specialized actions and value considerations should one belief system differ from another in admissible atom content. Who kills innocent women and children? The other side. . . .

At the plan level, there is also a great deal of common "knowledge." Who plans to be well liked? Almost everybody. Who plans long voyages? Diplomats and tourists. . . . Who plans to obtain secret information? Spies. . . . Who plans to assassinate American political leaders? Kooks and loners. . . . and so on. This last example makes clear, however, that subjective variations are quite possible. Although "kooks and loners" might be an accurate categorization in one belief system, "conspirators" would be more appropriate in another. That is, there is room for difference in the assignment of particular actors to particular types of plans, much more difference than is the case at the atom level.

At the theme level, subjective content is even more pronounced. Who cooperates with whom, who is in conflict with whom, who dominates, who is oppressed or put upon, who betrays obligations,—all of these are free to vary from one belief system to another. An interesting corollary of the identity of the actors appearing in certain themes is the identity of actors who do not appear, that is, who are deemed impossible to imagine in certain roles. For the chauvinist, and even many an ordinary citizen, it is impossible to imagine that his country oppresses other nations, for example. (The tenacious American myopia in Vietnam has stemmed in part from this kind of categorical inadmissibility, we would suppose.)

The foregoing remarks apply with even greater force at the script level. If a belief system is ideological, rather than analytical, it is especially committed to the assignment of particular actors to particular roles in its master script. This is partly what gives that script its partisan point of view (See also the section below on value).

When there are several scripts, many of the actors may be particularized, but conceivably there could also be generalized scripts (such as a playwright might have a stock of) which could accommodate a wide class of particular actors.

In brief, all levels of a structural hierarchy can display content variation from one to another belief system, but this variation is minimal at the atom level, and maximal at the script level.

3. VALUE

Once the actor is specified, the state designated by a given S-atom may potentially be assigned a value by the cognizer. If the actor is remote and/or the condition uninteresting, no value will be assigned, but if the actor is the cognizer himself or someone important to him, then interesting outcomes will be given either a positive or a negative value. This value will be positive when the self, or someone with whom the self is identified, is associated with a pleasant outcome; or when an opponent or disliked actor is associated with some negative outcome short of overkill. The value will be negative when the self, or someone with whom the self is identified, is associated with a negative outcome; or when an opponent or disliked actor is associated with a positive outcome.

The assignment of value affects all levels of a structure. Thus, plans successfully achieving (dis)valued S-atoms are (dis)valued. Themes in which both actors pursue (dis)valued plans are (dis)valued. Themes in which one protagonist is pursuing a valued plan, and the other a disvalued plan, permit the cognizer to "take sides," to hope that his side succeeds and the other side fails, and to feel the appropriate elation or despair when the outcomes are known.

Such *polarized themes* provide important orientation points for individual belief systems. They permit the system to interpret the value potential of previously unfamiliar actors and actions, by connecting them to one thematic pole or the other. We hypothesize a psychological tendency toward strong vigilance for cues identifying statements implying support or opposition of either the valued or disvalued actor of a polarized theme. Such statements would tend to be quickly noticed and would serve to readily amplify existing belief structures (e.g., by adding the speaker to the list of admissible actors in plans similar to the thematic plans). A case in point is the rather dramatic indignation which typically greets any criticism of a government in time of crisis, because it "gives aid and comfort to the enemy." One would expect different belief systems to differ in how touchy they were in this regard, according to the degree of elaboration and strength of value of their polarized themes (if any).

Since scripts are composed of themes, it is natural at this point to ask what configurations of valued, disvalued, and polarized themes one would expect to find in scripts. For a strong ideology, there almost certainly exists a polarized theme with a consequent disvalued theme, either negatively gated by a valued theme (as in the Cold War victory script) or followed in turn by a valued theme (as in the promise of a better life in the Hereafter). For analytic belief systems, there are no obvious constraints on the value configurations in scripts.

4. EXEMPLIFICATION

Different belief systems are differentially exposed to, and differentially retain, a variety of "facts." For our purposes, a fact is an event or series of events presumed real by the believer, exemplifying a structure at some level of the hierarchy.

Exemplification is common for atoms, since daily experience provides many examples of easily conceptualized actions and states. It is not necessarily true, however, that *all* atoms in the structural repertoire of the system are accompanied by knowledge of real examples. The system may be able to conceptualize an actor eating grasshoppers, let us say, or having hysterical blindness, without knowing of a single specific instance of the act or the state. One "hears that people have done it," or have had it. Some structures may be learned entirely symbolically rather than by induction from concrete examples, in other words. (The whole domain of the mode of learning of belief structures is fertile for psychological inquiry. For a study of certain features of induction from examples, cf. Abelson and Kanouse (1966) and Kanouse (1972).)

There is also the rare possibility of a fact being acknowledged without the prior existence of a structure in which to embed it (e.g., "Our side killed babies at My Lai"). The system may handle such an example by enlarging its structural repertoire, although if the example is embarrassing because it has unpleasant value implications, the new content-in-structure may not be allowed to proceed above the atom level of the hierarchy. ("Our side killed babies, but we didn't *plan* to kill babies like the other side does.")

At the plan level, exemplification is probably somewhat less frequent than at the atom level. One does not always understand the purposes of others, and many actions are observed without knowledge of outcome, or outcomes without knowledge of action. One can, however, induce examples of plans from examples of actions, or be told second-hand about examples of plans.

Direct observation becomes even less important at the theme level, because there is too much to observe at once for economical cognitive absorption. Induction from interrelated plans, and being told about thematic examples, become correspondingly more important. Themes are the stuff of anecdotes and journalism. The fantastic Clifford Irving caper is a marvelous example of a Deceit theme (closely related to the Betrayal theme of Figure 7.2). Thus themes need suffer no want of examples, although some themes in some belief systems may be thinly or not at all represented by examples.

Finally, scripts are probably not very densely represented by examples, although it would seem psychologically necessary for ideologies to promulgate at least one master example of the historical realization of the master script (and within that one master example several sub-examples using different shadings of theme content). Revolutionary ideologies have their favorite revolution to refer back to, whether Irish, French, Russian, Chinese, or whatever. The Cold War script, in addition to current parables such as the Czechoslovakia invasion and the Korean War, has a stark historical anchor in what might be called the "Munich model" ("Appease them, and you'll only whet their appetites and have to fight them later."). Of course a system lacking dialectic expertise may be fuzzy on the details of its historical script example; it is not necessary for the example to penetrate all the way down to the atom level in order for it to be invoked by the system at higher levels. Thus a system may have a rather loosely strung fabric of exemplifications throughout its hierarchy, the examples at lower levels possibly differing from those at higher levels for nested structures. More well-elaborated systems, whether ideological or analytic, would have more consistency among examples at different levels, providing yet another way in which belief systems may differ.

5. THE QUESTION OF OPERATION OF THE NEW SIMULATION

Part II of this paper has been about structure, not process. We have posited an elaborate potential system of hierarchical structural levels with well-determined composition rules at lower levels and looser rules at upper levels, with one system differing from the next in terms of admissible structures, content categories, value orientations, and exemplifications. We have not said how a simulation using this new system would work.

While a detailed treatment would be beyond the scope of the present paper, it is important to give some indication of our intentions. The business of levels creates complications, as there are many problems of communication between levels, as well as frequent ambiguities as to which level the system should work on. But at the same time, a well-constructed hierarchy provides opportunities for intelligent systemic response that were previously lacking; indeed, that was the whole reason for its construction. If we consider an example that was previously troublesome, we will see both the problems and the opportunities.

Suppose the Cold Warrior is asked whether it is credible that Red China built the Berlin Wall. (We deal here with a credibility question; the other more elaborate question types discussed in Part I involve all the same considerations, and more.) In order to make this situation interesting, we must suppose that the system has forgotten (or never knew) who built the Berlin Wall originally, but believes that it presently serves a function contrary to the interests of the Free World. The first thing the system might do is check at the atom level whether this type of structure is conceptually admissible: Can a country build a wall? Well, yes, there is no constraint on this actor-action pair to rule it out. In fact, if one next looks for examples, one may find that China once built the Great Wall, but there is no record in the system of who built the Berlin Wall.

Mildly encouraged to answer yes to the original question, the system next might search at a higher level. Are there general plans in which wall-building fits? (Yes, but this is not a very critical question). Are there plans for which Red China might be a plausible actor, in which this particular wall-building action would plausibly fit? Knowing that this action is causally connected to an outcome of Free World discomfort, the answer is definitely yes. Red China as a Communist actor might readily be thought to undertake an action distressing to the West, because in the view of a Cold Warrior system such is the nature of typical Communist planning. The previous simulation system would answer at this point that indeed Red China did build the Berlin Wall, that was exactly the sort of nasty thing Communist nations were always doing.

A more sophisticated system, however, should clearly go one step further. It should say, all right, building the Berlin Wall could easily be a Red Chinese plan (and they would certainly approve such a move), but could they actually have carried out such a project? The action of "building" has enabling conditions, the most pertinent of which is a "prox" condition, the proximity of the builder, the object built, and the building location. A program with any modicum of intelligence would now conclude that Red China, much as they would have liked to, could not have built the Berlin Wall because they are not close enough to the required location, and countries cannot be subjected to directional trans. Here, the response could be more subtle by calculating that someone else could have done it as agent for them (and the system could consult its knowledge of possible agents of Red China, etc.) or by finding other Communist nations satisfying the proximity conditions with or without agents such as soldiers. Thus, a well-formed total response might be, "I'm sorry, I don't have the historical information on who actually built the Berlin Wall. Red China certainly would have favored such an action harassing the West, but they are not close enough to have done it directly. Of course, they could always have had someone do it for them, or some other Communist power equally interested in damaging the Free World, such as Russia or East Germany, could have done it."

There are two important things to note about this example, which, while a bit fanciful, is certainly not atypical of the kinds of calculations a Cold Warrior system might be called upon to make. First, there are a lot of bits of knowledge included, in addition to the belief presumptions about Communism giving the system its Cold Warrior character. There is the conceptual compatibility information of whether a country can build a wall; there is the event memory for what countries have built what walls (in this example, with lacunae); also the specific information that the Berlin Wall embarrassed the West; there is a list of enabling conditions for the action "build"; finally (or not so finally, if the response is to be subtle) there must be a map or its equivalent, so that the non-proximity of China to Berlin could be calculated. This is a lot of information for a simple specific example, and of course the requirements would be compounded manyfold for any decent-sized conceptual vocabulary. There is really no way around it—there can be no veridical simulation of a belief system on a small scale.

Second, the hypothetical response process given above involves operations both "from the bottom up" and "from the top down." The system skips back and forth between levels, either looking for something that fits a specification, or for a specification that fits a something. (See Schank's discussion in Chapter 5 of the difference between "top down" parsers and "bottom up" parsers.) Although it is easy to construct any single example so as to minimize jumping between levels, there is no doubt that in general the belief system simulation will have to have a great deal of facility in inter-level communication.

Additional to the problems of how to communicate between levels are problems at what levels to operate. That is to say, a question itself may be phrased at either atom, plan, theme, or script level. But the response need not necessarily be at the same level as the question. The system can resort to generalizations in response to specifics, and may do so if it can comfortably find a general answer and has trouble translating the answer back down into specifics. We suspect that the response should be higher in the hierarchy when systemic values are at stake and/or when the given actor category occurs at the script level of the belief system. On the other hand, the system might churn out a lot of detailed exemplification in response to a general level question. We would suppose this to be likely when the actor is not categorized at the script level, but a number of event exemplifications about that actor are stored in memory.

These speculations are psychological assumptions about likely response tendencies depending both upon what the system knows and upon what the system assumes the questioner wants to know. Empirical investigation of assumptions such as these will have to proceed along with the implementation of the many facets of the indicated simulation.

MODELS OF MEMORY
AND COGNITION

Eight

The Memory We Must Have

Earl Hunt
The University of Washington

The fact of thought determines the form our brains might take. To comprehend we must translate sensory signals into messages, interpret the messages in the light of previous knowledge, and alter stored information to incorporate the meaning of new messages. How these acts might be accomplished has been a topic of speculation for the philosopher and a topic investigation for three scientists: the psychologist, the computer science specialist, and the linguist. The psychologist has gathered a substantial array of facts but has not marshalled them into a satisfactory theory. The linguist has produced a substantial theory, but it deals with the interpretation of one type of message and is more concerned with the analysis of form than the interpretation of content. Computer science specialists have attempted to develop machines which are capable of a rudimentary form of comprehension. Although their success has been modest by the standards of the most conservative science fiction, the effort has produced a store of concepts which figure heavily in today's discussions of cognition. These concepts have been used in a helter-skelter fashion for there has been little systematic consideration of how computing concepts might be pieced together into a single world view of the brain as an information processing machine.

Our work has been an attempt toward such an integration. The ideas proposed here do not provide a simulation of any specific behavior. Instead these ideas are intended as guides to the writing, evaluation, and analysis of specific simulation programs. Since the offering of such a guide is rather presumptuous, I must at least try to justify my goal. The designer of a computing system must make a series of basic decisions about the form of his effort. First he must choose the basic functional components and their relations to each other. In making this decision the designer states a *system architecture*. Communication between computing and information storage units will be accomplished by an *addressing system* with specific logical properties. Programmers using the computing system must decide upon a *data structure* to be used to represent the information on which their programs operate. The decisions which are made about system architecture, addressing technique, and data structure will determine the details of the algorithms used to accomplish specific computing tasks. Such considerations apply as much to the simulation of human behavior as to the calculation of a factor analysis. What I shall do is to propose some choices for architecture, addressing, and data structures that are reasonable in light of our knowledge of the physiology and psychology of cognition. No one would maintain that we know all there is to know about these topics, but on the other hand, we do know something. We may know enough to limit the frameworks within which specific simulations should be constructed.

The strongest possible statement of the goal of this paper is that it should define the set of computer simulations that are plausible given our current knowledge of psychology and physiology. There are three ways in which the set of plausible simulations might be delineated. The most obvious is a limitation on the elementary computing operations that the simulation programmer is permitted to use. This is analogous to the limitation placed on a conventional programmer by the order code of the computer or the constructs of the programming language which he has to use. Unfortunately we can make few statements about what is or is not a plausible simulation at this level. A second class of limitations is imposed by the computer architecture which the simulation implies. The simulation designer must decide what stations will exist for holding and transforming data, and what the flow of information and control between them will be. There is a great deal of relevant psychological literature at this level of abstraction. In fact, there is so much that I shall often arbitrarily assert a solution, rather than present details of the experimental evidence supporting it. Finally, as the earlier discussion indicated, the simulation programmer must decide upon the data structures to be used to represent within the program a picture of the external world. Computer science has devoted a great deal of thought to the question of data structure, as it turns out that a proper choice of data structure is one of the most influential decisions in determining the properties of an algorithm. It is not reasonable to suppose that man restructures his brain whenever he is faced with a new problem, so it is legitimate to ask what the data structures of the brain are. Here we find that computer science considerations can be used to sharpen the question, and that psychologists have gathered data which limits the range of possible answers.

System Architecture

In a previous paper I proposed a *distributed memory* model of the brain (Hunt, 1971). The basic idea in this model is that there are several distinct types of memory. It is quite likely that these are associated with different anatomical areas, although that is not logically implied by the model. The different memory areas are assumed to be organized into a system for controlling the flow of information which effectively decouples cognition from direct environmental demands. At the same time, this system makes possible the coding of present sensory input in terms of past experience. The basic structure of the model is shown in Figure 8.1. Information about sensory stimulation is funneled through a set of buffer memories into a central unit called *conscious memory*. At each stage in the buffering process the input information is recoded into progressively more meaningful units. For example, as part of the recoding process in reading we first distinguish lines from background, then letters from lines, and finally words from letters. These distinctions are not conscious; we read words. Prior to conscious attention, however, there has been a considerable amount of progressively higher level recoding. The buffer system is used to achieve the recoding, with a buffer memory area assigned to hold information at each stage. As the example illustrates, much of the buffer coding is under the control of long term memory (LTM). To continue the recoding example the buffering process will produce a *lexical string* of information in short term memory (STM), the first part of the conscious memory system. Interpretation of the lexical string produces a meaningful *semantic code* which is stored in intermediate term memory (ITM). It is important to realize that the semantic code is not thought of as the linguist's deep structure of a sentence. Rather, the semantic code is a picture of "what is going on at the time." Rumelhart, Lindsay, and Norman (1972) refer to this code as an *episode*. This is a good choice of a word, since what ITM holds is the episode of life currently

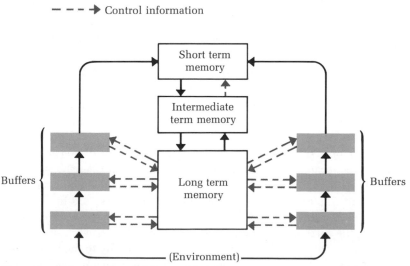

Figure 8.1 The Distributed Memory Model.

under examination. STM, by contrast, holds the identity of the information transmitting code just received. The episode is pieced together by addition of information from the environment through STM and by retrieval of amplifying information from LTM. The episode is not constructed solely by passive recording of messages from STM and LTM. It actively controls the interpretation and search processes required. What we recall at the moment and what we make of the environment before us both depend on what we think is going on.

An emphasis on buffering processes is useful when we wish to consider temporal distribution of activity during comprehension. It fails to deal with the spatial distribution of various cognitive functions. There is a great deal of evidence indicating that the left temporal lobe contains a number of areas required for the comprehension and generation of speech (Lenneberg, 1967, 1969; Geschwind, 1970). There is also evidence that the right side of the brain is responsible for the processing of "gestalt" activities, such as the recognition of faces and complicated line drawings (Lansdell, 1968; Milner, 1968). Unilateral dominance of certain intellectual tasks does not itself compel any great modification in the Distributed Memory model, since if all that lateral assymetry implied was that certain complex functions were carried out in particular areas of the brain, we could simply note that various areas of LTM were reserved for different processors. The situation is apparently more complex, since the side of the brain that is dominant for a particular task will exert control over the peripheral buffer operations associated with the task. Unilateral dominance effects in pattern analysis at the buffer level can be demonstrated in both the visual system (Rizzolatti, Umiltá, and Berlucchi, 1971; Umiltá. Frost, and Hyman, 1972) and in the auditory system (Day, Cutting, and Copeland, 1971). The exact nature of the effects in the visual system are complex, since one cannot always be sure to what extent subjects are responding to verbal codes for visual stimuli. The Day et. al. results, which are entirely confined to the auditory system, neatly illustrate the connection between lateral dominance and peripheral buffering, and do so in a way that points to an amplification of the memory model.

Day et al. used a variation on Broadbent's (1958) dichotic listening paradigm. Sounds were presented separately but almost simultaneously to each ear. Nine stimuli were used, the sounds created by combining the three phonemes /ba/, /ga/, and /da/ with three frequency levels. Thus a stimulus might be a medium pitched /ba/ or a high pitched /da/. The phonetic distinction between /ba/, /ga/, and /da/ is obviously one that is important in interpreting spoken English. Pitch, however, does not affect meaning in English speech except in a few special situations. Therefore one can look on the Day et al. stimuli as varying in two dimensions, only one of which is of importance in the comprehension of spoken English. Subjects were instructed either to report which syllable was heard first, thus requiring them to make a linguistic distinction, or to report the pitch of the first sound they heard. The accuracy of report was greatest for phoneme ordering if the first stimulus was in the right ear, while pitch ordering was most accurate if the first stimulus was in the left ear. Since the ears are primarily connected contralaterally to the brain, the right ear is an entry point for the left brain buffer system, and vice versa (Milner, 1962). Day *et. al.* interpreted their results as showing that even in a task which did not require linguistic analysis, speech relevant discriminations are processed on the left side of the brain.

The Day *et. al.* experiment and a number of other studies by Liberman and his associates (Mattingly, Liberman, Syrdal, and Hawles, 1971; Liberman, Mattingly, and Turvey, 1972) indicate that there is a separate speech processor for analyzing sounds in the context of speech signals. The Distributed Memory model must be amplified to handle this fact. As a first step, buffer channels within each sensory system must be assumed for each side of the brain. This produces left and right visual and auditory buffer systems. (A buffer system will be referred to by the side of the brain with which it is associated, rather than its anatomical locus.) Figure 8.2 shows the resulting configuration.

In the original presentation of buffer recoding (Hunt, 1971) the following steps were identified:

1. Information enters a sensory buffer, placing that buffer in a particular physical state.

2. The state of the buffer determines the location in LTM at which a search is begun for stored information that matches some portion of the buffer's current physical state.

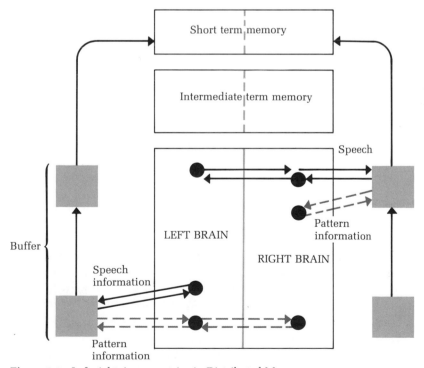

Figure 8.2 Left-right Assymmetries in Distributed Memory.

3. If the initial location contains information that matches the buffer contents, a match signal is sent upwards in the system to the next buffer. Otherwise the buffer is sent to a new physical state which depends upon the information previously in the buffer and the nature of the mismatch.

4. The new physical state of the buffer determines the next LTM location to be tested. The process continues as in steps 2-4 until a match is found.*

To amplify the model for laterality two further assumptions are added: that the location initially specified by the (sensorily controlled) buffer state is always on the same side of LTM as the buffer system, and that at each subsequent step the next location to be searched is, in some sense, physically close to the last location. These assumptions ensure that the matching process will begin on the same side as the buffer and gradually spread to the opposite side of the brain. Since the speech processor and speech information data are located on the left side, speech information in the left buffer can be identified more rapidly than speech information in the right buffer. Similarly, if the buffer information is concerned with form perception, data entering the right buffer will be analyzed more rapidly than data entering the left buffer.

The Day et. al. results can be considered in the light of the expanded model. Consistent with previous discussions of buffer and conscious memory functions, it is assumed that the observer has no conscious awareness of the stimuli, and thus cannot report that it has occurred, until all features of the signal reach the STM-ITM areas. Figure 8.2 shows the paths within LTM and the buffer areas that must be followed as data is passed upwards through the buffer system. Since speech stimuli in the right buffer and non-speech stimuli in the left buffer have longer paths to follow than non-speech stimuli in the right buffer and speech stimuli in the left, one would expect that if two stimuli were presented, simultaneously, to separate ears, the order of arrival of speech information in STM would be left-right, and for non-speech information right-left. This, of course, is in accord with results.

Day et al. used identical stimuli in each condition, varying only the instructions to discriminate speech or non-speech cues. How are we to account for the fact that the perception of the stimulus is unitary—i.e. that people hear single syllables of varying pitch—even though the results indicate that the order of arrival of information in STM depends upon the buffer to which the information is presented? The model postulates that the buffer system delivers a bundle of features to STM. A mechanism must be found for forming these features into a unitary percept. One reasonable assumption is that each feature is tagged with a marker giving time of delivery to STM and a second marker identifying the location of the feature in the sensory field. The second tag's distinctiveness probably varies with the buffer, reflecting our differential acuity in various perceptual systems. A single unit ("percept") is identified in STM if a group of features have similar, but not necessarily

*Many of the supporting arguments for the solutions which I shall assert here have been presented previously (Hunt, 1971).

identical, time and location tags. To answer the question "which sound came first" in the Day *et. al.* experiments the subjects would examine the time tags of either the phonetic or pitch features. To identify the sounds they heard, the subjects would look for pitch and phonetic features with common time and location tags. To answer the question "Which syllable began first?" they examined the time tags of the phonetic features of each percept; to answer the question "Which tone began first?" they examined the time tags of the pitch features.

If we are going to regard the buffer system and LTM as being strongly lateralized, the STM-ITM systems ought also to be regarded as lateralized and perhaps assymetrical in function. There is evidence from studies of the physiology of memory that this is indeed the case. Milner (1968, 1970, 1971) has surveyed a number of clinical reports of unilateral damage to the right or left hippocampus. Patients with left hippocampal damage have great difficulty fixing verbal information into long term memory, while patients with right hippocampal damage have somewhat less marked difficulty in fixing visual patterns. An almost complete loss of the ability to acquire new memories occurred in two patients suffering from bilateral hippocampal destruction (Milner, 1966, 1970).

The Implications of Architectural Models for Simulation

The remarks so far are most easily thought of as examples of the use of concepts from computing to order psychological observations. We can also use the Distributed Memory approach to make statements which are basic to psychological theory.

In explaining any task which requires that the subject react to his environment on a real time basis, the theoretician must specify which parts of memory are required for each subtask which the subject must complete. This forces the theory to deal with specifications of buffer sizes, the speed and complexity of coding within buffers, and the speed of information transfer between buffers. The simulation of paired associates learning offers a good case in point. While simulations of the learning of arbitrary associations between stimuli vary with the particular task under consideration, two themes run through most of the research. These are the idea of a discrimination tree for stimulus recognition (Feigenbaum, 1961) and the idea of a short term memory buffer in which the stimulus is held while its attributes are examined (Laughrey, 1969). It is generally assumed that these attributes are themselves the result of highly overlearned codings into letters or phonemes. The coded stimuli are contrasted to build a tree connecting the appropriate stimuli and responses. Feigenbaum (1970) has argued that the discrimination tree itself must be a data structure in intermediate term memory. On the other hand, the discrimination networks required to achieve the original stimulus coding before the stimulus reaches STM must be LTM data structures. Apparently the LTM discrimination trees are available to the buffer mechanisms, since rather complex letter and word recognition can occur without interfering with more central tasks. This has been shown by Posner and Boies (1971), in a study in which subjects were required to encode visually presented letters, while being ready to react to an auditorily presented stimulus. It was found that the encoding process itself could take place without affecting reaction time to the auditory stimulus, but that if the auditory stimulus was presented while the subject was trying to decide whether two visually presented stimuli were the same or different, then the latency to the auditory stimulus was increased. The matching task evidently competed with the auditory reaction task for STM memory space, whereas the complex encodings required only visual buffer memory.

It was previously noted that the timing considerations implicit in Figure 8.2 lead us to conclude that presentation of a stimulus to a Distributed Memory system will result in the delivery of a bundle of features to STM, all arising from the same stimulus but not all arriving in STM at the same time. We can represent each of these features as a triplet, $\langle t, s, c \rangle$, where t is the time of arrival of the triplet in STM, s is the source of the triplet in terms of the sensory channel on which it arrives, and c is the LTM code for the triplet. Now imagine a decision demon located in the STM area. How does this demon decide that two triplets, $\langle t_1, s_1, c_1 \rangle$ and $\langle t_2, s_2, c_2 \rangle$ arose from the same stimulus? The answer that was proposed is that the two triplets are assigned to the same stimulus if the time and source codes are sufficiently close. This conclusion commits one to the view that the effective STM stimulus is a vector of attributes, including a time tag location. Fortunately for consistency, this is a very popular view in current theories of memory.

A good deal has been made of the fact that speech is a very localized function. This can hardly be questioned, but what are its implications? To answer this question another question is proposed; under what conditions would speech localization be built into an electronic computing system? The question is not as silly as might appear, since in fact linguistic localization is built into large multiprogramming systems, such as are found in most university computing centers. The outside world of a large computing system consists of a series of jobs, each of which requires computing services. Some jobs are presented as directly executable machine instructions, but many first require translation from a user oriented language such as FORTRAN into machine language. If a large percentage of the jobs presented to the system require translation, special arrangements are usually made for the translation process. The commonest solution to the problem is to use a *core resident compiler*. A special area of the machine's primary memory is permanently assigned to the translation task. The necessary language processing programs are loaded into this memory area and remain there even when not being used. When a language analysis task is detected, the job requiring it is immediately moved to the core resident compiler's memory area, where the translation takes place. The memory area used is assigned to the translation by convention only; there is nothing special about the area's physical characteristics. Similarly, the language analysis programs cannot execute any machine instruction that is not also available to any other program.

An alternative solution to the language translation problem is called the *multiprocessor* solution. In this solution a special computing unit with features designed to be useful in language analysis is added to the hardware configuration of the computer. The various language processing routines needed (i.e. the compilers) are written as programs for the special processor. As before, whenever a job requests a language translation task, the job is immediately moved to the language processor's memory area. The processing programs, however, are different in kind from the other programs of the system since they have access to a unique computing unit and, perhaps, a memory with unique physical characteristics.

In modern computing the core resident compiler solution is by far the commonest solution to the translation process. This has no implication for psychology, since the choice has been dictated by engineering considerations.* What choice has Nature made in the design of the brain? This is an important question for Psychology for a number of reasons. If Nature has taken the same solution as the computer designer, then any memory capacity available to a language comprehender should also be available to a properly trained problem solver. Therefore we ought to assert that any data processing technique which can be shown to be logically necessary for the analysis of natural language must at least potentially be available for problem solving. On the other hand, if our brains use a physically different language processor, data processing operations which are available in language may not be available for thought in general. In particular, recursive computations appear to be basic to linguistic analysis. At least partly because of this, the importance of recursion in problem solving is sometimes stressed (Newell and Simon, 1961). There is no doubt that recursion is a basic operation in the identification of sentences. It has been found, however, that fairly simple non-recursive programs which classify objects on the basis of Boolean combinations of attributes can account for the data from a fairly wide variety of human concept learning experiments (Hunt, Marin, and Stone, 1966; Trabasso, Rollins and Shaugnessey, 1971; Williams, 1971). It is trivial to show that these programs cannot be used as sentence analyzers, but what is the force of this argument? Over the past few years in my own laboratory I and a number of associates have attempted to train normally intelligent college sophomores to perform graph searching tasks. We use a paradigm first developed by Hayes (1965). The subject memorizes a list of paired associates that implicitly defines a graph. For example, the list

> Tom-Bill
> Bill-Joe
> Bill-Bob

can easily be depicted as

> Tom .... Bill .... Joe
> :............ Bob

---

*It is possible that engineering advances will soon cause computer designers to shift to the multiprocessor solution.

After memorizing the list the subject is asked to search it in his mind, in order to retrieve some subset of the names in the graph. He is instructed *not* to repeat a name. The task should be quite easy if the subject can maintain a pushdown stack of locations visited. (Nilsson (1971) discusses a number of appropriate algorithms.) In fact, the task is not at all easy. Our subjects have to adopt the inefficient strategy of returning to a central point in the list, such as the list head, and finding new paths from that point. They are quite unable to use the pushdown principle, even when it is explained to them. Similar observations have been made about the use of memory in more complex problem solving (Newell and Simon, 1972).

In summary, the weight of the evidence from both anatomical studies and psychological observation seems to be that Nature has taken the multiprocessor approach to the language analysis program. The evidence, however, is much less firm than we would like it to be. Resolution of this question must be considered a basic question in Psychology and Physiology, since its answer will determine the relationship between thought and language. If the multiprocessor approach were to be proven to be the way in which we analyze language, this would not mean that language has nothing to do with thought. Certainly language provides a vehicle for the expression of some thoughts that could hardly be expressed in any other manner. Abstract mathematical reasoning is a good example. In other cases, however, thought may involve manipulation of sensory images and, thus, be basically non-linguistic. When we observe a person solving a problem we undoubtedly observe the product of both the linguistic and non-linguistic process. What we require is a model to account for the interplay between the two forms of problem solving, rather than a model which assumes that each of them occur autonomously. We shall return to this point subsequently, in the discussion of data structures. Before doing so another computer concept must be discussed. How does one area of the brain locate information stored in another area? The topic of memory addressing is dealt with in the next section.

Addressing Data in Memory

Modern theories of cognition focus attention on the selection, modification, and transfer of information from one memory area to another. Many of the effects of the traditional variables of experimental psychology, such as delay of reinforcement, magnitude of reinforcement, proactive and retroactive interference, and response generalization can be explained in these terms (Atkinson and Wickens, 1969). At some point we must specify the nature of the transfer mechanism. We cannot expect a precise answer since our knowledge of the physiology of memory is not complete. We do know enough to limit the class of possible addressing mechanisms, and we certainly know enough to establish the fact of a major functional difference between biological and electronic computers.

Consider a computing system in which memory area A contains information that is being actively manipulated by some attached processor, whereas area B contains a much larger store of currently unused records. In Distributed Memory the buffer systems and the STM-ITM 'conscious thought' areas correspond to area A, while LTM plays the role of area B. An addressing mechanism is required to write information from area A into area B, and to retrieve selected pieces of data from B for presentation to A. The precise information to be retrieved will be determined within the A area, the addressing mechanism must then find the data in B. In digital computers addressing is performed by explicit calculation of the locations in B which contain data required by A. In fact, a computer program can be thought of as a sequence of manipulations of the contents of prespecified memory locations. No one seriously proposes this scheme as a model for biological computing, but what is to take its place?

It has been proposed that biological memory is addressed by a *content addressing* (sometimes called *self-addressing*) mechanism (Norman, 1968; Shiffrin and Atkinson, 1969). In a content addressing system the representation of the information or part of the information in area A determines the location that is to be used to store the contents of A in B. Shiffrin and Atkinson give a good example of this . . . libraries use content addressing. A book on "Caulking methods used by the Pharaohs" will be placed in the Egyptian room. In more psychological terms, content addressing is an intuitively reasonable notion because it provides a selective encoding system that would be based on attention. Where we stored something would depend on how we viewed it at the time it came into conscious memory. To be more specific, the peripheral buffers produce a coded representation of the stimulus in STM. It is this code, not the original stimulus, which will be stored in LTM. Therefore any biases in the coding will be reflected later in biases in memory.

Only some of the STM code will be used to determine memory location. We can think of any stimulus which impinges on the sensors as giving rise to four sets of associated internal codes. The first set C_0, contains all memories (i.e. code words in LTM) which might be aroused by the stimulus. The second set, C_1, is the set of codes actually created by the buffering process and placed in STM. The third set, C_2, consists of the codes abstracted from the STM-ITM system and stored in LTM and constitutes the system's maximum memory of the stimulus. Logically, it is the *engram*, or memory representation of experience. Note that it might contain both codes from the buffering process and elaborations of the stimulus which resulted from processing in the STM-ITM system. Finally, we consider the set C_3 of codes which are used to determine the location of the engram in LTM. We shall want to allow for the possibility that the engram is stored in several locations, with several associated sets of location codes. Presumably the location code is a subset of the engram code itself ($C_3 \subseteq C_2$), although the engram code may not be a subset of the codes derived from the buffering system, since transformations may occur in the STM-ITM system. In recall, recreation of a C_3 code set suffices to locate one of the copies of the engram, thus retrieving a memory of the stimulus.

Content addressing can be used to account for a number of psychological phenomenon. Generalization and memory confusions occur if two distinct stimuli produce the same address codes. A failure to recognize previously presented stimuli occurs if a different coding function is used by the peripheral processors on two different presentations of the same stimulus. This effect has been shown in an interesting manner in two superficially quite different studies. Frost (1971) showed subjects line drawings which varied in semantic category (people, clothing, etc.) and in orientation (horizontal, vertical, slanted right or left). Subjects were led to expect either a recognition or recall test and were then tested to determine whether they had organized the material along semantic or visual lines. Subjects who were led to expect a recall test had organized memory on the basis of semantic cues, while subjects who had expected a recognition test used visual cues. G. Loftus (1971) has conducted a similar study using a continuous paired associates task. His results showed that the manner in which the subjects used the STM-ITM system was determined by the way in which they expected their material to be tested. There are probably wide individual differences in this respect. Hunt and Love (1972) found that one person with amazingly good memory relied almost exclusively on semantic cues when organizing the stimuli in Frost's study, even though the man was led to believe that he would be given a recognition test.

Content addressing as a psychological concept needs to be augmented by the idea of a *content area* consisting of LTM locations which share a common C_3 code. Such locations are thus tied together logically although not necessarily anatomically. If a C_3 code is created by the STM-ITM system, then this code can be used to access information in a content area. Evidently the access is serial. Shiffrin (1970) has shown that if we assume that retrieval is a two stage process, in which a memory area is accessed and its locations searched in a serial fashion, then we can account for a great deal of the data on free recall. Juola and Atkinson (1971) have extended this concept to recognition in a particularly nice manner. They determined the time required for subjects to make a decision in response to questions of the form "Is X a member of category Y" (for example, "Is a canary a bird?"). Previous studies by Landauer and Freedman (1968) had shown that the time required to answer such questions is determined by the number of items in the category. Juola and Atkinson varied the number of categories which might include the probe word. Thus they asked "Is a canary a . . . Waterfall, Airplane, or Bird?" (The answer to this question is "yes.") They found that the time required to answer was a linear function of the number of categories involved, but the slope of the function is about four times the slope of the function required to answer direct comparison questions, such as "Is a canary a . . . fox, eagle, canary." In terms of the Distributed Memory model the data is accounted for in the following steps:

1. The probe word ("canary") is recognized and stored in the STM-ITM system.

2. The category words (waterfall, airplane, bird) are recognized. Each provides a C_3 code which points to a logical location in memory. The items in that location are activated and compared with the term "canary" in the STM-ITM system. (Juola and Atkinson point out that their data do not indicate quite what the comparison process is.) If one of the comparisons is positive a flag is set in the STM-ITM system.

3. After the search is terminated the flag is checked. If it indicates that a positive match has been found the answer "yes" is given. Otherwise the subject answers "no."

A second argument for the content area model of memory addressing is provided by the clustering phenomenon. If a person is asked to recall a list of exemplars of various categories, such as *fox, potato, dog, beet,* free recall will be clustered by categories. For the example list, the order *fox, dog, potato, beet* would probably be observed. Clustering is what would be expected if the subject first located an area in which items within a category were stored, and then retrieved recently observed items within that category.

A major objection to content addressing in the straightforward manner in which it has been presented is that it does not lead to a reasonable physiological model. Presumably STM-ITM information is represented by an electrical code (i.e. by the firing state of some neurons in the brain), whereas LTM is almost certainly based upon chemical coding within the nervous system (Gurowitz, 1969). What does this imply for the logical system just described? The vector of components representing STM-ITM information (the C_2 code) must correspond to a state of electrical activity in the STM-ITM buffer system. For a content addressing mechanism to work as described, the physical state of each of the buffers and the STM must somehow be attached to a specific location in LTM. Such an extreme of anatomical localization does not seem plausible,* so an alternative addressing system will be proposed. It is a functional model based broadly on E. R. John's (1967, 1971, 1972) physiological model of memory addressing and retrieval. One need not, however, accept all the details of John's neurophysiology to accept the broader aspects of the model.

The mechanism will be called the *broadcast model* by analogy to a broadcast and recording system. Its basic assumption is that the decision to store an engram at a particular location is made not in the active buffer and STM-ITM areas, but rather in the LTM locations themselves. The LTM locations are thought of as sets of neurons whose activation *in a particular sequence* is a sufficient stimulus to drive the STM-ITM system into a given state. This drive state is the physiological substrate of the psychological phenomenon of recall. The neurons comprising an LTM location will be called a circuit. Note that a single neuron may participate in several circuits. Returning again to the fiction of a decision demon, suppose such a homunculus were stationed inside a neuron. The demon would be able to recognize the circuit that was attempting to drive his neuron by the characteristic sequence of spatial and temporal inputs to the neuron in which he resided.

The retrieval process will be considered first. At any time a circuit will have a current activity level associated with it. In effect, this is a measure of how closely the spontaneous activity of the various neurons in the circuit are in synchrony with the firing sequence they would go through if the circuit were to be activated. The individual neurons have within their cell structure an *activation record*, which is essentially an indication of how sensitive they are to the sequence of inputs which

---

*We could not store anything unless we had an area reserved for it. To return to Shiffrin and Atkinson's library example, what happens to the book on the Pharaoh if there is no Egyptian room? Another objection is that the idea of a content addressing system, if uncritically accepted, places upon a central process . . . selective attention to the stimulus . . . the burden of deciding where in the brain the engram will be located.

characterizes the circuit to them. (John (1967) discusses the physiology of the activation record in some detail.) When one of the neural memory areas (either the buffer or the STM-ITM system) becomes active it broadcasts a signal to all LTM locations to which it is anatomically connected. The spatial and temporal characteristics of this message will be determined by the physical state of the neural memory area which, in turn, will be determined by its previous state and by input from the environment. What happens next is best outlined by reference to Figure 8.3, which shows an active memory area broadcasting to a region of LTM containing three circuits, e_1, e_2, and e_3. Assume that circuit e_1 is at a low state of spontaneous activity when the broadcast is received. Thus it cannot be aroused unless there is an extremely close match between its prototype firing sequence and the sequence of stimuli impinging upon it. Therefore circuit e_1 is not aroused to the level at which it sends output back to the peripheral and STM-ITM systems. The fact of its being tested, however, may prime e_1 to respond to a weaker stimulus in the immediate future. Circuit e_2, on the other hand, is assumed to be at a high level of prior activity, but—because it does not match the input to it—it does not send a returning message. Circuit e_3 is both potentially active and sufficiently similar to the input to be aroused. Hence it begins to drive activity in active memory area A_1 and any other active area to which it may be connected. The information driven into the active memory area may often exceed the amount of information required from the active memory area in order to arouse the circuit. Thus we have a neurophysiological analog of the engram and retrieval codes (C_2 and C_3) referred to earlier. As a result

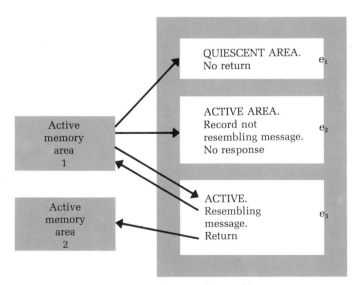

Figure 8.3 Information Transmission in a Braodcast Addressing System.

of the memory induced activity, the state of the active memory areas will have been changed. This—together with the changes in peripheral and conscious memory that are under stimulus control—will determine what memories are to be retrieved next.

The storage process will now be considered. John assumes that if a memory circuit is driven long enough, at a high enough level of activation, then the activation record of the individual neurons in the circuit will be changed to make them more sensitive to the circuit induced activity. Thus a circuit may be implanted in LTM by its being driven from STM-ITM or the buffer system, providing that the driving is sufficiently powerful and continued over a sufficiently long time. The Distributed Memory model assumes that such driving can be achieved only by the STM-ITM system, so that only information which reaches conscious memory can be retrieved later.

No attempt will be made to review the physiological evidence for this system, since several physiological mechanisms could produce a broadcast memory. There are a number of psychological points in favor of the proposed mechanism.

1. The broadcast model is a content addressing system because the internal representation of the stimulus in STM-ITM determines where it will be stored. Thus the broadcast model inherits the ability to explain any observations which fit the framework of a content addressing system, but without requiring commitment to an extreme view concerning anatomical localization of memory.

2. By using the broadcast model we have a mechanism for the transfer of information upward through the peripheral buffer system by arousal of circuits. Similarly, the broadcast mechanism can be used to account for the propagation of information through LTM in both storage and retrieval. Some of the possible paths of data arousal are shown in Figure 8.3.

3. A powerful argument can be made for the case that memories must be considered to vary in their strength (Wickelgren, 1970). In the broadcast model, strength of memory is represented in two distinct ways: in the number of circuits associated with a particular pattern of activity in the STM-ITM and buffer systems and, within the circuits, in the sensitivity of the activation records of the individual neurons. The latter determine how easy a circuit is to arouse.

4. The broadcast model predicts that memory searches will either be in sequence or in parallel, depending on what areas of peripheral and conscious memory are required for a particular task. LTM can be addressed by any of the active memories, and the fact of being addressed by one active memory can determine the ease with which a given circuit will be aroused by other active memory areas. These concepts are illustrated by two studies which might, at first glance, appear to be conflicting observations. Glucksberg and Cowen (1970) had subjects shadow prose presented to one ear while digits were presented in the other ear. Subsequent testing showed that memory for the digits persisted for a very brief time. In addition, subjects were unable to recall whether or not a digit had occurred unless they could also say what that digit was. These observations were taken as evidence that during shadowing the subjects kept the digits out of the STM-ITM system. But now consider a slightly different experiment. Lewis (1970) also asked subjects to shadow words presented

to one ear, but instead of digits he presented words of varying semantic relationship to the shadowed words into the "unattended" ear. Although the subjects did not report hearing the words in the unattended ear (as would be predicted from the Glucksberg and Cowen study) their reactions to the shadowed word were affected by the semantic relationship between the shadowed word and a simultaneously presented but allegedly unattended word.

To explain this within the broadcast model, consider the relationship between Figure 8.1 and Figure 8.3. Imagine that the left hand channel of Figure 8.1 represents an attended buffer and the right hand channel an unattended buffer. The unattended buffer, although closed off from the STM-ITM system, is still capable of broadcasting into LTM. Thus, in terms of the discussion of Figure 8.3, it can prime circuits to be ready to respond to stimuli in the attended buffer, either facilitating or interfering with the shadowing task.

The conclusion of this section is that our present evidence favors the conjecture that memory uses a content addressing system in which the buffer and STM-LTM active memory systems are capable of parallel addressing of LTM. Content addressing may be achieved by the broadcast method, which has as its basis a plausible but unproven physiological mechanism.

Data Structures in LTM: Basic Concepts

The logical organization of data in LTM is a topic which has attracted a great deal of speculation (Anderson and Bower, 1973; Quillian, 1968; Rumelhart, Lindsay, and Norman, 1972; Shiffrin, 1970; Winograd, 1971) in spite of, or perhaps because of, the difficulty of gathering definitive data. This section is an attempt to sharpen the issue by applying the data structure concepts developed for computing systems by Earley (1971) and Woods (1970) to psychological problems. Others have done this before. In particular, there is a great deal of similarity between the approach here and that of Rumelhart *et al.*

An information storage system consists of a set of basic records and a set of rules for accessing the records. Following Earley, the basic records will be referred to generically as *atoms*. These are the entities upon which basic operations of the information processing system may be performed. Each of these operations changes one or more atoms into another atom. The atoms are classified by the operations which may be applied to them.

These abstract and rather cryptic remarks may be made concrete by considering two examples, one from computer science and one from psychology. In FORTRAN programming the atoms are the variables and constants. The classes of atoms are the integer, real, and Boolean variables. The operations defining the types are the operations of integer and real arithmetic and the Boolean logical operations. Now consider the application of the same concepts to a study of visual imagery (Shepard and Metzler, 1971). Pairs of dimensional projections of three dimensional objects were displayed. The subject's task was to decide if the two dimensional pictures represented projections of two different three dimensional objects or projections of the same objects from different perspectives. The time required to make the judgment was linearly related to the angular rotation required to bring the two objects to the same perspective. The subjects behaved as if visual images were atoms and angular rotation was an operation applicable to the atomic type *visual image*.

In computing, a data structure is defined as a specification of the relations between atoms. An atom can be accessed from another atom if and only if there is some relation between the two of them; so a data structure is equivalent to an expression of how the basic data may be accessed. This concept can also be illustrated with examples from FORTRAN and Psychology. In FORTRAN programming the array is the commonest data structure. The ith element of an array is tied to the *i*-1st element by the successor function. In many psychological studies of semantic memory, the subset-superset relation has been assumed to play as basic a role in cognition as the successor function does in programming. Each item is assumed to be connected to its superset, as illustrated by the tie between *canary* and *bird*. Therefore access to supersets of *bird* from *canary* should occur via *bird*. It has been observed that it does, indeed, take longer to answer the question "Is a canary an animal?" than it does to answer "Is a canary a bird?" (Collins and Quillian, 1969). While it certainly is not true that one can be strict in requiring memory to obey the logical rules for set-superset relations*, it is possible to obtain orderly data indicating the strength of associations between category exemplars and category names (E. Loftus and Scheff, 1971). It is an open question whether the association strength or the frequency of co-occurrence of category names and exemplar names in English can account for the observed differences in reaction time when subjects are asked to answer questions about set membership (Wilkins, 1971). The exact nature of the link between terms, however, is somewhat beside the point in the present discussion. Some sort of link must be necessary. The system of links establishes the accessing rule, and thus defines the data structure.

Data structures can be represented as directed graphs with labeled arcs linking nodes to nodes and nodes to atoms. An example is shown in Box 8.1. The concept of a node is thus far undefined. Unlike atoms, nodes have meaning only in terms of their location in the data structure relative to other items. Although there is a loose correspondence between nodes and words or phrases in English, Rumelhart *et. al.*

Box 8.1   Hypothetical Graph of Data Structure based on Subset and 'Cont.' Relations.

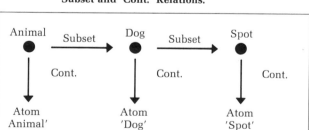

---

*Intuitively, how long would it take to answer the question "Is a canary a finch?"

point out that there are nodes that are required by a data structure but have no simple counterpart in English. Links specify the types of relation between nodes or between nodes and atom. Box 8.1 illustrates two particularly important links in a semantic memory, the *subset* link discussed previously and the *content* link which ties a node to an atom. An open and important question for psychology is the identification of the set of link types necessary for a reasonably rich data structure for cognition. Rumelhart et. al. suggest that link types exist for verbs, various classes of preposition (location, time), and for property and subset-superset relations. A specific link name, then, would itself refer to a node which defined the relation. This permits us to use qualified as well as directly named links, for instance as in the links between the nouns in

"John runs to the train."

and

"John runs quickly to the train."

Operations can be defined on data structures and substructures as well as on atoms. In general, however, quite a different sort of operator is required for a data structure than for an atom. Data structure operators alter the links between old data structures to form new ones, thus data structure operators can be thought of as the rules of inference of a cognitive system. In most computing applications such inferences are quite prosaic. For example, Earley (1971) defines the operations of "pushing" and "popping" items to and from a push down stack (PDS) by the graph transformation shown in Box 8.2. The same ideas can be applied in an hypothetical semantic memory. Box 8.3 illustrates a transformation defining the English language term "nephew" as a graph transformation. An interesting and important feature of this notation is that the transformation operator (the symbol $\Rightarrow$ in the graphs) can itself be thought of as a link between two data structures. Thus the operations permitted on a data structure may themselves be stored as part of the structure.

Box 8.2   Push Down List Operation Defined by Graph Transformations.

$$1 \qquad 0 \xrightarrow{\text{Next}} 2 \quad \Longleftrightarrow \quad 0 \xrightarrow{\text{Next}} 1 \xrightarrow{\text{Next}} 2$$

Push Down List Operation
Defined by Graph Transformations.
$\Longleftrightarrow$ indicates the transformation
is applicable in either direction.

$\Longleftrightarrow$ indicates the transformation is applicable in either direction.

Box 8.3   Example of a Semantic Net Change.

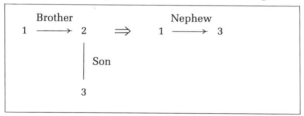

Cognition can be thought of as a sequence of operations that creates new data structures from old ones. The process of creation is controlled by the current contents of the STM-ITM ("conscious memory") system. Some mechanism is thus needed for choosing the sequence of operations which will be applied. Newell and Simon (1972) have suggested that a *production system* be applied to make the necessary choices. To understand what a production system is, consider a machine that has an *input string* of symbols, an internal data structure, an *output string*, and an ordered set of rules called *productions*. Each production consists of a pattern part and an action part. The pattern part describes a possible state (or set of states) of the input string and internal data structure. The machine scans down the ordered set of rules until a production is found whose pattern part matches the input string and data structure. The rearrangement specified by the action part is carried out, and the scan restarted at the initial position.

The use of a production system will be illustrated with a simple example from the analysis of programming languages, the field in which the idea of a production system was first developed (Gries, 1971). The example is of translation from conventional (infix) algebraic notation to prefix form, in which the operator precedes its operands. Assume a hypothetical machine whose internal data structure is PDS, with the operations of pushing and popping (Box 8.2) defined on it. The set of production rules to be used are all of the form

INPUT STATE; STACK STATE; OUTPUT STATE ⇒ INPUT STATE′;
STACK STATE; OUTPUT STATE′:

In stating the rules the symbol # will be used as a universal variable, so that the string A# means "A followed by anything," and is matched by any string with A as its leftmost member.

The rules are

R1 # OPERATOR ; # ; # → # ; OPERATOR #; #
R2 # VARIABLE; OPERATOR #; # → # ; #; OPERATOR VARIABLE #
R3 # VARIABLE; #; # → #; #; VARIABLE #

Suppose the input string is

$$A + B.$$

The translation to the prefix form, $+ A B$ would be as follows:

INPUT STRING	STACK	OUTPUT STRING	PRODUCTION MATCHED
$A + B$	0	0	3
$A +$	0	B	1
A	$+$	B	2
0	0	$+ A B$	Finished.

Note the importance of the order of the production rules. The example above will not work if rules R2 and R3 are interchanged.

The Psychologist can challenge the ideas presented here on two grounds: are they sufficient to account for cognitions of the complexity which we know humans exhibit and can they be connected to other useful concepts in psychology? The first question cannot really be answered by argument, one must use illustrations. Giving sufficient illustrations would never be possible, since no doubt the challenger could always construct a more complex example than any problem studied so far. On the other hand, there does exist some accumulated evidence. Newell and Simon (1972) have used production systems to simulate the protocols of human problem solvers working on "Scientific American" level puzzles. Winograd (1971) has established a connection between the data structure ideas presented here and techniques for mechanical theorem proving which, in principle, can be shown to be capable of answering any decidable question. The sufficiency question seems answered. The utility of the concepts for a psychological analysis still must be addressed.

Psychological Interpretations and Applications of Data Structure Concepts

The act of matching the pattern part of a production to an internal representation of the situation at hand must be primarily, if not exclusively, confined to the analysis of data in the STM-ITM system. This does not restrict our model of cognition to an examination of the memories we have already acquired. Newell and Simon point out that one of the things the action part of a production might direct is a search of the environment to determine whether a particular stimulus pattern could be brought to the focus of the problem solver's attention. In Distributed Memory terms this would drive the STM system into a state which would match a particular production. A second class of actions that a production might specify are actions associated with amplification or modification of LTM data structures. The Distributed Memory model makes the act of writing into memory a cognitive one; data is stored because a production's pattern has been matched. This is equivalent to saying that we remember something because we recognize it as having some relation to the cognitive acts (productions) we are attempting to execute. There is no place in the model for the storing of *semantic* material on the basis of simple repetition. This can be contrasted to the situation with respect to atomic information. Images are transferred to LTM by the broadcast technique and here, as has been pointed out, repetition or intense stimulation alone might be sufficient to store a new atom in memory.

To illustrate these ideas an example analysis of the sentence

John and Mary saw Sam

will be conducted. The data to be matched includes both the words in STM and the data structure in ITM. This latter structure will be called an *event*, since it is a picture of what is going on at the time rather than analysis of a single sentence. Box 8.4 shows the productions that will be used. These are productions that match and manipulate data structures, rather than strings of symbols. The step by step analysis is illustrated in Box 8.5. Going through each step in order:

1. "John" is placed in STM. The auditory image for "John" is retrieved, together with its associated link. This is recognized as a noun and proper name, and the reference to the *concept* John (not the word "John") is placed in ITM.

2. The "AND" construct with a noun is recognized by a similar process, retrieval of the reference to the auditory signal "and" and combination with a structure already in ITM to develop the incomplete noun phrase shown in Box 8.5b,

3. "Mary" is recognized, retrieved, and used to complete the noun phrase.

4. "Saw" is recognized and its associated node retrieved. This is found to be a verb, so an incomplete event is constructed—one in which an actor and an action have been identified, but the target of the action has not.

5. "Sam" is recognized. Since ITM is not empty, Production 1 applies rather than Production 4. The event structure is then completed.

Although the analysis has been phrased in terms of a combination of Newell and Simon's productions and Rumelhart *et. al.*'s data structures, the closest previously presented model in the literature is Schank's (1969) conceptual dependency analysis of the behavior of a listener. As in Schank's model, the listener in the Distributed Memory model is a constructor rather than a passive receiver of information. The LTM structures used to construct an ITM event structure at one moment play an active role in determining the interpretations which at the next moment will be made of external events. Consider the word "saw" in the example. In isolation this is either the past tense of the verb *to see* or it is a carpenter's tool. The acoustic image *saw* must be associated with both nodes in the lexical data structure. Within the context of the production rules of Box 8.4, however, only one of the structures associated with the word can be fit into the developing event. Therefore any other

Box 8.4   Semantic Productions.

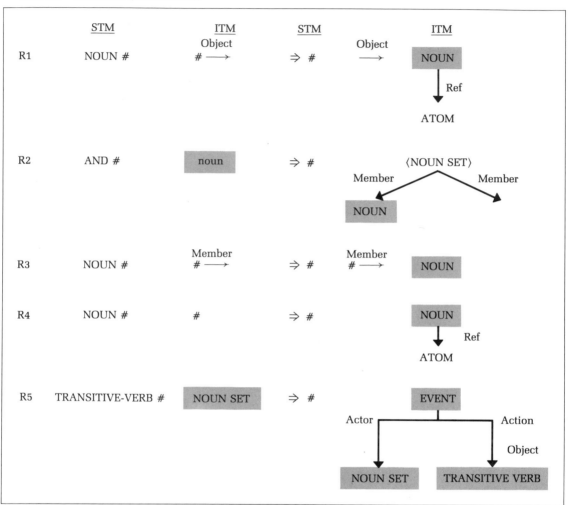

structure retrieved from LTM will be rejected by the linguistic processor associated with ITM.

The model of a listener as an event constructor has a number of interesting psychological implications. The main burden for message interpretation is placed on event construction, not on sentence analysis. Thus syntactic structures serve as aids in interpretation but are not the controlling factors. All the listener needs are sufficient cues to construct an event. This may not mean that the pattern match between STM-ITM structures and the pattern part of a production be exact; there may well be an internal interpretation of "close enough." This viewpoint assigns

Box 8.5 Successive Stages in Construction of an Event Structure.

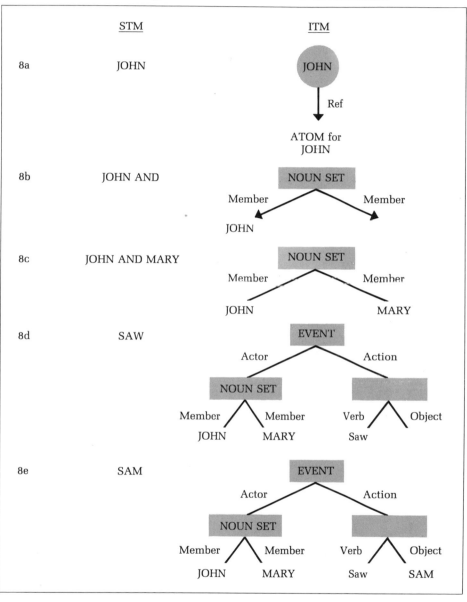

a much more subsidiary role to syntactical analysis than do most current theories of psycholinguistics.*

*It may be that syntactical structures are quite important in a psychological model of the speaker.

Another psychological observation is based on the way that distributed memory would have to handle ambiguities and "double takes" in speech. A data structure may have to be reinterpreted in the light of the structures that follow it. This is illustrated by the sentences

John shot his wife yesterday. He used Kodak Tri-X film.

Clearly the second sentence forces one to reconstruct the first. This can only be done if STM and ITM have retained sufficient data about the first structure recognized so that the new interpretation required by the second structure can be constructed. The example above is somewhat forced, and no doubt would be considered anomalous by most English speakers. To an extent, however, we have to guard against misinterpretations by keeping a record of partially interpreted data until we are certain that the interpretation is indeed correct and complete. The existence of such a strategy has been demonstrated empirically by Jarvella (1971). Suppose one is listening to a sequence of three clauses in connected discourse. Let the clauses be represented by A, B, C. The superordinate structure might be A (B C), as in the phrase

The confidence of Kofach was not unfounded. To stack the meeting for McDonald the union had even brought in outsiders.

or it might be (A B) C

Kofach was confident he would be able to stack the meeting for McDonald. The union had even brought in outsiders.

Recall of the B phrase is better in the A (B C) construction than in the (A B) C construction. Presumably this is because in A (B C) the words of the B clause must be kept available in STM until the C clause is interpreted. In (A B) C the construction of the larger (A B) event tells us that STM may be cleared.

An event structure in ITM may produce an associated image which will itself be composed of modifications of the images associated with the terms of the structure. There is evidence that repetition serves to strengthen the trace of the image, not the event structure itself. A number of experiments have shown that repetition of pairs of terms in discourse strengthens recall of those terms only if the context of the repetitions evokes the same or similar images (Bobrow, 1970; Jurca, 1971). Suppose a subject is shown simple sentence which form a complex event structure, as in

The earthquake started a rock slide.
The rock rolled down the hill.
The rock hit the hut on the lake.

then the compound sentence

The earthquake started a rock slide which rolled the rock down the hill to hit the hut on the lake.

is likely to be falsely recognized as having been presented even though it was not (Bransford and Franks, 1971). These observations strengthen the argument for a connection between the linguistic concept of an event data structure and memory for images. At the same time they raise a puzzling question. Abstract reasoning may not often take place in a psychological experiment, but it does occur in life. It has been amply demonstrated that it is difficult to remember or manipulate verbal statements that do not evoke images, but it is not impossible to do so (Paivio, 1971). We do have pure mathematicians who deal in number theory and there are other equally "non imagable" branches of law, politics, and philosophy. Are we to account for such thinking as a difference in kind?

Virtually every simulation of cognition which has been reported can be fit into the framework proposed here. In a trivial sense this is bound to be true, since every program can be described as a set of rules for manipulating data structures. Similarly, the assertion that simulations can be described in terms of production rules is also bound to be true since most, if not all, programming languages and the programs derived from them can be described by production systems (Gries, 1971). The argument must be not that it is possible, but that it is natural to use the concepts introduced here. The contention can be illustrated but not proven. One way to illustrate it is to show that the concepts can be used to reveal basic similarities between superficially different analyses of tasks.

Let us consider simulation models of paired associates learning (Feigenbaum, 1963) and concept learning (Hunt, Marin, and Stone, 1966; Williams, 1971), the use of concepts to classify objects (Trabasso, Rollins, and Shaugnessey, 1971), and decision making (Clarkson, 1963; Kleinmuntz, 1968).* In all the cited works the data structure that is manipulated is a tree of sequential decisions, and in each one the nodes of the tree are associated with attributes of the stimuli to be dealt with. In the concept learning and paired associates studies these attributes are physically identifiable properties of the stimulus, such as the name of a letter in a particular position in a trigram. In the decision making studies the stimulus attributes are themselves complex properties, such as medical diagnostic signs or categories of stock investments. The concept learning and paired associates learning studies deal with the construction of sequential decision procedures. In the concept learning and paired associates studies attention is focused on the construction of a sequential decision procedure in ITM (see, especially, Williams, 1971; and Feigenbaum, 1970). The two classes of simulation differ in how nodes are associated with particular stimulus attributes. In concept learning the decision is made on the basis of common features of identifiable subsets of stimuli, in the paired associates simulation individual stimuli are contrasted. The simulations of practical decision making in medical diagnosis (Kleinmuntz, 1968) and investment analysis (Clarkson, 1963) assume that the tree of decisions is resident in LTM at the beginning of the experiment. The target of the study was identification of a particular tree. In the concept utilization studies Trabasso et. al. defined the decision procedure for the

---

*The simulation of problem solving has deliberately been avoided because of the extensive discussion available elsewhere (Newell and Simon, 1972).

subjects verbally, but did not explicitly state it as a sequential procedure. By analyzing latencies in a classification task they were able to associate times with each step in the presumed classification process. The success of these widely varied simulations is strong evidence for the utility of the concept of a decision tree as a basic data structure in cognition.

Productions and pattern matching can be shown to have similarly wide applicability. Newell and Simon use production systems to simulate chess playing and problem solving at the "Scientific American puzzle" level. There are other studies in which production systems have been implied without the use of the "appropriate" terminology. Prytulak's (1971) analysis of the memorization of nonsense syllable lists can be looked at in this way. Prytulak proposed that when a nonsense syllable is shown the subject stores it as a word plus a transformation. Thus PYN is recalled as "Pin with Y in the middle." When a nonsense syllable is presented, the subject must find an appropriate word in his lexicon, which will then serve as a base to be remembered with the appropriate transformation, so that the nonsense syllable can be reconstructed as required. Prytulak assumed that each subject had a stack (i.e. ordered set) of transformations which he worked through in order to find the base. Prytulak's transformation stack could equally well be defined as an ordered set of productions. This is an example of the use of a production system in a task intuitively less complex than those studied by Newell and Simon. The implicit use of production systems in a task more complex than those considered by Newell and Simon can also be illustrated. Abelson and Reich (1969) have simulated the political analyses of a conservative American politician. They begin with a data structure that defines the politician's basic beliefs. These were stored as sets of assertions . . . e.g. "Liberals fear opposing communists." The program applied a set of rules for transforming a presented statement into a specific example of a general one. In a very simple example, substitution could be applied, which would transform "McCarthy speaks out against Vietnam war" into an example of the allegation about liberals. A number of more complex transformation rules were also available. These took the form of a match to input, followed by an alteration of a previously stored base of accepted statements. This is similar to the analyses of Box 8.4, in that the specific transformations applicable to an input statement were thus determined by the previously accepted statements of the data base. From the point of view of a production system analysis, the data base and set of productions were identical.*

Data structure concepts may also be used to develop a conjecture about the roles of semantic information processing and imagery in thought. The conjecture is based on the division of a data structure into nodes, links, and atoms. It has already been pointed out that the atoms ought to be regarded as basic engrams. As such, they would have to be laid down via a projection of data from the sensory projection areas into

---

*Winograd (1971) has developed the thesis that identity of data base and rules of inference is advisable in order to obtain good problem solving from any computing system, without regard to the system's plausibility as a simulation of human behavior.

the memory storage areas. In terms of the broadcast model an atom represents an engram which, when aroused, is capable of driving the STM into a state similar, in some sense, to the state that it was driven into by sensory data when the engram was constructed. Atoms, then, are identified with (perhaps generalized) images constructed either from sensory data or from an amalgamation of sensory input and atoms retrieved from memory. The latter is true when an image is constructed from the data structure of an event. We are capable of some non-trivial thoughts based solely upon the processing of atoms. The comparison of different projections of the same object, as in the Shepard and Metzler (1971) studies, is a good example. Since we can image the attachment of response images to sensory images, most of the tasks that psychologists have set for cats, pigeons, rats, and dogs could probably be handled by an information processing system capable of processing images only.

The nodes and links of a data structure, on the other hand, are only sensibly regarded as semantic structures. These structures play two roles. In a specific linguistic sense they provide the productions needed to transform an external language message into an internal data structure and vice versa. Internally, the productions of cognition are used to construct complex data structures and their associated images from simple ones. This is the sort of construction we mean when we speak of thinking.

The conjecture is, then, that there are two quite different types of memory. One is a memory for images. It is addressed by a broadcast mechanism, coded in terms of sensory inputs, and processed by a set of primitive transformations on images. The second memory is a semantic memory relating abstract linguistic concepts to each other. Pointers must exist to connect the terms of semantic memory to the engrams of image memory, but these pointers could quite well indicate that the basic records of the two types of memory reside in different locations. Semantic memory appears to be organized and addressed by a system of links that are addressed in series. There seems to be little chance of accounting for the data on the time required to retrieve semantically related terms in any other way, (Freedman and Loftus, 1971; Collins and Quillian, 1969, 1970; Landauer and Freedman, 1968; Juola and Atkinson, 1971). Therefore retrieving items from semantic memory must be by a search process rather than by a broadcast and reply system, although the nature of the search process remains obscure. We know even less about the rules for placing data into semantic memory. Perhaps systematic protocol analysis or simulation studies can help us most at this point. Newell and Simon (1972) make the point that a model of semantic memory must pass a *sufficiency test*. The structure must be powerful enough to accomplish those tasks which humans undoubtedly do. Logical analyses of natural language data processing indicate that the data structures of a language translator must permit recursive computation (Woods, 1970). Therefore we must assume that semantic memory permits operations on pushdown storage stacks.

Which of these memory systems is more complex? The question has a variety of answers. The logical interrelationships in semantic memory are certainly more sophisticated than in image memory, and the operations of semantic memory are more appealing as the operations of the "higher mental processes." Complexity, however, is a slippery concept.* The data structures of semantic memory could be realized by quite straightforward engineering principles. The associative memory systems required for the broadcast addressing technique are at or beyond the limits of modern technology (Foster, 1970). Intuitively the operations of searching for just the right word to fit into a sentence seem more like thought than the act of recognizing the face of a friend. From the viewpoint of a computer programmer, list processing programs are substantially easier to write than programs for processing pictorial data, and from the viewpoint of the computer designer the serial processing, Von Neuman machine which is sufficient for list processing is hopelessly inadequate when transformations on pictorial data are required. The problem is not just that the present day computer is a serial processor, either. Minsky and Papert (1969) have shown that there are definite limitations to the capabilities of interesting classes of simple parallel processors when the task requires analysis of geometric properties of stimuli. Our image memory may well be accompanied by a special image processor capable of executing rather complex analog processing operations on data derived either from sensory stimulation or from memory.

The last point to be made is that a two memory system is compatible with either the architecture of Distributed Memory or what little we know of the neuroanatomy of cognition. Image memory requires a long term memory area whose locations are capable of pattern matching, a broadcast system for memory addressing, and an STM-ITM system capable of receiving memory driven "sensory" projections. Various physiological theories assign these properties respectively to the right side of the cortex (Lansdell, 1968; Gazzaniga, 1969), the thalamic or limbic system (John, 1967, 1971) and the sensory projection areas (John, 1967). Semantic memory requires mechanisms for list searching and recursive computation (for language processing), and the capability of storing complex graphic data structures. Linguistic data processing is clearly associated with the left temporal cortex (Lenneberg, 1967, 1969; Geschwind, 1970). A number of clinical studies have associated failure to construct connections between more elementary ideas with the frontal lobe (Luria, 1966). Of course, such similarities between observations are only speculations. Each reader must decide whether they are interesting or not.

Conclusion

In a previous paper I asked "What kind of computer is Man?". On the basis of the evidence reviewed, a conjecture is in order. Man is describable as a dual processor, dual memory system with extensive input-output buffering within each system. The input-output system appears to have substantial peripheral computing power

---

*Computer science concepts cannot help us here. Minsky (1970) has pointed to an inadequate formulation of the notion of computational complexity in computers as one of the greatest drawbacks to advance in computer science. Certainly computational complexity in man is an equally difficult issue.

itself. But man is not modeled by a dual processor computer. The two processors of the brain are asymmetric. The semantic memory processor is a serial processor with a list structure memory. The image memory processor may very well be a sophisticated analog processor attached to an associative memory. When we propose models of cognition it would perhaps be advisable if we specified the relation of the model to this system architecture and its associated addressing system and data structure.

Acknowledgments

This research has been supported by the National Science Foundation Grant GB 25979. I would like to acknowledge the assistance I have received from my colleagues at the University of Washington, and in particular the assistance of Dr. Nancy Frost. The discussions and ideas proposed by my fellow participants in seminars on computer simulation were also of great help.

Nine

In Defense of Ad Hoc Systems

Robert K. Lindsay
The University of Michigan

Introduction

In 1959 and 1960 I developed a system of computer programs which I called SAD SAM. The original motivation for this work was an interest in how people understand ordinary language; a natural problem seemingly pertinent to this interest was the determination of a set of processes sufficient for answering questions about information presented in English. The availability of digital computers made possible the definition and study of processes in a way not before possible, and in this approach I saw promise of progress on the problem of automated question answering, and by that route, the hope of new insights into the larger issues. A few others at that time, and many others since then, have attempted to develop question-answering systems — sometimes for reasons similar to mine, sometimes for other reasons. None of these attempts has yielded impressive results, and it is now widely recognized that the task is far more difficult than we had imagined. It may be impossible.

By today's standards, SAD SAM is tiny indeed. It was developed on an IBM 650, a decimal machine of a mere 2000 words of main storage with an access time measured in milliseconds. The language used, IPL-V, was implemented in a manner that required searching magnetic tapes for most of the basic subroutines. Though the system was eventually run on an IBM 709, most of the debugging was done on the 650 while I hunched over the line printer checking the trace of each line of code. But at the time it seemed exciting and promising.

What SAD SAM did was this. An English sentence, limited to the 850 word vocabulary of Basic English, was read by the program. A parsing of this sentence was attempted by the first major portion of the program, SAD. If successful, the result was a tree which displayed approximately what is today called the surface structure of the sentence, in dependency analysis form. That is, a simple declarative sentence would be analyzed into subject, verb, and object, which in turn were analyzed into their constituents; the parsing tree had words, rather than syntactic classes, at its nodes, and the nodes were connected by directed edges denoting syntactic dependency. The strategy of analysis was based upon a left-to-right scan of the sentence, with predictions being made at each stage of what was to be looked for at subsequent stages. The construction used several cells of memory that could hold pieces of the tree and other symbols to flag the stages of the system. The program had the flavor, though not the coherence of an augmented transition network grammar, as developed by Woods (1970).

The sentences input could be about anything, but unless a sentence contained information about kinship relations, as signalled by the presence of certain kinship terms, nothing more became of it after the parsing tree was discovered (if it was). If kinship information were present, it was translated, by SAM, into facts of the form (xRy), where x and y were proper names and R was a kinship relation. These facts were then used to construct or add to a family tree graph that accumulated the kinship information presented during the run. Facts already encoded in the tree had no further effect; facts implied by facts supplied in sentences were "known" by virtue of the family tree mnemonic. A brief account of this program is given in Lindsay (1963).

Although miniature, SAD SAM embodied some design features which have subsequently gained acceptance, and some others which yet may gain acceptance:

1. SAD SAM sought to lay bare the structural relations implicit in the English input, rather than rely on statistical properties of text or simple associative connections, which was a strategy advocated by some early projects. SAD SAM produced what might be called phrase markers and semantic nets in today's jargon.

2. SAD SAM attended both to "syntactic" and "semantic" information [there is a good deal of confusion in the use of these terms — confusion into which I will not delve here — thus the sneer quotes]. However, the strategy then employed of processing first syntactic information (by SAD) and then semantic information (by SAM) is no doubt not always appropriate.

3. SAD, the syntactic portion, used heuristics to select the most probable syntactic parsing, rather than produce all possible parses. It was this feature which allowed it to succeed even though semantic analysis did not begin until a parse was available.

4. SAD SAM was goal oriented. It searched for information of a particular sort (kinship information) rather than attempting to extract all information and every nuance inherent in the input. It expected to hear certain things, and to be queried on just those things. This, I believe, is an essential feature of any intelligent system.

5. SAD SAM was based on psychologically plausible assumptions about storage and processing: limited short term memory, associative and hierarchically structured long term

memory, serial scan of inputs. These assumptions were taken seriously and guided the design of the system. This approach is not yet current, nor is it known to be the best strategy.

6. The system did not focus on the "meaning of a sentence" as the key to comprehension. The problem was viewed as that of growing and modifying an information structure represented in computer memory, and of extracting information from this structure. The structure was called a *map*, which together with *annexing* and *retrieval* processes comprised a *model* of the domain of discourse.

7. The major characteristic of comprehension was taken to be the ability to draw inferences from the inputs supplied, rather than merely to recall them verbatim on demand. One of the major obstacles to successful inferential capability was recognized to be the size of the combinatorial problem inherent in any formal deductive scheme. SAD SAM proposed as one weapon against this obstacle the use of appropriate models which could bear some of this burden, much as the diagrams of Euclidian geometry provide a powerful, though formally inessential aid in that classical deductive realm.

8. SAD SAM attempted to do what it could with what it was given. As such it was not sensitive to deviations from exact input formats; it did not have strong views on what was grammatical and what was not. SAD was not a pedant.

SAD SAM failed to capture the imagination of the computer science community, nonetheless. The failure may by and large be attributed to its seemingly *ad hoc* character. This character was in part real and in part merely apparent. The syntactic system was specified as a process, rather than as a set of rules (a generative grammar) characterizing a set of sentences, as was just becoming fashionable. Even today, but more so in 1960, a program is not a perspicuous description of the data it will handle; therefore the linguistic competence of my system could not readily be described. Its structure, however, was not *ad hoc* in the sense of being designed specifically for a limited set of special cases (in particular it was not based on a set of sentence "frames"), and the restriction to the vocabulary of Basic English was not a serious reduction of the magnitude of the problem. The system could deal, for its limited purposes, with some fairly complex sentences. But just what its limitations were, to this day I can not make precise. The problem was one of the state of the art of programming, not merely a tactical error of stating competence as process rather than as data-descriptive rule-set. Nonetheless, I do not wish to defend SAD at any length for much about it was incorrect.

The charge against SAM is better founded. As noted above, SAM was a system that examined the phrase markers produced by SAD, detected references to kinship facts, and constructed family trees as dictated by these facts. All this was quite straightforward. What intrigued me about family trees, however, were some properties which are very interesting and powerful. Having consciously remembered family structures through mental images of family trees for as long as I could recall, it seemed valuable to attempt to characterize just what it was that made them interesting or—as I came to say—*enriched* structures.

The basic feature is an important one: we can add facts one at a time in such a way that implications from *sets* of facts are *automatically* available in the structure, in just the form they would have taken had they been explicitly given. Thus, if (a is-the-mother-of b) and (a is-the-mother-of c) are given facts, the tree constructed makes available the additional fact (b is-the-sibling-of c). No additional memory is necessary, and no change in the process for retrieving facts is required. Further, the retrieval process is a lookup rather than a computation; retrieving the fact (b is-the-sibling-of c) is of exactly the same computational complexity irrespective of how the knowledge was gained. Furthermore, it is of course true that each name need only be represented by a single token in the computer memory, with labelled links denoting the relations between name tokens.

Although these properties are interesting and useful, they do indeed pertain only to family trees. Surely a system which works only with kinship relations is *ad hoc* to a fault, and thus interest in such a system is justifiably limited. SAD SAM was reasonably powerful as an inference maker, but it lacked generality.

Subsequent research has emphasized the value of generality in deductive abilities. The search for generality has usually taken the form of a search for general schemes of representation and general procedures for deduction. Two major trends may be seen. The clearer one is the suggestion that the first order predicate calculus be used as a representation language for natural language textual information and that deductions be effected by a general proof procedure, resolution. The second trend is the use of the so-called semantic net, in which relations are recorded in a linked memory scheme representation of a labelled, directed graph, that is appropriately formatted. For some propositions, the semantic net offers a more perspicuous translation than the first order predicate calculus. Notable among these are propositions which naturally translate into a higher order calculus; though these may in turn be translated into first order expression, the result is no longer a transparent rendition of the original. However, no general deductive procedure is available for semantic nets.

The price these general representations pay is lack of power. Put the other way, given a general representation, the research problem becomes that of developing deductive power (plus, of course, the task of translating from the input language into the general representation). In the case of semantic nets this problem has not yet yielded a clear direction. In the case of predicate calculus representations, resolution provides a clear direction for research. But even so the problem has not yet been solved, because the technique of resolution is — in any situation of interest — a huge combinatorial problem requiring extensive search through a large set of possible candidates. Furthermore, the reduction to a formal problem conceals whatever semantic clues might have been available in the original problem, and renders even more difficult the task of using such techniques as reasoning by analogy, planning, and the use of previous results. These difficulties may not be insurmountable, but they most certainly are problems for research, some of which is actively underway.

As suggested above, an alternative to either of these procedures is the recording of a critical subset of relational facts in a highly *structured* form which permits the retrieval of implied facts with exactly the same process by which the facts in the critical subset are retrieved. Another example will make clear the distinction between this approach and the predicate calculus plus formal inference approach.

Suppose we have a finite set of objects, say the first ten positive integers, and a strict simple ordering relation, less-than, defined on that set. The facts about this set of objects involving just the relation less-than, $<$, and its converse, greater-than, $>$, are 90 in number, including for example $(5 < 8)$, $(2 < 9)$, and $(6 > 3)$. A subset of nine facts $[1 < 2, 2 < 3, 3 < 4, \ldots , 9 < 10]$ together with the rules of inference $(x < y)$ & $(y < z) \rightarrow (x < z)$, $(x < y) \leftrightarrow$ not $(y < x)$, and $(x < y) \rightarrow (y > x)$, are sufficient for the purposes of storage and retrieval. Recording this information together with a procedure (perhaps resolution) for applying the rules of inference would be to use the general predicate calculus approach. On the other hand we might structure the information by storing the ordered string 1, 2, 3, 4, 5, 6, 7, 8, 9, 10 and employ the two retrieval processes (i) $(x < y)$ if and only if x precedes y in the structure, and (ii) $(x > y)$ if and only if y precedes x in the structure. (i) and (ii) work in the same manner for the critical set as for the remaining 81 facts. Of course the latter procedure works only for strict simple orderings.

The value of generality is uncontestable. However, there is more than one route to generality. One, as we have seen, is to employ a general scheme of representation. Another may be found at a higher level of abstraction. Rather than a general scheme of representation, we might seek a general scheme of devising special purpose representations: a general scheme for building *ad hoc* systems. This search would be similar in spirit to a search for a general language learning procedure which, under appropriate inputs and experiences, could learn English or French or German. The linguistic descriptions discovered for each language might, taken individually, appear *ad hoc*. But if this resulted in greater fluency in each language than could be achieved by a general representation encompassing all languages, the price might be worth paying.

A priori there is no way of telling which quest — that for a general representation or that for a general procedure for constructing special representations — will be more profitable. But since the former approach is in good hands, it may be worthwhile to examine how the latter might begin. If brought to a successful conclusion, we might then be able to produce enriched representations for specific applications and obtain a purchase on the problem of deductive power. It is at least plausible, and from my introspections compelling, that humans operate in this way — that their modes of thinking about chess, social organizations, water jug problems, getting around a city, and kinship structures bear little resemblance on the surface.

The remainder of this paper will not supply the system suggested. What follows is a description of some efforts in this direction carried out by myself and two of my students over the past decade.

The Problems to be Discussed

We will not be concerned with the problems of linguistic analysis, of mapping natural language expressions onto data structures. The focus here is on the problem of discovering data structures appropriate for a given type of data. The class of data structures will be limited to the class of labelled, directed graphs, whose representation in computer memory is now widely understood. The nodes of the graph will represent *objects* (people, numbers, things, or whatever) and the edges will represent binary relations between the two nodes connected with the label serving to distinguish different relations. Given an *initial data set* consisting of *facts* of the form (xR_iy), the construction of a graph (not necessarily connected) which encodes this set of facts is straightforward. We will call this graph the *ingenuous graph* for the given initial data set.

It may be the case that (a) some of the relations R_1, R_2, ... , R_n have interesting properties (e.g., symmetry, transitivity) or that (b) the set of relations $R = \{R_1, R_2, ... , R_n\}$ has interesting structure (e.g., some of the relations are identical, some can be expressed as compositions of others). If neither (a) nor (b) is true, the ingenuous graph is the best we can do, and in fact may not be worth bothering with. If (a) and/or (b) hold, it may be that the graph can be simplified or modified to achieve deductive advantages of the sort SAM enjoyed. To use kinship relations as the paradigm illustration, we may consider the initial data set given in Box 9.1. The ingenuous graph for this data set is given in Figure 9.1, and the corresponding family tree is given as Figure 9.2.

Problem One examines the case where a data set is based on only one relation, R, which has a known set of properties. The problem is to select an appropriate data structure which aids in deductions based on the set of properties. Roger Elliott has solved this problem for the cases with nine simple properties of relations, and this work will be described.

Box 9.1   An Initial Data Set of Kinship Facts.

GM	=	Grandfather	GF	=	Grandmother
PM	=	Father	PF	=	Mother
MM	=	Husband	MF	=	Wife
SM	=	Brother	SF	=	Sister
UM	=	Uncle	PN	=	Parent (neuter)

Fred	MM	Sue	Henry	SM	Bill
Fred	PM	Henry	Henry	SM	Barb
Fred	PM	Bill	Henry	PM	Cathy
Fred	PM	Barb	Bill	SM	Henry
Fred	GM	Cathy	Bill	SM	Barb
Fred	GM	Bob	Bill	UM	Cathy
Sue	MF	Fred	Bill	UM	Bob
Sue	PF	Henry	Barb	SF	Henry
Sue	PF	Bill	Barb	SF	Bill
Sue	PF	Barb	Barb	PF	Bob

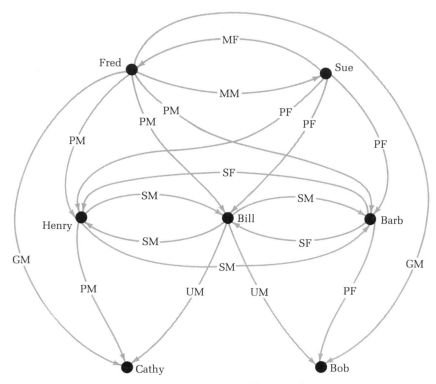

Figure 9.1 Ingenuous Graph for Facts from Table 9.1. (After Brown, 1972.)

Problem Two examines the case of more than one relation. The problem is to discover among the set of relations a subset of *atomic relations* in terms of which all the given relations may be defined. For example, all kinship relations may be defined in terms of Son, Daughter, Husband, and Wife. SAM knew this because he was built that way. Problem Two is to discover such structure, given only an initial data set. John Brown has worked on this problem, and his work will be described.

Problem Three is similar to Problem Two, except that the set of atomic relations need not be included within the set of relations found in the data set. Very little progress has been made on this problem. I will offer some suggestions for an approach.

Problem One

This problem is limited to a single relation, R, for which a set of properties, selected from a known, fixed set, is given. For example, take R to be an equivalence relation. That is, R is reflexive (for all x in the set of objects over which R is defined, xRx), symmetric (if xRy then yRx), and transitive (if xRy and yRz, then xRz). An equivalence relation partitions the set of objects into mutually exclusive equivalence

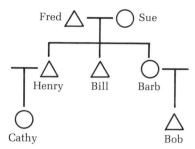

Figure 9.2 Family Tree for Facts
from Box 9.1; Sex is
indicated by the Shape
of Nodes. (After
Brown, 1972.)

classes. Thus an appropriate map in this case is a set of disconnected graphs, each connecting equivalent object nodes; an appropriate annexing process either (i) creates a new graph if neither object a nor object b has a corresponding node in the map as constituted when the fact (aRb) is presented, or (ii) combines the graph containing a with the graph containing b by connecting the a-node with the b-node if both exist, or (iii) if just one of a and b has a corresponding node in the existing map, a node for the other is created and connected to the previously existing node; an appropriate retrieval process answers "yes" to the query "(aRb)?" if and only if the a-node and b-node are both present in the same graph. Note the interdependence of annexing and retrieval processes. If the retrieval process in this example required that the a-node and b-node be directly connected as a necessary condition for a "yes" answer, the annexing process would have to totally connect each graph in the map. This variation would place the major computational burden on the retrieval process. Such trade-offs are characteristic, and may be exploited if something is known about the mix of declarative and interrogative inputs the system is to face, but we will not be concerned with these issues here.

Roger Elliott (1965) has analyzed this problem for all meaningful combinations of nine properties, and this work may serve as a model for similar efforts with other property sets. The properties and their definitions, as given by Elliott, are given in Box 9.2. The maximum number of subcases of Problem One for a set of nine properties is the number of subsets of a set with nine members: $2^9 = 512$. Clearly, however, not all of these are possible or distinct in the present example, since some of the properties are mutually exclusive (e.g., P-reflexive and irreflexive) and some combinations are redundant because some properties imply others (e.g., unlooped implies asymmetric). Elliott proved the results given in Box 9.3, and used these to demonstrate that exactly 32 unique combinations exist. These 32 are given in Table 9.1; equivalence relations, for example, are Type 17. Elliott then devised annexing and retrieval processes for each of these 32 Types. These processes are not the only ones possible, but they serve to illustrate the essentials of the solution. The annexing processes are capable of building several kinds of graphs. For example, a loop is a

---

Box 9.2   Definitions of Properties of Relations. (After Elliott, 1965.)

Property 1:   R   is p–reflexive if and only if
$(x,y) \in R \rightarrow (x,x) \in R$ and $(y,y) \in R$.

Property 2:   R   is irreflexive if and only if
$x \in A \rightarrow (x,x) \notin R$.

Property 3:   R   is p–symmetric if and only if
$R \nleq IA$ [$IA = \{(x,x) | x \in A\}$| and $(x,y) \in R \rightarrow (y,x) \in R$.

Property 4:   R   is asymmetric if and only if
$(x,y) \in R \rightarrow (y,x) \notin R$.

Property 5:   R   is p–transitive if and only if there exist
distinct elements $a,b,c \in A$ such that (a,b) and (b,c)
are elements of R and if for all $x,y,z \in A$
$(x,y) \in R$ and $(y,z) \in R \rightarrow (x,z) \in R$.

Property 6:   R   is one–follower if and only if R is
functional.

Property 7:   R   is one–leader if and only if R$*$ is
functional.

Property 8:   R   is noregrowth if and only if $(x,y) \in R$
implies that there exists no finite set $B \leq R$ such that
$(x,y) \notin B$ and
$B = \{(x,z_1), (z_1,z_2), \dots, (z_n,y)\}$.

Property 9:   R   is unlooped if and only if $(x,y) \in R$
implies there exists no finite set $B \leq R$ such that
$B = \{(y,z_1), (z_1,z_2), \dots, (z_n,x)\}$.

---

set of three or more nodes with exactly one connection "to" and exactly one connection "from" each, so that a closed loop is formed. This structure is one of the possible results of several different annexing processes. However, the effect of such a structure depends also on the retrieval process employed. Basically, retrieval processes are of two kinds: (i) a "yes" response to "(aRb)?" requires that a-node and b-node be *directly* connected; (ii) a "yes" response to "(aRb)?" requires only that a-node and b-node be connected, directly or through intermediary nodes.

To further illustrate, consider a Type 3 relation, having the properties irreflexive, asymmetric, 1-leader, unlooped, and noregrowth. As can be seen from an examination of Box 9.2, the properties 1-leader and unlooped imply the other three. The annexing process for fact (aRb) suggested by Elliott may be paraphrased as follows:

If a and b are identical, print "INCORRECT FACT" and exit.

If b-node is connected directly or indirectly to a-node, print "INCONSISTENT WITH MAP" and exit.

Box 9.3 Summary of Elliott's Lemmas.

```
p-reflexive  →  not irreflexive
irreflexive  →  not p-reflexive
asymmetric  →  irreflexive
asymmetric  →  irreflexive
p-transitive & irreflexive  →  asymmetric & unlooped
transitive & irreflexive & asymmetric  →  unlooped
p-symmetric & p-transitive  →  p-reflexive
1-leader  →  noregrowth
1-follower  →  noregrowth
noregrowth  →  not p-transitive
unlooped  →  asymmetric
not(noregrowth & p-reflexive & p-symmetric)
p-symmetric & 1-leader  →  1-follower
symmetric & 1-follower  →  1-leader
```

If a-node is directly connected to b-node, print "SUPERFLUOUS FACT" and exit.

If a-node is connected directly or indirectly to b-node, print "INCONSISTENT WITH MAP" and exit.

If b-node is back-connected to any node other than a-node, print "INCONSISTENT WITH MAP" and exit.

Otherwise, connect a-node to b-node, print "OK", and exit.

The corresponding retrieval process suggested by Elliot may be paraphrased as follows:

If a and b are identical, print "FALSE" and exit.

If b-node is connected directly or indirectly to a-node, print "FALSE" and exit.

If b-node is back-connected to any node other than a-node print "FALSE" and exit.

If a-node is directly connected to b-node, print "TRUE" and exit.

If a-node is connected directly or indirectly to b-node, print "FALSE" and exit.

Otherwise, print "INSUFFICIENT INFORMATION IN MAP" and exit.

The data structures constructed and interrogated by the above processes are trees. The trace shown in Box 9.4 illustrates the behavior of a system embodying these processes.

In this example the only queries "(aRb)?" which will yield a true answer are those for which the fact (aRb) was previously given; that is, inferences to true facts are all trivial. However, the retrieval process will inform us that certain facts are false even though this information was not explicitly provided. Only in cases involving the transitive property will we find examples of non-trivial inferences to

Table 9.1 The 32 Types of Relations for the Properties of Box 9.2. Italicized Properties are those from which the others follow. (After Elliott, 1965.)

Type		Properties	Type		Properties
R	R*	(R)	R	R*	(R)
1	1	irreflexive asymmetric *1-leader* *1-follower* *unlooped* *noregrowth*	2	3	irreflexive asymmetric *1-follower* *unlooped* noregrowth
3	2	irreflexive asymmetric *1-leader* *unlooped* noregrowth	4	4	irreflexive asymmetric *unlooped* *noregrowth*
5	5	irreflexive *asymmetric* *1-leader* *1-follower* noregrowth	6	8	irreflexive *asymmetric* *1-follower* noregrowth
7	10	*irreflexive* *1-follower* noregrowth	8	6	irreflexive *asymmetric* *1-leader* noregrowth
9	9	*irreflexive* *p-symmetric* *1-leader* *1-follower* noregrowth	10	7	*irreflexive* *1-leader* noregrowth
11	11	irreflexive *asymmetric* noregrowth	12	12	*irreflexive* *p-symmetric* noregrowth
13	13	*irreflexive* noregrowth	14	14	noregrowth *1-leader* *1-follower*
15	15	irreflexive *asymmetric* *p-transitive* unlooped	16	16	irreflexive asymmetric unlooped

Table 9.1 (continued)

Type		Properties	Type		Properties
R	R*	(R)	R	R*	(R)
17	17	p-reflexive p-symmetric p-transitive	18	18	p-reflexive p-transitive
19	19	p-transitive	20	20	irreflexive asymmetric
21	21	irreflexive p-symmetric	22	22	p-reflexive p-symmetric
23	23	p-symmetric	24	24	irreflexive
25	25	p-reflexive	26	26	none
27	27	p-symmetry noregrowth	28	28	noregrowth
29	30	noregrowth 1-leader	30	29	noregrowth 1-follower
31	31	irreflexive noregrowth 1-leader 1-follower	32	32	p-symmetry noregrowth 1-leader 1-follower

true facts. If, however, new relations S, T, etc. were defined as compositions of R, retrieval processes which would provide inferences to true and false facts concerning these new relations could sometimes be readily made. Information retrieval systems based upon these types of analyses of Problem One might be of practical interest, but the theoretical interest is clearly limited.

Problem Two

We wish to reduce the amount of information to be stored by taking advantage of redundancy. This can be done if the initial set of relations, in terms of which the initial data set is given, can be reduced to a smaller set from which the complete set may be recovered. This requires that some of the relations are definable in terms of others. Discovering such definitions from examination of the initial data set is thus the first step in discovering an atomic set of relations.

John Brown has devised a symbiotic program, called "The Monkey's Uncle," which deals with one important aspect of this general problem. The sense in which

Box 9.4 Behavior of Annexing and Retrieving Processes for a Type 3 Relation.

INPUT	OUTPUT	MAP
aRb	OK	a → b
cRd	OK	a → b
		c → d
eRf	OK	a → b
		c → d
		e → f
aRc	OK	a → b
		│
		→ c → d
		e → f
dRa	INCONSISTENT WITH MAP	(unchanged)
fRc		
cRf		
cRe	OK	a → b
		│
		→ c → d
		│
		→ e → f
aRd?	FALSE	
aRf?	FALSE	
eRa?	FALSE	
eRd?	FALSE	

a relation R is definable in terms of other relations R_1, R_2, etc. is limited to R's being constructed from R_1, R_2, etc., using (recursively) the operations of composition, disjunction, and converse. Thus ANCESTOR may be defined as PARENT *or* (ANCESTOR *of* PARENT), and DESCENDANT may be defined as *converse* of ANCESTOR. Using 'V' to denote disjunction, '/' to denote composition, and '∗' to denote converse, these definitions will be written ANCESTOR = PARENT V (ANCESTOR/PARENT), and DESCENDANT = ANCESTOR∗. The operations are defined as follows:

(i) The *composition* of R_1 and R_2:
For all x and y [(xR_1/R_2y) if and only if there exists a z such that (xR_1z) and (zR_2y)].

(ii) The *disjunction* of R_1 and R_2:
For all x and y [(xR_1VR_2y) if and only if (xR_1y) or (xR_2y)].

(iii) The *converse* of R:
For all x and y [$(xR∗y)$ if and only if (yRx)].

The basic computation used by The Monkey's Uncle is the determination of Labelled Path Sequences (LPS's). After constructing the ingenuous graph from the initial data set, each relation is considered in turn. For a given relation, a particular fact in the extension of that relation is selected. This determines two nodes in the ingenuous graph, corresponding to x and y in the selected fact (xRy). Any path from x to y in the graph is identified with the ordered set of relations labelling the edges traversed. Each such ordered set of relations is called an LPS for that fact. An LPS may contain converse relations, if an edge is traversed against its direction, and it may contain the relation R of the fact itself, but paths which contain loops (retrace themselves) are discounted.

Each fact involving relation R thus generates a set of LPS's; each LPS is a candidate definition of R as a composition of other relations and their converses. Clearly some of these candidates will be spurious, and the problem comes down to weeding these out while retaining those which work for all of the R-facts. Simply forming the intersection of all of the LPS sets would suffice except that the intersection may be null, if for example a disjunction was necessarily part of the definition. If this is so, then we would like to select a disjunction of the fewest terms. It may not always be that disjunctions of the least number of terms will lead to the optimum solution to the atomic set selection problem, but as a heuristic device, we would like to keep the number small. Even so, the task of finding the minimal disjunctions (there may be more than one) is computationally expensive, and other strategies are helpful. The Monkey's Uncle proceeds as follows: Intersect a pair of LPS sets, then intersect the next with the result, and so on until all have been intersected or until a null set is obtained. If the null set is obtained, use the intersection formed just prior to the production of the null set as one disjunct, and proceed in the same manner using only the remaining LPS sets. Clearly this strategy's outcome will depend critically on the order in which the LPS sets are considered. However, if there are N R-facts, there are N! orderings of LPS sets. We know of no good heuristics which will work for most problems. This is one place where symbiosis enters. The Monkey's Uncle will do the computations the user requests, so that the user may explore whatever intuitions or flashes of insight he is gifted with.

Given the set of candidate definitions thus formed — each consisting of a disjunction of compositions of relations and their converses — some may still be superfluous by virtue of their overgenerality. Thus while we are assured that each candidate definition works for each R-fact in the initial data set, there may be additional facts consistent with the definition which are not in the initial data set (and which are not proper inferences). Again the discovery of these is straightforward, but computationally expensive. Brown has employed the following heuristic to eliminate some of these overgeneral definitions.

The *inverse image* of x with respect to relation R is the set of all y such that there exists a z for which (xRz) and (yRz). The Monkey's Uncle computes the inverse image of x with respect to a selected R for the initial data set; it then computes the inverse image of x with respect to a candidate definition applied over the initial data set. If the inverse image of x with respect to the definition is not contained in the inverse image with respect to the given extension of R, for all x, then the definition is rejected. This heuristic will reject some overgeneral definitions, but not necessarily all of them.

To illustrate the effect of this heuristic, consider an example based on the family tree in Figure 9.3. The Monkey's Uncle conjectured the 15 definitions of "niece" given in Box 9.5. Consider the first definition, niece = cousin/daughter. A cousin-daughter path exists between every niece-uncle and niece-aunt pair in the tree; thus cousin-daughter remains as a candidate definition after the intersection procedure. However, this definition is not correct in our kinship system because a girl may be the niece of someone who has no daughter (or of someone who is childless, or not even married for that matter). In the initial data base, however, all potential aunts and uncles are married and have at least one daughter. Thus every niece in the data set is the cousin of the daughter of her aunt and uncle. However, not every cousin of a daughter is a niece: some are nephews (namely, "8" and "11"). Thus the definition is overgeneral even with respect to this data set, and this is reflected in the fact, among others, that the inverse image of 9 with respect to cousin/daughter [={8, 9, 10, 11, 12}] is not contained in the inverse image of 9 with respect to niece [={9, 10, 12}]. Eleven of 15 candidate definitions of "niece" are eliminated in this way, as indicated in Box 9.5.

Once we are in possession of a set of intensional definitions of each of the relations, we may begin determining a set of atomic relations, defined as a minimal subset of the initial set of relations which is sufficient to generate the entire initial set. The calculation may be accomplished in a straightforward manner by considering each subset of the initial set, starting with a subset of size 1 and progressing to the full set. There are 2^N such subsets for an initial set of N relations. The members of the candidate subset, of course, generate themselves. By examining the definitions of each of the other relations we find all those that can be generated directly by the candidate subset. Expanding the candidate subset by these, we iterate the process. If the set eventually expands to include the whole initial set, then the candidate subset is a generating set, and by virtue of the order in which the candidates are selected, the first such found is an atomic set. Of course it need not be

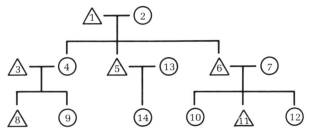

Figure 9.3   Family Tree for "Niece" Example of The
Monkey's Uncle (After Brown, 1972).

Box 9.5 Candidate Definitions of "Niece" produced by The Monkey's Uncle for Data based on Figure 9.3. Those Definitions eliminated by the Inverse Image Heuristic are indicated by †.

† Cousin/Daughter
† Cousin/Offspring
† Cousin/Daughter/Spouse
† Cousin/Cousin/Daughter
† Cousin/Cousin/Offspring
† Offspring/Uncle/Offspring
† Offspring/Uncle/Daughter
  Daughter/Uncle/Offspring
  Daughter/Uncle/Daughter
† Offspring/Aunt/Offspring
† Offspring/Aunt/Daughter
  Daughter/Aunt/Offspring
  Daughter/Aunt/Daughter
† Cousin/Cousin/Nephew
† Cousin/Offspring/Spouse

---

unique. Brown has devised some procedures for reducing the magnitude of these calculations. These procedures would be useful for large initial sets, particularly if the size of the atomic set turns out to be large also.

The Monkey's Uncle has been successfully applied to several initial data sets based on kinship relations. It was also applied to a data set that extensionally defines the accessibility relations between squares on a chess board for the various pieces. The program was then used to determine the definitions of the legal moves of the various pieces. These experiments are interesting to examine in detail because the initial data sets — devoid of our usual mental images of their underlying structures — are surprisingly complex and *prima facie* baffling. The discovery of the unifying "theories" of these data sets is thus an impressive simplification, even though these theories themselves contain no surprises for us.

Problem Three

Finally, we will consider the case where the atomic relations are not (all) among the set of initially given relations. Some rationale must thus be used to postulate new facts based on new relations. Our strategy is to (a) distinguish subsets of the set of names mentioned in the initial data set, and (b) define new relations which hold between all pairs of members of a common subset, or which map members of one subset onto members of another.

We have limited our formulation of the problem to what might be called purely syntactic considerations: there are only uninterpreted facts with which to work. One approach is to consider each fact to be a sentence of an unknown language; the initial data set is then a corpus from which we would generalize. Distinguishing subsets of names may be attempted by using the techniques of distributional analysis of linguistics. Names that enjoy similar privileges of occurrence in the "sentences" will be identified as members of a class, just as phonemes and syntactic classes are identified in natural languages on the basis of the contexts in which they appear.

To illustrate a simplified version of this approach, we return once more to kinship relations, but we now use an initial data base that does not involve the "atomic" relations of spouse and offspring, or the close derivative, sibling. See Figure 9.4. The representation used (a family tree) is the one we seek; the simple relations in terms of which all others are expressed are "spouse" and "offspring." We assume, however, that the only available information defines relations in terms of the compound relations "cousin," "grandparent," "sibling-in-law," and "neuter uncle," (i.e., aunt or uncle) which will be denoted by "C," "G," "S," and "U," respectively, where we drop the suffixes from our earlier notation. For the above module, the relations give rise to the following data set:

1. aCc	11. IIGa	21. FSH
2. bCc	12. IIGb	22. HSF
3. aCd	13. IGc	
4. bCd	14. IGd	23. GUa
5. cCa	15. IIGc	24. GUb
6. cCb	16. IIGd	25. HUa
7. dCa		26. HUb
8. dCb	17. ESH	27. EUc
	18. HSE	28. EUd
9. IGa	19. ESG	29. FUc
10. IGb	20. GSE	30. FUd

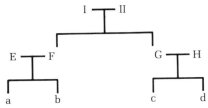

Figure 9.4 Graph for Illustration of Problem Three.

Let $R_1(x)$ be the set of relations in which name "x" may appear as the first name (as in xRy). Let $R_2(x)$ be the set of relations in which "x" may appear as the second name.

For our example, we can compute the following:

$$
\begin{aligned}
R_1(a) &= \{C\} & R_2(a) &= \{C, G, U\} \\
R_1(b) &= \{C\} & R_2(b) &= \{C, G, U\} \\
R_1(c) &= \{C\} & R_2(c) &= \{C, G, U\} \\
R_1(d) &= \{C\} & R_2(d) &= \{C, G, U\} \\
R_1(E) &= \{S, U\} & R_2(E) &= \{S\} \\
R_1(F) &= \{S, U\} & R_2(F) &= \{S\} \\
R_1(G) &= \{S, U\} & R_2(G) &= \{S\} \\
R_1(H) &= \{S, U\} & R_2(H) &= \{S\} \\
R_1(I) &= \{G\} & R_2(I) &= \emptyset = \text{the null set} \\
R_1(II) &= \{G\} & R_2(II) &= \emptyset
\end{aligned}
$$

The preceding characterization of the names yields a classification that is suggestive. For example, it suggests that a, b, c, and d may have a significant commonality; similarly for E, F, G, and H, and for I and II. However, we will need to distinguish the set {a,b} from the set {c,d} and the set {E,F} from the set {G,H}. To this end, let $C(x)$ be the "contexts" in which "x" may appear (a context is a relation and one name, such as "−Cc"). We then have the following.

$$
\begin{aligned}
C(a) &= \{-Cc, -Cd, IG-, IIG-, GU-, HU-\} \\
C(b) &= \{-Cc, -Cd, IG-, IIG-, GU-, HU-\} \\
C(c) &= \{-Ca, -Cb, IG-, IIG-, EU-, FU-\} \\
C(d) &= \{-Ca, -Cb, IG-, IIG-, EU-, FU-\} \\
C(E) &= \{-SH, -SG, HS-, GS-, -Uc, -Ud\} \\
C(F) &= \{-SH, \quad\quad HS-, \quad\quad -Uc, -Ud\} \\
C(G) &= \{-SE, \quad\quad ES-, \quad\quad -Ua, -Ub\} \\
C(H) &= \{-SE, -SF, ES-, FS-, -Ua, -Ub\} \\
C(I) &= \{-Ga, -Gb, -Gc, -Gd\} \\
C(II) &= \{-Ga, -Gb, -Gc, -Gd\}
\end{aligned}
$$

Since $C(a)$ and $C(b)$ are identical, as are $C(c)$ and $C(d)$, we may distinguish classes {a,b} and {c,d}. The identical contexts $C(I)$ and $C(II)$ give us no new information because {I,II} has already been identified. The remaining set {E,F,G,H} is more complex. To identify the sets {E,F} and {G,H} we note that $C(F)$ is a subset of $C(E)$, and $C(G)$ is a subset of $C(H)$. We may also note that under the permutation ((E,H), (F,G), (a,c), (b,d)), $C(E)$ maps into $C(H)$ and vice versa, and $C(F)$ maps into $C(G)$, and vice versa. This provides grounds for identifying the classes {E,H} and {F,G}.

Having identified these subsets, we first postulate new relations defined on each subset. This yields the following new facts.

aB_1b and bB_1a

cB_2d and dB_2c

IM_1II and IIM_1I

EM_2F and FM_2E

GM_3H and HM_3G

EZH and HZE

FB_3G and GB_3F

Two difficulties remain. First, we have not succeeded in discovering the off-spring relation. Second, although we have defined new relations between the siblings a and b, between the siblings c and d, and between the siblings F and G, these three relations, B_1, B_2, and B_3, are not identified as the same relation; the same is true for the three spouse relations defined, M_1, M_2, and M_3. [The spurious relation Z also has been defined, but this should be no serious problem.]

The first difficulty is successfully handled by a second basis for defining new relations. The initial data set includes relations that map some of our subsets onto others: the U relation maps {G,H} onto {a,b} and {E,F} onto {c,d} and the G relation maps {I,II} onto {a,b} and {c,d}. This suggests other relations which may be postulated: A relation we will call 0_1 maps {E,F} onto {a,b} and {G,H} onto {c,d} [we choose this as the same relation because of the symmetric roles played by this subset, i.e., {a,b} plays the same role in C(E) and C(F) that {c,d} plays in C(G) and C(H)]; relation 0_2 maps {I,II} onto {G,H} and {E,F}; relation 0_3 maps {I,II} onto {F,G}; and spurious relations (which we ignore here) map the remaining subsets onto one another.

These procedures have succeeded in identifying relations M_1 and M_2 between spouses, B_1 and B_2 between siblings, and 0_1, 0_2, and 0_3 between parents and off-spring, but we still have no basis for recognizing that M_1 and M_2 should be identified as the same relation, as should B_1 and B_2 and 0_1, 0_2, and 0_3.

On the basis of the information in the initial data set, it appears that there are no grounds for such unification. If the initial data set were based on a "deeper tree," —one that included more than three generations—the sorts of syntactic manipulations suggested might provide a basis for identifying the multiple offspring, spouse, and sibling relations except that the "boundary cases" (the top-most and bottom-most nodes of the tree) would be exceptions that would have to be recognized as such. To illustrate, consider the extended case illustrated in Figure 9.5.

This extension to the example adds the following facts to the initial data set.

31. 1C3	47. EG1	63. a'Sb	75. bU1
32. 1C4	48. EG2	64. bSa'	76. bU2
33. 2C3	49. FG1	65. a'Sb'	77. b'U1
34. 2C4	50. FG2	66. b'Sa'	78. b'U2
35. 3C1	51. EG3	67. aSb'	79. aU3
36. 4C1	52. EG4	68. b'Sa	80. aU4
37. 3C2	53. FG3	69. c'Sd	81. a'U3

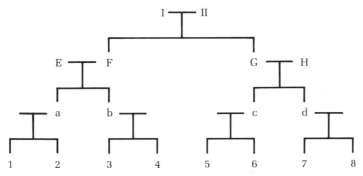

Figure 9.5 Graph for Illustration of Problem Three.

38. 4C2	54. FG4	70. dSc'	82. a'U4
39. 5C7	55. GG5	71. c'Sd'	83. dU5
40. 5C8	56. GG6	72. d'Sc'	84. dU6
41. 6C7	57. HG5	73. cSd'	85. d'U5
42. 6C8	58. HG6	74. d'Sc	86. d'U6
43. 7C5	59. GG7		87. cU7
44. 8C5	60. GG8		88. cU8
45. 7C6	61. HG7		89. c'U7
46. 8C6	62. HG8		90. c'U8

This extended data set leads to the distributional information given in Boxes 9.6 and 9.7.

Calculations of the same sort used in the previous example suffice to determine classes of names and define new relations as before. Given these newly defined relations as candidates for an identification process, we can see in the context information bases for making certain identifications, though these bases are rather obscure. For example, as we might expect, we note that I and II have the same grandchildren; it also happens that E has the same grandchildren as F, and G has the same grandchildren as H. On this basis, we might suppose that I and II, E and F, and G and H are related in the same way. Similar observations enable us to identify the various sibling relations: siblings have common neuter-uncles. The presence of this information should not obscure the difficulty of the problem. Our knowledge of the answer has guided our search for the pertinent information; the reader who approaches the data presented in a neutral, syntactic manner will find bases for many other guesses. Thus the problem of separating the wheat from the chaff can become quite difficult even in this simple example.

Once new relations are postulated and the facts they elicit are added to the initial data set, our problem reduces to Problem Two, for which the procedures of The Monkey's Uncle are applicable. Their success, however, will depend critically on how much chaff we have passed along.

Box 9.6   Distributional Data for Facts based on Figure 9.5.

$\underline{R}_1(1)$	= {C}		$\underline{R}_2(1)$	= {C,G,U}
$\underline{R}_1(2)$	= {C}		$\underline{R}_2(2)$	= {C,G,U}
$\underline{R}_1(3)$	= {C}		$\underline{R}_2(3)$	= {C,G,U}
$\underline{R}_1(4)$	= {C}		$\underline{R}_2(4)$	= {C,G,U}
$\underline{R}_1(5)$	= {C}		$\underline{R}_2(5)$	= {C,G,U}
$\underline{R}_1(6)$	= {C}		$\underline{R}_2(6)$	= {C,G,U}
$\underline{R}_1(7)$	= {C}		$\underline{R}_2(7)$	= {C,G,U}
$\underline{R}_1(8)$	= {C}		$\underline{R}_2(8)$	= {C,G,U}
$\underline{R}_1(a)$	= {C,S,U}		$\underline{R}_2(a)$	= {C,G,U,S}
$\underline{R}_1(b)$	= {C,S,U}		$\underline{R}_2(b)$	= {C,G,U,S}
$\underline{R}_1(c)$	= {C,S,U}		$R_2(c)$	= {C,G,U,S}
$\underline{R}_1(d)$	= {C,S,U}		$R_2(d)$	= {C,G,U,S}
$\underline{R}_1(a')$	= {S,U}		$\underline{R}_2(a')$	= {S}
$\underline{R}_1(b')$	= {S,U}		$R_2(b')$	= {S}
$\underline{R}_1(c')$	= {S,U}		$R_2(c')$	= {S}
$\underline{R}_1(d')$	= {S,U}		$R_2(d')$	= {S}
$\underline{R}_1(E)$	= {S,G}		$R_2(E)$	= {S}
$\underline{R}_1(F)$	= {S,G}		$\underline{R}_2(F)$	= {S}
$\underline{R}_1(G)$	= {S,G}		$\underline{R}_2(G)$	= {S}
$\underline{R}_1(H)$	= {S,G}		$R_2(H)$	= {S}
$\underline{R}_1(I)$	= {G}		$\underline{R}_2(I)$	= $\emptyset$
$\underline{R}_1(II)$	= {G}		$\underline{R}_2(II)$	= $\emptyset$

Comment

Many related problems readily come to mind, such as those due to noise or unreliability in the initial data set, and the difficulty of characterizing the notion of an adequately representative initial data set. The methods proposed are all sensitive to deviations of these sorts, and practical systems ought to embody appropriate counter-measures.

So here we have more problems than solutions. I think I have, however, illustrated what I mean by general schemes for finding *ad hoc* solutions. It should be plausible that such a route could lead to general cognitive abilities, at least to the extent that this is possible with digital models, even though these remarks have merely suggested some tentative first steps along such a route.

All three problems discussed deal with data structures of labelled, directed graphs. We have sought ways of constructing special graphs for special domains, but graphs remain the common vehicle of expression, as they have throughout most

---

Box 9.7   Distributional Data for Facts based on Figure 9.5

$\underline{C}(1)$ = {−C3, −C4, 3C−, 4C−, bU−, b'U−}
$\underline{C}(2)$ = {−C3, −C4, 3C−, 4C−, bU−, b'U−}
$\underline{C}(3)$ = {−C1, −C2, 1C−, 2C−, aU−, a'U−}
$\underline{C}(4)$ = {−C1, −C2, 1C−, 2C−, aU−, a'U−}
$\underline{C}(5)$ = {−C7, −C8, 7C−, 8C−, dU−, d'U−}
$\underline{C}(6)$ = {−C7, −C8, 7C−, 8C−, dU−, d'U−}
$\underline{C}(7)$ = {−C5, −C6, 5C−, 6C−, cU−, c'U−}
$\underline{C}(8)$ = {−C5, −C6, 5C−, 6C−, cU−, c'U−}
$\underline{C}(a)$ = {−Cc, −Cd, −Sb', −U3, −U4, IG−, IIG−, GU−, HU , b'S−}
$\underline{C}(b)$ = {−Cc, −Cd, −Sa', −U1, −U2, IG−, IIG−, GU−, HU−, a'S−}
$\underline{C}(c)$ = {−Ca, −Cb, −Sd', −U7, −U8, IG−, IIG−, EU−, FU−, d'S−}
$\underline{C}(d)$ = {−Ca, −Cb, −Sc', −U5, −U6, IG−, IIG−, EU−, FU−, c'S−}
$\underline{C}(a')$ = {−Sb', −Sb, −U3, −U4, b's−, bs−}
$\underline{C}(b')$ = {−Sa', −Sa, −U1, −U2, a'S−, aS−}
$\underline{C}(c')$ = {−Sd', −Sd, −U7, −U8, d'S−, dS−}
$\underline{C}(d')$ = {−Sc', −Sc, −U5, −U6, c'S−, cS−}
$\underline{C}(E)$ = {−SH, −SG, −G1, −G2, −G3, −G4, HS−, GS−, −Uc, −Ud}
$\underline{C}(F)$ = {−SH,   −G1, −G2, −G3, −G4, HS−,   −Uc, −Ud}
$\underline{C}(G)$ = {−SE,   −G5, −G6, −G7, −G8, ES−,   −Ua, −Ub}
$\underline{C}(H)$ = {−SE, −SF, −G5, −G6, −G7, −G8, ES−, FS−, −Ua, −Ub}
$\underline{C}(I)$ = {−Ga, −Gb, −Gc, −Gd}
$\underline{C}(II)$ = {−Ga, −Gb, −Gc, −Gd}

---

of the literature on data structures. It seems to me unarguable that humans are not thus restricted. At best, then, complete solutions to the problems posed here will provide methods for constructing *ad hoc* models of a limited class.

Another general class of data structures which is legion in our mental experience is visual space. Many of my images, and I assume many of your images, record themselves on a three dimensional blackboard over which the mind's eye scans. Sometimes discrete planar graphs appear there, but often not. The blackboard is both three-dimensional and continuous; it is my model of Euclidian space. Where it comes from I do not know, and seldom care; but its uses are many.

It is widely practised self-deception that the cognitive roles played by this blackboard may be understudied by discrete graphs, or by computations on finite sentences in formal languages. We play this game because we know how to manipulate discrete graphs and finite sentences of formal languages in our digital computer memories. We have no idea how to represent continuous three-dimensional visual space. Perhaps it can not be done in digital memory. If not, it would be good to know this so that we would stop kidding ourselves.

One suggestion, which I have not seen sufficiently explored, is to represent continuous space in a digital computer through the formalizations of analysis. This suggestion would not have us store a continuous map in the quasi-literal way we store a discrete graph, but would employ an active memory which would construct new, discrete loci as they are called for, using the axioms which define, say, metric or topological spaces. From the "outside," to the program annexing or retrieving information, the map would act as a continuous store, but the physical representation would be digital.

For example: If we wish the computer to deal with a dense set, say the rationals in the interval [0,1], it could deal with them as a finite but indefinitely expandable set. Whenever an argument or problem required consideration of a new element between two given elements, room would automatically be provided in the map as required by the axioms which define density. [The rationals may of course be "dealt with" in other, more familiar ways, through computations and formulas and theorems about rationals, but here we are concerned not with these things, but with "mental images" with which to conceive of the rationals and represent the rationals' specific problems.]

The leap from a one-dimensional dense set to three dimensional Euclidian metric space is rather large, but the leap to two dimensional topological space might be manageable. Here we would not need to deal with problems of distance and direction, but would be faced with problems of continuity and connectedness. Could such a map be simulated *sub rosa* by programs that place active axioms at the disposal of the problem-solving programs? If such maps, and others, could be so simulated, analogues of our three problems could be formulated to define the task of a yet more general system for devising *ad hoc* systems, and the case for *ad hoc* methods would be on firm ground.

Is there any good argument for the psychological plausibility of *ad hoc* conceptual systems, other than our illusive introspective judgments? Not really, but there are some things which can be said. One of the most striking characteristics of human behavior is its variability, both within and between persons. American experimental psychology has striven to eliminate such variability, first by studying more and more simple, stylized, contentless tasks, and finally by dealing with performance on simple measures *averaged* over college sophomore populations. Mathematical models, say of nonsense syllable learning, are clear examples of this methodology, but computer simulation models have not really come to any stronger confrontation with individual differences. In effect, the customary approach to individual differences is to throw in a parameter or two. We might call these "alpha" models, as in $P = \alpha E$: performance is a function of experience (time, trials, etc.), but varies among individuals, who have different values of alpha.

Process models do not immediately suggest explanations for the phenomena of individual differences, but they at least offer the potential richness needed. Even in a simple concept learning task (card-sorting experiment), success is highly dependent on the fit between specific tasks and specific strategies for generating and testing hypotheses. A subject who always first considers which hand the experimenter uses to display a concept exemplar before he considers the color of the cards, will do better in some experiments than others. This has been recognized, and recent attempts have sought to determine which strategy is most popular, rather than simply to clock success. It has turned out, however, that even in these highly contrived, simple combinatorial problems, subjects may differ widely in their strategies, and what is worse, a given subject's strategy is highly volatile. If any constancy is to be discovered in human performance, it surely will not take the form of a procedure which yields an unswerving strategy for a given task, and individual differences in performance will not be accounted for by a model which merely allows different subjects to run the same program at different speeds.

A heuristic program that is responsive to a multitude of features specific to a problem and to the momentary context offers hope of exhibiting variability commensurate with human behavior. Such a program tailor-makes its considerations to the task and setting, as people seem to do. With a general problem solving or cogitating program, the task must be translated into the program's language and thence treated formally. If performance is to be responsive to the idosyncracies of problem and setting, these too must be encodable into the program's formalism—a job most likely out of the question.

Many artificial intelligence researchers will be unmoved by these observations, as they are by most appeals to search for insights by studying psychological phenomena. After all, computers are different from people, and in some ways clearly superior. They can add faster, and remember less fallibly. Thus, the argument runs, powerful problem solvers need not and probably will not work on principles similar to humans. Problems may be solved by smashing through with syntactic methods—general methods which are not distracted by the human's peculiar affinity for irrelevant details and his *ad hoc* and idiosyncratic mental images. Perhaps. But until general procedures demonstrate convincing power, I will continue to bet on *ad hoc* procedures, and search for generality at a deeper level.

Ten

A Model for the Encoding of Experiential Information

Joseph D. Becker
Bolt, Beranek, and Newman, Inc.

I. Introduction

In the following pages I will propose a model for the encoding and use of primary (sensori-motor) experience. This model addresses the problem at the abstract, or "information-processing" level; it is not concerned with the physiological representation of experience in the brain, nor does it attempt to explain the functioning of any *particular* sensori-motor system. The model presented below will be called "JCM"—for reasons best left to the imagination of the reader.

The heart of JCM is a particular formal structure for representing information. Such a structure, called a "Schema", is essentially a sequence of observations in which one observation has gained predominant emphasis. To illustrate this very sketchily, let us suppose that a Schema has the form:

$$[\text{Sensation}_1 \rightarrow \text{Action}_1 \rightarrow \text{Action}_2 \Rightarrow \text{Sensation}_2]$$

The element "Sensation$_2$" is emphasized, as is shown by the big arrow, "$\Rightarrow$," preceding it. This Schema may be interpreted as saying, "Sensation$_1$, followed by Action$_1$, followed by Action$_2$, *leads to* Sensation$_2$." If an organism possesses this Schema in its memory, then whenever it encounters Sensation$_1$, it may seek to obtain Sensation$_2$ by performing Action$_1$ and Action$_2$ in that order.

In JCM, the process just sketched is woven into a large system of supporting processes. Among these are processes which encode experience into Schemata, processes which search the memory store for information relevant to a newly encountered situation, and processes which adapt past experience to new situations that are similar but not identical to the old. In addition, JCM contains a set of "information-refinement" processes, whose task is to compare a whole range of similar experiences and derive somehow the "essence" of those observations. The combined "essences" of an organism's past experiences will ultimately amount to an internalized model of the real world and its physical laws.

JCM attempts to formalize a number of processes which have not been treated formally by psychologists — and the majority of which have not been treated at all by workers in Artificial Intelligence. Moreover, this whole system of processes is modeled *within a single formalism.* The integration of several processes into a homogeneous system provides many insights that could not be obtained by modeling each process in isolation.

The subject of this investigation is the system of processes by which an organism stores and manipulates the experience it gains through interactions with its environment. This system might be said to occupy an "intermediate level" between the lowest and the highest forms of cognition.

The cognitive subsystem that we may call Low-Level Cognition (abbreviated LLC) consists of those processes which operate the sensori-motor interface between the organism and its world. These include sensory processes such as feature extraction and immediate sensory memory, and motor processes such as the feedback-loop control of muscular activity and the temporal coordination of motor acts. The processes of Low-Level Cognition characteristically are bound to particular modalities, and they make very limited use of the organism's acquired experience.

The processes of High-Level Cognition (or HLC) require an information-compression or "coding" system of some sort, which the organism uses to represent the essential features of himself, of the problem he desires to solve, and of the available methods for solving it. Included in HLC are the many functions of "thought," such as hypothetical and deductive reasoning, intentional remembering, and all nontrivial planning and problem solving. It appears that High-Level Cognition is found only in primates, and in certain people's dogs.

There remains a rather large group of cognitive processes, constituting the system of Intermediate-Level Cognition (or ILC), which are like the High-Level processes in that they make use of acquired experience, and yet are like Low-Level processes in that they operate with "unconscious" ease and swiftness. Intermediate-Level Cognition is what we do when we look around the room for the book we just set down somewhere, or when we drive a car, or when we turn on a faucet in order to get water, or when we understand what a friend is saying to us, or when we understand the friend's mood without his saying anything.

Intermediate-Level Cognition is the mainstay of our everyday existence. It is as ubiquitous as it is inconspicuous, and so we tend to overlook the fact that it needs explaining. But the need for a model of ILC has been brought home dramatically by our attempts to create "intelligent" machines. We can program computers to perform sensory feature extraction, and we can program them to play chess, but we have no idea how to program them to recognize a chair as such, or to predict what a person will do in a given situation. The smallest kitty-cat knows infinitely more about coping with the world than the most powerful computer program. Perhaps this is the most telling definition of Intermediate-Level Cognition.

II. An Example of Intermediate-Level Cognition

Since the following chapters describe the mechanisms of Intermediate-Level Cognition rather abstractly, it will be helpful to have in mind a particular example of how the model of these processes might function. The example below is intended only as an informal illustration, and not as an exposition or justification of the model. The notations and terminology introduced in the example are those that will be used throughout this chapter. If the reader is not interested in working through a somewhat protracted example, he should skip ahead directly to Section III.

Section II.A describes an artificial organism and its artificial world, and Section II.B shows how this organism might record and make use of the experience it gains from interacting with its environment.

II.A: An artificial sensori-motor system

In order for the model of Intermediate-Level Cognition to operate, there must be a set of Low-Level Cognitive processes supporting the model and a world to which the model can respond. Since our object of study is ILC itself, we will make do with a highly artificial model of the world and of Low-Level Cognition. The most important feature of the world described herein is that it has a non-trivial but non-overwhelming amount of physics. Otherwise, most of its details were chosen quite arbitrarily.

II.A.1: INTUITIVE DESCRIPTION OF THE ARTIFICIAL WORLD

The world we will be considering may be thought of as a smooth shelf 9 units long on which blocks may be placed and manipulated, as shown in Figure 10.1. There are two sorts of blocks: tall (2 units × 1 unit) rough white ones, and short (1 × 1) fuzzy black ones.

Our "organism" possesses a parallel-gripper type of hand that may open and close. The hand appears as a 1 × 1 red square; its arm is presumed to be invisible. The hand can range over the 9-unit length of the shelf, moving vertically or laterally in a 1-unit quanta. The hand may also "grope" to the left, right, or below; "groping" is thought of as a tiny motion which brings the hand into contact with any nearby surface in the given direction. The hand may feel the texture of any surface it is in contact with (including the shelf, which is smooth). The hand can push any block in front of it regardless of grip position or prior feeling, and blocks of course push other blocks.

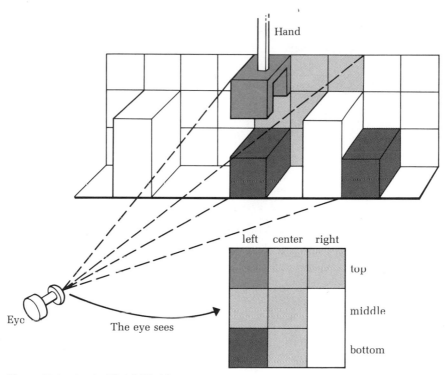

Figure 10.1 An Artificial World.

The organism possesses an eye whose field of view is 3 units by 3 units. The eye may shift to the right or left so as to view any 3×3 subspace of the 9×3 range of the hand, but we assume that eye always sees precisely a two-dimensional face of each object in its field of view. The eye detects only the colors projected onto its retina. (The background color is described simply as "none.")

This system provides a large number of interesting "laws" which the organism might learn by interacting with its environment. One such law is, "If I see a red square directly above a black square, then if I grope downward I will feel a fuzzy surface." When it has learned these general relationships which are implicit in its observations, the organism will essentially have assimilated the "physics" of the world it perceives.

II.A.2: MODELING THE SENSORI-MOTOR SYSTEM

THE ORGANIZATION OF THE SYSTEM. Let us now consider our organism and its world at the information-processing level. In Figure 10.2 we have a schematic representation of the world, the organism's systems of LLC and ILC, and the information flow among these components. As far as the organism is concerned, the world is

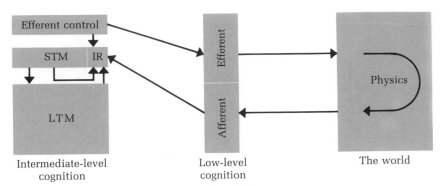

Figure 10.2 Information Flow in a Mind-world System.

nothing more than a set of rules which receives efferent activity from the organism and responds with afferent stimulation.

Since the "world" described in this section is itself only an artificial model, we need not deal with realities such as light waves or physical motions. Therefore, the processes of Low-Level Cognition, which serve to translate information between its "physical" form and its "mental" form, can be reduced to a trivial mapping: LLC serves merely to shuttle information back and forth between the model world and the model Intermediate-Level system. In any more realistic system, the efferent translation will include complex processes such as motor coordination, and the afferent translation will involve operations such as feature-extraction.

At the Intermediate Level, Figure 10.2 indicates three structures. The "Efferent Control" is a trivial function which, upon request from the ILC executive, issues a command into the world, and sends a copy of the command to Short-Term Memory (STM). The STM is essentially a stored sequence of features that are received from the sensory system, commands from the Efferent Control, and strings from Long-Term Memory (LTM). Information-units are said to enter the STM through its "Input Register" (IR). Information is stored in LTM as a network of sequences of features and commands.

THE UNIT OF INFORMATION. Throughout this chapter I will treat information as a discrete commodity. In this section I will briefly introduce the basic units of information that are used in JCM. Some theoretical issues surrounding this representation will be discussed in Section III.

In JCM, afferent and efferent information are represented in the same formalism. The unit of information is in the form of a predicate with arguments. A unit of this sort will be called a *Kernel*. I will denote a Kernel as a list of symbols (words) enclosed by angle brackets (standard n-tuple notation). For example, a typical Kernel in the artificial world system is:

⟨colorchange right bottom black red⟩

This Kernel reports the observation of a change in the color projected onto one of the cells of the organism's 3 × 3 retina. The first two argument-positions in this Kernel define the coordinates of the retinal cell, while the last two specify the old and new colors. Such Kernels may be thought of as resulting from a feature-extraction process performed by the organism's eye.

The elements within a Kernel are called *Nodes*. With respect to the translation performed by LLC, each Node corresponds to some well-defined aspect of the sensation or motor act. For example, the Node "red" presumably corresponds to some well-defined physical condition. However, within the Intermediate-Level system itself, a Node is characterized by its connections in the complex net-structure of Long-Term Memory—that is, it is defined by the totality of the information that is known about it. (The latter interpretation is derived from Quillian's notion of "unit" (1969).)

I will postulate the existence of two different types of afferent Kernels. Kernels from *differential* sensors indicate changes in conditions, and are generated only as the result of changes in the world. This means that if the organism wishes to attain some differential Kernel, it must perform a motor act, (which of course is not guaranteed to yield the desired result). Kernels from *static* sensors, by contrast, indicate the existence, value, degree, etc. of some ongoing condition, and are obtained by explicit interrogation of the appropriate sensor.

Correspondingly, the system has two types of efferent Kernels, namely *motor command* Kernels which control effectors, and *interrogation* Kernels which read out the static sensors. In order to make the distinctions among Kernels clearer in the notation, I will often place subscripts after Kernels to indicate their nature, according to:

⟨.....⟩ d = differential sensory Kernel
⟨.....⟩ s = static sensory Kernel
⟨.....⟩ m = motor command Kernel
⟨.....⟩ q = static sensor interrogation (efferent) Kernel

II.A.3: KERNELS OF THE ARTIFICIAL SENSORI-MOTOR SYSTEM

On the following pages is a list of the Kernels used in the sensori-motor system of the artificial organism described in Section II.A.1.

Motor Kernels

⟨raise⟩m	Raise the hand one unit
⟨lower⟩m	Lower the hand one unit
⟨movehand D⟩m	D is a direction: left or right
⟨grope DD⟩m	DD is a direction: left, right, or below
⟨grip⟩m	Close hand-grip
⟨release⟩m	Open hand-grip
⟨moveeye D⟩m	Shift eye one unit; D: left or right

Differential Sensory Kernels

⟨heightchange L⟩d   L is the new hand-level: top, middle, or bottom

⟨colorchange X Y OC NC⟩   Indicates change in a single retinal cell; X is a retinal abcissa: left, center, or right; Y is a retinal ordinate: top, middle, or bottom; OC is the old color: red, white, black, or none; NC is the new color

Pairs of Sensory-Interrogation/Static-Sensory Kernels

⟨handheight?⟩q

⟨handheight L⟩s   L: top, middle, or bottom

⟨handgrip?⟩q

⟨handgrip P⟩s   P is handgrip position: open or closed

⟨feel DD⟩q

⟨texture DD T⟩s   DD: left, right, below; T is a texture: smooth, rough, fuzzy, or none

⟨color? X Y⟩q

⟨color X Y C⟩s   X: left, center, right; Y: top, middle, bottom; C; red, white, black, none

There are many possible variants on this particular formalization, but this one serves to test several possible ways of relating action to sensation.

For any real organism some sensations are pleasant, and some are unpleasant. We may speak of the "drives" of the organism in terms of sensations that it seeks to attain or avoid. Unfortunately, there is no intuitively satisfactory way of assigning desirabilities to the sensory Kernels of the artificial organism that I have described. The problem is simple: What is the meaning of life to an organism consisting entirely of a hand, an eye, and a mind? For the sake of the discussion, let us arbitrarily assign a highly positive value to the situation in which the hand (i.e. the color red) is in the center of the visual field. That is, all Kernels will be neutral except those of form:

$$⟨color\ center\ middle\ red⟩\,s$$

and

$$⟨colorchange\ center\ middle\ C\ red⟩\,d$$

and these are highly desirable to the organism.

Thus, we have created an organism which seeks to look straight at its hand. Let us now see how it might gain the ability to do so.

II.B: An example of ILC: the encoding and application of an observed event

The example below will illustrate two phases of Intermediate-Level Cognition: (1) the organism's acquisition of some particular information through experience, and (2) its use of this information in responding later to a given situation. Many subsidiary processes in the ILC system are omitted in the example, although they are included in the formal model. Some of these processes are presented in Section V.

II.B.1: AN OBSERVATION IS RECORDED AS A "SCHEMA"

As Figure 10.2 indicates, the processes of ILC have access to a Short-Term Memory, which receives Kernels from the outside world, and which in addition receives a copy of all efferent Kernels. I will assume that the STM retains these Kernels in the order of their arrival. I will write a *Little Arrow* (" $\rightarrow$ ") between successive Kernels to denote their ordering (the Kernel to the left being the earlier).

Let us now consider a particular sequence of input Kernels that might be observed by our artificial organism. (The sequence we will consider was in fact produced by a computer simulation of the artificial world, where the organism was replaced by a random Kernel generator.) Below we have divided the Kernel sequence into groups consisting of an efferent Kernel and its consequences. The hand was initially in the center top cell of the eye's visual field.

Part of an Input Kernel Stream

> ... $\rightarrow$
> ⟨handgrip?⟩q $\rightarrow$ ⟨handgrip open⟩s $\rightarrow$
> ⟨grope below⟩m $\rightarrow$
> ⟨feel below⟩q $\rightarrow$ ⟨texture below none⟩s $\rightarrow$
> ⟨color? center middle⟩q $\rightarrow$ ⟨color center middle none⟩s $\rightarrow$
> ⟨lower⟩m $\rightarrow$ ⟨heightchange middle⟩d $\rightarrow$
>   ⟨colorchange center middle none red⟩d $\rightarrow$
>   ⟨colorchange center top red none⟩d $\rightarrow$
> ⟨handheight?⟩q $\rightarrow$ ⟨handheight middle⟩s $\rightarrow$
> ...

We will assume that the organism is completely naive at this point, meaning that it has no information in its Long-Term Memory to which it can relate the given input. All it can do, then, is store the observed sequence into LTM. This storage involves two small but non-trivial modifications of the input sequence.

When each Kernel arrives, it is inspected by a watchdog *Goal-Monitoring* process, which determines if it is pleasant, unpleasant, or neutral. In our sample input stream there is just one Kernel which is not neutral, namely ⟨colorchange center middle none red⟩d. Since the purpose of LTM storage is to provide a basis for future action, we may expect that desirable and undesirable Kernels will be emphasized in the LTM representation of the input stream. For simplicity, we may assume that each item in LTM storage is organized around a single Kernel of interest. Each information-item is designed to aid in the attainment (or avoidance) of its emphasized Kernel.

Once a single Kernel has been selected as the basis for storing a particular Kernel sequence, that sequence is conceptually divided in half near the designated Kernel. We might regard the first (left) half of the sequence as the "antecedents" to the special Kernel; the second (right) half might be regarded as the "consequences" of the antecedent conditions. In the absence of any previous knowledge concerning the observed events, the break will be placed just after the last efferent Kernel that preceded the designated sensory Kernel. In the notation, I will indicate the division of a Kernel sequence by means of a *Big Arrow* ("$\Rightarrow$"). Thus, the input sequence shown above will be modified to:

$$... \rightarrow$$
⟨color? center middle⟩q $\rightarrow$ ⟨color center middle none⟩s $\rightarrow$
⟨lower⟩m $\Rightarrow$ ⟨heightchange middle⟩d $\rightarrow$
⟨colorchange center middle none red⟩d $\rightarrow$
⟨colorchange center top red none⟩d $\rightarrow$ ...

The second modification that must be made to the input stream is less well-defined. In order to arrive at a bounded unit of LTM storage, it is necessary to choose a finite subsequence out of the indefinitely-extended input Kernel sequence. There do not appear to be any precise rules according to which this selection should be made. Fortunately — or rather, necessarily — the *information-refinement* processes of *Generalization* and *Differentiation* (see Section V.C) will later delete or add Kernels as is required in order to produce representations which are maximally successful in guiding future actions. Therefore we may assume the rough rule: Select a subsequence which includes several efferent Kernels preceding the pivotal sensory Kernel, but no efferent Kernels following it.

Applied to our example, this rule might yield the following schema as the information-unit to be stored (the boundaries of the unit are indicated by square brackets):

[⟨grope below⟩m $\rightarrow$ ⟨feel below⟩q $\rightarrow$ ⟨texture below none⟩s $\rightarrow$
⟨color? center middle⟩q $\rightarrow$ ⟨color center middle none⟩s $\rightarrow$
⟨lower⟩m $\Rightarrow$ ⟨heightchange middle⟩d $\rightarrow$
⟨colorchange center middle none red⟩d $\rightarrow$
⟨colorchange center top red none⟩d]

The unit of long-term information storage will be called a *Schema*. A *sensori-motor Schema* is one that has been encoded directly out of STM, and has not yet undergone any refinement processes. Such a Schema consists of a bounded sequence of sensori-motor Kernels, in the order of their arrival in STM, with a single "Big

Arrow" separating a noteworthy Kernel from its antecedent conditions. The relatively simple process we have just followed, which creates Sensori-Motor Schemata without the use of information from LTM, will be called *Unguided STM* → *LTM Encoding*. (In most cases, input information is encoded in terms of prior experience according to a more complex process, called *Guided STM* → *LTM Encoding*; see Section V.A).

The new Schema will be interwoven into the net-like associative structure of LTM, where it will await its use in guiding the organism's response to a new situation. We will now follow the process by which the Schema is so applied.

II.B.2: THE SCHEMA IS APPLIED TO A NEW SITUATION

We return to our organism at some indefinite time after the creation of the Schema described in the previous section (I will designate that particular Schema as "Schema S"). Let us suppose that, for whatever reason, the organism has just performed ⟨grope below⟩m and then ⟨feel below⟩q, and received ⟨texture below none⟩s in response. The Goal-Monitoring process which watches over the input stream will look up these Kernels and find them to be of neutral desirability. Now, in general a Kernel which is innocuous in itself may have *implications* which are of significance to the organism. Therefore the Goal-Monitoring process may (depending on several factors, such as the current cognitive load) seek to determine the implications of an input Kernel. The source of the rules by which these inferences are to be drawn is of course Long-Term Memory with its large network of learned Schemata.

The Goal-Monitoring process, having decided to investigate the new Kernel sequence ⟨grope below⟩m → ⟨feel below⟩q → ⟨texture below none⟩s, will call the *LTM-Search* process to seek a relevant Schema from LTM. In particular, the search will retrieve Schemata which begin with Kernels which are "similar" to the Kernels on which the search is based. Of course, Schema S begins with precisely this sequence, and therefore will be retrieved for application.

The application process is based on an implicit interpretation of the meaning of a Schema. A schema of form

$$[\text{Event}_1 \Rightarrow \text{Event}_2]$$

is taken to mean that the attainment of Event$_1$ is a sufficient condition for the attainment of Event$_2$. In accordance with this interpretation, the system asks itself two questions of any Schema which presents itself for application:

1. Has all of Event$_1$ been attained already?, and if not, then
2. Is Event$_2$ desirable?

In case Event$_1$ has already been attained in its entirety, the processing immediately enters its "prediction" phase. In case Event$_2$ is undesirable, the system will remain alert for the completion of Event$_1$ while of course doing nothing that would encourage that completion (the question of *forestalling* an undesirable event is somewhat more complex—see section V.B.3).

Our example illustrates the most interesting case, namely that in which Event$_1$ has not yet been completed, and in which the right side of the Schema is desirable (recall that Schema S contains the much-sought Kernel ⟨colorchange center middle none red⟩d). In this case the system will attempt to complete Event$_1$. The key to the Schema application process is that the remainder of the left side of the Schema is used as a program for the attainment of the desired right side.

In our example the remainder of the left side is: ⟨color? center middle⟩q ⟶ ⟨color center middle none⟩s ⟶ ⟨lower⟩m. The two efferent Kernels are immediately attainable, because as soon as such commands are issued, copies of them are automatically received in STM. In order to complete the match with the left side of Schema S, it remains only to obtain a match for the Kernel ⟨color center middle none⟩s. This can be achieved using a Schema of the form:

$$[\ \langle\text{color? X Y}\rangle q \Rightarrow \langle\text{color X Y C}\rangle s \ ].$$

Here the letters X, Y, and C stand for "dummy variables", formed by generalization (See section V.B.2). Let us assume that such a Schema is available at the time that the organism comes to seek ⟨color center middle none⟩s.

Now, when a Kernel must be sought indirectly as a subgoal, a *Goal-Pursuit* process institutes an LTM-Search for Schemata whose *right* sides contain a Kernel similar to the desired one. In our example, the subgoal Kernel ⟨color center middle red⟩s will certainly match the right side of the general Schema

$$[\ \langle\text{color? X Y}\rangle q \Rightarrow \langle\text{color X Y C}\rangle s \ ].$$

The match yields a correspondence X ⟷ center, Y ⟷ middle, C ⟷ red, so that the general Schema becomes instantiated as:

$$[\ \langle\text{color? center middle}\rangle q \Rightarrow \langle\text{color center middle red}\rangle s \ ].$$

Now *this* new Schema is applied, meaning that its left side is taken as a sequence of instructions for attaining the right side. In this example the left side happens to be trivial to attain, but it is clear that in general the pursuit of a subgoal may involve nested appeals to Goal-Pursuit.

If the Goal-Pursuit process is successful, it will eventually produce a sequence of efferent commands, which the organism may then execute. At this point the organism is *predicting* that this sequence of acts will bring it the sequence of results corresponding to the right side of the Schema that was applied. The input-monitoring process will then be on the watch for these Kernels, so that the successfulness of the prediction may be judged. In our example, the organism would execute ⟨color? center middle⟩q and, if this yielded ⟨color center middle none⟩s, it would do a ⟨lower⟩m. These commands might or might not bring it the desired ⟨colorchange center middle none red⟩d, depending on conditions which unfortunately were not tested in the left side of Schema S. Eventually, the Differentiation process might add these tests to Schema S, so that it would become a more accurate representation of the world, and a more useful rule for behavior.

The entire process discussed in this section is called *Schema-Application*. Its major subprocesses are the initial Goal-Monitoring, the recursive Goal-Pursuit, and the LTM-Search process.

III. Memory Structures

This section begins the description of the model JCM as it now stands. The model contains two memory structures, called Short-Term Memory (STM) and Long-Term Memory (LTM). The Short-Term Memory described in Section III.A corresponds well with Neisser's (1967) "Active Verbal Memory" and Norman's (1969) "Primary Memory," except that I do not believe this memory to be characteristically auditory. The Long-Term Memory described in Section III.B is everyone's long-term memory, but I should make it clear that many of the interesting phenomena open to introspection (as well as many of those discovered by Bartlett (1932)) result from recall-as-problem-solving, which is a High-Level process not included in JCM.

The general question of what is stored in long-term memory has been pursued much more fruitfully in the field of Artificial Intelligence than in the field of Psychology. In Section III.C, I will try to draw some general conclusions on this issue, with the help of notions taken from both fields.

III.A: Short-Term Memory

The function of Short-Term Memory is to retain a string of input Kernels so that they may be organized for storage into Long-Term Memory, or analyzed during the search for an appropriate response to the input. In the example from Section II, the original Kernel stream would be retained in STM until the Schema S had been formed, and later the new Kernel sequence

$$⟨\text{grope below}⟩m \longrightarrow ⟨\text{feel below}⟩q \longrightarrow ⟨\text{texture below none}⟩s$$

would be held in STM while Schema S was being matched to it.

The Short-Term Memory retains the input Kernels in their order of arrival. The STM must save this order information because it is often crucial to the meaning of a Schema, but this does not mean that the ordering of Kernels is forever immutable.

The order of arrival of a set of Kernels may eventually be found irrelevant by the process of Generalization (section V.B.2).

The primary source of input Kernels is external stimulation, as preprocessed by the Low-Level Cognitive system. Kernels may also be generated internally as copies of efferent commands, as products of the application of a Schema from LTM, or as the result of recycling within the STM (in the latter, we may say that the Kernel is recopied into the front of STM, so that the serial order of the old copy is preserved). I will assume that each Kernel in STM is "tagged" to indicate its source—this is necessary if an internal prediction is to be distinguishable from a confirming observation. Kernels which arise from Schema-Applications will bear *Confidence* weights, ranging between 0 and 1, which indicate how certain the system is of that prediction.

The watchdog "Goal-Monitoring" process performs certain operations on each Kernel as it arrives in STM. It will be convenient to think of the first "position" in STM as a place where scrutiny of a Kernel is especially easy. I will term the first location in STM the *Input Register* (or *IR*). Thus, when I say "a Kernel enters the Input Register," I mean that the Kernel enters Short-Term Memory, but I emphasize that it is to be subjected to Goal-Monitoring. (It is not entirely frivolous to think of the IR as the "fovea of the Mind's Eye," since it is effectively the focal point of Intermediate-Level processing. The recycling of a Kernel into the IR is analogous to an eye-movement designed to bring an object of interest back into the fovea.)

The Goal-Monitoring process rates each incoming Kernel for its relevance to the organism's goals—both the long-term goals, as represented by the innate desirability or undesirability of certain Kernels, and the short-term goals, which arise in the course of Schema-Applications. The rating that Goal-Monitoring assigns to each Kernel may be represented as a numerical weight attached to the Kernel, called the *Relevance* weight of the Kernel. Note that different occurrences of the same Kernel will in general differ in their Relevance, since the organism's short-term goals change over time. The Relevance weight of a Kernel in STM is of utmost importance in determining what processes will be applied to it, and what status it will have in LTM representation of the input stream (recall from Section II.B.1 that each sensori-motor Schema is organized around a highly-Relevant Kernel).

In summary, the Short-Term Memory consists of a set of Kernels ordered by their time of arrival, each bearing a tag indicating its source, a Confidence weight, and a Relevance weight. The first position of the STM is called the Input Register (IR).

(I should mention that the Short-Term Memory that I have just described is not the only form of temporary information storage required by the Intermediate-Level cognitive system. Many of the processes that I will describe require some form of "scratchpad" or administrative memory, so that they can keep track of what they are doing and what information they are manipulating. Moreover, there should be some sort of overall executive structure, perhaps a "goal tree," by which the system co-ordinates its activities and its resources. Although the maintenance of these memory structures is integral to the functioning of the system described here, their details will not be examined in this chapter.)

III.B: Long-Term Memory

The heart of JCM is the structure proposed here for Long-Term Memory. The formal devices that go into this structure are all derived from formalisms already available in the literature of Artificial Intelligence, but the selection and proper combination of these elements was not an easy task. Any information structure proposed for long-term memory must contribute elegance to the modeling of a sizeable number of different processes. The structure must be able to record sensori-motor experience, it must allow a means by which information relevant to a new situation may be rapidly retrieved, and the experimental record must be easily convertible into a sequence of appropriate actions. At the same time, the representation of a behavioral rule must allow various information-refinement processes to improve it on the basis of further experience, and the formalism must have the power to express the general laws that are the end-product of such refinement. In addition, the formalism must be capable of representing the hierarchical combination of concepts into larger concepts — including the organization of behavioral sequences into larger behavioral units. The representation must lead naturally to the synthesis or analysis of a hierarchically-constructed concept at the appropriate times, and in general it must cope with the appearance of the same information in many different guises. In short, a proposed structure for long-term storage is only as good as the process models that may be based on it.

The unit of long-term storage in JCM is the "Schema," which is used as a little "program" for the attainment of a certain goal (as illustrated in section II.B.2). The Schemata in LTM are woven together into a net-structure which corresponds to the associative nature of access to long-term memory. In the following sections I will describe the details of the LTM structure by building it up from its smallest elements. Figure 10.3 shows how these elements go together to form a typical Schema.

III.B.1: THE NODE

The *Node* is the atomic primitive of the memory structure, corresponding roughly to the intuitive notion of a "concept." As represented in JCM, every Node consists of a nest of two-way pointers or links. Each link joins the nest itself with a location within a Kernel, which in turn is located within a Schema in the LTM structure. I have attempted to illustrate what this definition means in Figure 10.4. For clarity in this figure I have drawn four minimal Schemata, consisting of two binary Kernels apiece, and in the center I have indicated only two of the Nodes occurring within these Schemata. Each node points to its occurrences within the four illustrated Schemata, as well as to all other occurrences not shown. The Schemata in turn are actually nothing more than highly-structured lists of pointers to Nodes. Between any two Schemata having a Node in common, the pointer-path from Schema-to-Node-to-Schema provides a direct two-way "association" between the two items of information. If the Schemata share more than one Node, or more than one occurrence of

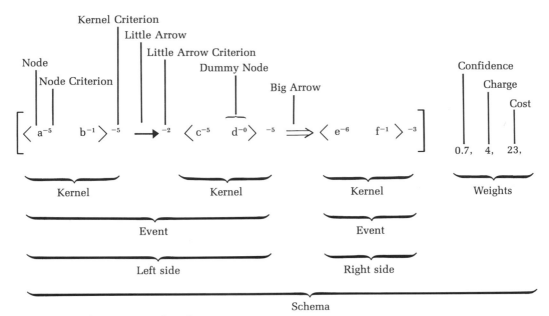

Figure 10.3   The Structure of a Schema.

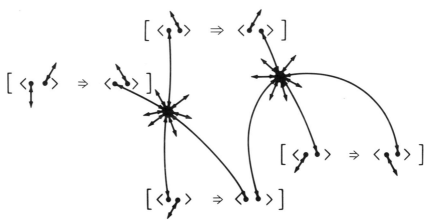

Figure 10.4   The Interconnection of Schemata via Nodes.

the same Node, they are associated by additional links. This device for providing associative structure is a minor adaptation of the "Type Node" (= Node) and "Token Node" (= occurrence) structure proposed by Quillian (1966).

   In the notation of this chapter, a Node is represented by a single symbol, often an English word. This notation is totally unsuggestive of the definition just given, but there seems to be no notational alternative. The reader should bear in mind that the actual definition of a node is in terms of associative structure.

INTERPRETATIONS OF THE ASSOCIATIVE STRUCTURE OF LTM. In its associative structuring for LTM, JCM asserts that two *items of information* (i.e., Schemata) that have something in common (i.e. a Node) have a direct association through that concept. Alternatively, we might say that two related concepts have an association *through the information that relates them.* What is significant is that, in either interpretation, JCM states that there is no "association" between concepts in Long-Term Memory except through specific information relating them. (The "Little Arrow" indicating sequence between Kernels might be regarded as a "directed association by temporal contiguity," but this sort of association exists only within a Schema.) Psychologists have often treated "associations" as the ultimate unit of memory, without asking what role they might play in the useful storage of information. But consider: What good does it do me to have an "association" between "Cynthia" and "QU2-9970," if I do not know that that is her telephone number? What good does it do me to have an "association" between "QU2-9970" and "telephone number", if I do not know that it is Cynthia's? Clearly, what I store is the *information* that Cynthia's telephone number is QU2-9970, and the three concepts are mutually associated through that fact itself.

When discussing the associative structure of LTM, we should recall that any information-processing "structure" is really a summary of the results of a *process.* We perform certain experiments on that black box, the mind, and we find that it behaves *as though* its long-term memory were structured as an associative net. Perhaps there are other, equally informative ways of summarizing the experimental results. At any rate, this way of phrasing the matter reminds us that the structures we propose are meaningful only in terms of the processes that operate on them. Thus, the "associative structure of Long-Term Memory" is really a characteristic of the memory-search process, which we will examine in (section IV.C).

III.B.2: THE KERNEL

The *Kernel* is the smallest formal structure capable of expressing an event or relation. Formally, a Kernel is an ordered n-tuple of Nodes. A kernel will be written as a list of Nodes enclosed in angle brackets, for example:

⟨color center top none⟩
⟨cat Lucifer⟩
⟨d82hf4 h46r5 k5grz⟩

A Kernel, by its presence in an observational record (Schema), indicates the occurrence of a condition whose "type" is given by the first Node in the Kernel, and whose parameters are given by the remaining Nodes.

As I indicated in section II.A.2, I will assume the existence of two sorts of sensory Kernels, Differential and Static, and of two sorts of efferent Kernels, Motor and Static-Sensor-Interrogation.

III.B.3: LITTLE ARROW AND THE EVENT

In a Schema that is the unrefined record of some observation, the Kernels are linearly ordered by their time of arrival in STM. This ordering relation will be represented by the symbol " $\rightarrow$ " called *Little Arrow,* placed between two Kernels so related. Thus, we will find ⟨a⟩ $\rightarrow$ ⟨b⟩ in a Schema only if ⟨a⟩ preceded ⟨b⟩ into STM. It is not necessarily true that ⟨a⟩ was the *immediate* predecessor of ⟨b⟩ (since we must be able to untangle sensations from several sources that happen to intermingle in STM).

As the result of the Generalization process, the order of arrival of a pair of Kernels may be found to be irrelevant. For example, the parts that make up an object may be noticed in any order, and in many cases the antecedent conditions of an implication need not be obtained in any particular order. In such cases, the irrelevant Little Arrows will be deleted by Generalization. Thus, in general the Kernels in a Schema are only *partially ordered* by Little Arrow. A partially-ordered set of Kernels will be called an *Event.*

An example of a linearly-ordered, sensori-motor Event is:

⟨grope below⟩ $\rightarrow$ ⟨feel below⟩ $\rightarrow$ ⟨texture below none⟩ $\rightarrow$ ⟨lower⟩.

In Events that are not linearly ordered, neighboring Kernels that are not ordered with respect to each other will simply be written adjacent to each other. Thus, a typical Event might look like:

⟨a⟩ ⟨b⟩ ⟨c⟩ $\rightarrow$ ⟨d⟩ $\rightarrow$ ⟨e⟩ ⟨f⟩ $\rightarrow$ ⟨g⟩

III.B.4: BIG ARROW AND THE SCHEMA

The *Schema,* which is the ultimate unit of information storage, is an ordered pair of events. The two Events in a Schema will be written between square brackets and separated by the symbol " $\Rightarrow$ ", called *Big Arrow,* as in:

[⟨grope left⟩ $\rightarrow$ ⟨color? left top⟩ $\Rightarrow$ ⟨color left top red⟩].

The first Event of the pair will be called the *Left Side* of the Schema; the second will be called the *Right Side.*

A Schema that constitutes the unrefined record of some experience is called a *sensori-motor Schema*. Because a sensori-motor Schema is derived by dividing a Kernel stream in two (recall II.B), the Big Arrow in a sensori-motor Schema replaces a Little Arrow ordering. Thus, Big Arrow arises as a strengthening of Little Arrow, and it retains this significance throughout all further processing of the Schema. A Big Arrow might be said to divide a Kernel stream into a "before" and an "after," or an "antecedent Event" and a "consequent Event."

When a Schema is applied, the consequent Event represents some *goal* of the organism — perhaps a long-term goal, or perhaps a short-term goal that was in force at the time the Schema was formed. The Left Side of the Schema is interpreted as an activity which was, in at least one case, sufficient to yield the goal represented by the Right Side. The purpose of the information-refinement processes (V.B) is to modify the Left Side until it contains the best possible specification of how to attain the Right Side.

In spirit, the Schema is similar to the "pattern-action rule" used in computer programming systems, but there is an important formal difference. The Right Side of a Schema contains the *goal* of the action, rather than the action itself. In fact, the Right Side of a Schema will never contain any efferent Kernels. The actions involved in applying a Schema are specified on the *Left* Side; they are executed by the Goal-Pursuit subprocess (IV.D). The object of applying the Schema, however, is the attainment of the goal, and not the performance of the actions per se. Thus, where a pattern-action rule might have the form

$$\text{condition} \Rightarrow \text{action,}$$

a Schema will generally be of the form

$$[\ \text{condition} \longrightarrow \text{action} \Rightarrow \text{result}\ ].$$

When a program is written in terms of pattern-action rules, the "goal" of each rule is *implicit* in the structure of the whole program. An organism, on the other hand, has no overall "program," so each of its "rules" must state its goal explicitly.

Formally, a Schema also resembles an "implication" in formal logic, or a "replacement rule" of the sort that has found many applications, from automata theory to linguistics. But again, the crucial characteristic of a Schema is that it is organized around the attainment of a particular goal. It is the pursuit of this goal that determines how the Schema is formed, how it is used, and how it is modified.

III.B.5: CRITERIALITY WEIGHTS

Consider the two observations, "Rupert is a fireman, and Rupert wears red suspenders" and "If X is a fireman, then X wears red suspenders." The second statement is a general law, of which the first is a particular instance. Let us suppose that it is truly a law of nature that all firemen wear red suspenders. Then when we observe that "Rupert is a fireman, and Rupert wears red suspenders," the essential phenomenon is really a relationship between firemanhood and the wearing of red suspenders—and *not* a special property of Rupert. In such a case, we will say that "Rupert" is not *criterial* in the first observation *with respect to* the general law expressed by the second.

Given two structures A and B, such that A is a substructure of B, the *Criteriality* of A with respect to an *application* (purpose, meaning, intent, etc.) of B is a measure of the degree to which the presence of A in B is required in order for B to succeed in that application. (In our example, the observation concerning firemen and red suspenders (= B) does not require the mention of Rupert (= A) in order to succeed as a statement of a general law of nature.) Since a Schema is organized around the attainment of a particular goal, we may discuss the criteriality of each constituent of the Schema with respect to that purpose. Put in these terms, the function of the information-refinement processes is to evaluate and record the criteriality of each substructure of a Schema with respect to the successful application of that Schema.

The formal model of a Schema must provide a means of recording the criteriality of each Node, Kernel, and Little Arrow in the Schema. I will assume that there is a numerical *Criteriality* weight attached to each of these sub-structures in every Schema. This assumption may seem rather extravagant, but without it a Schema could never rise above its origin as a direct recording of sensori-motor experience.

Criteriality weights will be represented as integers between 0 and 6 (the scale being quite arbitrary), where a Criteriality of 0 indicates the absolute irrelevance of a sub-structure, and a Criteriality of 6 indicates its absolute necessity. For the most part, Criteriality weights will not be shown in the notation, but when they are being discussed, they will be written as super-scripts to the appropriate sub-structure.

Node-Criterialities, Kernel-Criterialities, and Little-Arrow-Criterialities have slightly different properties. Little-Arrow-Criterialities are the simplest. As the Criteriality of a Little Arrow between two Kernels diminishes, the matching phase of the Schema-Application process (see sections II.B.2 and IV.B) becomes decreasingly concerned about matching those two Kernels in the indicated order. If the Criteriality of the Little Arrow should rise, the matching process would become increasingly strict about matching in the proper order.

Kernel-Criterialities differ from Little-Arrow-Criterialities in that they are allowed to assume *negative* values (so that their range is actually −6 to 6). A negative Criteriality indicates the importance of the *absence* of the given condition. Of course, the absence of a condition cannot be directly perceived, but must be inferred from the failure of some prediction dependent on the condition's presence. The process that performs such inferences is Differentiation (V.B.3). The magnitude of a Kernel's Criteriality determines the zeal with which the matching phase of Schema-Application will seek a match for it. If a Kernel attains a Criteriality of zero, it has been found to be irrelevant to the Schema it occurs in, so it is deleted. A major function of Generalization is simply to weed out the irrelevant Kernels that often appear in unrefined observations.

In contrast with the Little Arrow and the Kernel, a Node is not deleted if its Criteriality reaches zero. Each occurrence of a Node occupies an argument-position in a Kernel. If an occurrence of a Node attains zero Criteriality, this simply means that *any* value of that argument will satisfy the analogic matching process in Schema-Application. Nodes of zero Criteriality are called *Dummy Nodes*, since they behave much like dummy variables in mathematical notation: They may be matched to any other Node, but this matching must be consistent within any Schema.

The initial assignment of Criteriality weights, and the criteria by which they are later adjusted, will be discussed along with the appropriate processes (V.A and V.B).

Criteriality is a refinement of the general notion of the "relevance" of one structure to another. Although the concept of "relevance" is elusive and perhaps impossible to capture in its full generality, "criteriality" is sufficiently restricted to be capable of formalization. The criteriality measure is defined only when the one structure is a constituent of the other, and when the super-structure has a well-defined purpose. Even though criteriality is only a limited measure of "relevance," the maintenance of criteriality information is of the utmost importance in the goal-oriented storage of experience.

III.B.6: WEIGHTS ATTACHED TO SCHEMATA

My final addition to the LTM structure will be the postulation of certain weights that characterize a Schema as a whole. These weights are needed by the processes which manipulate Schemata, since these processes must in general choose among several Schemata that are candidates for processing. One such weight records the average *Cost* of matching the Left Side of the Schema, measured in some unit of effort. This measure will depend on the number of Kernels on the Left Side, the nature of the Kernels (e.g. Motor Kernels must be more expensive to execute than Sensory-Interrogation Kernels), the Criterialities involved, and so on.

More important than a Schema's Cost is the desirability of its consequence. If the organism finds itself applying some Schema whose consequence is highly undesirable, it will actually inhibit those actions which might complete the Schema, as well as choosing other Schemata to execute. The weight that indicates the desirability of a Schema's Right Side will be called its *Charge* (the term is adapted from Colby (1967)). A Schema's Charge may be positive or negative. It reflects the desirability of the individual Kernels of the Right Side, their Criterialities, the degree of certainty that the Right Side follows from the Left, and so on.

The application of a Schema is founded on the assumption that its Right Side will follow as a consequence of its Left Side, but of course there is no guarantee that this will in fact occur. The reliability of the "Big Arrow" relation in each Schema must be discovered by repeatedly applying the Schema, and keeping statistics as to its successes and failures. The resultant measure will be called the *Confidence* value attached to the Schema. We may think of the Confidence weight of a Schema as varying from 0.0 to 1.0, so that it represents the "*a priori* probability" that the Right Side will follow once the Left Side is obtained. Besides its obvious importance to the application of a Schema, the Confidence weight also allows the representation of qualified truths (e.g. "*Most* people who wear red suspenders are firemen").

To summarize the structure of Long-Term Memory: A Schema is an ordered pair of Events, joined by the Big Arrow relation. An Event is a set of Kernels partially ordered by the Little Arrow relation. A Kernel is an ordered n-tuple of Nodes. A Node is actually a nest of links which helps to weave the Schemata together into a complicated net structure. Nodes, Kernels, and Little Arrows bear numerical weights indicating their Criteriality to the Schemata they participate in. Schemata bear numerical weights estimating their Cost of application, their Charge, or importance to the organism's goals, and the Confidence with which the Schema may be used for prediction. Each Schema is organized around the attainment of a particular long- or short-term goal.

III.C: The pragmatics of memory systems

The memory system of JCM is "goal-oriented" because, in my view, organisms are goal-oriented. Unfortunately, psychologists have often chosen to study memory as a thing-in-itself, rather than as a part of an operating purposive system. Most psychological investigations of "memory" are conducted entirely without reference to the functions that memory must perform for the organism under consideration.

The purpose of Intermediate-Level Cognition is presumably to maintain the safety and comfort of the organism through the application of its previous experience to new situations. Figure 10.5 is intended to suggest the three elements of a memory *system* that can support Intermediate-Level Cognition. These three elements are: an *encoding process* which translates experience into some form which can be retained by the *storage structure* until it is transformed into action by the *application* process at an appropriate time. Notice that I have called this a memory *system*, emphasizing that from the information-processing point of view, there is no meaningful boundary between what we think of as a "static" stored representation and what we think of as dynamic processes of storage and retrieval.

It is an extremely poor idea, then, to think that memory is like a refrigerator, where we can put in a can of beer in the morning, and take out the same can of beer in the evening. We should not let the word "stored" imply to us that "things" of some sort are stashed away in memory, and we should not ask the nearly-meaningless ques-

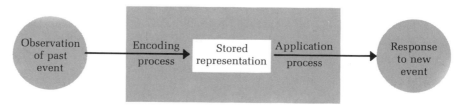

Figure 10.5   The Components of a Memory System.

tion, "What is stored?" Rather, we should try to think of the memory system in terms of its *behavior,* which is that it somehow enables the organism to function better in new situations on the basis of its past experience.

It seems that the best way that we have of conceiving of memory at present is to think of the "stored representation" as a sort of little computer program, and to think of the "application process" as an "interpreter" which causes this program to be executed. This is basically the way that a Schema is regarded in JCM; it gives us a feeling for the way in which a "static" representation can be latently dynamic. Still, this formalism preserves an artificial distinction between program and intepretation process; it invites us to think of Schemata as "things" which are shelved away in memory like cans of beer. I think we will have to put up with such misleading conceptualizations until we have the deep experience that will allow us to formulate better ones. Meanwhile, we should try as much as possible to think of memory as a *process* which is one among a system of processes dedicated to the organism's survival and well-being.

IV. The Process of Schema-Application

Schema-Application is the process that performs the primary function of Intermediate-Level Cognition. It applies a Schema from Long-Term Memory to the task of responding appropriately to some newly-acquired piece of information. A Schema is chosen for application if its Left Side closely matches the new input Event. The location of a suitable Schema is the responsibility of the Goal-Monitoring, Analogic-Matching, and LTM-Search subprocesses of Schema-Application. Once a Schema is chosen for application, the Goal-Pursuit subprocess attempts to complete the match with its Left Side. If the Left Side can be completely matched, the Event on the Right Side of the Schema is regarded as having been predicted or hypothesized — with a confidence given by the Confidence weight of the Schema.

The description given below is essentially an elaboration of what has just been said. Section IV.A provides a more detailed overall look at the process. The next three sections give the details of the Analogic-Matching, LTM-Search, and Goal-Pursuit subprocesses. Section IV.E describes how the predictions made by Schema-Application may be confirmed by later observations.

An extended example of Schema-Application is available for reference in section II.

IV.A: An overview of Schema-Application

The Schema-Application process may be said to fall into three phases:

PHASE I: AN INPUT KERNEL TRIGGERS THE SEARCH FOR A SCHEMA TO APPLY

STEP 1.1:   A Kernel $\langle a' \rangle$ enters the Input Register of Short-Term Memory. The Kernel is inspected by the Goal-Monitoring process, which makes a rough assessment of its relevance to the organism's long- and short-term goals, and assigns it a Relevance weight on this basis. Goal-Monitoring then computes a heuristic evaluation for the goal of deriving the consequences of the new Kernel ⟨a'⟩. The heuristic measure will increase with the Kernel's Relevance and Confidence weights.

STEP 1.2:   An LTM-Search is done to find Schemata whose Left Side begins with a Kernel similar to ⟨a'⟩. Such a Schema will have the general form:

$$[\; ⟨a⟩ \; (\rightarrow) \; ⟨b⟩ \; (\rightarrow) \; ⟨c⟩ \; (\rightarrow) \; ... \Rightarrow ⟨g⟩ \; (\rightarrow) \; ⟨h⟩ \; (\rightarrow) \; ... \;].$$

STEP 1.3:   Each candidate Schema is rated for its similarity to the new input by the Analogic-Matching process, which sets up a correspondence between the Kernels on the Left Side of the Schema and the Kernels found in STM (in particular, the new Kernel ⟨a'⟩ is matched with the old Kernel ⟨a⟩). A heuristic measure of the suitability of each candidate Schema is computed on the basis of its Analogic-match rating, and its Cost, Confidence, and Charge weights.

PHASE II: GOAL-PURSUIT SEEKS TO ATTAIN THE REMAINDER OF THE CANDIDATE-SCHEMA'S LEFT SIDE

STEP 2.1:   The application of a Schema is based on the assumption that attainment of the Left Side implies attainment of the Right Side. The remaining Kernels of the Left Side of the candidate Schema are therefore set up as ordered subgoals under the goal of applying the Schema. That is, if the candidate Schema is

$$[\; ⟨a⟩ \; (\rightarrow) \; ⟨b⟩ \; (\rightarrow) \; ⟨c⟩ \; (\rightarrow) \; ... \Rightarrow ⟨g⟩ \; (\rightarrow) \; ⟨h⟩ \; (\rightarrow) \; ... \;],$$

then Goal-Pursuit will be called upon to attain the Kernels ⟨b⟩, ⟨c⟩, etc. The heuristic measure for each of these subgoals is based on the Criteriality weight of the Kernel with respect to the Schema.

STEP 2.2:   Goal-Pursuit tries to find each subgoal Kernel in STM. Failing that, it uses LTM-Search to find Schemata which have the desired Kernel on the *Right* Side, and then attempts to apply *those* Schemata.

STEP 2.3:   Meanwhile, Goal-Monitoring is informed which Kernels are being sought, and stands ready to detect them when they enter the IR. The desired Kernels may be attained through the efforts of Goal-Pursuit or they may simply arrive fortuitously.

STEP 2.4:   When the entire Left Side of the Schema is finally matched, the inverse of the matching-Analogy is applied to the Right Side of the Schema. The resulting

Event "$\langle g' \rangle \rightarrow \langle h' \rangle$ ..." is entered into STM. It constitutes new input, which may form the basis for further Schema-Applications. The Confidence weights of the new, derived Kernels are based on the Confidence weight of the Schema that produced them. The Kernels are tagged as being internal in origin.

PHASE III: PREDICTED KERNELS ARE CONFIRMED

STEP 3.1: Goal-Monitoring takes cognizance of the conclusions that have been drawn from the applied Schema. It determines if those conclusions were already known and it waits to see if predicted Kernels in fact arrive.

STEP 3.2: On the basis of the success or failure of its predictions, the applied Schema is adjusted by the information-refinement processes. (The several processes that modify Long-Term Memory are not part of the Schema-Application process itself, so their discussion is relegated to section V.)

The process of Schema-Application is "input bound" at each phase. That is, each phase of Schema-Application requires some Kernel or Kernels to enter the IR before it can proceed. It might be useful to think of a whole goal-tree-full of Schema-Applications, all waiting for the Kernels they need. Goal-Monitoring intercepts new Kernels as they enter the STM and distributes them properly among the waiting Schema-Applications, as a mother bird distributes worms among its nestfull of hungry fledglings. Thus, individual Schema-Applications are "parallel" inasmuch as they exist in overlapping time-periods, but they are paced by the inputs to the IR, which may be strung out over time.

IV.B: Analogic-Matching

Viewed in the large, the purpose of Schema-Application is to make use of possible similarities between the current stream of observations and the past course of events. Of course, the present will never be *identical* with the past; their comparison must therefore involve some non-identity "mapping" between present and past events. Within JCM's formalism for representing events, the comparison between present and past can be expressed as a formal mapping between formal objects. I will call such a correspondence an *Analogy* between two Events.

An Analogy between two Events consists of *two* mappings, one of which establishes a correspondence between the *Kernels* of the two Events, and the other of which establishes a correspondence between their *Nodes*. Given a new Kernel stream and an old Schema, the mapping between Kernels might look something like:

New Kernels: $\langle a' \rangle \rightarrow \langle d' \rangle \rightarrow \langle f \rangle \rightarrow \langle c' \rangle \rightarrow \langle g' \rangle$

Old Schema: $[\ \langle a \rangle \rightarrow \langle b \rangle \rightarrow \langle c \rangle \rightarrow \langle d \rangle \Rightarrow \langle g \rangle\ ]$

The example above shows three extremely common phenomena which occur in the Analogic matching of Schemata: Kernel ⟨b⟩ of the Schema is not matched in the new Event; the new Event contains an interceding Kernel ⟨f⟩ which cannot be matched to the Schema; the Kernels ⟨c⟩ and ⟨d⟩ of the Schema are matched by ⟨c′⟩ and ⟨d′⟩ respectively, but the new Kernels occur in the reverse order. Yet a match ⟨g′⟩ for the goal ⟨g⟩ is nevertheless obtained. These facts about this Analogic mapping suggest that the presence of the Kernel ⟨b⟩ in the Schema is inessential—i.e. non-criterial— to the attainment of the goal ⟨g⟩, as is the relative order of Kernels ⟨c⟩ and ⟨d⟩. Perhaps the physical law that accounts for the appearance of ⟨g⟩ is really of the form

$$[\ \langle a \rangle \rightarrow \langle c \rangle \ \langle d \rangle \Rightarrow \langle g \rangle \ ].$$

It is the responsibility of the Generalization process (V.B.2) to draw such conclusions, and Analogic mappings form the prime evidence for Generalization.

The Kernels that are paired by an Analogic mapping need not be identical. They must have the same *first* Node, since only Kernels with the same first Node are comparable. The other Nodes, however, may differ, as in the following analogic mapping between Kernels:

New Kernel: <texture right rough>
                                        | | |
Kernel from Schema: <texture below fuzzy>.

Notice that the mapping between Nodes inside a Kernel cannot permute the order of Nodes, since the position of a Node within a Kernel corresponds to a particular "dimension" of that type of Kernel (e.g. direction, texture).

An Analogy, then, consists of a correspondence between Kernels, which further induces a correspondence between Nodes. I will require that the mapping between Nodes, considered over all Kernels in the Schema, be one-to-one. Thus, if the node "rough" is substituted for the Node "fuzzy" in one Kernel of a Schema, it must be substituted in all Kernels; conversely, "fuzzy" is the only Node that may be replaced by "rough" in that Analogy. The latter condition is perhaps a bit too strong, but it ensures that each Analogy will have an *inverse*.

The inverse of the Analogic match is used at the end of Phase II of Schema-Application. The typical Schema-Application might be diagrammed as:

New Events: Event$_1$′   (Event$_2$′)
                              ↓ A   ↑ $\overline{A}$
Old Schema: [Event$_1$ ⇒   Event$_2$].

An Analogy A is formed between the new Event "Event$_1$′" and the old Event$_1$. Then the "analogous" consequence is generated by applying $\overline{A}$, the inverse of Analogic mapping A, to the consequence Event$_2$ of Event$_1$. The predicted consequence Event$_2$' may or may not be confirmed in Phase III of the Schema-Application.

Analogic mappings are assigned numerical ratings which measure the satisfactoriness of the Analogy for the purposes of applying the given Schema. Clearly, the more nearly identical the new Event is to the Left Side of the Schema, the more satisfactory it is. More precisely, the rating of an Analogy depends on the Criteriality weights on each Node, Kernel, and Little Arrow in the Left Side of the Schema. An element with a Criteriality of 6 must be matched identically: an element with low Criteriality may be matched with anything (or with nothing).

IV.C: LTM-Search

When we recognize a visual scene, or when we understand a sentence, we are making use of a great deal of information that is retrieved from our Long-Term Memories. In most cases this retrieval is effortless, and in fact it usually goes unnoticed. The LTM-Search process discussed below is intended to model only these most straightforward, "unconscious" instances of recall.

LTM-Search is called for at two different stages in the Schema-Application process. In Step 1.2, an LTM-Search finds Schemata whose Left Sides match a new input Kernel, so that the consequences of that Kernel may be inferred. In Step 2.2, Goal-Pursuit uses LTM-Search to find Schemata whose Right Side contains a given goal-Kernel, so that that Kernel may be obtained. In either case, the input to LTM-Search is a single Kernel. This Kernel is recopied, if necessary, into the IR, since it is momentarily the "center of attention" of ILC.

In either use of LTM-Search, the output is a set of "candidate" Schemata which must be processed much further before their true applicability can be ascertained. In information-processing terms, the task of LTM-Search is not really one of "locating" information, but rather one of *selecting* Schemata which seem likely to be applicable to the given task. The notion of "likely" is formalized by a heuristic measure which LTM-Search computes for each Schema that it proposes as a candidate for application. The LTM-Search process thus has two stages: Stage I is the selection of a set of Schemata from LTM, and Stage II is the computation of a heuristic evaluation for these Schemata.

The initial selection of Stage I is made by means of the "associative structure" of Nodes (see III.B.1). Suppose that $\langle N_1\, N_2'\, \ldots\, N_n' \rangle$ is the Kernel on which the search is based. Then the Node N_1 is directly connected to all Schemata having Kernels of the form $\langle N_1\, N_2\, \ldots\, N_n \rangle$. Presumably no effort is required to "locate" these Schemata in LTM. The main task of Stage I is to weed out those Schemata in which the Kernel $\langle N_1\, N_2\, \ldots\, N_n \rangle$ occurs in the wrong position. The remaining Schemata are subjected to the heuristic evaluation.

The heuristic measure computed in Stage II is based on three factors: A measure of the "Analogic match" between the Kernels $\langle N_1\, N_2'\, \ldots\, N_n' \rangle$ and $\langle N_1\, N_2\, \ldots\, N_n \rangle$;

the Confidence weight of the Schema; and the Cost weight of the Schema. A possible formula for the Analogic match measure between Kernels is:

$$\text{Criteriality} (\langle N_1 \, N_2' \, \ldots \, N_n' \rangle)$$

$$\times \, \text{Criteriality} (\langle N_1 \, N_2 \, \ldots \, N_n \rangle)$$

$$\times \sum_{j=1}^{n} \text{Criteriality} (N_j) \times \text{Equal} (N_j', N_j)$$

where "Equal" is 1 if its arguments are identical, and 0 otherwise. Note, inside the summation, how the value of a Node-Node match varies with the Criteriality of the Node within the candidate Schema. In particular, a non-identical match with a Dummy Node (Criteriality = 0) is neither better nor worse than an identical match. As for the Schema's Confidence and Cost weights, the more Confident the Schema is, and the lower its Cost, the better it is as a candidate for application.

When the heuristic measures for each of the candidate Schemata have been computed, LTM-Search is finished. The process that called LTM-Search then establishes the candidates as subgoals, and pursues them according to their relative heuristic measures.

In this model, the major burden of LTM access is placed on the "structure" of the Node. As I have said, this "structure" is really equivalent to the *process* of finding all Kernels containing a given Node. It has no necessary relation to the physical structures that might contain Long-Term Memory, either in the brain or in a computer system. Although the "associative structure" of Nodes, or its equivalent process, is by any criterion a very expensive mechanism to employ, it is hard to imagine any parsimonious way of searching all of LTM for relevant Schemata in a very short time. This rapid search is an important characteristic of ILC in living systems, so it seems that we have little choice but to represent it as accurately as we can, even if this requires extravagant mechanisms.

The model I have proposed for LTM-Search is roughhewn, and I certainly would make no claims for its quantitative accuracy. It is intended only to model the following qualitative assertions about the type of information retrieval that serves Intermediate-Level Cognition:

a. The search process does not seek to locate a *particular* Schema, but instead delimits and evaluates a *set* of candidate Schemata. Further selection among these Schemata is left to the superordinate process that instituted the LTM-Search,

b. Only a tiny fraction of the Schemata in LTM are evaluated during any particular instance of LTM-Search, and

c. The subset of LTM to be evaluated is located extremely rapidly (i.e., in a time that is orders of magnitude smaller than the time required for a sequential testing of every Schema in LTM).

IV.D: Goal-Pursuit

The Goal-Pursuit process is responsible for obtaining the Kernels needed to complete the application of a Schema. There are four possible ways in which a desired Kernel might be obtained:

1. It might arrive in the IR fortuitously — i.e. not as the direct result of any activity on the part of the organism,

2. An efferent Kernel may be obtained by executing the corresponding command,

3. The Kernel might already be present in Short-Term Memory, or

4. It might be derivable as a consequence of some other set of Kernels, using a Schema from Long-Term Memory.

The first two cases present little difficulty. In the third case, the search proceeds "down" the STM, i.e. in order of decreasing recency. It may happen that a desired Kernel is found in STM, and yet *more recent* events may have invalidated it. This is one instance of what is called the "frame problem", namely the fact that any condition may have some logical or causal connection to any other. In such a case there are three possibilities:

a. The fact of invalidation may already have been noticed (through a Schema-Application made to the more recent Kernels when they arrived).

b. The validity of the located Kernel may for some reason come into question (e.g. if it is very crucial), and Schemata may at that time be applied to the more recent Kernels to see if they invalidate the old one, or

c. The invalidation may go unnoticed, in which case the organism simply makes the mistake of assuming that the condition has remained unchanged.

If Goal-Pursuit is unable to obtain the sought Kernel by luck, by fiat, or by linear search of STM, it must take the more drastic step of deriving the Kernel from other information. Goal-Pursuit calls for an LTM-Search based on the given Kernel, to find Schemata whose Right Side contains an Analogous Kernel. That is, if the sought Kernel is $\langle k' \rangle$, the LTM-Search will return candidates of the form:

$$[\langle g \rangle \ (\longrightarrow) \ \langle h \rangle \ (\longrightarrow) \ \langle i \rangle \ (\longrightarrow) \ \ldots \Rightarrow \langle j \rangle \ (\longrightarrow) \ \langle k \rangle \ (\longrightarrow) \ \ldots]$$

Then, in accordance with their heuristic measures, these candidates will be subjected to Schema-Application, which in turn will call on Goal-Pursuit to obtain matches for the Kernels $\langle g \rangle$, $\langle h \rangle$, $\langle i \rangle$, etc. With luck these Kernels will be obtained by one of the first three means listed above. Otherwise, another level of LTM-Search will be involved in attaining $\langle g \rangle$, $\langle h \rangle$, $\langle i \rangle$, etc.

In the application of a Schema, the Kernels of the Left Side represent an ordered set of subgoals. In general, however, neither the ordering nor any of the subgoals are absolutely necessary: both the Little Arrows and the Kernels themselves may vary in Criteriality. Furthermore, the Criteriality weight on any element of a Schema may be incorrect. For example, a Kernel may bear a Criteriality weight of 2 when in fact it is totally unnecessary to the Schema (Criteriality $= 0$). Because of these possibilities, the Criteriality weights on the Left Side are used only to *bias* the order in which Goal-Pursuit goes after subgoal-Kernels, but they do not determine it absolutely. For example, if the Left Side contains

$$\langle k_1 \rangle \xrightarrow{5} \langle k_2 \rangle$$

—i.e., two Kernels whose order is thought to be quite important—then little effort will be expended on attaining $\langle k_2 \rangle$ if progress on $\langle k_1 \rangle$ is poor. Yet, that little effort may in some cases suffice to yield $\langle k_2 \rangle$ before $\langle k_1 \rangle$. This reversal may cause the Schema-Application to fail (i.e. the Right Side may not follow, since the Left Side was not matched precisely); or the Schema may apply despite the reversal. Similarly, the effort allotted to the pursuit of a Kernel is a function of its Criteriality, yet even a low-Criteriality Kernel will occasionally prove unnecessary. In any case, the Schema-Adjustment process (V.B.1) will modify the Criteriality weights on the basis of the success or failure of the Schema-Application.

IV.E: The confirmation of derived kernels

Once the Left Side of A Schema is attained, the Kernels of the Right Side are entered into the IR in sequence. These Kernels are tagged to indicate that their origin is internal; they bear Confidence weights derived from the Confidence of the Schema and the Confidences of the Kernels that were used to match its Left Side. The Kernels that result from the application of a Schema may be regarded as "predicted" or "hypothetical" observations. Like any other new observation, a predicted or hypothetical Kernel is rated for its Relevance by Goal-Monitoring. Similarly, a derived Kernel may initiate further Schema-Applications and participate in the formation of new Schemata, just as any "real" Kernel might. The Confidence weight of the derived Kernel is very important here: a predicted or hypothetical observation whose Confidence is near 1.0 is almost as good as the real thing.

When any Kernel enters the IR, Goal-Monitoring searches through STM to see if that Kernel has already been observed recently. If two identical Kernels occur close together, and if one of them originated internally (a prediction) while the other originated externally (a "real" observation), then the predicted Kernel is said to be "confirmed." The Schema from which the prediction was derived is then said to have been successfully applied. If a derived Kernel passes out of STM without being confirmed, then the Schema which generated it is said to have failed in its prediction. The success or failure of a Schema's predictions is all-important to the information-refinement processes (V.B) that attempt to improve the Schema's trustworthiness.

The matching of two Kernels in STM is in general an Analogic match, rather than a test for strict identity. Therefore, "success" is graded, according to the Analogic-match measure between a Kernel and its "confirmation."

There are serious problems in identifying one Kernel with another that lie far deeper than the task of matching one with the other. Even if the two Kernels are completely identical, how is the system to know whether the two Kernels are genuinely redundant, or whether they represent two separate instances of the same observation? The question is pertinent to the case where identical *external* Kernels arrive in close succession, as well as to the confirmation of internally-generated predictions.

The general problem is: If STM contains a Kernel sequence of the form

$$\langle a \rangle \rightarrow \langle b \rangle \rightarrow \langle c \rangle \rightarrow \ldots \rightarrow \langle a \rangle$$

then is the second occurrence of Kernel $\langle a \rangle$ merely a repeat of the first, or is it an independent observation? Evidently the answer will depend on the relation between $\langle a \rangle$ and the intervening Kernels $\langle b \rangle$, $\langle c \rangle$, etc. If $\langle a \rangle$ is a static condition, perhaps $\langle b \rangle$, $\langle c \rangle$, etc. invalidate that condition, or perhaps $\langle a \rangle$ is invariant under the intervening activities. If $\langle a \rangle$ is differential, perhaps $\langle b \rangle$, $\langle c \rangle$, etc. cause a repetition of the events which led to the first occurrence of $\langle a \rangle$. These possibilities lead to very deep problems concerning the perception of change and of permanence.

V. Processes That Modify Long-Term Memory

Although Schema-Application and its subprocesses are directly responsible for putting an organism's experience to good use, Schema-Application cannot succeed unless the proper information is available in Long-Term Memory. The processes discussed in this section are responsible for maintaining the information in LTM in its most useful form. Although their influence is indirect, the processes that modify LTM are vital to the performance of the cognitive system. The importance of the LTM-modification processes arises in large part from the enormous quantity of information that must be stored in the Long-Term Memories of higher organisms. A human being collects experience for decades, yet in many situations he must respond properly to a new occurrence in a matter of seconds. Unless his experiences were properly collated, a person would spend all of his time testing out inapplicable Schemata.

In this chapter the LTM-modification processes are discussed under two headings: processes that encode experience, and processes that refine Schemata.

V.A: Processes that encode experience

Since an organism interprets its observations by applying Schemata to them, it will usually record its experience in a form dictated by its old Schemata. The process by which old Schemata organize new observations for storage will be discussed below as Guided STM → LTM Encoding. In a naive organism, or in an organism facing an unfamiliar situation, there may be no old Schemata to guide the recording of new observations. In such cases, the encoding must be made in accordance with less reliable principles, as in the process I call Unguided STM → LTM Encoding.

V.A.1: GUIDED STM → LTM ENCODING

In order for a sequence of Kernels to be converted into a Schema, two modifications must be made:

1. The sequence must be broken into "antecedent" and "consequent" Events by the insertion of a Big Arrow, and

2. Bounds must be inserted to make the Schema a small subsequence of the stream of observations.

In the case of Guided STM → LTM Encoding, both the Big Arrow and the bounds of the new Schema are inherited from an old Schema which was successfully applied to the input sequence.

The successful application of a Schema results in an Analogic mapping between new Kernels in Short-Term Memory and the Schema retrieved from Long-Term Memory. We have seen that this mapping might look something like:

New Kernels: $<a'> \rightarrow <d'> \rightarrow <f> \rightarrow <c'> \rightarrow <g'>$

Old Schema: $[<a> \rightarrow <b> \rightarrow <c> \rightarrow <d> \Rightarrow <g>]$

In recording the new observation, the Big Arrow and the outer bounds are simply inserted into the Kernel sequence at points corresponding to their locations in the old Schema. Thus, in the example above, the new Schema would be

$$[\langle a' \rangle \rightarrow \langle d' \rangle \rightarrow \langle f \rangle \rightarrow \langle c' \rangle \Rightarrow \langle g' \rangle]$$

The Node-Criteriality and Little-Arrow-Criteriality weights in the new Schema will be set to the neutral value of 3. The Kernel-Criteriality values, however, are based on the Relevance weights assigned to the Kernels by Goal-Monitoring at the time that they entered Short-Term Memory. Now, these Relevance weights depend in part on whether the Kernel was being sought as a short-term goal or as confirmation of a prediction. Thus, the Kernels $\langle d' \rangle$, $\langle c' \rangle$, and $\langle g' \rangle$ in the example will in general have higher Relevance weights than the unsought Kernel $\langle f \rangle$. It is likely that the first Kernel—$\langle a' \rangle$—also had a high Relevance weight, since it led to the Schema-Application in the first place. Hence an unmatched Kernel such as $\langle f \rangle$ will in general have a lower Criteriality in the new Schema than its fellows. In this way, the new Schema reflects both the properties of the new Event and the structure of the Schema to which it was assimilated.

The Charge weight of the new Schema is derived from the desirability of the Kernels on its Right Side. The Cost and Confidence weights are not established until the Schema has been applied.

V.A.2: UNGUIDED STM → LTM ENCODING

An extended example of Unguided STM → LTM Encoding was given in Section II.B.1. The process is identical to the Guided case, except there is no convenient source for the Big Arrow and the boundaries of the new Schema. These must be inserted by rough, unreliable rules. For example, a Big Arrow might be inserted after the last efferent Kernel preceding a highly Relevant Kernel. The boundaries might be extended to enclose neighboring Kernels that were not matched to any Schema (i.e. that were not "accounted for" by known Schemata).

There is also no reliable principle that specifies *when* Unguided STM → LTM Encoding may fruitfully be applied. Since the process has a rather low chance of producing a useful observation, it must be invoked very often in situations that are novel to the organism. Most of the Schemata created by Unguided STM → LTM Encoding will fail when applied, and hence attain low Confidence ratings, and therefore be tried less frequently. The few Schemata that do correspond to implications in the physical world will increase in Confidence, and become the basis for the organism's operational knowledge.

It might seem rather wasteful for the organism to create Schemata fairly indiscriminately and operate on the small percentage of lucky encodings, but "storage space" in LTM does not seem to be an expensive commodity in higher cognitive systems. In order for this strategy to work, however, the organism must have a delicate system for evaluating and choosing among Schemata on the basis of their past records of success, such that the meaningless Schemata rapidly disappear from contention. In addition, the organism must capitalize on the few valid Schemata it produces by amplifying and perfecting them until they converge to general, widely-applicable laws of behavior. The processes that hone Schemata on the wheel of experience form the topic of the next section.

V.B: Processes that Refine Schemata

V.B.1: Schema-adjustment

Schema-Adjustment is a simple process which recomputes a Schema's Cost and Confidence weights on the basis of its most recent Schema-Application. The Cost weight should eventually converge to the average cost of matching the Left Side of the Schema, measured in some appropriate unit of cognitive effort. The Confidence weight should converge to the ratio of successful confirmations of the Right Side to successful matchings of the Left Side (i.e. successes per trials).

The detailed structure of a Schema is refined by two processes which attend to the details of the Analogic match that mediated its last application. These processes will be called Generalization and Differentiation.

V.B.2: Generalization

The Generalization process is intimately bound to the notion of "criteriality". Let us recall the definition of criteriality from III.B.5: Given two structures A and B, such that A is a sub-structure of B, the *Criteriality* of A with respect to an application (purpose, meaning, intent, etc.) of B is a measure of the degree to which the presence of A in B is required in order for B to succeed in that application.

We will, of course, be concerned with the case where structure B is a Schema, whose "application" is the attainment of goals by means of Schema-Application. The function of Generalization is to discover the criteriality of each constituent (Node, Little Arrow, or Kernel) of a Schema with respect to the successful application of that Schema. The criterion that Generalization uses is as follows: If a constituent of the Schema participates (by being Analogically matched) in a successful application of the Schema, then that constituent is more likely to be criterial to the Schema; if a constituent goes unmatched, and the application is nevertheless successful, then that constituent is less likely to be criterial.

Thus, Generalization is invoked after the application of a Schema proves successful. We may assume that Generalization is applied after Guided STM → LTM Encoding, so that there is a new Schema recording the recent series of Events, as well as the original Schema that was applied. The Generalization process will produce yet another Schema: this Schema will be the same as the original except for appropriate adjustments to the Criteriality weights of the constituent Nodes, Little Arrows, and Kernels. The exact procedures for generalizing over Nodes, Little Arrows, and Kernels are somewhat different, so I will discuss each type of Generalization separately.

GENERALIZATION OVER NODES

Generalization over Nodes is based on the Node-to-Node correspondence that is established by the Analogic-Matching process (IV.B). A Node in the old Schema will be raised in Criteriality if it is mapped into *itself*, and lowered in Criteriality if it is mapped into any other Node. To take a very simple example, suppose that the old Schema were

$$[\ \langle \text{color? left bottom} \rangle \Rightarrow \langle \text{color left bottom red} \rangle \ ]$$

This schema might be applied to the new input Event

$$\langle \text{color? left middle} \rangle \rightarrow \langle \text{color left middle none} \rangle$$

which would then be converted into a Schema by Guided STM $\rightarrow$ LTM Encoding. The Analogic mapping between the two Schemata is simply:

New: [<color? left middle> $\Rightarrow$ <color left middle none>]

Old: [<color? left bottom> $\Rightarrow$ <color left bottom red>].

Now, let us assume for the sake of the example that a Node of the old Schema will have its Criteriality weight increased by unity if it is matched with itself, and decreased by unity if it is matched with some other Node. Let us also assume that all constituents initially had Criteriality weights of 3. These assumptions (which will hold for all examples in this section) are not intended to be realistic; the point here is simply to illustrate the main principles of the Generalization process. Under these assumptions, the new Schema produced by Generalization will be:

$$[\langle color?^4\ left^4\ bottom^2\rangle \Rightarrow \langle color^4\ left^4\ bottom^2\ red^2\rangle]$$

This new Schema will have a higher Confidence weight than either of the sensorimotor Schemata from which it was derived. Now, when a new copy of any of the Kernels $\langle$color? left bottom$\rangle$, $\langle$color? left middle$\rangle$, or $\langle$color? left top$\rangle$ enters the IR, all three of the above Schemata will compete for application to the new input. All other things being equal, it is the more general Schema that will be applied, because of its higher Confidence. The original sensori-motor Schemata will tend to sink into disuse.

As the generalized Schema is applied to more and more new Events, the Node "left" will rapidly lose the superior Criteriality that it fortuitously gained on the first Generalization. Eventually, the result will be a very high-Confidence Schema:

$$[\langle color?^6\ left^0\ bottom^0\rangle \Rightarrow \langle color^6\ left^0\ bottom^0\ red^0\rangle]$$

This highly-general Schema is equivalent to a statement of the form:

$$(\forall x)\ (\forall y)\ (\exists z)\ [\ \langle color?\ x\ y\rangle \Rightarrow \langle color\ x\ y\ z\rangle\ ]$$

In other words: "Whenever you interrogate the color of a particular retinal region, you will get back a static-sensory Kernel giving the color of that region."

Generalization over Nodes is the heart of the Generalization process. The most important characteristic of a "general" Schema is its ability to match many different Nodes that might occur in the same "context." This ability is provided by the Analogic-match measure function (discussed in IV.C), acting on the Dummy Nodes that Generalization produces. To put the matter another way, Generalization over Nodes is the process that allows ILC to "grow" its own *quantifiers* on the basis of its accumulated experience.

It is an assumption of JCM that the Kernels in a sensori-motor Schema are linearly ordered by their time of arrival in the IR. In many cases the relative order of two Kernels is actually irrelevant to the results recorded in the Schema; in other cases the ordering is essential to the validity of the Schema. The task of Generalization over Little Arrows is to discover the criteriality of the ordering between each pair of Kernels by comparing an old Schema with the new Schema that arises from its successful application. If the ordering of Kernels differs in the two Schemata, and yet both gave Analogous results, then the Criteriality weight of the corresponding Little Arrow can be reduced. If two Kernels occur in the same order in both Schemata, then the estimated Criteriality of the Little Arrow between them is increased. The following diagram indicates the results of Generalization over Little Arrows in a rather simple case:

$$\text{New:} \qquad [\ \langle a \rangle \xrightarrow{3} \langle c \rangle \xrightarrow{3} \langle b \rangle \Rightarrow \langle e \rangle \xrightarrow{3} \langle d \rangle\ ]$$

$$\text{Old:} \qquad [\ \langle a \rangle \xrightarrow{3} \langle b \rangle \xrightarrow{3} \langle c \rangle \Rightarrow \langle d \rangle \xrightarrow{3} \langle e \rangle\ ]$$

$$\text{Derived:} \qquad [\ \langle a \rangle \xrightarrow{4} \langle b \rangle \xrightarrow{2} \langle c \rangle \Rightarrow \langle d \rangle \xrightarrow{2} \langle e \rangle\ ]$$

$$\text{Ultimate:} \qquad [\ \langle a \rangle \xrightarrow{6} \langle b \rangle\ \langle c \rangle \Rightarrow \langle d \rangle\ \langle e \rangle\ ]$$

When a Little Arrow reaches a Criteriality value of zero, it is eliminated altogether. In this way it is possible to obtain partially ordered or completely unordered Events. We are quite used to thinking in terms of temporally-unordered relationships (e.g. the locations of pieces of furniture in a room are not thought of as being ordered), yet such conceptions, like quantifiers, cannot be derived from any single experiential record. Even though the serialism hypothesis of JCM is undoubtedly too strong, it remains true that our sensations are for the most part temporally ordered. Some experience-collating process is required if our internal models of the world are to be freed from the properties of our sensory systems.

One of the major tasks of Generalization is to eliminate Kernels which were recorded during a given observation, but which were in fact irrelevant to the course of events observed. The distinguishing property of such Kernels is that a Schema can be successfully applied without any match at all being found for its irrelevant Kernels. The diagram below shows a simple example in which two Kernels are eventually deleted from a Schema after continually failing to be matched in successful applications of the Schema:

New: $[\langle a \rangle \xrightarrow{3} \quad \langle c \rangle \xRightarrow{3} \quad \langle e \rangle^3]$

Old: $[\langle a \rangle \xrightarrow{3} \langle b \rangle \xrightarrow{3} \langle c \rangle \xRightarrow{3} \langle d \rangle \xrightarrow{3} \langle e \rangle^3]$

Derived: $[\langle a \rangle \xrightarrow{4} \langle b \rangle \xrightarrow{2} \langle c \rangle \xRightarrow{4} \langle d \rangle \xrightarrow{2} \langle e \rangle^4]$

Ultimate: $[\langle a \rangle \xrightarrow{6} \quad \langle c \rangle \xRightarrow{6} \quad \langle e \rangle^6]$

Kernels that attain a Criteriality value of zero are deleted, since Kernels of zero relevance do not belong in a Schema. Note that superfluous Kernels on the Right Side of a Schema are eliminated as are those on the Left Side. This will prevent misguided attempts to use the Schema in Goal-Pursuit (e.g. attempts to use the Schemata above for attaining the Kernel $\langle d \rangle$).

V.B.3: Differentiation

The Generalization process just discussed can be applied most fruitfully after *successful* Schema-Applications, and it can only *delete* elements of the given Schema. As seems only proper, there is a complementary process, which can be applied most fruitfully after unsuccessful Schema-Applications, and which can only *add* elements to the given Schema. This process is called Differentiation because it takes a Schema whose Left Side is insufficient to determine a unique resultant Event, and splits it into two or more Schemata whose antecedent conditions are more adequately specified.

When the Application of a Schema produces an unsuccessful prediction, there are two possible problems. The Schema may simply bear no correlation with any law by which the real world operates (such a case may be very common, since Unguided STM $\longrightarrow$ LTM Encoding will often produce meaningless encodings). On the other hand, the Schema may be correct but underspecified, so that its Left Side matches too broad a class of events. In the first case, the Schema will rarely succeed, and will have a very low Confidence value. In the second case, a Schema which applies *some* of the time will be accorded Generalization whenever it succeeds, and will attain a Confidence weight which converges to some number recognizably different from both 0 to 1. Therefore, these two types of unsuccessful Schemata are easily distinguishable on the basis of their Confidence weights. In the first case, no action need be wasted on the worthless Schema; in the second case, Differentiation may be applied to attain an even more reliable Schema.

In order to discuss Differentiation in general, I will use the symbols $E_0, E_1, \ldots , E_n$ to denote whole Events. A particular Event E_0 may have a large number of different possible consequences. When the organism has had enough experience with E_0, it will have encoded a set of Schemata:

$$[\ E_0 \Rightarrow E_1 \ ] \qquad \text{Confidence} = C_1$$
$$[\ E_0 \Rightarrow E_2 \ ] \qquad \text{Confidence} = C_2$$
$$\cdots$$
$$[\ E_0 \Rightarrow E_n \ ] \qquad \text{Confidence} = C_n$$

The C_j will have a sum that is nearly 1; it need not be extremely close to 1, since E_0 may have many improbable consequences that the organism has not observed.

Now, if the world is strictly deterministic, it cannot really be "the same" Event E_0 that has several possible consequences. The Schemata above must be lacking in the conditions that would distinguish among the various types of "Event E_0." The purpose of Differentiation is simply to add in the missing conditions E'_j — that is, to produce a new set of Schemata:

$$[\ E'_1 \longrightarrow E_0 \Rightarrow E_1 \ ] \qquad \text{Confidence} \approx 1$$
$$[\ E'_2 \longrightarrow E_0 \Rightarrow E_2 \ ] \qquad \text{Confidence} \approx 1$$
$$\cdots$$
$$[\ E'_n \longrightarrow E_0 \Rightarrow E_n \ ] \qquad \text{Confidence} \approx 1$$

In the general paradigm for Differentiation just given, it will often happen that one of the Confidence values, say C_1, is quite large, but that the remaining C_j for $2 < j \leq n$ are quite small — perhaps so small that the individual Schemata

$$[\ E_0 \Rightarrow E_j \ ] \ \text{for} \ 2 < j \leq n$$

are too unsuccessful to sustain themselves in memory. In such a case, the dominant Schema $[\ E_0 \Rightarrow E_1 \ ]$ may be "split" into the two Schemata

$$[\quad E_1' \longrightarrow E_0 \Rightarrow \quad E_1 \ ] \qquad \text{Confidence} \approx 1$$
$$[\ {\sim}E_1' \longrightarrow E_0 \Rightarrow {\sim}E_1 \ ] \qquad \text{Confidence} \approx 1$$

where the negation is supplied by Kernels of negative Criteriality. The "negative Schema" collects all the alternative results together into a Schema which is as important and reliable as the positive version.

There are other circumstances in which Differentiation may introduce negation. For example, suppose that Event E_1 is highly undesirable, while E_2 is quite neutral. Then the Schema

$$[\ E_2' \longrightarrow E_0 \Rightarrow E_2 \ ]$$

would be more useful in the form

$$[\ E_2' \rightarrow E_0 \Rightarrow \sim E_1 \ ]$$

which would have a higher Charge. This latter sort of Schema would be very useful for *forestalling* occurrences of the undesirable Event E_1, if the preconditions could be noticed in time.

Negation, like quantification and unorderedness, is extremely important in the representation of general information, and yet is not directly observable in a single sequence of events. Differentiation joins Generalization as a process that uses the *comparison* of individual occurrences to arrive at information about the world that is not derivable from any single observation.

At the same time, Differentiation and Generalization complement each other, by adding to or deleting from Schemata until they converge as closely as possible to the "true" laws by which the world operates.

VI. Concluding Remarks

The model presented in this chapter is based on a very simple idea: In essence it says that if B followed A in the past, an organism should remember that fact, so that the organism can expect B to follow A in the future. It's as simple as Modus Ponens.

But when we get down to cases, the working out of this idea is not at all simple. Considerable space has been given in this chapter to a number of subtle issues necessarily surrounding the application of past experience to new situations. Even more details can be found in a fuller treatment (Becker, 1970), including an executive process to coordinate the various sub-processes of Intermediate-Level Cognition, and some mechanisms for converting the dynamic experiential representation of the world into a static, "conceptual" model. Another whole nest of problems has been uncovered in the attempt to create a computer-simulated organism based on the ideas outlined in this chapter (Becker, 1972).

Why do these processes refuse to remain straightforward, un-subtle? I think that the answer lies simply in the sheer *amount* of experiential information that is available to any higher organism. With several complicated sensory systems operating constantly and with an environment rich in objects and physical laws, the organism has all it can do merely to keep track of its experience in an orderly way. Yet it must in addition sort out the crucial aspects of its experience from the mass of unimportant observations, and it must furthermore cope with the fact that no event is ever repeated in precisely the same way that it occurred originally.

The pressing facts of informational overabundance lead inevitably to mechanisms that extract *statistical* properties of the experiential stream. I have tried to stress these mechanisms in the present chapter (they are usually modeled in terms of numerical "weights"). In the last section, I showed how certain vital aspects of information-representation — namely quantification, negation, and atemporal re-lations — could be derived on the basis of statistical observations; indeed, there is no other way in which they can be discovered.

Thus the statistically-derived measures such as Confidence, Criteriality, and Cost should not be brushed aside as ornamental trimmings on an essentially deduc-tive model. This sort of information, and the processes based upon it, are absolutely necessary to any system that must deal with the immense variety of experiences that are encountered in real-world interactions. On the other hand, we cannot ignore the deductive, sequential aspects of Intermediate-Level Cognition, lest we return to the information-theoretic models of two decades ago. These models lacked the *procedural* mechanisms necessary for describing the coordinated, directed behavior of real organisms.

It seems that we will have to get used to models that embody both the deductive and the statistical aspects of behavior if we are ever to come to an understanding of the processing of experiential information in complex systems.

References

Abelson, R. P. 1968. Computer simulation of social behavior. In Lindzey and Aronson, Eds.; Vol. II. Reading, Mass.: Addison-Wesley.

Abelson, R. P. 1969. Psychological implication. In Abelson, *et al.*, Eds.

Abelson, R. P., E. Aronson, W. McGuire, T. Newcomb, M. Rosenberg, and P. Tannenbaum, Eds. 1968. *Theories of Cognitive Consistency*. New York: Rand-McNally.

Abelson, R. P. and J. D. Carroll. 1965. Computer simulation of individual belief systems. *American Behavioral Scientist 8*, 24–30.

Abelson, R. P. and D. E. Kanouse. 1966. The subjective acceptance of verbal generalizations. In Feldman, Ed., *Cognitive consistency: Motivational antecedents and behavioral consequents*. New York: Academic Press.

Abelson, R. P. and C. M. Reich. 1969. Implicational modules: A method for extracting meaning from input sentences. In Walker and Norton, Eds. 647–748.

Anderson, A. R. 1964. Introduction. In Anderson, Ed. *Minds and Machines*. Englewood Cliffs, N.J.: Prentice Hall.

Anderson, J. R. and G. Bower. 1973. *Human Associative Memory*. Washington D.C.: H. V. Winston and Co.

Anderson, N. H. 1968. A simple model for information integration. In Abelson, *et. al.*

Anscombe, G. E. M. 1958. Pretending. *Proc. of the Aristotelian Society*. Supplementary Volume XXXII.

Atkinson, R. C. and R. M. Shiffrin. 1968. Human memory: a proposed system. In Spence and Spence, Eds. *The Psychology of Learning and Motivation: Advances in research and theory*. Vol. 2. New York: Academic Press.

Atkinson, R. and T. Wickens. 1969. Human Memory and the Concept of Reinforcement. Institute for Math. Studies: Stanford Univ. Tech. Rept. #145.

Aune, B. and H. Feigl. 1966. On the mind-body problem. In Feyerabend and Maxwell.

Axelrod, R. How people make sense out of a complex world. *American Political Science Review*, (in press).

Bar-Hillel, Y. 1966. Talk at Carnegie-Mellon University on the role of logic in language.

Bar-Hillel, Y. 1970. Some reflections on the present outlook for high-quality machine translation. Mimeo, Univ. of Texas.

Baronofsky, S. 1970. Some heuristics for automatic detection and resolution of anaphora in discourse. M.A. Thesis, Dept. of Computer Science: Univ. of Texas at Austin.

Bartlett, F. C. 1932. *Remembering*. Cambridge, England: Cambridge University Press.

Becker, J. D. 1969. The modeling of simple analogic and inductive processes in a semantic memory system. In Walker and Norton, 655–668.

Becker, J. D. 1970. An information-processing model of Intermediate-Level Cognition Memo. No. 119, Stanford Artificial Intelligence Project, Computer Science Dept., Stanford Univ., Stanford, Ca. Also Report No. 2335, Cambridge, Mass.: Bolt Beranek and Newman, Inc.

Becker, J. D. 1972. "Robot" computer problem solving system. Final Progress Report. Cambridge, Mass.: Bolt Beranek and Newman, Inc.

Berloff, J. 1965. The identity hypothesis: a critique. In Symthies, Ed. *Brain and Mind*. Boston: Routledge and Kegan Paul.

Bierwisch, M. 1970. Semantics. In Lyons, Ed. *New Horizons in Linguistics*. London: Penguin Books.

Bobrow, D. 1967. Natural Language Input for a Computer Problem Solving System. In Minsky, 133–215.

Bobrow, S. A. 1970. Memory for words in sentences. *J. Verb. Learning and Verb. Behav.*, 9, 363–372.

Bolinger, D. 1965. The Atomization of Meaning. *Language* 41, #4.

Bower, G. H. 1967. A multicomponent theory of the memory trace. In Spence, Ed. *The Psychology of Learning and Motivation: Advances in research and theory*. Vol. 1. New York: Academic Press.

Bower, G. H. 1970. Organizational factors in memory. *Cogn. Psychol.*, 1 (1), 18–46.

Bransford, J. and J. Franks. 1971. The abstraction of linguistic ideas. *Cogn. Psychol.* 2, 331–350.

British Computer Society. 1971. Second International Joint Conference on Artificial Intelligence, Advance Papers of the Conference. London.

Broadbent, D. E. 1958. *Perception and Communication*. London: Pergamon Press.

Brown, J. S. 1972. A symbiotic theory formation system. Unpublished doctoral dissertation, The Univ. of Michigan.

Brown, R. and D. McNeill. 1966. The "Tip of the Tongue" phenomenon. *J. Verb. Learn. Verb. Behav.*, 5 (4), 325–337.

Bruner, J. S., J. J. Goodnow, and G. A. Austin. 1956. *A Study of Thinking*. New York: Wiley.

Bugelski, E., A. Kidd, and J. Segman. 1968. Image as a mediator in one-trial paired associate learning. *J. Experimental Psych.*, 76, 1, 69–73.

Bugelski, E., A. Kidd, and J. Segman. 1968 11; Self-timing in successive list. *J. Experimental Psych.*, 77, 2, 328–334.

Celce-Murcia, M. 1972. Paradigms for Sentence Recognition. Preprint from the author. Los Angeles: UCLA Dept. of Linguistics.

Celce-Murcia, M. 1972. English Comparatives. Ph.D. Thesis. Los Angeles: UCLA Dept. of Linguistics.

Chafe, W. L. 1970. *Meaning and the Structure of Language*. Chicago: Univ. of Chicago Press.

Charniak, E. 1972. Towards a model of children's story comprehension. Mimeo, MIT.

Chase, W. G. and H. A. Simon. 1973. Perception in chess. *Cogn. Psychol.* 4 (1), 55–81.

Chomsky, N. 1965. *Aspects of the Theory of Syntax*. Cambridge: The MIT Press.

Clark, H. H. 1969. Linguistic processes in deductive reasoning. *Psychol. Rev.*, 75, 4, 387–404.

Clarkson, G. 1963. A model of the trust investment process. In Feigenbaum and Feldman.

Clowes, M. B. 1971. Picture Descriptions. In Findler and Meltzer, Eds. *Artificial Intelligence and Heuristic Programming*. Edinburgh, U.K.: Edinburgh Univ. Press.

Colby, K. M. 1964. Experimental Treatment of Neurotic Computer Programs. *Archives of General Psychiatry*, 10, 220–227.

Colby, K. M. 1967. Computer simulation of change in personal belief systems. *Behav. Sci.,* 12, (3) 248–253.

Colby, K. M. and D. C. Smith. 1969. Dialogues between humans and an artificial belief system. In Walker and Norton.

Colby, K. M., L. Tesler, and H. Enea. 1969. Experiments with a Search Algorithm on the Data Base of a Human Belief Structure. In Walker and Norton.

Colby, K. M., S. Weber, and F. D. Hilf. 1971. Artificial Paranoia. *Artificial Intelligence,* 2, 1–25.

Colby, K. M., F. D. Hilf, S. Weber, and H. Kraemer. 1972. Turing-like Indistinguishability Tests for the Validation of a Computer Simulation of Paranoid Processes. *Artificial Intelligence,* 3, 199–221.

Coles, L. S. 1969. Talking with a robot in English. In Walker and Norton. Eds.

Collins, N. L. and D. Michie, Eds. 1967. *Machine Intelligence 1.* New York: American Elsevier.

Collins, A. and M. R. Quillian. 1969. Retrieval time from semantic memory. *J. Verb. Learn. and Verb. Behav.* 9, 240–247.

Collins, A. and M. R. Quillian. 1970. Does category size affect categorization time. *J. Verb. Learn. and Verb. Behav.* 9, 432–438.

Cyert, R. and J. March. 1963. *A Behavioral Theory of the Firm.* Englewood Cliffs, N.J.: Prentice-Hall.

Dale, E. and D. Michie, Eds. 1968. *Machine Intelligence 2.* New York: American Elsevier.

Day, R., J. Cutting, and P. Copeland. 1971. Perception of linguistic and non-linguistic dimensions of dichotic stimuli. Paper presented 12th Annual Meeting of the Psychonomic Society.

DeSoto, C., Albrecht, F. 1968. Conceptual good figures. In Abelson, *et. al.*

Diggory, S. Ed. 1972. *Information Processing in Children.* New York: Academic Press.

Ducasse, C. M. 1965. Minds, matter and bodies. In J. R. Smythies Ed. *Brain and Mind.* Boston: Routledge and Kegan Paul.

Earley, J. 1971. Toward an understanding of data structures. *Comm. Assoc. for Computing Machinery,* 10, 617–627.

Eastman, C. 1969. Cognitive processes and ill-defined problems. In Walker and Norton. Eds.

Elliott, R. W. 1965. A model for a fact retrieval system. Unpublished doctoral dissertation. The Univ. of Texas at Austin.

Ernst, G. and A. Newell. 1969. *GPS: A Case Study in Generality and Problem Solving.* New York: Academic Press.

Evans, T. 1964. An ALGOL compiler. *Annual Review of Automatic Programming,* Vol. 4, 87–124.

Evans, T. 1964. A program for the solution of geometric-analogy intelligence questions. In Minsky.

Feigenbaum, E. A. 1961. The simulation of verbal learning behavior. *Proc. Western Joint Comp. Conf.* 19, 121–132. Also in Feigenbaum and Feldman.

Feigenbaum, E. A. 1970. Information processing and memory. In Norman, D. A., Ed. *Models of Human Memory.* New York: Academic Press.

Feigenbaum, E. A. and J. Feldman, Eds. 1963. *Computers and Thought.* New York: McGraw-Hill.

Feigl, H. 1963. The "mental" and the "physical." In Feigl, Scriven and Maxwell, Eds. *Concepts, Theories and the Mind-body Problem*, Minnesota Studies in the Philosophy of Science, U. of Minnesota, 370–497.

Feldman, J. 1963. Simulation of behavior in binary choice experiments. In Feigenbaum and Feldman. Eds.

Feldman, J. A. 1967. First thoughts on grammatical inference. A.I. Memo No. 55, Stanford Univ., Stanford, Ca.

Feldman, J. A. 1972. Some decidability results in grammatical inference and complexity. In *Information and Control*. New York: Academic Press.

Feldman, J. A., G. M. Feldman, G. Falk, J. Pearlman, I. Sobel, and J. M. Tennenbaum. 1969. The Stanford hand-eye project. In Walker and Norton, 521–526a.

Feldman, J. A., K. Pingle, T. Binford, G. Falk, A. Kay, R. Paul, R. Sproull, and J. Tennenbaum. 1971. The use of vision and manipulation to solve the "instant insanity" puzzle. *Prereadings Second International Joint Conference on Artificial Intelligence*. London: British Computer Society.

Festinger, L. 1957. *A theory of cognitive dissonance*. Stanford, Ca.: Stanford Univ. Press.

Feyerabend, P. K. and G. Maxwell, Eds. 1966. *Mind, Matter, and Method*. Minneapolis: Univ. of Minnesota Press.

Fikes, R. 1969. A Heuristic Program for Solving Problems Stated as Non-deterministic Procedures. Unpub. Ph.D. Thesis, Carnegie-Mellon University.

Fillmore, C. J. 1968. "The Case for Case." In Bach and Harms, Eds. *Universals in Linguistic Theory*. Chicago: Holt, Rinehart and Winston, Inc.

Floyd, R. 1961. A descriptive language for symbol manipulation, *J. ACM*, 8, 579.

Floyd, R. 1967. Assigning meanings to programs. *Proc. Symp. Applied Mathematics*. Amer. Math. Soc., 19, 19–32.

Fodor, J. A. 1968. *Psychological Explanation*. New York: Random House.

Foster, C. 1970. *Computer Architecture*. New York: Van Nostrand Reinhold.

Freedman, J. and E. Loftus. 1971. The retrieval of words from long term memory. *J. Verb. Learn. and Verb. Behav.* 10, 107–115.

Freudenthal, H. 1962. *Lincos*. Amsterdam: North Holland.

Frost, N. H. 1971. Interaction of visual and semantic codes in long term memory. Unpub. Ph.D. Thesis, Univ. of Oregon.

Garner, W. R. 1970. Good patterns have few alternatives. *American Scientist*. 58, 34–42.

Gazzaniga, M. S. 1969. *The bisected brain*. New York: Academic Press.

Geschwind, N. 1970. The organization of language in the brain. *Science*, 170, 940–944.

Glucksberg, S. and Cowen, G. 1970. Memory for nonattended auditory material. *Cogn. Psychol.* 1, 149–156.

Goldman, N. 1973. "The Generation of English Sentences from a Deep Conceptual Base." Ph.D. Thesis, Computer Science Dept., Stanford Univ., Stanford, Ca.

Green, Cordell, 1969. "Application of Theorem Proving to Problem Solving." *Proceedings of the International Joint Conference on Artificial Intelligence*, Bedford, Mass., MITRE Corp. In Walker and Norton.

Green, C. and B. Raphael. 1969. Research on Intelligent Question Answering Systems. Proc. ACM 23rd National Conf., Princeton: Brandon Systems Press.

Gries, D. 1971. *Compiler Construction for digital computers*. New York: Wiley.

Gurowitz, E. 1969. *The molecular basis of memory*. Englewood Cliffs, N.J.: Prentice-Hall.

Haber, R. N., Ed. 1969. *Information Processing Approaches to Visual Perception*. New York: Holt, Rinehart and Winston.

Halliday, M. A. K. 1970. Functional diversity in language as seen from a consideration of modality and mood in English. *Foundations of Language*, 6, 322–361.

Hammond, K. R., and D. A. Summers. 1965. Cognitive dependence on linear and non-linear cues. *Psychol. Rev.*, 72, 215–224.

Harary, F., R. Z. Norman, and D. Cartwright. 1965. *Structural models: An introduction to the theory of directed graphs*. New York: Wiley.

Hayes, J. R. 1965. Problem topology and the solution process. *Journ. of Verb. Learn. and Verb. Behav.* 4, 371–379.

Hays, D. 1964. Dependency Theory: A formalism and some observations. *Language*, Vol. 40.

Heider, F. 1946. Attitudes and cognitive organization. *Journal of Psychology*, 21, 107–112.

Hempel, C. G. 1966. Recent problems of induction. In R. G. Colodny, Ed. *Mind and Cosmos*. Pittsburgh: Univ. of Pittsburgh Press.

Hewitt, C. 1969. PLANNER: A language for proving theorems in robots. In Walker and Norton. Eds.

Hewitt, C. 1971. Procedural embedding of knowledge in PLANNER. *Proceedings of the Second Joint Conference on Artificial Intelligence*, 167–182. London: British Computer Society.

Hudson, R. A. 1971. *English Complex Sentences*. Amsterdam: North-Holland.

Hunt, E. 1971. What kind of computer is man? *Cogn. Psychol.*, 2, 57–98.

Hunt, E. and L. T. Love, 1972. How good can memory be? In Melton and Martin, Eds. *Coding Processes in human memory*. Washington, D.C.: V. H. Winston and Sons.

Hunt, E. B., J. Marin, and P. J. Stone. *Experiments in induction*. New York: Academic Press.

Huttenlocher, J. 1968. Constructing spatial images: a strategy in reasoning. *Psychol. Rev.*, 75, 550–560.

Jarvella, R. C. 1971. Syntactic processing of connected speech. *J. Verb. Lrng. and Verb. Behav.* 10, 409–416.

Jacobs, R. A. and P. S. Rosenbaum. 1968. *English Transformational Grammar*. Waltham, Mass.: Blaisdell Publ. Co.

Jervis, R. 1973. (In Press). *Perception and international relations*.

John, E. R. 1967. *Mechanisms of Memory*. New York: Academic Press.

John, E. R. 1971. Brain mechanisms of memory. In J. McGaugh. *Psychobiology*. New York: Academic Press.

John, E. R. 1972. Switchboard versus statistical theories of learning and memory. *Science*, 177, 850–863.

Johnson, E. S. 1964. An information processing model of one kind of problem solving. *Psychol. Monographs*. Whole No. 581.

Jones, E. E., L. Rock, K. G. Shaver, G. R. Goethals, and L. M. Ward. 1968. Pattern of performance and ability attribution: an unexpected primacy effect. *J. of Personality and Soc. Psychol.*, 10, 317–340.

Joos, M. 1971. "Semantic Axiom number one." *Language*, 8, No. 2.

Juloa, J. F. and R. C. Atkinson. 1971. Memory scanning for words versus categories. *J. Verb. Learn. and Verb. Behav. 10*, 522–527.

Jurca, N. H. 1971. Recall of nouns in sentences as a function of noun and verb meaning changes. *J. Verb. Learn. and Verb. Behav.*, 10, 449–452.

Kahneman, D., and A. Tversky, 1972. Subjective probability: a judgement of representativeness. *Cogn. Psycholog.*

Kanouse, D. E. 1972. Language, labeling, and attribution. In E. E. Jones, *et al.*, Eds. *Attribution: Perceiving the causes of behavior.* New York: Academic Press.

Kaplan, R. 1971. Augmented Transition Networks as Psychological Models of Sentence Comprehension. *Second International Conference on Artificial Intelligence.* London: British Computer Society.

Katz, J. J. 1966. *The Philosophy of Language.* New York: Harper and Row.

Katz, J. J., and J. A. Fodor. 1963. The structure of a semantic theory. *Language,* 39, 2, 170–210.

Klein, S. 1965. Automatic Paraphrasing in Essay Format. *Mechanical Translation,* Vol. 8, 3 and 4.

Klein, S., *et. al.* 1968. The Autoling System. Tech. Report #43, Computer Science Dept., Univ. of Wisconsin, Madison.

Kleinmuntz, B. 1968. The processing of clinical information by man and machine. In Kleinmuntz, B., Ed. *Formal representation of human judgement.* New York: Wiley.

Kuhn, T. 1962. *The Structure of Scientific Revolutions.* Chicago: U. Chicago Press.

Kuno, S. 1965. "The predictive analyzer and a path elimination technique." *Comm. Assoc. for Computing Machinery,* 8, 687–698.

Kuno, S. and A. Oettinger. 1962. "Multiple Path Syntactic Analyzer" in *Information Processing.* North Holland Press: The Hague.

Lakoff, G. 1972. Linguistics and Natural Logic. In Davidson and Harman, Eds. *Semantics of Natural Language.* New York: Humanities Press.

Lamb, S. 1964. The Sememic Approach to Structural Semantics. *American Anthropologist* (special issue).

Lamb, S. 1966. *Outline of Stratificational Grammar.* Washington, D.C.: Georgetown Univ. Press.

Landauer, T. and J. Freedman. 1968. Information retrieval from long term memory: Category size and recognition time. *J. Verb. Learn. and Verb. Behav.* 1, 291–295.

Lansdell, H. 1968. Effect of temporal lobe ablations on two lateralized deficits. *Physiol. and Behav.* 3, 271–273.

Laughrey, K. 1969. Computer simulation of short term memory. A component decay model. In Spence and Bower, Eds. *Psychology of learning and motivation.* Vol. 3. New York: Academic Press.

Lenneberg, E. 1967. *The biological foundations of language.* New York: Wiley.

Lenneberg, E. H. 1969. On explaining language. *Science,* 164, 635–643.

Lenneberg, E. H., Ed. 1964. *New Directions in the Study of Language.* Cambridge: The MIT Press.

Lewis, J. L. 1970. Semantic processing of unattended messages using dichotic listening. *Journ. Exp. Psychol.* 85, 225–228.

Liberman, A., I. G. Mattingly, and M. T. Turvey. 1972. Language codes and memory codes. In Melton and Martin, Eds. *Coding processes in human memory.* Washington, D.C.: V. H. Winston and Sons.

Lindsay, R. K. 1963. Inferential memory as the basis of machines which understand natural thought. In Feigenbaum and Feldman.

Loftus, E. F. and R. W. Scheff, 1971. Categorization norms for fifty representative instances. *Journ. Exp. Psychol.*, 91, 355–365.

Loftus, G. R. 1971. Comparison of recognition and recall in a continuous memory task. *Journ. Exp. Psychol.* 91, 220–226.

Luce, R. D. and P. Suppes. 1965. Preference, Utility and Subjective Probability. In Luce, Bush, and Galanter, Eds. *Handbook of Mathematical Psychology.* Vol. III, 249–410. New York: Wiley.

Luria, A. R. 1966. *Higher cortical functions in man.* London: Tavistock.

McCarthy, J. and P. Hayes. 1969. Some Philosophical Problems from the standpoint of Artificial Intelligence. In *Machine Intelligence 4.* Edinburgh: Edinburgh Univ. Press.

MacKay, D. 1965. From mechanism to mind. In J. R. Smythies, Ed. 186. *Brain and Mind.* Boston: Routledge and Kegan Paul. 186.

Mandler, G. 1957. Organization and memory. In Spence and Spence, Eds. *The psychology of learning and motivation.* Vol. I. New York: Academic Press.

Manna, Z. 1969. Properties of programs and the first-order predicate calculus. *J. ACM,* 16, 2, 244–255.

Manna, Z. and J. Vuillemin. 1972. Five point approach to the theory of computation. *J. ACM,* 15, 528–536.

March, J. and H. A. Simon. 1958. *Organization.* New York: Wiley.

Mattingly, I., A. Liberman, A. Syrdal, and T. Hawles. 1971. Discrimination in speech and nonspeech modes. *Cogn. Psychol.* 2, 131–157.

Maxwell, G. and P. K. Feyerabend, Eds. 1966. *Mind, Matter and Method.* Minneapolis: Univ. of Minnesota Press.

Meehl, P. E. 1966. The Compleat Autocerebrescopist: A thought-experiment on Professor Feigl's mind-body identity thesis. In Feyerabend and Maxwell.

Michie, D. 1971. On not seeing things. Experimental Programming Reports #22, Univ. of Edinburgh.

Michie, D., Ed. 1969. *Machine Intelligence 3.* New York: American Elsevier.

Michie, D., Ed. 1970. *Machine Intelligence 4.* New York: American Elsevier.

Milgram, S. 1970. The experience of living in cities. *Science,* 167, 1461–1468.

Miller, G. A. 1956. The magical number seven, plus or minus two. *Psych. Rev.,* 63, 81–97.

Miller, G. A. 1962. Some psychological studies of grammar. *American Psychologist,* 17, November, 748–762.

Miller, G. A. and N. Chomsky. 1963. Introduction to the formal analysis of language; *also* Finitary models of language users. In Luce, Bush, and Galanter, Eds. *Handbook of Mathematical Psychology.* Vol. 2. New York: Wiley.

Miller, G. A., E. Galanter, and K. H. Pribram. 1960. *Plans and the structure of behavior.* New York: Holt, Rinehart, and Winston, Inc.

Milner, B. 1962. Laterality effects in audition. In Mountcastle, Ed. *Interhemispheric relations and cerebral dominance.* Baltimore: Johns Hopkins Press.

Milner, B. 1966. Amnesia following operation on the temporal lobes. In Zangwill and Whitty, Eds. *Amnesia.* London: Butterworths.

Milner, B. 1968. Visual recognition after right temporal lobe excision in man. *Neuropsychologica,* 6, 191–209.

Milner, B. 1970. Memory and the medial temporal regions of the brain. In Pribram and Broadbent, D. E. Eds. *Biology of Memory*. New York: Academic Press.

Milner, B. 1971. Interhemispheric differences in the localization of psychological processes in man. *BR: Medical Bull*. 27, 272–277.

Minsky, M. 1961. Steps toward artificial intelligence. *Proc. IEEE*. Reprinted in Feigenbaum and Feldman.

Minsky, M. 1967. *Computation: Finite and Infinite Machines*. Englewood Cliffs, N.J.: Prentice-Hall.

Minsky, M., Ed. 1968. *Semantic Information Processing*. Cambridge: The MIT Press.

Minsky, M. 1970. Form and computer science. *J. Assoc. for Comp. Machinery*. 17, 216–230.

Minsky, M., and S. Papert. 1969. *Perceptrons*. Cambridge: The MIT Press.

Montague, R. 1970. English as a formal language. In *Linguaggi nella Società e nella Tècnica*, Milan: Edizioni di Comunità.

Moses, J. 1968. Symbolic Integration. Unpub. Ph.D. Thesis, MIT.

Neisser, U. 1967. *Cognitive psychology*. New York: Appleton-Century-Crofts.

Newell, A. 1962. Learning, generality and problem solving. In M. Popplewell, Ed. *Proc. IFIPS Congress*.

Newell, A. 1967. *Studies in Problem Solving: Subject 3 on the arithmetic task DONALD + GERALD = ROBERT*. Pittsburgh: Carnegie Institute of Technology.

Newell, A. 1969. Heuristic Programming: Ill-structured problems. In Aronofsky, Ed. *Progress in Operations Research*. Vol. III, 360–414. New York: Wiley.

Newell, A. 1970. Remarks on the relationship between artificial intelligence and cognitive psychology. In Banerji and Mesarwic, Eds. *Theoretical approaches to Non-numerical Problem Solving*. Berlin: Springer-Verlag.

Newell, A. and G. Ernst. 1965. The search for generality. In Kalenich, Ed. *Proc. of IFIP Congress* 17–24, New York: Spartan Books.

Newell, A. and H. Simon. 1961. Computer simulation of human thinking. *Science*, 134, 2011–2017.

Newell, A. and H. A. Simon. 1963. GPS: A program that simulates human thought. In Feigenbaum and Feldman.

Newell, A. and H. A. Simon. 1965. An example of human chess play in the light of chess playing programs. In Weiner and Schade, Eds. *Progress in Biocybernetics*, Vol. 2, 19–75. New York: American Elsevier.

Newell, A. and H. A. Simon. 1967. Overview: memory and process in concept formation. In Kleinmuntz, Ed. 241–262. *Concepts and the Structure of Memory*, New York: Wiley.

Newell, A. and H. Simon. 1972. *Human Problem Solving*. Englewood Cliffs, N.J.: Prentice Hall.

Nida, E. and C. Taber. 1969. *The theory and practice of translation*. Leiden: Brill.

Nilsson, N. 1971. *Problem Solving Methods in Artificial Intelligence*. New York: McGraw-Hill.

Norman, D. A. 1968. Toward a theory of memory and attention. *Psychol. Rev*. 75, 522–536.

Norman, D. A. 1969. *Memory and Attention*. New York: Wiley.

Norman, D. A. and D. E. Rumelhart. 1970. A system for perception and memory. In Norman, Ed. *Models of Human Memory*, Academic Press.

Pavio, A. 1971. *Imagery and Verbal Processes*. New York: Holt, Rinehart, and Winston.

Palme, J. 1971. Making Computers Understand Natural Language. In Findler and Meltzer, Eds. *Artificial Intelligence and Heuristic Programming*. Edinburgh, U.K.: Edinburgh Univ. Press.

Posner, M. I. and S. Boies. 1971. Components of attention. *Psychol. Rev.*, 78, 391–408.

Preparata, F. and S. Ray. 1970. An Approach to Artificial Nonsymbolic Cognition. Coordinated Science Lab. Report R-478, Univ. of Ill., Urbana, Ill.

Prytulak, L. 1971. Natural language mediation. *Cogn. Psychol.* 2, 1–56.

Putnam, H. 1960. Minds and machines. In S. Hook, Ed. *Dimensions of Mind*, New York: New York Univ. Press.

Quillian, M. R. 1968. *Semantic Memory*. In Minsky (1968).

Quillian, M. R. 1969. The Teachable Language Comprehender: a simulation program and theory of language. *Comm. ACM*, 12 (8), 459–476.

Quinton, A. 1965. Mind and Matter. In J. R. Smythies, Ed. *Brain and Mind*. Boston: Routledge and Kegan Paul.

Rieger, C. 1973. Conceptual Memory. Ph.D. Thesis. Comp. Sci. Dept., Stanford Univ., Stanford, Ca.

Riesbeck, C. 1973. Computer Analysis of Natural Language in Context. Ph.D. Thesis. Computer Science Dept. Stanford Univ., Stanford, Ca.

Reitman, W. 1965. *Cognition and Thought*. New York: Wiley.

Rizzolatti, G., C. Umiltá, and G. Berlucchi. 1971. Opposite superiorities of the right and left cerebral hemispheres in discriminative reaction times to physiognomical and alphabetical material. *Brain*, 94, 431–442.

Robinson, J. A. 1967. A review of automatic theorem proving. *Proc. Symp. Applied Mathematics, Amer. Math. Sci.*

Rumelhart, D. E., P. H. Lindsay, and D. A. Norman. 1972. A process model for long term memory. In Tulving and Donaldson. *Organization and Memory*. New York: Academic Press.

Russell, S. 1972. Semantic Categories of Nominals for Conceptual Dependency Analysis of Natural Language. A.I. Memo-172. Comp. Sci. Dept., Stanford Univ., Stanford, Ca.

Sandewall, E. J. 1969. A Set-Oriented Property Structure Representation for Binary Relations. In Meltzer and Mitchie, Eds. *Machine Intelligence 5*. Edinburgh, U.K.: Edinburgh Univ. Press.

Sandewall, E. J. 1971. Representing natural language information in predicate calculus. *Machine Intelligence 6*. Edinburgh, U.K.: Edinburgh Univ. Press.

Schank, R. 1969. "A conceptual dependency representation for a computer-oriented semantics," A.I. Memo-83, Comp. Sci. Dept., Stanford Univ., Stanford, Ca.

Schank, R. 1971. "Finding the conceptual content and intention of an utterance in natural language conversation," Proc. 2nd Joint International Conference on A.I. London: British Computer Society.

Schank, R. 1971. Finding the conceptual content and intention in an utterance in natural language conversation. London: British Computer Society, 444–454.

Schank, R. 1972. Conceptual Dependency: A Theory of Natural Language Understanding. *Cogn. Psychol.*, Vol. 3, (4).

Schank, R. 1973. The Fourteen Primitive Actions and Their Inferences. A.I. Memo-183, Comp. Sci. Dept., Stanford Univ., Stanford, Ca.

Schank, R., N. Goldman, C. Rieger, and C. Riesbeck. 1972. Primitive Concepts Underlying Verbs of Thought. A.I. Memo-162, Comp. Sci. Dept., Stanford, Univ., Stanford, Ca.

Schank, R. and L. Tesler. 1970. A Conceptual Dependency Parser for Natural Language. In *Statistical Methods in Linguistics,* Vol. 6.

Schank, R. C., L. Tesler, and S. Weber. 1970. Spinoza II: Conceptual Case-Based Natural Language Analysis. *Stanford Artificial Intelligence Project Memo No. AIM-109,* Comp. Sci. Dept., Stanford Univ., Stanford, Ca.

Scriven, M. 1966. The limitations of the identity theory. In Feyerabend and Maxwell.

Scriven, M. 1972. The concept of comprehension. In Carroll and Freedle, Eds. *Language Comprehension.* Washington: J. V. Winston and Co.

Sellars, W. 1965. The identity approach to the mind-body problem. *Rev. Metaphysics XVIII,* 3. Reprinted in S. Hamshire, Ed. 1966. *Philosophy of Mind.* New York: Harper and Row.

Schackle, G. L. S. 1969. *Decision, Order and Time.* New York: Cambridge University Press.

Shapiro, M. J. and G. M. Bonham. 1973. (In press). Cognitive processes and foreign policy decision-making. *International Studies Quarterly.*

Shepard, R. N. and J. Metzler. 1971. Mental rotation of three dimensional objects. *Science,* 171, 701–703.

Shiffrin, R. 1970. Memory Search. In Norman, Ed. *Models of Human Memory.* New York: Academic Press.

Shiffrin, R. and R. Atkinson. 1969. Storage and retrieval processes in long term memory. *Psychol. Rev.* 56, 179–193.

Simmons, R. 1970. Natural Language Question Answering Systems: 1969. *Comm. ACM,* Vol. 13, #1.

Simmons, R. F. 1970. "Some Semantic Structures for Representing English Meanings." Tech. Report #NL-1, Comp. Sci. Dept., Univ. of Texas, Austin.

Simmons, R. and B. Bruce. 1971. "Some Relations between Predicate Calculus and Semantic Net Representations of Discourse." *Proc. 2nd International Joint Conference on Art. Intell.,* London: Brit. Comp. Soc.

Simmons, R. F. and J. Slocum. 1972. "Generating English Discourse from Semantic Nets" *Comm. ACM,* Vol. 15, #10.

Simon. H. A. 1966. Scientific discovery and the psychology of problem solving. In Colodny. *Mind and Cosmos.* Pittsburgh: Univ. of Pittsburgh Press.

Simon, H. A. 1969. *The Sciences of the Artificial.* Cambridge: The MIT Press.

Simon, H. A. and E. A. Feigenbaum. 1964. An information-processing theory of some effects of similarity, familiarization and meaningful in verbal learning. *J. Verb. Learn. and Verb. Behav.,* 3, 385–396.

Simon, H. A. and K. Kotovsky. 1963. Human acquisition of concepts for sequential patterns. *Psych. Rev.,* 70, 534–546.

Slagle, J. 1965. A multipurpose theorem proving heuristic program that learns. *Proc. IFIP Congress 65.* Vol. 2, 323–324. New York: Spartan Books.

Slagle, J. R. 1971. Artificial Intelligence: The heuristic programming approach. New York: McGraw-Hill.

Smith, F. and G. Miller, Eds. 1966. *The Genesis of Language.* Cambridge: The MIT Press.

Solberg, A. 1968. A Study of Decision Making: Job Choice. Ph.D. Thesis, Carnegie-Mellon University.

Spear, A. 1970. *Inside the Third Reich.* New York: Macmillan.

Sperling, G. 1960. The information available in brief visual presentation. *Psychol. Monographs,* 74, Whole No. 498.

Sussman, G., T. Winograd, and E. Charniak. 1970. Micro-planner reference manual. A.I. Memo 203, Artificial Intelligence Laboratory, MIT.

Swanson, D. W., P. J. Bohnert, and J. A. Smith. 1970. *The Paranoid.* Boston: Little, Brown and Co.

Thompson, S. A. 1971. The Deep Structure of Relative Clauses. In Fillmore and Langendoen, Eds. *Studies in Linguistic Semantics.* New York: Holt, Rinehart and Winston, Inc.

Tomkins, S. and S. Messick, Eds. 1963. *Computer Simulation of Personality.* New York: Wiley.

Trabasso, T., H. Rollins, and E. Shaugnessey. 1971. Storage and verification stages in processing concepts. *Cogn. Psychol.* 2, 239–289.

Turing, A. M. 1963. Computing Machinery and Intelligence. In Feigenbaum and Feldman.

Uhr, L., Ed. 1966. *Pattern Recognition.* New York: Wiley.

Umilita, C., N. Frost, and R. Hyman. 1972. Interhemispheric effects on choice reaction times for one-, two- and three-letter displays. *Journ. of Exper. Psychol.*

Waldinger, R. J. and R. C. T. Lee. 1969. PROW: A step toward automatic program writing. In Walker and Norton.

Walker, D. E. and L. M. Norton, Eds. 1969. *Proceedings of the International Joint Conference on Artificial Intelligence.* Boston: Mitre Corporation.

Wang, H. 1960. Towards mechanical mathematics. *IBM J. Research and Development.* 4.

Wang, H. 1965. Formalization and automatic theorem proving. *Proc. IFIP Congress 1965,* 1, 51.

Waterman, D. and A. Newell. 1971. Protocol analysis as a task for artificial intelligence. *Artificial Intelligence* 2, 285–318.

Waugh, N. C. and D. A. Norman. 1965. Primary memory. *Psychol. Rev.,* 72, 89–104.

Weizenbaum, J., 1966. ELIZA. *Comm. CM,* 9, 36–45.

Whitehead, A. N. and B. Russell. 1929. *Principia Mathematica.* Cambridge: Cambridge Univ. Press.

Wickelgren, W. 1970. Multitrace strength theory. In Norman, *Models of human memory.* New York: Academic Press.

Wilkins, A. J. 1971. Conjoint frequency, category size, and categorization time. *J. Verb. Lrng. and Verb. Behav.,* 10, 382–385.

Wilks, Y. 1968. On-line semantic analysis of English texts. *Mach. Trans. and Comp. Learn.*

Wilks, Y. 1971. Decidability and natural language. *Mind.*

Wilks, Y. 1971. *Grammar, meaning and the machine analysis of natural language.* Boston: Routledge and Kegan Paul.

Williams, D. 1969. Computer Program Organization induced by Problem Examples. Unpub. Ph.D. Thesis, Carnegie-Mellon Univ.

Williams, D. 1972. Computer program organization induced from problem examples. In H. A. Simon and L. Siklossy, Eds. *Representation and Meaning: Experiments with information processing systems.* Englewood Cliffs, N.J.: Prentice-Hall.

Williams, G. F. 1971. A model of memory in concept learning. *Cogn. Psychol.,* 2, 158–184.

Winikoff, A. 1967. Eye Movements and an Aid to Protocol Analysis of Problem Solving Behavior. Unpub. Ph.D. Thesis, Carnegie-Mellon Univ.

Winograd, T. 1972. *Understanding Natural Language.* New York: Academic Press.

Winograd, T. Procedures as a representation for data in a computer program for understanding natural language. MAC TR-84. M.I.T. Art. Intell. Lab. 1971. Ph.D. Thesis.

Woods, W. A. 1970. Transition network grammars for natural language analysis. *Comm. ACM,* 13, #10, 591–606.

Yntema, D. B. and W. S. Torgerson. 1961. Man-computer cooperation in decisions requiring common sense. *IEEE Transactions on Human Factors in Electronics,* HFE-2, 20–26.

Ziff, P. 1959. The feelings of robots. *Analysis,* XIX, 3. Reprinted in A. R. Anderson.

Name Index

Subject Index